Fodor's 96
Pocket Paris

Reprinted from *Fodor's Paris '96*

Fodor's Travel Publications, Inc.
New York • Toronto • London • Sydney • Auckland

Fodor's Pocket Paris

Editors: Kristen D. Perrault, Fionn Davenport
Editorial Contributors: Rob Andrews, Bob Blake, Simon Hewitt, Corinne LaBalme, Alexander Lobrano, Bevin McLaughlin, Tracy Patruno, Mary Ellen Schultz, M. T. Schwartzman, Dinah Spritzer
Creative Director: Fabrizio La Rocca
Cartographer: David Lindroth
Cover Photograph: Catherine Karnow/Woodfin Camp
Text Design: Between the Covers

Copyright

ISBN 0-679-02951-6

Special Sales

Fodor's Travel Publications are available at special discounts for bulk purchases for sales promotions or premiums. Special editions, including personalized covers, excerpts of existing guides, and corporate imprints, can be created in large quantities for special needs. For more information, contact your local bookseller or write to Special Markets, Fodor's Travel Publications, 201 East 50th Street, New York, NY 10022. Inquiries from Canada should be directed to your local Canadian bookseller or sent to Random House of Canada, Ltd., Marketing Department, 1265 Aerowood Drive, Mississauga, Ontario L4W 1B9. Inquiries from the United Kingdom should be sent to Fodor's Travel Publications, 20 Vauxhall Bridge Road, London SW1V 2SA.

MANUFACTURED IN THE UNITED STATES OF AMERICA
10 9 8 7 6 5 4 3 2 1

CONTENTS

ON THE ROAD WITH FODOR'S

AGOOD TRAVEL GUIDE is like a wonderful traveling companion. It's charming, it's brimming with sound recommendations and solid ideas, it pulls no punches in describing lodging and dining establishments, and it's consistently full of fascinating facts that make you view what you've traveled to see in a rich new light. In the creation of *Pocket Paris '96*, we at Fodor's have gone to great lengths to provide you with the very best of all possible traveling companions—and to make your trip the best of all possible vacations.

How to Use This Book

Organization

Chapter 1 comprises two sections chock-full of information about traveling in general and specifically at your destination. Both are in alphabetical order by topic. **Important Contacts** gives you addresses and telephone numbers of organizations and companies that offer destination-related services and detailed information or publications. Here's where you'll find information about how to get to Paris from wherever you are. **Smart Travel Tips,** the second section, gives you specific tips on how to get the most out of your

travels as well as information on how to accomplish what you need to in Paris.

Stars

Stars in the margin are used to denote highly recommended sights, attractions, hotels, and restaurants.

Credit Cards

The following abbreviations are used: **AE,** American Express; **DC,** Diners Club; **MC,** MasterCard; and **V,** Visa. Discover is not accepted outside the United States.

Please Write to Us

Everyone who has contributed to *Pocket Paris '96* has worked hard to make the text accurate. All prices and opening times are based on information supplied to us at press time, and the publisher cannot accept responsibility for any errors that may have occurred. The passage of time will bring changes, so it's always a good idea to call ahead and confirm information when it matters—particularly if you're making a detour to visit specific sights or attractions. When making reservations at a hotel or inn, be sure to mention if you have a disability or are traveling with children, if you prefer a private bath or a certain type of bed, or if you have specific dietary needs or any other concerns.

Were the restaurants we recommended as described? Did our hotel picks exceed your expectations? Did you find a museum we recommended a waste of time? Positive and negative, we would love your feedback. If you have complaints, we'll look into them and revise our entries when the facts warrant it. If there's a special place you've happened upon that we haven't included, we'll pass the information along to the writers so they can check it out. So please send us a letter or post card (we're at 201 East 50th Street, New York, NY 10022). We'll look forward to hearing from you. And in the meantime, have a wonderful trip!

Karen Cure

Karen Cure
Editorial Director

CAPTURING PARIS

YOU HAVE HEARD it said that "Paris would be great if it weren't for the Parisians." If a Frenchman says it, it means that he is determined to be provincial. But if it comes from a foreigner, it probably means that he or she has had an unfortunate linguistic encounter. It takes a certain nerve to try out one's French, no matter one's level. A former *New York Times* Paris bureau chief told me he got by only because his French was "audacious." Many foreigners, and I am one, are afraid of being laughed at. The cure for this is to make a faux pas so ridiculous that you can tell it on yourself. A young photographer friend of mine, for example, was trying to tell some French friends about his first date with a girl of good family and prim reputation. He thought he was telling them that he had kissed her good night— the polite peck. Instead, he was saying that he had bedded her the first night. They were impressed but incredulous.

Paris is the city where, once you are known, shopkeepers greet you coming and going and proprietors shake your hand as you leave their restaurants. It is the city where bus drivers may reopen the door for you if you come on the run, and where bellmen are sometimes too proud to linger for a tip.

Not that Parisians are perfect. There are the usual shady characters who populate our urbanized world. There are pickpockets, just to make you feel at home. *En garde!* Weapons are not often used in Paris crime, but thieves can be ingenious. A friend from Manhattan was the victim of a classic ploy. Sensing that his wallet had been lifted while he was standing in awe of Notre Dame, he whirled on the probable thief, a girl of about 12. To attest her innocence, she lifted her dress, revealing a totally naked body. Our friend was too flustered to pursue the matter further.

Paris is not France, but France would be unimaginable without Paris. Here, past and present co-exist, sometimes comfortably, sometimes uneasily. Children play house in the playground of the Cluny museum, on the spot where Romans took their leisure in baths 100 meters long.

Called Lutetia by the Romans but renamed for the Parisii, a Celtic tribe, Paris has been a settlement on the Seine for more than two millennia. Blood has flowed here as constantly as the river. Crossing the place de la Concorde, one still shivers at the thought of the 1,344 persons beheaded there by the guillotine, including King Louis XVI and Marie Antoinette. Tourists flock to the Sacré-Coeur, at once the ugliest and boldest church in Paris. It stands on a hill named Montmartre, for the Christian martyrs; one of them, Saint Denis, is said to have carried his severed head in his hands as he walked north out of the city in the third century. Joan of Arc was wounded in Paris in 1429, but it was another woman, Geneviève, a shepherdess from Nanterre, who became the special saint of Paris, having rallied the city against Attila the Hun. Today, students at the Sorbonne study in a reading room as long as a football field and high enough for a dropkick, in the library of her name. A department store, La Samaritaine, backs up against the church of St-Germain l'Auxerrois, from whose tower bells rang on the night of August 24, 1572, to signal the prearranged massacre of 3,000 Huguenots. A short walk away, at a Jewish restaurant called Goldenberg's in the heart of the Marais district, a minimassacre, on August 9, 1982, took the lives of six people at lunchtime.

Paris has a museum for every period and taste. Parisians argue museums as Americans fight over baseball teams. They tend either to loathe or love the Beaubourg, its red and blue insides exposed like an oil refinery. And unlike almost any other city, Paris's artistic life is closely tied to its political realities. The 14-year reign of President François Mitterrand will be forever remembered by the controversial "great works" he sponsored or inaugurated: the Musée d'Orsay, in a former railroad station; a new opera house, dominating place de la Bastille; the Great Arch, which lines up with the Arc de Triomphe; a new national library, housed in four glass towers; and the glass Pyramid, designed by I. M. Pei as the entrance to the grandly refurbished Louvre.

GREAT EXHIBITIONS are not limited to museums. The Grand Palais, a marvel of turn-of-the-century iron and glass construction, and its little neighbor of the same vintage, the Petit Palais, occasionally attract lines that stretch far down avenue Winston Churchill. As if those are not enough, the city has built another huge complex, a kind of fairground of halls, playgrounds, and theaters (one of which is enclosed in a shining sphere) on the site of the former slaughterhouses of La Villette, on the city's outskirts.

There are another dozen or so art museums. The Musée Guimet has Oriental art; the Marmottan is a mansion containing Monets and others. Museums have been created in the studios of Rodin, Delacroix, and Brancusi. Paris has major museums of anthropology, natural history, history, and science, and smaller ones dealing with everything from advertising and bread to urban transport and wine. The Musée Grévin, the waxworks museum on the boulevard Montmartre and in the Forum des Halles, is perhaps the most amusing of all.

If you're a nosy type, one who loves to poke and peek, a certain amount of respectful audacity will take you far in Paris. Instead of taking the guided tour at the Bourse, or stock exchange, you can try to talk your way into a look at the trading floor. Nearby, at the Bibliothèque Nationale, without a reader's card, you can look into the main reading room or the equally impressive periodicals room. For lawyers, a place of interest is the Palais de Justice, with courtrooms where black-robed judges and *avocats* hear and plead cases all day long. Just walking the halls there is a spectacle; one can tiptoe into courts in session. In the waiting rooms of the nearby Préfecture de Police, you will find scenes of poverty and desperation reminiscent of Daumier.

Some come to Paris just to eat. They come laden with research, with starred lists, credit cards, and calculated appetites. Many have done their homework well, with one or more of the useful books that devote themselves to mouth-watering descriptions of Parisian delicacies.

THE SHEER profusion of places to eat in Paris is staggering. There are thousands of places where one can get a cup of tea or coffee—*or* a glass of wine or beer—a convenience that is one of the finer attributes of French civilization. I go sometimes by hearsay, sometimes by looks, often by ambience. The *carte* posted at the door offers further clues, especially as to price. The same rules apply in Paris as elsewhere: One tends to pay for name and fame. Some places seem so cheap that one gets suspicious, but there is often more fun in a bistro than in an elegant two-star.

Next to dining, entertainment is the most appealing industry of Paris. The week begins on Wednesday with the appearance of *Pariscope*, one of the three weekly bibles for those who go out often. A typical issue will list the hundreds of films that play the cinemas in Paris and environs in an average week. It also lists revivals, film festivals, as well as screenings at the film libraries of the subsidized Beaubourg and Palais de Chaillot.

Paris is the home of the exile. It is here that Chopin came to compose, Picasso to paint, Joyce to write *Ulysses*. In Paris, even more than in London and New York, it is possible to live as a citizen of the world. It is almost possible to forget one's race, one's religion, almost possible to believe all men are brothers. Burnoose and sari, blue jeans and haute couture walk side by side. Gallic cynicism and *la vie en rose* go together. Victor Hugo aptly stated the message of Paris:

Cities are bibles of stone. This city possesses no single dome, roof, or pavement that does not convey some message of alliance and of union, and that does not offer some lesson, example, or advice. Let the people of all the world come to this prodigious alphabet of monuments, of tombs, and of trophies to learn peace and to unlearn the meaning of hatred. Let them be confident. For Paris has proven itself. To have once been Lutèce and to have become Paris—what could be a more magnificent symbol! To have been mud and to have become spirit!

— *John G. Morris*

John G. Morris has worked as a journalist for major American newspapers and magazines—the Washington Post, *the* New York Times, Life, Ladies' Home Journal, *and* National Geographic. *He is now writing his autobiography, to be published by Random House.*

x

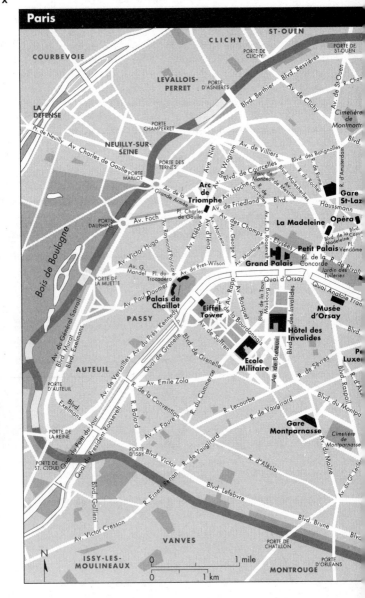

Paris

ST-OUEN
CLICHY
PORTE DE ST-OUEN
COURBEVOIE
LEVALLOIS-PERRET
PORTE DE CLICHY
Blvd. Berthier
Blvd. Bessières
Av. de St-Ouen
R. Char
PORTE D'ASNIERES
Blvd. des Batignolles
Cimetière de Montmartr
LA DEFENSE
PORTE CHAMPERRET
Av. de Villiers
Blvd.
R. d'Amsterdam
Pl. de Neuilly
Av. Charles de Gaulle
NEUILLY-SUR-SEINE
PORTE MAILLOT
PORTE DES TERNES
Av. Niel
Av. de Wagram
Blvd. de Courcelles
Blvd. Malesherbes
R. de Rome
R. du Rocher
Gare St-Laz
Av. de la Grande Armée
Arc de Triomphe
Av. Hoche
Parc de Monceau
Av. de Messine
Haussmann
PORTE DAUPHINE
Pl. Charles de Gaulle
Av. de Friedland
Blvd.
La Madeleine
Opéra
Av. Foch
Av. Kléber
Av. Marceau
Av. d'Iéna
Av. George V
Av. des Champs Élysées
Av. F.D. Roosevelt
Blvd. de la Capu
Blvd. de la Madeleine
Petit Palais
Pl. Vendôme
Av. Victor Hugo
Av. Raymond Poincaré
Av. Montaigne
Grand Palais
Pl. de la Concorde
R. de Rivoli
Jardin des Tuileries
Bois de Boulogne
Av. G. Mandel
Pl. du Trocadéro
Av. du Prés.-Wilson
Av. Rapp
Quai d'Orsay
Quai Anatole Fran
PORTE DE LA MUETTE
Av. Paul Doumer
Palais de Chaillot
Av. de la Bourdonnais
Blvd. de la Tour Maubourg
Musée d'Orsay
Blvd.
Eiffel Tower
PASSY
Av. du Prés. Kennedy
Av. de Suffren
Av. de Bosquet
des Invalides
Hôtel des Invalides
Av. du Général Sarrail
Blvd. Murat
Blvd. Exelmans
Quai de Grenelle
Blvd. de Grenelle
Av. de Breteuil
R. de Sèvres
Pe Luxe
AUTEUIL
Av. de Versailles
Ecole Militaire
PORTE D'AUTEUIL
R. de la Convention
Av. Emile Zola
R. du Commerce
R. Lecourbe
R. de Vaugirard
Blvd. Raspa
R. d'As
Blvd. Exelmans
R. Balard
R. F. Faure
Blvd. du Montpa
PORTE DE LA REINE
Quai du Pont du Jour
Av. de Versailles
Gare Montparnasse
Cimetière de Montparnasse
PORTE D'ISSY
Blvd. Victor
R. de Vaugirard
R. d'Alésia
Av. du Maine
Av. du Gl. Leclerc
PORTE DE ST-CLOUD
Quai du Président Roosevelt
R. Ernest Renan
Blvd. Lefebvre
Blvd. Galliéni
Blvd. Brune
Av. Victor Cresson
VANVES
PORTE DE CHATILLON
Blvd
PORTE D'ORLEANS
N
ISSY-LES-MOULINEAUX
0   1 mile
0   1 km
MONTROUGE

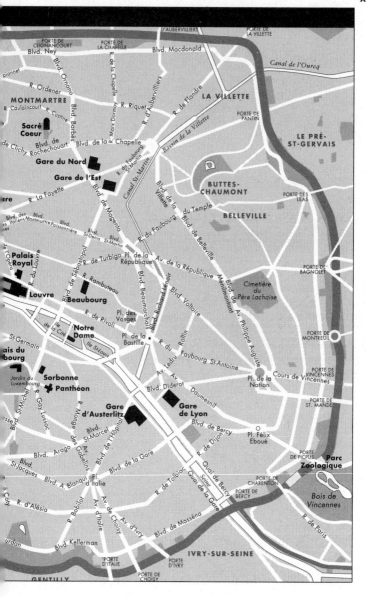

D'AUBERVILLIERS

PORTE DE
LA VILLETTE

PORTE DE
CLIGNANCOURT
Blvd. Ney

PORTE DE
LA CHAPELLE

Blvd. Macdonald

Canal de l'Ourcq

pionnet

Blvd. Ornano

R. de la Chapelle

R. Riquet

R. d'Aubervilliers

R. de Flandre

LA VILLETTE

R. Ordener

Marx Dormoy

MONTMARTRE

R. Caulaincourt

R. Custine

Blvd. Barbès

Bassin de la Villette

PORTE DE
PANTIN

LE PRÉ-
ST-GERVAIS

Sacré
Coeur

Blvd. de
Rochechouart

Blvd. de Clichy

Blvd. de la Chapelle

R. de Faubourg St-Martin

Canal St-Martin

Gare du Nord

Blvd. de la Villette

BUTTES-
CHAUMONT

PORTE DES
LILAS

Gare de l'Est

R. La Fayette

Blvd. de Magenta

du Temple

BELLEVILLE

R. du Faubourg

Blvd. de Belleville

Blvd. des Italiens
Montmartre
Poissonnière

Blvd.
St-Denis

Blvd.
St-Martin

R. de Turbigo

Pl. de la
République

Av. de la République

Ménilmontant

PORTE DE
BAGNOLET

de l'Opéra

R. du Louvre

Palais
Royal

R. de Sébastopol

R. Rambuteau

Blvd. Beaumarchais

Blvd. Richard Lenoir

Blvd. Voltaire

Cimetière
du
Père Lachaise

Av. Philippe Auguste

Louvre

Beaubourg

R. de Rivoli

Pl. des
Vosges

Notre
Dame

Île de la Cité

Île St-Louis

Pl. de la
Bastille

R. du

Rollin

Faubourg St-Antoine

PORTE DE
MONTREUIL

St-Germain

ais du
bourg

Jardin du
Luxembourg

Sorbonne

Panthéon

Av. Ledru

Av.

Av. Daumesnil

Cours de Vincennes

PORTE DE
VINCENNES

Pl. de la
Nation

Blvd. St-Michel

R. Gay Lussac

R. Monge
des Gobelins

Gare
d'Austerlitz

Blvd. Diderot

Gare
de Lyon

PORTE DE
ST. MANDE

sse

Blvd.
St-Marcel

Blvd. de l'Hôpital

Blvd. de Bercy

Blvd. Arago

Av.

Blvd. de la Gare

R. de Dijon

Pl. Félix
Eboué

PORTE
DE PICPUS

Parc
Zoologique

Blvd.
St-Jacques

Blvd. A. Blanqui

Pl.
d'Italie

R. de Tolbiac

Quai de Bercy

Quai de la Gare

PORTE DE
CHARENTON

Bois de
Vincennes

Cóty

R. d'Alésia

R. Bobillot

Av. d'Italie

Av. d'Ivry

Seine

PORTE DE
BERCY

urdan

Blvd. Kellerman

IVRY-SUR-SEINE

R. de Paris

GENTILLY

PORTE
D'ITALIE

PORTE DE
CHOISY

PORTE
D'IVRY

Blvd. de Masséna

1 Essential Information

IMPORTANT CONTACTS

An Alphabetical Listing of Publications, Organizations, and Companies That Will Help You Before, During, and After Your Trip

AIR TRAVEL

Flying time is 7 hours from New York, 9½ hours from Chicago, and 11 hours from Los Angeles.

AIRPORT TRANSFERS

One company that will pick you up at either Paris airport and drive you directly to your destination—for less than the cost of a taxi—is **Paris Airports Service** (☎ 49–62–78–78).

CARRIERS

FROM THE U.S.➤ The airlines that serve Paris from various major U.S. cities include **Air France** (☎ 800/237–2747), **American Airlines** (☎ 800/433–7300), **Continental** (☎ 800/231–0856), **Delta** (☎ 800/241–4141), **Northwest** (☎ 800/225–2525), **TWA** (☎ 800/892–4141), **United** (☎ 800/538–2929), and **USAir** (☎ 800/428–4322). Most local reservations offices close their phone lines after 10 PM and on Sundays.

FROM THE U.K.➤ **Air France** (☎ 0181/742–6600) and **British Airways** (☎ 0181/897–4000) offer service from London's Heathrow Airport to Paris every hour to two hours. The cost of round-trip tickets is almost halved if you purchase them 14 days in advance and stay over on a Saturday night. There are up to eight **Air France** flights daily, except weekends, to Paris from London's most central airport, London City, in the Docklands area.

Other airlines with regular scheduled flights from London to Paris include **British Midland** (☎ 0181/754-7231) and **Air U.K.** (☎ 0345/666–777). Except on Sunday, there are several daily flights (mostly Air France and BA) direct to Paris from Manchester, Bristol, and Birmingham, and up to four from Glasgow, Edinburgh, Aberdeen, Cardiff, Belfast, Newcastle, East Midlands (near Nottingham), and Southampton.

BICYCLING

You can hire bikes in the Bois de Boulogne (Jardin d'Acclimatation), Bois de Vincennes, some RER stations, and from the Bateaux-Mouches embarkation point by place de l'Alma. Or try **Paris-Vélo** (2 rue du Fer à Moulin, 5e, ☎ 43–37–59–22). Rental rates vary from about 90 to 140 francs per day, 160 to 220 francs per weekend, and 420 to 500 francs per week, depending on the

type of bike. There is about a
1,000-franc deposit for rental,
which can be put on a credit card.

BUS TRAVEL
Eurolines (52 Grosvenor Gardens,
London SW1W 0AU, ☎ 0171/
730–0202) operates a nightly service from London's Victoria
Coach Station, via the Dover–
Calais ferry, to Paris. Departures
are at 9 AM, arriving at 6:15 PM;
noon, arriving at 9:45 PM; and 9
PM, arriving at 7:15 AM. Fares are
£52 round-trip (under-25 youth
pass £49), £31 one-way. **Hoverspeed** (International Hoverport,
Marine Parade, Dover CT17 9TG,
☎ 01304/240241) offers up to
four daily departures from Victoria Coach Station. Fares are £55
round-trip, £38 one-way. Reservations can be made in person at any
National Express office or at the
Coach Travel Centre (13 Regent
Street, London SW1 4LR). Call to
make credit-card reservations (☎
0171/824–8657).

CAR RENTAL
Major car-rental companies represented in Paris include **Avis**
(☎ 800/331–1212, 800/879–
2847 in Canada), **Budget** (☎ 800/
527–0700, 0800/181–181 in the
U.K.), **Hertz** (☎ 800/654–3131,
800/263–0600 in Canada,
0181/679–1799 in the U.K.), and
National (☎ 800/227–3876,
0181/950–5050 in the U.K.,
where it is known as Europcar).
Rates in Paris begin at $180 a

week for an economy car with unlimited mileage. This does not include VAT tax, which at 18.6% is
among the highest in Europe.

THE CHANNEL TUNNEL
For information, contact **Le Shuttle** (☎ 01345/353535 in the U.K.,
800/388-3876 in the U.S.), which
transports cars, or **Eurostar**
(☎ 0171/922–4486 in the U.K.,
800/942–4866 in the U.S.), the
high-speed train service between
London (Waterloo) and Paris
(Gare du Nord). Eurostar tickets
are avilable in the U.K. through
InterCity Europe, the international
wing of BritRail (London Victoria
Station, ☎ 0171/834-2345 or
0171/828–8092 for credit-card
bookings), and in the United
States through **Rail Europe**
(☎ 800/942–4866) and **BritRail
Travel** (1500 Broadway, New
York, NY 10036, ☎ 800/677–
8585).

CUSTOMS
U.S. CITIZENS
The **U.S. Customs Service** (Box
7407, Washington, DC 20044,
☎ 202/927–6724) can answer
questions on duty-free limits and
publishes a helpful brochure,
"Know Before You Go." For information on registering foreign-
made articles, call 202/927–0540.

CANADIANS
Contact **Revenue Canada** (2265
St. Laurent Blvd. S, Ottawa, On-
tario, K1G 4K3, ☎ 613/993–

0534) for a copy of the free
brochure **"I Declare/Je Déclare"**
and for details on duties that exceed the standard duty-free limit.

U.K. CITIZENS

HM Customs and Excise (Dorset
House, Stamford St., London SE1
9NG, ☎ 0171/202–4227) can answer questions about U.K. customs regulations and publishes
"A Guide for Travellers," detailing
standard procedures and import
rules.

FOR TRAVELERS
WITH DISABILITIES

PUBLICATIONS

An RER and métro access guide is
available from the Paris Transit
Authority (RATP) kiosk (pl. de la
Madeleine, 8e, ☎ 40–46–42–
17). Ask for the free brochure
Touristes Quand Même at the
main tourist office (127 av. des
Champs-Elysées) for detailed
information about wheelchair
accessibility.

EMBASSIES

U.S. Embassy (2 av. Gabriel, 8e,
☎ 42–96–12–02). **Canadian Embassy** (35 av. Montaigne, 8e,
☎ 44–43–29–00). **British Embassy**
(35 rue du Fbg St-Honoré, 8e,
☎ 42–66–91–42).

EMERGENCIES

Police (☎ 17). **Ambulance** (☎ 15
or 45–67–50–50). **Doctor** (☎ 47–
07–77–77). **Dentist** (☎ 43–37–
·51–00).

24-HOUR PHARMACIES

Dhéry (Galerie des Champs, 84 av.
des Champs-Elysées, 8e, ☎ 45–
62–02–41) is open 24 hours.
Drugstore Publicis (corner of blvd.
St-Germain and rue de Rennes,
6e) is open daily until 2 AM. **Phar-
macie des Arts** (106 blvd. Montparnasse, 14e) is open daily until
midnight.

FERRY AND
HOVERCRAFT TRAVEL

DOVER–CALAIS

Ticket prices for ferries vary
widely depending on the number
of passengers in a group, the size
of the car, the season and time of
day, and the length of your trip.
Call one of the ferry service reservation offices for more exact information. **P&O European Ferries**
(Channel House, Channel View
Rd., Dover, Kent CT17 9TJ, ☎
0181/575–8555) has up to 20
sailings a day; the crossing takes
about 75 minutes. **Sealink** (Char-
ter House, Park St., Ashford, Kent
TN24 8EX, ☎ 01233/646801)
operates up to 25 sailings a day;
the crossing takes about 90 minutes. **Hoverspeed** (International
Hoverport, Marine Parade, Dover

CT17 9TG, ☎ 01304/240241)
operates up to 15 crossings a day
by Hovercraft and catamaran. The
crossings take 35 minutes (Hovercraft) or 55 minutes (catamaran).

FOLKESTONE-BOULOGNE
Hoverspeed (*see* Ferry and Hovercraft Travel, *above*) is the sole operator on this route, with six
40-minute crossings a day.

NEWHAVEN-DIEPPE
Sealink has as many as four sailings a day, and the crossing takes
four hours.

PORTSMOUTH-LE HAVRE
P&O European Ferries has up to
three sailings a day, and the crossing takes 5¾ hours by day, 7 by
night.

RAMSGATE-DUNKERQUE
Sally Line (Argyle Centre, York
St., Ramsgate, Kent CT11 9DS,
☎ 01843/595522) has up to six
2½-hour crossings a day.

HEALTH ISSUES

HOSPITALS
The American Hospital (63 bd. Victor Hugo, Neuilly, ☎ 47–45–71–
00) has a 24-hour emergency
service. **The Hertford British Hospital** (3 rue Barbès, Levallois-Perret,
☎ 47–58–13–12) also offers a
24-hour service.

MONEY MATTERS

ATMS
For specific foreign **Cirrus** locations, call 800/424–7787; for for-

eign Plus locations, consult the
Plus directory at your local bank.

CURRENCY EXCHANGE
If your bank doesn't exchange
currency, contact **Thomas Cook
Currency Services** (41 E. 42nd St.,
New York, NY 10017, or 511
Madison Ave., New York, NY
10022, ☎ 212/757–6915 or
800/223–7373 for locations) or
Ruesch International (☎ 800/424–
2923 for locations).

WIRING FUNDS
Funds can be wired via **American
Express MoneyGram℠** (☎ 800/
926–9400 from the U.S. and
Canada for locations and information) or **Western Union** (☎ 800/
325–6000 for agent locations or
to send using MasterCard or Visa,
800/321–2923 in Canada).

PASSPORTS AND VISAS

U.S. CITIZENS
For fees, documentation requirements, and other information, call
the **Office of Passport Services**
information line (☎ 202/647–
0518).

CANADIANS
For fees, documentation requirements, and other information, call
the Ministry of Foreign Affairs
and International Trade's **Passport
Office** (☎ 819/994–3500 or 800/
567–6868).

U.K. CITIZENS
For fees, documentation requirements, and to get an emergency

passport, call the **London passport office** (☎ 0171/271–3000).

PHONE MATTERS

The country code for France is 33. For local access numbers abroad, contact **AT&T** USA Direct (☎ 800/874–4000), **MCI** Call USA (☎ 800/444–4444), or **Sprint** Express (☎ 800/793–1153).

RAIL TRAVEL

Paris has six international rail stations: **Gare du Nord** (northern France, northern Europe, and England via Calais or Boulogne); **Gare St-Lazare** (Normandy, England via Dieppe); **Gare de l'Est** (Strasbourg, Luxembourg, Basle, and central Europe); **Gare de Lyon** (Lyon, Marseille, the Riviera, Geneva, Italy); and **Gare d'Austerlitz** (Loire Valley, southwest France, Spain). Note that Gare Montparnasse has taken over as the main terminus for trains bound for southwest France since the introduction of the new TGV-Atlantique service. You can call for **train information** (☎ 45–82–50–50) from any station and can reserve tickets in any Paris station, irrespective of destination. Go to the Grandes Lignes counter for travel within France and to the Billets Internationaux desk if you're heading out of the country.

British Rail (☎ 071/834–2345) has four daily departures from London's Victoria Station, all linking with the Dover–Calais/Boulogne ferry services

through to Paris. There is also an overnight service on the Newhaven–Dieppe ferry. Journey time is about eight hours. Credit-card bookings are accepted by phone or in person at a British Rail Travel Centre.

TOURS

BIKE TOURS

Paris by Cycle (78 rue Ouest, 14e, ☎ 43–35–28–63) organizes daily bike tours around Paris and its environs (Versailles, Chantilly, and Fontainebleau) for about 200 francs (including lunch and insurance, with an additional 120 francs for bike rental).

BOAT TOURS

Boat trips along the Seine run throughout the day and evening, and many include lunch or dinner. **Bateaux-Mouches** (Pont de l'Alma, 8e, ☎ 42–25–96–10) boats depart from the Pont de l'Alma (Right Bank) 10–noon, 2–7, and 8:30–10:30. The price is 40 francs, 20 francs for children under 14. Lunch is served on the 1 PM boat and costs 300 francs (150 francs children under 12). Dinner on the 8:30 service costs 500 francs (reservations required). Wine and service are included in the lunch and dinner prices.

Bateaux Parisiens–Tour Eiffel (Pont d'Iéna, 7e, ☎ 44–11–33–44) boats depart from the Pont d'Iéna (Left Bank) every half hour in summer and every hour in winter, starting at 10 AM (the last boat leaves at 6 PM). The price is 45 francs during the day (20 francs children under 12). Lunch service costs 300 francs (200 francs children under 12). Dinner cruises on the 8 PM service cost 550 francs. Wine and gratuities are included in the lunch and dinner prices.

ORIENTATION TOURS

The two largest bus tour operators are **Cityrama** (4 pl. des Pyramides, 1er, ☎ 44–55–61–00) and **Paris Vision** (214 rue de Rivoli, 1er, ☎ 42–60–31–25). For a more intimate—albeit expensive—tour of the city, Cityrama also runs several minibus excursions per day.

The **RATP** (Paris Transport Authority, pl. de la Madeleine, 8e, and 53 bis quai des Grands-Augustins, 6e, ☎ 40–46–42–17) has many guide-accompanied excursions in and around Paris. Both its Tourist Service at place de la Madeleine (to the right of the church as you face it) and the office on quai des Grands-Augustins are open daily 9–5.

Other tour companies include **American Express** (11 rue Scribe, 9e, ☎ 47–77–77–07), **Air France** (119 av. des Champs-Elysées, 8e, ☎ 44–08–24–24), and **Wagons-Lits** (32 rue du Quatre-Septembre, 2e, ☎ 42–66–15–80).

PERSONAL GUIDES

Espaces Limousine (18 rue Vignon, 9e, ☎ 42–65–63–16) and **Paris Bus** (16 av. du Château, Vincennes, ☎ 43–65–55–55) have limousines and minibuses (taking up to seven passengers) that will take you around Paris and its environs for a minimum of three hours. Reservations are required. The cost is about 250 francs per hour.

SPECIAL-INTEREST TOURS

Cityrama and **Paris Vision** (*see* Orientation Tours, *above*) offer a variety of thematic tours ("Historic Paris," "Modern Paris," "Paris-by-Night") lasting from 2½ hours to all day and costing between 150 and 300 francs (more if a cabaret show is included).

WALKING TOURS

You can get information on walking tours by contacting the **Caisse Nationale des Monuments Historiques** (Bureau des Visites/Conférences, Hôtel de Sully, 62 rue St-Antoine, 4e, ☎ 44–61–20–00), which publishes a small booklet every two months listing all upcoming tours.

STUDENTS

For a detailed listing of deals for students in Paris, ask for the brochure **"Jeunes á Paris"** from the main tourist office (127 av. des Champs-Elysées, ☎ 49–52–53–54). Also try **Usit Voyages** (12 rue Vivienne, 2e, ☎ 42–96–15–88), a travel agency specializing in youth travel, for current information.

PUBLICATIONS

See the *Berkeley Guide to Paris*
($12; Fodor's Travel Publications,
800/533–6478 or from book-
stores).

VISITOR INFORMATION

IN PARIS

The main **Paris Tourist Office** (127
av. des Champs-Elysées, 75008
Paris, ☎ 49–52–53–54) is open
daily 9–8. There are also offices
at all main train stations, except
Gare St-Lazare. Dial 49–52–53–
56 for recorded information in
English (updated weekly).

IN THE U.S.

For a free packet of information,
call the **French Government Tourist
Office** at 900/990–0040 (50¢ per
minute). Or write one of the
tourist offices at 444 Madison
Ave., 16th Floor, New York, NY
10020; 676 N. Michigan Ave.,
Chicago, IL 60611, ☎ 312/751–
7800; or 9454 Wilshire Blvd.,
Beverly Hills, CA 90212.

IN CANADA

1981 McGill College Ave., Suite
490, Montreal, Québec H3A 2W9,
☎ 514/288–4264; 30 St. Patrick
St., Suite 700, Toronto, Ontario
M5T 3A3, ☎ 416/593–4723.

IN THE U.K.

178 Piccadilly, London W1V 0AL,
☎ 0891/244–123 weekdays 9
AM–10 PM, Sat. 9 AM–5 PM. There
is a charge for this call.

WEATHER

For current weather and forecasts,
plus the local time and helpful
travel tips, call the **Weather Channel Connection** (☎ 900/932–8437;
95¢ per minute) from a touch-
tone phone.

SMART TRAVEL TIPS

Basic Information on Traveling in Paris and Savvy Tips to Make Your Trip a Breeze

AIR TRAVEL

If time is an issue, **always look for nonstop flights,** which require no change of plane and make no stops. If possible, **avoid connecting flights,** which stop at least once and can involve a change of plane, although the flight number remains the same; if the first leg is late, the second waits.

AIRPORT TRANSFERS

CHARLES DE GAULLE (ROISSY)

From the Charles de Gaulle airport, **the easiest way to get into Paris is on the RER-B line,** the suburban express train. A new station was opened right beneath Terminal 2 in 1994. Trains to central Paris (Les Halles, St-Michel, Luxembourg) leave every 15 minutes. The fare (including métro connection) is 44 francs, and journey time is about 30 minutes. Buses operated by Air France run every 15 minutes between Charles de Gaulle airport and the Arc de Triomphe, with a stop at the Air France air terminal at Porte Maillot. The fare is 48 francs, and journey time is about 40 minutes. The Roissybus, operated by the Paris Transit Authority, has buses every 15 minutes to rue Scribe at the Opéra; cost is 35 francs. Rush-hour traffic can make this trip slow and frustrat-

ing. Taxis are readily available. Journey time is around 30 minutes, depending on the traffic, and the fare is around 200 francs. For substantially less, Paris Airports Service will meet you on arrival at either Paris airport and drive you to your destination.

ORLY AIRPORT

There are two simple ways of getting to Paris from Orly by train. The most economical is to **take the free shuttle bus from the terminal to the train station,** where you can pick up the RER-C line, the suburban express train. Trains to Paris leave every 15 minutes. The fare is 40 francs, and journey time is about 28 minutes. Or you can **take the new shuttle-train service, Orlyval,** which runs between the Antony RER-B station and Orly airport every 7 minutes. The fare to downtown Paris is 50 francs. Air France buses run every 12 minutes between Orly airport and the Air France air terminal at Les Invalides on the Left Bank. The fare is 32 francs, and journey time is between 30 and 60 minutes, depending on traffic. The Paris Transit Authority's Orlybus leaves every 15 minutes for the Denfert-Rochereau métro station; cost is 30 francs. Taxis take around 25 minutes in light traffic; the fare will be about 160 francs.

BUS TRAVEL

Travel by bus is a convenient, scenic way to get around the city, although it's slower than the métro. Paris buses are green single-deckers; route number and destination are marked in front and with major stopping-places along the sides. Most routes operate from 6 AM to 8:30 PM; some continue to midnight. Ten *Noctambus,* or night buses, operate hourly (1:30–5:30 AM) between Châtelet and various nearby suburbs; they can be stopped by hailing them at any point on their route. The brown bus shelters, topped by red and yellow circular signs, contain timetables and route maps.

The bus accepts métro tickets, or you can buy a single ticket on board. You need to show (but not punch) weekly, monthly, and *Paris-Visite/Formule 1* (*see* Métro, *below*) tickets to the driver as you get on. If you have individual tickets, you should state your destination and be prepared to punch one or more tickets in the red and gray machines on board the bus.

THE CHANNEL TUNNEL

The Channel Tunnel provides the fastest route across the Channel—25 minutes from Folkestone to Calais, or 60 minutes from motorway to motorway. It consists of two large 50-kilometer-long (31-mile-long) tunnels for trains, one in each direction, linked by a smaller tunnel running between them.

Le Shuttle, a special car, bus, and truck train, operates continuously, with trains departing every 15 minutes at peak times and at least once an hour through the night. No reservations are necessary, although tickets may be purchased in advance from travel agents. Most passengers travel in their own car, staying with the vehicle throughout the "crossing," with progress updates via radio and display screens. Motorcyclists park their bikes in a separate section with its own passenger compartment, while foot passengers must book passage by coach. At press time, prices for a one-day roundtrip ticket began at £107–£154 for a car and its occupants. Prices for a five-day roundtrip ticket began at £115.

Eurostar operates high-speed passenger-only trains, which whisk riders between new stations in Paris (Gare du Nord) and London (Waterloo) in 3 hours and between London and Brussels (Midi) in 3¼ hours. At press time, fares were $154 for a one-way, first-class ticket and $123 for an economy fare.

The Tunnel is reached from exit 11a of the M20/A20. Tickets for either Tunnel service can be purchased in advance (*see* Important Contacts, *above.*)

CUSTOMS AND DUTIES

IN PARIS

If you're coming from outside the European Union, you may import duty free: (1) 200 cigarettes or 100 cigarillos or 50 cigars or 250 grams of tobacco (twice that if you live outside Europe); (2) 2 liters of wine and, in addition, (a) 1 liter of alcohol over 22% volume (most spirits) or (b) 2 liters of alcohol under 22% volume (fortified or sparkling wine) or (c) 2 more liters of table wine; (3) 50 milliliters of perfume and 250 milliliters of toilet water; (4) 200 grams of coffee, 100 grams of tea; and (5) other goods to the value of 300 francs (100 francs for those under 15).

If you're arriving from an EU country, you may be required to declare all goods and prove that anything over the standard limit is for personal consumption. Since January 1993, however, there is no longer any limit or customs tariff imposed on goods carried within the EU.

Any amount of French or foreign currency may be brought into France, but foreign currencies converted into francs may be reconverted into a foreign currency only up to the equivalent of 5,000 francs.

BACK HOME

In the U.S.➤ You may bring home $400 worth of foreign goods duty-free if you've been out of the country for at least 48 hours and haven't already used the $400 exemption, or any part of it, in the past 30 days.

Travelers 21 or older may bring back one liter of alcohol duty-free, provided the beverage laws of the state through which they reenter the United States allow it. In addition, 100 non-Cuban cigars and 200 cigarettes are allowed, regardless of your age. Antiques and works of art more than 100 years old are duty-free.

Duty-free, travelers may mail packages valued at up to $200 to themselves and up to $100 to others, with a limit of one parcel per addressee per day (and no alcohol or tobacco products or perfume valued at more than $5); outside, identify the package as being for personal use or an unsolicited gift, specifying the contents and their retail value. Mailed items do not count as part of your exemption.

In Canada➤ Once per calendar year, when you've been out of Canada for at least seven days, you may bring in C$300 worth of goods duty-free. If you've been away less than seven days but more than 48 hours, the duty-free exemption drops to C$100 but can be claimed any number of times (as can a C$20 duty-free exemption for absences of 24 hours or more). You cannot combine the yearly and 48-hour exemptions, use the C$300 exemption only partially (to save the balance for a later trip), or pool exemptions with family members. Goods claimed under the C$300 exemption may follow you by mail; those claimed under the lesser exemptions must accompany you.

Alcohol and tobacco products may be included in the yearly and 48-hour exemptions but not in the 24-hour exemption. If you meet the age requirements of the province through which you reenter Canada, you may bring in, duty-free, 1.14 liters (40 imperial ounces) of wine or liquor *or* two dozen 12-ounce cans or bottles of beer or ale. If you are 16 or older, you may bring in, duty-free, 200 cigarettes, 50 cigars or cigarillos, and 400 tobacco sticks or 400 grams of manufactured tobacco. Alcohol and tobacco must accompany you on your return.

An unlimited number of gifts valued up to C$60 each may be mailed to Canada duty-free. These do not count as part of your exemption. Label the package "Unsolicited Gift—Value under $60." Alcohol and tobacco are excluded.

IN THE U.K.➤ If your journey was wholly within EU countries, you no longer need to pass through customs when you return to the United Kingdom. If you plan to bring large quantities of alcohol or tobacco, check in advance on EU limits.

DRIVING

There are a number of different driving routes to Paris. The **Dover–Calais route** includes the shortest Channel crossing; the **Newhaven–Dieppe** route requires a longer Channel crossing but a shorter drive through France.

Driving distances from the French ports to Paris are as follows: from Calais, 290 kilometers (180 miles); from Boulogne, 243 kilometers (151 miles); from Dieppe, 193 kilometers (120 miles); from Dunkerque, 257 kilometers (160 miles). The fastest routes to Paris from each port are via the N43, A26, and A1 from Calais; via the N1 from Boulogne; via the N15 from Le Havre; via the D915 and N1 from Dieppe; and via the A25 and A1 from Dunkerque.

INSURANCE

Travel insurance can protect your investment, replace your luggage and its contents, or provide for medical coverage should you fall ill during your trip. Most tour operators, travel agents, and insurance agents sell specialized health-and-accident, flight, trip-cancellation, and luggage insurance as well as comprehensive policies with some or all of these features. Before you make any purchase, **review your existing health and homeowner policies** to find out whether they cover expenses incurred while traveling.

BAGGAGE

Airline liability for your baggage is limited to $1,250 per person on domestic flights. On international flights, the airlines' liability is $9.07 per pound or $20 per kilogram for checked baggage (roughly $640 per 70-pound bag) and $400 per passenger for unchecked baggage. However, this excludes valuable items such as jewelry and cameras that are listed in your ticket's fine print. You can buy additional insurance from the airline at check-in, but first **see if your homeowner's policy covers lost luggage.**

MAIL

Post offices, or PTT, are scattered throughout every arrondissement and are recognizable by a yellow sign. They are usually open weekdays 8 AM–noon and 2:30–7 PM, Saturday 8 AM–noon. The main office, at 52 rue du Louvre in the first arrondissement, is open 24 hours.

RATES

Airmail letters to the United States and Canada cost 4.30 francs for 20 grams, 7.90 francs for 40 grams, and 12.50 francs for 60 grams. Letters to the United Kingdom cost 2.80 francs for up to 20 grams, as they do within France. Postcards cost 2.80 francs within France and EU countries, and 4.30 francs to the United States and Canada. Stamps can be bought in post offices and cafés sporting a red TABAC sign.

RECEIVING MAIL

If you're uncertain where you'll be staying, have mail sent to American Express (if you're a card member) or to Poste Restante at any post office.

MÉTRO

Métro stations are recognizable either by a large yellow *M* within a circle or by the distinctive curly green Art Nouveau railings and archway bearing the full title (Métropolitain). **The métro is the most efficient way to get around Paris** and is so clearly marked at all points that it's easy to find your way without having to ask directions.

There are 13 métro lines crisscrossing Paris and the suburbs, and you are seldom more than 500 yards from the nearest station. It is essential to **know the name of the last station on the line you take,** as this name appears on all signs. A connection (you can make as many as you like on one ticket) is called a *correspondance*. At junction stations, illuminated orange signs bearing the name of the line terminus appear over the correct corridors for each *correspondance*. Illuminated blue signs marked *sortie* indicate the station exit.

The métro service starts at 5:30 AM and continues until 1:15 AM, when the last train on each line reaches its terminus. Some lines and stations in the less salubrious parts of Paris are a bit risky at night, in particular Lines 2 and 13. But in general, the métro is relatively safe throughout, providing you don't walk around with your wallet hanging out of your back pocket and (especially women) **don't travel alone late at night.** The biggest nuisances you're likely to come across will be the wine-swigging *clochards* (tramps) blurting out drunken songs as they bed down on platform benches.

The métro network connects at several points in Paris with the RER (*Réseau Express Régional,* or the Regional Express Network). RER trains, which race across Paris from suburb to suburb, are a sort of supersonic métro and can be great time-savers.

All métro tickets and passes are valid for RER *and* bus travel within Paris. Métro tickets cost 7 francs each; a *carnet* (10 tickets for 41 francs) is a better value. If you're staying for a week or more and plan to use the métro frequently, the best deal is the weekly (*coupon jaune*) or monthly (*carte orange*) ticket, sold according to zone. Zones 1 and 2 cover the entire métro network; tickets cost 63 francs a week or 219 francs a month. If you plan to take suburban trains to visit places in the Ile-de-France, consider a four-zone (Versailles, St-Germain-en-Laye; 113 francs a week) or six-zone (Rambouillet, Fontainebleau; 150 francs a week) ticket. For these weekly/monthly tickets, you will need a pass (available from rail and major métro stations) and a passport-size photograph.

Alternatively, there are one-day (*Formule 1*) and three- and five-day (*Paris Visite*) unlimited travel tickets for the métro, bus, and RER. Their advantage is that, unlike the *coupon jaune,* which is good from Monday morning to Sunday evening, *Formule 1* and *Paris Visite* passes are valid starting any day of the week and also give you discounts on a limited number of museums and tourist attractions. The price is 38 (one-day), 95 (three-day), and 150 (five-day) francs for Paris only; 95, 210, and 285 francs, respectively, for suburbs including Versailles, St-Germain-en-Laye, and Disneyland Paris.

Access to métro and RER platforms is through an automatic ticket barrier. Slide your ticket in and pick it up as it pops out. Be certain to **keep your ticket during your journey;** you'll need it to leave the RER system.

MONEY AND EXPENSES

The unit of currency in France is the franc, which is divided into 100 centimes. The bills are 500, 200, 100, and 50 francs. Coins are 20, 10, 5, 2, and 1 francs and 50, 20, 10, and 5 centimes. At press time (early 1995), the exchange rate was 5.3 francs to the dollar and 8.4 francs to the pound. Inflation in France has continued to average less than a modest annual 3% increase in recent years.

EXCHANGING CURRENCY

For the most favorable rates, **change money at _bureaux de change,_** which charge no commission. Some banks also offer good exchange rates. You won't do as well at exchange booths in airports, rail, and bus stations, nor in hotels, restaurants, and stores, although you may find their hours more convenient. To avoid lines at airport exchange booths, **get a small amount of currency before you leave home.**

COSTS

As in most capital cities, life in Paris is more expensive than anywhere else in the country (except the Riviera). **Avoid the obvious tourist traps** so you will not have to pay extravagant rates. Places where you can be virtually certain to shop, eat, and stay without overpaying include the streets surrounding Montmartre (not the Butte, or hilltop, itself); the St-Michel/Sorbonne area on the Left Bank; the mazelike streets around Les Halles and the Marais in central Paris; and the Bastille area and eastern Paris.

SAMPLE COSTS➤ A cup of coffee, standing at a bar, costs 5 francs; if you sit, it will cost from 10 francs. A glass of beer costs from 8 francs

standing at the bar and from 12 francs if you're seated. A soft drink costs between 7 francs and 14 francs; a ham sandwich between 14 francs and 20 francs. Expect to pay 30–35 francs for a short taxi ride.

TAXES

HOTEL➤ Restaurant and hotel prices must by law include taxes and service charges: If these appear as additional items on your bill, you should complain.

SALES➤ All taxes must be included in affixed prices in France.

VAT➤ Value added tax (known in France as TVA), at a standard rate of 18.6%, is included in the price of many goods, but foreigners are often entitled to a refund.

OPENING AND CLOSING TIMES

Banks are open weekdays, but there's no strict pattern to their hours of business. Generally, they're open from 9:30 to 4:30 or 5. Some banks close for lunch between 12:30 and 2.

Most Paris **museums** close one day a week—usually either Monday or Tuesday—and on national holidays. Usually, they're open from 10 to 5 or 6. A few museums close for lunch (noon–2) and are open Sundays only in the afternoon.

Large **shops** are open from 9 or 9:30 to 6 or 7 and don't close at lunchtime. Smaller shops often open earlier (8 AM) but take a lengthy lunch break (1–3); small food shops are often open Sunday mornings, 9–1. Some corner grocery stores will stay open until about 10 PM. Most shops close all day Sunday, except in the Marais, where shops are closed Monday.

NATIONAL HOLIDAYS

With 11 national holidays (*jours feriés*) and five weeks of paid vacation, the French have their share of repose. In May, there is a holiday nearly every week, so be prepared for stores, banks, and museums to shut their doors for days at a time. Bastille Day (July 14) is observed in true French form, with an annual military parade down the Champs-Elysées and a fireworks display, usually at Trocadéro.

January 1 (New Year's Day); April 8 (Easter Monday); May 1 (Labor Day); May 8 (VE Day); May 16 (Ascension); May 27 (Pentecost Monday); July 14 (Bastille Day); August 15 (Assumption); November 1 (All Saints); November 11 (Armistice); December 25 (Christmas).

PACKING FOR PARIS

Pack light: Although you'll usually have no trouble finding a baggage cart at the airport, luggage restrictions on international flights are tight. What you pack depends more on the time of year than on any particular dress code. It can

rain a fair amount in Paris, even in the summer, so **consider bringing a raincoat and umbrella.** Otherwise, pack as you would for a major American city: formal clothes for formal restaurants and nightclubs, casual clothes elsewhere. Jeans are as popular in Paris as anywhere and are perfectly acceptable for sightseeing and informal dining. However, a jeans-and-sneakers outfit will raise eyebrows at the theater, at expensive restaurants, and when visiting French families.

Wear sturdy walking shoes for sightseeing: Paris is full of cobblestone streets, and many historic buildings are surrounded by gravel paths. To protect yourself against purse snatchers and pickpockets, take a handbag with long straps that you can sling across your body, bandolier-style, with a zippered compartment for your money and passport—French law requires that you carry identification at all times.

Bring an extra pair of eyeglasses or contact lenses in your carry-on luggage, and if you have a health problem, **pack enough medication** to last the trip or have your doctor write a prescription using the drug's generic name, because brand names vary from country to country (you'll then need a prescription from a doctor in the country you're visiting). In case your bags go astray, **don't put prescription drugs or valuables in luggage to be checked.** To avoid problems with customs officials, carry medications in original packaging. Also don't forget the addresses of offices that handle refunds of lost traveler's checks.

ELECTRICITY

To use your U.S.-purchased electric-powered equipment, **bring a converter and an adapter.** The electrical current in Paris is 220 volts, 50 cycles alternating current (AC); wall outlets take two round prongs.

If your appliances are dual voltage, you'll need only an adapter. Hotels sometimes have 110-volt outlets for low-wattage appliances marked "For Shavers Only" near the sink; don't use them for high-wattage appliances like blow-dryers. If your laptop computer is older, carry a converter; new laptops operate equally well on 110 and 220 volts, so you need only an adapter.

LUGGAGE

REGULATIONS➤ Free airline baggage allowances depend on the airline, the route, and the class of your ticket; ask in advance. In general, on domestic flights and on international flights between the United States and foreign destinations, you are entitled to check two bags—neither exceeding 62 inches, or 158 centimeters (length + width + height), or weighing more than 70 pounds (32 kilograms). A third piece may be brought aboard; its total dimen-

sions are generally limited to less than 45 inches (114 centimeters), so it will fit easily under the seat in front of you or in the overhead compartment. In the United States, the Federal Aviation Administration gives airlines broad latitude to limit carry-on allowances and tailor them to different aircraft and operational conditions. Charges for excess, oversize, or overweight pieces vary.

If you are flying between two foreign destinations, note that baggage allowances may be determined not by piece but by weight—generally 88 pounds (40 kilograms) in first class, 66 pounds (30 kilograms) in business class, and 44 pounds (20 kilograms) in economy. If your flight between two cities abroad *connects* with your transatlantic or transpacific flight, the piece method still applies.

SAFEGUARDING YOUR LUGGAGE➤ Before leaving home, **itemize your bags' contents** and their worth, and label them with your name, address, and phone number. (If you use your home address, cover it so that potential thieves can't see it.) Inside your bag, **pack a copy of your itinerary.** At check-in, **make sure that your bag is correctly tagged** with the airport's three-letter destination code. If your bags arrive damaged or not at all, file a written report with the airline before leaving the airport.

PASSPORTS AND VISAS

If you don't already have one, **get a passport.** While traveling, **keep one photocopy of the data page** separate from your wallet and leave another copy with someone at home. If you lose your passport, promptly call the nearest embassy or consulate and the local police; having the data page can speed replacement.

U.S. CITIZENS

All U.S. citizens, even infants, need a valid passport to enter France for stays of up to 90 days. New and renewal application forms are available at any of the 13 U.S. Passport Agency offices and at some post offices and courthouses. Passports are usually mailed within four weeks; allow five weeks or more in spring and summer.

CANADIANS

You need a valid passport to enter France for stays of up to 90 days. Application forms are available at 28 regional passport offices as well as post offices and travel agencies. Whether for a first or a subsequent passport, you must apply in person. Children under 16 may be included on a parent's passport but must have their own to travel alone. Passports are valid for five years and are usually mailed within two to three weeks of application.

U.K. CITIZENS

Citizens of the United Kingdom need a valid passport to enter France for stays of up to 90 days. Applications for new and renewal passports are available from main post offices as well as at the passport offices, located in Belfast, Glasgow, Liverpool, London, Newport, and Peterborough. You may apply in person at all passport offices or by mail to all except the London office. Children under 16 may travel on an accompanying parent's passport. All passports are valid for 10 years. Allow a month for processing.

TAXIS

Paris taxis may not have the charm of their London counterparts—there is no standard vehicle or color—but they're cheaper. Daytime rates (7 AM–7 PM) within Paris are around 2.80 francs per kilometer, and nighttime rates are around 4.50 francs. There is a basic hire charge of 12 francs for all rides, and a 6-franc supplement per piece of luggage. Rates outside the city limits are about 40% higher. Waiting time is charged at roughly 110 francs per hour. **Ask your hotel or restaurant to call for a taxi or go to the nearest taxi station** (you can find one every couple of blocks); cabs with their signs lit can be hailed but are annoyingly difficult to spot. Note that taxis seldom take more than three people at a time. **Tip the driver about 10%.**

TELEPHONES

LOCAL CALLS
The French telephone system is modern and efficient. A local call costs 80 centimes for every three minutes. Call-boxes are plentiful; they're found at post offices and often in cafés.

Most French pay phones are now operated by cards (*télécartes*), which you can buy from post offices and some *tabacs* (the cost is 40 francs for 50 units; 96 francs for 120 units). These cards will save you money and hassle. In cafés you can still find pay phones that operate with 1-, 2-, and 5-franc coins (1 franc for local calls). Lift the receiver, place your coin(s) in the appropriate slots, and dial. Unused coins are returned when you hang up. All French phone numbers have eight digits; a code is required only when calling Paris from outside the city (add 16–1 for Paris) and when calling outside the city from Paris (add 16, then the number).

LONG DISTANCE
Dial 19 and wait for the tone, then dial the country code (1 for the United States and Canada, 44 for the United Kingdom) and the area code (minus any initial 0) and number. Expect to be overcharged if you make calls from your hotel. Approximate daytime rates, per minute, are 7 francs to the United States and Canada; 4 francs to the United Kingdom;

reduced rates, per minute, are 5 francs (2 AM–noon) to the United States and Canada or 6 francs (weekdays 8 PM–2 AM, weekends and public holidays noon–2 AM); and 3 francs to the United Kingdom (before 8 AM and after 9:30 PM).

The international services of AT&T, MCI, and Sprint make calling home relatively convenient and let you avoid hotel surcharges. Typically, you dial a local telephone number to use these services. Before you go, **find out the local access codes** for your destinations.

OPERATORS AND INFORMATION
To find a number within France or to request information, dial 12. For international inquiries, dial 19–33 plus the country code.

TOURS

ORIENTATION TOURS
Bus tours of Paris offer a good introduction to the city, though complaints of dull and confusing narration are not infrequent. Their tours start from the place des Pyramides, across from the Louvre end of the Tuileries Gardens. Tours are generally in double-decker buses with either a live or tape-recorded commentary (English, of course, is available) and last two hours. Expect to pay about 150 francs.

Excursions are also available on minibuses, which have a maximum capacity of eight people and can pick up or drop off at hotels. The cost is 210 francs for a 2-hour tour, 350 francs for 3 hours. Reservations are necessary.

For those who prefer to sightsee at their own pace, **Parisbus,** a red double decker with nine pick-up and drop-off points around Paris, allows you to discover the city's main tourist sites independently. Tours start from Trocadéro at 10:20 AM and depart every 50 minutes until 5. Tickets are good for two days and cost 120 francs for adults, 60 francs for children under 12.

BOAT TRIPS

Boat trips along the Seine, usually lasting about an hour, are a must for the first-time visitor. Many boats have powerful floodlights to illuminate riverbank buildings; on some, you can also lunch or wine and dine—book ahead.

WALKING TOURS

There are plenty of guided tours of specific areas of Paris, often concentrating on a historical or architectural topic—"Restored Mansions of the Marais," "Private Walled Gardens in St-Germain," or "Secret Parts of the Invalides." Tours are often restricted to 30 people and are popular with Parisians as well as tourists. They are accompanied by guides whose enthusiasm and dedication is invariably exemplary, though most are French and may

not be able to communicate their enthusiasm to you in English. These potential linguistic problems are more than outweighed by the chance to see Paris in a new light and to visit buildings and monuments that are not usually open to the public. Charges vary between 40 and 60 francs, depending on fees that may be needed to visit certain buildings. Tours last around two hours and are generally held in the afternoons, starting at 2:30 or 3. Details are published in the weekly magazines *Pariscope* and *L'Officiel des Spectacles* under the heading "Conférences." In most cases, you must simply turn up at the meeting point (usually listed as "RV" or "rendezvous"), but it's best to get there early in case of restriction on numbers. For visits to some private mansions, you may be asked to show identification, so be sure to have your passport with you.

WHEN TO GO

The major tourist season in France stretches from Easter to mid-September, but **Paris has much to offer at every season.** Paris in the early spring can be disappointingly damp; June is delightful, with good weather and plenty of cultural and other attractions. July and August can be sultry and dusty. Moreover, many restaurants, theaters, and small shops close for at least four weeks in summer.

September is ideal. Cultural life revives after the summer break, and sunny weather often continues through the first half of October. The ballet and theater are in full swing in November, but the weather is part wet-and-cold, part bright-and-sunny.

December is dominated by the *fêtes de fin d'année* (end-of-year festivities), with splendid displays in food shops and restaurants and a busy theater, ballet, and opera season into January. February and March are the worst months, weatherwise, but with the coming of Easter, Paris starts looking beautiful again.

CLIMATE

What follow are the average daily maximum and minimum temperatures for Paris.

Climate in Paris

Jan.	43F	6C	May	68F	20C	Sept.	70F	21C
	34	1		49	10		53	12
Feb.	45F	7C	June	73F	23C	Oct.	60F	16C
	34	1		55	13		46	8
Mar.	54F	12C	July	76F	25C	Nov.	50F	10C
	39	4		58	14		40	5
Apr.	60F	16C	Aug.	75F	24C	Dec.	44F	7C
	43	6		58	14		36	2

Paris Arrondissemonts

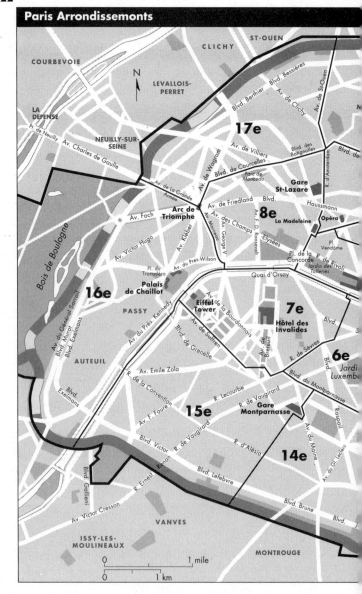

COURBEVOIE

CLICHY

ST-OUEN

LEVALLOIS-PERRET

N

LA DEFENSE

Pt. de Neuilly

Av. Charles de Gaulle

NEUILLY-SUR-SEINE

Blvd. Berthier

Av. de Clichy

Av. de St-Ouen

Blvd. Bessières

17e

Av. de Villiers

Blvd. des Batignolles

Blvd. de

Av. de Wagram

Blvd. de Courcelles

R. d'Amsterdam

Av. de la Grande Armée

Parc de Monceau

Gare St-Lazare

Av. Foch

Arc de Triomphe

Av. de Friedland

Blvd.

Haussmann

Av. Victor Hugo

Av. Kléber

Av. des Champs

Av. Marceau

Av. George V

Av. F. D. Roosevelt

-Elysées

8e

La Madeleine

Opéra

Pl. Vendôme

Bois de Boulogne

Pl. du Trocadéro

Av. du Prés. Wilson

Pl. de la Concorde

R. de Rivoli

Jardin des Tuileries

Quai d'Orsay

Palais de Chaillot

16e

PASSY

Eiffel Tower

Av. de la Bourdonnais

7e

Hôtel des Invalides

Blvd.

Av. du Prés. Kennedy

Av. de Suffren

Blvd. de Grenelle

Av. de Breteuil

R. de Sèvres

6e

Jardi Luxemb

Av. du Général Sarrail

Blvd. Murat

Blvd. Exelmans

AUTEUIL

Av. Emile Zola

R. de la Convention

R. Lecourbe

R. de Vaugirard

Blvd. du Montparnasse

Raspail

Blvd. Exelmans

Av. F. Faure

15e

R. de Vaugirard

Gare Montparnasse

Av. du Maine

Blvd. Galliéni

Blvd. Victor

R. de Vaugirard

R. d'Alésia

14e

R. Ernest Renan

Blvd. Lefebvre

Av. du Gl. Leclerc

Av. Victor Cresson

VANVES

Blvd. Brune

Blvd.

ISSY-LES-MOULINEAUX

MONTROUGE

0 — 1 mile

0 — 1 km

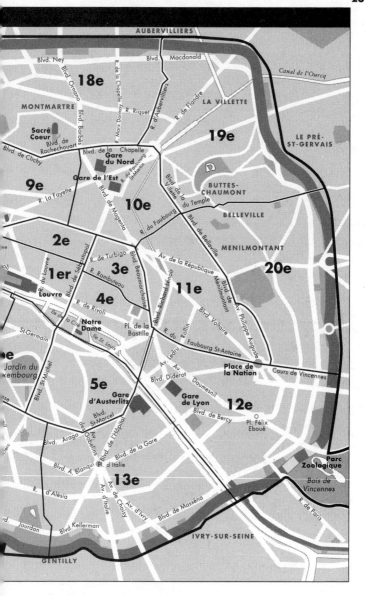

Paris Métro

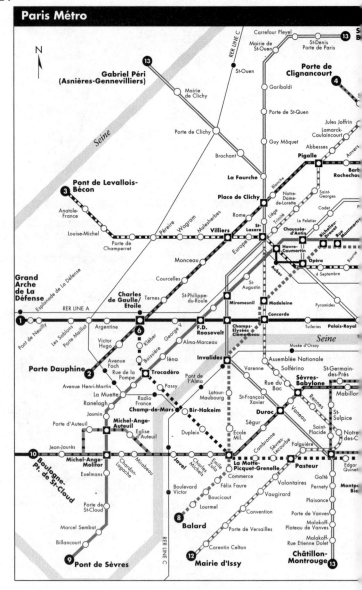

N

Carrefour Pleyel
13
St-Denis
Porte de Paris
Mairie de
St-Ouen
RER LINE C
St-Ouen

Porte de
Clignancourt
4

Gabriel Péri
(Asnières-Gennevilliers)
13

Garibaldi

Mairie
de Clichy

Porte de St-Ouen

Jules Joffrin
Lamarck-
Caulaincourt
Abbesses
Guy Môquet

Porte de Clichy

Brochant
La Fourche
Pigalle
Barbè
Rochechou
Anvers
Blanche

Place de Clichy
Notre-
Dame-
de-Lorette
Saint-
Georges

Pont de Levallois-
Bécon
3

Anatole-
France
Rome
Liège
Trinité
Le Peletier
Cadet
Richelieu-
Drouot
Rue
Montmartr

Louise-Michel
Péreire
Wagram
Malesherbes
Villiers
St-
Lazare
Chaussée-
d'Antin

Porte de
Champerret
Europe
Havre-
Caumartin
Opéra
Bours

Monceau
St-Augustin
Auber
Opéra
4 Septembre

Courcelles
St-Philippe-
du-Roule
Miromesnil
Madeleine
Pyramides

Grand
Arche
de La
Défense
Esplanade de La Défense
Charles
de Gaulle/
Étoile
Ternes
Concorde
RER LINE A
Tuileries
Palais-Royal

1
Pont de Neuilly
Les Sablons
Porte Maillot
Argentine
6
George V
F.D.
Roosevelt
Champs-
Élysées
Clémenceau
Seine

Victor
Hugo
Kléber
Alma-Marceau
Musée d'Orsay

Porte Dauphine
2
Avenue
Foch
Boissière
Iéna
Invalides
Assemblée Nationale
St-Germain-
des-Prés

Rue de la
Pompe
Trocadéro
Varenne
Solférino

Avenue Henri-Martin
Passy
Pont
de
l'Alma
Rue du
Bac
Sèvres-
Babylone
Mabillor

La Muette
Radio
France
St-François
Xavier
Rennes
St-
Sulpice

Ranelagh
Champ-de-Mars
Bir-Hakeim
Latour-
Maubourg
Duroc
Saint-
Placide
Notre
des-C

Jasmin
Michel-Ange-
Auteuil
Ségur
Vaneau

Porte d'Auteuil
Église
d'Auteuil
Dupleix
École
Mil.
Cambronne
Sèvres-
Lecourbe
Falguière

Jean-Jaurès
10
Michel-Ange-
Molitor
Chardon-
Lagache
Mirabeau
Javel
Charles
Michels
La Motte-
Picquet-Grenelle
Pasteur
Edgar
Quinet

Exelmans
Émile
Zola
Commerce
Volontaires
Gaîté
Pernety
Montp
Bie

Porte de
St-Cloud
Boulevard
Victor
Félix Faure
Vaugirard
Plaisance

Boulogne-
Pt. de St-Cloud
Boucicaut
Convention
Porte de Vanves
Malakoff-
Plateau de Vanves

Marcel Sembat
8
Balard
Lourmel
Porte de Versailles
Malakoff-
Rue Etienne Dolet

Billancourt
RER LINE C
Corentin Celton
Châtillon-
Montrouge
13

9
Pont de Sèvres
12
Mairie d'Issy

Seine

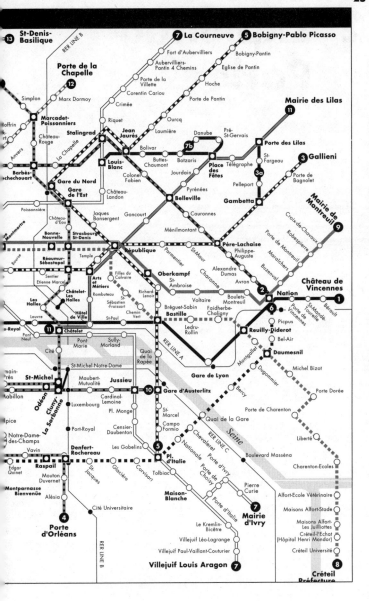

2 Exploring Paris

A **CITY OF VAST,** noble perspectives and winding, hidden streets, Paris remains a combination of the pompous and the intimate. Whether you've come looking for sheer physical beauty, cultural and artistic diversions, world-famous dining and shopping, history, or simply local color, you will find it here in abundance.

Updated by Simon Hewitt

The French capital is also, for the tourist, a practical city: It is relatively small as capitals go, with many of its major sites and museums within walking distance of one another. The city's principal tourist axis is less than four miles long, running parallel to the north bank of the Seine from the Arc de Triomphe to the Bastille. In fact, the best method of getting to know Paris is on foot, although public transportation—particularly the métro subway system—is excellent. Buy a *Plan de Paris* booklet: a city map-guide with a street-name index that also shows métro stations. Note that all métro stations have a detailed neighborhood map just inside the entrance.

Paris owes both its development and much of its visual appeal to the river Seine, which weaves through its heart. Each bank of the Seine has its own personality; the *Rive Droite* (Right Bank), with its spacious boulevards and formal buildings, generally has a more sober and genteel feeling to it than the more carefree and bohemian *Rive Gauche* (Left Bank) to the south. The historical and geographical heart of the city is Notre Dame Cathedral on the Ile de la Cité, the larger of the Seine's two islands (the other is the Ile St-Louis).

Monuments and museums are sometimes closed for lunch, usually between 12 and 2, and one day a week, usually Monday or Tuesday. Check before you set off. And don't forget that cafés in Paris are open all day long. They are a great boon to foot-weary tourists in need of a coffee, a beer, or a sandwich. *Boulangeries* (bakeries) are another reliable source of sustenance.

We've divided our coverage of Paris into six tours, but there are several "musts" that any first-time visitor to Paris should try not to miss: the Eiffel Tower, the Champs-

Elysées, the Louvre, and Notre Dame. It must be said, however, that a visit to Paris will never be quite as simple as a quick look at a few landmarks. Every *quartier* has its own treasures, and travelers should adopt the process of discovery—a very pleasant prospect in this most elegant of French cities.

THE HISTORIC HEART

Numbers in the margin correspond to points of interest on the Historic Heart map.

Of the two islands in the Seine—the Ile St-Louis (*see* The Marais and Ile St-Louis, *below*) and the Ile de la Cité—it is the Ile de la Cité that forms the historic heart of Paris. It was here, for obvious reasons of defense, and in the hope of controlling the trade that passed along the Seine, that the earliest inhabitants of Paris, the Gaulish tribe of the Parisii, settled in about 250 BC. They called their little home Lutetia, meaning "settlement surrounded by water." Whereas the Ile St-Louis is today largely residential, the Ile de la Cité remains deeply historic, the result not just of more than 2,000 years of habitation, but of the fact that this is the site of the most important and one of the most beautiful churches in France—the great brooding cathedral of Notre Dame. Few of the island's other medieval buildings have survived to the present, most having fallen victim to town planner Baron Haussmann's ambitious rebuilding of the city in the mid-19th century. But among the rare survivors are the jewel-like Sainte-Chapelle, a vision of shimmering stained glass, and the Conciergerie, the grim former city prison.

Another major attraction on this tour—the Louvre, recently renovated—came into existence in the mid-13th century, when Philippe-Auguste built it as a fortress to protect the city's western flank. It was not until pleasure-loving François I began a partial rebuilding of this original rude fortress in the early 16th century that today's Louvre began gradually to take shape. A succession of French rulers was responsible for this immense, symmetrical structure, now the largest museum in the world, as well as the easiest to get lost in.

If Notre Dame and the Louvre represent Church and State, respectively, the third major attraction we cover—Les Halles (pronounced *lay al*)—stands for the common man. For centuries, this was Paris's central market, replenished by an army of wagons and later, trucks, which caused astounding traffic jams in the city's already congested streets. The market was closed in 1969 and replaced by a striking shopping mall, the Forum. The surrounding streets have since undergone a transformation, much like the neighboring Marais, with shops, cafés, restaurants, and chic apartment buildings.

Old and new blend and clash in Paris, contrasts that are hard to escape as you follow this tour. The brash modernity of the Forum, for example, stands in contrast to the august church of St-Eustache nearby. The Louvre itself has not been spared controversy: While Louis XIV's harmoniously imposing Cour Carrée, one of the supreme architectural achievements of his reign, has been painstakingly restored and thousands of cobblestones have been laid in place of tarmac, a mixture of awe and outrage has greeted the glass pyramid on the opposite side of the complex. Similarly, the incongruous black-and-white columns in the classical courtyard of Richelieu's neighboring Palais Royal present a further case of architectural vandalism—or daring modernity, depending on your point of view.

Toward the Louvre

The tour begins at the western tip of the Ile de la Cité, at the sedate **Square du Vert Galant.** Nothing is controversial here, not even the statue of the Vert Galant himself, literally the vigorous—by which was really meant the amorous—adventurer, Henri IV, sitting foursquare on his horse. Henri, King of France from 1589 until his assassination in 1610, was something of a dashing figure, by turns ruthless and charming, a stern upholder of the absolute rights of monarchy, and a notorious womanizer. He is probably best remembered for his cynical remark that *Paris vaut bien une messe* ("Paris is worth a mass"), a reference to his readiness to renounce his Protestantism as a condition of gaining the throne of predominantly Catholic France, and

30

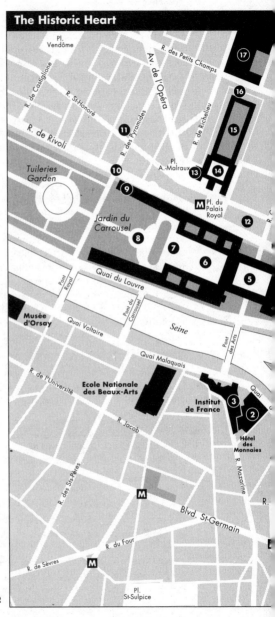

The Historic Heart

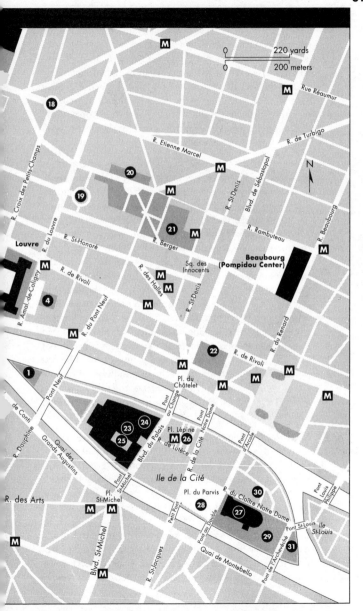

M

0   220 yards
0   200 meters

Rue Réaumur

18

R. Etienne Marcel

R. de Turbigo

M

20

R. St-Denis

Blvd. de Sébastopol

R. Beaubourg

N

19

R. Croix des Petits-Champs

R. du Louvre

R. St-Honoré

21

R. Berger

M

R. Rambuteau

M

**Beaubourg
(Pompidou Center)**

Louvre

M

R. Amal-de-Coligny

R. de Rivoli

4

R. des Halles

Sq. des
Innocents

M

R. St-Denis

R. du Renard

M

R. du Pont Neuf

M

22

R. de Rivoli

M

M

1

Pont Neuf

Pl. du
Châtelet

Pont au Change

Pont Notre Dame

M

M

M

de Conti

R. Dauphine

Quai des
Grands Augustins

23   24

Blvd. du Palais

25

Pl. Lépine

M   26

de Lutèce

R. de la Cité

Pont d'Arcole

Ile de la Cité

Pont Louis Philippe

R. des Arts

Pl.
St-Michel

Pont St-Michel

Petit Pont

Pl. du Parvis

28

R. du Cloître Notre Dame

30

27

29

M

Blvd. St-Michel

Pont au Double

Pont St-Louis   Ile
St-Louis

31

M

M

R. St-Jacques

Quai de Montebello

Pont de l'Archevêché

indeed of being allowed to enter the city. A measure of his canny statesmanship was provided by his enactment of the Edict of Nantes in 1598, by which French Protestants were accorded (almost) equal rights with their Catholic counterparts. It was Louis XIV's renunciation of the Edict nearly 100 years later that led to the massive Huguenot exodus from France, greatly to the economic disadvantage of the country. The square itself is a fine spot to linger on a sunny afternoon. It is also the departure point for the glass-topped *vedette* tour boats on the Seine. *Métro: Pont Neuf.*

Crossing the Ile de la Cité, just behind the Vert Galant, is the oldest bridge in Paris, confusingly called the **Pont Neuf,** or New Bridge. It was completed in the early 17th century and was the first bridge in the city to be built without houses lining either side. Visible to the north of the river is the large-windowed **Samaritaine** department store with its panoramic rooftop café. We, however, are heading along the bridge in the other direction, turning right onto quai de Conti to the

❷ **Hôtel des Monnaies,** the national mint. Louis XVI transferred the Royal Mint to this imposing mansion in the late 18th century. Although the mint was moved to Pessac, near Bordeaux, in 1973, weights and measures, medals, and limited-edition coins are still made here. In June 1988, an enlarged **Musée de la Monnaie** opened so that the vast collection of coins, documents, engravings, and paintings could be displayed. The workshops are on the second floor. *11 quai de Conti.* ☛ *20 frs adults, 15 frs students and senior citizens, under 16 free; Sun. 15 frs adults, under 16 free.* ☉ *Tues., Thurs.–Sun. 1–6, Wed. 1–9. Métro: Pont-Neuf.*

❸ Next door is the **Institut de France.** With its distinctive dome and commanding position over the quai at the foot of the Pont des Arts, it is not only one of France's most revered cultural institutions but also one of the Left Bank's most impressive waterside sights. The **Académie Française,** the oldest of the five academies that comprise the Institut de France, was created by Cardinal Richelieu in 1635. Its first major task was to edit the French dictionary; today, among other functions, it is still charged with safeguarding the purity of the French language. *Guided visits are reserved for cultural associations only. Métro: Pont-Neuf.*

Head across the Seine via the elegant iron-and-wood **Pont des Arts** footbridge, which provides delightful views of the Ile de la Cité, to the newly cleaned facades of the Louvre. But, before entering, turn right onto the Quai du Louvre, left onto the tiny rue de l'Amiral de Coligny, and duck into ❹ the church of **St-Germain l'Auxerrois.** This was the French royal family's Paris church, used by them right up to 1789, in the days before the Revolution, when the Louvre was a palace rather than a museum. The fluid stonework of the facade reveals the influence of 15th-century Flamboyant Gothic, the final, exuberant fling of the Gothic before the classical takeover of the Renaissance. Notice the unusually wide windows in the nave, light flooding through them, and the equally unusual double aisles. *Métro: Louvre-Rivoli.*

The Louvre

The Louvre colonnade across the road from St-Germain l'Auxerrois screens one of Europe's most dazzling court- ❺ yards, the **Cour Carrée,** a monumental, harmonious, and superbly rhythmical ensemble. It has something of the as- sured feel of an Oxford or Cambridge quadrangle, though on a much grander scale. In the **crypt** under it, excavated in 1984, sections of the defensive towers of the original, 13th-century fortress can be seen.

If you saunter through the courtyard and pass under the **Pavillon de l'Horloge**—the Clock Tower—you will come face to face with the Louvre's most controversial develop- ❻ ment, I. M. Pei's notorious **Great Pyramid,** surrounded by three smaller pyramids in the Cour Napoléon. Unveiled in March of 1989, it's more than just a grandiloquent gesture, a desire on the part of President François Mitterrand, who commissioned it, to make his mark on the city. First, the pyramid provides a new, and much needed, entrance to the Louvre; it also houses a large museum shop, café, and restaurant. Second, it acts as the terminal point for the most celebrated city view in Europe, a majestic vista stretching through the Arc du Carrousel, the Tuileries Gardens, across place de la Concorde, up the Champs-Elysées to the tow- ering Arc de Triomphe, and ending at the giant modern arch at La Défense, 2½ miles more to the west.

The pyramids mark only the first phase of the **Grand Louvre project,** a plan for the restoration of the museum launched by Mitterand in 1981, projected to reach a total cost of $1.3 billion by its completion in 1996. In November 1993, exactly 200 years since the Louvre first opened its doors to the public, Mitterand cut the ribbon on the second phase of construction. This included first of all the renovation of the **Richelieu wing** on the north side of the Cour Napoléon. Built between 1852 and 1857 by Napoléon III and grudgingly vacated in 1989 by the Ministry of Finance, the wing was gutted and reconstructed by Pei and his French associates and reopened to house over 12,000 artworks, nearly a third of them brought out from storage. The wing contains principally the Islamic and Mesopotamian art collections, French sculpture and painting, and Napoléon III's sumptuous apartments lovingly restored to their full

❼ ostentatious glory. Second was the opening of the **Carrousel du Louvre,** a subterranean shopping complex centered around an inverted glass pyramid, containing a wide range of stores, a food court, spaces for fashion shows, an auditorium, and a huge parking garage. The third and final phase of the Grand Louvre project is slated to be finished in 1996, a much-needed improvement of lighting and air-conditioning throughout the museum, while on the exterior the remaining facades will be restored and cleaned. In addition, the Tuileries Gardens are being redesigned and a pedestrian bridge built to connect the Louvre with the Musée d'Orsay.

Paintings, drawings, antiquities, sculpture, furniture, coins, jewelry—the quality and the sheer variety are intimidating. The number-one attraction for most is Leonardo da Vinci's enigmatic **Mona Lisa,** "La Joconde" to the French. But there are numerous other works of equal quality. The collections are divided into seven sections: Oriental antiquities, Egýptian antiquities, Greek and Roman antiquities, sculpture, objets d'art, paintings, and prints and drawings. Try to make repeat visits—the Louvre is half-price on Sundays and after 3 PM on other days. Study the plans at the entrance to get your bearings, and pick up a map to take with you. *Palais du Louvre,* ☎ *40–20–53–17 for information.* ☛ *40 frs adults, 20 frs 18–25 years, over 60, after*

3 PM *and Sun.; children under 18 free.* ☉ *Thurs.–Sun. 9–6, Mon. and Wed. 9* AM*–9:45* PM*. Some sections open limited days. Métro: Palais-Royal.*

TIME OUT   The recently opened **Carrousel du Louvre,** the subterranean shopping complex on the west side of the museum, features a mall–style food court with a selection of 13 food counters ranging from brasserie–style to Italian to Chinese food. For something more refined, if you can make it to the Tuileries, stop at **Angelina** (226 rue de Rivoli). Founded in 1903, this elegant salon de thé is famous for its "L'Africain"—a cup of hot chocolate so thick you'll need a fork to eat it (irresistible even in the summer). Non-chocoholics can select from a dizzying assortment of pastries and other goodies.

North of the Louvre

Stretching westward from the main entrance to the Louvre and the Great Pyramid is an expanse of stately, formal gardens. This is the **Jardin des Tuileries** (*see* Toward place de la Concorde, *below*), or Tuileries Gardens, currently undergoing a renovation that will restore the fountains, statues, and shady groves to their condition under Louis-Philippe and Napoléon III by the end of 1996. Leading to them is

❽ the **Arc du Carrousel,** a small relation of the distant Arc de Triomphe and, like its big brother, put up by Napoléon. To the north, in the Pavillon de Marsan, the northernmost wing

❾ of the Louvre, is the **Musée des Arts Décoratifs,** which houses over 50,000 objects charting the course of French furniture and applied arts through the centuries. The Musée de la Publicité, with its collection of 50,000 posters, stages temporary exhibits. *107 rue de Rivoli.* ☛ *16 frs.* ☉ *Wed.–Sat. 12:30–6, Sun. noon–6. Métro: Palais-Royal.*

Running the length of the Louvre's northern side is Napoléon's elegant, arcaded **rue de Rivoli,** a street whose generally dull tourist shops add little to their surroundings.

❿ Cross it and you're in **place des Pyramides** and face-to-face with its gilded statue of Joan of Arc on horseback. The square is a focal point for city tour buses.

11 Walk up rue des Pyramides and take the first left, rue St-Honoré, to the Baroque church of **St-Roch.** The church was begun in 1653 but completed only in the 1730s, the decade of the coolly classical facade. Classical playwright Corneille (1606–1684) is buried here; a commemorative plaque honoring him is located at the left of the entrance. It's worth having a look inside the church to see the bombastically baroque altarpiece in the circular Lady Chapel at the far end.

12 Double back along rue St-Honoré to place du Palais-Royal. On the far side of the square, opposite the Louvre, is the **Louvre des Antiquaires,** a chic shopping mall housing upscale antiques shops. It's a minimuseum in itself. Its stylish, glass-walled corridors deserve a browse whether you intend to buy or not.

13 Walk back through place du Palais Royal to place André-Malraux, with its exuberant fountains. The Opéra building is visible down the avenue of the same name, while, on one corner of the square, at rue de Richelieu, is the **Comédie Française.** This theater is the time-honored setting for performances of classical French drama, with tragedies by Racine and Corneille and comedies by Molière regularly on the bill. The building itself dates from 1790, but the Comédie Française company was created by that most theatrical of French monarchs, Louis XIV, back in 1680. Those who understand French and who have a taste for the mannered, declamatory style of French acting—it's a far cry from method acting—will appreciate an evening here. (*See* Chapter 6, The Arts and Nightlife, for details on how to get tickets.)

14 To the right of the theater is the unobtrusive entrance to the gardens of the **Palais-Royal.** The buildings of this former palace—royal only in that all-powerful Cardinal Richelieu (1585–1642) magnanimously bequeathed them to Louis XIII—date from the 1630s. In his early days as king, Louis XIV preferred the relative intimacy of the Palais-Royal to the intimidating splendor of the Louvre. He soon decided, though, that his own intimidating splendor warranted a more majestic setting; hence, of course, that final word in un-intimacy, Versailles.

Today, the Palais-Royal is home to the French Ministry of Culture and is not open to the public. But don't miss the
⑮ **Jardin du Palais-Royal,** gardens bordered by arcades harboring discreet boutiques and divided by rows of perfectly trimmed little trees. They are a surprisingly little-known oasis in the heart of the city. It's hard to imagine anywhere more delightful for dozing in the afternoon sun. As you walk into the gardens, there's not much chance that you'll miss the black-and-white striped columns in the courtyard or the revolving silver spheres that slither around in the two fountains at either end, the controversial work of architect Daniel Buren. Walk up to the end, away from the main palace, and peek into the opulent, Belle Epoque, glass-lined interior of
⑯ **Le Grand Véfour.** This is more than just one of the swankiest restaurants in the city; it's probably the most sumptuously appointed, too (*see* Chapter 4, Dining).

Just north of here, on rue de Richelieu, stands France's na-
⑰ tional library, the **Bibliothèque Nationale.** It contains more than 7 million printed volumes. A copy of every book and periodical printed in France must, by law, be sent here. Visitors can admire Robert de Cotte's 18th-century courtyard and peep into the 19th-century reading room. The library galleries stage exhibits from time to time from the collections. *58 rue de Richelieu.* ☉ *Daily 9–8. Métro: Bourse.*

From the library, walk southeast along rue des Petits-
⑱ Champs to the circular **place des Victoires.** It was laid out in 1685 by Mansart, a leading proponent of 17th-century French classicism, in honor of the military victories of Louis XIV, that indefatigible warrior whose near-continuous battles may have brought much prestige to his country but came perilously close to bringing it to bankruptcy, too. Louis is shown prancing on a plunging steed in the center of the square; it's a copy, put up in 1822 to replace the original one destroyed in the Revolution. You'll find some of the city's most upscale fashion shops here and on the surrounding streets.

Head south down rue Croix des Petits-Champs. You'll pass the undistinguished bulk of the Banque de France on your right. The second street on the left leads to the circular, 18th-
⑲ century **Bourse du Commerce,** or Commercial Exchange.

Alongside it is a 100-foot-high fluted column, all that remains of a mansion built here in 1572 for Catherine de Médicis. The column is said to have been used as a platform for stargazing by Catherine's astrologer, Ruggieri.

20 You don't need to scale Ruggieri's column to be able to spot the bulky outline of the church of **St-Eustache,** away to the northeast. Since the demolition of the 19th-century iron and glass market halls at the beginning of the '70s, an act that has since come to be seen as little short of vandalism, St-Eustache has reemerged as a dominant element on the central Paris skyline. It is a huge church, the "cathedral" of Les Halles, built as the market people's Right Bank reply to Notre Dame on the Ile de la Cité. St-Eustache dates from a couple of hundred years later than Notre Dame. With the exception of the feeble west front, added between 1754 and 1788, construction lasted from 1532 to 1637, spanning the twilight of Gothic and the rise of the Renaissance. *2 rue du Jour,* ☎ *46–27–89–21 for concert information.* ☉ *Daily. Métro: Les Halles.*

21 The once-grimy facades of the buildings facing Les Halles have been expensively spruced up to reflect the mood of the shiny **Forum des Halles,** the multilevel mall. Just how long the plastic, concrete, glass, and mock-marble of this gaudy mall will stay shiny is anyone's guess. Much of the complex is already showing signs of wear and tear, a state of affairs not much helped by the hordes of down-and-outs who invade it toward dusk. Nonetheless, the multitude of shops gathered at the Forum makes it somewhere no serious shopper will want to miss. The sweeping white staircase and glass reflections of the central courtyard have a certain photogenic appeal.

Leave by square des Innocents to the southeast; its 16th-century Renaissance fountain has recently been restored. As you make your way toward boulevard de Sébastopol, you can see the futuristic funnels of Beaubourg jutting above the surrounding buildings (*see* The Marais and Ile St-Louis, *below*). Head south, toward the Seine. Just before you reach place du Châtelet on the river, you'll see the

22 **Tour St-Jacques** to your left. This richly worked, 170-foot stump, now used for meteorological purposes and not open to the public, is all that remains of a 16th-century church destroyed in 1797. *Métro: Châtelet.*

The Ile de la Cité

From place du Châtelet, cross back over the Seine on the Pont au Change to the Ile de la Cité. To your right looms
㉓ the imposing **Palais de Justice,** the Law Courts, built by Baron Haussmann in his characteristically weighty classical style about 1860. You can wander around the building, watching the bustle of the lawyers, or attend a court hearing. But the real interest here is the medieval part of the complex, spared by Haussmann in his otherwise wholesale destruction of the lesser medieval buildings of the Ile de la Cité. There are two buildings you'll want to see: the Conciergerie and the Sainte-Chapelle. *Métro: Cité.*

㉔ The **Conciergerie,** the northernmost part of the complex, was originally part of the royal palace on the island. Most people know it, however, as a prison, the grim place of confinement for Danton, Robespierre, and, most famously, Marie Antoinette during the French Revolution. From here, all three, and countless others who fell foul of the Revolutionary leaders, were taken off to place de la Concorde and the guillotine. Inside, you'll see the guardroom, complete with hefty Gothic vaulting and intricately carved columns, and the Salle des Gens d'Armes, an even more striking example of Gothic monumentality. From there, a short corridor leads to the kitchen, with its four vast fireplaces. Those with a yen to throw a really memorable party can rent the room. The cells, including that in which Marie Antoinette was held, and the chapel, where objects connected with the ill-fated queen are displayed, complete the tour.
☛ *26 frs adults, 17 frs students and senior citizens. Joint ticket with Sainte-Chapelle: 40 frs.* ☉ *Daily 9:30–6:30; winter, daily 10–4:30.*

The other perennial crowd puller in the Palais de Justice is
㉕ the **Sainte-Chapelle,** the Holy Chapel. It was built by the genial and pious Louis IX (1226–1270), whose good works ensured his subsequent canonization. He constructed it to house what he took to be the Crown of Thorns from Christ's crucifixion and fragments of the True Cross, all of

which he had bought from the impoverished Emperor Baldwin of Constantinople at phenomenal expense. Architecturally, for all its delicate and ornate exterior decoration—notice the open latticework of the pencil-like *flèche,* or spire, on the roof—the design of the building is simplicity itself. In essence, it's no more than a thin, rectangular box, much taller than it is wide. But think of it first and foremost as an oversize reliquary, an ornate medieval casket designed to house holy relics.

The building is actually two chapels in one. The plainer, first-floor chapel, made gloomy by insensitive mid-19th-century restorations (which could do with restoration themselves), was for servants and lowly members of the court. The upper chapel, infinitely more spectacular, was for the king and more important members of the court. This is what you come to see. You reach it up a dark spiral staircase. Here, again, some clumsy 19th-century work has added a deadening touch, but the glory of the chapel—the stained glass—is spectacularly intact. The chapel is airy and diaphanous, the walls glowing and sparkling as light plays on the windows. Notice how the walls, in fact, consist of at least twice as much glass as masonry: The entire aim of the architects was to provide the maximum amount of window space. The Sainte-Chapelle is one of the supreme achievements of the Middle Ages and will be a highlight of your visit to Paris. Come early in the day to avoid the dutiful crowds that trudge around it. Better still, try to attend one of the regular, candle-lit concerts given here. ☎ *43–54–30–09 for concert information.* ☛ *26 frs adults, 17 frs students and senior citizens. Joint ticket with Conciergerie: 40 frs.* ⊙ *Daily 9:30–6:30; winter, daily 10–6. Métro: Cité.*

㉖ Take rue de Lutèce opposite the Palais de Justice down to place Louis Lépine and the bustling **Marché aux Fleurs,** the flower market. There's an astoundingly wide range of flowers on sale and, on Sundays, there are birds, too—everything from sparrows to swans. ⊙ *Daily 9–7. Métro: Cité.*

Notre Dame

Around the corner, looming above the large, traffic-free place du Parvis (*kilometre zéro* to the French, the spot from which all distances to and from the city are officially measured), is the most enduring symbol of Paris, its historic and

㉗ geographic heart, the **Cathédrale Notre Dame.** The building was started in 1163, with an army of stonemasons, carpenters, and sculptors working on a site that had previously seen a Roman temple, an early Christian basilica, and a Romanesque church. The chancel and altar were consecrated in 1182, but the magnificent sculptures surrounding the main doors were not put into position until 1240. The north tower was finished 10 years later. Full-scale restoration started in the middle of the century, the most conspicuous result of which was the construction of the spire, the *flèche,* over the roof. It was then, too, that Haussmann demolished the warren of little buildings in front of the cathedral, creating the place du Parvis. ☛ *Free. Métro: Cité.*

㉘ The **Crypte Archéologique,** the archaeological museum under the square, contains remains unearthed during excavations here in the 1960s. Slides and models detail the history of the Ile de la Cité. The foundations of the 3rd-century Gallo-Roman rampart and of the 6th-century Merovingian church can also be seen. *Place du Parvis.* ☛ *26 frs adults (40 frs including tower of Notre Dame), 17 frs ages 18–24 and over 60, 6 frs ages 7–17.* ☉ *Daily 10–6:30; winter, daily 10–5. Métro: Cité.*

Visit the Place du Parvis early in the morning, when the cathedral is at its lightest and least crowded. You come first to the massive, 12th-century columns supporting the twin towers. Look down the nave to the transepts—the arms of the church—where, at the south (right) entrance to the chancel, you'll glimpse the haunting, 12th-century statue of Notre Dame de Paris, Our Lady of Paris. The chancel itself owes parts of its decoration to a vow taken by Louis XIII in 1638. Still without an heir after 23 years of marriage, he promised to dedicate the entire country to the Virgin Mary if his queen produced a son. When the longed-for event came to pass, Louis set about redecorating the chancel and choir.

On the south side of the chancel is the **Treasury,** with a collection of garments, reliquaries, and silver and gold plate.

☛ *15 frs adults, 10 frs students and senior citizens, 5 frs children.* ☉ *Weekdays 9:30–6.*

The 387-step climb to the top of the **towers** is worth the effort for a close-up of the famous gargoyles—most of them added in the 19th century—and the expansive view over the city. *Entrance via north tower.* ☛ *31 frs adults, 20 frs students and senior citizens.* ☉ *Daily 9:30–12:15 and 2–6; winter, daily 10–5.*

㉙ On the subject of views, no visit to Notre Dame is complete without a walk behind the cathedral to **Square Jean XXIII,** located between the river and the building. It offers a breathtaking sight of the east end of the cathedral, ringed by flying buttresses, surmounted by the spire. From here, the building seems to float above the Seine like some vast, stone ship.

㉚ If your interest in the cathedral is not yet sated, duck into the **Musée Notre Dame.** It displays paintings, engravings, medallions, and other objects and documents, all of which trace the cathedral's history. *10 rue du Cloître-Notre-Dame.* ☛ *12 frs adults, 6 frs students and senior citizens, 4 frs children under 14.* ☉ *Wed. and weekends 2:30–6. Métro: Cité.*

㉛ There's a final pilgrimage you may like to make on the Ile de la Cité to the **Mémorial de la Déportation,** at square de l'Ile-de-France, on the eastern tip of the island. Here, in what was once the city morgue, you'll find the modern crypt, dedicated to those French men and women who died in Nazi concentration camps. You may wish to visit the quiet garden above it. ☛ *Free.* ☉ *Daily 9–6; winter, daily 9–dusk.*

THE MARAIS AND ILE ST-LOUIS

Numbers in the margin correspond to points of interest on the Marais and Ile St-Louis map.

This tour includes two of the oldest and most historic neighborhoods in Paris: the Marais—once a marshy area north of the Seine, today about the most sought-after residential and business district of the city—and the Ile St-Louis, the smaller of the two islands in the Seine. It also includes a side trip to the Bastille, site of the infamous prison stormed on July 14, 1789, an event that came to symbolize the beginning of the French Revolution. Largely in commemoration of the bicentennial of the Revolution in 1989, the Bastille area has been renovated.

Renovation is one of the key notes of this tour, especially around the Marais; the word *marais,* incidentally, means marsh or swamp. Well into the '70s, this was one of the city's poorest areas, filled with dilapidated tenement buildings and squalid courtyards. Today, most of the Marais's spectacular *hôtels particuliers*—loosely, "mansions," onetime residences of aristocratic families—have been restored and transformed into museums. Even the formerly run-down streets of the Jewish quarter, around the rue des Rosiers, are showing signs of gentrification with the displacement of kosher butchers and family storefronts by trendy clothing boutiques and cafés. The area's regeneration was sparked by the building of Beaubourg, arguably Europe's most vibrant—and architecturally whimsical—cultural center. The gracious architecture of the 17th and early 18th centuries, however, sets the tone for the rest of the Marais. Try to visit during the Festival du Marais, held every June and July, when concerts, theater, and ballet are performed.

Hôtel de Ville to Beaubourg

❶ Begin your tour at the **Hôtel de Ville,** the city hall, overlooking the Seine. In the Commune of 1871, the Hôtel de Ville was burned to the ground. Today's exuberant building, based closely on the Renaissance original, went up between 1874 and 1884. In 1944, following the liberation of Paris from Nazi rule, General de Gaulle took over the leadership of France here. *Métro: Hôtel-de-Ville.*

From the Hôtel de Ville, head north across rue de Rivoli and up rue du Temple. On your right, you'll pass one of
❷ the city's most popular department stores, the **Bazar de l'Hôtel de Ville,** or BHV, as it's known locally. The first street on your left, rue de la Verrerie, will take you down to rue
❸ St-Martin and the church of **St-Merri,** an ornate mid-16th-century structure. Its dark late-Gothic–style interior can be fun to explore, though it contains nothing of outstanding

44

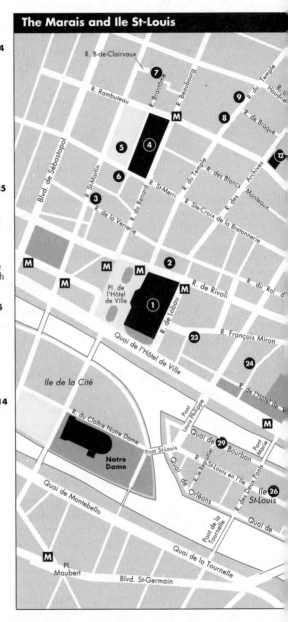

The Marais and Ile St-Louis

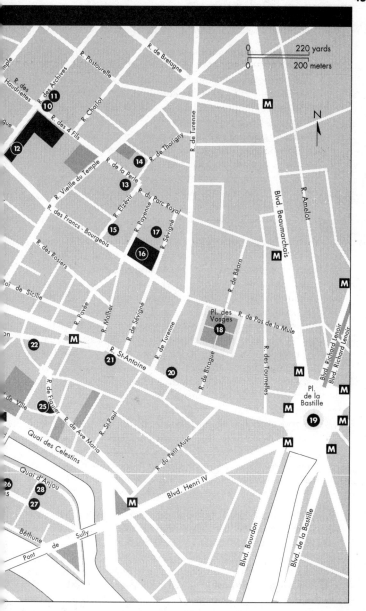

R. de Bretagne

0 ___ 220 yards
0 ___ 200 meters

R. Pastourelle

mple

R. des Archives

R. des Haudriettes

11
10

R. Charlot

que

R. des 4 Fils

M

12

R. de Turenne

N

R. Vieille du Temple

R. de la Perle

R. de Thorigny

14

Blvd. Beaumarchais

R. Amelot

13

R. Elzévir

R. du Parc Royal

R. des Francs - Bourgeois

R. Payenne

R. de Sévigné

15

17

16

R. des Rosiers

M

R. de Béarn

Roi de Sicile

R. Pavée

R. Malher

R. de Sévigné

R. de Turenne

Pl. des Vosges

R. de Pas de la Mule

18

on

22

M

R. de Birague

Blvd. Richard Lenoir
Blvd. Richard Lenoir

R. des Tournelles

R. St-Antoine

21

20

M

M

M

Pl. de la Bastille

19

M

R. de Ville

R. de Figuier

25

R. de Ave Maria

R. St-Paul

R. du Petit Musc

M

M

Quai des Celestins

M

26
s

Quai d'Anjou

28

27

Blvd. Henri IV

Béthune   de   Sully

Pont

Blvd. Bourdon

Blvd. de la Bastille

interest. You may find the upscale stores, restaurants, and galleries of rue St-Martin more diverting.

4 The **Beaubourg/Pompidou Center** or, to give it its full name, the Centre National d'Art et de Culture Georges-Pompidou (known to Parisians simply as Beaubourg), is next. Georges Pompidou (1911–1974) was the president of France who inaugurated the project. If nothing else, Beaubourg is an exuberant melting pot of culture, which casts its net far and wide: Anything goes here. The center hosts an innovative and challenging series of exhibits, in addition to housing the largest collection of modern art in the world. Unveiled in 1977, Beaubourg is by far the most popular museum in the world, attracting upward of 8 million visitors a year; but it has begun to show its age in no uncertain terms.

5 You'll approach the center across **plateau Beaubourg,** a substantial square that slopes gently down toward the main entrance. In summer, it's thronged with musicians, mime artists, dancers, fire-eaters, acrobats, and other performers. Probably the single most popular thing to do at Beaubourg is to ride the escalator up to the roof, with the Parisian skyline unfolding as you are carried through its clear plastic piping. There is a sizable restaurant and café on the roof. The major highlight inside is the modern art museum (Musée National d'Art Moderne) on the fourth floor. The emphasis is largely on French artists; American painters and sculptors are conspicuous by their absence. Movie buffs will want to take in the cinémathèque, a movie theater showing near-continuous programs of classic films from the world over. *Plateau Beaubourg,* ☎ *42–77–12–33.* ☛ *Plateau Beaubourg free. Art museum: 30 frs, 20–30 frs for special exhibitions.* ☉ *Wed.–Mon. noon–10 PM, weekends 10 AM–10 PM; closed Tues. Guided tours in English weekdays 3:30, weekends 11 during summer and Christmas seasons only. Métro: Rambuteau.*

On the right side of Beaubourg (as you're facing it) is a large digital clock, dubbed the "Genitron." Inaugurated by President François Mitterrand in 1987, it counts down the seconds to the year 2000 at what seems like an apocalyptic pace. From here you can turn right into the café-lined **6** **square Igor Stravinsky,** backed by the church of St-Merri—

you'll delight in the lively, eponymous fountain animated by the colorful and imaginative sculptures of French artist Niki de Saint-Phalle, together with the aquatic mechanisms of Jean Tinguely.

You'll see the more obvious of the area's historical highlights if you take rue Rambuteau, which runs along the north side of Beaubourg (to your left as you face the building). **7** The **Quartier de l'Horloge,** the Clock Quarter, opens off the plateau here. An entire city block has been rebuilt, and, though its shops and cafés make a brave attempt to bring it to life, it retains a resolutely artificial quality. The mechanical clock around the corner on rue Bernard de Clairvaux will amuse kids, however.

Around the Marais

You are now poised to plunge into the elegant heart of the Marais. You won't be able to get into many of the historic homes here—the private hôtels particuliers—but this won't stop you from admiring their stately facades. And don't be afraid to push through the heavy formal doors—or *portes cochères*—to glimpse the discreet courtyards that lurk behind them.

From the Clock Quarter, continue down rue Rambuteau **8** and take a left at rue du Temple, to the **Hôtel de Saint-Aignan** at No. 71, built in 1640. At press time it was undergoing restoration, with plans to reopen in 1996 as the Museum of Jewish Art & History. A few doors up, at No. **9** 79, is the **Hôtel de Montmor,** dating from the same period. It was once the scene of an influential literary salon—a part-social and part-literary group—that met here on an impromptu basis and included the philosopher Descartes (1596–1650) and the playwright Molière (1622–1673). Note the huge windows and intricate ironwork on the second-floor balcony.

10 Head east on rue des Haudriettes to the little-known **Musée de la Chasse et de la Nature,** housed in one of the Marais's most stately mansions, the Hôtel de Guénégaud. The collections include a series of immense 17th- and 18th-century pictures of dead animals, artfully arranged, as well as a wide variety of guns and stuffed animals. *60 rue des Archives,* ☎ *42–72–86–43.* ☛ *25 frs adults, 5 frs under 16.* ☉ *Wed.–Mon. 10–12:30 and 1:30–5:30. Métro: Rambuteau.*

Next door, at 58 rue des Archives, two fairytale towers stand ⑪ on either side of the Gothic entrance (1380) to the **Hôtel de Clisson.** In the mid-15th century this was the Paris base of the Duke of Bedford, regent of France after Henry V's demise, during the English occupation of Paris, a phase of the Hundred Years War that lasted from 1420 to 1435. At the end of the 17th century, it was bought by the glamorous princess of Soubise, a grande dame of Parisian literary society. She later moved into the neighboring Hôtel de Soubise, now the **Archives Nationales.** Its collections today form part ⑫ of the **Musée de l'Histoire de France,** whose entrance is at the far end of the courtyard. *60 rue des Francs-Bourgeois,* ☎ *40–27–62–18.* ☛ *15 frs adults, under 18 free.* ☉ *Wed.–Mon. 1:45–5:45. Métro: Rambuteau.*

Continue east on rue des Francs-Bourgeois past the Crédit Municipal (the city's official, grandiose pawnbroking concern), the Domarais restaurant (housed in a circular 18th-century chamber originally used for auctions), and the church Notre-Dame des Blancs-Manteaux, with its superb inlaid pulpit. Turn left onto rue Vieille du Temple and pass the Hôtel de Rohan (on your left, on the corner), built for the archbishop of Strasbourg in 1705. Turn right onto rue ⑬ de la Perle and walk down to the **Musée de la Serrure,** the Lock Museum. It's sometimes also called the **Musée Bricard,** a name you'll recognize on many French locks and keys. The sumptuous building in which the collections are housed is perhaps more interesting than the assembled locks and keys within; it was built in 1685 by Bruand, the architect of Les Invalides (*see* From Orsay to Trocadéro, *below*). But those with a taste for fine craftsmanship will appreciate the intricacy and ingenuity of many of the older locks. One represents an early security system—it would shoot anyone who tried to open it with the wrong key. *1 rue de la Perle,* ☎ *42–77–79–62.* ☛ *20 frs adults, under 18 free.* ☉ *Weekdays 2–5; closed weekends.*

From here it is but a step to the Hôtel Salé, today the
(14) Musée Picasso, opened in the fall of 1985 and so far showing no signs of losing its immense popularity. What's no-
table about the collection—other than the fact that it's the
largest collection of works by Picasso in the world—is that
these were works that Picasso himself owned; works, in other
words, that he especially valued. There are pictures from
every period of his life, adding up to a grand total of 230
paintings, 1,500 drawings, and nearly 1,700 prints, as well
as works by Cézanne, Miró, Renoir, Braque, Degas, Matisse, and others. If you have any serious interest in Picasso,
this is not a place you'd want to miss. The palatial surroundings of the Hôtel Salé add greatly to the pleasures of
a visit. *5 rue de Thorigny,* ☎ *42–71–25–21.* ☛ *26 frs adults,
17 frs 18–25, under 18 free; Sun. 17 frs for everyone.* ☺
Thurs.–Mon. 9:30–6. Métro: St-Sébastien.

Head back down rue de Thorigny and cross to rue Elzévir,
(15) opposite. Halfway down on the left is the **Musée Cognacq-
Jay,** opened here in 1990 after being transferred from its
original home on boulevard des Capucines near the Opéra.
The museum is devoted to the arts of the 18th century and
contains outstanding furniture, porcelain, and paintings (notably by Watteau, Boucher, and Tiepolo). *8 rue Elzévir,*
☎ *40–27–07–21.* ☛ *17 frs adults, 9 frs students and senior citizens.* ☺ *Tues.–Sun. 10–5:30. Métro: St-Paul.*

Continue down rue Elzévir to **rue des Francs-Bourgeois.** Its
name—Street of the Free Citizens—comes from the homes
for the poor, or almshouses, built here in the 14th century,
whose inhabitants were so impoverished that they were allowed to be "free" of taxes. In marked contrast to the
(16) street's earlier poverty, the substantial **Hôtel Carnavalet**
became the scene, in the late 17th century, of the most brilliant salon in Paris, presided over by Madame de Sévigné.
She is best known for the hundreds of letters she wrote to
her daughter during her life; they've become one of the most
enduring chronicles of French high society in the 17th century, and the Carnavalet was her home for the last 20 years
of her life. In 1880, the hotel was transformed into the **Musée
Carnavalet,** or Musée Historique de la Ville de Paris. As
part of the mammoth celebrations for the bicentennial of
the French Revolution, in July 1989, the museum annexed

⑰ the neighboring **Hôtel Peletier St-Fargeau.** Together the two museums chronicle the entire history of the city of Paris, with material dating from the city's origins until 1789 housed in the Hôtel Carnavalet, and objects from that time to the present in the Hôtel Peletier St-Fargeau. *23 rue de Sévigné,* ☎ *42–72–21–13.* ☛ *27 frs adults, 19 frs students and senior citizens.* ⊙ *Tues.–Sun. 10–5:30. Métro: St-Paul.*

Now walk a minute or two farther along rue des Francs-
⑱ Bourgeois to **place des Vosges.** Place des Vosges, or place Royale as it was originally known, is the oldest square in Paris. Laid out by Henri IV at the beginning of the 17th century, it is the model on which all later city squares are based. The combination of symmetrical town houses and the trim green square, bisected in the center by gravel paths and edged with plane trees, makes place des Vosges one of the more pleasant places to spend a hot summer's afternoon in the city.

You can tour the **Maison de Victor Hugo** at No. 6, where the French author lived between 1832 and 1848. The collections here may appeal only to those with a specialized knowledge of the workaholic French writer. ☛ *15 frs adults, 6.50 frs students.* ⊙ *Tues.–Sun. 10–5:40. Métro: Chemin-Vert.*

Around the Bastille

From place des Vosges, follow rue de Pas de la Mule and turn right down boulevard Beaumarchais until you reach
⑲ **place de la Bastille,** site of the infamous prison destroyed at the beginning of the French Revolution. Until 1988, there was little more to see here than a huge traffic circle and the **Colonne de Juillet,** the July Column. As part of the country-wide celebrations for July 1989, the bicentennial of the French Revolution, the **Opéra de la Bastille** (opera house) was erected on the south side of the square. Designed by Argentinian-born Carlos Ott, it seats more than 3,000 and boasts five moving stages. This ambitious project has inspired substantial redevelopment on the surrounding streets, especially along rue de Lappe—once a haunt of Edith Piaf—and rue de la Roquette.

The Bastille, or, more properly, the Bastille St-Antoine, was a massive building, protected by eight immense towers and a wide moat (its ground plan is marked by paving stones set into the modern square). It was built by Charles V in the late 14th century. He intended it not as a prison but as a fortress to guard the eastern entrance to the city. By the reign of Louis XIII (1610–1643), however, the Bastille was used almost exclusively to house political prisoners. Voltaire, the Marquis de Sade, and the mysterious Man in the Iron Mask were all incarcerated here, along with many other unfortunates. It was this obviously political role—specifically, the fact that the prisoners were nearly always held by order of the king—that led the "furious mob" (in all probability no more than a largely unarmed rabble) to break into the prison on July 14, 1789, and kill the governor, steal what firearms they could find, and free the seven remaining prisoners.

Toward the Ile St-Louis

There's more of the Marais to be visited between place de la Bastille and the Ile St-Louis, the last leg of this tour. Take ❷⓿ wide rue St-Antoine to the **Hôtel de Sully,** site of the **Caisse Nationale des Monuments Historiques,** the principal office for the administration of French historic monuments. Guided visits to sites and buildings all across the city begin here, though all are conducted in French. Still, it's worth stopping here to look at the stately, 17th-century courtyard with its richly carved windows and lavish ornamentation. The bookshop just inside the gate has a wide range of publications on Paris, many of them in English (open daily 10–12:45 and 1:45–6). You can also wander around the gardens. *Métro: St-Paul.*

Those with a fondness for the Baroque should duck into ❷❶ the early 17th-century church of **St-Paul-St-Louis,** a few blocks west on rue St-Antoine. Its abundant decoration, which would be easier to appreciate if the church were cleaned, is typical of the Baroque taste for opulent detail.

❷❷ The **Hôtel de Beauvais,** on rue François Miron, is a Renaissance-era hôtel particulier dating from 1655. It was built for one Pierre de Beauvais and financed largely by a series of discreet payments from the king, Louis XIV. These surprisingly generous payments—the Sun King was normally parsimonious toward courtiers—were de Beauvais's reward for having turned a blind eye to the activities of his wife, Catherine-Henriette Bellier, in educating the young monarch in matters sexual. Louis, who came to the throne in 1643 at the age of 4, was 14 at the time Catherine-Henriette gave him the benefit of her wide experience; she was 40.

Continue down rue François Miron. Just before the Hôtel
㉓ de Ville is the site of one of the first churches in Paris, **St-Gervais-St-Protais,** named after two Roman soldiers martyred by the Emperor Nero in the 1st century AD. The original church—no trace remains of it now—was built in the 7th century. The present church, a riot of Flamboyant-style decoration, went up between 1494 and 1598, making it one of the last Gothic constructions in the country. Pause to look at the facade, constructed between 1616 and 1621. Where the interior is late Gothic, the exterior is one of the earliest examples of classical, or Renaissance, style in France. The church hosts occasional organ and choral concerts. ☎ 47–26–78–38 *for concert information.* ☺ *Tues.–Sun. 6:30 AM–8 PM. Métro: Hôtel-de-Ville.*

Don't cross the Seine to the Ile St-Louis yet: Take rue de l'Hôtel de Ville and turn left on rue Geoffroy l'Asnier. At
㉔ No. 17 is the **Memorial of the Unknown Jewish Martyr,** erected in March, 1992—50 years after the first convoy of deportees left France—to honor the memory of the six million Jews who died "without graves." The monument is part of the **Center for Contemporary Jewish Documentation (CDJC);** its archives, library, and gallery, which hosts temporary exhibitions, are open to the public. In the basement of the building is a dramatic underground crypt where a huge black marble star of David contains the ashes of victims from death camps in Poland and Austria. *17 rue Geoffroy l'Asnier, 4e,* ☎ *42–77–44–72.* ☛ *12 frs.* ☺ *Sun.–Fri. 10–1 and 2–5:30. Métro: Pont Marie.*

Continue along rue de l'Hôtel de Ville to where it meets
㉕ rue de Figuier. The painstakingly restored **Hôtel de Sens** (1474) on the corner is one of a handful of Parisian homes to have survived since the Middle Ages. With its pointed

corner towers, Gothic porch, and richly carved decorative details, it is a strange mixture, half defensive stronghold, half fairytale château. Its best-known occupants were Henri IV and his queen, Marguérite, philanderers both. While Henri dallied with his mistresses—he is said to have had 56—at a series of royal palaces, Marguérite entertained her almost equally large number of lovers here. Today the building houses a fine arts library, the **Bibliothéque Forney.** ☛ *Free.* ☉ *Tues.–Fri. 1:30–8:30, Sat. 10–8:30. Métro: Pont Marie.*

The Ile St-Louis

❷❻ Cross pont Marie to the **Ile St-Louis,** the smaller of the two islands in the heart of Paris, linked to the Ile de la Cité by pont St-Louis. The contrast between the islands is striking, considering how close they are. Whereas the Ile de la Cité, the oldest continuously inhabited part of the city, is steeped in history and dotted with dignified, old buildings, the Ile St-Louis is a discreet residential district, something of an extension of the Marais. Once thought to be an unimportant backwater and an area curiously out-of-sync with the rest of the city, the Ile St-Louis is now a highly desirable address.

The most striking feature of the island is its architectural unity, which stems from the efforts of a group of early 17th-century property speculators. At that time, there were two islands here, the Ile Notre Dame and Ile aux Vaches—the cows' island, a reference to its use as grazing land. The speculators, led by an energetic engineer named Christophe Marie (after whom the pont Marie was named), bought the two islands, joined them together, and divided the newly formed Ile St-Louis into building plots. Louis Le Vau (1612–1670), the leading Baroque architect in France, was commissioned to put up a series of imposing town houses, and by 1664 the project was largely complete.

There are three things you'll want to do here. One is to walk
❷❼ along **rue St-Louis en l'Ile,** which runs the length of the island. People still talk about its quaint, village-street feel, although this village street is now lined with a high-pow-

ered array of designer boutiques and a constant throng of
tourists patrolling its length.

TIME OUT **Berthillon** has become a byword for amazing ice cream.
Cafés all over the Ile St-Louis sell its glamorous products, but
the place to come is still the little shop on rue St-Louis en
l'Ile. Expect to wait in line. *31 rue St-Louis en l'Ile. Closed
Mon. and Tues.*

28 The second place to visit is the **Hôtel de Lauzun.** It was built
in about 1650 for Charles Gruyn, who accumulated an im-
mense fortune as a supplier of goods to the French army,
but who landed in jail before the house was even completed.
In the 19th century, the revolutionary critic and visionary
poet Charles Baudelaire (1821–1867) had an apartment
here, where he kept a personal cache of stuffed snakes and
crocodiles. In 1848, the poet Théophile Gautier (1811–1872)
moved in, making it the meeting place of the Club des
Haschischines, the Hashish-Eaters' Club. Now the building is used for receptions by the mayor of Paris. *17 quai
d'Anjou,* ☎ *43–54–27–14.* ☛ *22 frs.* ☉ *Easter–Oct.,
weekends only 10–5:30. Métro: Pont Marie.*

29 The third and most popular attraction is a walk along the
quays. The most lively, **quai de Bourbon,** is at the western
end, facing the Ile de la Cité. There are views of Notre Dame
from here and of the Hôtel de Ville and church of St-Gervais-St-Protais on the Right Bank. It can be an almost eerie
spot in the winter, when it becomes deserted. In the summer, rows of baking bodies attest to its enduring popularity as the city's favorite sunbathing spot. **No. 19** marks the
former atelier of female sculptor and Rodin contemporary
Camille Claudel, who worked here from 1899 to 1913.

FROM THE ARC DE TRIOMPHE
TO THE OPÉRA

*Numbers in the margin correspond to points of interest on
the Arc de Triomphe to the Opéra map.*

This tour takes in grand, opulent Paris: the Paris of imposing
vistas, long, arrow-straight streets, and plush hotels and jew-

elers. It begins at the Arc de Triomphe, standing foursquare
at the top of the most famous street in the city, the Champs-
Elysées. You'll want to explore both its commercial upper
half and its verdant lower section. The hinterland of the
Champs-Elysées, made up of the imposing streets leading
off it, is equally stylish. You're within striking distance of
the Seine here (and a ride on a Bateau Mouche) to the south,
and the cheerful, crowded Faubourg St-Honoré to the
north. This is not so much an area for museums as for win-
dow-shopping and monument-gazing. Dazzling vistas open
up from place de la Concorde, place de la Madeleine, and
L'Etoile.

Local charm is not, however, a feature of this exclusive sec-
tor of western Paris, occupying principally the 8th Arrondissement. It's beautiful and rich—and a little impersonal.
Visit during the day, and head elsewhere in search of
Parisian ambience and an affordable meal in the evening.

The Arc de Triomphe and Champs-Elysées

Place Charles de Gaulle is known by Parisians as **L'Etoile,**
the star—a reference to the streets that fan out from it. It
is one of Europe's most chaotic traffic circles, and short of
a death-defying dash, your only way of getting to the Arc
de Triomphe in the middle is to take an underground passage from the Champs-Elysées or avenue de la Grande
Armée.

❶ The colossal, 164-foot **Arc de Triomphe** was planned by
Napoléon—who believed himself to be the direct heir to
the Roman emperors—to celebrate his military successes.
Unfortunately, Napoléon's strategic and architectural visions
were not entirely on the same plane, and the Arc de Triomphe proved something of a white elephant. When it
was required for the triumphal entry of his new empress,
Marie-Louise, into Paris in 1810, it was still only a few feet
high. To save face, a dummy arch of painted canvas was
put up.

The view from the top illustrates the star effect of the 12
radiating avenues and enables you to admire the vista down
the Champs-Elysées toward place de la Concorde and the

The Arc de Triomphe to the Opéra

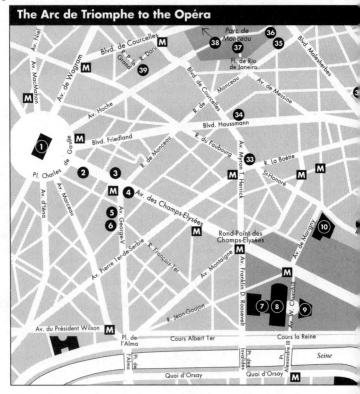

Arc de
Triomphe, **1**

Atelier de
Gustave
Moreau, **29**

Crillon, **18**

Eglise de la
Madeleine, **12**

Fauchon, **14**

Fouquet's, **4**

Galeries
Lafayette, **25**

Gare
St-Lazare, **30**

George V, **6**

Grand Palais, **8**

Hédiard, **15**

Jardin des
Tuileries, **21**

Lido, **3**

Marks &
Spencer, **27**

Maxim's, **16**

Musée
Cernuschi, **36**

Musée de
l'Orangerie, **20**

Musée de Jeu de
Paume, **19**

Musée
Jacque-
mart-André, **34**

Musée
Jean-Jacques
Henner, **38**

distant Louvre. In the other direction, you can see down avenue de la Grande Armée toward La Défense and its severe modern arch, surrounded by imposing glass and concrete towers. There is a small museum halfway up the arch devoted to its history. France's Unknown Soldier is buried beneath the archway; the flame is rekindled every evening at 6:30. *Pl. Charles-de-Gaulle.* ☛ *31 frs adults, 21 frs students and senior citizens, 10 frs under 18.* ☉ *Daily 10–5:30; winter, daily 10–5. Closed public holidays. Métro: Etoile.*

The cosmopolitan pulse of Paris beats strongest on the gracefully sloping, 1¼-mile-long **Champs-Elysées.** It was originally laid out in the 1660s by the landscape gardener Le Nôtre as a garden sweeping away from the Tuileries, but you will see few signs of these pastoral origins as you stroll past the cafés, restaurants, airline offices, car showrooms, movie theaters, and chic arcades that occupy its upper half. In 1994 the City of Paris completed an ambitious reconstruction program to reestablish this once glorious thoroughfare as one of the world's most beautiful avenues. The result: extra trees, broader sidewalks, coordinated designer street-furniture (everything from benches and lighting to traffic lights, telephone booths and trash cans), Art Nouveau newsstands, underground parking to alleviate congestion, and a clampdown on garish storefronts.

❷ Start off by stopping in at the main **Paris Tourist Office** at No. 127. It's at the Arc de Triomphe end of the Champs-Elysées, on the right-hand side as you arrive from Etoile. It is an invaluable source of information on accommodations, places to visit, and entertainment—both in Paris and in the surrounding Ile-de-France region. ☉ *Oct.–May, daily 9–8; June–Sept., weekdays 9–9; winter, Sun. 9–6. Métro: Etoile.*

The Champs-Elysées occupies a central role in French national celebrations. It is the site of vast ceremonies on July 14, France's national, or Bastille, day, and November 11, Armistice Day. It also witnesses the finish of the Tour de France bicycle race on the fourth Sunday of July. Its trees are often decked with the French *tricolore* and foreign flags to mark visits from heads of state.

Three hundred yards down on the left, at 116b, is the fa-
❸ mous **Lido** nightclub: Foot-stomping melodies in French and
English and champagne-soaked, topless razzmatazz pack
❹ in the crowds every night. In contrast is the nearby **Fouquet's,** an 1898 landmark restaurant-café that still caters
to a highbrow clientele (though the outdoor café is thronged
with tourists in the summertime). Swing by the red-awninged
❺ **Prince de Galles** (Prince of Wales) and the blue-awninged
❻ **George V,** two of the city's top hotels on avenue George V,
a right-hand turn off the Champs-Elysées. Continue down
the Champs-Elysées to the Rond-Point and turn right onto
the spacious avenue Franklin D. Roosevelt. Halfway down
❼ is the entrance to the **Palais de la Découverte** (Palace of Discovery), whose scientific and technological exhibits include
working models and a planetarium. *Av. Franklin D. Roosevelt.* ☛ *25 frs adults, 15 frs extra for planetarium; 15 frs
under 18, 10 frs extra for planetarium.* ☉ *Tues.–Sat. 9:30–
6, Sun. 10–7. Métro: Champs Elysées Clemenceau.*

This "Palace of Discovery" occupies the rear half of the
❽ **Grand Palais.** With its curved glass roof, the Grand Palais
is unmistakable when approached from either the Seine or
the Champs-Elysées and forms an attractive duo with the
Petit Palais on the other side of avenue Winston Churchill.
Both these stone buildings, adorned with mosaics and
sculpted friezes, seem robust and venerable. In fact, they
were erected with indecent haste prior to the Paris World
Fair of 1900. Today, the atmospheric iron and glass interior of the Grand Palais plays host to major exhibitions,
but was closed for urgent renovation in 1994 and the date
of reopening had not been announced as of press time. Admire the view from the palaces across the Alexandre III bridge
toward the Hôtel des Invalides. *Av. Winston Churchill.
Métro: Champs Elysées Clemenceau.*

❾ The **Petit Palais** has a beautifully presented permanent collection of French painting and furniture, with splendid
canvases by Courbet and Bouguereau. Temporary exhibits
are often held here, too. The sprawling entrance gallery contains several enormous turn-of-the-century paintings on
its walls and ceilings. *Av. Winston Churchill.* ☛ *26 frs
adults, 14 frs students and senior citizens.* ☉ *Tues.–Sun. 10–
5:30. Métro: Champs Elysées Clemenceau.*

Head up Avenue Winston Churchill, cross the Champs-Elysées, and continue on avenue de Marigny to rue du Faubourg St-Honoré, a prestigious address in the world of luxury fashion and art galleries. You'll soon spot plenty of both, but may be perplexed at the presence of crash barriers and stern policemen. Their mission: to protect the French president in the **Palais de l'Elysée.** This "palace," where the head of state lives, works, and receives official visitors, was originally constructed as a private mansion in 1718. Although you catch a glimpse of the palace forecourt and facade through the Faubourg St-Honoré gateway, it is difficult to get much idea of the building's size or of the extensive gardens that stretch back to the Champs-Elysées. The French government—the Conseil des Ministres—attends to public affairs when it meets here each Wednesday morning. *Not open to the public. Métro: Miromesnil.*

Toward place de la Concorde

St. Michael's English Church, close to the British Embassy on rue du Faubourg St-Honoré, is a modern building whose ugliness is redeemed by the warmth of the welcome afforded to all visitors, English-speaking ones in particular. *5 rue d'Aguesseau,* ☎ *47–42–70–88. Services Thurs. 12:45 and Sun. 10:30 (with Sunday school) and 6:30; supervised nursery for younger children in the morning. Métro: Madeleine.*

Continue down rue du Faubourg St-Honoré to rue d'Anglas, turn left, then take the first right through an archway into Cité Berryer, a newly restored courtyard with several trendy boutiques. This leads to rue Royale, a classy street lined with jewelry stores that links place de la Concorde to the **Eglise de la Madeleine,** a sturdy neo-classical edifice that was nearly selected as Paris's first train station (the site of what is now the Gare St-Lazare, just up the road, was eventually chosen). With its rows of uncompromising columns, the Madeleine looks more like a Greek temple than a Christian church. Inside, the only natural light comes from three shallow domes. The church was designed in 1814 but not consecrated until 1842. The portico's majestic Corinthian colonnade supports a gigantic pediment with a sculptured frieze of the Last Judgment, restored to original glory in 1992. ⊙ *Mon.–Sat. 7:30–7, Sun. 8–7. Métro: Madeleine.*

Alongside the Madeleine, between the church and L'Ecluse, ⑬ is a **ticket kiosk** (open Tues.–Sat. 12:30–8) selling tickets for same-day theater performances at greatly reduced prices. ⑭ ⑮ Behind the church are **Fauchon** and **Hédiard,** two stylish delicatessens that are the ultimate in posh nosh. At the end ⑯ of the rue Royale is the legendary **Maxim's** restaurant. Unless you choose to eat here—an expensive and not always rewarding experience—you won't be able to see the interior decor, a riot of crimson velvets and florid Art Nouveau furniture.

There is a striking contrast between the sunless, locked-in feel of the high-walled rue Royale and the broad, airy **place** ⑰ **de la Concorde.** This huge square can also be approached from the Champs-Elysées: The flower beds, chestnut trees, and sandy sidewalks of the avenue's lower section are reminders of its original leafy elegance. Place de la Concorde was built in the 1770s, but there was nothing in the way of peace or concord about its early years. Between 1793 and 1795, it was the scene of over a thousand deaths by guillotine; victims included Louis XVI, Marie Antoinette, Danton, and Robespierre. The obelisk, a present from the viceroy of Egypt, was erected in 1833. The handsome, symmetrical, 18th-century buildings facing the square in⑱clude the deluxe hotel **Crillon,** though there's nothing so vulgar as a sign to identify it—just an inscribed marble plaque above the doorway.

Facing one side of place de la Concorde are the **Tuileries Gardens.** Two smallish buildings stand sentinel here. To ⑲ the north, nearer rue de Rivoli, is the **Musée du Jeu de Paume,** fondly known to many as the former home of the Impressionists (now in the Musée d'Orsay). After extensive renovation, the Jeu de Paume reopened in 1991 as a home to brash temporary exhibits of contemporary art. The other, identical building, nearer the Seine, is the recently re⑳stored **Musée de l'Orangerie,** containing some early 20th-century paintings by Monet (including his vast, eight-paneled *Water Lilies*), Renoir, and other Impressionists. *Place de la Concorde.* ☛ *Jeu de Paume: 35 frs adults, 25 frs students* *and senior citizens. L'Orangerie: 27 frs adults, 18 frs students and senior citizens.* ☉ *Jeu de Paume: Tues. noon–9:30, Wed.–Fri. noon–7, weekends 10–7. L'Orangerie: Wed.–Mon. 9:45–5:15, closed Tues. Métro: Concorde.*

㉑ As gardens go, the newly renovated **Jardin des Tuileries** are typically French: formal and neatly patterned, with statues, rows of trees, and gravel paths. It is a charming place to stroll and survey the surrounding cityscape; you may see a string quartet or jugglers entertaining large crowds on weekends. To the north is the disciplined, arcaded rue de Rivoli; to the south, the Seine and the gold-hued Musée d'Orsay with its enormous clocks; to the west, the Champs-Elysées and Arc de Triomphe; to the east, the Arc du Carrousel and the Louvre, with its glass pyramid.

Place Vendôme and the Opéra

㉒ **Place Vendôme,** north of the Tuileries Gardens, one of the world's most opulent squares, benefited in 1992 from a facelift that included new granite pavement, Second Empire–style street lamps, and an underground garage. Mansart's rhythmic, perfectly proportioned example of 17th-century urban architecture has shone in all its golden-stoned splendor since being cleaned a few years ago. Many other things shine here, too—in jewelers' display windows and on the dresses of guests of the top-ranking **Ritz** hotel. Napoléon had the square's central column made from the melted bronze of 1,200 cannons captured at the battle of Austerlitz in 1805. That's him standing vigilantly at the top. Painter Gustave Courbet headed the Revolutionary hooligans who, in 1871, toppled the column and shattered it into thousands of metallic pieces. *Métro: Tuileries.*

㉓ Cross the square and take rue des Capucines on your left to boulevard des Capucines. The **Olympia** music hall is still going strong, though it has lost some of the luster it acquired as the stage for such great postwar singers as Edith Piaf and Jacques Brel.

TIME OUT There are few grander cafés in Paris than the **Café de la Paix,** on the corner of place de l'Opéra. This is a good place to people-watch, or just to slow down; but expect the prices to be as grand as the setting.

㉔ The **Opéra,** begun in 1862 by Charles Garnier at the behest of Napoléon III, was not completed until 1875, five years after the emperor's political demise. It is often said to typify the Second Empire–style of architecture, which is to say that it is a pompous hodgepodge of styles, imbued with as much subtlety as a Wagnerian cymbal crash. After paying the entry fee, you can stroll around at leisure. The monumental foyer and staircase are boisterously impressive, a stage in their own right, where, on first nights, celebrities preen and prance. If the lavishly upholstered auditorium (ceiling painted by Marc Chagall in 1964) seems small, it is only because the stage is the largest in the world—over 11,000 square yards, with room for up to 450 performers. ☛ *30 frs adults, 18 frs students and senior citizens.* ☉ *Daily 10–4:30, but closed occasionally for rehearsals; call 47–42–57–50 to check. Métro: Opéra.*

Around the Opéra

㉕ Behind the Opéra are the *grands magasins,* Paris's most renowned department stores. The nearer of the two, the **Galeries Lafayette,** is the more outstanding, if only because of its vast, shimmering, turn-of-the-century glass dome. The **㉖** domes at the corners of **Printemps,** farther along boulevard Haussmann, to the left, can be best appreciated from the outside; there is a splendid view from the store's rooftop **㉗** cafeteria. **Marks & Spencer,** across the road, provides a brave outpost for British goods, such as ginger biscuits, bacon rashers, and Cheddar cheese. *Métro: Havre-Caumartin.*

㉘ The **Trinité** church, 300 yards north of the Opéra via rue de Mogador, is not an unworthy 19th-century effort at neo-Renaissance style. Its central tower is of dubious aesthetic merit but is a recognizable feature in the Paris skyline. The church was built in the 1860s and is fronted by a pleasant garden. *Métro: Trinité.*

㉙ The nearby **Atelier de Gustave Moreau** was the town house and studio of painter Gustave Moreau (1826–1898), doyen of the Symbolist movement that strove to convey ideas through images. Many of the ideas Moreau was trying to express remain obscure to the general public, however, even though the artist provided explanatory texts. But most onlookers will be content admiring his extravagant colors and flights of fantasy, which reveal the influence of Persian and Indian miniatures. Fantastic details cover every inch of his canvases, and his canvases cover every inch of wall space, making a trip to the museum one of the strangest artistic experiences in Paris. Go on a sunny day, if possible; the low lighting can strain the eyes even more than Moreau's paintings. *14 rue de la Rochefoucauld.* ☛ *17 frs adults, 11 frs students and senior citizens, under 18 free.* ☉ *Thurs.–Sun. 10–12:45 and 2–5:15, Mon. and Wed. 11–5:15. Métro: Trinité.*

30 Rue St-Lazare leads west from the Trinité to the **Gare St-Lazare,** whose imposing 19th-century facade has been restored. In the days of steam and smoke, the station was an inspiration to several Impressionist painters, notably Monet. Note an eccentric sculpture to the right of the facade—a higgledy-piggledy accumulation of clocks.

31 From the southwestern corner of the train station, head down rue Pasquier to the leafy, intimate **Square Louis XVI** on boulevard Haussmann. This is perhaps the nearest Paris gets to a verdant, London-style square—if you discount the bombastic mausoleum in the middle. The unkempt chapel marks the initial burial site of Louis XVI and Marie Antoinette after their turns at the guillotine on place de la Concorde. *Métro: St-Augustin.* ☉ *Daily 10–noon and 2–6; winter, daily 10–4.*

Before leaving the square, take a look at the gleaming 1930s-style facade of the bank at the southeast corner of rue Pasquier and rue Mathurins (bordering the square). It has some amusing stone carvings halfway up, representing various exotic animals.

32 A mighty dome is the most striking feature of the innovative iron-and-stone church of **St-Augustin,** dexterously constructed in the 1860s within the confines of an awkward, V-shaped site. The use of metal girders obviated the need for exterior buttressing. The dome is bulky but well-proportioned and contains some grimy but competent frescoes by the popular 19th-century French artist William Bouguereau. *Métro: St-Augustin.*

If you're in a hurry, or have had your fill of churches and museums, head west along boulevard Haussmann and turn right up avenue de Messine to Parc Monceau (*see below*).

㉝ Otherwise, take rue La Boétie off place St-Augustin to **St-Philippe du Roule,** built by Chalgrin between 1769 and 1784. Its austere classical portico dominates a busy square. The best thing inside this dimly lit church is the 19th-century fresco above the altar by Théodore Chassériau, featuring the Descent from the Cross. *Métro: St-Philippe-du-Roule.*

Make your way back to boulevard Haussmann via avenue

㉞ Myron T. Herrick. The **Musée Jacquemart-André** features Italian Renaissance and 18th-century art in a dazzlingly furnished, late-19th-century mansion. *158 blvd. Haussmann,* ☎ *42–89–04–91.* ☛ *18 frs.* ☉ *Wed.–Sun. 1–6. Métro: St-Philippe-du-Roule.*

Rue de Courcelles and a right on rue de Monceau will lead to place de Rio de Janeiro. Before venturing into the Parc Monceau just down avenue Ruysdaël, continue along rue

㉟ de Monceau to the **Musée Nissim de Camondo.** Inside, you will find the stylish interior of an aristocratic Parisian mansion in the style of Louis XVI, dating from the last days of the regal Ancien Régime. *63 rue de Monceau.* ☛ *20 frs adults, 14 frs students and senior citizens.* ☉ *Wed.–Sun. 10–noon and 2–5. Métro: Monceau.*

Rue de Monceau and boulevard Malesherbes lead to the

㊱ **Musée Cernuschi,** whose collection of Chinese art ranges from neolithic pottery (3rd century BC) to funeral statuary, painted 8th-century silks, and contemporary paintings. *7 av. Velasquez.* ☛ *17 frs adults, 9 frs students and senior citizens.* ☉ *Tues.–Sun. 10–5:40. Métro: Monceau.*

㊲ The **Parc Monceau,** which can be entered from avenue Velasquez, off boulevard Malesherbes, was laid out as a private park in 1778 and retains some of the fanciful elements then in vogue, including mock ruins and a phony pyramid. In 1797, Garnerin, the world's first-recorded parachutist, staged a landing in the park. The rotunda, known as the

Chartres Pavilion, was originally a tollhouse and has well-worked iron gates.

Leave the Parc Monceau by these gates and follow rue
38 Phalsbourg and avenue de Villiers to the **Musée Jean-Jacques Henner.** Henner (1829–1905), a nearly forgotten Alsatian artist, here receives a sumptuous tribute. His obsessive fondness for milky-skinned, auburn-haired female nudes is displayed in hundreds of drawings and paintings on the three floors of this gracious museum. *43 av. de Villiers.* ☛ *14 frs adults, 10 frs students, senior citizens, and on Sun.* ☯ *Tues.–Sun. 10–noon and 2–5. Métro: Malesherbes.*

Boulevard de Courcelles, which runs along the north side of the Parc Monceau, leads west to rue Pierre-le-Grand (Peter the Great Street). At the far end of that street, at 12 rue Daru, loom the unlikely gilt onion domes of the Russian
39 Orthodox cathedral of **St-Alexandre Nevsky,** erected in neo-Byzantine style in 1860. Inside, the wall of icons that divides the church in two creates an atmosphere seldom found in Roman Catholic or Protestant churches. *Métro: Courcelles.*

FROM ORSAY TO TROCADÉRO

Numbers in the margin correspond to points of interest on the Orsay to Trocadéro map.

The Left Bank has two faces: the cozy, ramshackle Latin Quarter (*see* The Left Bank, *below*) and the spacious, stately 7th arrondissement. This tour covers the latter, then heads back across the Seine for a look at the museums and attractions clustered around the place du Trocadéro. The latest addition to the area is already the most popular: the Musée d'Orsay. Crowds flock to this stylishly converted train station to see the Impressionists, but also discover important examples of other schools of 19th- and early 20th-century art.

The atmosphere of the 7th arrondissement is set by the National Assembly, down the river from Orsay, opposite place de la Concorde. French deputies meet here to hammer out laws and insult each other. They resume more civilized attitudes when they return to the luxurious ministries that dot the nearby streets. The most famous is the Hôtel Matignon, official residence of the French prime minister.

The majestic scale of many of the area's buildings is totally in character with the daddy of them all, the Invalides. Like the Champ de Mars nearby, the esplanade in front of the Invalides was once used as a parade ground for Napoléon's troops. In a coffin beneath the Invalides dome, M. Bonaparte dreams on.

Musée d'Orsay

❶ The **Musée d'Orsay** opened in December 1986. It is devoted to the arts (mainly French) produced between 1848 and 1914, and its collections are intended to form a bridge between the classical collections of the Louvre and the modern collections of Beaubourg. The building began in 1900 as a train station for routes between Paris and the southwest of France. By 1939, the Gare d'Orsay had become too small for mainline travel, and intercity trains were transferred to the Gare d'Austerlitz. Gare d'Orsay became a suburban terminus until, in the 1960s, it closed for good. After various temporary uses (a theater, an auction house, and a setting for Orson Welles' movie, *The Trial,* based on Kafka's novel), the building was set for demolition. However, the destruction of the 19th-century Les Halles (market halls) across the Seine provoked a furor among conservationists, and in the late 1970s, President Giscard d'Estaing, with an eye firmly on establishing his place in the annals of French culture, ordered Orsay to be transformed into a museum. The architects Pierre Colboc, Renaud Bardou, and Jean-Paul Philippon were commissioned to remodel the building, while Gae Aulenti, known for her renovation of the Palazzo Grassi in Venice, was hired to redesign the interior.

The chief artistic attraction is the Impressionists, whose works are displayed on the top floor, next to the museum café. Renoir, Sisley, Pissarro, and Monet are all well represented. Highlights for many visitors are Monet's *Poppy Field* and Renoir's *Le Moulin de la Galette.* The Post-Im-

Orsay to Trocadéro

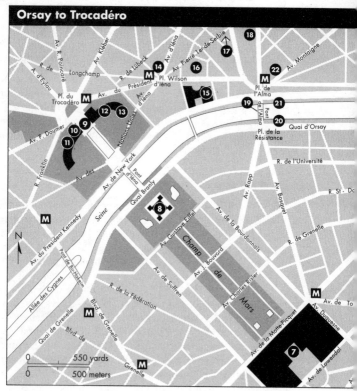

American
Cathedral of the
Holy Trinity, **18**

Bateaux
Mouches, **21**

Ecole
Militaire, **7**

Eiffel Tower, **8**

Hôtel des
Invalides, **6**

Hôtel
Matingnon, **4**

Les Egouts, **20**

Musée d'Art
Moderne de la
Ville de Paris, **15**

Musée de la
Légion
d'Honneur, **2**

Musée de la
Marine, **11**

Musée de
l'Homme, **10**

Musée des
Monuments
Français, **12**

Musée d'Orsay, **1**

Musée du
Cinema Henri
Langlois, **13**

Musée
Guimet, **14**

Musée Rodin, **5**

Palais
Bourbon, **3**

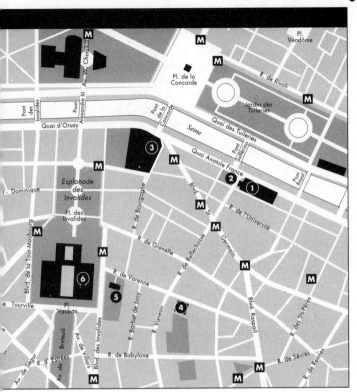

pressionists—Cézanne, van Gogh, Gauguin, and Toulouse-Lautrec—are all also represented on this floor.

On the first floor, you'll find the work of Manet and the delicate nuances of Degas. Pride of place, at least in art historical terms, goes to Manet's *Déjeuner sur l'Herbe,* the painting that scandalized Paris in 1863. Another reworking by Manet of a classical motif is his reclining nude, *Olympia.* Gazing boldly out from the canvas, she was more than respectable 19th-century Parisian proprieties could stand.

Those who prefer more correct academic paintings should look at Puvis de Chavannes's larger-than-life, classical canvases. The pale, limpid beauty of his figures is enjoying considerable attention after years of neglect. Those who are excited by more modern developments will make for the early 20th-century Fauves (meaning wild beasts, the name given them by an outraged critic in 1905)—particularly Matisse, Derain, and Vlaminck.

Sculpture at the Orsay means, first and foremost, Rodin (though there's more to enjoy at the Musée Rodin, *see below*). Two further highlights are the faithfully restored Belle Epoque restaurant and the model of the entire Opéra quarter, displayed beneath a glass floor.

The Musée d'Orsay, otherwise known as M.O., is one of Paris's star attractions. Crowds are smaller at lunchtime and on Thursday evenings. *1 rue de Bellechasse.* ☛ *35 frs adults, 24 frs students and senior citizens and on Sun., under 18 free.* ⊙ *Tues.–Sat. 10–6, Thurs. 10–9:30, and Sun. 9–6. RER: Musée d'Orsay. Métro: Solférino.*

② Across from the Musée d'Orsay stands the **Musée de la Légion d'Honneur.** French and foreign decorations are displayed in this stylish mansion by the Seine (officially known as the Hôtel de Salm). The original building, constructed in 1786, burned during the Commune in 1871 and was rebuilt in 1878. *2 rue de Bellechasse.* ☛ *10 frs adults, 5 frs students and senior citizens.* ⊙ *Tues.–Sun. 2–5. Métro: Solférino.*

Toward the Invalides

Continue westward along the left bank of the Seine to the
❸ 18th-century **Palais Bourbon** (directly across from place de
la Concorde), home of the Assemblée Nationale (French Par-
liament). The colonnaded facade, commissioned by
Napoléon, is a sparkling sight after a recent cleaning program. There is a fine view from the steps across to place
de la Concorde and the church of the Madeleine. *Not open
to the public.*

The quiet, distinguished 18th-century streets behind the
Palais Bourbon are filled with embassies and ministries. The
most famous, reached via rue de Bourgogne and rue de
❹ Varenne, is the **Hôtel Matignon,** residence of the French Prime
Minister, and Left Bank counterpart to the President's
Elysée Palace. "Matignon" was built in 1721 but has
housed heads of government only since 1958. From 1888
to 1914, it was the embassy of the Austro-Hungarian Empire. *57 rue de Varenne. Neither house nor garden is open
to the public. Métro: Varenne.*

A few doors down at **No. 53** you can pay your respects to
American novelist Edith Wharton, who lived and worked
here from 1910 to 1920. She wrote of her abode, "My years
of Paris life were spent entirely in the rue de Varenne—rich
years, crowded and happy years."

Another glorious town house along rue de Varenne is the
❺ Hôtel Biron, better known as the **Musée Rodin.** The splendid house, with its spacious vestibule, broad staircase, and
light, airy rooms, retains much of its 18th-century atmosphere and makes a handsome setting for the sculpture of
Auguste Rodin (1840–1917). You'll doubtless recognize the
seated *Thinker,* with his elbow resting on his knee, and the
passionate *Kiss.* There is also an outstanding white marble bust of Austrian composer *Gustav Mahler,* as well as
numerous examples of Rodin's obsession with hands and
erotic subjects.

The second-floor rooms, which contain some fine paintings
by Rodin's friend Eugène Carrière (1849–1906), afford
views of the large garden behind the house. Don't go without visiting the garden: It is exceptional both for its rose

bushes (over 2,000 of them, representing 100 varieties)
and for its sculpture, including a powerful statue of the novelist Balzac and the despairing group of medieval city fathers known as the *Burghers of Calais. 77 rue de Varenne.*
Métro: Varenne. ☛ 27 frs, 18 frs Sun. ⊙ Easter–Oct.,
Tues.–Sun. 10–6; Nov.–Easter, Tues.–Sun. 10–5.

❻ From the Rodin Museum, you can see the **Hôtel des Invalides,** along rue de Varenne. It was founded by Louis XIV
in 1674 to house wounded (or "invalid") veterans. Although no more than a handful of old soldiers live at the
Invalides today, the military link remains in the form of the
Musée de l'Armée—one of the world's foremost military
museums—with a vast, albeit somewhat musty, collection
of arms, armor, uniforms, banners, and military pictures
down through the ages.

The **Musée des Plans-Reliefs,** housed on the fifth floor of
the right-hand wing, contains a fascinating collection of scale
models of French towns made to illustrate the fortifications
planned by Vauban in the 17th century. (Vauban was a superb military engineer who worked under Louis XIV.) The
largest and most impressive is Strasbourg, which takes up
an entire room. Not all of Vauban's models are here, however. As part of a cultural decentralization program, France's
socialist government of the early 1980s decided to pack the
models (which had languished for years in dusty neglect)
off to Lille in northern France. Only half the models had
been shifted when a conservative government returned to
office in 1986 and called for their return. Ex-Prime Minister Pierre Mauroy, the socialist mayor of Lille, refused,
however, and the impasse seems set to continue.

The museums are not the only reason for visiting the Invalides. The building itself is an outstanding monumental
ensemble in late-17th-century Baroque, designed by Bruand
and Mansart. The main, cobbled courtyard is a fitting
scene for the parades and ceremonies still occasionally held
here. The most impressive dome in Paris towers over the
Eglise du Dôme (church of the Dome). Before stopping
here, however, visit the 17th-century **Eglise St-Louis des Invalides,** the Invalides's original church, and the site of the
first performance of Berlioz's *Requiem* in 1837.

The Dôme church was built onto the end of Eglise St-Louis but was blocked off from it in 1793—no great pity perhaps, as the two buildings are vastly different in style and scale. It was designed by Mansart and built between 1677 and 1735. The remains of Napoléon are here, in a series of no fewer than six coffins, one inside the next, within a bombastic tomb of red porphyry, ringed by low reliefs and a dozen statues symbolizing Napoléon's campaigns. Among others commemorated in the church are French World War I hero Marshal Foch; Napoléon's brother Joseph, erstwhile king of Spain; and fortification-builder Vauban, whose heart was brought to the Invalides at Napoléon's behest. *Hôtel des Invalides.* ☛ *34 frs adults, 24 frs children and senior citizens.* ☼ *Daily 10–6; winter, daily 10–5.* Metro: St-François-Xavier.

Cross the pleasant lawns outside the Dôme church to place Vauban. Follow avenue de Tourville to the right, and turn left onto avenue de la Motte-Picquet.

The Eiffel Tower and the Trocadéro

7 A few minutes' walk will bring you face-to-face with the Eiffel Tower. Spare a thought for the **Ecole Militaire** on your left; it is 18th-century architecture at its most harmonious. It is still in use as a military academy and therefore not open to the public.

8 The pleasant expanse of the **Champ de Mars** makes an ideal approach to the **Eiffel Tower,** whose colossal bulk (it's far bigger and sturdier than pictures suggest) becomes evident the nearer you get. It was built by Gustave Eiffel for the World Exhibition of 1889, the centennial of the French Revolution, and was still in good shape to celebrate its own 100th birthday. Recent restoration hasn't made the elevators any faster (lines are inevitable), but the nocturnal illumination is fantastic—every girder highlighted in glorious detail.

Such was Eiffel's engineering wizardry that even in the strongest winds his tower never sways more than 4½ inches. Today, it is Paris's best-known landmark and exudes a feeling of permanence. As you stand beneath its huge legs, you may have trouble believing that it nearly became 7,000 tons of scrap-iron when its concession expired in 1909. Only its potential use as a radio antenna saved the day; it now bristles with a forest of radio and television transmitters. If you're full of energy, stride up the stairs as far as the third deck. If you want to go to the top, you'll have to take the elevator. The view at 1,000 feet may not beat that from the Tour Maine-Montparnasse (*see* The Left Bank, *below*), but the setting makes it considerably more romantic. *Pont d'Iéna.* ☛ *By elevator: 2nd floor, 20 frs; 3rd floor, 36 frs; 4th floor, 53 frs. By foot: 2nd and 3rd floors only, 12 frs.* ☼ *July–Aug., daily 9 AM–midnight; Sept.–June, daily 9 AM–11 PM. RER: Champ de Mars. Métro: Bir-Hakeim.*

Just across the Pont d'Iena from the Eiffel Tower, on the **⑨** heights of Trocadéro, is the muscular, sandy-colored **Palais de Chaillot**—a cultural center built in the 1930s to replace a Moorish-style building constructed for the World Exhibition of 1878. The gardens between the Palais de Chaillot and the Seine contain an aquarium and some dramatic fountains. The terrace between the two wings of the palace offers a wonderful view of the Eiffel Tower.

The Palais de Chaillot contains four large museums, two in each wing. In the left wing (as you approach from the Seine) are the Musée de l'Homme and the Musée de la Ma- **⑩** rine. The **Musée de l'Homme,** on the second and third floors, is an earnest anthropological museum with arti- facts, costumes, and domestic tools from around the world, **⑪** dating from prehistoric times to the recent past. The **Musée de la Marine,** on the first floor, is a maritime museum with a salty collection of ship models and seafaring parapher- nalia, illustrating French naval history right up to the age of the nuclear submarine. ☛ *Musée de l'Homme: 25 frs adults, 15 frs children; Musée de la Marine: 31 frs adults, 16 frs senior citizens, students, and children.* ☼ *Musée de l'Homme: Wed.–Mon. 9:45–5; Musée de la Marine: Wed.–Mon. 10–6. Métro: Trocadéro.*

⑫ The other wing is dominated by the **Musée des Monuments Français,** an excellent introduction to French medieval ar- chitecture. This museum was founded in 1879 by architect- restorer Viollet-le-Duc (the man responsible for the extensive

renovation of Notre Dame). It pays tribute to French buildings, mainly of the Romanesque and Gothic periods (roughly
1000–1500), in the form of painstaking copies of statues,
columns, archways, and frescoes. It is easy to imagine yourself strolling among ruins as you pass through the first-floor
gallery. Substantial sections of a number of French churches
and cathedrals are represented here, notably Chartres and
Vézelay. Mural and ceiling paintings—copies of works in
churches around the country—dominate the other three
floors. The **Musée du Cinéma Henri Langlois,** located in the
basement of this wing, traces the history of motion pictures
since the 1880s. Henri Langlois devoted his life to collecting the memorabilia contained in this museum, which include scripts, photos, costumes, and Louis Lumière's first
movie camera, dating from 1895. ☛ *Musée des Monuments
Français: 21 frs, 14 frs on Sun; Musée du Cinéma Henri
Langlois: 25 frs.* ☉ *Musée des Monuments Français:
Wed.–Mon. 10–6; Musée du Cinéma Henri Langlois:
Wed.–Mon; guided tours only, at 10, 11, 2, 3, 4 and 5.*

The area around the Palais de Chaillot is a veritable feast
for museum lovers. The **Musée Guimet** (down avenue du
Président Wilson, at place d'Iéna) has three floors of Indo-
Chinese and Far Eastern art, and the largest collection of
Cambodian art this side of Cambodia. The museum was
founded by the Lyonnais industrialist Emile Guimet, who
traveled around the world in the late 19th century amass-
ing priceless objets d'art. Among the museum's bewilder-
ing variety of exhibits are stone buddhas, Chinese bronzes,
ceramics, and painted screens. *6 pl. d'Iéna.* ☛ *26 frs adults,
17 frs students and senior citizens.* ☉ *Wed.–Mon. 9:45–
6. Métro: Iéna.*

The museum recently opened a new gallery, the **Hotel Hei-
delbach–Guimet,** a minute's walk down avenue d'Iéna,
which features Buddhist art from China and Japan. *19 av.
d'Iena.* ☛ *26 frs.* ☉ *Wed.–Mon. 9:45–6. Métro: Iéna.*

The **Musée d'Art Moderne de la Ville de Paris,** further down
avenue Wilson on the opposite side, has both temporary exhibits and a permanent collection of modern art, continuing where the Musée d'Orsay leaves off. Among the earliest
works are Fauvist paintings by Vlaminck and Derain, fol-

lowed by Picasso's early experiments in Cubism. No other
Paris museum exudes such a feeling of space and light. Its
vast, unobtrusive, white-walled galleries provide an ideal
background for the bold statements of 20th-century art.
Loudest and largest are the canvases of Robert Delaunay.
11 av. du Président Wilson. ☛ *15 frs, half-price on Sun. for
permanent exhibitions only. Prices vary for special exhibitions.* ☉ *Tues.–Sun. 10–5:30, Wed. 10–8:30. Métro: Iéna.*

⑯ Across from the Museum (the entrance is around the corner on avenue Pierre Ier de Serbie) is the **Palais Galliera,**
home of the small and some would say overpriced Museum
of Fashion and Costume. This stylish, late-19th-century town
house hosts rotating exhibits of costume, design, and accessories, usually based on a single theme. *10 av. Pierre-
Ier-de-Serbie.* ☛ *26 frs adults, 17 frs students and senior
citizens.* ☉ *Tues.–Sun. 10–5:40. Métro: Iéna.*

⑰ Continue along avenue Pierre Ier de Serbie and turn left on
avenue Marceau to the church of **St-Pierre de Chaillot.** The
monumental frieze above the entrance, depicting scenes from
the life of St. Peter, is the work of Henri Bouchard and dates
from 1937.

⑱ Rue Pierre Ier de Serbie eventually intersects avenue George
V; turn right toward the slender spire of the **American
Cathedral of the Holy Trinity,** built by G. S. Street between
1885 and 1888. ☉ *Weekdays 9–12:30 and 2–5, Sat. 9–
noon. Services: weekdays 9 AM, Sun. 9 AM and 11 AM; Sun.
school and nursery. Guided tours Sun. and Wed. 12:30.
Métro: Alma Marceau.*

Walk down to the bottom of the avenue, passing the **Crazy
Horse Saloon** across the avenue at No. 12, one of Paris's
most enduring and spectacular nightspots, to place de
l'Alma and the Seine.

⑲ The **Pont de l'Alma** (Alma bridge) is best known for the
chunky stone "Zouave" statue carved into one of the pillars. Zouaves were Algerian infantrymen recruited into the
French army who were famous for their bravura and colorful uniforms. Parisians use him to judge the level of the
Seine during heavy rains:

Just across the Alma bridge, on the left, is the entrance to
② **Les Egouts,** the Paris sewers (☛ 25 frs adults, 20 frs students and senior citizens; ⊘ Sat.–Wed. 11–5). Brave the
unpleasant—though tolerable—smell and follow the underground passages and footbridges along the sewers'
banks. Signs note the streets above you, and detailed panels and displays illuminate the history of waste disposal in
Paris, which boasts the second largest sewer system in the
world (after Chicago's). If you prefer a less malodorous tour
of the city, stay on the Right Bank and head down the sloping side road to the left of the bridge, for the embarkation
② point of the **Bateaux Mouches.** These popular motorboats
set off every half hour, heading east to the Ile St-Louis and
then back west, past the Eiffel Tower, as far as the Allée
des Cygnes and its miniature version of the Statue of Liberty. *Métro: Alma Marceau.*

Stylish avenue Montaigne, home to several top fashion
houses, leads from the Seine back toward the Champs-
② Elysées. The facade of the **Théâtre des Champs-Elysées** is
a forerunner of the Art Deco style. The theater dates from
1913 and was the first major building in France to be constructed in reinforced concrete. *15 av. Montaigne. Métro:
Alma Marceau.*

THE LEFT BANK

*Numbers in the margin correspond to points of interest on
the Left Bank map.*

References to the Left Bank have never lost their power to
evoke the most piquant of all images of Paris. Although the
bohemian strain the area once nurtured has lost much of
its vigor, people who choose it today as a place to live or
work are, in effect, turning their backs on the formality and
staidness of the Right Bank.

The Latin Quarter is the geographic and cerebral hub of
the Left Bank, populated mainly by Sorbonne students and
academics who fill the air of the cafés with their ideas—
and their tobacco smoke. (The university began as a theological school in the Middle Ages and later became the
headquarters of the University of Paris; in 1968, the stu-

dent revolution here had an explosive effect on French politics, resulting in major reforms in the education system.) The name Latin Quarter comes from the university tradition of studying and speaking in Latin, a tradition that disappeared during the Revolution.

St-Michel to St-Germain

❶ **Place St-Michel,** named for the grandiose fountain at its hub depicting St-Michel striking down the dragon, is a good starting point for exploring the rich slice of Parisian life that the Left Bank offers. Leave your itineraries at home, and wander along the neighboring streets lined with restaurants, cafés, galleries, old bookshops, and all sorts of clothing stores, from tiny boutiques to haute couture showrooms. *Métro: St-Michel.*

Pick up the pedestrian rue St-André des Arts at the south-❷ west corner of place St-Michel. **Studio St-André des Arts,** at No. 30, is one of Paris's most popular experimental cinemas. Just before you reach the Carrefour de Buci cross-❸ roads at the end of the street, turn onto the **Cour du Commerce St-André.** Jean-Paul Marat printed his revolutionary newspaper, *L'Ami du Peuple,* at No. 8; and it was here that Dr. Guillotin conceived the idea for a new, "humane" method of execution that was used during the Revolution—it was rumored that he practiced it on sheep first—and that remained the means of executing convicted murderers in France until President Mitterrand abolished it in 1981.

Down a small passageway on the left stands one of the few remaining towers of the 12th-century fortress wall built by ❹ Philippe-Auguste. The passage leads you to the **Cour de Rohan,** a series of three cloistered courtyards that were part of the hôtel of the archbishops of Rouen, established in the 15th century; the name has been corrupted over the years to Rohan.

Rejoin the Cour du Commerce St-André and continue to ❺ the **Carrefour de Buci,** once a notorious Left Bank landmark. By the 18th century, it contained a gallows, an execution stake, and an iron collar for punishing troublemakers. In

September 1792, the Revolutionary army used this daunting site to enroll its first volunteers, and many Royalists and priests lost their heads here during the bloody course of the Revolution. There's nothing sinister, however, about the Carrefour today. Brightly colored flowers spill onto the sidewalk at the **Grange à Buci** flower shop, on the corner of rue Grégoire-de-Tours. **Rue de Buci** has one of the best markets in Paris. ☺ *Tues.–Sun. 7:30 AM–1 PM. Métro: Mabillon.*

Several interesting, smaller streets of some historical significance radiate from the Carrefour. **Rue de l'Ancienne-Comédie,** which cuts through to the busy place de l'Odéon, is so named because it was the first home of the now legendary French theater company, the Comédie Française. The street was named in 1770, the very year the Comédie left for the Tuileries palace. The company moved again later to the Odéon, before heading to its present home by the Palais-Royal (*see* The Historic Heart, *above*).

Across the street from the company's first home (No. 14) is the oldest café in Paris, **Le Procope.** Opened in 1686 by an Italian named Francesco Procopio (only three years before the Odéon itself opened), it has been a watering hole for many of Paris's most famous literary sons and daughters over the centuries; Diderot, Voltaire, Balzac, George Sand, Victor Hugo, and Oscar Wilde were some of its more famous regulars.

Stretching north from the Carrefour de Buci toward the Seine is the **rue Dauphine,** the street that singer Juliet Greco put on the map when she opened the Tabou jazz club here at No. 33 in the '50s. It attracted a group of young intellectuals who were to become known as the Zazous, a St-Germain movement promoting the jazz culture, complete with all-night parties and free love. You may still find jazz played here, but the club is a shadow of its former self.

Take rue Mazarine, the next street emanating from the Carrefour de Buci (west of rue Dauphine), then turn left onto rue J. Callot, continue to the end, and take next left into tiny **rue Visconti,** which has a lot of history packed into its short length. In the 16th century, it was known as Paris's Little Geneva—named after Europe's foremost Protestant

80

The Left Bank

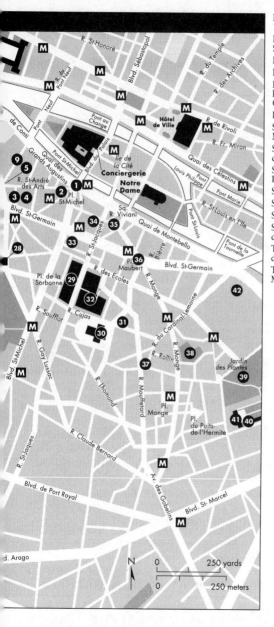

city—because of the Protestant ghetto that formed here. Racine, one of France's greatest playwrights and tragic poets, lived at No. 24 until his death in 1699. Balzac set up a printing shop at No. 17 in 1826, and the fiery Romantic artist Eugène Delacroix (1798–1863) worked here from 1836 to 1844.

TIME OUT   The terrace at **La Palette** (43 rue de Seine) beckons as soon as you reach the rue de Seine, at the end of rue Callot. This popular café has long been a favorite haunt of Beaux Arts students.

Follow rue Visconti west to rue Bonaparte; here stands the ⑪ **Ecole Nationale des Beaux-Arts,** whose students can usually be seen painting and sketching on the nearby quais and bridges. The school—today the breeding ground for France's foremost painters, sculptors, and architects—was once the site of a convent, founded in 1608 by Marguerite de Valois, the first wife of Henri IV. During the Revolution, the convent was turned into a depot for works of art salvaged from the monuments that were under threat of destruction by impassioned mobs. Only the church and cloister remained, however, when the Beaux-Arts school was established in 1816. Allow yourself time to wander into the courtyard and galleries of the school to see the casts and copies of the statues that were once stored here, or stop in at one of the temporary exhibitions of professors' and students' works. *14 rue Bonaparte.* ⊗ *Daily 1–7. Métro: St-Germain-des-Prés.*

Head back down rue Bonaparte, swing right, and follow pretty rue Jacob, where both Wagner and Stendhal once lived, across rue des Saints-Pères, where it changes to rue de l'Université. You are now in the Carré Rive Gauche, the Left Bank's concentrated quarter-mile of art dealers and galleries. *Galleries are usually open 10–12:30 and 2–6, closed Mon. Métro: St-Germain-des-Prés.*

Double back along rue Jacob until you meet rue de Fürstemberg on your right. This leads to the quiet place Fürstemberg, bedecked with white globe lamps and catalpa trees. ⑫ Here is **Atelier Delacroix,** Delacroix's former studio, containing only a paltry collection of sketches and drawings by the artist; the garden at the rear of the studio is almost as interesting. Nonetheless, those who feel the need to pay homage to France's foremost Romantic painter will want to make the pilgrimage. *6 place Fürstemberg.* ☛ *12 frs adults, 7 frs ages 18–25 and over 60, 7 frs on Sun.* ⊘ *Wed.–Mon. 9:45–5:15. Métro: St-Germain-des-Prés.*

Follow rue de Fürstemberg south to rue de l'Abbaye; turn
⑬ right to reach **St-Germain-des-Prés,** Paris's oldest church, which began as a shelter for a relic of the True Cross brought back from Spain in AD 542. Behind it, rue de l'Abbaye runs alongside the former Abbey palace, dating from AD 990 and once part of a powerful Benedictine abbey. The chancel was enlarged and the church then consecrated by Pope Alexander III in 1163. The church stages superb organ concerts and recitals; programs are displayed outside and in the weekly periodicals *Officiel des Spectacles* and *Pariscope.* ⊘ *Weekdays 8–7:30; weekends 8–9. Métro: St-Germain-des-Prés.*

Across the cobbled place St-Germain-des-Prés stands the
⑭ celebrated **Les Deux Magots** café, named after the grotesque Chinese figures, or *magots,* inside. It still thrives on its post–World War II reputation as one of the Left Bank's prime meeting places for the intelligentsia. Though the Deux Magots remains crowded day and night, these days you're more likely to rub shoulders with tourists than with philosophers. Yet those in search of the mysterious glamour of the Left Bank can do no better than to station themselves at one of the sidewalk tables—or at a window table on a wintry day—to watch the passing parade.

In the postwar years, Jean-Paul Sartre and Simone de Beauvoir would meet "the family" two doors down at the **Café de Flore** on boulevard St-Germain. "The family" was de Beauvoir's name for their close-knit group, which included fellow-graduates from the prestigious Ecole Normale Supérieure and writers from Gaston Gallimard's publishing house in the nearby rue Sébastien-Bottin. Along with
⑯ the Deux Magots and the pricey **Brasserie Lipp** across the street, where politicians and show-biz types come to wine and dine (after being "passed" by the doorman), it is a scenic spot that never lacks for action.

Turn left after Brasserie Lipp down rue du Dragon to the

⑰ carrefour de La Croix Rouge, with its mighty bronze **Centaur** by the contemporary sculptor, César. Take rue du Vieux-Colombier to place St-Sulpice. This newly renovated square is ringed with cafés, and Yves St-Laurent's famous Rive Gauche store is at No. 6. Looming over the square is

⑱ the enormous 17th-century church of **St-Sulpice.** The 18th-century facade was never finished, and its unequal towers add a playful touch to an otherwise sober design. The interior is baldly impersonal, however, despite the magnificent Delacroix frescoes—notably Jacob wrestling with the angel—in the first chapel on your right. If you now pick up the long, boutique-filled rue de Rennes and follow it south, you'll soon arrive in the heart of Montparnasse. *Métro: St-Sulpice.*

Montparnasse

With the growth of Paris as a business and tourist capital, commercialization seems to have filled any area where departing residents and businesses have created a vacuum. Nowhere else is this more true than in and around the vaulting, concrete space and starkly functionalist buildings that have come to rule Montparnasse. Seeing it now, it is difficult to believe that in the years after World War I, Montparnasse replaced Montmartre as *the* place in which Parisian artists came to live.

⑲ The opening of the 59-story **Tour Maine-Montparnasse** in 1973 forever changed the face of this painters' and poets' haunt. (The name Montparnasse itself came from some 17th-century students who christened the area after Mount Parnassus, the home of Apollo, leader of the Muses.) The tower was part of a vast redevelopment plan that aimed to make the area one of Paris's premier business and shopping districts. Fifty-two floors of the tower are taken up by offices, while a vast commercial complex, including a Galeries Lafayette department store, spreads over the first floor. Although it is uninspiring by day, it becomes a neon-lit beacon for the area at night. As Europe's tallest high rise, it affords stupendous views of Paris; on a clear day, you can see for 30 miles. (There's a snack bar and cafeteria on

Reality check. Call home.

AT&T USADirect® and World Connect.®
The fast, easy way to call most anywhere.

Take out AT&T Calling Card or your local calling card.** Lift phone. Dial AT&T Access Number for country you're calling from. Connect to English-speaking operator or voice prompt. Reach the States or over 200 countries. Talk. Say goodbye. Hang up. Resume vacation.

Austria⁺†††	022-903-011	Portugal†	05017-1-288
Belgium*	0-800-100-10	Romania*	01-800-4288
Czech Republic*	00-420-00101	Russia⁺†(Moscow)	155-5042
Denmark	8001-0010	Slovak Rep.*	00-420-00101
Finland	9800-100-10	Spain●	900-99-00-11
France	19-0011	Sweden	020-795-611
Germany	0130-0010	Switzerland*	155-00-11
Greece*	00-800-1311	Turkey*	00-800-12277
Hungary*	00◊-800-01111	United Kingdom	0500-89-0011
Ireland	1-800-550-000		
Italy*	172-1011		
Luxembourg	0-800-0111		
Netherlands*	06-022-9111		
Norway	800-190-11		
Poland†♦¹	0◊010-480-0111		

AT&T
Your True Choice

**You can also call collect or use most U.S. local calling cards. Countries in bold face permit country-to-country calling in addition to calls to the U.S. World Connect® prices consist of USADirect® rates plus an additional charge based on the country you are calling. Collect calling available to the U.S. only. *Public phones require coin or card. †Limited availability. †††Public phones require local coin payment during call. ♦ Not available from public phones. ◊Await second dial tone. ¹Dial 010-480-0111 from major Warsaw hotels. ●Calling available to most European countries. ©1995 AT&T.

For a free wallet sized card of all AT&T Access Numbers, call: 1-800-241-5555.

All the best trips start with **Fodor's**.

the 56th floor; if you go to the top-floor bar for drinks, the ride up is free.) It also claims to have the fastest elevator in Europe! ☛ *40 frs adults, 32 frs students and senior citizens, 24 frs ages 5–14.* ☺ *Daily 9:30 AM–10:30 PM. Métro: Montparnasse Bienvenüe.*

20 Immediately north of the tower is **place du 18 Juin 1940,** part of what was once the old Montparnasse train station and a significant spot in Parisian World War II history. It is named for the date of the radio speech Charles de Gaulle made, from London, urging the French to continue resisting the Germans after the fall of the country to Nazi Germany in May 1940. In August 1944, the German military governor, Dietrich von Choltitz, surrendered to the Allies here, ignoring Hitler's orders to destroy the city as he withdrew; the French General Philippe Leclerc subsequently used it as his headquarters.

To the south, **Gare Montparnasse,** with its huge glass facade, serves Chartres, Versailles, and the west of France. The high-speed *TGV Atlantique* leaves here for Brittany (Rennes and Nantes) and the southwest (Bordeaux, via Tours, Poitiers, and Angoulême). The **Jardin Atlantique,** a small designer park built over the tracks (it opened in 1994), contains benches for weary travelers sweating through a stopover, and features an assortment of trees from all countries that—appropriately—border on the Atlantic ocean.

21 The **Cimetière de Montparnasse** (Montparnasse cemetery) contains many of the quarter's most illustrious residents, buried only a stone's throw away from where they worked and played. It is not at all a picturesque cemetery (with the exception of the old windmill in the corner, which used to be a student tavern) but seeing the names of some of its inhabitants—Baudelaire, Maupassant, Saint-Saëns, and the industrialist André Citroën—may make the visit worthwhile.

From here you may wish to head south 300 yards to place Denfert Rochereau and visit the extensive underground
22 labyrith of **catacombs** (*denfert* is a corruption of the word for hell, *enfer*) built by the Romans, tunneling under much of the Left Bank and into the near suburbs. They were subsequently used to store millions of skeletons from disused

graveyards; then, during World War II, they became the headquarters of the French Resistance. You are well advised to
take a flashlight with you. ☛ *27 frs adults, 15 frs students
and senior citizens.* ⊙ *Tues.–Fri. 2–4, weekends 9–11 and
2–4. Guided tours on Wed. at 2:45; 20 frs extra. Métro
and RER: Denfert Rochereau.*

Montparnasse's bohemian aura has dwindled to almost
nothing, yet the area hops at night as *the* place in Paris to
find movies of every description, many of them shown in their
original language. Back up boulevard Raspail and west on
Montparnasse, across from the Vavin métro station, are two
of the better-known gathering places of Montparnasse's heyday, the **Dôme** and **La Coupole** brasseries. La Coupole opened
in 1927 as a bar-restaurant-dance hall and soon became a
home away from home for some of the area's most famous
residents, such as Apollinaire, Max Jacob, Cocteau, Satie,
Stravinsky, and the ubiquitous Hemingway.

Across the boulevard are two more celebrated Montparnasse cafés, the **Sélect** and the **Rotonde.** Rue Vavin leads to
the Jardin du Luxembourg. But stay on boulevard du Montparnasse for the intersection with boulevard St-Michel,
where the verdant avenue de l'Observatoire begins its long
sweep up to the Luxembourg gardens. Here you'll find perhaps the most famous bastion of the Left Bank café culture, the **Closerie des Lilas.** Now a pricey bar-restaurant,
the Closerie remains a staple on all literary tours of Paris
not least because of the commemorative plaques fastened
onto the bar, marking the places where renowned person-
ages sat—Baudelaire, Verlaine, Hemingway, and Apollinaire
are just a few of the names. Although the lilacs (*lilas*) have
gone from the terrace, it is still a pretty place, opening onto
the luxuriant green of the surrounding parkland, and as
crowded in the summer as it ever was in the '30s.

The vista from the Closerie includes the **Observatoire de
Paris** (Paris Observatory) to the south, built in 1667 under
Louis XIV by architect Claude Perrault. Its four facades were
built to align with the four cardinal points—north, south,
east, and west—and its southern wall is the determining point
for Paris's official latitude, 48° 50′11″N. French time was

based on this Paris meridian until 1911, when the country decided to adopt the international Greenwich Meridian.

A tree-lined alley leads along avenue de l'Observatoire past Davioud's **Fontaine de l'Observatoire** (Observatory Fountain), built in 1873 and decked with four statues representing the four quarters of the globe. Look north from here and you'll have a captivating view of Montmartre and Sacré-Coeur, with the Luxembourg Gardens in the foreground.

Palais du Luxembourg

The **Jardin du Luxembourg** (the Luxembourg Gardens) is one of the city's few large parks. Its fountains, ponds, trim hedges, precisely planted rows of trees, and gravel walks are typical of the French fondness for formal gardens. At the far end is the **Palais du Luxembourg,** gray and imposing, built, like the park, for Maria de' Medici, widow of Henri IV, at the beginning of the 17th century. The palace remained royal property until the Revolution, when the state took it over and used it as a prison. Danton, the painter David, and Thomas Paine were all detained here. Today, it is the site of the French Senate and is not open to the public. *Métro: Odéon, RER: Luxembourg.*

The **Théâtre National de l'Odéon,** set at the north end of the Luxembourg Gardens, was established in 1792 to house the Comédiens Français troupe. The structure you see today replaced the original theater, which was destroyed by fire in 1807. Since World War II, it has specialized in 20th-century productions. It was the base for Jean-Louis Barrault's and Madeleine Renaud's theater company, the Théâtre de France, until they fell out of favor with the authorities for their alleged role in spurring on the student revolutionaries in May 1968. Today, the Théâtre de l'Odéon is the French home of the Theater of Europe and stages some excellent productions by major foreign companies.

The Sorbonne and the Latin Quarter

If you follow rue de Vaugirard (the longest street in Paris) one block east to boulevard St-Michel, you will soon be at the **place de la Sorbonne,** the hub of the Latin Quarter and nerve center of the student population that has always held such sway over Left Bank life. The square is dominated by the Eglise de la Sorbonne, whose outstanding exterior features are its cupola and 10 Corinthian columns. Inside is the white marble tomb of Cardinal Richelieu. (The church is open to the public only during exhibitions and cultural events.) The university buildings of La Sorbonne are spread out around the church from rue Cujas down to the visitor's entrance on rue des Ecoles.

㉙ The **Sorbonne** is the oldest university in Paris—indeed, one of the oldest in Europe—and has for centuries been one of France's principal institutions of higher learning. It is named after Robert de Sorbon, a medieval canon who founded a theological college here in 1253 for 16 students. By the 17th century, the church and university buildings were becoming dilapidated, so Cardinal Richelieu undertook to have them restored; the present-day Sorbonne campus is largely a result of that restoration. Despite changes in the neighborhood, the maze of amphitheaters, lecture rooms, and laboratories, and the surrounding courtyards and narrow streets, still have a hallowed air. For a glimpse of a more recent relic of Sorbonne history, look for Puvis de Chavannes's painting of the *Sacred Wood* in the main lecture hall, a major meeting point during the tumultuous student upheavals of 1968, and now a university landmark.

Behind the Sorbonne, bordering its eastern reach, is the rue St-Jacques. The street climbs south toward the rue Souf-flot, named to honor the man who built the vast, domed
㉚ church called the **Panthéon,** set atop place du Panthéon. One of Paris's most physically overwhelming sites—it was commissioned by Louis XV as a mark of gratitude for his recovery from a grave illness in 1744—the Panthéon is now a monument to France's most glorious historical figures, and is renowned for Puvis de Chavannes's monumental frescoes and the crypt, which holds the remains of Voltaire, Zola, Rousseau, and dozens of French statesmen, military heroes, and thinkers. In 1789—the year the church was completed—its windows were blocked by order of the Revolutionary Constituent Assembly, and they have remained that way ever since, adding to its sepulchral gloom. The dome, which weighs about 10,000 tons, is best appreciated

from a distance. ☛ *26 frs adults, 17 frs ages 18–25, 6 frs ages 7–17.* ☼ *Daily 10–5:30. Métro: Cardinal-Lemoine.*

③ Diagonally across from the Panthéon on the corner of rue Clovis and rue Cujas stands the striking **St-Etienne-du-Mont.** This mainly 16th-century church's ornate facade combines Gothic, Baroque, and Renaissance elements. Inside, the fretted rood screen is the only one of its kind in Paris. Note the uneven-floored chapel behind the choir, which can be reached via a cloister containing some exquisite stained glass dating from the 17th century.

㉜ Up rue St-Jacques again and across from the Sorbonne are the **Lycée Louis-le-Grand** (Molière, Voltaire, and Robespierre studied here) and the elite **Collège de France,** whose grounds continue around the corner onto rue des Ecoles. In 1530, François I created this school as the College of Three Languages, which taught High Latin, Greek, and Hebrew, and any other subjects eschewed by academics at the Sorbonne. Diagonally across from the college, on the other side of rue des Ecoles, is the **square Paul-Painlevé;** behind it lies the entrance to the inimitable Hôtel et Musée National du Moyen-Age.

㉝ Built on the site of the city's enormous old Roman baths, the **Musée National du Moyen-Age** (formerly the **Musée de Cluny**) is housed in a 15th-century mansion that originally belonged to monks of the Cluny Abbey in Burgundy. The remains of the baths that can still be seen are what survived a sacking by Barbarians in the 4th century. But the real reason people come to the Cluny is for its tapestry collection. The most famous series of all is the graceful *Dame à la Licorne,* or *Lady and the Unicorn,* woven in the 15th or 16th century, probably in the southern Netherlands. And if the tapestries themselves aren't enough at which to marvel, there is also an exhibition of decorative arts from the Middle Ages, a vaulted chapel, and a deep, cloistered courtyard with mullioned windows, set off by the *Boatmen's Pillar,* Paris's oldest sculpture, at its center. ☛ *27 frs, 18 frs students and senior citizens and on Sun.* ☼ *Wed.–Mon. 9:45–5:45. Métro: Cluny–La Sorbonne.*

Above boulevard St-Germain, rue St-Jacques reaches toward the Seine, bringing you past the elegant proportions of the

❸❹ church of **St-Séverin.** Rebuilt in the 16th century and noted for its width and its Flamboyant Gothic style, the church dominates a close-knit Left Bank neighborhood filled with quiet squares and pedestrian streets. In the 11th century, it was the parish church for the entire Left Bank. Louis XIV's cousin, a capricious woman known simply as the Grande Mademoiselle, adopted St-Séverin when she tired of the St-Sulpice church; she then spent vast sums getting Le Brun to modernize the chancel. Note the splendidly deviant spiraling column in the forest of pillars behind the altar. ☺ *Weekdays 11–5:30, Sat. 11–10. Métro: St-Michel.*

Running riot around the relative quiet of St-Séverin are streets filled with restaurants of every description, serving everything from souvlaki-to-go to five-course haute cuisine. There is definitely something for every budget here. Rue de la Huchette is the most heavily trafficked of the restaurant streets and especially good for its selection of cheaper Greek food houses and Tunisian patisseries.

❸❺ Cross to the other side of rue St-Jacques. In Square René Viviani, which surrounds the church of **St-Julien-le-Pauvre,** stands an acacia tree that is supposed to be the oldest tree in Paris (although it has a rival claim from another acacia at the Jardin des Plantes). This tree-filled square also gives you one of the more spectacular views of Notre Dame. The tiny church here was built at the same time as Notre Dame (1165–1220), on a site where a whole succession of chapels once stood. The church belongs to a Greek Orthodox order today, but was originally named for St. Julian, bishop of Le Mans, who was nicknamed "Le Pauvre" after he gave all his money away.

Behind the church, to the east, are the tiny, elegant streets of the **Maubert** district, bordered by quai de Montebello and boulevard St-Germain. Rue de Bièvre, once filled with tanneries (the Bièvre River flows underneath), used to be guarded at both ends to protect François Mitterrand's private residence.

Public meetings and demonstrations have been held in place Maubert ever since the Middle Ages. Nowadays, most gatherings are held inside or in front of the elegantly
❸❻ Art Deco **Palais de la Mutualité,** on the corner of the square,

also a venue for jazz, pop, and rock concerts. On Tuesdays, Thursdays, and Saturdays, it is transformed into a colorful outdoor food market.

③⑦ Head down rue Monge, turn right onto rue du Cardinal-Lemoine, and you'll find yourself at the minute **place de la Contrescarpe.** It doesn't start to swing until after dusk, when its cafés and bars fill up. During the day, the square looks almost provincial, as Parisians flock to the daily market on rue Mouffetard. There are restaurants and cafés of every description on rue Mouffetard, and if you get here at lunchtime, you may want to buy yourself the makings for an alfresco lunch and take it to the unconventional picnic spot provided by the nearby Gallo-Roman ruin of the **③⑧ Arènes de Lutèce;** it begins on rue Monge, just past the end of rue Rollin. The ancient arena was discovered only in 1869 and has since been excavated and landscaped to reveal parts of the original Roman amphitheater. This site and the remains of the baths at the Cluny constitute the only extant evidence of the powerful Roman city of Lutetia that flourished here in the 3rd century. It is also one of the lesser-known delights of the Left Bank, so you are not likely to find it crowded. *Métro: Monge.*

③⑨ The **Jardin des Plantes,** reached via rue de Navarre and rue Lacépède, is an enormous swath of greenery containing spacious botanical gardens and a number of natural history museums. It is stocked with plants dating back to the first collections here in the 17th century, and has been enhanced ever since by subsequent generations of devoted French botanists. It claims to shelter Paris's oldest tree, an *acacia robinia,* planted in 1636. There is also a small, old-fashioned zoo here (☞ 25 francs; open daily 9–5); an alpine garden; an aquarium; a maze; and a number of hothouses. Three natural history museums are at the far side of the gardens: The **Musée Entomologique** is devoted to insects, the **④⓪ Musée Paléontologique** exhibits fossils and pre-historic animals, and the **Musée Minéralogique** houses an impressive collection of rocks and minerals. ☞ *12–25 frs.* ☉ *Museums: Wed.–Mon. 9–11:45 and 1–4:45, weekends 2–4:45. Garden: daily 7:30–sunset. Métro: Monge.*

41 The **Grande Galerie de l'Evolution,** next door to the museums, reopened amidst popular acclaim in 1994. This vast, handsome glass-and-iron structure, built, like the Eiffel Tower, in 1889 but abandoned in the 1960s, contains one of the world's finest collections of stuffed animals, including a section devoted to extinct and endangered species. There's a reconstituted *dodo*—only a foot actually remains of this cumbersome, flightless bird from Madagascar— and a miniature South African zebra, the *quagga,* which disappeared earlier this century. Stunning lighting effects include push-button spotlighting and a roof that changes color to suggest storms, twilight, or hot savannah sun. ☛ *40 frs, 30 frs before 2 PM.* ☉ *Wed.–Mon. 10–6, Thurs. 10– 10. Métro: Monge.*

TIME OUT At the back of the gardens, in place du Puits-de-l'Hermite, you can drink a restorative cup of sweet mint tea in **La Mosquée,** a beautiful white mosque, complete with minaret. Once inside, you'll be convinced that you must be elsewhere than the Left Bank of Paris. The students from the nearby Jussieu and Censier universities pack themselves into the Moslem restaurant here, which serves copious quantities of couscous. The sunken garden and tiled patios are open to the public (the prayer rooms are not) and so are the *hammams,* or Turkish baths. ☛ *15 frs for guided tour, 65 frs for Turkish baths.* ☉ *Baths: daily 11 am–8 pm; Fri. and Sun. men only; Mon., Wed., Thurs., and Sat. women only. Guided tours of mosque Sat.–Thurs. 10–noon and 2–5:30. Métro: Monge.*

In 1988, Paris's large Arab population gained another base:
42 the huge **Institut du Monde Arabe,** which overlooks the Seine on quai St-Bernard, just beyond Université Jussieu. Jean Nouvel's harmonious mixture of Arabic and European styles in a striking glass and steel edifice was greeted with enthusiasm when the center first opened. Note on the building's south side the 240 shutter-like apertures that open and close to regulate light exposure. It contains a sound and image center, a vast library and documentation center, and an excellent art museum containing an array of Arab-Islamic art, textiles, and ceramics, with exhibits on Arabic mathematics, astronomy, and medicine. Glass elevators

will take you to the ninth floor, where you can sip tea on the roof and enjoy (yet another) memorable view over the Seine and Notre Dame. *23 quai St-Bernard.* ☞ *Free.* ☉ *Tues.–Sun. 10–6. Métro: Sully-Morland.*

MONTMARTRE

Numbers in the margin correspond to points of interest on the Montmartre map.

On a dramatic rise above the city is Montmartre, site of the Sacré-Coeur basilica and home to a once-thriving artistic community, a heritage recalled today chiefly by the gangs of third-rate painters clustered in the area's most famous square, the place du Tertre. Despite their presence, and the fact that the fabled nightlife of old Montmartre has fizzled down to some glitzy nightclubs and porn shows, Montmartre still exudes a sense of history, a timeless quality infused with that hard-to-define Gallic charm.

Visiting Montmartre means negotiating a lot of steep streets and flights of steps. If the prospect of trudging up and down them is daunting, you can tour parts of Montmartre by public transportation, aboard the Promotrain or the Montmartrobus. The Promotrain offers daily 40-minute guided tours of Montmartre between 10 AM and midnight. The cost is 25 francs, 15 francs for children under 12, and departures are from outside the Moulin Rouge on place Blanche. The Montmartrobus is a regular city bus that runs around Montmartre for the price of a métro ticket. It departs from place Pigalle. If you're visiting only Sacré-Coeur, take the funicular that runs up the hill to the church near Anvers métro station.

Exploring Montmartre

❶ Begin your tour at **place Blanche,** site of the Moulin Rouge. Place Blanche—White Square—takes its name from the clouds of chalky dust churned up by the windmills that once dotted Montmartre (or *La Butte,* meaning "mound" or "hillock"). They were set up here not just because the hill was a good place to catch the wind—at over 300 feet, it's

Montmartre

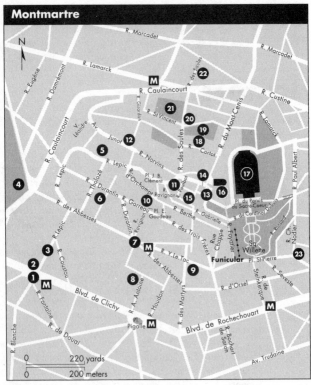

0 ⊢———————⊣ 220 yards
0 ⊢———————⊣ 200 meters

the highest point in the city—but because Montmartre was covered with wheat fields and quarries right up to the end of the 19th century. The carts carrying away the wheat and crushed stone trundled across place Blanche, turning the square white as they passed. Today, only two of the original 20 windmills are intact. A number have been converted

② to other uses, none more famous than the **Moulin Rouge,** or Red Windmill, built in 1885 and turned into a dance hall in 1900. It was a genuinely wild place in its early days, immortalized by Toulouse-Lautrec in his boldly simple posters and paintings. It's still trading shamelessly on the notion of Paris as a city of sin: If you fancy a Vegas-style night out, with computerized light shows and troupes of bare-breasted women sporting feather headdresses, this is the place to go (*see* Chapter 6, The Arts and Nightlife). The cancan, by the way—still a regular feature here—was considerably more raunchy when Lautrec was around.

For a taste of something more authentically French, walk

③ past the Moulin Rouge, up **rue Lepic,** site of one of the most colorful and tempting food markets in Paris (closed Mon.). *Métro: Blanche.*

Turn left onto rue Joseph de Maistre and walk along to

④ **Cimetière de Montmartre** (Montmartre cemetery). It's by no means as romantic or as large as the better known Père Lachaise cemetery in the east of the city, but it contains the graves of many prominent French men and women, including the 18th-century painters Greuze and Fragonard; Degas; and Adolphe Sax, inventor of the saxophone. The Russian ballet dancer Nijinsky is also buried here.

Walk back along rue Joseph de Maistre (it turns into rue des Abbesses once you pass rue Lepic). Rue Tholozé, the second street on the left, was once a path over the hill, the

⑤ oldest in Montmartre. It leads to the **Moulin de la Galette,** one of the two remaining windmills in Montmartre, which

⑥ has been unromantically rebuilt. To reach it, you pass **Studio 28.** This seems to be no more than a generic little movie theater, but when opened in 1928, it was the first purposely built *art et essai,* or experimental theater, in the world. Over the years, the movies of such directors as Jean Cocteau,

François Truffaut, and Orson Welles have often been shown here before their official premieres.

7 Return to rue des Abbesses, turn left, and walk to **place des Abbesses.** The little square is typical of the kind of picturesque and slightly countrified style that has made Montmartre famous. The entrance to the métro station, a curving, sensuous mass of delicate iron, is one of a handful of original Art Nouveau stations left in Paris. The austere, red-brick **church of St-Jean l'Evangéliste** (1904) is worth a look, too. It was one of the first concrete buildings in France; the brick had to be added later to soothe offended locals. The **café St-Jean,** next to it, is a popular local meeting place, crowded on weekends. *Métro: Abbesses.*

There are two competing attractions just off the square. Theater buffs should head down the tiny rue André-Antoine.
8 At No. 37, you'll see what was originally the **Théâtre Libre,** or Free Theater, founded in 1887 by André Antoine and immensely influential in popularizing the work of iconoclastic young playwrights such as Ibsen and Strindberg. The other attraction is **rue Yvonne-le-Tac,** scene of a vital event in Montmartre's early history and linked to the disputed story of how this quarter got its name. Some say the name Montmartre comes from the Roman temple to Mercury that was once here, called the Mound of Mercury or *Mons Mercurii.* Others contend that it was an adaptation of *Mons Martyrum,* a name inspired by the burial here of Paris's first bishop, St-Denis. The popular version of his martyrdom is that he was beheaded by the Romans in AD 250, but arose to carry his severed head from rue Yvonne-le-Tac to a place 4 miles to the north, an area now known as St-Denis. He is com-
9 memorated by the 19th-century **Chapelle du Martyre** at No. 9, built over the spot where he is said to have been executed. It was in the crypt of the original chapel here that St. Ignatius of Loyola founded the Jesuit order in 1540, a decisive step in the efforts of the Catholic Church to reassert its authority in the face of the Protestant Reformation.

From rue Yvonne-le-Tac, retrace your steps through place des Abbesses. Take rue Ravignan on the right, climbing to the summit via place Emile-Goudeau, an enchanting little
10 cobbled square. Your goal is the **Bateau-Lavoir,** or Boat Wash

House, at its northern edge. Montmartre poet Max Jacob coined the name for the old building on this site, which burned down in 1970. First of all, he said, it resembled a boat. Second, the warren of artists' studios within was always cluttered and paint-splattered, and looked to be in perpetual need of a good hosing down. The new building also contains art studios, but, if you didn't know its history, you'd probably walk right past it; it is the epitome of poured concrete drabness. It was in the original Bateau-Lavoir that painters Picasso and Braque, early this century, made their first bold stabs at the concept of Cubism—a move that paved the way for abstract painting.

Continue up the hill to place Jean-Baptiste Clément. The Italian painter and sculptor Modigliani (1884–1920) had a studio here at No. 7. Some have claimed he was the greatest Italian artist of the 20th century, the man who fused the genius of the Italian Renaissance with the modernity of Cézanne and Picasso. He claimed that he would drink himself to death—he eventually did—and chose the right part of town to do it in. This was one of the wildest areas of Montmartre. Its bistros and cabarets have mostly gone now, though, and only the **Moulin de Paris** still reflects a glimmer of the old atmosphere. Look for the octagonal tower at the north end of the square; it's all that's left of Montmartre's first water tower, built around 1840 to boost the area's feeble water supply.

Rue Norvins, formerly rue des Moulins, runs behind and parallel to the north end of the square. Turn left along it to reach stylish avenue Junot, site of the **Cité Internationale des Arts** (International Residence of the Arts), where the city authorities rent out studios to artists from all over the world. Retrace your steps back to rue Norvins and continue east past the bars and tourist shops, until you reach place du Tertre.

Place du Tertre (*tertre* means hillock) regains its village atmosphere only in the winter, when the somber buildings gather in the grays of the Parisian light and the plane tree branches sketch traceries against the sky. At any other time of year, you'll have to fight your way through the crowds to the southern end of the square and the breathtaking view over the city. The real drawback is the swarm of artists clamoring to dash off your portrait. Most are licensed to be there, and, like taxi drivers, their prices are officially fixed. But there is no shortage of con men, sketch pads in hand, who will charge whatever they think they can get away with. If one produces a picture of you without having first asked, you're under no obligation to buy it, though that's not to say you won't have to argue your case. It's best just to walk away.

⑭ La Mère Catherine, the restaurant at the northern end of the square, has an honored place in French culinary history. It was a favorite with the Russian cossacks who occupied Paris in 1814 after Napoléon had been exiled to the island of Elba. Little did they know that when they banged on the tables and shouted *"bistro,"* the Russian word for "quick," they were inventing a new breed of French restaurant. For a restaurant catering almost entirely to the tourist trade, La Mère Catherine is surprisingly good, though prices are high for what's offered.

TIME OUT   **Patachou,** opened in 1987, sounds the one classy note on place du Tertre (at No. 9). It offers exquisite, if expensive, cakes and teas.

⑮ Around the corner on rue Poulbot, the **Espace Dali** houses 25 sculptures and more than 300 prints of works by Salvador Dali, who once kept a studio in the area. The museum's atmosphere is meant to approximate the surreal experience, with black walls, low lighting, and a new-agey musical score—punctuated by recordings of Dali's own voice. If you're interested in seeing some of Dali's less-familiar works, including a series of sculptures and bronzes, a visit will prove worthwhile. *11 rue Poulbot,* ☎ *42–64–40–10.* ☛ *35 frs adults, 25 frs students and senior citizens.* ☼ *Daily 10–6; summer, daily 10–8. Métro: Abbesses.*

It was in place du Tertre in March 1871 that one of the most destructively violent episodes in French history began, one that colored French political life for generations. Despite popular images of later-19th-century France—and Paris especially—as carefree and prosperous, for much of this period the country was desperately divided into two camps: an ever more vocal and militant underclass, motivated by resentment of what they considered an elitist government, and a reactionary and fearful bourgeoisie and ruling class. It was a conflict that went back at least as far as the French Revolution at the end of the 18th century, and one that twice flared into outbreaks of civil war and rebellion, in 1832 and 1848, as the country oscillated between republican and imperial forms of government. In 1870, France, under the leadership of an opportunistic but feeble Napoléon III (nephew of the great Napoléon), was drawn into a disastrous war with Bismarck's Prussia, which was rapidly growing into one of the most formidable military powers in Europe. (Soon after, Prussia was to dominate a newly united and aggressive Germany.) In September that year, Prussia invaded France, surrounded Paris, and laid siege to it. After four months of appalling suffering the new government under French statesman Adolphe Thiers capitulated. Although mass starvation seemed imminent, fears that Thiers would restore an imperial rather than a republican government caused Parisians to refuse to surrender their arms to him. Thiers then ordered that the guns at Montmartre be captured by loyal government forces. Insurgents responded by shooting the two generals ordered to retake the guns. Almost immediately, barricades were thrown up across the city streets, and the fighting began in earnest. The antimonarchists formed the Commune, which for three heady months ruled Paris. In May, from his base at Versailles, Thiers ordered the city retaken. Estimates as to the numbers killed in the fighting vary greatly. Some say 4,000 Communards lost their lives; others claim 20,000. No one, however, doubts that upward of 10,000 Communards were executed by government troops after the collapse of the Commune.

In expiation for this bloodshed, the French government decided, in 1873 (after the downfall of Thiers), to build the basilica of the Sacré-Coeur. It was to be a sort of national guilt offering. Before visiting this landmark, walk to the **16** church of **St-Pierre de Montmartre** at the east side of place du Tertre. It's one of the oldest churches in the city, built in the 12th century as the abbey church of a substantial Benedictine monastery. It's been remodeled on a number of occasions down through the years, and the 18th-century facade, built under Louis XIV, contrasts uncomfortably with the mostly medieval interior. Its setting is awkward, too: The bulk of the Sacré-Coeur looms directly behind it.

⓱ The **Basilique du Sacré-Coeur,** begun in 1873 and completed in 1910 (though not consecrated until 1919), symbolized the return of relative self-confidence to late-19th-century Paris after the turmoil of the Commune. Even so, the building was to some extent a reflection of political divisions within the country. It was largely financed by French Catholics fearful of an anticlerical backlash and determined to make a grand statement on behalf of the Church. Stylistically, the Sacré-Coeur borrows elements from Romanesque and Byzantine models, fusing them under its distinctive Oriental dome. Built on a grand scale, the effect is strangely disjointed and unsettling, rather as if the building had been designed by an architect of railway stations, with a pronounced taste for exoticism. (The architect, Abadie, died in 1884, long before the church was finished.) The gloomy, cavernous interior is worth visiting for its golden mosaics; climb to the top of the dome for the view over Paris. *Métro: Anvers.*

More of Montmartre beckons north and west of the Sacré-Coeur. Take rue du Mont-Cenis (west of the basilica) down
⓲ to rue Cortot, site of the **Musée du Vieux Montmartre.** Like the Bateau-Lavoir, the building that is now the museum sheltered an illustrious group of painters, writers, and assorted cabaret artists in its heyday toward the end of the 19th century. Foremost among them were Renoir—he painted the *Moulin de la Galette,* an archetypical Parisian scene of sun-drenched revels, while he lived here—and Maurice Utrillo, Montmartre painter par excellence. Almost the best thing about the museum, however, is the view over
⓳ the tiny **vineyard** on neighboring rue des Saules, the only vineyard in Paris, which still produces a symbolic 125 gallons of wine every year. It's hardly vintage stuff, but there are predictably bacchanalian celebrations during the October harvest. *Musée du Vieux Montmartre, 12 rue Cortot.* ☛ *25 frs adults, 20 frs students and senior citizens.* ☯ *Tues.–Sun. 11–6. Métro: Lamarck Caulaincourt.*

There's an equally famous Montmartre landmark on the
⓴ corner of rue St-Vincent, just down the road: the **Lapin Agile.**

It's a bar-cabaret and originally one of the raunchiest haunts in Montmartre. Today, it manages against all odds to preserve at least something of its earlier flavor, unlike the Moulin Rouge. It got its curious name—it means the Nimble Rabbit—when the owner, André Gill, hung a sign outside (you can see it now in the Musée du Vieux Montmartre) of a laughing rabbit jumping out of a saucepan clutching a wine bottle. In those days, the place was still tamely called La Campagne (The Countryside). Once the sign went up, locals rebaptized the place Lapin à Gill, which, translated, means Gill's rabbit. When in 1886 it was sold to cabaret singer Jules Jouy, he called it the Lapin Agile, which has the same pronunciation in French as Lapin à Gill. In 1903, the premises were bought by the most celebrated cabaret entrepreneur of them all, Aristide Bruand, portrayed by Toulouse-Lautrec in a series of famous posters.

㉑ Behind the Lapin Agile is the **St-Vincent Cemetery;** the entrance is off little rue Lucien-Gaulard. It's a tiny graveyard, but serious students of Montmartre might want to visit to see Utrillo's burial place.

㉒ Continue north on rue des Saules, across busy rue Caulaincourt, to reach the **Musée d'Art Juif,** the Museum of Jewish Art. It contains devotional items, models of synagogues, and works by Pissarro and Marc Chagall. *42 rue des Saules.* ☛ *30 frs adults, 20 frs students and senior citizens.* ⊘ *Sun.–Thurs. 3–6. Closed Aug. Métro: Lamarck Caulaincourt.*

There are several routes you can take back over Montmartre's hill. Luxurious avenue Junot, from which you'll see the villa Léandre, one of Montmartre's most charming side streets, makes for a picturesque return from the area around the cemetery and the museum. Alternatively, you can turn east onto rue Lamarck, past several good restaurants, to circle around the quieter side of the Sacré-Coeur basilica. If you then take the little stairpath named after Utrillo down
㉓ to rue Paul Albert, you'll come upon the **Marché St-Pierre** (St. Pierre Market), the perfect place to rummage for old clothes and fabrics. Prices are low. ⊘ *Tues.–Sun. 8–1.*

Take rue de Steinkerque, opposite the foot of the Sacré-Coeur gardens, then turn right onto boulevard de Rochechouart and continue down to **Place Pigalle** to complete your tour of Montmartre. Despite the area's reputation as a tawdry red-light district, a number of trendy clubs have opened here (*see* Chapter 6, The Arts and Nightlife). If you choose to visit at night, however, be aware that dubious characters and lewd sex shows still prevail.

3 Shopping

WINDOW-SHOPPING is one of Paris's great spectator sports. Tastefully displayed wares—luscious cream-filled éclairs, lacy lingerie, rare artwork, gleaming copper pots—entice the eye and awaken the imagination. And shopping is one of the city's greatest pastimes, a chance to mix with Parisians and feel the heartbeat of the country. Who can understand the magic of French cuisine until they've explored a French open-air produce market on a weekend morning? Or resist the thrill of seeing a Chanel evening gown displayed in its own glossy Paris boutique—where the doorknobs are shaped like Chanel crystal perfume bottle stoppers?

By Corinne
LaBalme

Opéra Area

Au Printemps (64 blvd. Haussmann, 9e, ☎ 42–82–50–00, métro Havre–Caumartin or Opéra or Auber) is a glittery three-store complex that includes "La Maison," for housewares and furniture; "La Mode," for ladies and children; and "Brummel," a six-floor emporium devoted to menswear. Flo Prestige, the celebrated Parisian brasserie chain, caters the in-house restaurants.

Galeries Lafayette (40 blvd. Haussmann, 9e, ☎ 42–82–34–56, métro Chaussée d'Antin or Opéra or Havre–Caumartin; Centre Commercial Montparnasse, 15e, ☎ 45–38–52–87, métro Montparnasse–Bienvenüe) spices up its elegant Parisian aura with periodic exhibits featuring crafts from exotic countries. Be sure and look up while in the main store: The glorious Belle Epoque stained-glass dome is a Paris landmark. Stylish private-label fashions (Briefing and Jodphur) offer good value, and the elegant floor-wide gourmet shop includes several sophisticated wine bars.

Marks & Spencer (35 blvd. Haussmann, 9e, métro Havre–Caumartin or Auber or Opéra, ☎ 47–42–42–91; 88 rue de Rivoli, 4e, ☎ 44–61–08–00, métro Hôtel de Ville) is a British store chiefly noted for its moderately priced sportswear and its excellent English grocery and take-out food service. A new five-floor outlet opened in 1994 on rue de Rivoli.

Louvre–Pont Neuf Area
La Samaritaine (19 rue de la Monnaie, 1er, ☎ 40–41–20–20, métro Pont–Neuf or Châtelet), a sprawling four-store complex, is rapidly shedding its fusty, grandmotherly image. Especially good for kitchen supplies, housewares, and furniture, it's famous for its rooftop snackbar that offers a marvelous view of Notre Dame.

Hôtel de Ville/Marais Area
Bazar de l'Hôtel de Ville (52–64 rue de Rivoli, 4e, ☎ 42–74–90–00, métro Hôtel de Ville), affectionately called BHV, houses an enormous basement hardware store that sells everything from doorknobs to cement mixers! The fashion offerings are minimal, but BHV is noteworthy for quality household goods, home decor materials, and office supplies.

Left Bank
Au Bon Marché (22 rue de Sèvres, 7e, ☎ 44–39–80–00, métro Sèvres–Babylone), founded in 1852, is chiefly known for linens, table settings, and high-quality furniture. La Grande Epicerie, a grocery store and deli here, is a gourmet's delight, and the sleek restaurant was designed by jet-set decorator Andrée Putman. The basement is a treasure trove for books, records, and arty gifts.

Budget
Most Parisians dash into their neighborhood **Monoprix** or **Prisunic** stores—with branches throughout the city—at least once a week. These handy shops stock inexpensive cosmetics, toothpaste, groceries, toys, typing paper, bathmats—a little of everything.

Specialty Shops

Antiques
Louvre des Antiquaires (2 pl. du Palais-Royal, 1er, métro Palais Royal), is an elegant multifloor complex where 250 of Paris's leading dealers showcase their rarest objects.

Bags and Luggage
La Bagagerie (41 rue du Four, 6e, ☎ 45–48–85–88, métro Mabillon; 11 rue du Fbg. St-Honoré, 8e, ☎ 47–42–79–13, métro Concorde; 12 rue Tronchet, 8e, ☎ 42–65–03–

106

A la Mère de Famille, **28**

Agnès b., **34**

Annick Goutal, **16**

Au Bain Marie, **11**

Au Bon Marché, **40**

Au Nain Bleu, **14**

Au Printemps, **23**

La Bagagerie, **15, 21, 42**

Bazar de l'Hôtel de Ville, **38**

Bouchara, **25**

Brummel, **26**

Cartier, **19**

Chanel, **17, 3**

Chantal Thomass, **31**

Charvet, **36**

Christian Dior, **6**

Christian Lacroix, **7**

Fauchon, **20**

FNAC (Forum des Halles), **37**

Galerie Vivienne, **30**

Galeries Lafayette, **26**

Guerlain, **1**

Hédiard, **9**

Hermès, **10**

Inès de la Fressange, **5**

Jean-Paul Gaultier, **29**

La Samaritaine, **39**

Lalique, **12**

Laurent Mercadel, **22**

Louvre de Antiquaires, **36**

Marks & Spencer, **24**

Natari, **18**

Passage Jouffroy, **27**

Poilâne, **43**

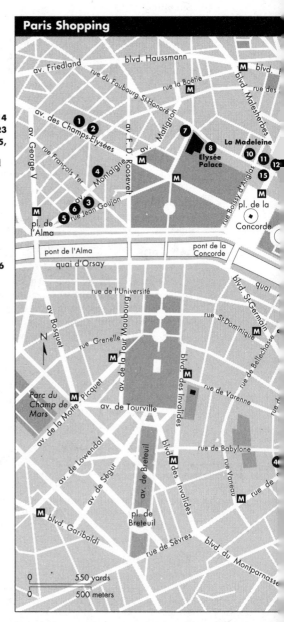

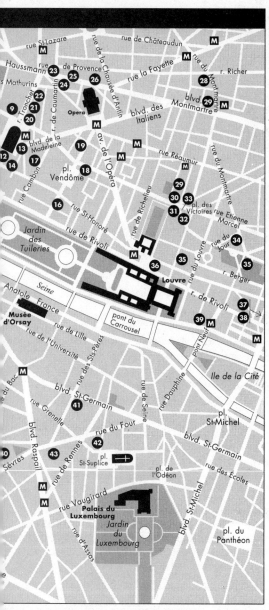

40, métro Madeleine) features brightly colored bags and belts with youthful style and moderate prices.

Hermès (24 rue du Fbg. St-Honoré, 8e, ☎ 40–17–47–17, métro Concorde) was established as a saddlery in 1837 but since went on to scarves and more: Its most famous leather creation is the eternally chic Kelly bag, created for Grace Kelly. Prices are astronomical.

Clothing (Women's)

CLASSIC CHIC

Chanel (42 av. Montaigne, 8e, ☎ 47–23–74–12, métro Franklin D. Roosevelt; 31 rue Cambon, 1er, ☎ 42–86–28–00, métro Tuileries) has experienced a radical transformation under Karl Lagerfeld, who has added leather, chains, and string bikinis to classic tweed suits and accessories.

Christian Dior (30 av. Montaigne, 8e, ☎ 40–73–54–44, métro Franklin D. Roosevelt) is a pearl gray palace selling women's fashions, menswear, perfumes, jewelry, lingerie, furs, leather goods, porcelain, and gifts. The cosmopolitan women's wear is created by the Italian designer Gianfranco Ferré.

TRENDSETTERS

Christian Lacroix (26 av. Montaigne, 8e, ☎ 47–20–68–95, métro Franklin D. Roosevelt; 73 rue du Fbg. St-Honoré, 8e, ☎ 42–65–79–08, métro Champs Elysées Clemenceau; 2–4 pl. St-Sulpice, 6e, ☎ 46–33–48–95, métro St-Sulpice) turns haute couture into a Provençal carnival with daring cuts and candy-coated colors.

Jean-Paul Gaultier (6 rue Vivienne, 2e, ☎ 42–86–05–05, métro Bourse or Palais Royal), Madonna's clothier, specializes in outrageously attention-getting garments for men and women. The less-expensive "Junior" line is sold at 30 rue Fbg. Saint Antoine, 11e, métro Bastille.

Thierry Mugler (10 pl. des Victoires, 2e, ☎ 42–60–06–37, métro Bourse or Palais Royal; 49 av. Montaigne, 8e, ☎ 47–23–37–62, métro Franklin D. Roosevelt), with kinky lace-up dresses and sexy cat-suits, keeps fans coming back for more—menswear is next door at No. 8.

CHIC AND CASUAL

Agnès b. (3, 6, and 10 rue du Jour, 1er, ☎ 45–08–46–56, métro Les Halles) has knitwear separates that are wardrobe basics for young Parisians. The teenage "Lolita" line is sold at No. 10.

Inès de la Fressange (14 av. Montaigne, 8e, ☎ 47–23–08–94, métro Franklin D. Roosevelt), the former Chanel supermodel, creates casual looks based on evergreen V-neck sweaters and slim, velvet jeans. The costume jewelry—with de la Fressange's signature oak leaf pattern—is always light-hearted and charming. Whimsical gift items (like the "stop smoking please" ashtray) are also good bets.

Sonia Rykiel (175 blvd. St-Germain, 6e, ☎ 49–54–60–60, métro St-Germain-des-Prés; 79 rue du Fbg. St-Honoré, 8e, ☎ 42–65–20–81, métro Concorde) singlehandedly made cotton velour into a recognized fashion statement. At the annual sales, the lines go around the block.

Suzette Idier (9 rue de Birague, 4e, ☎ 42–77–72–52, métro St-Paul) runs an intimate, pocket-size boutique chockful of sexy cocktail gowns, colorful daywear, and all the latest accessories. Madame Idier, who travels frequently to Asia and America, takes special care to find fabrics and styles that pack easily and are suitable for various climates.

Clothing (Men's)

Brummel (Au Printemps department store, 64 blvd. Haussmann, 9e, ☎ 42–82–50–00, métro Havre-Caumartin or Opéa or Auber) is Paris's menswear fashion leader: six floors of suits, sportswear, underwear, coats, ties, and accessories in all price ranges.

Charvet (28 pl. Vendôme, 1er, ☎ 42–60–30–70, métro Opéra) is the Parisian equivalent of a London tailor or New York's Brooks Brothers: a conservative, aristocratic institution famed for made-to-measure shirts and exquisite ties and accessories.

Fabrics

Bouchara (54 blvd. Haussmann, 9e, ☎ 42–80–66–95, métro Auber) sells top-quality apparel and upholstery fabrics.

Food

BREAD

Poilâne (8 rue du Cherche-Midi, 6e, ☎ 45–48–42–59, métro St-Sulpice) produces the most famous bread in the world. The chewy sourdough loaves are sold in hundreds of Paris restaurants and shops and are airmailed to United States and Tokyo restaurants every day.

CANDY AND CHOCOLATE

A la Mère de Famille (35 rue du Fbg. Montmartre, 9e, ☎ 47–70–83–69, métro Cadet) is an enchanting shop specializing in old-fashioned bonbons, sugar candy, and more.

GOURMET SHOPS

Fauchon (26–28–30 pl. de la Madeleine, 8e, ☎ 47–42–60–11, métro Madeleine), established in 1886, sells prestigious house brands of paté, honey, jelly, and private label champagne. Hard-to-find foreign foods (US pancake mix, British lemon curd) are also stocked. The pastry and chocolates are particularly delectable and can be sampled in the casual cafeteria.

Jewelry

Cartier (7 and 23 pl. Vendôme, 1er, ☎ 42–61–55–55, métro Opéra) has two less formal "Les Must" boutiques, which carry lighters, pens, watches, key-chains, and other gift items.

Lingerie

Chantal Thomass (1 rue Vivienne, 1er, ☎ 40–15–02–36, métro Bourse or Palais Royal) sets the right mood for her trademark black-lace hosiery, satin corsets, and feather-trimmed negligees in this plush, pink velvet boutique that resembles a Victorian bordello.

Natari (7 pl. Vendôme, 1er, ☎ 42–96–22–94, métro Opéra or Concorde) seduces all, with selections for every pocketbook. Movie-star lingerie and peignoir sets come in pure silk or washable synthetic versions.

Music/Records

FNAC (Forum des Halles, 1er, ☎ 40–41–40–00, métro Les Halles; 26 av. Ternes, 17e, ☎ 44–09–18–00, métro Ternes; 136 rue de Rennes, 6e, ☎ 49–54–30–00, métro St-Placide) is a high-profile French chain selling music, books, and photo, TV, and audio equipment.

Virgin Megastore (52–60 av. des Champs-Elysées, 8e, ☎ 49–53–50–00, métro Franklin D. Roosevelt; Carrousel du Louvre mall, 99 rue de Rivoli, 1er, ☎ 49–53–52–90, métro Palais-Royal) has acres of CDs and tapes—everything from classic to rap—plus a book division.

Perfumes

Annick Goutal (14 rue de Castiglione, 1er, ☎ 42–60–52–82, métro Concorde) sells this exclusive signature perfume line.

Guerlain (68 av. des Champs-Elysées, 8e, ☎ 47–89–71–84, métro Franklin D. Roosevelt; 47 rue Bonaparte, 6e, ☎ 43–26–71–19, métro Mabillon) boutiques are the only authorized Paris outlets for legendary perfumes like Shalimar, Jicky, Vol de Nuit, Mitsouko, and Chamade.

Scarves

Hermès (24 rue du Fbg. St-Honoré, 8e, ☎ 40–17–47–17, métro Madeleine) clocks a scarf sale every 20 seconds before the Christmas holidays! The all-silk *carrés*—truly fashion icons—are legendary for their brilliant colors and intricate designs, which change yearly.

Shoes

Laurent Mercadel (31 rue Tronchet, 8e, ☎ 42–66–00–48, métro Opéra; 3 pl. des Victoires, 1er, ☎ 45–08–84–44, métro Palais-Royal) offers classic styles—for both men and women—updated with unusual accents.

Stéphane Kélian (23 blvd. de la Madeleine, 1er, ☎ 42–96–01–84, métro Madeleine; 6 pl. des Victoires, 2e, ☎ 42–61–60–74, métro Palais-Royal) creates chic, high-style, comfortable shoes for men and women.

Tablewares

CHINA AND CRYSTAL

Au Bain Marie (10 rue Boissy d'Anglas, 8e, ☎ 42–66–59–74, métro Concorde) is an enchanted kingdom for amateur and professional cooks. Come here for crockery, porcelain, and a world-class collection of cookbooks.

Lalique (11 rue Royale, 8e, ☎ 42–66–52–40, métro Madeleine) crystal vases and statuettes are prized for their sinuous, romantic forms and delicate design.

Toys

Au Nain Bleu (406–410 rue St-Honoré, 8e, ☎ 42–60–39–01, métro Concorde) is a high-price wonderland, with elaborate dollhouses, miniature sports cars, and enchanting hand-carved rocking horses.

Shopping Arcades

Paris's 19th-century commercial arcades, called *passages,* are the forerunners of the modern shopping mall. Glass roofs, decorative pillers, and inlaid mosaic floors give these spaces great charm. Shops range from the avant-garde (Gaultier and Yukii Tori designs in the luxurious Galerie Vivienne) to the genteel (embroidery supplies and satin ribbons at Le Bonheur des Dames in the Passage Jouffroy). The major arcades are conveniently located in the central 1st and 2nd arrondissements on the Right Bank. The patient browser will find all sorts of dusty curiosity shops tucked into the alleys, holding such items as rare stamps, secondhand books, and even antique canes.

Galerie Vivienne (4 rue des Petits-Champs, 2e, métro Bourse), between the Stock Exchange (Bourse) and the Palais-Royal, has a range of interesting shops and an excellent tearoom, and is home to Cave Legrand, a quality wine shop.

Passage Jouffroy (12 blvd. Montmartre, 9e, métro Montmartre) has shops selling toys, postcards, antique canes, perfumes, original cosmetics, and dried flowers: Try Pain d'Epices (No. 29) and Au Bonheur des Dames (No. 39).

Markets

Food Markets
Paris's open-air food markets are among the city's most colorful attractions. Every *quartier* (district) has one, although many are open only a few days each week. Sunday morn-

ing, till 1 PM, is usually a good time to go; Monday is the day these markets are likely to be closed.

Many of the better-known markets are in areas you'd visit for sightseeing; our favorites are on **rue de Buci** (6e, métro Odéon; open daily); **rue Mouffetard** (5e, métro Monge; best on weekends), and **rue Lepic** in Montmartre (métro Blanche; best on weekends). The **Marché d'Aligre** (12e, métro Ledru-Rollin; open Sat., Sun., and Mon. mornings) is a bit farther out, beyond the Bastille on rue d'Aligre, but you won't see many tourists in this less-affluent area of town, and Parisians from all over the city know it and love it. The prices come tumbling down as the morning draws to a close.

Flea Markets

Le Marché aux Puces (métro Porte de Clignancourt; open weekends and Monday) on Paris's northern boundary still attracts the crowds, but its once unbeatable prices are now a feature of the past. This century-old labyrinth of alleyways packed with antiques dealers' booths and junk stalls now spreads for over a square mile. Early birds often pick up the most worthwhile loot. But be warned—if there's one place in Paris where you need to know how to barter, this is it! For lunch, stop for mussels and fries in one of the rough-and-ready cafés.

Flower and Bird Markets

Paris's main flower market is located right in the heart of the city on the Ile de la Cité, between Notre Dame and the Palais de Justice (métro Cité). It's open every day except Sunday, when a bird market takes its place, and Monday, when it's closed.

4 Dining

By Robert
Noah

Updated
by
Alexander
Lobrano

WHETHER YOUR DREAM meal is savoring truffle-studded foie gras from Limoges china, or breaking the crust of a steaming cassoulet in a thick crockery bowl, you can find it in Paris. For most visitors, the prospect of eating here is exciting; for many, it's the main reason for a trip. It's certainly possible to have a bad meal here. Yet the city's restaurants exist principally for the demanding Parisians themselves, for whom every meal is—if not a way of life—certainly an event worthy of their undivided attention.

Generally, Paris restaurants are open from noon to about 2, and from 7:30 or 8 to 10 or 10:30. Brasseries have longer hours and often serve all day and late into the evening; some are open 24 hours. The iconoclastic wine bars do as they want, frequently serving hot food only through lunch and cold assortments of charcuterie and cheese until a late-afternoon or early evening close.

Because restaurants are open for only a few set hours for lunch and dinner, and because meals are much longer affairs here than they are in the United States, we urge you to make reservations. Most wine bars do not take reservations; reservations are also unnecessary for brasserie and café meals at odd hours. In the reviews below, we have indicated where reservations are advised or required (and when booking weeks or months in advance is necessary), and where reservations are not accepted. If you want nonsmoking, make this clear; the mandatory nonsmoking area is sometimes limited to a very few tables.

Although prices include tax and tip (*service compris* or *prix nets*), pocket change left on the table in simple places, or an additional 5% in better restaurants, is appreciated.

CATEGORY	COST*
$$$$	over 550 frs
$$$	300 frs–550 frs
$$	175 frs–300 frs
$	under 175 frs

*per person, including tax and service but not drinks

1st Arrondissement (Louvre)

$$$$ Le Grand Véfour. Luminaries from Napoléon to Colette to
Jean Cocteau have frequented this intimate address under
the arcades of the Palais-Royal; you can request to be
seated at their preferred table. This sumptuously decorated
restaurant, with its mirrored ceiling and painted glass panels, is perhaps the prettiest in Paris, and its 18th-century
origins make it one of the oldest. Chef Guy Martin impresses
with his unique blend of sophisticated yet rustic dishes, including roast lamb in a juice of herbs. ✕ *17 rue Beaujolais,* ☎ *42–96–56–27. Reservations 1 wk in advance
advised. Jacket and tie. AE, DC, MC, V. Closed weekends
and Aug. Métro: Palais-Royal.*

$$–$$$ Chez Pauline. This restaurant near the Palais Royal has be-
★   come a neighborhood institution. The setting, with wood-
paneled walls, is warm and welcoming. Chef André Gelin
has been here for decades and his touch is sure and swift.
Dishes are bourgeois, old-fashioned, and delicious; try the
oysters in cream sauce. The wine list is filled with classic
Burgundies. The lunch menu provides good value. ✕ *5 rue
Villedo,* ☎ *42–96–20–70. Reservations advised. AE, MC,
V. Closed Sat. dinner, Sun., and 2 wks in Aug. Métro: Pyramides or Palais-Royal.*

$–$$ Aux Crus de Bourgogne. The din of a happy crowd fills this
delightful, old-fashioned bistro with bright lights and red-
checkered tablecloths. It opened in 1932 and quickly became
popular by serving two luxury items—foie gras and cold lobster with homemade mayonnaise—at surprisingly low prices,
a tradition that happily continues. Among the bistro classics on the menu, the *boeuf au gros sel* (beef boiled in bouil-
lon with vegetables and garnished with rock salt) and *confit
de canard* (duck confit) are very satisfying. Tempting desserts
include fruit tarts, flan, and chocolate mousse. ✕ *3 rue
Bachaumont,* ☎ *42–33–48–24. Reservations advised. V.
Closed weekends and Aug. Métro: Sentier.*

$–$$ La Tour du Montlhéry. When the centuries-old Les Halles
marketplace became an aseptic shopping mall, many neighborhood bistros closed or went upscale. With sagging
wood-beamed ceilings, red-checkered tablecloths, and exposed brick walls lined with imaginative portraits, the
Montlhéry has managed to hang on to the old market feel.

If you don't mind passing under hanging samples of your future meal (sausages, etc.) on your way into the dining room, jovial waiters will serve you simple grilled food. Try the *côte de boeuf* and wash it down with a good Beaujolais. ✗ *5 rue des Prouvaires,* ☎ *42–36–21–82. Reservations advised. MC, V. Closed weekends and July 14–Aug. 15. Métro: Les Halles.*

2nd Arrondissement (Stock Exchange)

$$–$$$ **Pile ou Face.** This restaurant serves the most interesting and creative food around the Stock Exchange. Housed on two floors in a narrow building, it offers an intimate setting for discussing big business. The cooking is inventive, the service attentive. Try the rabbit paté or the scrambled eggs with mushrooms, then move on to the sweetbreads and the exquisite roast chicken. ✗ *52 bis rue de Notre Dame des Victoires,* ☎ *42–33–64–33. Reservations advised. MC, V. Closed weekends and Aug. Métro: Bourse.*

$$ **Brissemoret.** There's a lot of timeless Parisian ambience in this pocket-sized bistro with only nine tables. It's crowded to capacity at lunch and dinner—25 diners in a real pinch—but the dinner crowd is more relaxed and cosmopolitan than the stockbrokers and journalists who come at noon. Feast on fresh artichoke hearts, veal in lemon, sautéed duck breast garnished with clementines, and crème caramel. ✗ *5 rue St-Marc,* ☎ *42–36–91–72. Reservations essential. V. Closed weekends. Métro: Bourse.*

$ **Café Runtz.** Next to the Salle Favart in a neighborhood once
★ full of theaters, this friendly bistro with rich *boiseries* (woodwork) and photos of customers from the entertainment industry serves up an Alsatian feel and cuisine. Tasty, hearty dishes include Gruyère salad, onion tart, choucroute, and fresh fruit tarts. Order a *pichet* of Riesling or other Alsatian wine. ✗ *16 rue Favart,* ☎ *42–96–69–86. Reservations advised. AE, MC, V. Closed weekends and Aug. Métro: Richelieu-Drouot.*

3rd Arrondissement (Le Marais/Beaubourg)

$ **Au Bascou.** Gregarious proprietor Jean-Guy Lousteau enthusiastically shares his knowledge of the wines of south-

Paris Dining

L'Arpège, **35**	Aux Fins Gourmets, **32**	Brissemoret, **16**	Le Grand Véfour, **34**
Astier, **18**	Baracane, **19**	Café Runtz, **12**	Guy Savoy, **4**
Au Bascou, **17**	La Bastide Odéon, **28**	La Cagouille, **30**	Ledoyen, **7**
Auberge Etchegorry, **24**	Bofinger, **21**	Campagne et Provence, **25**	L'Os à Moëlle, **36**
Au Trou Gascon, **22**	Les Bookinistes, **29**	Chardenoux, **20**	Le Petit Plat, **1**
Aux Crus de Bourgogne, **15**	Brasserie Flo, **14**	Chartier, **9**	Le Petit Yvan, **6**
		Chez Bruno, **13**	Pile ou Face, **11**
		Chez Pauline **10**	

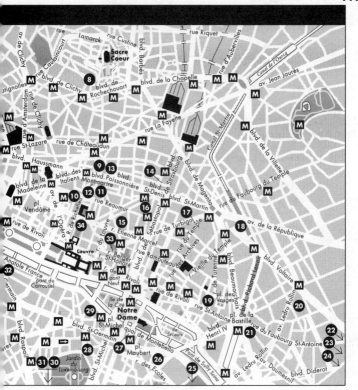

Prunier, **3**
La Régalade, **31**
Le Restaurant, **8**
Taillevent, **5**
La Timonerie, **26**
La Tour de
Montlhéry, **33**
La Tout Petit
Plat, **27**

Le Vivarois, **2**
Les
Zygomates, **23**

western France at this fashionable little bistro with a simple but imaginative decor, including mosaics of broken mirror. The sturdy, savory cuisine of the Basque country stars on the menu, and the country ham, cod with broccoli purée, and sautéed baby squid are particularly flavorful. ✕ *38 rue Reaumur,* ☎ *42–72–69–25. Reservations advised. MC, V. Closed weekends. Métro: Arts et Metiers.*

4th Arrondissement (Le Marais/Ile St-Louis)

$$ **Bofinger.** Founded in 1864, this may be Paris's oldest brasserie. It's also one of the prettiest, with its authentic Belle Epoque decor, white linen tablecloths, black leather banquettes, and beautiful stained-glass dome (ask to be seated on the main floor). The menu offers excellent shellfish and choucroute (including a lighter version with fish), and there's a large selection of Alsatian beers. Only steps from the place de la Bastille, and open until 1 AM, Bofinger makes a good postopera rendezvous. ✕ *5 rue de la Bastille,* ☎ *42–27–87–82. Reservations advised. AE, DC, MC, V. Métro: Bastille.*

$ **Baracane.** The owner oversees the menu, full of the robust
★ specialties of his native southwest France, including rabbit confit, veal tongue, and pear poached in wine and cassis. This small, simple place is one of the best values in the Marais district; a reasonable dinner menu and cheaper menu at lunch keep the Baracane solidly affordable. Service is friendly. ✕ *38 rue des Tournelles,* ☎ *42–71–43–33. Reservations advised. MC, V. Closed Sun. No Sat. lunch. Métro: Bastille.*

5th Arrondissement (Latin Quarter)

$$–$$$ **La Timonerie.** This small, elegant restaurant along the quai
★ avoids all theatrics and sticks to fine cooking. Philippe de Givenchy works with a small staff and his creations are consistently interesting and well-executed. In his hands, a simple dish such as rosemary and lemon mackerel is turned into a high-class eating experience. ✕ *35 quai de la Tournelle,* ☎ *43–25–44–42. Reservations advised. Jacket and tie. MC, V. Closed Sun. and Mon. Métro: Maubert-Mutalité.*

$$ **Campagne et Provence.** The talented young owners of the
★ Miravile (4th Arr.) also run this small establishment on the

quai across from Notre Dame. The fresh, colorful, Provençal-inspired cuisine includes ratatouille and vegetables stuffed with cod brandade. The wine list includes reasonably priced regional wines. ✕ *25 quai de la Tournelle,* ☎ *43–54–05–17. Reservations advised. MC, V. Closed Sun. No lunch Mon., Sat. Métro: Maubert-Mutualité.*

$ **Le Tout Petit Plat.** This charming and conveniently located wine bar where the food's as good as the wine occupies the tiny former quarters of the very popular Le Petit Plat (*see* 15th arr., *below*). All the dishes are paired with a suggested glass of wine, allowing you to discover such mellifluous combinations as a plate of country ham, nutty *tête de moine* (monk's head cheese), and a glass of crisp, white Vouvray. Other savory, light offerings include tomatoes and fennel Provençale, and a delicious stewed chicken with five spices. ✕ *3 rue des Grands Degrés,* ☎ *40–46–85–34. Reservations advised. MC, V. Closed Thurs. Métro: Maubert-Mutualité.*

6th Arrondissement (Luxembourg)

$$ **La Bastide Odéon.** This little corner of Provence in Paris is
★ just a few steps from the Luxembourg Gardens. The cooking of southern France continues to increase its popularity in the capital, and this sunny yellow room with old oak tables and chairs is one of the best places to sample the soothing Mediterranean food. Chef Gilles Ajuelos, formerly of Michel Rostang's kitchen at Le Bistrot d'à Côté, is a fine fish cook who also prepares wonderful pastas, such as tagliatelle in *pistou* (basil and pine nuts) with wild mushrooms, and main courses like peppered tuna steak with ratatouille or roast cod with capers. The best bet on the slightly pricey wine list is the red Côteaux du Tricastin. ✕ *7 rue Corneille,* ☎ *43–26–03–65. Reservations advised. MC, V. Closed weekends. Métro: Odéon or RER: Luxembourg.*

$$ **Les Bookinistes.** Talented chef Guy Savoy's fifth bistro
★ annex—his first on the Left Bank—is a big success with the locals. The cheery postmodern room is painted peach, with red, blue, and yellow wall sconces, and it looks out on the Seine. The menu of French country cooking changes seasonally, and might include a mussel and pumpkin soup, ravioli stuffed with chicken and celery, or baby chicken roasted

in a casserole with root vegetables. The reasonable prices are challenged by a somewhat pricey wine list. The service is friendly and efficient. ✕ *53 Quai des Grands-Augustins, ☎ 43–25–45–94. Reservations advised. AE, DC, MC, V. Closed Sun. No Sat. lunch. Métro: St-Michel.*

7th Arrondissement (Invalides)

$$$$ **L'Arpège.** This small, striking restaurant one block from
★ the Rodin Museum is currently one of the most talked-about of Paris's restaurants. Young chef-owner Alain Passard's cuisine is both original (lobster/turnip starter in a sweet-sour vinaigrette, stuffed sweet tomato) and classic (beef Burgundy, pressed duck). The problem here is inconsistency: one sublime meal followed by a mediocre experience. With its curving, hand-crafted wood panels and wrought-iron window frames, the decor is unusually minimalist. The staff, although young and energetic, sometimes falls behind. The fixed-price lunch is a steal. ✕ *84 rue de Varenne, ☎ 45–51–47–33. Reservations advised. AE, DC, MC, V. Closed Sat., Aug. No Sun. lunch. Métro: Varenne.*

$ **Aux Fins Gourmets.** What would the western end of boulevard St-Germain be without this comforting bistro? Solid country dishes prevail: *pipérade* (a mixture of eggs, peppers, onions, tomatoes, and garlic), duck confit, and cassoulet. Pastries come from the excellent Peltier shop. In warm weather, dinner or lunch on the terrace, under the shady plane trees, is a delight. ✕ *213 blvd. St-Germain, ☎ 42–22–06–57. Reservations advised. No credit cards. Closed Sun., Aug. No Mon. lunch. Métro: Bac.*

8th Arrondissement (Champs-Elysées)

$$$$ **Ledoyen.** Chef Ghislaine Arabien is the most talked about
★ up-and-coming chef in Paris. She sets gastronomic fashion by concentrating on northern French cuisine, and creates specialties featuring beer sauces, including *coquilles St-Jacques à la bière.* The elegant restaurant, with its gilded ceilings and walls, plush armchairs, and tables with candelabra, is set in a posh location off the Champs-Elysées near place de la Concorde. ✕ *1 av. du Tuit, on the Carré des Champs-Elysées, ☎ 47–42–23–23. Reservations es-*

sential. AE, DC, MC, V. Closed weekends. Métro: Place de la Concorde or Champs Elysées Clemenceau.

$$$$ **Taillevent.** Many say it's the best restaurant in Paris. Within
★ the paneled main dining rooms of this mid-19th-century mansion you will find exceptional service that is never over-bearing, a stellar wine list, and the tempered classic cuisine of young chef Philippe Legendre. Among his signature dishes are lobster boudin and lamb with cabbage. Pastry chef Gilles Bajolle is one of the finest in Paris. Try his *nougatine glacée aux poires* (thin layers of nougat, pastry, and pear sherbet) or tarte Tatin with quince. ✕ *15 rue Lamennais,* ☎ *45–63–39–94. Reservations 3–4 wks in advance essential. Jacket and tie. AE, MC, V. Closed weekends, Aug. Métro: Charles de Gaulle/Etoile.*

$ **Le Petit Yvan.** Personable Yvan, much loved by fashionable Paris, has opened a new annex to his other eponymous restaurant nearby. The decor (unremarkable, but comfortable and casual) and menu are both simpler than at his star-studded main outpost, but this place is exceptional and has become very stylish for lunch. The prix-fixe menu offers very good value and might include such dishes as lemon-marinated salmon and steak tartare. ✕ *1 bis rue Jean-Mermoz,* ☎ *42–89–49–65. Reservations advised. MC, V. Closed Sun. No Sat. lunch. Métro: St-Philippe-du-Roule.*

9th Arrondissement (Opéra)

$ **Chartier.** People come here more for the bonhomie than the food, which is often rather ordinary. This cavernous turn-of-the-century restaurant enjoys a huge following among the budget-minded, including students, solitary bachelors, and tourists. You may find yourself sharing a table with strangers as you study the long, old-fashioned menu of such favorites as hard-boiled eggs with mayonnaise, pâté, and roast veal with spinach. ✕ *7 rue du Faubourg-Montmartre,* ☎ *47–70–86–29. No reservations. No credit cards. Métro: Rue Montmartre.*

$ **Chez Bruno.** In a theater neighborhood with few good, inexpensive restaurants, this jazzy bistro stands out. The dim interior, photos and posters, and soft music all bow to jazz. A solid 79-franc menu gets you three courses that change daily; 130 francs will buy you homemade foie gras with the house special of fondu Bourguignonne. There's also an interesting, inexpensive afternoon tea with a good selection of pastries. ✗ *5 rue Bergère,* ☏ *45–23–24–42. Reservations advised. AE, MC, V. Closed Sun. No Sat. lunch. Métro: Rue Montmartre.*

10th Arrondissement (République)

$$ Brasserie Flo. This, the first of brasserie king Jean-Paul Bucher's seven Paris addresses, is hard to find down its passageway near the Gare de l'Est, but worth the effort. The rich wood- and stained-glass interior is typically Alsatian, the service enthusiastic, and the brasserie standards such as shellfish, steak tartare, and choucroute savory. Order one of the carafes of Alsatian wine. It's open until 1:30 AM, with a special night-owl menu from 11 PM. ✗ *7 cour des Petites Ecuries,* ☏ *47–70–13–59. Reservations advised. AE, DC, MC, V. Métro: Château d'Eau.*

11th Arrondissement (Bastille)

$$ Chardenoux. A bit off the beaten track but well worth the
★ effort, this cosy neighborhood bistro with amber walls, etched-glass windows, dark bentwood furniture, tile floors, and a long zinc bar attracts a cross section of savvy Parisians with its first-rate traditional cooking. Start with one of the delicious salads, such as the green beans and foie gras, and then try the veal chop with morels, or a game dish. Savory desserts and a nicely chosen wine list with several excellent Côtes-du-Rhônes complete the experience. ✗ *1 rue Jules-Valles,* ☏ *43–71–49–52. Reservations advised. AE, V. Closed weekends and Aug. Métro: Charonne.*

$ Astier. You'll find remarkable value at this pleasant restaurant, where the menu is prix-fixe (there's no à la carte). Among high-quality seasonal dishes, try mussel soup with saffron, fricassée of beef cheeks, and plum clafoutis. Service can be rushed, but the enthusiastic crowd does not seem to mind. Study the excellent wine list, which has some surprising buys. ✗ *44 rue Jean-Pierre Timbaud,* ☏ *43–57–16–35. Reservations advised. AE, MC, V. Closed weekends, Aug. Métro: Parmentier.*

12th Arrondissement (Gare de Lyon)

$$$ Au Trou Gascon. The success of this Belle Epoque establishment off the place Daumesnil enabled owner Alain Dutournier to open the now-renowned Carré des Feuillants (1st arr.). He's still the owner here, too, and continues to serve his personal version of the cuisine of Gascony, a region of outstanding ham, foie gras, lamb, and poultry. His white chocolate mousse is now a classic. ✕ *40 rue Taine,* ☎ *43–44–34–26. Reservations advised. AE, DC, MC, V. Closed weekends, Christmas wk, Aug. Métro: Daumesnil.*

$ Les Zygomates. When this handsome old butcher's shop with marble counters was converted into a bistro a few years ago, it became instantly popular with a local, young, more-dash-than-cash crowd. Since it's deep in a part of the city few tourists venture to, you'll find yourself surrounded by Parisians, and if you don't speak French, the menu pages in the back of this guide will be a help. You'll experience delicious modern bistro food like a terrine of rabbit with tarragon, chicken in cream with chives, and a very fairly priced catch-of-the-day selection. ✕ *7 rue Capri,* ☎ *40-19–93–04. Reservations advised. V. Closed Sun., Sat. June–Sept., 1st 3 wks Aug. No Sat. lunch Oct.–May. Métro: Michel-Bizot or Daumesnil.*

13th Arrondissement (Les Gobelins)

$$ Auberge Etchegorry. Pull up a chair under the rafters festooned with braids of dried peppers and garlic, cured ham and sausages, and experience the lively flavors of traditional Basque country cooking in Paris. This friendly spot serves up generous portions of Basque classics like pipérade, along with other southern favorites like paella and a succulent pan-sautéed duck breast with wild mushrooms. ✕ *41 rue Croulebarbe,* ☎ *43-31–63–05. Reservations advised. AE, DC, V. Closed Sun. Métro: Corvisart or Gobelins.*

14th Arrondissement (Montparnasse)

$$$ La Cagouille. This is one of the best fish restaurants in Paris. Though Gérard Allemandou's intimate and very successful *bistro à poissons* overlooks the somewhat sterile place

Brancusi, Parisians continue to flock here for his intriguingly Zen-like cooking: Few sauces or adornments mask the fresh, clean flavors of fish—from elegant sole and turbot to more pedestrian sardines and mackerel. An aquarium and a long wooden bar are almost the only decoration in the large, simple, modern dining room. Besides its excellent wine list, La Cagouille has the finest collection of Cognacs in the city. There's a large terrace for warm-weather dining. ✕ *10–12 pl. Brancusi,* ☎ *43–22–09–01. Reservations advised. AE, MC, V. Métro: Gaîté.*

$ **La Régalade.** This is one of the most talked about new restaurants in Paris. The location, in a remote, colorless residential
★ neighborhood is a nuisance, but Yves Camdeborde's cooking is stunning. Although a veteran of the Crillon, he has kept his prices remarkably low—$35 for a three-course feast. Tables are booked far in advance, but service does continue until midnight, and you can often sneak in late in the evening. ✕ *49 av. Jean-Moulin,* ☎ *45–45–68–58. Reservations 1 month in advance advised. MC, V. Closed Sun., Mon., Aug. No Sat. lunch. Métro: Alesia.*

15th Arrondissement (Front de Seine)

$ **L'Os à Moëlle.** It's unlikely that you'll go away hungry. This small, popular bistro serves a very good value six-course dinner menu—starter, soup, fish, meat, cheese, and dessert—that changes daily; portions are generous (there's no à la carte). A sample menu might include white-bean soup, a country terrine of pork with peppers, rouget, sautéed veal, cheese with a small salad, and a delicious clafoutis of apples and rhubarb. At lunchtime, the à la carte menu is similarly good. With an excellent list of fairly-priced wines, your bill will stay comfortably low. ✕ *3 rue Vasco-de-Gama,* ☎ *45–57–27–27. Reservations essential. MC, V. Closed Sun., Mon. Métro: Balard.*

$ **Le Petit Plat.** Originally squeezed into a tiny space in the Latin Quarter (*see* Le Tout Petit Plat, 5th arr., *above*), this bistro was so popular that the owners found a bit more space in a quiet residential area; it's still small, but now the feel is intimate rather than crowded. The kitchen turns out generous portions of the slightly urbanized French country cooking that Parisians are currently mad about: Try the terrine of rabbit in tarragon aspic, sausage with potato salad in shallot vinaigrette, or roast chicken with sautéed mushrooms. The excellent wine list was selected by Henri Gault of Gault-Millau, the famous French food guide (his daughter is one of the three owners). ✗ *45 av. Emile-Zola,* ☏ *45–78–24–20. Reservations advised. V. Closed Mon. No Tues. lunch. Métro: Charles-Michel.*

16th Arrondissement (Trocadéro/Bois de Boulogne)

$$$$
★

Le Vivarois. Chef–owner Claude Peyrot is one of the most inspired and creative of contemporary French chefs, though his cooking can be uneven. He is a master with fish and puff pastry, his *bavarois* of red bell pepper (a creamy, molded concoction) is oft-imitated, and his original dishes shine: scallops with sesame and ginger, *rissolette* (small meat patty) of lamb's feet with artichokes and basil, and chocolate soufflé with chicory ice cream. Service is not always up to par. ✗ *192 av. Victor Hugo,* ☏ *45–04–04–31. Reservations advised. AE, DC, MC, V. Closed weekends, Aug. Métro: Rue de la Pompe.*

$$–$$$

Prunier. When Prunier reopened in late 1994, Parisians were thrilled to find that one of their favorite and most glamorous restaurants had not only been sensitively renovated— the famous Art Deco mosaics have never looked better—but that the kitchen, too, had been resurrected with skill and creativity. Founded in 1925, this was one of the best—and surely the prettiest—seafood restaurants in Paris for more than 50 years. Now the white marble counters again display impeccably fresh shellfish like precious jewelry, and the kitchen not only excels at classic French fish cooking, but has added some variety, with dishes like a *Saintongeaise* plate—raw oysters with grilled sausages—as eaten in Bordeaux. The pan-fried langoustines and turbot in hollandaise sauce are superb. The well-balanced wine list echoes director Jean-Claude Vrinat's acclaimed cellar at his other restaurant, Taillevent. No reservations are needed for the raw bar on the main level, but book for lunch or dinner in the upstairs dining room. ✗ *16 Avenue Victor Hugo,* ☏ *44–17–35–85. Reservations advised for main dining room. Jacket and tie. AE, DC, MC, V. Closed Sun., Mon. Métro: Etoile.*

17th Arrondissement (Monceau/Clichy)

$$$$ **Guy Savoy.** Guy Savoy is one of a handful of top chefs in
Paris today, and his four bistros have not managed to dis-
tract him too much from his handsome luxury restaurant
near the Arc de Triomphe. Savoy's oysters in aspic, sea bass
with spices, and poached and grilled pigeon reveal the
magnitude of his talent. His mille-feuille is a contemporary
classic. ✕ *18 rue Troyon,* ☎ *43–80–40–61. Reservations
advised. AE, MC, V. Closed Sun. No Sat. lunch. Métro:
Charles de Gaulle–Etoile.*

18th Arrondissement (Montmartre)

$$ **Le Restaurant.** Here's a real oasis just steps from the Place
Pigalle, an area where it's not easy to find a good meal. The
simply decorated storefront dining room is popular with
the artists and media types who've been quietly moving into
this otherwise touristy and slightly tawdry neighborhood.
The food's interesting and generally good; try the omelet
of oysters, and lamb with fennel and black olives. For
dessert, the shortbread tart filled with melted chocolate is
delicious. The service is often slow, though, especially on
weekends. ✕ *32 rue Veron,* ☎ *42–23–06–22. Reserva-
tions advised. AE, MC, V. Closed Mon. Métro: Abbesses.*

5 Lodging

OUR CRITERIA when selecting the hotels reviewed below were quality, location, and—where possible—character.

Updated
by Corinne
LaBalme

Generally, there are more Right Bank hotels offering luxury—or at any rate formality—than there are on the Left Bank, where hotels tend to be smaller but often loaded with character. Despite the huge choice of hotels here, you should always reserve well in advance, especially if you're determined to stay in a specific hotel. You can do this by telephoning ahead, then writing or faxing for confirmation. If you are asked to send a deposit, make sure you discuss refund policies before mailing your check or money order. Always ask for some form of written confirmation of your reservation, detailing the duration of your stay, the price, location and type of your room (single or double, twin beds or double), and bathroom (*see below*).

Despite widespread improvement, many Paris hotels still have idiosyncracies—some charming, others less so. Rooms are not always perfectly square, floors not always perfectly flat. The standard French double bed is slightly smaller than its American counterpart. The most enduring example of quirkiness is French plumbing, which sometimes looks like avant-garde sculpture. Shared toilets or bathrooms down the hall, though increasingly rare, are still found in many modest establishments. Never assume that what is billed as a bathroom (*salle de bain*) will necessarily contain a tub. Some rooms have toilets (what the French call *wc* or *cabinet de toilet*), some have bidets only—but no tub or shower. Others have a shower but no toilet, and still others have only washstands. Our reviews indicate the number of rooms with full bath facilities including tub (*baignoire*) or shower (*douche*), and number of rooms with shared baths. Make sure you know what you are getting when you book.

Almost all Paris hotels charge extra for breakfast, with prices ranging from 30 francs to over 100 francs per person in luxury establishments. Hotels generally assume you will be having breakfast there, and will add the breakfast charge to your bill automatically. If you don't want to have breakfast at the hotel, say so when you check in. For anything more than the standard Continental breakfast of *café au lait* (coffee with hot milk) and *baguette* (bread) or croissants, the price will be higher.

You'll notice that the French government grades hotels from four-star deluxe to one star, and that the stars appear on a shield on the hotel's facade. Theoretically, the ratings depend on amenities and price. They can be misleading, however, since many hotels prefer to be understarred for tax reasons. Many two- and three-star establishments offer excellent price-to-quality ratios. We list hotels by price, but often a hotel in a certain price category will have a few rooms that are less expensive; it's worthwhile to ask. Rates must be posted in all rooms, and all extra charges clearly shown. A nominal *séjour* tax (per person, per night) was introduced in 1994 to pay for increased promotion of tourism in Paris.

Unless otherwise stated, the hotels reviewed below have elevators, rooms have TVs and telephones, and English is spoken. Additional facilities, such as restaurants and health clubs, are listed at the end of each review.

CATEGORY	COST*
$$$$	over 1,200 frs
$$$	750 frs–1,200 frs
$$	450 frs–750 frs
$	under 450 frs

All prices are for a standard double room, including tax and service.

1st Arrondissement (Louvre)

$$$$ **Inter-Continental.** An aura of elegant luxury reigns throughout this exquisite late-19th-century hotel, one of the largest of the city's top hotels. It was designed by the architect of the Paris Opéra, Charles Garnier, and three of its gilt and stuccoed public rooms are official historic monuments. Spacious guest rooms overlook quiet inner courtyards. In summer, breakfast on the patio is a delicious experience. Service is impeccable. ⌨ *3 rue de Castiglione, 75001,* ☎ *44–77–11–11,* 𝔽𝔸𝕏 *44–77–14–60. 378 rooms with bath, 72 suites. 2 restaurants, bar. AE, DC, MC, V. Métro: Concorde.*

132

Paris Lodging

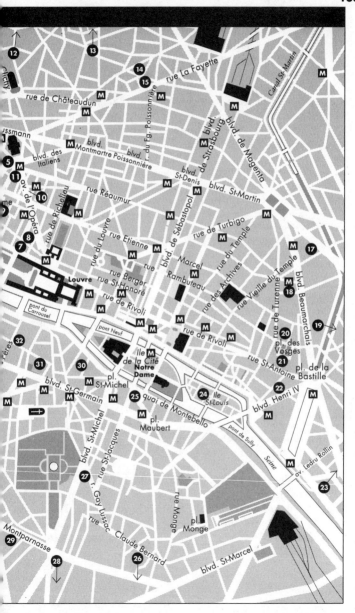

$$$$ **Ritz.** Surrounded by the city's finest jewelers, the Ritz is the
★   crowning gem on the sparkling place Vendôme. Festooned
           with gilt and ormolu, dripping with crystal chandeliers
           and tapestries, and swathed in heavy silk, this dazzling
           hotel, which opened in 1896, is the epitome of fin-de-siè-
           cle Paris. It's surprisingly intimate, too. The hotel has no
           lobby, for the express purpose of discouraging paparazzi
           and sightseers who could annoy the privileged clientele. Leg-
           endary suites are named after ritzy former residents like Mar-
           cel Proust and Coco Chanel. The famous Hemingway Bar
           (which the writer claimed to have "liberated" in 1944) re-
           opened in 1994. The handsome Vendôme Bar and the Es-
           padon restaurant remain elite meeting spots, and the
           lower-level health club has a magnificent indoor swim-
           ming pool surrounded by bucolic frescoes and towering
           columns. There's warm-weather seating in the charming ad-
           jacent garden. ⊠ *15 pl. Vendôme, 75001,* ☎ *42–60–38–
           30,* FAX *42–86–00–91. 142 rooms with bath, 45 suites. 2
           restaurants, 2 bars, indoor pool, beauty salon, health club,
           shops. AE, DC, MC, V. Métro: Madeleine.*

$$$ **Normandy.** The Belle Epoque decor, warm welcome, and
           central location near the Palais-Royal and theaters make
           this hotel a fine choice. Rooms are comfortable and indi-
           vidually decorated. Some are much smaller than others, and
           a handful of the least expensive have shower only. A won-
           derful wood-paneled bar with roaring fireplace is fre-
           quented by hotel guests and well-heeled theatergoers. ⊠ *7
           rue de l'Echelle, 75001,* ☎ *42–60–30–21,* FAX *42–60–45–
           81. 116 rooms with bath, 6 with shower, 7 suites. Restau-
           rant, bar. AE, DC, MC, V. Métro: Pyramides.*

$$ **Londres Stockholm.** An appealing combination of charac-
           ter and comfort singles out this small hotel. The lobby has
           300-year-old exposed oak beams, statues in niches, and rus-
           tic-looking stone walls. The rough-cast white walls in the
           rooms are offset by deep red carpeting. There's no restau-
           rant or bar, but limited room service is available. The ele-
           vator doesn't go to the ground floor. ⊠ *13 rue St-Roch,
           75001,* ☎ *42–60–15–62,* FAX *42–60–16–00. 29 rooms with
           bath, 2 with shower. AE, MC, V. Métro: Pyramides.*

2nd Arrondissement (Stock Exchange)

$$ **Gaillon-Opéra.** The oak beams, stone walls, and marble tiles
★ of the Gaillon-Opéra single it out as one of the most charm-
ing hotels in the Opéra neighborhood. The plants through-
out and a flower-filled patio also delight. ☎ *9 rue Gaillon,
75002,* ☎ *47–42–47–74,* ℻ *47–42–01–23. 26 rooms with
bath, 1 suite. AE, DC, MC, V. Métro: Opéra.*

$$ **Choiseul-Opéra.** The no-frills, functional decor keeps prices
low at this centrally located hotel between the Opéra and the
Place Vendôme. Twin rooms are large for this price range; remodeled rooms on the first floor are more expensive. Service
is relaxed but efficient, and the staff are happy to try out their
English on guests. The famed expatriate watering hole, Harry's
Bar, is right next door. ☎ *1 rue Daunou, 75002,* ☎ *42–61–
70–41,* ℻ *42–86–91–96. 28 rooms with bath, 14 with
shower, 2 suites. AE, DC, MC, V. Métro: Opéra.*

3rd Arrondissement (Le Marais/Beaubourg)

$$$$ **Pavillon de la Reine.** The 17th-century place des Vosges is
★ the setting for the best hotel in the Marais, built around
two flower-filled courtyards behind the historic Queen's
Pavilion. Although this cozy mansion looks old, it was actually reconstructed from scratch in 1986 following original plans and using period timbers, rough-hewn paving
stones, Louis XIII fireplaces, and antiques. Ask for a du-
plex with French windows overlooking the first courtyard
(there are no rooms overlooking the place des Vosges).
Breakfast is served in a vaulted cellar. ☎ *28 pl. des Vosges, 75003,* ☎ *42–77–96–40,* ℻ *42–77–63–06. 31
rooms with bath, 24 suites. Free parking. AE, DC, MC, V.
Métro: Chemin Vert.*

$ **Hôtel du Marais.** On the edge of the Marais, this small hotel
in a restored turn-of-the-century building is near the Bastille
Opéra and the Picasso Museum. For extremely reasonable
rates you get amenities generally reserved for more expensive hotels, such as minibars and color TVs in rooms.
Some rooms have exposed beams; all are functional, sound-
proofed, and clean. ☎ *2 bis rue Commines, 75003,* ☎ *48–
87–78–27,* ℻ *48–87–09–01. 12 rooms with bath, 27 with
shower. AE, MC, V. Métro: Filles-du-Calvaire.*

4th Arrondissement (Le Marais/Ile St-Louis)

$$$ **Deux-Iles.** This converted 17th-century mansion on the Ile
★ St-Louis has long won plaudits for charm and comfort.
Flowers and plants are scattered around the stunning hall.
The fabric-hung rooms, though small, have exposed beams
and are fresh and airy. Ask for a room overlooking the lit-
tle garden courtyard. The lounge is dominated by a fine chim-
neypiece and doubles as a bar. ☎ *59 rue St-Louis-en-l'Ile,
75004,* ☎ *43–26–13–35,* FAX *43–29–60–25. 8 rooms with
bath, 9 with shower. No credit cards. Métro: Pont-Marie.*

$ **Castex.** This family-run, two-star hotel in a 19th-century
★ building is a real find. Rooms are squeaky clean. The decor
is strictly functional, but the extremely friendly owners
and rock-bottom prices mean the Castex is often fully
booked months ahead. There's a large American clientele.
The eight least expensive rooms, two per floor, share toi-
lets on the immaculate, well-lit landings. There's no elevator,
and TV is in the lobby only. ☎ *5 rue Castex, 75004,* ☎
42–72–31–52, FAX *42–72–57–91. 4 rooms with bath, 23
with shower. MC, V. Métro: Bastille.*

$ **Place des Vosges.** A loyal American clientele swears by this
small, historic hotel on a charming street just off the
exquisite square of the same name. Oak-beamed ceilings
and rough-hewn stone in public areas and some of the
guest rooms add to the atmosphere. Ask for the top-floor
room, the hotel's largest, with a view of Marais rooftops.
Some rooms, the size of walk-in closets, are less expensive.
There's a welcoming little breakfast room. ☎ *12 rue de Bi-
rague, 75004,* ☎ *42–72–60–46,* FAX *42–72–02–64. 11
rooms with bath, 5 with shower. AE, DC, V. Métro: Bastille.*

5th Arrondissement (Latin Quarter)

$$ **Elysa Luxembourg.** The Elysa is what the French call *un hôtel
★ de charme.* Though the building is not large, most rooms
are surprisingly spacious, and all are exquisitely maintained
and refurbished yearly. Cream-colored furniture is set against
pale blue or pink fabrics. You'll find a minibar in every room
and a breakfast lounge serving Continental or buffet break-
fasts. This is one of the rare hotels in the city with a sauna.
☎ *6 rue Gay Lussac, 75005,* ☎ *43–25–31–74,* FAX *46–34–*

56–27. 25 rooms with bath, 5 with shower. Sauna. AE, MC, V. Métro: Luxembourg.

$ **Esméralda.** One either loves it or hates it. The Esméralda, which boasts a fine (though noisy) location in a fusty 17th-century building across from Notre Dame, is famed for its cozy, eccentric charm. Some closet-size rooms are nearly overpowered by gaudy imitation antiques. Request a room with a view of the cathedral. Animal lovers will enjoy the friendly dogs and cats that snooze in the lobby. Single rooms with showers on the landings are very cheap. ☎ *4 rue St-Julien-le-Pauvre, 75005, ☎ 43–54–19–20, ꜰꜰ 40–51–00–68. 15 rooms with bath, 4 with shower on the landing. No credit cards. Métro: St-Michel.*

6th Arrondissement (Luxembourg)

$$$$ **Relais Christine.** The Relais Christine is one of the most ap-
★ pealing of the Left Bank hotels, impeccably luxurious yet oozing charm. The hotel is located on a quiet street between the Seine and the boulevard St-Germain and occupies some precious 16th-century cloisters. The best rooms overlook the central lawn. All are spacious and comfortable, particularly the duplexes on the upper floors. Air-conditioning and double-glazed windows add to their appeal. There's no restaurant, and only guests may use the bar. ☎ *3 rue Christine, 75006, ☎ 43–26–71–80, ꜰꜰ 43–26–89–38. 36 rooms, 6 suites, 12 duplexes, all with bath. Bar, air-conditioning, free parking. AE, DC, MC, V. Métro: St-Michel.*

$$$ **Hôtel d'Angleterre.** Some claim the Hôtel d'Angleterre is the ultimate Left Bank hotel—a little small and shabby, but elegant and perfectly (albeit snobbishly) managed. The 18th-century building was originally the British ambassador's residence; later, Hemingway made it his Paris home. Room sizes and rates vary greatly, though all rooms are individually decorated. Some are imposingly formal, others are homey and plain. Ask for one overlooking the courtyard. ☎ *44 rue Jacob, 75006, ☎ 42–60–34–72, ꜰꜰ 42–60–16–93. 26 rooms with bath, 3 suites. Bar. AE, DC, MC, V. Métro: St-Germain-des-Prés.*

$$–$$$ **Marronniers.** Accessed through an appealing courtyard off the chic rue Jacob, the Marronniers is a sentimental favorite for many budget-conscious tourists. The management re-

cently conducted a room-by-room renovation to clean up the cobwebs that had started to obscure the hotel's charm, and air-conditioning was installed. (Good news: Prices have stayed roughly the same.) The salon-breakfast room, in a glassed-in veranda, is an oasis of calm and greenery. ⌂ *21 rue Jacob, 75006,* ☎ *43–25–30–60,* ⊠ *40–46–83–56. 17 rooms with bath, 20 with shower. Bar, air-conditioning. No credit cards. Métro: St-Germain-des-Prés.*

7th Arrondissement (Invalides)

$$$$ **Duc de Saint-Simon.** Set back from a peaceful little street
★ leading to boulevard St-Germain, the Saint-Simon is both quaint and classy. Parts of the building date back to the 17th century, others date from the 18th. Try for one of the rooms with a terrace; they look over the courtyard and neighboring gardens. There's a pleasant bar and a cellar lounge for breakfast. The regular doubles are significantly less expensive than the suites. ⌂ *14 rue St-Simon, 75007,* ☎ *45–48–35–66,* ⊠ *45–48–68–25. 29 rooms with bath, 5 suites. Bar. No credit cards. Métro: Bac.*

$$$ **Université.** This appealingly converted 17th-century town
★ house is located between boulevard St-Germain and the Seine. Rooms have their original fireplaces and are decorated with English and French antiques. Ask for one of the two rooms with a terrace on the fifth floor. Though there's no restaurant, you can rent the vaulted cellar for parties. Rooms with shower are moderately priced. ⌂ *22 rue de l'Université, 75007,* ☎ *42–61–09–39,* ⊠ *42–60–40–84. 20 rooms with bath, 7 with shower. AE, MC, V. Métro: St-Germain-des-Prés.*

$ **Champ de Mars.** This simple, clean two-star hotel has one-star prices. Don't expect luxury or atmosphere, just a nondescript room for a very good deal, in a nice neighborhood near the Eiffel Tower and Invalides. ⌂ *7 rue du Champ de Mars, 75007,* ☎ *45–51–52–30. 19 rooms with bath, 6 with shower. MC, V. Métro: Ecole Militaire.*

8th Arrondissement (Champs-Elysées)

$$$$ **Crillon.** The Crillon is the crème de la crème of Paris's
★ "palace" hotels, set as it is in two 18th-century town houses

on the place de la Concorde, site of the French Revolution's infamous guillotine. Marie-Antoinette, who met her end there, took singing lessons at the Hôtel de Crillon, where one of the original *grands appartements,* now sumptuous salons protected by the French National Historic Landmark Commission, has been named for the Queen. Guests must pay dearly for a suite with a balcony overlooking the great square, with seemingly all of Paris at their feet. Lesser mortals still get magnificent digs, individually decorated with Rococo and Directoire antiques, crystal and gilt wall sconces, and gold fittings. Most double rooms have separate sitting rooms, and the bathrooms, stocked with wonderful Annick Goutal toiletries, are clad in marble. The sheer quantity of the marble downstairs—in the lobby, the adjacent lounge, and especially the grand, top-rated Les Ambassadeurs restaurant—is staggering. The staff anticipates your every need. ☎ *10 pl. de la Concorde, 75008,* ☎ *44– 71–15–00,* FAX *44–71–15–02. 120 rooms with bath, 43 suites. 2 restaurants, 2 bars, shop. AE, DC, MC, V. Métro: Concorde.*

$$$ **Bradford-Elysées.** The turn-of-the-century Bradford-Elysées, now affiliated with the Best Western chain, has an appealing, old-fashioned feel. An old wooden elevator carries you from the flower-filled lobby to the spacious, comfortable rooms, some equipped with Louis XVI–style furniture, brass beds, and fireplaces. All guest rooms were repainted and decorated with new bedspreads and draperies in 1995. Some rooms with shower are less expensive between early December and mid-March. ☎ *10 rue St-Philippe-du-Roule, 75008,* ☎ *45–63–20–20,* FAX *45–63–20–07. 34 rooms with bath, 12 with shower, 2 suites. Bar. AE, DC, MC, V. Métro: St-Philippe-du-Roule.*

★ **Argenson.** This friendly, family-run hotel provides what may well be the best value in the swanky 8th arrondissement. Some of the city's greatest sights are just a 10-minute walk away. Old furniture, molded ceilings, and skillful flower arrangements add to the charm. Ongoing room-by-room renovation means new bathrooms in many. The best rooms have full bath, but they are pricier; reserve well in advance for one of these. The smallest rooms have shared baths. ☎ *15 rue d'Argenson, 75008,* ☎ *42–65–16–87,* FAX *47–42–*

02–06. 5 rooms with bath, 19 with shower, 3 with shared bath. MC, V. Métro: Miromesnil.

9th Arrondissement (Opéra)

$$$$ Grand Hotel Inter-Continental. Paris's biggest luxury hotel has endless hallways and a facade that seems as long as the Louvre. This 1862 gem sparkles like new. The grand salon's Art Deco dome and the painted ceilings of the Opéra and Café de la Paix restaurants are registered landmarks. Rooms are spacious and light, decorated in Art Nouveau style with pastel colors. The famed Café de la Paix is one of the city's great people-watching spots. ☎ *2 rue Scribe, 75009,* ☎ *40–07–32–32,* FAX *42–66–12–51. 470 rooms with bath, 23 suites. 3 restaurants, 2 bars, health club, shops, parking (fee). AE, DC, MC, V. Métro: Opéra.*

$$ Hôtel du Pré. Slightly off the beaten track, this three-star hotel is near the pretty square Montholon. Its reasonable prices, charming and sunny public areas, comfortable rooms done in summery colors, and large bathrooms make it a very good deal. The owners also run the equally good Relais du Pré and Résidence du Pré on the same street (at numbers 16 and 15). ☎ *10 rue Pierre-Sémard, 75009,* ☎ *42–81–37–11,* FAX *40–23–98–28. 22 rooms with bath, 19 with shower. Bar. AE, DC, MC, V. Métro: Poissonière.*

$ Riboutté-Lafayette. This small, cozy two-star hotel in a 19th-century building near the busy rue La Fayette is family-run and filled with charming bric-a-brac and old furniture. The clean, sunny rooms are decorated in pastel colors, and those on the top floor have sloping ceilings. ☎ *5 rue Riboutté, 75009,* ☎ *47–70–62–36,* FAX *48–00–91–50. 15 rooms with bath, 9 with shower. AE, MC, V. Métro: Cadet.*

11th Arrondissement (Bastille)

$$ Méridional. The lobby may be a bit garish, but the rooms at this three-star hotel are comfortable and quiet, decorated in earth tones or floral prints. The 19th-century building, on a handsome but busy tree-lined boulevard, is a five-minute walk from either the Bastille or the Marais. ☎ *36 blvd. Richard Lenoir, 75011,* ☎ *48–05–75–00,* FAX *43–57–*

42–85. *26 rooms with bath, 10 with shower. AE, DC, MC, V. Métro: Bréguet-Sabin.*

$ **Résidence Alhambra.** The Alhambra's gleaming white ex-
★ terior, backyard garden, and flower-filled window boxes provide a bright spot in an otherwise drab neighborhood. The
hotel is on the edge of the historical Marais quarter and is
conveniently close to five Métro lines. The smallish guest
rooms are painted in fresh pastel or cool ivory shades;
most rooms have color TV. The lobby is filled with plants
and leather armchairs. ▦ *11 bis–13 rue de Malte, 75011,*
☎ *47–00–35–52,* ℻ *43–57–98–75. 10 rooms with bath,
48 with shower. MC, V. Métro: République.*

12th Arrondissement (Gare de Lyon)

$ **Modern Hôtel-Lyon.** Built in 1903, this cozy, family-run hotel
is conviently located between the Bastille and the Gare de
Lyon. Rooms are freshly decorated in pastel tones of blue
and lavender. The owners are friendly and helpful. ▦ *3
rue Parrot, 75012,* ☎ *43–43–41–52,* ℻ *43–43–81–16.
36 rooms with bath, 12 with shower. Bar. AE, DC, MC,
V. Métro: Gare de Lyon.*

13th Arrondissement (Les Gobelins)

$ **Résidence les Gobelins.** Five minutes' walk from the Latin
Quarter, this simple, small two-star hotel on a quiet street
offers pleasant rooms decorated in warm, coordinated colors. The breakfast room faces a small flower-filled garden.
▦ *9 rue des Gobelins, 75013,* ☎ *47–07–26–90,* ℻ *43–
31–44–05. 18 rooms with bath, 14 with shower. AE, MC,
V. Métro: Gobelins.*

14th Arrondissement (Montparnasse)

$$$ **Raspail.** The rooms in this recently remodeled art deco
★ hotel are named after the artists who made Montparnasse
the art capital of the world in the '20s and '30s. All are dec-
orated in pastel colors and have TV with CNN and built-
in hairdryers; five offer spectacular panoramic views of
Montparnasse and the Eiffel Tower. Most rooms are at the
low end of this price category. ▦ *203 blvd. Raspail, 75014,*

☎ *43–20–62–86*, FAX *43–20–50–79. 28 rooms with bath, 10 with shower. Air-conditioning, in-room safes, minibars. AE, DC, MC, V. Métro: Raspail.*

$ Midi. Don't be put off by the nondescript facade and reception area; most of the rooms here are adequately furnished, and those facing the street are both large and quiet. This hotel is close to both Montparnasse and the Latin Quarter, and there are Métro and RER stations nearby. 🖭 *4 av. Réné-Coty, 75014,* ☎ *43–27–23–25,* FAX *43–21–24–58. 20 rooms with bath, 21 with shower, 9 with shared bath. MC, V. Métro: Denfert-Rochereau.*

16th Arrondissement (Trocadéro/ Bois de Boulogne)

$$$$ Parc Victor Hugo. The newest (1992) luxury hotel on the
  ★ Right Bank, decorated in cozy chintz by Nina Campbell, is a gracious tribute to English country-house charm. Rooms are perfumed by floral potpourri and have sleek lighting and up-to-date amenities (TV with CNN, air-conditioning). A gourmet plus: the celebrated Jamin/Robuchon restaurant is right next door. 🖭 *55-57 av. Raymond-Poincaré, 75116,* ☎ *44–05–66–66,* FAX *44–05–66–00. 104 rooms with bath, 11 suites. Restaurant, bar, air-conditioning, no-smoking floor, room service, in-room VCRs, parking (fee). AE, DC, MC, V. Métro: Victor Hugo.*

18th Arrondissement (Montmartre)

$ Regyn's Montmartre. Despite small rooms, this owner-run hotel on Montmartre's place des Abbesses provides simple, comfortable accommodations. A predominantly young clientele and a relaxed atmosphere have made this an attractive choice for some. Try for one of the rooms on the upper floors, with great views of either the Eiffel Tower or Sacré Coeur. 🖭 *18 pl. des Abbesses, 75018,* ☎ *42–54–45–21,* FAX *42–23–76–69. 14 rooms with bath, 8 with shower. In-room safes. AE, MC, V. Métro: Abbesses.*

$ Utrillo. The Utrillo is on a quiet side street at the foot of Montmartre, quite near the colorful rue Lepic markets. The decor is appealing, with prints and a marble-topped breakfast table in every room. Because white paint and fabrics are used throughout, the hotel seems light, clean, and more spacious than it actually is. Two rooms (numbers 61 and 63) have views of the Eiffel Tower. ☎ *7 rue Aristide-Bruant, 75018, ☎ 42–58–13–44, FAX 42–23–93–88. 5 rooms with bath, 25 with shower. Sauna. AE, DC, MC, V. Métro: Blanche.*

6 The Arts and Nightlife

THE ARTS

THE WEEKLY MAGAZINES *Pariscope, L'Officiel des Spectacles,* and *Figaroscope* (a supplement to *Le Figaro* newspaper) are published every Wednesday and give detailed entertainment listings. The Paris Tourist Office has set up a **24-hour hot line** (☎ 49–52–53–56) in English with information about weekly events. The best place to buy tickets is at the venue itself. Half-price tickets for many same-day theater performances are available at the **Kiosque Théâtre** (across from 15 place de la Madeleine; open Tues.–Sat. 12:30–8, Sun. 12:30–6); expect a line. There's another branch at Châtelet RER station (closed Sun.).

Updated by Simon Hewitt

Classical Music

Salle Pleyel (252 rue du Fbg. St-Honoré, 8e, ☎ 45–61–53–00, métro Ternes), near the Arc de Triomphe, was Paris's principal home of classical music before the new Opéra de la Bastille opened. The Paris Symphony Orchestra and other leading international orchestras still play here regularly. Paris may not be as richly endowed as New York or London when it comes to orchestral music, but the city compensates with a never-ending stream of inexpensive lunchtime and evening concerts in churches, ranging from organ recitals to choral music. **Sainte-Chapelle** (blvd. du Palais, 1er, ☎ 43–54–30–09, métro Cité) holds outstanding candlelit concerts—make reservations well in advance. **Notre Dame** (Ile de la Cité, ☎ 42–34–56–10, métro Cité) is another church where you can combine sightseeing with good listening.

Museums are another place to find concerts in the classical mode, especially **Le Musée d'Orsay** (1 rue de Bellechasse, 7e, ☎ 45–49–48–14, RER Musée d'Orsay), which regularly holds small-scale concerts (song cycles, piano recitals, or chamber music) at lunchtime or in the early evening.

Opera

L'Opéra Bastille (pl. de la Bastille, ☎ 44–73–13–00, métro Bastille) has taken over the role as Paris's main opera house from L'Opéra Garnier. It's had its share of start-up and management problems, and many feel it is not living up to its promise of grand opera at affordable prices (which range from 60 to 570 francs). **Théâtre Musical de Paris** (2 pl. du Châtelet, 1er, ☎ 40–28–28–28, métro Châtelet), better known as the Théâtre du Châtelet, offers opera and ballet for a wider audience, at more reasonable prices.

Rock Concerts

Unlike French jazz, French rock is not generally considered to be on par with its American and British cousins. Even so, Paris is a great place to catch some of your favorite groups, because concert halls tend to be smaller and tickets less expensive. Most places charge from 90 to 120 francs for entrance and get going around 11 PM. **Palais Omnisports de Paris–Bercy** (rue de Bercy, 12e, ☎ 44–68–44–68, métro Bercy) is a larger venue where you'll find leading English and American groups. **Zenith** (Parc de la Villette, 19e, ☎ 42–08–60–00, métro Porte-de-Pantin) is a large hall located in eastern Paris; check posters and papers for details.

Dance

L'Opéra Garnier (pl. de l'Opéra, 9e, ☎ 47–42–53–71, métro Opéra) hosts the highlights of the Paris dance year. In addition to being the sumptuous home of the well-reputed Paris Ballet, (French ballet superstar Patrick Dupont is the reigning artistic director), it also bills dozens of major foreign troupes ranging from classical to modern. The **Palais des Congrès** (pl. de la Porte Maillot, 17e, ☎ 40–68–00–05, métro Porte Maillot) is a large, modern hall where the unadventurous program is aimed at a family audience. The **Palais des Sports** (pl. de la Porte de Versailles, 15e, ☎ 48–28–40–48, métro Porte de Versailles), a circular building dating from the 1970s, often stages ballet.

Theater

Bouffes du Nord (37 bis blvd. de la Chapelle, 10e, ☎ 46–07–34–50, métro La Chapelle) offers wonderful experimental productions. Other avant-garde theater is found further south, in the Marais and the Bastille neighborhoods. **Café de la Gare** (41 rue du Temple, 4e, ☎ 42–78–52–51, métro Rambuteau) is a fun spot to experience a particularly Parisian form of theater, the *café-théâtre*—a mixture of satirical sketches and variety show riddled with slapstick humor and viewed in a café setting. You should have a good grasp of French. A pricier option is **Chez Michou** (80 rue des Martyrs, 18e, ☎ 46–06–16–04, métro Abbesses).

Movies

There are hundreds of movie theaters in the city, and a number of them, especially in principal tourist areas such as the Champs-Elysées and the boulevard des Italiens near the Opéra, run English films. Check the *Officiel du Spectacle* or *Pariscope* for a movie of your choice. Look for the initials "v.o.," which mean *version originale;* i.e., not subtitled or dubbed. Cinema admission runs from 40 francs to 50 francs; there are reduced rates on Mondays and, in some cinemas, for morning shows. Most theaters will post two show times: the first is the *séance,* or period of commercials and previews, and sometimes short films. The feature presentation usually starts 10–25 minutes later.

The Champs-Elysées bristles with cinemas, among them the **Gaumont Marignan** (No. 27, ☎ 43–59–92–82, métro Franklin D. Roosevelt), **Gaumont Ambassade** (No. 50, ☎ 43–59–19–08, métro Franklin D. Roosevelt), **Gaumont Champs-Elysées** (No. 66, ☎ 43–59–04–67, métro Franklin D. Roosevelt), **Publicis** (No. 129, ☎ 47–20–76–23, métro Etoile), and the **Club Gaumont** (2 Rond-Point, ☎ 43–59–31–97, métro Franklin D. Roosevelt). Big-screen fanatics should try the **Gaumont Grand Ecran** (30 pl. d'Italie, 13e, ☎ 45–88–88–03, métro Place d'Italie), the **Max Linder Panorama** (24 blvd. Poissonnière, 9e, ☎ 48–24–00–47, métro Rue Montmartre), the **Kinopanorama** (60 av. de la Motte-Piquet, 15e, ☎ 43–06–50–53, métro La Motte Picquet Grenelle), or the **Grand Rex** (1 blvd. Poissonnière, 2e,

☎ 42–36–83–93, métro Bonne-Nouvelle), which sometimes doubles as a rock venue.

On the Left Bank, the Action chain of cinemas, including the **Action Ecoles** (23 rue des Ecoles, 5e, ☎ 43–25–72–07, métro Maubert-Mutualité), **Action Rive Gauche** (5 rue des Ecoles, 5e, ☎ 43–54–47–62, métro Cardinal Lemoine), and **Action Christine** (4 rue Christine, 6e, ☎ 43–29–11–30, métro St-Michel), show offbeat films and reruns; so do the **Studio Galande** (42 rue Galande, 5e, ☎ 43–26–94–08, métro St-Michel), the **Saint-André-des-Arts** (30 rue Saint-André-des-Arts, 6e, ☎ 43–26–48–18, métro St-Michel), and the **Lucernaire Forum** (53 rue Notre-Dame-des-Champs, 6e, ☎ 42–22–26–50, métro Vavin). The Chinese-style **La Pagode** (57 rue de Babylone, 7e, ☎ 36–68–75–07, métro St-Fraçois-Xavier) is a national monument, and well worth a visit.

NIGHTLIFE

The French are definitely nightbirds, though these days that means smart, elegant *bars de nuit* rather than frenetic dance clubs. The Champs-Elysées, that ubiquitous cabaret land, is making a comeback, though the clientele remains predominantly foreign. The tawdry Pigalle and down-at-the-heels Bastille areas are trendy these days, and the Left Bank boasts a bit of everything. During the week, people are usually home after closing hours at 2 AM, but weekends mean late-night partying.

Boîtes de Nuit

The more upscale Paris *boîtes de nuits* (nightclubs) tend to be both expensive (1,000 francs for a bottle of gin or whiskey) and private—in other words, you'll usually need to know someone who's a member in order to get through the door. Dance clubs aren't as hot as they once were; you'll find more Parisians seeking moody little cocktail bars these days. Clubs stay open until the wee hours; call ahead for admission prices.

Les Bains (7 rue du Bourg-l'Abbé, 3e, ☎ 48–87–01–80, métro Etienne Marcel), a forever-trendy hot spot, is hard to access;

it helps to be famous—or look like a model. **Le Balajo** (9 rue de Lappe, 11e, ☎ 47–00–07–87, métro Bastille) is an old Java ballroom that specializes in salsa and techno. **La Chapelle des Lombards** (19 rue de Lappe, 11e, ☎ 43–57–24–24, métro Bastille) goes for an Afro-Cuban beat.

Bars

Café de la Plage (59 rue de Charonne, 11e, ☎ 47–00–91–60, métro Ledru-Rollin) has jazz in the cellar and Guinness at the bar. **La Casbah** (18 rue de la Forge-Royale, 11e, ☎ 43–71–71–89, métro Faidherbe-Chaligny) is both a bar and dance club with a touch of Casablanca. **China Club** (50 rue de Charenton, 12e, ☎ 43–43–82–02, métro Ledru-Rollin) is a trendy bar with an Orient Express theme. **Le Piston Pelican** (15 rue de Bagnolet, 20e, ☎ 43–70–93–98, métro Alexandre-Dumas), a favorite among Beaux-Arts students, has a laid-back ambience and occasional live music. **Lili la Tigresse** (98 rue Blanche, 9e, ☎ 48–74–08–25, métro Blanche) is a sexy, velvet-lined bar with bar-top dancers and a trendy crowd. **Moloko** (26 rue Fontaine, 9e, ☎ 48–74–50–26, métro Blanche), a smoky late-night bar with a small dance floor, is a popular spot.

Gay and Lesbian Bars and Clubs

Amnesia Café's (42 rue Vieille du Temple, 4e, ☎ 42–72–16–94, métro Rambuteau) under-lit bar and art deco ceiling paintings attract a young, yuppie gay and lesbian crowd. **Club 18** (18 rue de Beaujolais, 1er, ☎ 42–97–41–49, métro Pyramides), the oldest gay disco in Paris, took on a modern look in 1993 and is as popular and casual as ever, particularly on theme nights. **La Champmesle** (4 rue Chabanais, 2e, ☎ 42–96–85–20, métro Bourse) is the hub of lesbian nightlife with a back room reserved for women only.

Pubs

L'Académie de la Bière (88 bis blvd. de Port-Royal, 5e, ☎ 43–54–66–65, RER Port-Royal) serves more than 100 foreign brews to accompany good french fries and *moules marinière* (mussels cooked in white wine). **Bar Belge** (75 av. de Saint-Ouen, 17e, ☎ 46–27–41–01, métro Guy Mô-

quet) is an authentically noisy Flemish drinking spot.
Connolly's Corner (12 rue Mirbel, 5e, ☎ 43–31–94–22,
métro Censier-Daubenton) has a dart board and the best
pint of Murphy's in Paris. Don't wear a tie, or the end
will be snipped off and stuck on the wall. **Kitty O'Shea's**
(10 rue des Capucines, 2e, ☎ 40–15–08–08, métro
Opéra) is the perfect spot to quaff Guinness in an Irish
mode. **The Mayflower** (49 rue Descartes, 5e, ☎ 43–54–
56–47, métro Cardinal Lemoine) is a classy, Left Bank
spot, British-style.

Jazz Clubs

The French take jazz seriously, and Paris is one of the great
jazz cities of the world, with plenty of variety, including
some fine, distinctive local coloring. (You're in Europe now,
so why insist on American performers?) For nightly sched-
ules, consult the specialty magazines *Jazz Hot* or *Jazz Magazine*. Remember that nothing gets going till 10 or 11 PM,
and that entry prices can vary widely from about 40 francs
to over 100 francs.

On the Left Bank, **Le Bilboquet** (13 rue Saint-Benoît, 6e,
☎ 45–48–81–84, métro St-Germain-des-Prés) plays main-
stream jazz in a faded Belle Epoque decor. **Caveau de la
Huchette** (5 rue de la Huchette, 5e, ☎ 43–26–65–05, métro
St-Michel) is a smoke-filled shrine to the Dixieland beat.
Montana (28 rue Saint-Benoît, 6e, ☎ 44–39–71–00,
métro St-Germain-des-Prés) is a well-known spot for jazz
lovers. **La Villa** (29 rue Jacob, 6e, ☎ 43–26–60–00, métro
St-Germain-des-Prés), a newcomer on the jazz scene, has
been attracting serious musicians.

On the Right Bank, **Au Duc des Lombards** (42 rue des
Lombards, 1er, ☎ 42–33–22–88, métro Les Halles) is an
ill-lit, romantic venue. **Le Baiser Salé** (58 rue des Lombards,
1er, ☎ 42–33–37–71, métro Les Halles) attracts a younger
crowd. **The Lionel Hampton Jazz Club** (81 blvd. Gouvion-
St-Cyr, 17e, ☎ 40–68–30–42, métro Porte Maillot), at the
Meridien Hotel near Porte Maillot, also boasts top jazz
artists. **New Morning** (7 rue des Petites-Ecuries, 10e, ☎ 45–
23–51–41, métro Château-d'Eau) is a premier spot for serious jazz fans; the mood can be reverential.

Cabaret.

Paris's nightclubs are household names, shunned by wordly Parisians and beloved of foreign tourists, who flock to the shows. Prices can range from 200 francs (simple admission plus one drink) to more than 700 francs (dinner plus show). For 350–500 francs, you can get a good seat plus half a bottle of champagne.

L'Ane Rouge (3 rue Laugier, 17e, ☎ 43–80–79–97, métro Ternes) is a typical French cabaret playing to a mixed Parisian and foreign crowd, where the emphasis is on laughs and entertainment, with a host of singers, magicians, comedians, and ventriloquists. **Au Lapin Agile** (22 rue des Saules, 18e, ☎ 46–06–85–87, métro Lamarck Caulaincourt) considers itself the "doyen of cabarets," and Picasso once paid for a meal with one of his paintings; the setting in Montmartre is touristy but picturesque. **Le Crazy Horse** (12 av. George V, 8e, ☎ 47–23–32–32, métro Alma-Marceau) is one of the best known clubs for pretty girls and dance routines: lots of humor and lots less clothes. **Les Folies Bergère** (32 rue Richer, 9e, ☎ 44–79–98–98, métro Cadet), a legend since the days of Manet, reopened at the end of 1993 after closing briefly due to financial trouble; the new-and-improved cabaret includes ornate costumes, masterful lighting, and a show that returns to its music hall origins. **Le Lido** (116 bis av. des Champs-Elysées, 8e, ☎ 40–76–56–10, métro George V) stars the famous Bluebell Girls and underwent a spectacular $10 million face-lift in 1994. The owners now claim no show this side of Las Vegas can rival for it for special effects. **Le Moulin Rouge** (pl. Blanche, 18e, ☎ 46–06–00–19, métro Blanche), that old favorite in Montmartre, mingles the can-can and crocodiles in an extravagant spectacle.

Casino

Casino d'Enghien (☎ 34–12–90–00), the nearest public casino, is by the lake at Enghien-les-Bains, 10 miles to the north of Paris.

INDEX

NOTES

PRAISE FOR HARRY TURTLEDOVE
AND HIS NOVELS

"The maven of alternate history."
— *The San Diego Union-Tribune*

"Turtledove creates a whole intricate biosphere with a some-how breathable atmosphere." — *The New Yorker*

"Full of gravitas and speculative heft."
— *The Wall Street Journal*

"[Turtledove] provides brain candy for history buffs."
— *Sacramento News & Review*

"Turtledove has a knack for creating well-rounded charac-ters who epitomize the time he describes, whether in works of alternative history or speculative fiction."
— *Library Journal*

"Turtledove is a master of operating on a grand scale, using interconnected stories of individuals to tell a much larger tale." — *The Maine Edge*

"[Turtledove] remains the top guru of the alternative-his-torical universe." — *Alternative Worlds*

continued . . .

"Whether he's going for humor or pathos, action
commentary, Turtledove's research is always solid,
ulation thoughtful, and his execution professional."
— *Publishers Weekly*

"Alternate history is Turtledove's field and no one explores
the possibilities in such depth as he does."
— Lisa DuMond, SF Site

"Harry Turtledove is a historian by training and [is] a masterful teller of tales." — SciFiDimensions

HARRY TURTLEDOVE

JOE STEELE

A ROC BOOK

ROC
Published by New American Library,
an imprint of Penguin Random House LLC
375 Hudson Street, New York, New York 10014

This book is a publication of New American Library. Previously published in a
Roc hardcover edition.

First Roc Mass Market Printing, December 2015

For more information about Penguin Random House, visit penguin.com.

ISBN 978-0-451-47219-9

Printed in the United States of America
10 9 8 7 6 5 4 3 2 1

Penguin
Random
House

Joe Steele is for Janis Ian.

The novel *Joe Steele* has a plotline derived from the short story "Joe Steele," which appeared in *Stars: Original Stories Based on the Songs of Janis Ian*, edited by Janis Ian and Mike Resnick (DAW Books: New York, 2001). In "god & the fbi," Janis wrote "Stalin was a Democrat . . ." I started wondering how and why Stalin might have become a Democrat, and the story grew from there. So that's one reason why I've dedicated the novel to her.

But wait! There's more! When I was a teenager, still living at home, I listened to Janis' music and read the article about her in *Life*. (She was a teenager, still living at home, then, too.) I never dreamt then that I might one day meet her. I *really* never dreamt then that we might become friends. That we have means a lot to me in a lot of different ways. So thanks, Janis. Thanks for everything. This one's for you.

I

Charlie Sullivan never expected to meet Joe Steele in the service elevator of a cheap hotel only a couple of blocks from the Chicago Stadium. The AP stringer gaped at the Presidential candidate when Steele boarded on the second floor. Charlie had slipped the boss cook a buck, so he got on and off in the kitchen as he pleased.

"You're—him!" Charlie blurted when Joe Steele and one of his aides strode into the car. Long-standing tradition said that candidates stayed away from the convention till it nominated them . . . if it did.

Governor Franklin Roosevelt, Steele's main rival for the Democratic nomination in this summer of America's discontent, was still in the Executive Mansion in Albany. Charlie's older brother, Mike, who wrote for the *New York Post*, was covering him there. Roosevelt's operatives worked the Stadium hotels and bars just as hard as Joe Steele's, though. They glad-handed. They promised. They spread favors around.

"I am him," the Congressman from California agreed. His smile didn't reach his eyes. Charlie Sullivan was a scrawny five-eight, but he overtopped Joe Steele by three inches. Steele stood straight, though, so you might not notice how short he was. That his henchman, a cold-looking fellow named Vince Scriabin, was about the same size also helped.

"But . . . What are you doing in town?" Charlie asked.

The elevator door groaned shut. Joe Steele punched the button for 5. Then he scratched at his mustache. It was bushy and graying; he was in his early fifties. His hair, also iron-gray, gave a little at the temples. He had bad skin—

either he'd had horrible pimples or he'd got through a mild case of smallpox. His eyes were an interesting color, a yellow-brown that almost put you in mind of a hunting animal.

"Officially, I'm in Fresno," he said as the elevator lurched upward. That fierce, hawklike stare burned into Charlie. "You might embarrass me if you wrote that I was here."

Vince Scriabin eyed Charlie, too, as if fitting him for a coffin. Scriabin also wore a mustache, an anemic one that looked all the more so beside Joe Steele's. He had wire-framed glasses and combed dark, greasy hair over a widening bald spot. People said he was very bad news. Except for the scowl, you couldn't tell by looking.

Joe Steele's stare, though less outwardly tough, worried Charlie more. Or it would have, if he'd been on FDR's side. But he said, "We need some changes—need 'em bad. Roosevelt talks big, but I think you're more likely to deliver."

"I am." Joe Steele nodded. He wasn't a big man, but he had a big head. "Four years ago, Hoover promised two chickens in every pot and two cars in every garage. And what did he give us? Two chickens in every garage!" Despite the big mustache, Charlie saw his lip twist.

Charlie laughed as the service elevator opened. "Good one, Congressman!" he said. "Don't worry about me. I'll keep my trap shut."

"I wasn't worrying." Joe Steele stepped out of the little car. "Come on, Vince. Let's see what kind of deal we can fix with John." Scriabin followed him. The door groaned shut again. The elevator lurched up toward Charlie's seventh-floor room.

His mind whirred all the way there. You couldn't find a more common name than John. But John Nance Garner, the Speaker of the House from Texas, also had a Presidential yen, and controlled his state's delegation as well as other votes from the Deep South. He wasn't likely to land the top spot on the ticket. Swinging him one way or the other could get expensive for Steele or Roosevelt.

Roosevelt had never known a day's want in his life. His family went back to before New Amsterdam turned into New York. His cousin Theodore had been Governor ahead of him, and had served almost two full terms as President after the turn of the century.

Joe Steele was a different story. His folks got out of the Russian Empire and into America only a few months before he was born. He became a citizen well ahead of them. As a kid, he picked grapes under Fresno's hot sun, and few suns came hotter.

He hadn't been born Joe Steele. He'd changed his name when he went from farm laborer to labor agitator. The real handle sounded like a drunken sneeze. Several relatives still wore it.

Not all prices were payable in cash, of course. John Nance Garner might want as much power as he could get if he couldn't be President. Veep? Supreme Court Justice? Secretary of War?

Charlie Sullivan laughed as he strode down the hall to the sweltering top-floor room. He wasn't just building castles in the air, he was digging out their foundations before he built them. Not only didn't he know what Garner wanted, he didn't know whether Joe Steele and Scriabin had been talking about him to begin with.

The first thing he did when he went inside was to pull the cord that started the ceiling fan spinning. The fan stirred the hot, humid air a little, but didn't cool it.

Chicago Stadium was just as bad. No, worse—Chicago Stadium was packed full of shouting, sweating people. A handful of trains, restaurants, and movie houses boasted refrigerated air-conditioning. The new scientific marvel got you too cold in summer, as central heating made you sweat in January.

But air-conditioning didn't exist at the Chicago Stadium. Inside the massive amphitheater, you roasted as God had intended. If you walked around with an apple in your mouth, someone would stick a fork in you and eat you.

And too many Democrats knew more about politics than they did about Ivory or Palmolive or Mum. Some doused themselves in aftershave to try to hide the problem. The cure might have been worse than the disease. Or, when you remembered how some of the other politicos smelled, it might not.

Charlie eyed the Remington portable that sat on a nightstand by the bed. It didn't quite lie about its name; he'd lugged it here without rupturing himself. He sure wouldn't haul it to the convention floor, though. If he dropped it out the window, it would make a big hole in the sidewalk. And it would drive any passerby into the ground like a hammer driving a nail.

"Nope," he said. For the floor, he had notebooks and pencils. Reporters would have covered Lincoln's nomination in Chicago the same way. They would have given their copy to telegraphers the same way, too, though he could also phone his in.

He could make a splash if he reported that Joe Steele was in town to fight for the nomination in person. He suspected his brother would have. Mike liked FDR more than Charlie did.

Whoever nabbed the Democratic nomination this summer would take the oath of office in Washington next March. The Republicans were dead men walking. Poor stupid bastards, they were the only ones who didn't know it.

They'd elected Herbert Hoover in a landslide in 1928. When Wall Street crashed a year later, the land slid, all right. Hoover meant well. Even Charlie Sullivan, who couldn't stand him, wouldn't have argued that. No doubt the fellow who'd rearranged the deck chairs on the *Titanic* after it hit the iceberg did, too.

No, when your name stuck to the shantytowns full of people who had nowhere better to live, you wouldn't win a second term. Yet the Republican faithful had gathered here in June to nominate him again. Charlie wondered if they'd bothered looking outside of Chicago Stadium before they did.

He stuck a straw hat on his head and rode down on the regular elevator. His clothes would stick to him by the time he got to the Stadium. Why give them a head start by taking the stairs?

No sign of Joe Steele in the lobby. Through air blue with cigarette smoke, Charlie did spot Vince Scriabin and Lazar Kagan, another of Steele's wheeler-dealers, bending the ear of some corn-fed Midwestern politician. He was pretty sure

Scriabin saw him, too, but Steele's man never let on. Scriabin wasn't anyone you'd want to play cards against.

Lighting a Chesterfield of his own, Charlie hurried west along Washington Boulevard toward the Chicago Stadium. He went by Union Park on the way. An old man sat on a park bench, tossing crumbs to pigeons and squirrels. Maybe he was making time go by. Then again, maybe he was hunting tonight's supper.

Charlie didn't look behind him when he tossed away his cigarette butt. Somebody would pick it up. You didn't want to take a man's pride, watching him do something like that. He wouldn't want you to see what he was reduced to, either.

Two ragged men slept under the trees. A bottle lay near one. By that, and by his stubble, he might have been sleeping on the grass for years. The other guy, who used a crumpled fedora for a pillow, was younger and neater. If he didn't have some kind of hard-luck story to tell, Charlie would have been amazed.

He also didn't look back at a thirtyish woman who gave him the eye. Some gals thought they had no better way to get by. It wasn't as if Charlie had never seen the inside of a sporting house. This poor, drab sister only gave him the blues, though.

He walked past a tailor's shop with a GOING OUT OF BUSINESS! sign in the window. Next door stood a shuttered bank. Close to forty banks had gone under in a local panic earlier in the year. They wouldn't be the last, either. These days, Charlie kept his money under his mattress. Thieves with masks seemed a smaller risk than the ones who wore green eyeshades.

Chicago Stadium was the biggest indoor arena in the country. The red-brick pile had a gently curving roofline. Lots of American flags flew from it any day of the week. With the convention there, they'd draped it with so much red-white-and-blue bunting, it might as well have been gift-wrapped.

Cops and reporters and politicians milled around outside. Charlie thought of the line Will Rogers used to fracture audiences all over the country: *I am not a member of any organized political party. I am a Democrat.* The scene here lived up to, or down to, it all too well.

"Press pass," a flatfoot growled at him.

"For Chrissake, Eddie," Charlie said—they'd had coffee and donuts together plenty of times when he wrote for a Chicago paper.

"Press pass," Eddie repeated. "I gotta log that I'm doin' it for everybody." A disgusted look on his face, he showed a notebook of his own. Bureaucrats were taking over the world.

Charlie displayed the press pass. The cop scribbled and waved him on. The first thing he saw when he got inside was Huey Long, as comfortable as anyone could be in there with a white linen suit and a blue silk shirt, laying down the law to someone much bigger in an undertaker's suit of black wool. Listening to Huey made the man even less happy than baking in that outfit.

Whenever Charlie saw the Kingfish, lines about the jawbone of an ass jumped into his mind. Long made such an easy target. He couldn't possibly be as big a buffoon as he seemed . . . could he?

A loud brass band blaring away and a demonstration much less spontaneous than it looked turned the floor to chaos. The great state of Texas—as if there could be any other kind at a convention—had just nominated its favorite son, John Nance Garner. No, it had placed his name in nomination. No, it had proudly placed his name in nomination. People seeking clear English at a gathering like this commonly needed to pay a sin tax on account of their leaders' syntax.

If a demonstration got big enough and rowdy enough, it could sweep previously undecided delegates along in its wake. It could, yes, but the odds were poor, especially at the Democrats' national clambake. The Democrats still hung on to the two-thirds rule.

Two delegates out of three had to agree on the Presidential candidate. If they didn't, the Democrats had no candidate. *Will Rogers isn't kidding,* Charlie thought as the demonstration began to lose steam.

The two-thirds rule had been around a long time. In

1860, the Democratic Party fractured because Stephen Douglas couldn't get over the hump. That let Lincoln win with a plurality far from a majority. Secession and civil war soon followed.

One might think that memories of such a disaster would scuttle the rule. One might, but one would be wrong. Just eight years earlier, in 1924, the Donkeys needed 103 ballots to nominate John W. Davis. By the time they got done, he was a national laughingstock. Calvin Coolidge walloped him in November.

The only Democratic President this century was Woodrow Wilson. He won the first time because Teddy Roosevelt's revolt split the GOP, and—barely—got reelected when he said he'd keep America away from the Great War . . . a promise he danced on less than a year later. Aside from that, the Democrats might as well have been short-pants kids swinging against Lefty Grove.

But they'd win this time. They couldn't very well not win this time. They might pluck Trotsky out of Red Russia and run him against Hoover. They'd win anyway, probably in a walk.

Somebody from Wisconsin was making a speech for Joe Steele. Why Wisconsin? It had to come down to courting delegates. "Joe Steele has a plan for this country! Joe Steele will set this country right!" the Congressman on the podium shouted.

People yelled themselves hoarse. Joe Steele did have a plan: a Four Year Plan, straightening things out through his first term. And Franklin D. Roosevelt offered the American people a New Deal, one he claimed would be better than the bad old deal they had now.

Hoover had no plan. Hoover stood for the old deal that had left the country in the ditch. He was making it up as he went along. He didn't even bother pretending he wasn't. He was about as political as a pine stump. No wonder he wouldn't win.

When the guy from the great state of Wisconsin proudly placed the name of Joe Steele in nomination for the office of President of the United States of America, the place went nuts. Confetti and straw hats flew. A new brass band did terrible things to "California, Here I Come." People snake-danced through the aisles screaming, "Joe Steele! Joe Steele! Joe Steele!"

Not everybody got caught up in the orchestrated frenzy. Big Jim Farley kept the New York delegation in line for Governor Roosevelt. He was FDR's field boss, the way Vince Scriabin was for Joe Steele. Roosevelt's other chief sachem, Lou Howe, hadn't left his Madison Avenue office for a hick town like Chicago. That was how you heard it from Joe Steele's troops, anyway.

Roosevelt's people told a different story—surprise! They reminded people that Howe was an invalid, and didn't travel. They also claimed he made a better pol by remote control than most people who pumped your hand and breathed bourbon into your face.

You heard all kinds of things, depending on whose story you listened to at any given moment. Never having met Lou Howe, Charlie didn't know what to think about him. *Gotta ask Mike next time I talk to him or shoot him a wire,* the reporter thought.

There stood Farley by the aisle, thumbs dug into the front pockets of his trousers. He couldn't have radiated any more disgust if Typhoid Mary were prancing past him. Not even the suntanned California girls who made up part of the Golden State's delegation wiped the scowl off his jowly mug.

Charlie slipped between two dancers and bawled a question into Big Jim's imperfectly shell-like ear. Then he bawled it again, louder: "What do you think of this show of strength?"

"It's all bullshit, Charlie, piled up like in the stockyards," Farley shouted back.

Like any good politico, he was endlessly cynical. Even more than most, he made a point of knowing—and of making sure Roosevelt seemed to know—any reporter or legislator or preacher or fat cat he ran into. Charlie had heard he kept files on everyone he met so he and FDR would never get caught short. He didn't know if that was true, but he wouldn't have been surprised.

He also wasn't surprised at the answer. "C'mon, Jim," he said. "Give me something I can write for a family paper."

Farley said something about Joe Steele and a ewe that wasn't printable but sure as hell was funny. Then, he added, "You can say I said it was much sound and fury, signifying nothing. That's what it is, and that makes me sound smarter than I am."

He was sandbagging, of course. Charlie knew very few people smarter than Jim Farley. He wasn't sure Franklin D. Roosevelt was one of them, either. But Farley didn't have his own political ambitions. He worked to put his boss over the top—and he did just-one-of-the-boys better than the aristocratic Roosevelt could.

After scrawling the answer in shorthand, Charlie asked, "How many ballots d'you think they'll need this time around?"

Farley scowled. That was a serious question. "It won't be a few," he said at last, reluctantly. "But we'll come out on top in the end. People don't care how long the gal's in the delivery room. They just want to see the baby."

Charlie wrote that down, too. Big Jim gave terrific quotes when he kept them clean. Then, spotting Stas Mikoian in the Joe Steele conga line, Charlie hurried after him. The Armenian was another of Steele's campaign stalwarts. They'd met in Fresno, and stuck together after Steele went to Washington.

Mikoian might not have been as clever as Farley, but he was no dope. His brother was one of Donald Douglas' top aeronautical engineers in Long Beach, so brains ran in the family. Dancing along next to him, Charlie asked, "How do things look?"

"We'll have a long night once the balloting starts," Mikoian said, echoing Farley's prediction. "We'll have a long two or three days, chances are. But we'll win in the end."

He sounded as confident as Big Jim. Smart or not, one of them was talking through his hat. In ordinary times, Charlie would have figured Roosevelt had the edge. The Roosevelts had been important while Joe Steele's folks—and those of most of his aides—were nobodies under the Tsar. FDR served as Assistant Secretary of the Navy when Wilson was President. He'd fought infantile paralysis to a standstill. How could you help admiring somebody like that?

You couldn't. But these times were far from ordinary. Maybe they needed somebody without history behind him. Maybe Joe Steele's upstarts had the moxie to go toe-to-toe with the well-tailored guys who'd been finagling since the Year One.

Actually, Stas Mikoian seemed pretty well tailored himself. The straw boater didn't go with his sober gray suit, but you put on silly stuff like that when you joined a demonstration.

"Count on it," Mikoian said, dancing all the while and never losing the beat. "Joe Steele's our next President."

A sly Armenian. And Lazar Kagan was a sly Hebe. And Vince Scriabin was a plenty sly whatever he was. Were they sly enough to lick FDR and his all-American veterans?

The chairman rapped loudly for order. Microphones and loudspeakers made the gavel sound like a rifle. "Come to order! The convention will come to order!" the chairman shouted.

Oh, yeah? Charlie thought from his seat in the stands. The floor went on bubbling like a crab boil. You just had to pour in some salt and spices, peel the Democrats out of their shells, and eat 'em before they got cold.

Bang! Bang! "The convention *will* come to order!" the chairman repeated, his voice poised between hope and despair. "The sergeant-at-arms has the authority to evict unruly delegates. Come to order, folks! We've got a new President to choose!"

That turned the trick. The delegates' cheers echoed from the low dome of the ceiling. Somebody on the podium patted the chairman on the back. Beaming, the big shot positioned himself in front of the microphone again. "The secretary will call the roll of the states," he said in his best dramatic tones, and then stood aside so the secretary could do just that.

Charlie figured the secretary actually knew what he was doing. No one so scrawny and bland and insignificant could have found himself in such an important place unless he did.

He knew the alphabet, and started at the top: "Alabama!"

The leader of the Alabama delegation made his way to the floor microphone. "Mr. Secretary," he boomed in a drawl thick enough to slice, "the great and sovereign state of Alabama casts the entirety of its voting total for that splendid and honorable American patriot, Senator Hugo D. Black!"

"Alabama casts fifty-seven votes for Senator Black," the secretary said. It was no coincidence that the Senator was from Alabama. The secretary continued, "Alaska!"

Alaska wasn't a state. Neither was the Canal Zone or Guam or Hawaii or Puerto Rico or the Virgin Islands or Washington, D.C. They couldn't vote in the general election. They all could help—a little—in picking who would run.

Down the roll the secretary went. Along with plenty of other spectators, Charlie totted up the first-ballot totals. They'd look good in his story. They wouldn't mean anything, though. Favorite sons like Senator Black still littered the field. They let states wheel and deal to their hearts' content.

At the end of that first ballot, Joe Steele had a twenty-three-vote lead on FDR. At the end of the second, Roosevelt had an eight-vote edge on the California Congressman. After the third, Joe Steele was back in front by thirteen and a half votes.

A half-hour recess followed the third ballot. The gloves came off then. Most states were bound to favorite sons for three ballots, though a few had to stick with them through five. The fourth ballot would start to show where the strength really lay.

Or it would have, had it shown anything. Franklin D. Roosevelt and Joe Steele wound up in a dead heat. Charlie whistled softly to himself. What were the odds of that?

Roosevelt took a tiny lead on the fifth ballot, and lost it on the sixth. Favorite sons bled votes to the two front-runners, though neither had gained a majority, much less two-thirds.

Huey Long stayed in the fight. He had not a delegate

from north of the Mason-Dixon Line, but he'd picked up votes from lesser Southern candidates like Hugo Black. The Kingfish could dicker with the bigger fish from Yankeeland. Since he hadn't a prayer of winning the nomination, no one seemed to mind his cutting capers on the convention floor.

Jim Farley paid him a courtesy call. Two ballots later, so did Stas Mikoian. Long preened and posed. Hardly anyone admired him more than he admired himself. He wasn't just Kingfish, not for the duration. He had hopes of being kingmaker, too.

Ballot followed ballot. Tobacco smoke thickened the air. So did the growing fug of badly bathed, sweating pols. Most of the party's anointed were in their shirtsleeves after a while, and most of the shirts had spreading stains at the armpits.

Charlie recorded each count, wondering whether Huey Long's total plus that of one of the major candidates would reach the magic number. It didn't look as though that would happen any time soon, though. Everyone had said Joe Steele and FDR were as close as two rivals could get. For once, everyone seemed to be right.

As if plucking the thought from his mind, another reporter asked, "How many ballots did they need to nominate Davis?"

"A hundred and three," Charlie said with sour satisfaction.

"Christ!" the other man said. "They're liable to do it again. If anything gives Hoover a fighting chance, this is it."

"Yeah. If anything. But nothing does," Charlie replied. The other reporter laughed, as if he were kidding.

They balloted through the night. Gray predawn light showed in the Stadium's small number of small windows—they were there more for decoration than to let the sun shine in. At last, the chairman came up to the microphone and said, "A motion to adjourn till one this afternoon will be favorably entertained. Such a motion is always in order."

Half a dozen men proposed the motion. Several dozen seconded it. It passed by acclamation. Delegates and members of the Fourth Estate staggered out into the muggy morning twilight.

A newsboy hawked copies of the *Chicago Tribune*. He bawled the front-page headline: "No candidate yet!" Charlie didn't think that would tell the Democratic movers and shakers much they didn't already know.

He ate bacon and eggs and drank strong coffee at a greasy spoon on the way back to his hotel. Coffee or no, in his room he put his alarm clock too far from the bed for him to kill it without getting up.

Mike Sullivan didn't like going up to Albany to cover Governor Roosevelt. He didn't like *having* to go to Albany to cover FDR. He was an inch taller and two years older than Charlie—two years grumpier, they both liked to say. Mike had a perfectly good apartment in Greenwich Village. As far as he was concerned, if the state of New York had to have a governor and a legislature, it could damn well stash them in New York City, which was where it put everything that mattered.

But no. He had to leave his cat and his girlfriend and come upstate to the front edge of nowhere if he needed to report on Franklin D. Roosevelt. (To him, the middle of nowhere lay about halfway between Syracuse and Rochester.)

Massachusetts did things right. The big city there was Boston, and it was also the state capital. But an amazing number of states, even ones with proper cities, plopped their capitals in towns that barely showed up on the map. Pennsylvania was run from Harrisburg, even though it boasted Philadelphia and Pittsburgh. California had San Francisco and Los Angeles, but it was run from Sacramento. Portland and Seattle didn't tell Oregon and Washington what to do; Eugene and Olympia did.

The list went on. Tallahassee, Florida. Annapolis, Maryland. Springfield, Illinois. Jefferson City, Missouri. Frankfort, Kentucky. Not one a place you'd visit unless you had to.

Albany met that description. It did to Mike, anyway. It wasn't a tiny village. It had something like 130,000 people in it. But when you came from a city of 7,000,000, give or take a few, 130,000 were barely enough to notice, even if one of them had a better than decent chance of becoming the next President.

Plenty of reporters camped around the big red-brick

State Executive Mansion on the corner of Eagle and Elm. To keep them happy, Roosevelt held a press conference the morning after the Democrats started balloting. The press room was on the ground floor of the Executive Mansion. Despite the electric lamps that lit the chamber and the lectern with the microphone, it seemed to Mike to come straight out of the Victorian age, when the mansion was built. The building's modern conveniences were, and obviously were, later additions.

Roosevelt already stood behind the lectern when his flunkies let the reporters into the room. With the braces on his legs, he could stand, and even take a halting step or two, but that was it. Somebody would have had to help him into place there. He didn't care for outsiders to watch him getting helped that way. He and his flunkies *really* didn't care for anyone photographing him getting helped that way. Mike understood why they didn't. It made him look weak, which was the last thing anyone aiming for the White House wanted.

"Hello, boys!" Roosevelt said. Mike thought the Governor's rich tenor voice had an accent almost as affected as the cigarette holder jutting from his mouth. Somehow, though, FDR got away with the holder and with the old-boy accent where a lesser man would have been laughed at. Behind the gold frames of his spectacles, his eyes twinkled. "Nothing much to talk about today, is there? Not as though Chicago's given us any news."

He got the laugh he'd surely been looking for. "How many ballots do you think it'll take, Governor?" asked a reporter Mike had never seen before—surely an out-of-stater.

"You know, Roy, I haven't even worried about that," FDR said. The men in the press room laughed again, this time in disbelief. Mike chuckled along with everybody else, but he also saw that Roosevelt knew who the reporter was even if he didn't. Roosevelt hardly ever missed that kind of trick—and the attention to detail paid off. Looking wounded but smiling at the same time, the Governor held up a hand. "Honest injun, I haven't. We'll get where we want to go in the end, and nothing else matters."

"Joe Steele will have something to say about that," another newshawk called.

Franklin Roosevelt shrugged. He had broad, strong shoulders. He swam a lot for physical therapy—and, usually where no one could see him, he used crutches. "It's a free country, Grover. He can say whatever he wants. But just because he says it, that doesn't make it so." There was, or seemed to be, a certain edge to his tone.

Hearing that, Mike asked, "What *do* you think of his Four Year Plan, Governor?"

"Ah, Mr. Sullivan." No surprise that Roosevelt knew who Mike was. "What do I think of it? I think he thinks the American people want someone—need someone—to tell them what to do. In some distant European lands, that may perhaps be true. But I am confident that here in the United States we are able to look out for ourselves better than he thinks. I believe my New Deal will let us do that, help us do that, better than anything he's proposed while still cleaning up the mess Mr. Hoover has left us."

Most of the reporters scrawled down the response, probably without thinking about it much. But one of Mike's eyebrows quirked as he wrote. If that wasn't a dig at Joe Steele for coming out of tyrannical Russia, he'd never heard one. It was a polite dig, a well-disguised dig, but a dig all the same. The words behind the words were something like *He doesn't really understand how America works.* Maybe it was true, maybe not. Digs didn't have to be to sting. That Trotsky's modern Russia was even more tyrannical than the one Joe Steele's parents had left only gave it a sharper point.

Quickly, Mike tried a follow-up question: "If you get the nomination, sir, what do you think Joe Steele will do?"

Roosevelt smiled his patrician smile. "He's represented the people of his farm district for a long time now. He can probably get the nomination there again."

After that, nobody asked whether there'd be a place for Joe Steele in a Franklin D. Roosevelt administration. FDR hadn't said *Go back and tend to your raisins* in so many words, but he might as well have. A low hum rose from the press corps, so Mike wasn't the only one who got it. No, Roosevelt didn't love Joe Steele, not even a little bit.

And how did Joe Steele feel about Roosevelt? In Albany, that didn't seem important enough to worry about. The *Post* got a whacking good story, though.

Moving the alarm clock proved smart: Charlie squashed his hat trying to make the clock shut up. He staggered down the stairs and out the door. He grabbed more java on the way back to the Stadium. By the time he got there, he made a pretty fair ventriloquist's dummy of his real self. *Progress,* he thought.

In the lobby, somebody said, "What I really wanna do is pour a pitcher of ice water over my head." Charlie was already sweating, and the new session's politicking hadn't started. If he'd seen a pitcher of ice water he could have grabbed, he might have done it, suit and cigarettes and notebooks be damned.

At one on the dot, the chairman gaveled the convention to order. "I will summon the secretary, and we shall proceed to the twenty-sixth ballot," he said.

"Twenty-seventh!" The cry came from several places.

The chairman did summon the secretary, and briefly consulted with him. "The twenty-seventh ballot—excuse me," he said with a wry grin. "Time flies when you're having fun."

They balloted through the night again. In the votes before midnight, Joe Steele forged ahead, a few votes this round, a few more the next. But when the wee smalls rolled around, FDR started gaining again. He kept gaining till the sky lightened once more. This time, Stas Mikoian moved to adjourn.

Roosevelt's backers didn't object—they had to eat and drink and sleep (and perhaps even piss and bathe) like anyone else. But they were jubilant as they walked out into the new day. Things finally looked to be rolling their way. The people who liked Joe Steele most seemed glummest.

Charlie shoehorned himself into that diner for another breakfast. At the counter next to him, one delegate said to another, "If Long throws his weight FDR's way . . ."

"Yeah," the second man said miserably. "I'd almost sooner keep Hoover than see Huey as VP. Almost."

"If Huey is, Roosevelt better watch his back but good," the first fellow said. His buddy nodded. So did Charlie, not that they paid him any mind. Anyone who trusted Huey Long needed to have his head examined—and his life insurance paid up.

One cup of coffee turned into three. Three turned into a trip to the men's room. The diner had pay phones on one wall of the hallway leading back there. Vince Scriabin fed quarters into a telephone as Charlie walked by: a long-distance call.

There were lines at both urinals. Plenty of Democrats unloaded the coffee they'd taken aboard the past few hours. Charlie waited, then eased himself. He got out of the john as fast as he could; the aroma didn't make you want to linger.

At the telephone, Scriabin had got through. "Yeah," he was saying. "Take care of it—tonight. You let it go, it'll be too late." He sounded like a politician. Tomorrow was always too late. He added, "That son of a bitch'll be sorry he ever messed with us." Then he hung up and headed for the restroom himself.

Anybody thought twice before crossing Joe Steele. Ever since he got on the Fresno city council, he'd been his friends' best friend and his enemies' worst enemy. Charlie wondered who was getting paid back now. He also wondered whether Scriabin thought he needed to hurry now because his man trailed. If Roosevelt won, Joe Steele's revenge wouldn't be anything to fear so much.

The fight wasn't over yet, though. FDR had come back to take the lead. Joe Steele could rally, too. Mikoian and Kagan and Scriabin would do everything they knew how to do to make that happen. Charlie wondered if Joe Steele's men knew enough.

II

They'd be at it again tonight, out there in Chicago. They'd already gone through fifty-odd ballots. You had to wonder whether the Democrats owned a death wish. They claimed they'd run things better than the GOP had. Considering how deep the Depression was, that didn't seem like a high bar to jump. But if they couldn't even settle on a nominee, didn't you have to wonder what kind of job they'd do once they finally wrapped their sweaty palms around the steering wheel?

Some people would say so. Herbert Hoover sure would, as often and as loud as he knew how. But who'd believed Hoover since Wall Street rammed an iceberg and sank on Black Tuesday? Mike Sullivan knew he didn't. Precious few people did.

So here he was in Albany, still keeping tabs on FDR for the *Post*. Reporters from half the papers in the country seemed to be here. They jammed hotels and boarding-houses. They filled the town's indifferent restaurants and technically illicit saloons. They followed one another around, each hoping the next was on to something juicy. They told one another lies over card games and in barber shops.

Roosevelt was coy about the invasion. Except for the press conference, he stayed secluded with Eleanor on the second floor—the living quarters—of the State Executive Mansion. The way it looked to Mike, staying secluded with Eleanor Roosevelt was within shouting distance of a fate worse than death. If you had to seclude yourself, couldn't you at least do it with somebody cute?

Had he been back in New York City, he could have

watched the Yankees or the Giants or the Dodgers (well, actually the Giants were out of town). Here, the Albany Senators of the Eastern League were taking on the New Haven Profs at Hawkins Stadium on Broadway in the village of Menands, a couple of miles north of downtown Albany. Ticket prices ran from half a buck in the bleachers to $1.10 for the best seat in the house.

He went to a game that night. Hawkins Stadium had something Yankee Stadium, the Polo Grounds, and Ebbets Field couldn't match. They played baseball under the lights in Albany (um, in Menands). The big leagues didn't want to put them in. This was the first night game Mike had ever seen.

The crowd was somewhere around 4,000—not half bad for a midseason game between two Class A teams going nowhere. The second-division Giants might not have drawn as many. They were so rotten, John McGraw had finally called it a career after thirty years at their helm.

New Haven won the game, 6-4, sending the local fans home unhappy. Mike had no rooting interest in either team. The night game was enough of an attraction all by itself. He looked at his watch as he left the ballpark. Half past ten. He'd walk down Broadway and be back at his hotel a few minutes after eleven. It had a radio in the lobby. He could listen to the bloodletting from Chicago for a while. If they chose Roosevelt there, the new nominee would almost have to make a statement in the morning.

He was nearly to the hotel—just south of the state capitol, as a matter of fact—when fire-engine sirens started wailing like damned souls. Three of the long red machines roared past him, one after another, their flashing lights warning ordinary cars off the road. Police black-and-whites followed hard on the fire engines' heels.

The engines he saw weren't the only ones he heard, either—nowhere close. Albany had itself a four-alarm fire, sure as the devil. And sure as the devil, he saw the flames ahead, a little farther inland from the Hudson than he was. He started to run. It wasn't the story he'd come to cover, which didn't mean it couldn't be big.

Plenty of people were running toward the fire. "Isn't that the Mansion?" one man called to another.

"'Fraid it is," the second man said.

"Which mansion?" Mike asked, panting. They said cigarettes played hell with your wind. For once, they knew what they were talking about.

"Executive Mansion. Governor's mansion. FDR's mansion," the two fellows said, not really in chorus. One of them added, "He's up there on the second floor, how's he supposed to get out?"

"Jesus Christ!" Mike crossed himself. He couldn't remember the last time he'd heard Mass or gone to confession, but sometimes what you took for granted when you were a kid came out at the oddest moments.

"Yeah, wouldn't that screw the pooch?" said one of the guys trotting along with him.

"In spades, doubled and redoubled," the other one put in.

Landscaped grounds surrounded the Executive Mansion, which stood well back from the street. Some of the trees near the Governor's residence were on fire, too. But the big two-story building might as well have exploded into flame. Mike couldn't have got there more than ten minutes after the first sirens began to scream. All the same, fire engulfed the mansion. Anybody could see it would burn to the ground, and soon. Flames taller than a man leaped from almost every window.

Silhouetted against that inferno, the fire engines didn't look so long and impressive any more. And the streams of water the firemen aimed at the blaze also seemed punier than they should have. Eyeing that, Mike decided it wasn't his imagination. He shoved his way through the crowd till he found himself standing beside a burly guy in a heavy canvas coat and a broad-brimmed rubber helmet. "Shouldn't you have got more water pressure than this?" he shouted.

"Most places, yeah, but maybe not around here," the fireman said. "You gotta remember, everything around here is old as the hills. They built this thing during the Civil War. I bet it didn't have no plumbing then—just thundermugs and outhouses, and a well to get typhoid from. Even the gas got added on later. And the electricity?" He smacked his forehead with the heel of his right hand.

Mike had noticed the same thing when Roosevelt gave

his press conference. "You think that's how the fire started?" he asked.

"I dunno. However it started, it's goin' great guns, ain't it?" The fireman shrugged broad shoulders. "I don't gotta figure out what happened. I just gotta try an' put it out. The how and the what, they're for the guys from the arson patrol."

"Was it arson?" Mike demanded.

"I dunno," the fireman said again. "When one burns this big and this hot, though, we'd poke around even if it was a bunch of empty offices and not the Executive Mansion."

"Did anybody . . . get caught in the fire?"

The fireman scowled at Mike as if, for the first time, he'd asked a really dumb question. And so he must have, because the man said, "A housemaid got out, and a nigger cook from the kitchen busted a window and jumped out with his pants on fire. Everybody else who was in there . . . Christ have mercy on their souls, that's all I can tell ya." As Mike had, he crossed himself.

"Oh, my Lord." Hearing it that way was like a kick in the belly. "Roosevelt was inside, wasn't he? Franklin and Eleanor both, I mean."

"That's what we heard when we rolled, uh-huh." The fireman nodded. "If they were, though, it's gonna take a while to find 'em, on account of all the other shit that's burning, pardon my French. Even when we do, they'll be like charcoal. Sorry, but that's how it is. Won't hardly be enough of 'em left to bury."

I come to bury Caesar, not to praise him. Shakespeare chimed inside Mike's head. Well, FDR would never be Caesar now. "I wasn't thinking about burying them," Mike said, which was half true, anyhow. "I was thinking, now who gets the Democratic nomination?"

Once more, the fireman eyed him as if he were a moron. "Joe Steele does," the man said. "Who else is left now?"

When you asked it like that, the answer was simple. With Franklin D. Roosevelt out of the picture, no one else was left now, no one at all.

The movement from ballot to ballot at the Chicago Stadium reminded Charlie Sullivan of the Western Front in

1918. You couldn't see much movement from one day to the next then, but after a while the French and English and Americans were always going forward and the Kaiser's boys were always going back. Roosevelt kept moving forward here, and Joe Steele kept falling back. Sooner or later, the trickle would turn to a flood, and retreat to rout. Later was starting to look more and more like sooner, too.

Charlie saw the exact moment when everything changed. A spotty-faced kid tore onto the convention floor at a speed an Olympic sprinter might have envied. He dashed straight for the New York delegation and huddled with Big Jim Farley.

Farley clapped both hands to his head and spun away: an operatic gesture of despair. The anguished bellow he let out might have come straight from grand opera, too. He asked the kid something. The answer he got made him spin away again.

His next shout had words in it: "Mister Chairman! *Mister Chairman!*"

Although the secretary was calling the roll for the umpty-umpth time, the chairman motioned for him to pause. "The chair recognizes the distinguished delegate from New York."

"Thank you, Mr. Chairman. I—" Jim Farley's chin sagged down to his chest. His voice broke. For a moment, Charlie didn't think he'd be able to go on. Then, visibly gathering himself, Farley did: "Mr. Chairman, I have the inexpressibly sad duty of informing you and the convention that Governor and Mrs. Roosevelt have perished in a quickly spreading fire at the Executive Mansion in Albany. The Governor, of course, was confined to his wheelchair and did not have a chance of escaping the flames."

Delegates on the floor and gawkers in the stands all cried out in horror. Charlie tried to imagine Roosevelt's final moments, trapped in that chair as fire swept over him. Shuddering, he wished he hadn't. The most you could hope for was that it ended pretty fast.

Stas Mikoian and Lazar Kagan were with the rest of the California delegation. They looked as shocked and as devastated as anyone else on the floor, regardless of which candidate he backed. Mikoian in particular went white as a sheet and swayed where he stood. Like a lot of people down there and in the stands, he made the sign of the cross. With a reporter's gift for noting useless details, Charlie saw that he shaped the horizontal stroke from right to left, not from left to right the way a Roman Catholic would.

Charlie looked around the floor for Vince Scriabin. He couldn't spot Joe Steele's other California henchman. Maybe that was because Scriabin had the kind of face and build you forgot five seconds after you saw them. He seemed so ordinary, he blended into any crowd like a chameleon.

Or maybe Charlie didn't see him because he wasn't there. A chill ran through Charlie as he remembered the chunk of Scriabin's phone call he'd overheard early this morning—or a million years ago, depending on how you looked at things.

Take care of it—tonight, he'd said. *You let it go, it'll be too late.* By the money he fed into the telephone, he was calling long-distance.

Where was he calling, exactly? Who was on the other end of the line? What did Vince want him to take care of? Why might it be too late if that other fellow waited?

The obvious answer Charlie saw scared the piss out of him. He didn't want to believe Joe Steele or his backers could imagine anything like that, much less do it. He had no proof at all, as he knew perfectly well. He didn't even have what anybody would call a suspicion. He had a possibility, a coincidence. Only that, and nothing more.

Some of the moans and groans and cries of grief around him shaped themselves into a different kind of noise inside his head. What it sounded like was a goose walking over his grave.

Vince Scriabin had noticed him, there in the hallway leading back to that greasy spoon's john. How much did Vince think he'd overheard? Would Vince figure he could add two and two and come up with four? If Vince did, what was he liable to do about it?

If this wasn't all moonshine, Scriabin had just arranged to have Joe Steele's main rival roasted all black and crispy, like a ham forgotten in the oven. After that, getting rid of a reporter would be no more than snipping off a loose end. People who knew too much were some of the most inconvenient people in the world.

If this wasn't all moonshine. If Vince Scriabin hadn't been talking about something else altogether. If he had been talking about something else, Charlie was just borrowing trouble. *As if I don't have enough already,* he thought. *Yeah, as if!*

Nobody was going to come after him right this minute. He wasn't sure of much, but he was sure of that. Cautiously, the chairman asked, "Mr. Farley, what do you and your people have in mind for the delegates who have been supporting Governor Roosevelt?"

"We would have liked to continue as we were going, to win the nomination here and to win the White House in November," Farley said, every word full of unshed tears. "Obviously, that . . . will not happen now. Just as obviously, our party still needs to win the general election. This being so, Governor Roosevelt's delegates are released from any pledges they may have made, and are free to follow the dictates of their several consciences."

Before the chairman could say anything or even ply his gavel, one of Huey Long's wheeler-dealers moved for a one-hour recess. He got it; hardly anyone opposed him. He still thought the Kingfish could make headway against Joe Steele, then. Charlie would have bet double eagles against dill pickles that he was nutty as a Christmas fruitcake, but he deserved the chance to try—the chance to fail.

Try the Long backers did. Fail they did, too, gruesomely. The delegates from outside the old Confederacy who wanted to have anything to do with Huey Long didn't make anybody need to take off his shoes to count them. And a Mississippi Congressman who sported buttons for John Nance Garner and Joe Steele waved his cigar and shouted, "How about we win an election for a change, hey?"

That put it in terms even another Congressman could understand. A few minutes after three in the morning, on the convention's sixty-first ballot, West Virginia's votes lifted Joe Steele over the two-thirds mark. Come November, he'd face Hoover.

Blizzards of confetti blew through the Chicago Stadium. Delegates scaled straw hats. Some of them flew for amazing distances. Charlie watched one sail past the chairman's left ear. That worthy, affronted, moved his head a little to avoid the collision.

Charlie wasn't affronted. He was entranced. *If you could make a toy that glided so well, you'd be a millionaire in a month,* he thought. The band played "California, Here I Come" and "You Are My Sunshine."

The enchantment of flying straw hats didn't perk Charlie up for long. Neither did the thought of becoming a millionaire in a month. For once, he couldn't get excited about kicking Herbert Hoover out of Washington in November with a tin can tied to his tail. He wondered if he'd still be alive in a month, let alone in the dim and distant future of November.

Someone knocked on the door to Charlie's hotel room. Whoever the son of a bitch was, he wouldn't quit, either. Opening one eye a slit, Charlie peered toward the alarm clock ticking on the dresser against the far wall. It was a quarter past eight. To somebody covering a political convention, a knock at this heathen hour felt too much like the midnight visits that brought panic in Trotsky's Russia.

Yawning and cussing at the same time, Charlie lurched to the door. He threw it wide. Whoever was out there, he'd give him a good, jagged piece of his mind.

But he didn't. In the hallway, neatly groomed and dressed, stood Vince Scriabin. The only thing that came out of Charlie's mouth was "Ulp."

"Good morning," Scriabin said, as if they hadn't last seen each other when the fixer was arranging something horrible (unless, of course, he wasn't doing that at all).

"Morning," Charlie managed. It was an improvement on *Ulp*, if only a small one.

"Joe Steele would like to see you in his room in fifteen minutes," Scriabin said. "It's 573." He touched the brim of his homburg, nodded, and walked away.

"Jesus!" Charlie said as he shut the door. His heart thumped like a drum. He'd half—more than half—expected Scriabin to pull a snub-nosed .38 from an inside pocket and fill him full of holes. A—breakfast?—invitation from the candidate? His crystal ball hadn't shown him anything about that.

Gotta get it fixed, he thought vaguely. He had to fix himself up, too, and in a hurry. He stuck a new Gillette Blue Blade in his razor and scraped stubble from his cheeks and chin and upper lip. He threw on some clothes, dragged a comb through his sandy hair, and went down to 573.

When he knocked, Lazar Kagan let him in. The round-faced Jew hadn't shaved yet this morning. "It's a great day for America," Kagan said.

"I think so, too," Charlie answered. He might have sounded heartier if he hadn't walked past Vince Scriabin at just the wrong moment, but how hearty was anyone likely to sound before he had his coffee?

Joe Steele was sipping from a cup. The pot perked lazily on a hot plate. A tray of scrambled eggs and another full of sausages sat above cans of Sterno. A loaf of bread lay beside a plugged-in toaster.

Scriabin and Mikoian were also there with their boss. No other reporters were. Charlie didn't know whether that was good news or bad. "Congratulations on winning the nomination," he said.

"Thanks. Thanks very much." Joe Steele set down the coffee cup. He came over to shake Charlie's hand. He had a strong grip. He might not be a large man, but his hands were good-sized. "Believe me, Charlie, this is not the way I wanted to do it."

"I guess not!" Charlie exclaimed. Of course the Californian would have wanted to take the prize without anything happening to Franklin D. Roosevelt. He would have wanted to beat the stuffing out of the Governor of New York. He probably wouldn't have been able to do that, but it didn't matter any more.

Joe Steele waved to the spread. "Help yourself to anything," he said.

"Thank you. Don't mind if I do." Charlie wondered if he

needed a food taster, the way kings had in the old days. If he did, he had several, because the candidate and his aides had already had some breakfast. Kagan and Joe Steele took more along with Charlie.

After Charlie had had coffee and a cigarette and had got outside of some breakfast, he asked Steele, "What can I do for you this morning?"

The Congressman from California smoked a pipe. Getting it going let him pause before he answered. Charlie watched him—studied him—while he fiddled with it. His face gave away nothing. You could peer into his eyes forever, and all you'd see would be eyes. Whatever was going on behind them, Joe Steele would know and you wouldn't.

After a couple of puffs of smoke floated up to the ceiling, the candidate said, "I wanted to tell you how well you've done, how fair you've been, covering the campaign up till now. I've noticed, believe me."

"I'm glad," Charlie said. When a politician told you you'd been fair, he meant you'd backed him. Well, Charlie had. He'd thought Joe Steele could set the country right if anybody could. He still wanted to think so. It wasn't so easy now, not when he wondered what Vince Scriabin had talked about on that long-distance call.

And when a politician said *Believe me*, you had to have rocks in your head if you did. Any reporter worth the crappy wage he got learned that in a hurry.

Joe Steele looked at Charlie. Looking back, Charlie saw . . . eyes. Eyes and that proud nose and the bushy mustache under it. Whatever Joe Steele was thinking, the façade didn't give it away.

"As long as you keep writing such good stories, no one in my camp will have anything to complain about," the candidate said.

Stas Mikoian grinned. When he had his color, as he did now, his teeth flashed against his dark skin. "Of course, people in political campaigns never complain about the stories reporters write," he said.

"Of course," Charlie said, with a lopsided smile of his own.

"Well, then," Joe Steele said. He opened a nightstand

drawer and pulled out a squat bottle of amber glass. The writing on the label was not in an alphabet Charlie could read. Steele pulled the cork and poured a slug from the bottle into each coffee cup. Charlie sniffed curiously. Brandy of some kind—apricot, he thought—and strong, unless he missed his guess.

"To winning!" Vince Scriabin said. They clinked cups as if they held wine glasses. Charlie sipped. Yes, even cut with coffee, that stuff would put hair on your chest. It would probably put hair on your chest if you were a girl.

"Winning is the most important thing, yes," Joe Steele said. His henchmen nodded in unison, almost as if a single will animated the three of them. More slowly, with all of the other men watching him, Charlie followed suit. He didn't know what he'd expected when Vince Scriabin summoned him here. Or maybe he did know, but he didn't want to think about it.

Whatever he'd expected, this wasn't it. This was better. Much better.

Mike Sullivan didn't know what he'd done to deserve—or rather, to get stuck with—covering Franklin Roosevelt's funeral. No, he knew, all right. By accident, he'd covered the Governor's incineration for the *Post*. Having him at the burial would neatly finish things off. Too many editors thought like that.

Hyde Park was a hamlet on the Hudson, about halfway between New York City and Albany. Roosevelt had been born here. He would go to his eternal rest, and Eleanor with him, behind the house where he'd come into the world.

The house was a mansion. A lot of fancy buildings in Hyde Park were connected to the Roosevelts one way or another. FDR always played down his patrician roots in public. If you were going to go anywhere in politics, you had to act like an ordinary joe, even—maybe especially—if you weren't. You had to gobble hot dogs, and get mustard all over your face while you did it.

But the people who came to bury Franklin Delano Roosevelt were rich and elegant and proud. They weren't on constant public display, and weren't so used to disguising wealth and power. They wore expensive, stylish clothes, somber for the occasion, and wore them well. They stood straight. When they talked, Mike heard more *which*es and *whom*s than he would have in a month of Sundays from hoi polloi, and almost all of them fit the grammar.

When Roosevelt's relatives and friends talked, Mike also heard, or thought he heard, a certain well-modulated anger and frustration in their voices. They'd been sure one of theirs would get something they felt equally sure he deserved. Now, instead, he was getting what all men got in the end: a plot of earth six feet by three feet by six.

"Can you imagine it?" a handsome young man said to a nice-looking girl whose sculptured features were partly obscured by a black veil. "Now it looks as though that damned raisin picker will be President of the United States."

"I wouldn't mind so much if he'd won fair and square at the convention—not that I think he would have," she answered. "But to have it taken away like this—"

"They say it wasn't arson," the young man said.

"They say they can't prove it was arson," she corrected him. "It's not the same thing."

He clucked in mild reproof. "As long as they can't prove it, we have to go on as if it wasn't," he said. "If we start seeing conspiracies behind every accident, we might as well be living in Mexico or Paraguay or some place like that."

"But what if the conspiracies are really there?" she asked.

Mike stepped away before he heard the young man's answer. He didn't want them to think he was eavesdropping, even if he was. Not hearing how that conversation ended didn't much matter, anyhow. He listened to bits of half a dozen others not very different before the service started.

The Episcopal bishop presiding over the funeral wore vestments that looked a lot like their Roman Catholic equivalents. Mike had voted for Al Smith in 1928, and knew Charlie had, too. The walloping Hoover gave Smith convinced Mike no Catholic would be elected President in his lifetime, if ever.

Of course, when you looked at how things had turned out under Hoover, you had to wonder how Al Smith could have done worse. It sure wouldn't have been easy. But here Hoover was, up for a second term. Like so many generals in the Great War, the Republicans seemed to be reinforcing failure.

And here crippled Franklin and homely Eleanor were, side by side in closed coffins because nobody wanted to look at the charred bits the firemen and undertakers thought were their remains. The bishop ignored that as far as he could. As countless clergymen of all denominations had before him and would long after he was dust himself, he took his text from the Book of John: "I am the resurrection and the life: he that believeth in me, though he were dead, yet shall he live: And whosoever liveth and believeth in me shall never die."

What could you say after that? Anyone who believed it would be consoled. Anyone who didn't . . . Well, chances were you couldn't say anything that would console unbelievers. They would say it didn't mean a goddamn thing, and how were you supposed to tell them they were wrong?

The bishop did his best: "Franklin and Eleanor were snatched away from us all untimely. They might have done great things in this world had they been allowed to remain longer. They were true servants of mankind, and were on the brink of finding ways to serve commensurate with their talents and abilities. But Almighty God, from Whom spring all things, in His ineffable wisdom chose otherwise, and His judgments are true and righteous altogether, blessed be His holy Name."

"Amen," murmured the man next to Mike. Mike missed the sonorous Latin of the Catholic graveside service. Just because it was so hard for a layman to understand, it added importance and mystery to the rite. He supposed the Episcopal cleric was doing as well as a man could hope to do when he was stuck with plain old mundane English.

He was if the fire that killed the Roosevelts was a horrible accident, anyhow. If it was something else—if they really might as well have been living in Mexico or Paraguay—that was a different story. Then it wasn't God's will being done: it was the will of some rival of Franklin Roosevelt's.

Or was it? If you honestly believed God's judgments

were true and righteous altogether, wouldn't you also believe He had placed the impulse to roast FDR to a charcoal briquette in the arsonist's mind and then allowed the bastard's plan to succeed? Wouldn't you believe God had let Roosevelt roast in his wheelchair so the world as a whole could become a better place?

Mike Sullivan couldn't make himself believe any of that. He had trouble thinking any of the mourners, or even the Episcopal bishop, could believe it. Accidents? Yeah, you could blame accidents on God—hell, insurance policies called them "acts of God." Murder? Unh-unh. Murder was a thing that sprang from man, not from God.

"Let us pray for the souls of Franklin and Eleanor," the bishop said, and bowed his head. Along with the mourners and the rest of the reporters, Mike followed suit. He doubted whether prayer would do any good. On the other hand, he didn't see how it could hurt.

Down into the fresh-dug holes that scarred the green, green grass went the two caskets. FDR and Eleanor would lie side by side forever. Whether they would care about it . . . If you believed they would, you also believed they found themselves in a better place now. Mike did his best, and wished his best were better.

Dirt thudded down onto the coffins' lids as the gravediggers started undoing what they'd done. Mike's lips skinned back from his teeth in a soundless snarl. He'd always thought that was the loneliest sound in the world. It left you all by yourself against mortality, and it reminded you mortality always won in the end.

The pretty girl in the black veil spoke to her young man: "Sweet Jesus Christ, but I want a cocktail!" He nodded. If they weren't feeling the same thing Mike was, he would have been amazed.

He took a notebook out of his pocket and scribbled notes that only he and the God Who probably wasn't presiding over this ceremony had any hope of reading. That told the people around him he was a reporter, not one of their prosperous selves. Some moved away from him, as if he carried a nasty, possibly catching disease. Others seemed intrigued.

They were more intrigued when they found out he'd witnessed the fire. "What did you think it was?" asked a middle-aged man whose horsey features put Mike in mind of Eleanor Roosevelt.

Mike could only spread his hands. "It was a heck of a big fire, that's what," he said. "I have no idea what touched it off. I didn't see it start, and I didn't see anybody running away from the Executive Mansion if there was anybody."

"They stole the nomination from Franklin," the horse-faced man said bitterly. "They stole it, and they murdered him. That stinking Rooshan from California, he's the one behind it. He learned from the Reds, I bet."

"Sir, that's the kind of charge it's better not to make unless you can prove it," Mike said.

"How am I supposed to prove it? You do something like that, you'd better be able to cover your tracks," the mourner said. "But I'd sooner see Hoover win again than that Joe Steele so-and-so. Hoover's an idiot, sure, but I never heard he wasn't an honest idiot."

"Don't put Cousin Lou in the paper, please," a svelte blond woman said. "He's terribly upset. We all are, of course, but he's taking it very hard."

"I understand." Mike didn't intend to put those wild charges in his story. He'd meant what he said—unless you could prove them, you were throwing grenades without aiming. Things were bad enough already. He didn't want to make them any worse.

III

As far as Mike Sullivan was concerned, dinner at Hop Sing Chop Suey was like meeting on neutral ground. Stella Morandini laughed when he said so. "You're right," she said. "No spaghetti, no ravioli—but no corned beef and cabbage and potatoes, either."

"There you go, babe." Mike nodded. "They've still got some kind of noodles here, though, so your side's probably ahead on points."

"Noodles doused in this waddayacallit? Soy sauce? Forget it, Mike—that's not Italian." Stella was a little tiny gal, only an inch or two over five feet. She wasn't shy about coming out with what she thought, though. That was one of the things that drew Mike to her. He'd never had any use for shrinking violets.

Her folks were from the Old Country. They wanted her to tie the knot with a *paisan*, preferably with one from the village south of Naples they'd come from. Like Mike, Stella was no damn good at doing what other people wanted.

His folks were almost as disgusted that he was going with a dago as hers were that she was dating a mick. They weren't just as disgusted because they'd been in the States a couple of generations longer—and because Charlie's fiancée was Jewish. That really gave them something to grouse about.

Stella sipped tea from one of the small, funny handleless cups the chop-suey joint used. It wasn't as if she might not have gone out with a sheeny or two herself. She was a secretary at a theatrical booking agency, and almost all the guys she worked for were Jews. She didn't speak much Yiddish, but she'd learned to understand it in self-defense.

Mike waved to the waiter. "Can we have another couple of fried shrimp, please?" he said.

"Sure thing." The waiter wasn't Chinese. He was tall and blond and skinny as a soda straw, and he swished. Fruit or not, he was a good waiter. He hustled back to the kitchen and brought them in nothing flat.

Just as he set them down, Charlie and Esther Polgar walked into Hop Sing's. Mike and Stella both waved; his brother and almost-sister-in-law sat down at the table with them. Esther had wavy red hair and a pointed chin. Her mother and father had brought her to America from Budapest when she was a little girl, bare months before the Great War started.

She grabbed one of the fried shrimp. Charlie snagged the other one. "Of all the nerve!" Mike said in mock indignation.

"Yeah." Stella wagged a finger at Esther. "Those things aren't even kosher."

"They're delicious, is what they are," Esther answered.

"We're gonna need a couple of more fried shrimp," Mike told the waiter. "And another pot of tea, and more chop suey, too." He glanced at his brother. "Unless you can make supper out of our scraps. That's what you get for showing up late."

"We get to have you watch us while we eat, too," Charlie said. "Not that we care."

The waiter hurried back to the kitchen again. He put a lot of hip action into his walk. If he wasn't careful, the vice squad would land on him like a ton of bricks one of these days. He wasn't a bad guy—not the sort of queer who annoyed normal people in the hope that they shared his vice. As long as he didn't, Mike was willing to live and let live.

"Not much been going on since we saw each other last," Charlie said. His smile lifted only one side of his mouth. "Hardly anything, matter of fact."

"Joe Steele getting nominated? Roosevelt going up in smoke? Uh-huh—hardly anything," Mike said.

"You forgot Garner getting the nod for VP," Charlie said.

"Mm, I guess I did," Mike said after a little thought. "Wouldn't you?"

"You guys are terrible," Esther said. "You're worse when you're together, too, 'cause you play off each other."

"Now that you're both here, I've got a question for the two of you," Stella said. "The Executive Mansion burning down like it did—do you think that was an accident?"

"I was there, and I still can't tell you one way or the other. Neither can the arson inspector, and he knows all kinds of things I don't," Mike answered. "As long as nobody can prove anything, I think we've got to give Joe Steele the benefit of the doubt. Herbert Hoover, too, as long as we're talking about people who might want to see Roosevelt dead."

He looked across the table at his brother. Stella and Esther eyed Charlie, too. Charlie kept quiet. He looked down at the crumbs and little grease spots on the plate that had held the fried shrimp. Silence till it got uncomfortable. At last, Esther remarked, "You're not saying anything, Charlie."

"I know," Charlie said.

"How come?"

He started not to say anything again—or some more, depending on how you looked at the language. Then he seemed to change his mind, and made a small production out of lighting a cigarette. After that, he did answer: "Because a bunch of people here may hear me. They're people I don't know, people I can't trust. Maybe after dinner we can find a cozy place, a quiet place. Then . . ." His voice trailed off.

"Do you really think it matters if someone you don't know overhears you?" Stella asked.

"Yes." Charlie bit off the single grudged word.

There didn't seem to be much to say to that. Mike didn't try to say anything. He watched his brother shovel food into his chowlock . . . much the same way he had himself not long before. Esther ate more sedately. When they got done, Mike threw a dollar bill, a half, and a couple of dimes on the table. The two couples walked out of Hop Sing's together.

"Where now?" Stella said.

"Back to my place," Mike replied in tones that brooked

no argument. "It's closest. And I don't have any spies in there."

"You hope you don't," Charlie said. Mike let that go. It was either let it go or get dragged into an argument that had nothing to do with what he really wanted to hear.

The Village was . . . the Village. A Red stood on a soapbox and harangued a ten-at-night crowd that consisted of three drunks, a hooker, and a yawning cop who seemed much too lazy to oppress the proletariat. Posters touting Joe Steele and Norman Thomas sprouted like toadstools on walls and fences. Herbert Hoover's backers had posted no bills in this part of town. They saved them for districts where somebody might look at them before he tore them down.

Under a streetlamp, a sad-looking woman in frayed clothes hawked a crate of her worldly goods in lieu of selling herself. Mike thought that was a good idea. She'd get more for the novels and knickknacks and bits of cheap silver plate than she would for her tired, skinny body, and she wouldn't want to slit her wrists come morning.

Mike's apartment was crowded for one. Four made it claustrophobic, especially when three of them started smoking. He didn't care. He had a bottle of moonshine that claimed it was bourbon. It wasn't, but it would light you up. He poured good shots into four glasses that didn't match, added ice cubes, and handed them around.

"Give," he barked at Charlie.

Give his brother did. "I can't prove a damn thing," Charlie finished. "I don't know who Vince Scriabin was talking to, or where the guy was, or what Vince told him to do, or even if he did it. I don't *know* a thing—but I sure do wonder." He finished the rotgut at a gulp, then stared at the glass in astonishment. "Suffering Jesus! That's awful! Gimme another one, will ya?"

Mike handed him the second drink. His own head was whirling, too, more from what he'd heard than from the bad whiskey. "Let me get this straight," he said. "Scriabin calls . . . somebody . . . somewhere. He says to take care of it that night, because waiting would foul it up. And that night the Executive Mansion goes up in smoke."

"That's about the size of it," Charlie agreed. Mike built himself a fresh drink, too. He needed it, no matter how lousy the hooch was.

Stella and Esther were both staring at Charlie. Mike got the idea that Charlie hadn't said anything to Esther about this till now. "You guys are sitting on the biggest story since Booth shot Lincoln," she said. "Maybe since Aaron Burr shot Hamilton. You're just sitting on it."

"Don't blame me," Mike said. "I'm just hearing it now, too."

"I don't know what we're sitting on," Charlie said. "Maybe it's an egg. Maybe it's a china doorknob, and nothing'll ever hatch out of it. For all I can prove, Scriabin has a bookie in California who's giving him grief." He took another healthy swig from the glass. "I ever say they call Vince the Hammer?"

"Tough guy, huh?" Stella said.

Charlie shook his head. "He looks like a pencil-necked bookkeeper. A bruiser with that kind of handle, he's gonna be bad news, sure. But a scrawny little guy like Scriabin? You call *him* the Hammer, you can bet he'll be ten times worse than the heavyweight."

"You're scared," Mike said in wonder.

"You bet I am!" his brother said. "If you ever had anything to do with Scriabin, you would be, too. If I write a story that says he did this and that, 'cause Joe Steele told him to, it's bad enough if he comes after me 'cause I'm wrong. If he comes after me 'cause I'm right . . . Way I've got things set up now, you and Esther split my life insurance."

"I don't want your life insurance!" Esther said.

"Me, neither," Mike added.

"I wouldn't want it, either. It comes to about fifteen bucks apiece for you guys," Charlie said. "But that's where we are. Joe Steele's gonna be the next President unless he gets hit by lightning or something. But there's at least a chance that's because he fried Franklin and Eleanor like a couple of pork chops."

Stella thrust her glass at Mike. "Make me another drink, too." Esther held hers out as well.

They killed that bottle, and another one that claimed it

was scotch. Mike felt awful in the morning, and the hangover was the least of it.

The first Tuesday after the first Monday in November.
Charlie wondered how and why the Founding Fathers
had chosen that particular day to hold a Presidential election. For most of the time since the Civil War, America had
been a reliably Republican country. It had been. By all the
signs, it wasn't any more. The polls back East had closed.
Joe Steele and the Democrats held commanding leads almost everywhere. They were taking states they hadn't won
in living memory. And it wasn't just Joe Steele trouncing
Herbert Hoover. Steele had coattails.

The Congress that came in with Hoover four years earlier had 270 Republicans and only 165 Democrats and
Farmer-Labor men in the House, fifty-six Republicans
and forty Democrats and Farmer-Labor men in the Senate. The one that came in two years later, after the Depression crashed down, was perfectly split in the Senate,
while the Democrats and their Minnesota allies owned a
minuscule one-vote edge in the House.

This one . . . Not all the votes were counted, of course.
But it looked as if the Democrats and the Farmer-Labor
Party would dominate the House by better than two to one,
maybe close to three to one. Their majority in the Senate
wouldn't be so enormous: only one Senator in three was
running this year. They'd have a majority, though, and a big
one.

And so the victory party at the Fresno Memorial Auditorium was going full blast. The auditorium, built to com-
memorate the dead from the Great War, was hardly out of
its box—it had opened earlier in the year. It was concrete
and modern, all sharp angles, with nods to the classical style
in the square columns that made up the main entranceway.
For a town of just over 50,000, it was huge: it took up a
whole city block.

Up on the balcony of the auditorium was the Fresno
County Historical Museum. Charlie didn't see a lot of people going up there. The ones who did were mostly couples
of courting age. He wasn't sure, but he would have bet they

were more interested in finding privacy than in looking over gold-mining equipment from seventy-five years before.

Down on the main floor, a band that looked to be full of Armenians played jazz. Straight off of Bourbon Street, it wasn't. Charlie wondered what a colored fellow from New Orleans would have thought of it. Not much, he figured. But the musicians did the best they could, and the campaign workers cutting a rug weren't complaining.

That might have been because of the punch filling half a dozen big cut-glass bowls. Joe Steele had said he favored repealing the Eighteenth Amendment. Prohibition was on the way out, but remained officially in effect. That punch had fruit juice in it for cosmetic purposes. Fruit juice or not, though, it was damn near strong enough to run an auto engine.

A Democratic State Senator came to the microphone to announce a Democratic Congressional victory in Colorado. The people who'd come for politics and not just a good time let out a cheer. The others went on dancing and drinking.

A few minutes later, another California politico stepped up to the mike. "Ladies and gentlemen!" he shouted. "Ladies and gentlemen!" He sounded as if he were announcing the Friday night fights. "Ladies and gentlemen, it is my great privilege and distinct honor to introduce to you the Vice President–elect of the United States, John Nance Garner of the great state of Texas!"

More people cheered as Garner shambled up to the microphone. Controlling the Texas delegation had won him the second spot on the ticket, even if he couldn't parlay it all the way to the top. His bulbous red nose said that not all the stories about his drinking habits were lies from his enemies.

He had big, knobby hands, the hands of a man who'd worked hard all his life. He held them up in triumph now. "Friends, we went and did it!" he shouted, his drawl thick as barbecue sauce. "Herbert Hoover can go and do whatever he pleases from here on out, 'cause he won't be doing it to America any more!"

He got a real hand then, and basked in it like an old soft-shelled turtle basking on a rock in the sun. "Now we're gonna do it to America!" shouted someone else who'd taken a good deal of antifreeze on board.

"That's right!" Garner began. Then he caught himself and shook his head. "No, doggone it! That's *not* right. We're gonna do things for America, not to it. You wait and see, folks. You won't recognize this place once Joe Steele gets to work on it."

They cheered him again, even though you could take that more than one way. As if by magic, Stas Mikoian materialized alongside Charlie. "Joe Steele will speak in a little while," he said. "He'll take away whatever bad taste that drunken old fool leaves behind."

"When you win so big, nothing leaves a bad taste," Charlie said. He couldn't ask Mikoian what he knew about Franklin Roosevelt's untimely demise. He was sure Mikoian didn't know anything. Nobody who did know could have turned so pale on the convention floor in July.

Charlie looked around for Vince Scriabin. He didn't see Joe Steele's Hammer. Asking Scriabin that question might bring out an interesting answer. Or it might be the last really dumb thing Charlie ever got a chance to do. Not seeing him might be good luck rather than bad.

Or I might be imagining things, making up a story where there isn't one. Charlie had been trying to convince himself of the same thing ever since the convention. On good days, he managed to do it for a little while. On bad days, he couldn't come close. On bad days, he told himself it wouldn't matter once Joe Steele took the oath of office. Now he had to hope he was right.

Mike Sullivan stood on the White House lawn, waiting for Herbert Hoover and Joe Steele to come out and ride together to the new President's inauguration. It was almost warm and almost spring: Saturday, March 4, 1933. The lawn still looked winter brown; only a few shoots of new green grass pushed up through the old dead stuff.

This was the last time a President would take office five months after he won the election. The states had just ratified the Twentieth Amendment. From now on, January 20 would become Inauguration Day. Winter for sure then, not that it was usually so bad down here in Washington. With telephones and radio, with trains and cars and even planes, things moved faster than they had when the Founding Fathers first framed the Constitution.

A military band struck up the national anthem. As if he were at a baseball game, Mike took off his hat and held it over his heart. A door opened on the White House's column-fronted entrance. The President and the President-elect walked out side by side.

Hoover, a big man, stood several inches taller than Joe Steele. He didn't tower over his successor by quite so much as Mike had thought he would. Had Joe Steele put lifts in his shoes? If he had, they were good ones; Mike couldn't be sure at a glance, the way you could with a lot of elevator oxfords.

One thing that did make Hoover seem taller was his black silk top hat. He also wore white tie and a tailcoat. He might have been an Allied leader dictating terms to defeated Germany at Versailles in 1919. Or he might have been one of the European diplomats who dickered the Treaty of Berlin between Russia and Turkey forty years earlier.

Joe Steele, by contrast, was unmistakably a man of the twentieth century, not the nineteenth. Yes, he had on a black suit and a white shirt, but they were the kind of clothes a druggist might have worn to dinner. The shirt's collar was stand-and-fall; it wasn't a wing collar. He wore a plain black necktie, not a fancy white bow tie. And on his head sat not a topper, not even a fedora, but a gray herringbone tweed cap.

Hoover's clothes said *I'm important. I have money. I tell other people what to do.* Joe Steele's outfit delivered the opposite message, and delivered it loud and clear. His suit said *I'm an ordinary guy. I'm getting dressed up because I have to.* Wearing a cloth cap with the suit added *But I don't think it's all that important even so.*

All around Mike, people gasped when they saw what the new President had chosen to put on. "Shameful!" somebody muttered. "No, he has no shame," someone else replied. Mike chuckled to himself. If those reporters weren't a couple of old-guard Republicans from somewhere like Philadelphia or Boston, he would have been surprised. Whenever folks like that deigned to notice the world changing around them, they, like Queen Victoria, were Not Amused.

Well, Queen Victoria had been dead for a long time now. He wondered whether the rock-ribbed (and rock-headed) GOP stalwarts had noticed yet.

Photographers snapped away. Flash bulbs popped. Joe Steele genially touched the brim of his scandalous cap. Hoover looked as if he were sucking on a lemon. He'd looked that way in every photo of him taken since November that Mike had seen.

Behind the men came their wives. Lou Hoover had been the only woman majoring in geology at Stanford while Herbert Hoover studied there. She remained a handsome woman forty years later, and wore a gown in which she might have greeted the King and Queen of England. Betty Steele's dress looked as if it came from the Montgomery Ward catalogue—from one of the nicer pages there, but still. . . . Any middle-aged, middle-class woman with some small sense of style could have chosen and afforded it.

She looked less happy than she might have. From what Charlie had heard, she often did. She and Joe Steele had lost two young children to diphtheria within days of each other, and never had any more. He poured his energy into politics after that. She didn't seem to have much.

More photographs recorded the outgoing and incoming First Ladies for posterity. No one close enough for Mike to overhear sneered about Betty Steele's clothes. People had used up their indignation on her husband.

The two Presidential couples got into a long open car for the ride to the swearing-in ceremony on the Mall. Reporters and photographers scrambled for the cars that would follow the fancy limousine to the formal inauguration. No one reserved seats in those; getting aboard reminded Mike of a rugby scrum. He managed to grab a seat next to the driver of a Model A. He felt like a tinned sardine, but at least he could go on.

Smoke rose from small fires in Lafayette Park, across the street from the White House. People who had nowhere else to live made encampments there. No doubt they hoped it gave the President something to think about when he looked out the window. By all the things Hoover hadn't done in his unhappy term, he didn't look out that window very often.

The Bonus Army had camped in several places near the Mall till Hoover ordered General MacArthur to clear them out. Clear them the Army did, with fire and bayonets and tear gas. Anyone who wasn't rich sympathized with the hapless victims, not with their oppressors in uniform. Hoover seemed to have done everything he could to dig his own political grave and jump on in.

What about Roosevelt? Mike wondered for the thousandth time. The arson inspector didn't say the Executive Mansion had had help burning down. He didn't say it hadn't. He said he couldn't prove it had. Charlie had tried to run down phone records to see if Vince Scriabin was talking to anybody in Albany early that morning. No matter how much cash he spread around, he had no luck. Those records "weren't available." Had someone made them disappear? If anyone had, nobody who knew would say so. Another dead end—as dead as FDR.

Crowds lined the streets to watch the new man in the White House go by. Some of the people in the crowd were the lawyers and talkers who catered to Congress—and to whom Congress had always catered. Money talked in Washington, the same as it did everywhere else. Money talked louder in Washington than it did in a lot of other places, to tell you the truth.

Mike could recognize *those* people right away. They mostly didn't dress as fancy as Herbert and Lou Hoover. They didn't, but they could have. The quality of a haircut, the cut of a suit jacket, the glint of real gold links when somebody shot a cuff . . . Mike knew the signs, sure as hell.

Most of the people who watched Joe Steele go to take the oath, though, were the ordinary folks who made Washington run. Butchers, bakers, waitresses, secretaries, sign-painters, cake decorators, housewives—people like that were out in force. Since it was Saturday, lots of them had brought their kids along so they could say they'd seen a President once upon a time.

Some of the people in the crowd were colored. Washington had rich colored folks, but most of them were even poorer than the whites. They cleaned and kept house for the city's prosperous whites, and raised their children for them, too. No Jim Crow laws on the sidewalks. They could mix and mingle with the folks who thought they were their betters—as long as they stayed polite about it, of course.

Plenty of people on the sidewalk were out of work. Mike knew the signs: the shabby clothes, the bad shaves, most of all the pinched mouths and worried eyes. Unemployment stalked whites and Negroes alike. It brought its own odd kind of equality: when you didn't have a job, everybody who did was better off than you were. A rising tide might lift all boats. The ebbing tide in America since Wall Street crashed had left millions of boats stranded on the beach.

Colored men and women who were out of work eyed Joe Steele with a painful kind of hope: painful not least because hope was something they'd been scared to feel and even more scared to show. But he was different from Hoover. He'd made them believe their worries were his worries, not just unpleasant noises in another room. If that turned out to be one more lie, chances were they wouldn't just be disappointed. They'd be furious.

That same mix of people, rich and poor, white and black, packed the temporary bleachers on the Mall. Some construction firm or another had given day laborers work to run them up. Those same workers, or a different set, would get paid to knock them down after the ceremony ended.

One of the bleachers, the one right behind the podium with the microphones, was full of Congressmen and Cabinet members and Supreme Court justices and other movers and shakers. The one next closest was for reporters and photographers. Mike piled out of the Model A as unceremoniously as he'd got in. He grabbed himself a pretty good seat.

On the podium, awaiting Joe Steele's arrival, stood Charles Evans Hughes. The Chief Justice seemed from even further back in time than President Hoover. Partly, that sprang from his flowing black judicial robes. And it was partly because of his neatly groomed but still luxuriant white beard. Most men who'd worn beards before the Great War were dead, and the fashion had died with them. Hughes and his whiskers lingered still.

Mike rubbed his own clean-shaven chin. He had a nick on the side of his jaw. Even when you didn't slice yourself, shaving every day was a time-wasting pain in the neck. He wondered why beards had ever gone out of style.

More to the point, he wondered what Charles Evans Hughes was thinking as he waited on the podium. Chief Justice was a pinnacle of sorts. But Hughes had almost—almost!—taken the Presidential oath instead of giving it. He'd gone to sleep on election night in 1916 positive he'd licked Woodrow Wilson. Only when California's disappointing returns came in the next day did he find out he'd lost.

Nimbly, his cap under his arm now, Joe Steele hopped up onto the podium with the Chief Justice. "Are you ready to take the oath, Mr. President?" Hughes asked.

"Yes, sir. I am." Steele's baritone had the flat lack of regional accent so common in California, the lack of accent that was a kind of accent in itself. Underneath that plain, plain General American lay a hint—no, a ghost—of something harsh and guttural, something that didn't belong to English at all.

"All right, then. We shall proceed. Repeat after me: "'I'—state your full legal name."

"I, Joseph Vissarion Steele—"

"'—do solemnly swear that I will faithfully execute the Office of President of the United States, and will to the best of my Ability, preserve, protect and defend the Constitution of the United States.'"

Hughes broke the oath down into chunks a few words long. Phrase by phrase, Joe Steele echoed it. When they'd both finished, Hughes held out his hand. "Congratulations, President Steele!"

"Thank you, Mr. Chief Justice." Joe Steele held on to Hughes' hand for a few extra seconds so the photographers could immortalize the moment. Applause from the bleachers washed over the two of them. There sat Herbert Hoover politely clapping for his successor when he could have wanted nothing more than to take the oath of office again himself. Democracy was a strange and sometimes wondrous thing.

Chief Justice Hughes descended from the podium and took his place next to the now ex-President. Joe Steele put the cloth cap back on his head and stuck reading glasses on his nose before he fiddled with his mike for a moment, positioning it just the way he wanted it. He held his notes on cards in his left hand, and glanced down at them every once in a while. For the most part, though, he knew what he intended to say.

"This country is in trouble," he began bluntly. "You know that. I know that. We all know that. If everything was great in the United States, you wouldn't have elected me. You do not elect people like me when everything is great. You elect important people, fine-talking people, people like President Hoover or Governor Roosevelt, God have mercy on his soul."

Mike looked over at Herbert Hoover. He was scowling, but he'd been scowling all day long. It wasn't as if Joe Steele were wrong. It was more that he was saying what someone with better manners wouldn't have mentioned.

"I grew up on a farm outside of Fresno," the new President went on. "I worked with my hands in the fields. My father and mother came to America because they wanted a better life for themselves and their children than they could hope for where they used to live. Millions of people listening to me today can say the same thing."

He paused. Applause came from the bleachers full of ordinary people—and, Mike noticed, from the one full of reporters and photographers. It also came from the bleachers full of government officials, but more slowly and grudgingly.

Joe Steele nodded to himself, as if that didn't surprise him one bit. "And I had a better life," he said. "I managed to study law, and to start my own practice. I said what I thought needed saying about how things were in my home town. Some people there thought the things I was saying deserved to be said. They talked me into running for the city council, and then for Congress, and Fresno sent me—me, a son of immigrants!—to Washington."

More applause. Some Representatives and Senators were self-made men, but there as anywhere old family and old money didn't hurt.

"When I look at the country now, I see it is not the way it was when I grew up," Steele said. "We are in trouble. We do not have a better life than we did before. Things are bad now, and they are getting worse day by day, month by month, year by year. When I saw that, and when I was sure I saw it, that is when I decided to run for President. The way it looked to me was, I could not do anything else. Someone has to set things right, here in the United States. The people who were in power were not doing it. I decided I had to be the one who did."

He wasn't a great speaker. He didn't make Mike want to charge out and do whatever he said. Hitler had basically talked his way to power in Germany a couple of months earlier. But Joe Steele did show a confidence not so very different from the German dictator's.

And, like Hitler, he was taking charge in a country that had just got knocked through the ropes. People would give him the benefit of the doubt for a while because of that.

"So we will have jobs in my administration," Joe Steele said. "Labor is a matter of honor, a matter of fame, a matter of valor and heroism. Without jobs, all else fails. People of America, I tell you—*we will have jobs!*"

Surely not all the people in the bleachers who cheered themselves hoarse had no job right now. Just as surely, a lot of them were out of work. Again, the stands full of government functionaries cheered more slowly and less enthusiastically than ones full of ordinary folks.

"I can be rough. I can be harsh. But I am only rough and harsh toward those who harm the people of this great country," Joe Steele said. "What is my duty? To do my job and to fight for the people. Quitting is not in my character. Whatever I have to do, I will do it."

How did Franklin D. Roosevelt feel about that? He knew Joe Steele wasn't kidding, anyhow. And a whole fat lot of good knowing did him. Mike shivered, though the day wasn't cold.

"We will do whatever we have to do to get the United States on its feet again. You cannot set things to rights while you have silk gloves on." The President held up his hairy hands. He wasn't wearing gloves of any kind. He went on, "The ones who wear silk gloves, they use them to take from ordinary people without leaving any fingerprints. When banks fail, they steal the people's money. Have you ever seen a hungry banker? Has anyone in the history of the world ever seen a hungry banker? If I have to choose between the people and the bankers, I will choose the people. We will nationalize the banks and save the people's money."

This time, the applause nearly blasted him off the podium. Ever since the big stock crash, banks had failed by the hundreds—no, by the thousands. And every time a bank went under, the depositors who'd put money into it and couldn't pull the cash out fast enough went down the drain with it. Everybody who was listening to him had either lost money that way him- or herself or knew someone else who had. Bankers were some of the most hated people in the whole country these days.

Mike looked over to the stands full of officials. Herbert Hoover was shaking his head, and he wasn't the only one. He didn't understand the nerve Joe Steele had struck. That he didn't understand was one big reason he hadn't won his second term.

President Hoover had tried to ignore the building whirlwind—and it had swept him away. President Steele would try to ride it. He'd have trouble doing worse. Mike feared he'd also have trouble doing better.

IV

Charlie Sullivan and a couple of other reporters watched Senator Carter Glass walk into the White House to confer with Joe Steele. Joe Steele had summoned Congress to a special session. Winning the kind of majority he had in the House made getting what he wanted easier.

President Steele didn't have that kind of majority in the Senate. And a lot of Southern Democrats were more conservative than Republicans from the rest of the country. Carter Glass, a Virginian, was a case in point. He'd been born before the Civil War started, and apparently hadn't changed his views a great deal since. He loudly opposed nationalizing the banking system. Since he'd been Secretary of the Treasury in the Wilson administration, his views counted.

One of the other newsmen, a skinny cub with the impressive handle of Virginius Dabney, was from the *Richmond Times*. "I've got a dollar that says Joe Steele won't make him change his mind," he said, lighting a Camel.

"You're on," Charlie said at once. They shook hands to make things official.

The kid from Virginia was in a gloating mood. "I'm gonna buy myself a nice dinner with your dollar," he said. "You've got no idea what a pigheaded old coot Carter Glass has turned into. Neither does the President, or he would've picked somebody else to try to get around the logjam in the Senate."

"Well, you could be right," Charlie said.

"Damn right, I'm right," Dabney broke in.

"Hang on. I wasn't done yet." Charlie held up his right hand, palm out, like a cop stopping traffic. "You could be right, but don't get too sure yet. Carter Glass never had to deal with anybody like Joe Steele before, either."

Virginius Dabney blew out a stream of smoke. "It won't matter. Glass'll just keep saying no. He'll get as loud as he reckons he needs to. He'll go on about Trotsky and the Reds, and maybe about Hitler and the Nazis, too. Then he'll say no some more. He doesn't reckon the Federal government's got the right to do this."

"One of the guys who doesn't reckon Washington has the right to shake it after a leak, huh?" Charlie said with a sour chuckle.

"That's him," Dabney said, not without pride. "States' rights all the way." By the way he answered, he was a states' rights man himself. He was a white Southerner. Not all of them filled that bill, but most of them did.

You couldn't argue with them. Oh, you could, but you'd only waste your time. Charlie didn't waste any of his. Instead, he said, "Let me scrounge one of your cigarettes, okay?"

"Sure." Dabney handed him the pack and even gave him a match. Camels were stronger than Charlie's usual Chesterfields, but he didn't complain. He'd gone to France in 1918, though too late to see combat. With what they smoked over there, he was amazed that German poison gas had bothered them.

After about an hour and fifteen minutes, Carter Glass came out of the White House. He always looked kind of weathered. He was in his mid-seventies; he'd come by it honestly. Now . . . Now Charlie wasn't sure what he was seeing. Unless he was imagining things, Glass looked as if he'd just walked into a haymaker from Primo Carnera. The giant Italian wasn't heavyweight champ just yet, but he had a fight with Jack Sharkey set for the end of June.

"Senator Glass!" Charlie called. "Did the President bring you around to his way of thinking, Senator?"

Glass flinched at the question, as if he were afraid Primo Carnera would belt him again. He took a deep breath, like a man coming off the canvas and trying to stay upright. "After some discussion with President Steele, I have decided that the nationalization bill is, ah, a worthy piece of legislation. I intend to vote for it, and I will work with the President to persuade my colleagues to support it as well. Right now, that's all I have to say. Excuse me."

He scuttled away. Up till that moment, Charlie had always thought T. S. Eliot stretched language past the breaking point when he compared a man to a pair of ragged claws. If ever a man walked like a dejected crab, it was Carter Glass.

Charlie held out his hand. "Pay up."

Virginius Dabney was still gaping after the Senator from his home state. "Dog my cats," he said softly, more to himself than to Charlie. He took out his billfold, fumbled, and pulled out an engraved portrait of George Washington. "Here y'are. I wouldn't have believed it if I didn't see it with my own eyes. The President, he's got some big mojo working."

After pocketing the dollar, Charlie said, "Some big what?"

"Mojo," Dabney repeated. "It's nigger slang. Means something like magic power. I can't think of anything else that would make Carter Glass turn on a dime like that."

"Mojo, huh? Have to remember that," Charlie said. "But didn't I tell you Joe Steele had a way of getting what he wanted?"

"You told me. I didn't believe you. Nobody who knows anything about Glass would've believed you."

A couple of other recalcitrant Senators went to confer with the President. When they came out of the White House, they were all for nationalization, too. Charlie didn't see them emerge, so he didn't know whether they looked as steamrollered as Carter Glass had. He figured it was likely, though. Joe Steele could be mighty persuasive. Look how well he'd persuaded Franklin Roosevelt, after all.

The Senators remained among the living. Like Carter Glass, though, they had their change of heart. With their loud new support, the nationalization bill passed the Senate by almost as big a margin as it had in the House.

Joe Steele went on the radio to talk to the American people. "We are heading in the right direction at last," he said. "Some folks make money when others are miserable. A few want to wreck all the progress the rest support. We almost had that kind of trouble over this bill. But I talked sense to a few men who didn't see things quite the right way at first. Most of them took another look and decided going along would be a better idea. I'm glad they did. We need to get behind the country and push so we can start it going. If some push at the wrong end, that won't work so well. We're all together on this one, though. We are now."

Since he was speaking from the White House, no one on the program tried to tell him he was wrong. Hardly anyone anywhere tried to tell Joe Steele he was wrong at first. He was doing something, or trying to do something, about the mess. Herbert Hoover had treated the Depression the way the Victorians treated sex—he didn't look at it, and he hoped it would just go away.

That hadn't worked for the Victorians, and it hadn't worked for him, either. They were mostly dead, and he'd lost the election. For a politician, that was the fate worse than death.

Even a reporter who came into Washington only every so often knew where the people who worked in the White House ate and drank. Charlie went to half a dozen of those places. He talked to more than half a dozen people who typed things and filed things and answered wires and telephone calls. And they all told him they didn't know how Joe Steele got Carter Glass and the other Senators who'd opposed the bill that nationalized the banks to turn around and vote for it.

He plied them with liquor. Even more to the point, he plied them with money. It was the Associated Press' money, so he didn't have to be chintzy with it. It didn't help. They went right on telling him they didn't know. Frustrated, he yelped, "Well, who the hell does, then?"

Most of them didn't even know who knew. Charlie knew what that meant: Joe Steele wasn't just good at holding his cards close to his chest. He was terrific at it. One or two people suggested that Charlie might talk to Kagan or to Mikoian or to Scriabin.

He could have figured that out for himself when the wells he drilled at lower levels came up dry. He pretty much had figured it out, in fact. Vince Scriabin still scared the crap out of him. Lazar Kagan's moon of a face was as near unreadable as made no difference. That left Stas Mikoian. Of the President's longtime henchmen, he seemed the most approachable.

Chances were Charlie didn't get a phone call from Mikoian completely by coincidence. "I hear you've been trying to find out a few things," the Armenian said after they got through the hellos and how-are-yous.

"Didn't know that was against the rules for a reporter," Charlie said.

Mikoian laughed. Charlie judged Scriabin would have got mad. He couldn't guess about Kagan, or about what the Jew's reaction would have meant. Yeah, Stas was the most human of the three. "Why don't you have dinner with me tonight?" Mikoian said. "We can talk about it there."

"Sounds great. Where do you want to go?" Charlie asked.

"There's a chop house called Rudy's, across Ninth from the Gayety," Mikoian answered. "See you there about eight?"

"Okay." Charlie eyed the phone in bemusement as he hung up. The Gayety was Washington's leading burlesque house. Was Stas only using it as a geographical reference point, or was he human all kinds of ways? Charlie, of course, had never ogled a stripper in his life. Of course.

Nothing wrong with Rudy's, though. It gave off an aura of quiet class. The air smelled of grilled meat and expensive cigars. A gray-haired colored waiter escorted Charlie to a booth. "Mr. Mikoian is expecting you, sir," he murmured.

Stas stood up to shake hands. He had a dark drink in a tall glass. "Rum and Coke," he said, seeing Charlie's eye fall on it. "They get the rum straight from Cuba."

"Sounds great," Charlie said, as he had on the telephone. The rum *was* smooth, and they didn't stint on it. He chose lamb chops from the menu; Mikoian ordered a medium-rare T-bone.

The Armenian steepled his fingers and looked across the table at Charlie. "I can tell you what you want to know," he said.

"But there's a catch," Charlie said. "There's always a catch."

"Yes, there's always a catch," Mikoian agreed. "Anyone more than six years old knows that. You'd be surprised how many people in Washington don't."

"Would I? Maybe not," Charlie said. "Tell me what the catch is, and I'll tell you whether I want to go on. If I don't, we'll have a nice dinner and talk about what kind of chance the Senators have for the pennant."

"Pretty decent chance this year, I think," Mikoian said. "But all right—fair enough. The catch is, you can't write about any of what I tell you. The President doesn't mind if you know. He says you've always been fair to him—certainly fairer than your brother has. But politics is like sausage-making: you don't want to watch how it's done."

"That's Bismarck."

"Uh-huh. He knew what he was talking about, too. He mostly did."

Charlie considered. "I could just lie to you, you know," he remarked.

"Oh, sure. And you'd have a story. But the President would know you weren't someone he could trust. So is one story worth selling him out?"

You asked that kind of question whenever you made a dubious deal. Another question also surfaced in Charlie's mind. *Do I want to go on Joe Steele's black list for any reason under the sun?* He knew damn well he didn't. He sighed. "Tell me."

Stas Mikoian didn't even smile. He also didn't talk right away, because the waiter brought their meals then. Charlie didn't think anything could go better with lamb than mint jelly. When he said so, Mikoian did grin. "I'd argue for garlic myself, but you're Irish and I'm Armenian. What it really comes down to is what you got used to when you were growing up."

"That's about the size of it." Charlie chewed, then nodded. "This is mighty good. How's your steak?"

"It's fine. Hard to go wrong with anything at Rudy's. They've been here a long time, and you can see why." Stas Mikoian cut another bite and ate it. He sipped from his rum and Coke. "Shall I tell you about Senator Glass?"

"I wish you would."

"He's a fine Virginian. Comes from a good family. Back when he was a boy, they owned slaves. Not after the Civil War, naturally, but they still had colored people working for them. Before he went off to college, they had this pretty little maid called Emma, Emma . . . well, you don't need to know her last name. You won't be writing a story about this."

"That's right." Charlie got a little farther down his own drink. "Can I guess where this is going?"

"You probably can. Sometimes boys from families like that learn the facts of life from a maid or a cook. Carter Glass did. And nine months later he learned more about the facts of life than he thought he would when he gave her a tumble. Had himself what they call a high-yaller little boy." He spoke the Southern phrase as if it came from a foreign language.

"Did he try to pretend the whole thing never happened?" Charlie asked.

"No. He was a gentleman. He—or his family—took care of Emma and the baby. It wasn't fancy, but it was quite a bit better than nothing. The boy got as good an education as a colored kid in Virginia could. He's a teacher there. He has children of his own. They're doing well for themselves—as well as colored people can in that part of the country. And one of the reasons they're doing well is that they never, ever let on that they're related to Carter Glass."

"So it was a family secret, you're saying?"

"That's right. That's what I'm saying." Mikoian raised a dark, bushy eyebrow. "Senator Glass was interested in keeping it a family secret, too. We were able to oblige him— and he was able to oblige us."

"I guess he was." Charlie lifted a forefinger. The waiter appeared as if by magic. "I'd like another rum and Coke, please."

"So would I," Stas said.

"Comin' right up, gentlemen." The waiter went off to get them.

Charlie aimed that forefinger at Mikoian like the barrel of a pistol. "How did you—how did Joe Steele—discover the old family secret?"

"We could see who the leaders were in the faction that was trying to obstruct us," Mikoian said. "We did a little poking around to see if any of them had skeletons in the closet. And what do you know? Carter Glass did."

The waiter returned with their drinks on an enameled tray. He ceremoniously set them down, then disappeared again. After he was gone, Charlie said, "You did a little poking around?"

"That's right." Mikoian's eyes twinkled.

"You personally? Or Joe Steele personally? Or was it maybe Lazar Kagan?"

That twinkle got sparklier. "You're a funny fellow, you know? There's a smart young guy in the Justice Department's Bureau of Investigation who goes after these things like a bulldog. He takes a bite, and he won't let go. He even looks kind of like a bulldog—he's stocky and not too handsome and he's got an underslung jaw. He dug up what we wanted to know."

Charlie named it: "The dirt."

"Uh-huh, the dirt." Stas Mikoian's smile invited Charlie to share the joke. "Go on, tell me nobody else ever did anything like this before in the whole history of politics. Go ahead. I dare you." He leaned back against the booth's brass-button leather upholstery and waited.

"Don't be silly. You know I can't do that," Charlie said. Joe Steele and his underlings might play rougher than most people did, but blackmail had always been part of the game. By the nature of things, it wasn't a part that got talked about much. But it was there.

Mikoian was still smiling. "You're an honest man. I knew you were. That's why I talked the boss into letting me level with you."

Which might be true and might be grease to slick Charlie up some more. "Well, thanks," Charlie said, trying not to show how pleased he was. "And you didn't need to worry— that's not the kind of story I could print."

"Oh, you never know," Stas Mikoian said. "We have plenty of enemies, people trying to stop us from doing anything just because we're the ones who are doing it—or because they're making money the way things are now. You think we play dirty? Some of the things they do . . ."

"Get you fellas some dessert?" the waiter asked. "Some vanilla ice cream, or maybe scrumptious lemon-meringue pie?"

They ate dessert. Mikoian put money on the table. "Trying to bribe a member of the working press, are you?" Charlie said, and then, with a sheepish grin, "Thanks."

"Any time," Stas Mikoian answered easily. "Any old time at all."

The hallway that led back to the records room of the Albany Fire Department was as black as the inside of King Tut's tomb the year before Howard Carter found it. Only a flashlight beam pierced the gloom. The clerk who carried the flashlight was more nervous than Carter had been. He had no ancient Egyptian curses to worry about. His fear was more concrete.

"If they ever find out I let you in here, they'll fire me faster than you can say Jack Robinson," he whispered.

He'd said the same thing three times before. Mike Sullivan was sick of hearing it. "They won't fire you," he whispered. He'd had to pay the clerk fifty dollars of the *New York Post*'s money to get him to come here at two in the morning. He didn't think the *Post* was paying him enough to listen to all the pissing and moaning.

A brass doorknob gleamed in the skinny beam. "They're in there," the clerk whispered. He shifted the flashlight to his left hand. Keys clinked as he pulled a key ring from his pocket. He found the one he wanted, but the beam kept sliding away from the lock when he tried to use it.

"Here. I'll hold the light." Mike took it away from him before he could say no. The clerk managed to open the door then, though he almost wet his pants at the click the key made turning in the lock.

They went inside. The clerk closed the door after them. Since the room full of filing cabinets had no windows, Mike flipped the switch and turned on the overhead light. The clerk had more conniptions.

"Easy, man. Easy," Mike said. "Nobody can see through the walls. Now—where's the report on the Executive Mansion fire?"

"This cabinet here," the clerk answered. The filing cabinet also had a lock. "See—hot stuff," the man said. Mike almost told him not to tell jokes, but decided he wouldn't appreciate the advice. The clerk found the smaller key that unlocked the man-tall wooden cabinet.

He slid out the second drawer and extracted a fat manila folder. STATE EXECUTIVE MANSION FIRE, said a typewritten label stuck to the tab. It also gave the date of the fire. "Thanks." Mike grabbed it from him and started flipping through it.

In lifeless bureaucratic prose, it told him how the fire had been reported, and how engines from several firehouses had converged on the scene. It told how the firemen had battled the flames, how some people in the mansion managed to escape, and how others, including Governor and Mrs. Roosevelt, hadn't.

There were photographs of the scene, and of the victims. Mike bit his lip hard, looking at those. A man who'd burned to death was not a pretty sight. He flipped on through the folder, looking for one thing in particular.

He didn't find it. "Where's the arson report?" he asked the clerk. He wanted to see exactly how the inspector had decided he couldn't decide whether the fire's start had had help. But he couldn't find it.

The clerk frowned. "Everything should be there." He quickly went through the folder, too. "Huh," he said. "I'm sure it was in there when I filed this one. Let me see something." He pawed through the folders between which the one detailing the Executive Mansion fire had rested. He also looked in the drawer itself, in case the arson report had somehow slipped out. He had no luck anywhere. "Huh," he said again. "Isn't that funny? I know it was there—I remember the heading."

"Did you read any of it?" Mike asked.

"No." The clerk shook his head. "I was just making sure the report was complete before I filed it." How many times had he done that with reports no one would ever want to

look at again? Not this one. This one had answers to important questions—among which was, had somebody got to the
arson inspector? It might have had answers to those questions, anyhow. It didn't now. The vital piece was missing.

"Who else would have a copy of that report?" Mike
asked.

"I'm sure Mr. Kincaid would have kept one for his personal files," the clerk replied. "He's a very thorough man,
Mr. Kincaid."

"You don't know where those personal files are?"

"In his house, I expect. Probably in a fireproof cabinet,
Mr. Kincaid being in the line of work he's in."

"Uh-huh." Mike swore under his breath. If he wanted to
get into the arson inspector's personal files, a money-
hungry clerk wouldn't cut it. He'd need a second-story man.

"Can we get out of here, please?" Even fidgety, the clerk
stayed polite. "I've done everything for you I promised I
would. I can't help it if the report's not there."

"Yeah, let's go." Mike didn't want to get hit with a
breaking-and-entering rap any more than the clerk did.
When you were after stuff as politically explosive as that
arson report might be, you didn't want to get caught. And
somebody else had been after it, too, and had got it before
he had. He didn't believe for a second that it had just fallen
out of the manila folder. No, somebody'd lifted it, whether
because of what it said or because of what it didn't say he
couldn't guess without seeing it.

They left the room. The clerk locked the door after
them—you didn't want to forget to tend to details. They
made their getaway. The building didn't have any alarms.
No one had imagined anybody would want to sneak away
with Albany Fire Department records. You never could tell
when imagination would fall short of reality. It had this
time.

Sneakiness failing, Mike tried the direct approach. He
did his best to interview Fire Department Lieutenant Jere-
miah V. Kincaid, who had produced the report. His best
turned out not to be good enough. Lieutenant Kincaid's
secretary, an uncommonly pretty girl, told him, "Lieutenant
Kincaid doesn't talk to reporters."

"Why not?" Mike asked. "Isn't that part of his job?"

"His job is to investigate," she answered. "It isn't to publicize."

"Son of a gun," he said, in lieu of something more heartfelt. "Well, does the Albany Fire Department have a Public Information Officer or anybody else who *is* supposed to talk to reporters?"

The Albany Fire Department did. His name was Kermit Witherspoon. He wasn't at his post. His wife had just had a baby boy, and he was using vacation time to be with her. No one wanted to tell Mike where he lived. Mike found out for himself. He was no great threat to Sherlock Holmes. But the Albany telephone book gave him all the clues he needed—not a hell of a lot of Kermit Witherspoons lived within the city limits.

When he knocked on the front door, a baby inside the white clapboard house started to cry. Junior had a good set of lungs. A harried-looking man answered the knock. "Are you Kermit Witherspoon?" Mike asked.

"That's right. Who are you?"

"Mike Sullivan. I write for the *New York Post*." Mike handed him a card. It was much more convincing than simply saying who he was and what he did. "I'd like to ask you some questions about Lieutenant Kincaid's report on the Executive Mansion fire."

Witherspoon's face froze. "That happened almost a year ago now. I've talked to I don't know how many reporters. I don't have anything new to say to anybody, so I've stopped talking. It isn't news any more."

"It still could be. Can you tell me why Kincaid wouldn't state whether he thought the fire was arson or not?"

"I'm afraid I don't remember the details, Mr., uh, Sullivan," Witherspoon answered. "You'd do better asking Lieutenant Kincaid."

"He says he's not talking, either."

"There you are, then."

"Yeah, here I am—up a dead end. And I shouldn't be. This was a public tragedy, Lieutenant Witherspoon. What happened at the Executive Mansion shouldn't be a secret."

"I can't do anything about that, I'm afraid."

From inside, the baby's wails got louder. "Kermit, can you give me a hand here?" a woman called. "Who are you talking to, anyway?"

"A peddler." Witherspoon closed the door in Mike's face. He locked it, too. Mike stood on the front porch for a moment, then turned and walked away.

Stella Morandini gnawed meat off a purple-red sweet-and-sour pork rib at Hop Sing's. She eyed Mike. "You know what'll happen if you write a story like that?" she said.

"A little piece of the truth will come out," he answered, and bit into a fried shrimp. "Not a big piece, 'cause it's buried pretty deep, but a little one. That's better than no truth at all."

"You can't prove any of it."

"I can prove what people aren't saying, what they won't say. I can prove that reports that ought to be part of the public record have walked with Jesus—or with somebody. Somebody's hiding things. People don't do that unless they've got a darn good reason to."

"Yeah." She nodded. "And who would those people be?"

"Has to be Joe Steele, or the so-and-sos who work for him. He's the one who stood to get the most when Roosevelt cooked."

"Okay. Say you're right. Say he did all that stuff," Stella said. "So you write a story that says he oughta be in Sing Sing, not the White House. So what does he do to you right after that?"

"Uh—" Mike stopped with what was left of that fried shrimp halfway to his mouth. Till that moment, that he might put himself in danger with a story like that had never crossed his mind. He wondered why not. *'Cause you're stupid, that's why.* Joe Steele didn't stop at anything to get what he wanted. Charlie had laughed when he told how the President blackmailed Senators into voting his way. Mike didn't think it was so funny, especially now.

Stella nodded. "'Uh' is right, Mike. This isn't a game, or it won't be if you write a story like that. You're playing for keeps."

When you strike at a king, you must kill him. Mike didn't remember offhand who'd said that. Bartlett's would. Who-ever'd said it, he'd known what he was talking about. Be-cause if you didn't kill the king you'd struck at, he'd do some striking of his own.

He ate the rest of the shrimp. "Gotta do it, sweetie. Do you want somebody that, that cold-blooded and merciless running the country? As bad as Trotsky and Hitler, you ask me."

"You're gonna land in more *tsuris* than you know what to do with." Yes, she spent a lot of time working around Jews. So did Mike, who had no trouble with the Yiddish.

He wrote the story anyway. One of the Jews he worked around was Stan Feldman, the managing editor of the *Post*. Feldman called Mike into the cramped little office where he turned stories into newspapers. Pictures of scantily clad girls lined one wall. The office stank of stale cigar smoke.

Feldman jabbed a finger at Mike's piece. "I'm not gonna run this," he said. "Get me some real evidence and maybe I will. But nothing is just—nothing."

"It's not just nothing," Mike said. "It's nothing where there ought to be something. That's not the same thing."

"It's not enough, either," the editor answered. "Show me something and I may change my mind. Something real, not *This ought to be here and it isn't, so they're all a bunch of crooks.*"

"But—" Mike spread his hands. "If I can see it, Stan, other people will be able to see it, too."

"I can see it. Seeing it's not good enough, not for some-thing like this," Feldman said. "You have to nail it down tight, so there's no possible doubt. If you don't, we'll have more libel suits than Hart Schaffner and Marx has of the kind with two pairs of pants."

"Funny. Ha, ha. See how hard I'm laughing?"

Feldman lit another nasty cheroot. "I ain't laughing, ei-ther, Mike. We can't run it like it is, and that's flat. Besides, we're a Democratic paper, remember? This kind of stuff, it sounds like Father Coughlin. Ever hear of giving somebody the benefit of the doubt?"

"Sure, where there's a doubt to give the benefit of. Is

there, with Joe Steele? Some of the things I've heard from Washington—" He stopped there. He'd heard those from his brother. Charlie'd got them off the record, and passed them along even further off the record. They weren't for other people's ears.

"He's better than Hoover. So he's not as slick as Roosevelt woulda been. So what?" Feldman said. "He's getting stuff done. He's putting people to work, and he's putting the rich bastards in their place. You can't make an omelette without breaking eggs."

"'They that can give up essential liberty to obtain a little temporary safety deserve neither liberty nor safety,'" Mike said. Ben Franklin always sounded better than some dumb cliché.

Ben Franklin sounded enough better than the cliché to make Stan Feldman turn red. "I'm not giving up essential anything, except a story that doesn't prove what it needs to. Show me the proof and we'll go on from there. In the meantime, haven't you got something to write about besides Joe Steele?"

"Nothing as important."

"So go write about something that ain't important. Go on. Beat it. I've wasted too much time on you already."

Muttering, Mike left. *Go write about something that ain't important.* Now there was a battle cry to send a reporter rushing to his typewriter! Yeah, the cub who covered a Long Island flower show knew his deathless prose would never make the history books. He still wrote better if he wrote as though those roses and peonies were as important as Mussolini and Picasso.

"You okay, Mike?" another reporter asked. "You look like you could use some Bromo-Seltzer or something."

"Got anything in your desk that'll cure me of humanity, Hank?" Mike said.

Instead of Benjamin Franklin, Hank quoted Dorothy Parker: "'Guns aren't lawful;/ Nooses give;/ Gas smells awful;/ You might as well live.'"

"Heh," Mike said. But then he chuckled in genuine appreciation. "Okay, that's pretty good. Thanks."

"Any time, man. Seriously, though, what's eating you? Is it anything I can help you with?"

"Not unless you want to charge in there and convince Stan to run a story I just wrote. He doesn't think I did enough to tie the can to Joe Steele's tail."

Hank whistled, soft and low. "You don't think small, do you?"

"Who, me?"

"Yeah, you. You better watch yourself, is all I've got to say."

"Everybody keeps telling me that." Mike knew it was good advice, too. The safe, sane, calculating part of him did, anyhow. But how safe, sane, and calculating should you be when you were sure the President knocked off his main rival for the nomination when it looked as if he was going to lose? Was anybody who did something like that fit to lead the land of the free and the home of the brave?

The problem was, most people didn't want to believe it. Easier to think Roosevelt died in some sad accident. Then you wouldn't have to wonder about yourself when you voted to toss Herbert Hoover on the rubbish heap of the past. And people had voted that way. Joe Steele got one of the biggest wins in the history of the USA, the kind of win that would change politics for years to come.

It would unless people decided Joe Steele was a murderer, anyway. Would they impeach him and throw him out of office? Or would they just not reelect him? But that would bring back the Republicans. Wasn't the cure worse than the disease? Wouldn't most people think it was?

So they went by on the other side of the road. They turned their eyes away from the burnt bodies in the ditch. Pharisees, the lot of 'em. *I'll show them what Joe Steele did*, Mike thought. *I'll show them whether they want to see it or not.*

V

During the special session, Joe Steele fed bills to the leaders of the House and Senate one after another. After the brief pause at nationalizing the banks, those bills went through, lickety-split—the advantage of winning an election by a landslide, and the advantage of putting the fear of God (or at least of embarrassment) into Representatives and Senators. More new laws regulated Wall Street. They tried to make sure financiers' foibles didn't send the economy crashing down in ruins again. Bills regulating banks did their best to keep the bankers from lending money they didn't have.

Charlie Sullivan got calluses on the tips of his index fingers banging out stories about the start of the President's Four Year Plan. He had plenty to write about. Every day, Joe Steele seemed to sign a bill that would have been a good year's work in ordinary times. On a lively day, he'd sign two or three bills like that.

The country's never going to be the same seemed to be the theme of the special session. Bills regulated what management could do to labor. More bills set out how labor could and couldn't dicker with management. There were massive public-works programs. Roads, canals, tunnels, airstrips . . . Joe Steele had swarms of hungry men—and not a few hungry women—eager to dig in with a shovel or swing a pick in exchange for three square meals, a place to sleep, and a little cash in their pockets now and then.

Foreclosures and dust storms meant big stretches of farmland in the Midwest lay idle. Joe Steele's bill set up community farms on abandoned land. People lived on the land together, worked it all together, and shared whatever they got from the crops they raised. The Republicans asked how that was any different from what was going on in Russia.

Joe Steele went on the radio to answer them. "Some people would rather keep the country hungry and farmers out of work," he said. "If you want to see food on the table and men proud of what they do, let your Senators and Representatives know about it." The people who listened to him must have done that, because the farm bill passed with all the others.

After it did, Charlie took a few days off so he could go back up to New York and marry Esther Polgar. Mike was his best man. At the reception, Mike asked him, "Do you really like that SOB so much? I swear to God, he murdered Roosevelt to get the nomination."

"If you can prove it, I'll worry about it then," Charlie answered. "In the meantime, he's doing the country good. People have hope again. When Hoover was sitting there twiddling his thumbs, everybody just wanted to lay down and die."

"Lie down," Mike said automatically.

Charlie thumbed his nose at him. "You didn't put on that monkey suit to be my copy editor."

Mike laughed, but not for long. "One of the reasons nobody can prove anything is that a lot of the paperwork's gone and disappeared. That tells you something right there, or it does if you're not a cheerleader for the bum in the White House."

"I'm no cheerleader, dammit." Charlie wasn't kidding around any more, either. "I watched Mikoian on the convention floor when news came of the fire in Albany. He almost dropped dead. Nobody's that good an actor."

"And you heard Scriabin order it, too."

"I heard Scriabin on the phone talking about something. I don't know what any more than you do. They deserve the benefit of the doubt."

Mike took a deep breath, blew it out, and then took another one. "Okay. It's your wedding. I don't want to fight with you on your big day. But it sure seems you're banging Joe Steele's drum for him with those stories you keep cranking out."

"The bills are important. They'll help clean up the mess we're in. I don't care if the Devil wrote them. They're still good bills."

"Who says the Devil didn't?" Mike said. Charlie threw up his hands and went over to the bar for another bourbon. He didn't want to fight with his brother, either, not on a day like this.

Esther had a fresh drink in her hand, too. "What were you and Mike going on about?" she asked.

"Nothing that has anything to do with you, babe," he said, and kissed her. "Just dumb old politics."

"He really can't stand the President, can he? That's so funny—it's not like he's a Republican or anything."

"He doesn't trust him," Charlie said, which was putting it mildly. To his relief, the band Esther's folks had hired started going through its paces. He gulped his bourbon and led Esther out onto the dance floor. "C'mon, Mrs. Sullivan. Let's cut a rug." If he was dancing, he didn't have to think about his brother or Joe Steele or anything else.

"Mrs. Sullivan. I like that." Esther smiled at him. She spread the fingers of her left hand so the tiny diamond in her wedding ring sparkled. "I've got to get used to it, but I like it."

"You better get used to it. You'll be wearing it the next fifty or sixty years." He leaned close to whisper in her ear: "And tonight you won't be wearing anything else." She squeaked and made as if to hit him, but they were grinning at each other.

They honeymooned at Niagara Falls. It was not too far and not too expensive. Charlie didn't much care where they went. He didn't plan on seeing much besides the hotel room they'd rented any which way. He and Esther did finally go to the Falls the day before they were supposed to head back to New York City and Charlie to continue to Washington and to find a bigger apartment than the cramped place he'd had up till then.

The Falls were impressive. Damned if he'd admit it, Charlie spoke to his new wife in a mock-gruff growl: "I wouldn't even know what this place looks like if you hadn't worn me out."

This time, Esther did hit him. No one around them paid any attention. A lot of the people gaping at the Falls were young couples too tired from honeymooning to do any more of it right that minute. One of these days before too long, Charlie figured, Mike and Stella would come here, too. He wondered how much of Niagara they'd see.

"Ladies and gentlemen, live from the White House in Washington, D.C., the President of the United States." The radio announcer had the rich, slightly plummy tones of an actor who'd spent a lot of time in first-rate vaudeville and a few short stretches in Broadway flops.

Charlie noticed the hamminess but didn't fuss about it. At least half the leading radio announcers sounded like this guy. Besides, Charlie wasn't inclined to fuss about anything then. He liked the new apartment. He could walk through the living room with a good chance of evading the shin-eating coffee table. More space did make a difference. He could grab Esther and go to bed with her whenever he felt like it, too. That also made a difference, one much more pleasant than that which came from a larger front room.

"This is Joe Steele." The President didn't sound like a pretty good actor. He sounded like someone who should have been a tough guy but had somehow ended up with an education instead. His voice held a faint rasp. Some of that might have come from the pipe he smoked. The rest he would have had anyway. Anybody who didn't hear the don't-mess-with-me in his voice wasn't listening hard enough. To Charlie, it was as unmistakable as the warning buzz of a rattlesnake's tail.

"I want to talk to you tonight about my bill for electrifying the Tennessee Valley," Joe Steele said. "It's an important bill. It will build dams up and down the river. The dams will give thousands of people jobs for years. They will stop the floods that have drowned the lowlands in those parts every so often since only Indians lived there. And the electricity the dams generate will bring millions of people into the twentieth century."

The President paused to cough. "Only when the farmer is surrounded by electrical wiring will he fully become an

American citizen. The biggest hope and weapon for our country is industry, and making the farmer part of industry. It is impossible to base construction on two different foundations, on the foundation of large-scale and highly concentrated industry, and on the foundation of very fragmented and extremely backward agriculture. Systematically and persistently, we must place agriculture on a new technical basis, and raise it to the level of an industry."

He coughed again. He used that cough, Charlie realized, as a kind of punctuation mark to show when he was moving from one idea to another. "This is also the logic behind my new system of community farms. But in the Tennessee Valley, some men have grown rich by keeping most farmers poor and backward. They are trying to bottle up the bill authorizing the dams and the electrical industry so they can hold on to their control of them. I wanted to talk to you on the radio tonight to ask you to urge your Representative and Senator to support the Tennessee Valley electrification project. This is *your* government. Its leaders have to listen to *your* will. If they don't, we will throw them on the ashheap of history, where they belong. Thank you, and good night."

"That was President Joe Steele, speaking from the White House," the announcer said. "We'll be right back after this important message."

The important message plugged a brand of coffee that, to Charlie, tasted like Mississippi mud. Lighting a Chesterfield, he asked Esther, "What did you think of the speech, sweetie?"

"Let me have one of those, please," she said. He tossed her the pack. After she lit up, she went on, "I noticed something interesting at the end."

"Like what?"

"He said '*your* government.' He said 'the leaders will listen to *your* will.' But then he said *we* would throw them out if they didn't. Not *you* would—*we* would."

"Are you sure?" Charlie asked. "I didn't catch that."

"I'm positive." Esther nodded emphatically.

"Okay," Charlie said. His wife was nobody's dope. He wouldn't have wanted anything to do with her—well, no, she was pretty enough that he might have wanted something to do with her, but he wouldn't have wanted to marry her—if she had been. He did a little thinking himself. "Probably just political talk. He doesn't want people going after Senators by themselves or anything. That's too much like the Bonus Army."

"Maybe." Esther's cheeks hollowed as she sucked in smoke. She didn't sound a hundred percent convinced, but she didn't argue about it, either. She was easy to get along with. Charlie tried to be the same way, but he had more trouble with it than his wife seemed to.

Whatever Joe Steele meant by switching between *you* and *we*, the speech did what he wanted it to do. It scared the living bejesus out of the people in Congress who were trying to block the bill.

That amused Lazar Kagan. The President's moonfaced aide and Charlie met for lunch at a little Italian restaurant a few blocks from 1600 Pennsylvania Avenue. Charlie ordered spaghetti and meatballs; Kagan chose lasagna. As they started to eat, Joe Steele's underling said, "I would have got the spaghetti, too, only I never have been able to twirl it worth a damn."

Charlie eyed him. He decided Kagan wasn't kidding. "It's not that important," he said. "You could just cut up the noodles and eat 'em with your fork. Plenty of people do— it's easier. I sure wouldn't care."

"You might not," Kagan said, "but the waiter would laugh at me behind my back. So would the dago who runs this joint. If you can't do it so it looks good, you should do something else instead."

That made Charlie eye him again. Kagan seemed perfectly serious. "Is that the kind of thing you tell the President?" Charlie asked, a hint of laughter in his voice so Kagan could laugh, too, and tell him he was full of baloney.

But the Jew nodded. "Not that I need to tell him very often. He's the one who taught me that. Take the Tennessee Valley bill. The President wanted people to let their Congressmen hear from them, right?"

"Sure." Charlie nodded, too. "So?"

"So . . . You haven't heard this from me, you know. This doesn't go in your next story. This is background."

"Sure," Charlie said again, not without some reluctance. Yes, you heard things off the record. That was part of the business. If you broke one source's trust, you risked losing all your sources. If your source had the President's ear, you risked more than that. Sometimes you had to take those risks. More often, you were a sponge. You soaked up what you heard. It might flavor what you wrote, but it wouldn't show up there.

Lazar Kagan ate lasagna as daintily as a cat might have. Dabbing at his full lips with a napkin, he said, "So we make sure the reactionaries hear from the people. The people don't have good handwriting and they don't spell very well, but they sure know what they want. They want dams and electricity in the Tennessee Valley, that's what."

"Wait a minute." Charlie stopped, a twirled forkful of spaghetti in tomato sauce and Parmesan cheese halfway to his mouth. "Are you telling me you cooked up some of those letters?"

"I didn't say that. You said that," Kagan answered, which was what any sensible official would have said in place of *yes*.

"Well, no wonder it's background." Charlie would have been more surprised had he been more shocked. Yes, it was a cheap trick. Yes, it was a sleazy trick. No, it wasn't a new trick. The ancient Greeks had probably used it, scratching their messages on potsherds with nails. Charlie found the next question to ask: "So how's it working?"

"Just fine, thank you very much. They'll report the bill out of committee day after tomorrow. And that isn't background. You can use it."

"And help make it come true." Charlie knew the mysterious ways in which politics often moved.

"Well, maybe. With a little luck." Kagan's voice was bland.

"Why are you telling *me*?" Charlie asked.

"The President likes you," Lazar Kagan said. When Charlie let out a startled yip of laughter, the Jew nodded.

"He does. He thinks you give him a fair shake. That's all he wants, for people to give him a fair shake. He wishes your brother would do the same thing."

Which meant what, exactly? *Make your brother come around and we'll keep feeding you good stories?* Something like that, anyway. Carefully, Charlie said, "Mike writes what he writes, that's all. We quit trying to make each other do stuff about the time we started to shave."

"I have a brother, too. He's a tailor in Bakersfield. So I know what you mean," Kagan said. "I was just telling you what Joe Steele thought."

"Thanks. It's good to know," Charlie said, which was bound to be true in all kinds of ways.

The Tennessee Valley program was the last important bill to go through Joe Steele's special session of Congress. Almost everything the President proposed passed. Although none of Joe Steele's aides would admit it, even off the record, Charlie had the feeling that the few bills which failed were ones the President offered just so they *could* fail. That was a mark of a smart, sly politico—give the lawmakers a few things they could shoot down and they wouldn't worry so much about the rest.

And what did pass was enough and then some. Wall Street operators screeched that the new rules squeezed them like anacondas. So did construction companies in the road- and dam-building businesses. So did union bosses who didn't fancy federally ordered cooling-off periods interrupting their strikes.

You could tell whose ox was being gored by the bellows that came from it. A gored ox might gore back. A gored construction-company executive reached for a lawyer instead. That produced less blood and more noise.

Almost before the ink dried on some of Joe Steele's legislative signatures, Federal judges started ruling the bills unconstitutional. Naturally, Federal lawyers appealed those rulings. Charlie had never found Federal lawyers particularly appealing, but he knew where they got their marching orders.

So did they, and also which side their bread was buttered

on. Anyone who worked for Joe Steele could see the bene-
fits of keeping him happy. The appeals that came out of the
Attorney General's office were uncommonly vehement
and uncommonly urgent. The programs passed in Joe
Steele's special Congressional session zoomed up toward
the Supreme Court as if shot from a battlewagon's big guns.

And the Supreme Court listened to arguments for both
sides, and then it deliberated. Since the turn of the century, the
Democrats had had only eight years to appoint Supreme
Court justices. The rest of the time, the White House lay in
Republican hands. Herbert Hoover might have lost the latest
election, but the Supreme Court didn't care. To a good many
of the justices enshrined in their chamber in the Capitol, even
Hoover was a dangerous liberal.

Which, in their eyes, made Joe Steele . . . well, what, exactly? Not Trotsky, maybe. Not the Antichrist, maybe. Then
again, maybe not. To say the Supreme Court was suspicious
of any changes to the economic life of the country beggared the power of language.

The justices tossed out one of his relief bills: they said it
exceeded the Federal government's authority. They said
the same thing about the bill that regulated Wall Street.
And they said the same thing about the one that limited
management's ability to coerce labor.

Charlie dutifully hammered out stories about the Supreme Court decisions. And he hammered out stories
about the President's reaction to the Supreme Court decisions. He had access to Joe Steele's closest cronies. He had
it, and he used it.

"No, the President isn't happy," Stas Mikoian told him.
"The President doesn't like it when nine old fools try to
torpedo the recovery."

"Can I quote you on that?" Charlie asked.

Mikoian started to nod, but checked himself. "I'm afraid
you'd better not," he said regretfully. "If it gets back to the
nine old fools, they'll really show the President how hard
they can screw him."

Since Charlie was sure Stas had that straight, he just
clucked and said, "That isn't how they teach you things
work in your civics class."

"Things in a civics class work fine," Mikoian answered. "But we aren't in a civics class right now. We're in Washington, dammit. And so are those bastards in the black robes."

When Charlie talked with Vince Scriabin at the White House a couple of weeks later—right after the Supreme Court said the Federal government had no business sticking its snoot into banking regulation, either—the little man they called the Hammer was even blunter than Mikoian had been. "The justices want to bang heads with Joe Steele?" he said. "They'd better have harder heads than I think they do—that's all I've got to tell you."

"What can the President do?" Charlie asked. "The Supreme Court is a separate branch of government. Until they start dropping dead so he can choose his own men, he can't make them call his laws constitutional."

Scriabin leaned back in his swivel chair. It squeaked. The lightbulb in the ceiling fixture flashed off the oval lenses of his wire-framed spectacles. For a few seconds, it turned them big and yellow, so that he might have had an owl's fierce, predatory eyes rather than his own. He could have been preening when he scratched his closely trimmed little mustache. "Nobody elected them," he said in a deadly voice. "If they think they can block what the people want, they'd better think again."

He didn't mean *what the people want*. He meant *what Joe Steele wants*. The two weren't quite the same, but Charlie could see that Scriabin would never admit there was a difference. Anything Joe Steele wanted, the Hammer wanted, too. Anything at all.

"What can Joe Steele do?" Charlie asked again. He didn't think the Capitol would go up in flames and barbecue Charles Evans Hughes and his robed comrades. It crossed his mind, but he didn't believe it. *Mike would,* he thought.

When Vince Scriabin leaned toward Charlie once more, he looked like a small, mild-mannered man, not something that hunted through the night on silent wings. "He'll take care of it," the aide said, and his voice held complete assurance. "Nobody stops Joe Steele, not when he gets going."

That seemed to be the end of that interview. As Charlie

was leaving the White House, he paused to take his umbrella from the stand—it was raining outside. In came a jowly young man whose square head and underslung jaw reminded Charlie of a mastiff. His face was vaguely familiar, but Charlie couldn't hang a name on him. Whoever he was, he wore a sharp fedora and a double-breasted suit that didn't go with his stocky frame.

"Excuse me," he murmured as he closed his own umbrella and thrust it into the polished brass stand. His voice was surprisingly high. He hurried off to whatever appointment he had.

"Who is that fellow?" Charlie asked Scriabin.

Joe Steele's aide smiled a thin smile. "Believe it or not, his name is Hoover."

"Ripley wouldn't believe that!" Charlie said with a snort.

"It's true anyway. He's an investigator in the Justice Department. He's smarter than you'd think from his mug, too. The only thing I wonder about sometimes is whether he's too smart for his own good."

He had to be the guy Mikoian had mentioned a little while before. His look was right—bulldog came closer than mastiff—and so was his job. "What's he doing here today?" Charlie asked.

"I don't know." Scriabin shrugged narrow shoulders. "The President wanted to see him. When Joe Steele sends for you, you come." That last was certainly true. Saying no to Joe Steele was like saying no to a bulldozer. You could say it, sure, but how much good would that do you? As for Scriabin's shrug, Charlie took it with a grain of salt about the size of the Polo Grounds. What was Scriabin there for, if not to know his boss' mind?

Of course, knowing it and talking about it were also two different things. Even talking about it with a reporter in the White House's good graces might not be what the President wanted. Evidently it wasn't, because Vince Scriabin kept his thin lips buttoned tight. With a shrug of his own, Charlie walked out into the rain. He popped the umbrella open. It was coming down harder than it had when he got there.

* * *

Charlie soaked up the last of the gravy from the beef stew on his plate with the heel of a loaf of bread. He smiled across the table at Esther. "That was mighty good," he said, patting his belly to show he meant it.

"I've done worse," she agreed.

"Hey, you're getting the hang of it," Charlie said. Her cooking had been on the catch-as-catch-can side when they got married. Since what he'd called cooking was heating up a can of hash, he couldn't get too critical.

"It's not hard. It's not nearly as hard as running an office," she said—she'd been an administrative assistant before they tied the knot. "It just takes practice, that's all, like anything else." She lit an after-dinner cigarette and blew smoke up at the ceiling. "Charlie?"

"What's cookin', babe?" He knew something was by the way she said his name.

"Would you mind if I look for part-time office work here?"

He frowned. "I'm bringing in enough money. We won't put the Du Ponts outa business any time soon, but we're doing okay."

"I know we are," she said quickly. "It's not for the money, not really, even though a little extra never hurt anybody. It's just . . . I don't know. I kind of feel like I'm rattling around the apartment when you aren't home, and you aren't home a lot of the time."

She'd held her job, held it and done it well, when millions and millions of people lost theirs. If she hadn't done it well, she would have lost it. She might have lost it no matter how well she did it. She was used to going out and taking care of things on her own. But even if she was . . . "I don't want people thinking I can't support you," Charlie said.

"It wouldn't be like that. Honest to Pete, it wouldn't," Esther said. "Before the market crashed, people might've thought that way. Not any more, though. Everybody knows you latch on to anything you can get, 'cause you may be out of work again tomorrow."

"You really want to do this."

She heard that it wasn't a question. "Yeah, I do. I'm all

by myself here. My friends are back in New York. I'd like to get to know people, not just sit in the chair and read sappy novels and listen to the radio all day."

If he told her no, she'd do things his way, or he thought she would. But she wouldn't be happy about it. He didn't need to be Hercule Poirot to have the little gray cells to figure that out. Right now, the apartment probably seemed like a little gray cell to her. Telling her she should stay in it would only cause trouble down the line. Charlie didn't like trouble, not nearly so much as Mike did. He never had.

And so he sighed, not too loud and not too sorrowfully, and said, "Okey-doke. Go ahead and do it. But when you land something, try and get home in time to have dinner on the table for me. Deal?"

"Deal!" She must have expected him to tell her no, because she jumped at the bargain.

Not only did she jump at it, she celebrated it by fixing gin-and-tonics for them. The gin was strong, but that was as much as it had going for it. Charlie sighed again, on a different note this time. "Tastes like it came from somebody's bathtub—or his chemistry set."

"I bet it did," Esther said. "That bottle's from before Repeal. Still not much good stuff on the shelves."

"What there is is expensive, too." Charlie took another sip. "Well, we can drink this. When it's gone, we'll get more, that's all."

"I don't mind the radio so much when I've got company," Esther said. "After I do the dishes, we can listen for a while, have another drink while we do."

"And who knows what'll happen then, huh?" He leered at her.

She glanced back out of the corner of her eye. "Who knows?"

Some nice, romantic music would have been great. But when Charlie turned on the set and the tubes had warmed up, what he got were commercials for soap and shampoo and then one of those smooth-voiced announcers going, "We interrupt our regularly scheduled broadcast so we may bring you an address from the President of the United States."

"What's he going to talk about?" Esther asked.

"Beats me," Charlie answered.

He would have gone on from there, but the President's voice came out of the radio: "This is Joe Steele." He didn't sound smooth. He never did, but tonight even less so than usual. "I need to talk to you tonight because the country has a problem. There are nine old men sitting in a dusty old chamber in the Capitol who think they have the power to do whatever they want with the hopes and dreams of Americans everywhere."

"Uh-oh," Esther said.

"Yeah." Charlie couldn't have put it better himself. When Joe Steele went after something or somebody, he didn't do it halfway.

"You elected the new Congress—you did, the people of the United States," the President went on. Charlie thought he heard cold fury in the voice coming out of the radio. Or Joe Steele might just have been a good actor. How could you know for sure? "You elected the new Congress, and you elected me. I've done everything I know how to do to try to get our country back on its feet again. Congress— well, most of Congress—has helped me by passing the laws that set up my Four Year Plan."

Even when he was mostly talking about something else, he couldn't resist throwing a dart or two at the conservatives the election hadn't swept out of Washington. Whatever else you did, you didn't want to get on his bad side.

"But no one elected the nine old fools in their black robes who sit in their musty room and dare to stop the people's progress," Joe Steele growled. "Why are they doing that? What can they want? They are hurting the country. They are *wrecking* the country. How could any loyal American say that the laws we need to fix what is broken go against the Constitution? There has to be something wrong, something horribly wrong, with anyone who would do that. I don't know what it is, but I tell you this—I'm going to find out."

He kept on for a while after that, but he was firing at the same targets over and over. When he signed off, the announcer sounded faintly stunned and more than faintly relieved to turn the airwaves over to a jazz band.

Charlie and Esther stared at each other. "Wow," Charlie said.

"Wow is right," Esther said. "You could see what he was doing when he went after the Congressmen who were stalling his bills. But what's the point to hammering the Supreme Court like that?"

"I don't know," Charlie answered. "Joe Steele said it himself—nobody elected them. If people write them angry letters, you think they'll care? Not likely. The only way justices leave the Supreme Court is feet first. Once they're there, they're there. The rest of the country's stuck with 'em."

"They could—waddayacallit—impeach them," Esther said. But even she didn't sound as if she believed it would happen.

Neither did Charlie. "You practically have to catch somebody taking bribes on his front lawn to get rid of him that way. The Supreme Court justices aren't doing anything like that, and Joe Steele's got to know it. It's politics, that's all it is. You can't impeach somebody just on account of politics."

"Andrew Johnson," Esther said. "I remember from high school history."

"Uh-huh. But they couldn't throw him out of office, and they had at least as big a bulge in Congress as Joe Steele does."

"Maybe Joe Steele thinks that, if the justices find out how many people can't stand them, they'll start taking a different look at the Constitution," Esther said.

"It could happen. It makes more sense than anything else I can think of—I'll tell you that," Charlie said. "But it could backfire on him, too. They're liable to dig in their heels and toss out all of his laws just because they're his. He's got pride, but so do they."

"Nothing we can do about it except try not to get stuck in the gears when they grind together," Esther said.

"No, there's one more thing I can do," Charlie said.

"Like what?"

"Talk to the White House people tomorrow and see if they know what Joe Steele has in mind. Scriabin didn't the last time I was there—or if he did, he didn't let on. He's got the deadest pan you ever saw. But I'll see what I can pry out of Kagan and Mikoian. Mikoian could be a regular guy if he didn't keep looking over his shoulder so much."

"That's tomorrow," Esther said archly. "What do you intend to do tonight?"

"The wench grows bold," Charlie said. "I expect I'll think of something." And he did.

He had less luck when he called at the White House the next morning. That Justice Department investigator named Hoover was just leaving as Charlie walked in. Hoover smiled at him on the way out. Had Charlie been a kid, that smile would have scared him out of a year's growth. Hoover had one of those faces that seemed only a little south of ordinary in repose or angry. When he smiled, he made you want to run away.

Charlie said as much to Stas Mikoian. He made Mikoian laugh. Nothing frightening about Mikoian when he did; he was handsome in a swarthy, strong-nosed way. "We don't work with Hoover because he's pretty," Stas said.

"Why do you work with him, then?" If he gave Charlie an opening, Charlie'd run through it.

"Because he's one of those people who can take care of things," Mikoian replied.

"What's that supposed to mean?"

"What it says," answered jesting Stas, and would not stay for more questions.

VI

Time went on, and time went on, and time went on some more. The papers had a field day with Joe Steele's speech. They split pretty much down the middle between backing him and calling him a would-be Hitler or Trotsky. That amused Charlie. "I can see calling him one name or the other, but both?" he said to Esther. "If you call him both, then he's somewhere between the two of them. Seems to me that's the right place to be."

"Well, it's hard to get left of Trotsky or right of Hitler," his wife answered, which was bound to be true. Then she went on, "They're both dictators, though, whether they fly the red flag or the swastika. I think that's what the editorial writers were getting at, or aiming at, anyway."

"Huh," Charlie said: a thoughtful grunt. He looked her over in a way unusual for him—altogether untinged by desire. "I sure didn't marry a dummy when I tied the knot with you, did I?"

"I hope not." Esther left it right there. She would toot her own horn sometimes, but never very loud.

After a while, the papers forgot about the speech. To a newspaperman, everything was a nine days' wonder. You reported it, you screamed about it, and then you stopped talking about it because you were too busy screaming about the next nine days' wonder. Charlie understood that a lot of what he wrote, he wrote on the wind. He didn't let it bother him. His bills were paid, he didn't owe anybody in the world a dime (Mike owed him fifteen bucks, and had since not long after the Treaty of Versailles. Charlie wasn't holding his breath about collecting.), and he couldn't think of anything he'd sooner be doing.

He was at the AP office, writing a story about a Congressman from Mississippi who'd never heard of discretion, when the phone on his desk rang. He grabbed it halfway through the second chime. "Sullivan," he barked, hoping for more dirt about the way the Congressman soaked up campaign cash like a greedy sponge.

"Hello, Sullivan." The voice on the other end of the line obviously knew him, but he didn't recognize it right away. It didn't give him a chance to, either, for it continued, "If you're outside the north end of the Capitol tomorrow morning a little before ten o'clock, you'll see something interesting."

"Oh, yeah? What?" he said, but he was talking to a dead line. He took longer to realize that than he might have, too. Swearing under his breath, he hung up.

"What's going on?" asked the newshawk at the next desk.

"Don't know. Crank call, I think." Charlie didn't want anyone else at the Capitol to see—and to write about—whatever there was to see.

"Sometimes I hate telephones," the other reporter said. "They're handy and all, but Christ, they can be annoying."

"You got that right," Charlie said. The other guy—his name was Zach Stark—kept on bellyaching. Charlie listened with less than half an ear. He kept playing the phone call in his mind, over and over again. He hadn't recognized the voice, but he kept feeling he should have.

He couldn't place it, though, so he went back to the story of the Congressman on the take. His stomach rumbled. He was hungry—he should have knocked off for lunch twenty minutes earlier and headed for a diner.

A diner . . . He remembered that one in Chicago going on two years earlier now, the one he'd gone to after the Democrats balloted through the night and broke up in the morning without a nominee. He remembered Vince Scriabin talking into the pay phone in the hallway when he went back to take a leak.

Sure as hell, that was the voice he'd heard just now. So something was cooking, or would be at the Capitol tomorrow morning. The little guy they called the Hammer wouldn't call just to pass the time of day. He wouldn't waste time with a practical joke, either. Charlie could imagine Stas Mikoian doing that, but not Scriabin. As far as Charlie could tell, Scriabin had had his sense of humor surgically removed when he was nine.

Somehow, Charlie would have bet the mansion he didn't own that Scriabin had dropped a nickel in a telephone today, too. It didn't sound like the kind of call that ought to come from the White House. It also didn't sound like the kind of call that ought to be traceable to the White House.

Which meant . . . Who the hell could say what it meant? Had Scriabin wanted him to know, the cold-blooded little bastard would have done more explaining. No, Scriabin wanted him to come see for himself. And Scriabin knew damn well he would, too.

Charlie didn't like being so easy to jerk around. But he would have liked *not* getting that call even less. He didn't want anybody scooping him. And he particularly didn't want Vince Scriabin to help anybody scoop him. He knew too well the Hammer would be chuckling to himself while he did it. Screwing a reporter was almost as much fun as pulling the wings off flies.

Charlie stood outside of the Capitol, waiting for whatever he was waiting for. Inside, Congress was in session and the Supreme Court was deliberating, however little Joe Steele liked that. A new building especially for the court was going up a few blocks away, but it wouldn't be ready to use for another year.

Just on the off chance, Charlie'd brought a photographer with him, a stocky, bald guy named Louie Pappas. Louie had the habit of gnawing on a cigar without ever lighting it. Maybe he wanted to split the difference between smoking and chewing tobacco. Maybe he was simply on the peculiar side.

"So what exactly's going on here?" he asked Charlie.

"I don't know. That's what we're here to find out," Charlie answered. "If it turns out to be nothing, I'll buy you lunch."

"Okay. I'll let you," Louie said. "Not freezing my nuts off

out here, anyhow. Spring's on the way." The air was still cool, but did give promise of warming up some. Hopeful green leaves were starting to show up on what had been bare, bony twigs. Robins hopped across dirt, keeping an eye peeled for worms. Of course, they did that all through the winter, too, so it didn't prove much. Louie pointed at Charlie's watch. "What time you got?"

"Quarter after nine—almost twenty after." Like any halfway decent reporter, Charlie was compulsively early.

A silver-painted panel truck stopped near them. A crew got out and pulled a newsreel camera and tripod from the back. "How about that?" Louie said.

"Yeah, how about that?" Charlie echoed tonelessly. Vince Scriabin must have had more than one nickel in his pocket when he ducked into that telephone booth. Charlie still didn't know what they were waiting for, but now he was sure it would be a story worth writing about.

Louie pointed up Capitol Street. "Look—here comes the parade." The dead cigar twitched in his mouth.

Not all the cars were the same make. Some were Fords, some Chevrolets, while a big, lordly Packard led them. But they all plainly belonged together. They pulled to a stop with that lead Packard—surprise!—right behind the newsreel van.

Doors flew open. Out of the lead Packard sprang the Hoover who wasn't Herbert. He wore a dark blue pin-striped suit and a pale gray fedora that marked him as a commander like a ship captain's white-crowned cap. In his right hand he carried a gleaming revolver.

More men jumped from the plebeian cars. All their hats were dark. Some of them had pistols, too. Others cradled Tommy guns with big drum magazines full of death. Most of them looked to be advancing on forty. Unless Charlie missed his guess, they would have gone Over There in the Great War, and gone over the top, too. Their faces had that hard, ready-for-anything look.

Hoover waved them forward. "Come on, men!" he shouted. "We'll clean out that nest of vipers, all right!"

As the newsreel cameraman cranked away and Louie snapped photo after photo, Hoover and his followers (They had to come from the Department of Justice, didn't they? Well, didn't they?) charged into the Capitol. After a couple of seconds of dithering, Charlie charged after them. He didn't *think* a gun battle would break out in one of the two great centers of the Federal government. He sure hoped not.

Inside the North Small Rotunda, a cop who looked almost old enough to have fought on one side or the other at Pickett's Charge wagged a finger at Hoover and said, "What do you think you're doing in here with all that firepower?"

"I'm doing the nation's business, that's what!" Hoover snapped. He waved a piece of paper that might have been a warrant or might have been his laundry list. "Get out of our way, pop, or you'll be sorry."

The flummoxed cop retreated. Hoover and his men advanced: north into the Supreme Court Rotunda and then, with no ceremony whatever, into the maroon-draped, semicircular Supreme Court Chamber. Charlie heard the lawyer arguing his case before the nine justices let out an undignified squawk and then fall silent. In that lawyer's shoes, Charlie figured he would have shut up, too.

Chief Justice Charles Evans Hughes glowered down from the bench at Hoover and his gun-toting followers. "What is the meaning of this?" Hughes demanded, a normally meaningless question more serious than usual because it was plain he had no idea what the meaning of this was.

Hoover waved that paper again. "I have warrants here for the arrest of four Associate Justices," he answered, not without pride.

Hughes stared at him. The Chief Justice's reading glasses made his eyes look even bigger than they would have anyway. "You're out of your mind!" he exclaimed.

"The Devil, I am," Hoover said cheerfully. "Associate Justice Willis Van Devanter. Associate Justice James Clark McReynolds. Associate Justice George Sutherland. And Associate Justice Pierce Butler." He read out the names and titles with somber relish.

All four men named yelled abuse at him till Charles Evans Hughes raised a hand and calmed the tumult. "This is ridiculous. Absurd," Hughes said. "What possible charge could you bring against these men?"

Was that the tiniest smirk on Hoover's face? "Treason, Your Honor," he said, and turned back to his pistoleers and Tommy gunners. "Grab them, boys, and take them away."

Supreme Court justices—almost half the court—handcuffed while still in their judicial robes and shoved into motorcars by Justice Department soldiers carrying trench brooms? Now that was a sensation! Louie Pappas snapped away. The newsreel guy slapped in a fresh roll of film so he could get all the juicy action.

And Charlie interviewed Hoover. Hoover turned out to be John Edgar, and went by J. Edgar. "Yes, treason," J. Edgar Hoover said in his high-pitched rasp. "They have given aid and comfort to the enemies of the United States. That's how the Constitution defines treason."

"But . . . who are the enemies of the United States?" Charlie asked. "Last I looked, we weren't at war with anybody."

"Not in the declared sense of the word. Not in the shooting sense of the word," Hoover . . . admitted? No, he denied it, because he went on, "We have enemies anyway, Mr. Sullivan. There are plenty of countries in Europe that hate the American way of life and want to do everything they know how to do to tear it down. That's the truth, the whole truth, and nothing but the truth." He stuck his chin out even farther than usual, as if defying Charlie to disagree with him.

Charlie didn't, or not exactly. He was too busy wondering how this Hoover—J. Edgar Hoover—knew his name, and why. He also wondered some other things. "These Supreme Court justices, they're in cahoots with countries on the far side of the Atlantic?"

"That's what the warrant says, Mr. Sullivan." Oh, yes, Hoover knew his name, all right. That did worry him.

"Are they in cahoots with the Reds in Russia, or the Nazis in Germany, or maybe with Mussolini?"

"It will all come out in the proceedings against them, Mr. Sullivan. I promise you, it will all come out in the proceedings against them." Hoover sounded very sure of himself. He turned to holler to his men: "Take them away! Take them to prison!"

Off went the cars with the justices—the prisoners—in them. "How happy do you think the American people will be when they learn you've arrested close to half the Supreme Court?" Charlie asked.

"I don't think they'll be happy at all," J. Edgar Hoover said. "I think they'll be angry that such important people could betray the country this way. I think that's how anybody with even one drop of loyal American blood in his veins will feel."

Charlie hadn't meant the question like that. Politicians made a living by answering questions in ways that worked to their advantage. Charlie hadn't thought a Justice Department investigator would have learned how to be slippery like that.

"Can you tell me how you found out that the justices did—or were supposed to have done—the things you're accusing them of?" Charlie asked.

"Information was developed. Leads were pursued. Evidence was accumulated—painstakingly accumulated. I can absolutely assure you that the investigation was one of the most thorough in the history of the Department of Justice. I can't go into all the details, because I don't want to prejudice the proceedings. When things start, you'll be impressed. All of America will be impressed. I guarantee you it will."

He could assure and guarantee as much as he wanted, especially when he didn't talk about the evidence to back his assurances and guarantees. Charlie tried again: "Who tipped you off? How did the Department of Justice find out about what you say the Supreme Court justices were up to?"

"For obvious reasons, Mr. Sullivan, I can't discuss our sources without compromising them," Hoover said primly.

"Okay. Fine," Charlie said. "Let me give you a different question, then. Is it a coincidence that the justices you just arrested are the justices who voted against the President's bills the most often and called them unconstitutional?"

"No, it's not a coincidence," J. Edgar Hoover said. Charlie's jaw fell; he'd looked for anything but that blunt agree-ment. A battering ram in pinstripes, Hoover thumped Charlie's chest with a blunt forefinger and plowed ahead: "Those crooks have been working to tear down the country any way they can. Blocking legislation that helps us dig our way out of our hole is an important way to keep us weak and poor and divided."

"I . . . see." Charlie scribbled in his notebook. This was explosive stuff—if they could prove it. "Is that the line of reasoning you're going to present when the justices go to trial?"

Hoover shrugged football-player shoulders. "I'm only an investigator, Mr. Sullivan. I'm not the prosecutor who will try the case. So I'm afraid I'm the wrong fella to ask about that."

Tell me another one, Charlie thought. If anything about J. Edgar Hoover was crystal clear, it was how much he admired J. Edgar Hoover. If he was po'-mouthing himself, he had to be doing it so he could duck the question.

But Charlie didn't see how he could push Hoover without putting his back up and making him pull his head into his shell. Sometimes the best thing you could do was quit while you were even if not ahead. "Thanks for your time, then," he said. "Can we get a few more pictures, please?"

Using *please* and *thank you* was more important than keeping your car well greased. Charlie waved Louie forward. Hoover grinned and smirked for the camera. He was much more alarming when he did that than when the usual scowl stayed on his blunt mug. The scowl, you felt, belonged there. The more cheerful expressions seemed as phony, and as nourishing, as a plaster-of-Paris ham.

Hoover got back into the Packard. The driver whisked him away. "Holy crap, Charlie," Louie said.

"You said a mouthful," Charlie answered. "You get some good shots?"

"Oh, you bet I did," the photographer said. "Only thing I'm worried about is if what's-his-name—J. Edgar—busted my lens there at the end. Talk about homely!"

"He won't win Miss America any time soon," Charlie agreed. "Don't let him hear you say so, that's all. Otherwise, you'll wind up in the cell across the hall from the Supreme Court."

"Listen, Charlie, I done a bunch o' stupid things in my time, but I ain't never been dumb enough to give a flatfoot an excuse to work out on me. Too many times, them sonsabitches don't even need one," Louie said. "And that Hoover character, he's a heap big chief flatfoot, him and his chrome-plated roscoe." The photographer spat on the sidewalk to show what he thought of that.

"There you go," Charlie said. "Let's get back to the office. You give 'em your pictures, and I'll write the piece that goes with 'em."

Naturally, the arrests of the Supreme Court Four caused banner headlines to flower in newspapers from sea to shining sea. Just as naturally, the papers split on party lines. The ones that backed Joe Steele called the justices the worst traitors since Benedict Arnold—if not since Judas Iscariot. The ones that didn't like the President called him even worse.

It came out . . . somehow . . . that the foreign country the justices were said to be working for was Germany. In Berlin, William L. Shirer asked Adolf Hitler what he thought of the justices' arrest. The *Führer*, he reported, looked at him as if he'd lost his marbles. "Except for Hollywood, I pay no attention to the United States," Hitler answered. "As for these judges, are they Jews?"

"Not so far as I know," Shirer said.

Hitler shrugged. "Well, perhaps they need purging even so." Not too much later, during the Night of the Long Knives, he showed he knew everything he needed to know about purges.

Meanwhile, the Supreme Court Four and their lawyers demanded writs of *habeas corpus* so they could appear in court and try to show that they'd been improperly arrested and imprisoned. A judge on the U.S. Court of Appeals refused to issue the writs. So did the judges of the U.S. District Court for Washington.

That fed fresh conniptions. Everybody who didn't like Joe Steele quoted Article I, Section 9 of the Constitution: *The privilege of the Writ of Habeas Corpus shall not be suspended, unless when in Cases of Rebellion or Invasion the public Safety may require it.*

The judges, of course, were judges, and didn't have to explain why they did what they did. Joe Steele didn't *have* to explain anything, either. His stern face didn't encourage people who hankered for explanations. But he did talk to reporters not long after the Associate Justices went to their cells.

"I don't know what everyone is getting so excited about," he said. "It's not as if *habeas corpus* hasn't been suspended before. Lincoln did it, for instance."

"That was during a rebellion!" Three reporters shouted the same thing at the same time. Charlie was one of them, as much to see what Joe Steele would do as for any other reason. Poking the animal behind the bars to make it jump and roar wasn't always a reporter's smallest pleasure.

Joe Steele didn't jump or roar. He made a small production of filling his pipe and getting it going. After sending up some smoke signals, he said, "Friends, I have news for you. The Constitution is not a suicide pact. As Lincoln asked when Chief Justice Taney complained about his suspension of *habeas corpus*, 'Are all the laws, but one, to go unexecuted, and the government itself go to pieces, lest that one be violated?' The men who have been arrested are a clear and present danger to the United States. They must not be set at liberty to subvert the country further until proceedings against them are complete."

Walter Lippmann looked ready to blow a gasket. "Lincoln did what he did during the Civil War!" the liberal columnist called. "We aren't at war now!"

"No?" Joe Steele puffed some more. He turned his head toward Lippmann, his expression as opaque as usual. "Isn't the United States at war against hunger, and against poverty, and against want? Aren't those four justices fighting for the enemy?"

"That has nothing to do with treason, or with spying for Germany," Lippmann said. "And we're at peace with Germany."

"The Attorney General will show in the proceedings against these men how they follow Hitler's lead and take Hitler's money," Joe Steele answered. "And we were at war with Germany not so long ago, and we may be again one day, if Hitler stays on the road he is walking. Not all enemies openly declare themselves beforehand."

"You're dancing on the Constitution for your own purposes!" Lippmann exclaimed.

Puff. Puff. "I don't think so, Mr. Lippmann," Joe Steele said coolly. "I have the responsibility. All you have is a deadline. I am not sorry the writs of *habeas corpus* were denied. Those men will keep hurting the country if they are set free, or else run away to their Nazi paymasters."

All you have is a deadline. That was the best answer Charlie had heard from a man in power to a poking, prodding reporter. Still . . . "You won't change your mind?" Charlie asked.

For the first time at the press conference, Joe Steele looked honestly surprised. "Change my mind? Of course not." The idea might never have occurred to him before. His voice firmed as he went on, "The four traitors from the Supreme Court will stay in prison until proceedings against them go forward."

And that was about as much that as anything was ever likely to be.

*H*ABEAS *C*ORPUS DENIED AGAIN! shouted the *New York Post*. The smaller subhead was PRESIDENT SAYS SUPREME COURT TRAITORS TO STAY JAILED TILL TRIALS. Mike Sullivan eyed the words in the newspaper that paid his salary as if they belonged to some language other than English.

He went through the whole story, which even quoted a couple of questions from his brother. He was shaking his head before he got halfway down, and shaking it more than ever by the time he tossed the paper down on his desk. "Man," he said. "Man, oh, man."

He was working on a piece about a Wall Street brokerage house where money kept disappearing into thin air . . . and into brokers' pockets. He couldn't keep his mind on his writing. He picked up the paper and read the story about Joe Steele's press conference over and over. If *habeas corpus* went bye-bye . . .

"If *habeas corpus* goes bye-bye, we're all screwed. Every

one of us," he said at lunch that day. The stuffed cabbage on his plate left something to be desired. The Goulash House was around the corner from the *Post*'s offices, and was cheap and quick. Good? That could be a different story. Sometimes you'd rather talk than eat.

"Have his carcase," one of the other reporters said between forkfuls of Wiener schnitzel.

"Not funny, Ken," Mike said.

"Hey, I thought it was," Ken said. "That's the name of the Dorothy Sayers mystery from a coupla years ago, remember?"

"Um—" Mike hoped he looked sheepish, because he felt that way. "I forgot all about it, to tell you the truth. Stella likes whodunits, but I go in more for adventure stuff."

Ken turned to the guy behind the counter. "Hey, Jules, draw me a Falstaff, willya?"

Jules, Mike happened to know, was really named Gyula. "I vill do dat," he said—his accent sounded just like Bela Lugosi's, only he didn't have pointy teeth or turn into a bat. Mike had never seen him turn into a bat, anyhow.

The reporter chuckled to himself, but not for long. Nothing seemed funny in light of the day's big story. "I'm not kidding," Mike said. "Honest to God, Joe Steele wants to make like Mussolini or Hitler. Without *habeas corpus*, he can throw anybody in the can for as long as he wants and lose the key."

Ken swigged from his beer. "He can, sure, but will he? Why would he? You put people in jail for no reason, you get all their friends and relations ticked off at you and you lose the next election."

"So what's he doing, then?" Mike demanded.

"You ask me, he's putting the old squeeze play on the Supreme Court," Ken answered. "They bounced some laws of his, and he's telling them there's a price for everything even if they do wear those black robes. It'll all have a happy ending, just like in the movies."

That was the first explanation of the arrests besides the notion that Joe Steele was a hatching tyrant that made any kind of sense to Mike. But he said, "I bet he starts a forest fire when he wants to light a cigarette, too."

Ken chuckled. "C'mon—you know he smokes a pipe."

If they'd been back in the newsroom, Mike would have given him the finger. In a restaurant, even one as crummy as the Goulash House, he held back. All he said was, "You shoulda been a lawyer or a barber. You're good for nothing but splitting hairs."

"Har-de-har-har. See how hard I'm laughing?" Ken slid a couple of quarters across the counter. Jules/Gyula started to give him a nickel back, but he waved it away. He poked Mike. "See you in paradise."

"Hold on. I'm coming." Mike took one more bite, paid the counterman, and escaped the Goulash House.

He still had trouble getting anywhere with the latest Wall Street story after he went back to his beat-up desk. Stan Feldman, not seeing it when he wanted it, breathed down his neck, which was one of the things editors were for. "Sorry, Stan," Mike said, and meant it, because he took pride in getting work done on deadline. "The whole thing with Joe Steele's thrown me for a loop."

"Well, you better straighten up and fly right." When dealing with a story that wasn't there, Feldman had all the warmth and understanding of an undertaker or a principal.

"Story may not be as good as I wanted it to be." Mike spread his hands in apology.

"*Good* I can live without sometimes," his editor answered. "The story, I can't. Get it on my desk by half past four."

Mike got it on his desk by half past four. It wasn't as good as he wished it would have been. The only reason it was even as good as it was was that he knew how to put stories together. He could do it while most of his brain was chewing on something else. *Let's hear it for experience,* he thought.

He wanted to work on something important, dammit, something that would get him remembered. The brokerage-house story wasn't it. He'd had hopes for the piece when he sailed into it, but it was just one more tale of greed. The world had seen too many of them lately. They'd helped spark the Depression, and they kept popping up in its aftermath. Greed was as common a driver as sex—too common to make most of the stories about it very interesting.

Greed for power, now . . . If Ken was right, Joe Steele was playing rougher than a President had any business playing. *And if Ken's wrong, then I'm right,* Mike thought. *And if I'm right, we're in even more trouble than we were when the market crashed.*

The kid from the mailroom threw an envelope on Mike's desk. "What's this?" Mike asked.

"I dunno." The kid was steady, but not long on brains. "Somethin' for you."

"Okay. I'll investigate." Mike pulled his letter-opener out of the top drawer. It was overqualified for its job: it was a saw-toothed German bayonet from the Great War, as long as a young sword, the kind the hero in *All Quiet on the Western Front* said you needed to grind down because Entente soldiers would kill you if they caught you with it.

It bit into yellow-brown heavy paper as readily as it would have torn through flesh. Inside were four typewritten sheets stapled together. Paperclipped to them was a note. *I finally found this—never mind where,* it said. *With everything that's going on in Washington these days, it's extra interesting.*

The note was unsigned. Mike pulled the envelope out of the wastebasket. It had no return address. But it was postmarked in Menands, the little town next door to Albany where the minor-league team played its games.

And the four typewritten pages were the missing arson inspector's report on the fire that gutted the Executive Mansion and killed Franklin D. Roosevelt in the summer of 1932. So Mike could make a pretty good guess about who'd sent it to him. But it would only be a guess—he couldn't prove a thing. That had to be just the way the clerk in the Albany Fire Department wanted it.

Mike dove into the report headfirst. When he came up again on the other side, he was blowing like a whale. No wonder the arson report had vanished from the file! It didn't quite say the fire *had* been set. It mentioned the possibility of liquor bottles or rubbing alcohol helping the flames spread so fast. But it sure implied that the conflagration and the way it engulfed the old building weren't accidental.

Whistling tunelessly between his teeth, Mike picked up the report and took it into Stan's office. He dropped it on the editor's desk. Stan was on the phone. He glanced down at the report. Then he took a longer look and stiffened. "Al?" he said. "Listen, lemme call you back in a little while." He hung up. Glaring at Mike, he asked, "Where the hell'd you get *this*?"

"A little bird dropped it in the mailbox," Mike said.

"Some little bird. Jesus!" Stan went through the report faster than Mike had. When he looked up again, he said, "What do you want to do with it?" Then he took a pint of Old Crow out of his own desk drawer, swigged, and offered Mike the bourbon. Mike drank, too. He needed it.

"I want to get it out there," he said when he could breathe again—straight bourbon on an empty stomach in midmorning wasn't something he did every day. "People have the right to know how Roosevelt died. When you add in what my brother heard the morning before—"

Stan held up a hand like a traffic cop. "You can't write that, on account you can't prove it connects. Your brother didn't hear what's-his-face go, 'Okay, cook Roosevelt tonight.' He just heard him say, 'Take care of it'—whatever *it* is." He slammed the report with his fist. "Not even all the way sure it was arson. Probably, the guy says, but not for sure."

"Even probably is dynamite." The Old Crow seemed to make Mike's wits work double-quick. "How about this? I write about the report, and I make sure I leave the probably in. Then I write about how Franklin Roosevelt and Joe Steele were locking horns for the nomination summer before last, how Roosevelt was edging ahead and might've won if he didn't burn to a crisp. I won't say that I think Joe Steele and his merry men had anything to do with the fire, but you'll be able to read between the lines if you want to."

Stan studied him. Then the editor took another knock from the bottle, a bigger one this time. "No matter how careful you write it, you're gonna be in deep shit as soon as it comes out. So will I."

"I won't make any accusations. If you think I do, you'll take 'em out," Mike said.

"Even so," Stan said. "Joe Steele and his boys, they've got a memory like an elephant for anybody who does 'em dirt. And you're already on their list from before, don't forget."

"So?" Mike shrugged. "If we let 'em scare us out of doing our job, they've already won, right?"

Stan cast a longing look at the flat-sided bottle of Old Crow, but didn't drink again. "Easy to talk brave when you aren't really putting anything on the line," he remarked, not quite apropos of nothing. He eyed the bourbon one more time, then sighed and shook his head. "Go write the goddamn story. Maybe I'll run it, or maybe I'll can it. Right now, I've got no idea. Go on—get the hell outa here."

As Mike left, he saw the editor pick up the telephone. *Getting back to his bookie or whoever that was,* he thought. He ran a sheet of paper into the Underwood upright and pounded away. Words flowed out of him. This wasn't hard labor, the way the brokerage story had been. If Someone put him on earth, it was to do something like this.

He laid the story on Stan's desk after stashing a carbon where it wouldn't be easy to find. An hour later, the managing editor walked by his desk. He nodded and raised his right thumb. "Now the fun starts," he said.

"About time," Mike answered. He wondered if he meant it. Well, he'd get the chance to find out.

VII

When Lazar Kagan called Charlie to the White House, it might be anything. When Stas Mikoian wanted to meet with him, what came from that was more likely than not to be interesting. And when Vince Scriabin told him to get his tail down to the President's residence, chances were Joe Steele was steamed at him.

Charlie knew why Joe Steele was steamed, too, though he figured he would do better to seem taken by surprise. So when the man they called the Hammer slammed his fist down on a copy of the *New York Post* from three days earlier and growled, "Have you seen this crap from your brother?" Charlie just shook his head. Scriabin shoved the paper across his desk. "Well, look at it, then."

It didn't come right out and accuse Joe Steele of roasting marshmallows in the flames while Franklin Roosevelt sizzled. Then again, you didn't need to be Lord Peter Wimsey to see what Mike was driving at.

"I don't know what you want me to do about it," Charlie said when he got done. "Mike is Mike, and I'm me. I didn't have anything to do with this." That was true, and then again it wasn't. If Charlie hadn't overheard Scriabin in that diner, and if he hadn't told Mike about it, his brother wouldn't have been able to invite the people who read his story to connect the dots.

Scriabin remained coldly furious. Like the man he worked for, he was scarier for not making a show of losing his temper. "I know you didn't," he said now. "You'd be sorry if you did." Charlie gulped, and hoped it didn't show. Scriabin went on, "Your brother had better think twice before he libels the President of the United States."

"There's no libel in this," Charlie said.

"Saying things you know to be untrue, saying them with malice, is libel even when you say them about a public figure," Scriabin insisted.

"There's no libel," Charlie said once more. "He quotes the arson inspector's report. That says the fire might have been set or it might not. He says that Joe Steele was just about sure of the nomination after Roosevelt died. Both those things are true. But he doesn't say anywhere that Joe Steele had anything to do with starting the fire."

Vince Scriabin stared at him, pudgy face hard as a stone. "I know he is your brother. I make allowances for that. I know your own stories have been more fair and balanced toward this administration. I also make allowances for that. But if your brother writes another piece that is so monumentally prejudiced against the President and everything he's working to accomplish, there will be no allowances left to make. Do you understand me?"

"I hear you," Charlie answered.

"All right," Scriabin said. "Make sure your brother understands me, too. Have you got that?"

"Oh, yes." Charlie nodded. "You're coming in loud and clear."

"Good." Vince Scriabin spat the word out. "I do not want anyone to have any doubts whatsoever about how we view this . . . trash. Now get the hell out of here."

Charlie made his exit. As if he were walking out of a police station, he was glad he *could* make his exit. The back of his shirt was wet with sweat, and it hadn't sprung from Washington humidity. He'd never had that narrow-escape feeling walking out of the White House before. He hoped to heaven he never did again.

The sun wasn't over the yardarm yet. Charlie didn't give a damn. He ducked into the nearest bar and ordered himself a double bourbon. If anything would smooth him out of his jitters, that ought to do it.

"There you go, sonny," said the white-haired man two stools down from him. "Two or three more of those and you'll be a man before your mother."

By the way he talked and by the empty glasses on the bar in front of him, he'd already had at least two or three more. *What the hell business is it of yours?* Charlie started to ask. But then he recognized the other barfly. "Mr. Vice President!" he exclaimed.

John Nance Garner nodded. "You got me, sonny," he said, the bourbon only thickening his Texas drawl. "And a hell of a git you got. I was Speaker of the House before Joe Steele tapped me. Remember? Speaker! That was a real job, by Jesus! Not like this one." He nodded to the bartender. "Fill me up again, Roy."

"Comin' up, Cactus Jack." The colored man made him another tall bourbon. John L. Lewis had called Garner a poker-playing, whiskey-drinking, evil old man. Charlie didn't know about the other attributes, but drink whiskey Garner could.

"What's wrong with being Vice President?" Charlie asked. "You're a heartbeat away from the White House. That's what everybody says—a heartbeat away."

"A heartbeat away, and further'n the moon," Garner said. "Thing with being Vice President is, you don't *do* anything. You sit there an' grow moss, like I'm doin' here. Sure got nothin' better to do. I tell you, bein' Vice President ain't worth a bucket of warm piss."

"What would you do if you were President? How do you like the job Joe Steele is doing?" Charlie hadn't expected to run into Garner, but he'd take advantage of it now that he had.

The Vice President's eyes were narrow to begin with. They gimleted more now. "You won't get me to say anything bad about him, kiddo," he replied. "I may be drunk, but I ain't that drunk—or that stupid. He's a man you don't want to get on the wrong side of."

"Really? I never would have guessed," Charlie said, deadpan.

For a second, Garner took that literally. Then he chuckled and coughed, shifting all the smoker's phlegm in his chest. "That's right. You're one of those reporter bastards. You know all about Joe Steele, or you reckon you do." He chuckled and coughed some more. The horrible sound made Charlie want to swear off cigarettes for life. "Yeah, you reckon you do—but you'll find out."

The proceedings against the Supreme Court Four opened that autumn. They opened suddenly, in fact, before a military tribunal, only a few days after J. Edgar Hoover—that man again!—announced an arrest in the kidnapping of the Lindbergh baby more than two years earlier. Charlie wondered if the timing of the two events was a coincidence. A cynical newspaperman? Him? Even he laughed at himself.

He wondered about the fellow J. Edgar Hoover arrested, too. Bruno Hauptmann was a German in the USA illegally. He had a criminal record back in the *Vaterland*. Considering how Joe Steele felt about Adolf Hitler, couldn't he be a sucker who got caught in a net way bigger than he was?

And, considering that the four justices were accused of plotting with the Nazis, couldn't arresting a German for the Lindbergh kidnapping be set up to show that you couldn't trust a kraut no matter what—and that you couldn't trust any Americans who had much to do with krauts? Again, Charlie didn't know about that. He couldn't prove it. But he did some more wondering.

He did that wondering very quietly, either by himself or with Esther. None of it got into the bull sessions that political reporters had among themselves or with the big wheels they covered. Not even liberal doses of bourbon made his tongue slip. He noticed he might not be the only one who wasn't saying everything he might have had on his mind. It was a careful time. Everybody seemed to do his best to walk on eggshells without breaking them.

Charlie also didn't do any wondering that Mike could hear or read. Mike, of course, could get ideas on his own, but Charlie didn't want to give him any. A small but noisy segment of the press hated Joe Steele and everything he did. To those folks, Mike was a hero, a man who'd uncovered secrets and pulled the blankets away from dark plots.

Joe Steele's backers tagged Mike for a hateful, lying skunk. Anyone would think they'd listened to Vince Scriabin, or something. And the vast majority of Americans paid no attention to the name of Mike Sullivan. Times were still tough. They tried to get by from one day to the next, and didn't worry about anything much past Tuesday's supper or the month's rent.

The Attorney General was a tough-talking Polack prosecutor from Chicago named Andy Wyszynski. He wasn't leery of taking on spectacular cases. He'd been part of the legal team that tried to convict Belva Gaertner when she shot her lover. Belva not only walked, but one of the reporters wrote a hit play about her. Wyszynski's comment after the verdict was, "Juries are full of jerks."

From everything Charlie had seen, Wyszynski wasn't wrong, even if the crack didn't endear him to the sob sisters. He wasn't the endearing sort. A big, fleshy man, he had a face like a clenched fist. Like Vince Scriabin and like Joe Steele himself, he wasn't a man you wanted mad at you.

He'd learned a thing or three from that Roaring Twenties trial. Then, the prosecution let the defense set the agenda. They thought they had an open-and-shut case. As a matter of fact, they did, but Belva's lawyer wouldn't let them shut it.

This time, Wyszynski rolled out the heavy artillery before the military judges were chosen. He showed off for the newspapers. He had all kinds of things to show off, too. Wires back and forth between Berlin and Washington. Letters in German on swastika stationery with generals' illegible signatures. Stacks of swastika-bedizened Reichsmarks, some still in bank wrappers with German writing in Gothic letters on them. Bank transactions showing Reichsmarks converted into dollars. All kinds of good stuff.

Like the rest of the Washington press corps, Charlie wrote stories about the goodies Wyszynski showed off. Among themselves, the reporters were more skeptical. "In a real trial, a lot of that shit wouldn't even get admitted," said one who'd done a lot of crime stories. "In this military tribunal thing, though, who the hell knows?"

"How come it isn't a real trial?" another man asked. "On account of they're scared they'd lose it if it was one?"

"There's more to it than that," Charlie said. "They tried treason cases with military tribunals during the Civil War, so they've got some precedent."

The other reporter looked at him. "You'd know that stuff. You're the teacher's pet, right? It's your bad, bad brother who keeps getting paddled."

"Hey, fuck you, Bill," Charlie said. "You think I'm the teacher's pet, we can step outside and talk about it."

Bill started to get up from his barstool. Another reporter put a hand on his arm. "Take it easy. Charlie's okay."

"Nobody who has anything good to say about that lying so-and-so in the White House is okay, you ask me," Bill said.

"Well, who asked you? Sit back down and have another drink. You sound like you could use one."

Having another drink struck Charlie as a good idea, too. It often did. After he got half of it down, he said, "Even if it is a military tribunal, I think it'll be interesting. They'll have to let the press in. If they let the press in, they'll have to give the justices lawyers and let 'em speak their piece. And when they do that, all bets are off. Those guys were all lawyers themselves before they were judges. Probably fifty-fifty they can talk their way out of everything."

"*You* say that?" Bill sounded as if he didn't trust his ears.

"Why wouldn't I?" Charlie returned.

"'Cause . . . Ah, shit. Maybe I had you wrong."

"This round's on me, boys!" Charlie sang out. People whooped and pounded him on the back. He went on, "I'll do the same thing next time Bill admits he's wrong, too. That oughta be—oh, I dunno, about 1947. Or 1948."

"Up yours, Sullivan," Bill said. But he let Charlie buy him a drink.

You could hold a military tribunal anywhere. Military courts, by the nature of things, had to be portable. Andy Wyszynski—or perhaps Joe Steele—chose to hold this one in the lobby of the District Court Building on Indiana Avenue. The lobby gave reporters and photographers and newsreel cameramen plenty of room to work. Sure enough, this proceeding would get as much publicity as the government could give it.

In front of the District Court Building's somewhat beat-up classical façade stood a statue of Abraham Lincoln. Charlie pointed to it on the way in. "Betcha that statue's another reason they're trying the justices here. Remember how Joe Steele went on and on about Lincoln and treason and *habeas corpus*—I mean, no *habeas corpus*—during the Civil War?"

"Sure do." Louie Pappas nodded. "Betcha you're right." The dead cigar in the photographer's mouth twitched every time he talked.

Up the broad flight of stairs they went. The walls of the lobby were of tan plaster. The floor was marble. The officers of the tribunal had already taken their places behind a table on a dais. The chairman was a Navy officer. A neat sign announced his name: Captain Spruance. The other three military judges belonged to the Army: Colonel Marshall, Major Bradley, and Major Eisenhower. Each man had a microphone in front of his place, no doubt for the benefit of the newsreels.

Attorney General Wyszynski sat at the prosecutors' table, drinking coffee and talking in a low voice with an aide. Two lawyers from the American Civil Liberties Union muttered to each other at the defense table. One looked quite snappy; the other wore the loudest checked suit Charlie'd ever seen. Of the Supreme Court Four there was as yet no sign.

More reporters and photographers filed in to fill their assigned sections. "We will begin at ten o'clock sharp," Captain Spruance said, his voice soft even with a mike. He looked more like a minister or a professor than a military man. Colonel Marshall had that professorial look, too. Spruance went on, "No one from the press will be admitted after that. And we must have silence from the observers. Anyone creating a disturbance will be ejected and will not be allowed to return for the duration of the proceeding."

Military policemen, shore patrolmen, and U.S. marshals from the Justice Department stood ready to do whatever he told them to do. Charlie intended to keep his trap shut. He wouldn't have been surprised if somebody raised a ruckus, though.

At ten o'clock on the dot, Captain Spruance said, "Let the tribunal be sealed." The doors were closed and locked. A late-arriving reporter banged on them in vain. Through the banging, Spruance continued, "Let the accused be brought before the tribunal."

He looked to the left. Charlie's gaze, and everyone else's, followed his. A door opened. The newsreel cameras swung towards it. This would be the first time anyone but their jailers had set eyes on the Supreme Court Four since their spectacular arrest.

Out they came, Justices McReynolds, Butler, Sutherland, and Van Deventer. They all wore suits of good cut and somber gray or blue or black wool. Charlie thought they looked thinner than they had when they were taken away, but he wasn't sure. They'd worn robes then, which might have expanded their outline. He was pretty sure they were paler than they had been. Wherever Joe Steele had stowed them, they hadn't got to sunbathe there. He saw no lumps or bruises that might have shown rough treatment, though.

MPs with Tommy guns shepherded the accused men to their table. As they sat, the ACLU lawyer in the horrible clothes whispered something to Justice McReynolds. Whatever answer he got, it made him do a double take Harpo Marx would have been proud of. He whispered again.

After a moment, Captain Spruance said, "The accused will rise." The men obeyed. "State your names for the record," he told them.

"James McReynolds."

"Pierce Butler."

"Associate Justice George Sutherland."

"Willis Van Deventer."

To the chief petty officer transcribing the testimony, Spruance said, "Yeoman, you will disregard the title claimed by the accused Sutherland."

"Aye, aye, sir," the yeoman replied.

"Be seated," Spruance told the Supreme Court Four. They sat once more. He went on, "You are all accused of treason against the United States, of collusion with a foreign power, and of perverting your high office to the detriment of the American people. Mr. McReynolds, how say you to these charges?"

"May it please Your Honor—" Justice McReynolds began.

Captain Spruance held up a hand. "This is a military proceeding, not a court of law in the strict sense of the words. You will address me as *sir*."

"Yes, sir." McReynolds licked his lips, then went on with no expression in his voice: "May it please you, sir, I wish to plead guilty and to throw myself on the mercy of the court—uh, the tribunal."

Both ACLU lawyers sprang into the air as if they'd just sat on long, sharp tacks. Several reporters and cameramen exclaimed as well. Charlie wouldn't have sworn that he wasn't one of them. Of all the things he and everybody else had looked for, a guilty plea was the last one. Or maybe somebody had looked for it—at the prosecutors' table, Attorney General Wyszynski leaned back in his chair and looked like a cat blowing a couple of feathers off its nose.

Spruance might not have presided over a court of law per se, but they'd issued him a gavel anyhow. He used it vigorously. "We will have order here," he said. "Remember my earlier warning. Disruptive persons will be ejected." Still, he made no move to signal to his enforcers.

"Sir," said the ACLU man in the dreadful suit, "I object to this so-called confession. It's obviously coerced, and—"

"It's no such thing." Andy Wyszynski spoke for the first time. He sounded amused, and didn't bother leaning forward.

Bang! Spruance used the gavel again. "That will be enough of that from both of you. We can get to the bottom of this. Mr. McReynolds, are you admitting your guilt of your own free will?"

McReynolds licked his lips again. "Yes, sir," he said quietly.

"Has anyone coerced you into doing so?"

"No, sir," McReynolds said.

"After your arrest, have you received adequate treatment, given the understanding that incarceration is not and cannot be a rest cure?"

"Yes, sir."

"Very well." Spruance turned to the yeoman. "You will record that Mr. McReynolds has admitted his guilt to the charges raised against him, has done so freely and without coercion, has been treated acceptably while imprisoned, and has asked mercy of the tribunal."

"Aye, aye, sir." The yeoman's pencil flashed across the page.

"All right, then." Captain Spruance sounded satisfied with the way things were going, if not exactly pleased. Charlie got the feeling Spruance seldom sounded pleased about anything. The Navy four-striper looked back to the table where the Supreme Court Four sat. "Mr. Butler, how say you to these charges?"

Pierce Butler took a deep breath. "Sir, I plead guilty and throw myself on the tribunal's mercy."

Again, the defense lawyers tried to object. Again, Captain Spruance overrode them. Again, he asked the justice whether his confession was voluntary and whether he'd been treated all right while behind bars. Like McReynolds, Butler affirmed that it was and that he had been. Attorney General Wyszynski looked even more smug than he had before.

Spruance asked Justice Sutherland and Justice Van Deventer how they answered the charges leveled against them. Each in turn confessed his guilt and begged the tribunal for mercy. Each said he confessed of his own free will and that he hadn't been mistreated since his arrest. The yeoman recorded the guilty pleas one by one.

The ACLU lawyer with the bad taste in clothes said, "Sir, I find these confessions utterly unbelievable."

"Do you?" Spruance said. "The men deny coercion. By their appearance, they have not been abused. I find myself compelled to credit them." He pointed to the reporters and to the newsreel cameras. "The American people will see them soon enough. I think their view of the matter will accord with mine, Mr. Levine."

"It's *Le-veen*, sir, not *Le-vine*," the lawyer said.

"Pardon me." Spruance tossed him the tiny victory, then went on to more important things: "Mr. McReynolds, would you care to explain to the tribunal why you chose to betray your country and your oath? You are not obliged to do so, but you may if you desire to. Perhaps you will offer mitigating circumstances."

"Thank you, sir," McReynolds said. "Yes, I would like to speak. We did what we did because we felt we had to stop Joe Steele at any cost and wreck everything he was doing. We thought—we think—Joe Steele is the American Trotsky."

Butler, Sutherland, and Van Deventer nodded almost in unison. McReynolds' words caused a fresh stir and buzz among the onlookers. Captain Spruance gaveled it down. Charlie had all he could do to keep from giggling. If the Supreme Court Four really believed that, they were a lot dumber than he'd given them credit for. Joe Steele hated Trotsky even more than he hated Hitler. His beef with Hitler was political. With Trotsky, it was personal. If Joe Steele could have bashed out the boss Red's brains with an ice axe, Charlie was convinced he would have done it.

Spruance might have been talking about the weather when he asked, "So you felt you had to stop him by any means necessary, whether legitimate or illegitimate?"

"Yes, sir," McReynolds repeated. "We could see that his programs were going to build up the country. He would get reelected, and reelected, and reelected again. He would be able to set up a tyranny over the United States."

"And so you conspired with a foreign tyrant against him?"

"Yes, sir. We wanted to keep the United States a democracy no matter what." If James McReynolds tried to sound proud of himself, he could have done better.

Justice Sutherland did do pride better. "We weren't the only ones, either," he put in, as smoothly as if responding to a cue.

"I beg your pardon?" Captain Spruance said.

"We weren't the only ones," Sutherland said once more. "Plenty of good, loyal Americans helped us try to put Joe Steele's head on the wall."

"Good, loyal Americans, you say?" Spruance rubbed his impeccably shaved chin. "Will you name those good, loyal Americans for me?" He didn't sound like someone putting quotation marks around the phrase. He said it the same way Sutherland had.

"Yes, sir," said the justice—ex-justice now, Charlie supposed—and confessed traitor. Levine and the other ACLU lawyer tried to stop him. He waved them away. Charlie heard him say, "What difference does it make now?" He wasn't sure the newsreel recordings would pick that up.

"Will you name them?" Spruance asked once more when Sutherland didn't go on right away.

"Yes, sir. One was Senator Long, from Louisiana. Another was Father Coughlin."

That loosed a hawk, or a whole flock of hawks, among the pigeons. Captain Spruance had to rap loudly for order. It didn't help much. Huey Long had been sniping at Joe Steele ever since Steele got the nomination the Kingfish wanted. Father Coughlin was a radio preacher from Michigan. Politically, he stood a little to the right of Attila the Hun, but millions of people listened to him. You could see how he might like *der Führer* better than the President.

"You've taken that down?" Spruance asked the yeoman.

"Yes, sir, I have." The CPO looked and sounded a little flabbergasted himself.

"I'm sure that will be the subject of further investigation," Spruance said. "I now declare a recess until two o'clock this afternoon so that the gentlemen of the press can file their stories and eat and so the members of this tribunal can consider the fate of the four men sitting at the defendants' table." Down came the gavel one more time.

Charlie sprinted for a telephone booth. As soon as someone picked up the other end of the line, he started dictating. Half a dozen other men in cheap suits and fedoras were doing the same thing along the bank of phones. The doors for most of the booths were open. That let Charlie hear how the rest of the reporters, like him, sounded more coherent and better organized than they did in ordinary conversation. They'd all had to do this before, a great many times. Like writing, it was a skill that improved with practice.

When Charlie stopped shoving in nickels and hung up, two guys behind him got into a wrestling match over who'd use the phone next. He grabbed Louie and headed for the cafeteria in the basement. He'd eaten there only once before. As soon as he bit into his turkey sandwich, he remembered why.

Louie'd got roast beef, and didn't look any happier with it. "Holy Jesus, Charlie!" he said with his mouth full. "I mean, holy jumping Jesus!" He swallowed heroically.

"That's about the size of it," Charlie agreed.

"They confessed," the photographer said. "I mean, they *confessed*. I knew they'd tell Joe Steele to piss up a rope. I *knew* it. Only they didn't."

"They sure didn't. They fingered some other big shots who can't stand him, either." Charlie kept eating the sandwich even if it was lousy. "And they didn't look like J. Edgar Hoover was giving 'em the third degree. They just decided to sing."

"Like canaries." Louie lowered his voice: "You believe 'em? You believe all that treason malarkey's legit?"

"I believe anybody who sets out to prove it isn't will have a tough time doing it unless the justices take back their confessions," Charlie said.

Louie chewed on that, literally and metaphorically. Then he nodded. "Yeah, that's about the size of it. I bet Father Coughlin's spitting rivets right now." Well, he might have said *spitting*.

Charlie didn't get such a good seat when the tribunal reconvened. Other reporters had either eaten faster or skipped lunch. He'd made it to a phone in a hurry. He wouldn't complain about this.

At two o'clock straight up, Captain Spruance gaveled the proceedings back into session. "We have reached a decision in this case," he said. "Are the defendants ready to hear it?"

If any of the four Associate Justices wasn't ready, he didn't say so.

"Very well," Spruance continued. "Because of their confessions earlier today and because of the evidence against them, evidence they did not seek to contest, we find them guilty of the crime of treason against the United States of America." He turned to the Army officers sitting at his left hand. "Is that not our unanimous decision, gentlemen?"

"It is," chorused Colonel Marshall, Major Bradley, and Major Eisenhower.

"Furthermore," Spruance said, "we sentence the defendants to death, the sentence to be carried out by firing squad." Willis Van Deventer slumped in his seat. The other three sat unmoving. Captain Spruance looked at the other officers again. "Is *that* not our unanimous decision, gentlemen?"

"It is," they said together.

Levine bounced to his feet. "This is a kangaroo court, nothing else but! We'll appeal this outrageous verdict!"

"Who to? The Supreme Court?" Over at the prosecutors' table, Andy Wyszynski went into gales of laughter. The ACLU lawyer stared at him, pop-eyed. Wyszynski rubbed it in some more: "Or maybe you'll appeal to the President?" Oh, how he laughed!

He laughed until Captain Spruance brought down the gavel. "Mr. Attorney General, your display is unseemly."

"Sorry, sir." Wyszynski didn't sound sorry. He didn't look sorry, either. But he did stop openly gloating.

Soldiers, sailors, and U.S. marshals took the convicted traitors away. The reporters scrambled to file their new stories. Charlie wondered how many late editions would sport a one-word headline: DEATH!

He wondered some other things, too. But that didn't matter, or not very much. If the accused men admitted that they'd done what they were accused of, and if you couldn't prove they'd been forced to admit it, what could anybody do? Not much, not that Charlie could see. And questions without good answers seemed all too much like questions better left unasked.

"Take it easy, Mike." Stella sounded scared. "You'll blow a gasket if you don't relax."

"Somebody needs to blow a gasket, by God," Mike said savagely. "They were railroaded. They must've been railroaded—nobody in his right mind would confess to anything like that. I bet they got plenty of rubber hoses and castor oil and water up the nose. You don't need to leave marks to hurt somebody so bad he'll say anything you want. Ask Mussolini . . . uh, no offense."

Stella Morandini said something incandescent about *il Duce* in the language she'd learned at her mother's knee. Then she went back to English: "But you know, even here in the Village a lot of people think the Supreme Court Four are guilty as sin."

Mike did know that. It left him depressed, if not neurotic. "You know what it proves?" he said.

"What?" Stella asked, as she knew she should.

"It proves a lot of people are goddamn imbeciles, that's what." Mike made as if to tear out his hair. "Ahh . . . ! What I really need to do is go on a six-day bender, stay so pickled I can't even remember all the different ways this country's going to the dogs." He started for the kitchen to see what he had in the way of booze. In his apartment, nothing was more than a few steps from anything else.

"Wait," Stella said.

"How come? What could be better than getting smashed?"

He didn't think she'd have an answer for that, but she started taking off her clothes. He paused to reconsider. Making love wouldn't give him six days of forgetfulness, but it also wouldn't leave him wishing he were dead afterwards. In his haste to join her, he popped a button off his shirt.

His bed was of the Murphy persuasion. Instead of shoving a chair and an end table out of the way to use it, they made do with the sofa. Still straddling him in the afterglow, her face on his shoulder, she asked, "Happier now?"

"Some ways, sure." He patted her behind. "Others, not so much. The country's still a mess."

"What can you do about it?"

"I've been doing what I can—and look how far it's got me," he answered. "What happened today, that makes me want to go out in the streets and start throwing bombs at police stations. Then they'll hang a treason rap on me, too."

"I don't think I'll let you have your pants back," Stella said seriously. "You can't go out and throw bombs without pants."

"You're right. Somebody would arrest me." Mike laughed. It was either laugh or push Stella off him and go pound his head against the wall. The noise from that would make the neighbors complain. Besides, Stella was far and away the best thing he had going for him, and she had been for a while. Wasn't it about time he figured out what he needed to do about that? "Hon," he said, "you want to marry me?"

Her eyes widened. "What brought that on?"

"A rush of brains to the head, I hope. Do you?"

"Sure," she said. "My mother's gonna fall over, you know. She was sure you wouldn't ever ask me. She figured you were just using me to have fun. 'He's a *man*,' she says, 'and you know the only thing *men* want.'"

"I've never just used you to have fun, and that isn't the only thing I want you for," Mike said. Then he spoiled his foursquare stand for virtue by patting her again. "It's pretty darn nice, though, isn't it?"

"I wouldn't be in this compromising position if I didn't think so."

"You didn't compromise, sweetie. You cooperated. There's a difference."

"So what do we do once we tie the knot? Do we live happily ever after, like in the fairy tales?"

"We live as happily ever after as Joe Steele will let us," Mike said. Stella poked him in the ribs. He supposed he deserved it, but he hadn't been kidding even so.

VIII

Since Levine and the ACLU couldn't come up with any better ideas, they did appeal the death sentences of the Supreme Court Four to Joe Steele. Levine also published the letter in the papers. In it, he asked the President to spare the lives "of four dedicated public servants whose differences with him over fine points of law were perhaps unfairly perceived as differences over public policy."

Pointing to the letter in the *Washington Post*, Esther asked Charlie, "Do you think it will do any good?"

He sighed and shook his head. "Nope. It might, if they just kept making decisions he didn't go for. But this whole treason business . . . He can't look like he's letting them get away with that."

"Oh, come on!" she said. "How much of that do you believe? How much of that can anybody believe?"

"I'll tell you—I don't know what to believe," Charlie answered. "Mike thinks it's a bunch of hooey, too. But he wasn't there. I was. Would you confess to something that horrible, something you had to know would get you the death penalty, unless you did . . . some of it, anyway?"

"See? Even you have trouble swallowing the whole thing." To Charlie's relief, his wife didn't push it any further. Instead, she pointed to the paper again and asked, "What do you think Joe Steele will do about it?"

"I don't think he'll do anything till the whole Louisiana mess gets straightened out, and God only knows how long that'll take," Charlie answered.

On the strength of George Sutherland's accusations, Attorney General Wyszynski had got warrants against Father Coughlin and Huey Long. The rabble-rousing priest had gone meekly into custody, showing off his bracelets for the reporters swarming around his Michigan radio studio and quoting the Twenty-third Psalm: "'The Lord is my shepherd; I shall not want. He maketh me to lie down in green pastures: he leadeth me beside the still waters. . . . Yea, though I walk through the valley of the shadow of death, I will fear no evil: for thou art with me.'"

That sounded very pretty. It also left him behind bars. No judge would grant bail or issue him a writ of *habeas corpus*. Eventually, Joe Steele and Andy Wyszynski would try him or send him before a tribunal or do whatever they did to him. Meanwhile . . .

Meanwhile, Huey Long was kicking up a ruckus. Unlike Father Coughlin, the Kingfish didn't sit around waiting to get jugged. As soon as he heard that Sutherland had taken his name in vain, he drove to Washington National Airport, chartered a Ford Trimotor, and flew off to Baton Rouge.

Nobody arrested him there. Even Federal officials in Louisiana kowtowed to the Kingfish. And from Louisiana, Long bellowed defiance at Joe Steele and at the other forty-seven states. "If that lying, cheating fool infesting the White House wants a new War of Yankee Aggression, let him start it!" the Senator roared. "He may fire the first shot, but the American people will fire the last one—at him! Everybody who's against Joe Steele ought to be for me!"

What he didn't seem to realize was that, if the choice lay between him and the President, most people outside Louisiana came down on Joe Steele's side. Yeah, Joe Steele was cold and crafty. Everybody knew that. But most people also thought he had his head screwed on tight. Outside of Louisiana, Huey Long came off as something between a buffoon and a raving loony.

When Joe Steele went on the radio, he sounded like a reasonable man. "No one is going to start another Civil War," he said. He had his name for the late unpleasantness, as Huey Long had *his*. Joe Steele's was the one more Americans used, though. He continued, "But we will have the laws obeyed. A warrant for Senator Long's arrest on serious charges has been issued. It will be served at the earliest opportunity."

The Kingfish's next radio speech amounted to *Nyah, nyah, nyah—you can't catch me!* Charlie listened to it and shook his head in reluctant admiration. "He's got moxie—you have to give him that."

"If he gets people laughing at Joe Steele, that's his best chance," Esther said. "Then nobody will want the government to get tough." It looked the same way to Charlie.

Huey Long traveled around Louisiana making speeches, too. He had to keep the juices flowing there—if his own state turned against him, his goose went into the oven. He traveled with enough bodyguards to fight a small war. They wouldn't have won against Federal troops, but they would have put up a scrap. And they definitely helped keep Louisiana in line.

None of which did the Senator any good when he spoke in front of the Alexandria city hall. A sniper at least half a mile away fired one shot. The .30-06 round went in the Kingfish's left ear and came out just below his right ear, bringing half his brain with it. He was dead before he hit the sidewalk.

His bodyguards went nuts. Some of them did run in the direction from which the shot had come. Others started firing in that direction. Still others, in a frenzy of grief and horror and rage, emptied their revolvers into the crowd that had been listening to Long. More than twenty people, including eleven women and an eight-year-old girl, died in the barrage and in the stampede that followed.

No one caught the assassin. At lunch a few days later, Louie Pappas remarked to Charlie, "My brother is a gunnery sergeant in the Marines."

"Is that so?" Charlie said around a mouthful of ham and cheese.

"Uh-huh. He was in France in 1918—he was just a PFC then. He says he knew plenty of guys in the Corps who coulda done what the fella in Louisiana did."

"Oh, yeah?" Charlie said. The photographer nodded. Charlie asked, "Is he saying a leatherneck *did* punch Huey's ticket for him?"

"Nah. How could he say that? He wasn't there." Louie was eating liverwurst and onions: a sandwich to make skunks turn tail. "Only that it coulda been."

"How about that?" Charlie said. He waved to the counter-man. "Hey, can you get me another Coke, please?"

Mike knew why Stan had put him on a train to Baton Rouge to cover Huey Long's funeral. He was a reporter who had a reputation for going after Joe Steele. If he went after him some more, it would just be icing on the cake, not a whole new cake. Joe Steele and his flunkies already couldn't stand him. *I'm expendable,* Mike thought, not without pride.

The funeral made him think of nothing so much as the ones banana republics threw for dead military dictators. Baton Rouge was decked in black crepe. U.S. flags flew at half staff. Sometimes they flew upside down, an old, old signal of distress.

What must have been a couple of hundred thousand people, almost all in black, lined up in front of the grand new state capitol to file past Long's body. The new Capitol had gone up while the Kingfish was Governor of Louisiana. The old one, a Gothic horror out of Sir Walter Scott, stood empty and unloved a few blocks south and a little west, by the banks of the Mississippi. Along with other reporters, Mike climbed the forty-eight steps—one for each state, and recording its name and admission date—and passed through the fifty-foot-tall bronze doors into the rotunda.

Long's coffin lay in the center of the rotunda. It was double, copper inside of bronze, and had a glass top to let people peer down at the tuxedoed corpse. The pillows on which Long's head rested had been built up on the right side so no one would have to contemplate the ruins of that side of his head.

Mourners filed by in a continuous stream, rich and poor, men and women, whites and even some Negroes. Some of them had the look of people who were there because they thought being there would do them some good. More seemed genuinely sorry their eccentric kingpin was gone.

At least four mourners turned to the reporters and said, "Joe Steele did this." Mike wouldn't have been a bit surprised, but he thought they needed to get hold of the gunman to nail that down. It hadn't happened yet. The sloppy and grandiose feel of Louisiana made Mike wonder if it ever would.

A hellfire-brimstone-and-damnation minister preached the funeral oration. "We were robbed of our sun! We were robbed of our moon! Washington stole the stars from our sky!" he thundered. "God will smite those who foully slew him and those who plotted his destruction! They will go into the lake of burning lava and cook for all eternity! Huey Long will look down on them from heaven, and he will laugh to see their suffering. He will laugh, for he has been translated to bliss eternal!"

"That's right!" someone in the crowd shouted, as if in a Holy Roller church.

"The mustachioed serpent in the White House will not escape, for the judgments of the Lord are true and righteous altogether," the preacher went on. He got more responses to that, and an angry rumble that made the hair on the back of Mike's neck try to stand on end. "No, he will not get free of God's ineffable judgment, for his lying charges against the lion of Louisiana were what set Senator Long's death in motion. There is blood on his hands—blood, I say!"

Mike absently wondered how any serpent outside the Garden of Eden—even a mustachioed one—could have hands, bloody or not. The preacher went right on talking around accusing Joe Steele of ordering Long's murder. Was that prudence or fear? Was there a difference?

Some in the crowd were less restrained. "String up that son of a bitch in the White House!" a man hollered, and it became a rolling, throbbing chorus. Mike had never seen a funeral turn into a riot, and hoped to keep his record intact.

They buried the Kingfish on the lawn in front of the capitol. There were about enough flowers for a Rose Parade and a half. As Mike wrote up some of the more florid floral displays, he wondered how much all this was costing. Certainly in the hundreds of thousands, probably in the millions. It came straight out of the pockets of everybody in Depression-strapped Louisiana.

He had to wait till after midnight to file his story. Baton Rouge just didn't have enough telegraph and telephone lines to cope with all the reporters who had descended on it. Once he'd sent it on to New York, he found himself three stiff drinks—which seemed easy enough to do—and went to bed.

The only reason he didn't feel as if he was escaping a foreign country when his eastbound train left Louisiana was that he didn't have to stop and show his passport and clear customs. *Foreign country, nothing,* he decided. He might as well have been on a different world.

Stella met him at Penn Station. "How'd it go?" she asked him.

He thought about it. "I'll tell you," he said at last. "Going to that funeral made me embarrassed to be against Joe Steele. Embarrassed by the company I was keeping, I mean."

"Embarrassed enough to stop?"

Mike thought some more. Then he shook his head. "Nah. It's a dirty job, but somebody's gotta do it. And somebody's gotta do it right, 'cause they sure weren't down there."

Joe Steele didn't comment about Huey Long's demise till the Senator from Louisiana was six feet under. Then he went on the radio to say, "I regret Senator Long's death at the hands of another. The Justice Department will make every effort to work closely with Louisiana's authorities to track down Senator Long's killer and to give him the punishment he deserves. We have known since the days of Lincoln that assassination has no place in the American political system."

"First Roosevelt, now Long, and he says that?" Esther demanded.

"He says it," Charlie answered wearily. They'd gone round this barn before. "We don't know for sure what happened either time."

"Do I have to connect the dots for you?" his wife asked.

"You—" Charlie stopped.

He stopped because Joe Steele was talking again. The President had paused much longer than a professional radio performer would have; maybe he was fiddling with his pipe. "I also regret Senator Long's untimely death because he was not able to answer the charges leveled against him. He would have received the hearing he deserved."

"What does *that* mean?" Esther said.

Charlie hushed her this time—the President hadn't stopped. "You will also know that I have been given a request for clemency on behalf of the four Supreme Court justices who confessed in an open hearing to treason on behalf of the Nazis. I am not a cruel man—"

"Ha!" Esther broke in.

"—but I find I cannot grant this request. If I did, it would only encourage others to plot against America. The sentence the military tribunal found fitting for their crimes will be carried out tomorrow morning. I hope I will not have to approve any more sentences like that, but I will do my Constitutional duty to keep the United States safe and secure. Thank you, and good night."

"Tomorrow morning," Esther said. "Now that Huey's gone, he's not wasting any time, is he?"

"If it were done when 'tis done, then 'twere well it were done quickly." Charlie had read a lot of Shakespeare. Not only did he enjoy it, but he thought it rubbed off on his writing.

Esther startled him by carrying on the quotation: "If the assassination could trammel up the consequence, and catch with his surcease success; that but this blow might be the be-all and the end-all here." Giggling at his flummoxed expression, she added, "I was Lady Macbeth my senior year of high school. I can do it in Yiddish, too. Well, some of it—been a while."

Before he could answer, the phone rang. When he picked it up, Lazar Kagan was on the other end of the connection. For a split second, Charlie wondered whether Kagan could do *Macbeth* in Yiddish. Then Joe Steele's factotum said, "Do you want to witness the executions tomorrow?"

That was about the last thing Charlie wanted. He said "Yes" anyhow. This was part of history. Not even Aaron Burr had been convicted of treason. Kagan told him where the firing squads would do their jobs: across the Potomac in Arlington, between the Washington Airport and the Roaches Run Waterfowl Sanctuary. If you had to do something like that near the capital, they'd found a good place for it. The airport wasn't busy, and only the occasional bird-watcher came out to peer at the ducks and egrets in the sanctuary.

Charlie didn't like getting out there at five in the morning. Joe Steele's officials took the idea of "shot at sunrise" too seriously, as far as he was concerned. But, fortified by three cups of sludgy coffee, he made it on time. Hitting your mark was as important for a reporter as for an actor.

Four squads of soldiers waited in front of posts driven into the soft ground. Charlie talked with the first lieutenant in charge of them. "One rifle in each squad has a blank cartridge," the young officer explained. "The guys can think they didn't kill anyone if they want to."

A few minutes later, a khaki-painted panel truck pulled up. Soldiers took the four convicted traitors out of the back and shackled one to each post. They offered blindfolds; Butler declined his. Then they pinned a white paper circle to the center of each man's coarse cotton prison shirt.

"Squads, take your marks!" the lieutenant said briskly. The soldiers did. It went off almost the way it would have in a movie. "Ready . . . Aim . . . Fire!" The rifles roared and flashed. McReynolds let out a gurgling shriek. The others slumped in silence.

The lieutenant waited a couple of minutes, then felt McReynolds for a pulse. "He's gone. That's good," he said. "I would've had to finish him otherwise." He patted the .45 on his belt. He checked the other justices, too. They were also dead. The soldiers who'd brought them wrapped their bodies in waterproof shelter halves and put them into the truck again.

"What will happen to them now?" Charlie asked.

"They'll go back to their families for burial," the lieutenant said. "I think there will be a request to keep services small and private. I don't know what will happen if the families disobey."

"Thanks." Charlie wrote down the reply. Then he asked, "How do *you* feel about being here this morning?"

"Sir, I'm just doing my job. That's how you have to look at

things, isn't it? They gave me the orders. I followed them. To-morrow I'll do something else."

As Mike had been best man for Charlie, so Charlie was best man for Mike. Esther was one of Stella's brides-maids, along with two of Stella's sisters and a first cousin. From what Mike told Charlie, Stella's folks had grumbled about a Jewish bridesmaid at a Catholic wedding, but he and Stella managed to sweeten them up. Charlie didn't tell Esther anything about that, and Stella's father and mother stayed polite to her, if not exactly warm. That was their good luck. She would have gone off like a bomb if they'd said anything about her religion.

The reception was at a Knights of Columbus hall two doors down from the church. Since Stella's folks were foot-ing the bill, the chow was Italian. So was the band. One of the trumpeters and a sax player looked as if they might be made men. Since Charlie was there as brother of the groom and not as a reporter, he didn't ask them. He made a point of not asking them, in fact.

He toasted Mike and Stella with Chianti. "Health, wealth, long life, happiness, kids!" he said. You couldn't go wrong with those. Everybody raised a cheer and everybody drank.

After Stella mashed wedding cake in Mike's face, he came over to Charlie and said, "What do you think our chances are?" His cheeks were flushed. He'd been drinking pretty hard, and not just Italian red wine.

"Hey, you've got a job and a pretty girl," Charlie an-swered. "That puts you ahead of most people right there."

"Till I go up in front of one of those goddamn treason tribunals, anyway," Mike said.

"Mike . . . This isn't the time or the place," Charlie said.

"Everybody says that. Everybody says that all the stinkin' time," Mike snarled. "And everybody'll keep on saying it till we're as bad off and as much under the gun as the poor bastards in Italy or Germany or Russia."

Charlie held a full glass of wine. He wanted to pour it over his brother's hot head, but people would talk. In lieu of starting trouble, he said, "Honest to God, Mike, it's not gonna come to anything like that."

"No, huh? Ask Roosevelt what he thinks. Ask Huey Long, too. Huey was as crazy as the people who liked him, and that's really saying something. But what did it get him in the end? A cemetery plot on the front lawn on his gaudy, overpriced, oversized capitol."

"A cemetery plot is all any of us gets in the end," Charlie said quietly.

"Yeah, yeah." Mike sounded impatient—and drunk as an owl. "But you want to get it later, not sooner. Joe Steele wanted Huey to get it sooner, and the Kingfish, he's in the cold, cold ground."

"They still haven't found who shot Long." Charlie felt as if he were reprising scenes he'd already played with Esther.

"Huey's storm troopers and the Louisiana cops, they couldn't find their ass with both hands," Mike said with a fine curl of the lip. "And when Joe Steele's Department of Justice is down there giving them a boost, you think anybody'll go pointing fingers back at the big chief in the White House?" He cackled laughter bitter enough to make people stare at him.

"Mike, what I think is, you're at your wedding. You need to pay more attention to Stella and less attention to Steele."

"Doggone it, Charlie, *nobody* wants to pay attention to what Steele's doing to the country. Everybody looks the other way because the economy seems a little better than it did right after the crash. Not good, but a little better. And Steele grabs a bit of power here and a bit more there, and pretty soon he'll hold all the strings. And everybody else'll have to dance when he pulls them."

"Why don't you go dance, man, no strings attached? Like I told you, that's what you're here for. If you want to go after Joe Steele some more when you're back from your honeymoon, okay, you'll do that. In the meantime, enjoy yourself. *Dum vivimus, vivamus!*"

"'While we live, let us live.' Good luck!" Mike said, but then, suddenly grinning, "I wonder what ever happened to Sister Mary Ignatia."

"Nothing good, I hope," Charlie said. The large, strong,

stern nun was so old, Latin might have been her native language. She'd carried a ruler and inflicted the language and flattened knuckles on both of them.

"Who was the one with the mustache? Was that Sister Bernadette?" Mike asked.

"No—Sister Susanna." Charlie happily chattered about teachers from years gone by. His brother was definitely buggy when it came to Joe Steele. Anything that distracted him from the President looked good to Charlie.

When Charlie went out onto the parquet dance floor with Esther a little later, she asked him, "What was going on there? Looked like Mike was getting kind of excited."

"Maybe a little." If Charlie minimized for his wife, he might be able to minimize for himself, too. "But I managed to calm him down." That, he was pretty sure about. Mike was dancing with Stella, and seemed happy enough.

"More politics?" Esther asked.

"Yeah. He looks at Joe Steele the same way you do, only more so. You know that."

He hoped he would get Esther to back away, but his wife was made of stern stuff. "There's a difference," she said.

"Like what?"

"If I don't like the President, what do I do? I talk to you. If Mike doesn't like him, he writes a story that says so, and thousands—maybe millions—of people know about it. Joe Steele knows about it, and so do his men."

"They may know about it, but what can they do about it? We still have freedom of the press in this country," Charlie said.

Esther didn't answer. She let him imagine all the things someone who didn't like what a reporter had to say might do. He was sure the things he imagined were worse than anything she might have said. He'd always had more imagination than was good for him.

So, like a man flicking a light switch, he deliberately turned it off. Sometimes you did better taking the world as you found it and not troubling yourself about moonshine and vapors and ghosties and ghoulies and things that went bump in the night. You couldn't do anything about those even if they happened to be real. Mike and Stella would be going bump in the night tonight. Charlie could hope they had a ton of fun doing it. He could, and he did.

Mike seemed to be playing the same kind of mental games with himself. He didn't talk about Joe Steele any more during the reception. He laughed and joked and looked like somebody having a good time at his wedding. If he wasn't, he didn't let anyone else see that. With any luck, he didn't let himself see it, either.

Stella seemed to be having a good time, too. But when Charlie danced with her, she whispered in his ear: "Don't let Mike do anything too crazy, okay?"

"How am I supposed to stop him?" Charlie whispered back. "And why don't you take care of it? You're his wife now, remember, not just his girlfriend."

"That doesn't mean I know anything about newspapers. You do. He has to take you seriously."

Charlie laughed out loud, there on the dance floor. "I'm his little brother. He hasn't taken me seriously since the day I was born. If you think he'll start now, I'm sorry, but you're out of luck."

"I married him. That makes me lucky. I want to stay lucky for a while, if you know what I mean."

"Sure." Charlie left it there. Everybody wanted to stay lucky for a while. Just because you wanted it didn't mean you would get it. Hardly anybody managed that. But it wasn't the kind of thing you pointed out to a bride on her wedding day. Chances were she'd see for herself all too soon.

Andy Wyszynski ordered Father Coughlin brought back to Washington, D.C., for his hearing before a military tribunal. He scheduled the hearing for the lobby of the District Court Building: the place where the Supreme Court Four had met their fate.

In a press conference, Wyszynski said, "I wish he'd kept his nose out of politics, that's all. I'm a Catholic myself. Most of you know I am. I don't like the idea that a priest could betray his country. He should have stuck with God's things. Those are what priests are for. When he started messing with Caesar's, that's when he got in trouble."

"Joe Steele didn't mind when Father Coughlin backed him in the election," Walter Lippmann said. "He didn't mind when Coughlin supported some of his early programs, either."

One of the Attorney General's bushy eyebrows twitched. But Wyszynski answered calmly enough: "The President wouldn't have minded if Father Coughlin campaigned for Herbert Hoover."

"No?" Lippmann said. Charlie wondered the same thing. Joe Steele wanted people behind him, not pushing against him.

But Wyszynski said "No" and sounded like a man who meant it. He went on, "Herbert Hoover is an American, a loyal American. He is not someone who has thrown in his lot with tyrants from overseas. Father Coughlin is. We will show that he is at the upcoming tribunal."

"Will he confess, the way the Supreme Court Four did?" a reporter asked.

"I have no idea," Wyszynski answered. "If he does, that will simplify things. If he doesn't, we will prove the case to the satisfaction of the members of the military tribunal."

"What if they acquit him?" the newshound persisted.

Both of Andy Wyszynski's eyebrows sprang toward his hairline then. If Charlie was any judge, that meant the possibility had never occurred to him. After a shrug, though, he responded smoothly enough: "If they do, then they do, that's all. I think it would be a shame, because Father Coughlin has shown that he's the enemy of everything the USA stands for. But I didn't win every case in Chicago, and I don't know whether I'll win every case here."

A slicked-down Army colonel named Walter Short headed the tribunal. Also on it were a Navy captain named Halsey, an Army Air Corps major called Carl Spatz (he pronounced it *spots*, not *spats*), and an Army Air Corps first lieutenant with the interesting handle of Nathan Bedford Forrest III. Only his eyebrows reminded Charlie of his Confederate ancestor.

Charlie and Louie had the good sense to get to the District Court Building early. The crush was a little less overwhelming than it had been for the Associate Justices' hearing. Coughlin wasn't a government figure, and this wasn't the first such proceeding.

The ACLU lawyer named Levine was one of Father Coughlin's defense attorneys. He had on another godawful jacket, and a scarlet bow tie with bright blue polka dots that almost made it seem sedate by comparison. His companion, in pinstriped charcoal gray with a white shirt and a discreet maroon four-in-hand, was next to invisible beside him.

At the prosecutors' table, Andy Wyszynski might have been the most relaxed man in the place. He smoked a cigarette, told a joke that made an aide wince, and generally seemed without a care in the world. If he wasn't ready for anything Coughlin might do or say, he didn't let on.

Colonel Short gaveled for order at ten sharp. "Close those doors," he barked at the MPs and shore patrolmen by the entrance. "Let's get on with it—the sooner the better." He pointed to U.S. marshals at the edge of the lobby. "Bring in the prisoner, you men."

He was the kind of officer Charlie disliked on sight. He owned a mean mouth, he used too much grease on his thinning hair, and, unlike Captain Spruance at the last tribunal, he had routineer stamped all over him.

In came Father Coughlin, handcuffed and herded along. He was in his mid-forties, the map of Ireland on his face. Wire-rimmed glasses aided his bright blue eyes. He had a shock, almost a quiff, of brown hair. In place of a clerical dog collar, he wore prison clothes.

"State your name for the record," Short told him.

"I am Charles Edward Coughlin, sir."

"Well, Mister Coughlin—"

"I prefer Father Coughlin, sir."

"Well, Mister Coughlin," Walter Short repeated with sour relish, "you are charged with doing the business of foreign countries seeking to weaken and destroy the United States of America and with doing it for money—with the crime of high treason, in other words. How say you to the charges, Mister Coughlin?"

Levine reached out toward the priest. He must have believed everyone deserved legal help, because Coughlin ranted about wicked, greedy Jewish bankers with as much gusto as he tore into Joe Steele. Levine didn't want the priest to admit the charges. He wanted to fight.

In a voice almost too soft to hear even with the microphone, Father Coughlin said, "For the benefit of those who once believed in me, I find that I have no choice but to plead guilty, sir. I beg the tribunal for leniency for my sins, which the almighty God will also judge."

A sigh wafted through the lobby. It was nothing like the amazement the audience had shown when the Supreme Court Four pleaded guilty. Walter Short used the gavel with officious energy just the same. He asked whether Coughlin was confessing voluntarily, whether he'd been coerced, and whether he'd been treated all right while behind bars. Coughlin gave each question the expected answer.

"All right, then." Colonel Short sounded pleased with himself, and with how things were going. He turned to the other officers. "We've heard the prisoner confess. We know the charges against him. Do we need to waste a lot of time haggling over the sentence we pass?"

Halsey and Spatz sat silent. Forrest said, "Only one penalty for a crime like his—one that makes sure he never does it again."

"Well put, Lieutenant. Well put." Short eyed his fellow judges again. "Does anyone think anything less than the supreme penalty fits the crime?" If anyone did, he kept quiet about it. Short swung back to the radio priest. "For the crime of treason, which you have openly admitted in this tribunal, you are sentenced to die by the firing squad at a time and place the Attorney General or the President shall designate."

Coughlin managed a nod. "We'll appeal this!" Levine shouted.

"You have the right," Walter Short admitted grudgingly.

"Good luck," Wyszynski added with a chuckle. The Supreme Court was back in business, with four new justices named by Joe Steele. Papers that didn't like the President were already calling them the Rubber Stamps. They didn't seem likely to bite the hand that could arrest them.

"We *will* appeal," Levine said. "The real truth needs to come out."

"The real truth has come out, admitted by Mister Coughlin," Short said. "And, since it has, this tribunal's business is concluded. We stand adjourned." He used the gavel one more time.

"They're getting better at this," Louie said as the assembly broke up. "Today, we don't even gotta hurry back from lunch."

"Yeah," Charlie said. He had no use for the priest. Whether Coughlin had done what he'd admitted doing might be a different question. If Charlie couldn't prove that one way or the other, though, what was he supposed to do? Going along with the record as it came out in the tribunal might not be the bravest thing, but it was definitely the safest. And that was how Charlie wrote the story.

Appeal Levine did. The Supreme Court played safe, too. It declined to hear the appeal, saying it lacked jurisdiction over verdicts from military tribunals. Undaunted, Levine asked Joe Steele for clemency. As Charlie expected, the President went on the radio to say he wouldn't grant it. Charlie didn't expect Joe Steele to quote Lincoln again, but he did: "'Must I shoot a simple-minded deserter, while I must not touch a hair of a wily agitator who induces him to desert?'" The question was disturbingly good.

No political kerfuffle delayed Father Coughlin's shuffle off this mortal coil. A few days after Joe Steele rejected the appeal, Charlie got the phone call from Kagan he dreaded. The next morning, yawning despite coffee, he went to Arlington, to the open ground by the Roaches Run Waterfowl Sanctuary. Only one post driven into the earth this time. Only one waiting firing squad.

Coughlin died as well as a man could. He refused a blindfold. Where Joe Steele had quoted Lincoln, he quoted Luke: "'Father, forgive them; for they know not what they do,'" he said, nodding toward the soldiers with Springfields.

That made no difference in how things came out, of course. The men who'd brought him shackled him to the post. The lieutenant in charge of the firing squad ordered his soldiers into place. He went through the commands that were becoming familiar to Charlie: "Ready . . . Aim . . ."

Courage perhaps failing him at last, Father Coughlin began to gabble out a Hail Mary: *Ave—"*

"Fire!" the lieutenant shouted, and the rifles barked together. Coughlin fell silent forever. Proving he'd studied Latin, too, the junior officer added, *"Ave atque vale."*

And he gave Charlie a headline that ran from coast to coast: AVE ATQUE VOLLEY.

IX

Some bills go through Congress with people having conniptions about them even before they're fully drafted. Others come in, as it were, under assumed names, so nobody understands what they're all about till they take effect. Sometimes, people don't fully realize what they're all about till years after they take effect. The Fourteenth Amendment to the Constitution was one of those sleepers.

Another one—maybe on a smaller scale, but, then again, maybe not, too—was a proposal of Joe Steele's with the innocuous, even soporific, title "A Bill Providing Labor for the Reconstruction of Facilities in States Adversely Affected by Weather During the Recent Economic Contraction." It allowed the Federal government to draft prisoners out of local, state, and U.S. lockups and put them to work in the Midwest and Rocky Mountain states building roads and bridges and dams and canals and pretty much anything else anybody thought needed building.

It passed the House before Mike noticed it at all. Even then, he wouldn't have if he hadn't read a column about it in the *New York Times*. The columnist seemed of two minds about the bill. *No one can deny that a great deal of building and rebuilding needs to be done between Oklahoma and Utah,* he wrote. *Not only the Depression but also the storms that created the Dust Bowl have ravaged America's midsection. Yet when the country as a whole finds chain gangs in the South distasteful, we may wonder at the wisdom of creating Federal chain gangs over such an enormous region. Would we not be better served by reducing this form of punishment than by expanding it?*

Mike took the *Times* piece to his editor. "How come we haven't done anything with this?" he asked.

Stan skimmed the column. "How come? I'll tell you how come. 'Cause I never heard of it till right now. Go chase down the text of the bill and see what it's all about. Once we find out what it really says, we'll figure out what to do and whether we need to do anything."

"Okay." As far as Mike was concerned, any excuse for a trip to the New York Public Library was a good one. He always felt smarter every time he walked up the steps and passed between the two big library lions. Just because he felt smarter didn't mean he was, but he liked the feeling even so.

He'd heard that something like 11,000 people used the enormous central building on Fifth Avenue every day. The library's collection was grander than any but that of the Library of Congress. Mike knew where the shelf upon shelf of the *Congressional Record* lived. He pawed through indices in recent fascicules till he found the bill.

Naturally, it was written in governmentese, a dialect that thought it was English but was in fact a far more degraded tongue. Mike had to pan for meaning the way the Forty-Niners had panned for gold. He sifted through tons of mud and gunk and gravel to win a precious few nuggets. Notes filled page after page of his spiral-bound notebook.

When he put the fascicule back on the shelf, he was shaking his head. He paid another nickel to ride the subway back to the *Post*'s headquarters on West Street. The seventeen-story pile of buff brick was as familiar to him as his face in the mirror when he shaved every morning.

"Well?" Stan said when Mike walked into his office again.

"Well," Mike said, "you know that German prison camp called Dachau, where Hitler throws anybody he doesn't happen to like?"

"Personally, no. But I have heard of it," Stan said. "So?"

"So if Joe Steele grabs this law and runs with it as far as he can go, he'll be able to make as many prison camps as he wants, all over the Midwest. He can pull people out of jails and put them to work. I didn't see anything in the bill that limits how long he can hold them and keep them busy. That may be in there—I went through it pretty fast. But if it is, I didn't spot it."

"How sure are you that it isn't?" Stan Feldman asked.

"Oh, about ninety-five percent. It's the kind of thing that ought to jump out at you if it's the law."

"All right, then. Write it up and we'll get it out there. Maybe the Senate will come through for us, or maybe we're only spinning our wheels. But if we don't stand up and show people what's going on, they almost deserve what they get."

Mike banged away for all he was worth. Like his brother, he was a two-fingered typist. Also like his brother, he was as fast and accurate as most people who typed by touch. His headline was LAND OF THE FREE AND HOME OF THE LABOR CAMP?

Stan made one change in it—he turned the question mark into an exclamation point. He didn't make many more changes in the story. The ambiguous one in the *New York Times* hadn't gained much traction. The *Post* had a reputation for all kinds of things, but ambiguity wasn't any of them.

"What I really want us to do is get people like Will Rogers and Walter Winchell talking about this bill," Mike said. "If they can get folks mad at it or laughing at it, it won't pass."

"You hope it won't," his editor replied. "Nobody ever went broke underestimating the intelligence of the American people—"

"Thank you, H. L. Mencken," Mike broke in.

"—and that goes double for the Senate," Stan finished, unfazed. "Well, we're still in there swinging. Maybe the whole country will come to its senses and boot Joe Steele the hell out next year."

"Maybe." Mike did his best to sound as if he believed it. But he had the bad feeling his best might not be good enough.

Charlie was cranking out a story about the Daughters of the American Revolution when the phone on his desk rang. He reached for the telephone with something like relief. Writing what he was writing was about as creative as pouring cement for a new sidewalk. Very little brain was engaged doing either. Any excuse for a break seemed a good one.

"This is Charlie Sullivan," he said.

"Scriabin, at the White House," a harsh voice said in his ear. "Get over here."

"On my way," Charlie said. Scriabin hung up on him. Even the clunk sounded harsh. He wondered why he obeyed so automatically, but not for long. Vince Scriabin never sounded happy, but he rarely sounded as irked as he did right now. Something had struck a nerve on Pennsylvania Avenue. Charlie didn't know that it had anything to do with Mike, but he had the feeling it might. Mike couldn't resist taking potshots at the White House. One of these days, the White House would shoot back. Having seen firing squads in action lately, Charlie hoped like hell he wasn't being literal.

"What's cooking?" another desk man asked as he grabbed his fedora.

"Something at the White House," Charlie asked. "Dunno what yet. I'll find out when I get there."

The guards at the entrance were expecting him. "Scriabin said you'd be coming," one said. If the Hammer impressed him, he hid it well. He'd seen aides come and go before. "Head straight for his office. He's waiting for you."

So Scriabin was. On his desk lay a copy of the *New York Post* from the day before yesterday. He slammed his small, pale fist down on an article headlined LAND OF THE FREE AND HOME OF THE LABOR CAMP! "What do you have to say about this?" he snapped.

"That I haven't seen it yet," Charlie answered—reasonably, he thought.

"Well, look at it, then. And tell me why your brother distorts everything Joe Steele is trying to do."

Charlie read the article. Like most people in Washington, he'd paid no attention to the bill. He hadn't spotted the column in the *New York Times* that Mike mentioned, either. When he finished, he looked up and asked Scriabin, "Okay, what's your side of the story?"

"It's simple." Scriabin spread his hands. Even though they were pale, their backs were thatched with dark, wiry hair. He had five o'clock shadow, too, even if it was only half past ten. "We have, in jails and prisons across the country, thousands and thousands of young, healthy men sitting behind bars. Women, too. What are they doing? Sitting there eating their heads off. With this legislation, we can use their labor for socially important purposes. Your brother makes it sound like we're going to turn them into galley slaves or something." His glare said that was partly— more likely mostly—Charlie's fault.

"Hey, for one thing, I'm not my brother's keeper," Charlie said.

"Someone needs to be," Scriabin said.

"And for another thing, it sounds to me like he has a point," Charlie went on. Joe Steele's aide looked death and destruction at him. He plowed ahead anyhow: "Suppose you swiped a couple of baseball gloves and you're doing sixty days in a county jail somewhere. This would put you out in the middle of nowhere at hard labor for as long as they feel like keeping you if Mike has things straight."

"Yes. If," Scriabin said scornfully. "But the provision of proportionality is included in the legislation whether your brother bothered to notice it or not."

"Okay. Pull out a copy and show it to me," Charlie said.

He got another first-rate glare from Vince Scriabin. Then the Hammer opened a desk drawer, grabbed a printed copy—it was at least as fat as a spicy crime pulp you could buy at a newsstand—and thumbed through it. After a minute or two, he grunted in triumph and pointed to a paragraph halfway down a page. "Here you go."

Charlie read it. The gobbledygook was thick even by Washington standards. But it said, or he thought it said, nobody could be kept at labor in a Federal establishment beyond the terms of his original sentence unless he violated the regulations of the camp where he was assigned.

"What about that?" Charlie asked, doing some pointing of his own.

"What about it?" Scriabin returned. "If you keep breaking rules, you deserve more punishment. Be reasonable,

Sullivan. It is an inch. Your fool of a brother thinks we will use it to take a mile. But it is only an inch."

Mike was a hothead. Charlie knew that. A fool, however, he was not. If he saw the possibility of something, that possibility was there. Whether it would turn real might be a different question. Trying to turn the conversation, Charlie asked, "What do you want from me, anyhow?"

"A piece pointing out the positive features of this legislation might be appropriate," Scriabin said. "That area *does* need restoration. Who could possibly doubt it? This is a way to accomplish that at minimal expense. It may even help reform criminals. At the least, it will keep them far away from new trouble. I ask you—where is the wickedness in that?"

"When you put it that way . . ." Charlie said slowly.

"I do put it that way. So does the bill," Scriabin answered. "Anyone who isn't biased against us should be able to see that."

"Why do you want me to do it?" Charlie asked. A story like that out of his typewriter would only make trouble with Mike. Didn't they have enough already?

But Vince Scriabin said, "Partly to show the world that at least someone in the Sullivan clan can be a sensible human being and not see things that aren't there like a drunken stumblebum with the DTs."

Mike didn't see things that weren't there. Charlie knew him too well to believe that for a minute. He could be seeing things that might not be there. Anybody could do that; imagination was part of the human condition. One of the things Charlie could see right now was a door slammed in his face hard enough to smash his nose if he told Joe Steele's flunky to take a long walk off a short pier. If he didn't do the administration a favor now and then, he couldn't expect it to do any for him. No less than any other segment of mankind, Washington ran on that kind of barter.

He sighed. He made a production of lighting a cigarette (Joe Steele's pipe was better for that). He blew out smoke. Having stalled as long as he could, he mumbled, "I'll take care of it." He was a reporter, not a hero.

Had Vince Scriabin been a proper politician, he would

have glad-handed Charlie till Charlie felt good, or at least
not so bad, about doing what he saw he had to do. But the
Hammer was an aide. He didn't have to worry about getting elected. He was prickly, not greasy. He grudged Charlie
a nod. "Okay. Good." He shoved the *Post* at him. "Take this
with you. If it stays here, I'll use it in the bathroom."

"Nice to see you're still as charming as ever," Charlie
said, and had the small pleasure of walking out while Scriabin scratched his head.

He wrote the story. Where Mike had painted the bill as
black as he could, Charlie chose pastels. He went on about
the ruination of the Dust Bowl. He went on about how
empty the states where the bill would take effect were, and
about how much they needed labor. He talked about how
the criminals who would be doing the labor were paying
their debt to society. He put in so much sugar, if he were a
diabetic he would have needed an insulin shot.

He wondered if he was laying it on too thick, if the White
House would think he was mocking it by singing its praises
too loudly. He also wondered if he really was doing that.
You could insult somebody by calling him sweetie just as
well as you could by calling him a son of a bitch.

But the story ran in papers from Bangor to San Diego. A
few days after it did, he got a call from the White House at
home. It wasn't Scriabin this time. It was Stas Mikoian.
"Good job, Charlie!" the Armenian said. "The wires and
letters coming into the Senate about the bill are running
close to four to one for it."

"They are?" Charlie said. "How do you know?"

Mikoian laughed. "We have ways. You bet we do."

He didn't say what they were. Did someone report to
Joe Steele from every Senator's office? Did the President
have spies in the mailroom at the Capitol? Did somebody
in the Western Union office tally every telegram as it came
off the wire? Charlie had trouble believing that, but he had
just as much trouble not believing Mikoian. Vince Scriabin,
without a doubt, would lie straight-faced. Mikoian seemed
much more at home with the truth.

Which meant . . . what? Suppose you were one of the
minority, someone who didn't like Joe Steele's bill. Would a

cop or a Justice Department agent knock on your door or rough you up on the street? Charlie shook his head. This was America, not one of those sorry countries far away across the sea. That kind of thing couldn't happen here.

"Anyhow," Mikoian went on, his voice warm and genial, "Joe Steele's pleased with what you did. He told me to say thanks, so I am. See you."

"What was that all about?" Esther asked as Charlie hung up.

"That was the White House—Mikoian." If Charlie sounded dazed, well, he felt that way, too. "Joe Steele liked my piece."

"Is that good or bad?"

"Probably." Charlie walked into the kitchen and fixed himself a stiff drink.

A week later, the bill for reconstructing the Midwest passed the Senate. Joe Steele signed it into law. Charlie was one of the reporters he invited to cover the signing ceremony. J. Edgar Hoover stood at the President's right hand while Joe Steele put on his John Hancock. Hoover looked even happier about the law than his boss did. Seeing Hoover happy made Charlie wonder how big a mistake he'd made.

France didn't lose all its royalists after the French Revolution, or after Napoleon, or even after the founding of the Third Revolution. France had royalists to this day, still convinced a Bourbon ought to be ruling from the palace of Versailles. People said about the French royalists that they'd learned nothing and that they understood nothing.

America didn't have royalists—well, except for those who worshiped home-run hitters and movie stars. But nobody, not even the worshipers, wanted to see a movie star as President. That didn't mean the USA did without people who'd learned nothing and who understood nothing. On this side of the Atlantic, they called them Republicans.

As the election of 1936 began to rise over the horizon, the GOP seemed intent on pretending that Joe Steele's first term had never happened. The Elephants might better have been called the Ostriches, so intent were they on sticking their heads in the sand. When Hitler marched the *Reichswehr* into the Rhineland in March, not one of the leading GOP candidates said a word about it. It happened, after all, on the faraway planet called Europe.

Joe Steele spoke up. Charlie noticed that. Unlike most Republican politicos, Joe Steele didn't come from a family American for generations. His parents had made the trip. The Old Country still meant something to him, as it did to millions of his countrymen.

"With this move, Adolf Hitler has torn up the Treaty of Locarno," he said in a radio address. "Germany was not forced to sign that treaty. She did so of her own free will. And now German and French soldiers stare at each other across the Rhine, rifles in their hands. If France had moved, she might have toppled Hitler. The United States would have backed her by all means short of war. I am afraid it's too late now."

From across the Atlantic, the *Führer* thumbed his nose at the President. For all Charlie knew, they both enjoyed it. They could call each other as many names as they pleased. Neither was in any position to go after the other. "Joe Steele understands nothing of the national will or of national self-determination," Hitler bellowed. "No one has ever told him he does not have the right to fortify his frontier."

"Good neighbors don't need forts," Joe Steele retorted. "Our border with Canada is three thousand miles long, without a fort on either side of it. Trust counts for more in keeping the peace than concrete and cannons."

Every bit of that flew straight over the Republicans' heads. They wanted to turn the clock back to 1931. (Actually, they wanted to turn it back to 1928 and prosperity, but no one seemed to know how to bring that off.) In one of his articles about the state of the GOP, Charlie quoted Mr. Dooley, a wit from the turn of the century: *Th' raypublican party broke ye, but now that ye're down we'll not turn a could shoulder to ye. Come in an' we'll keep ye—broke.*

He got a phone call from a chuckling Stas Mikoian about that one. And he also got a rebuttal of sorts from Westbrook Pegler. The *Chicago Tribune* columnist had supported Joe Steele over Hoover in 1932, but soon soured. Now nothing the President did was any good to him. He threw Mr. Dooley back in Charlie's face—and in Joe Steele's, too: *A man that'd expict to thrain lobsters to fly in a year is called a loonytic; but a man that thinks men can be tu-rrned into angels be an iliction is call a rayformer an' remains at large.*

Charlie laughed in spite of himself when he saw Pegler's piece. So did Esther, when he showed it to her. "He got you, Charlie," she said, which Charlie couldn't very well deny. But then she added, "I bet even Joe Steele thinks that's funny."

"Nope." Charlie shook his head. "Mikoian may. Joe Steele and Scriabin, though, they don't laugh at a whole bunch."

He hied himself off to Cleveland to watch the Republicans pick someone to run against the President. Herbert Hoover wanted another crack at Joe Steele. However big a death wish the GOP owned, it wasn't that big. The convention nominated Governor Alfred Landon of Kansas on the first ballot. For a running mate, the delegates gave him Chicago newspaper publisher Frank Knox (he put out the *Daily News*, not the *Tribune*).

Landon was in his late forties. He was better-looking than Joe Steele; he might have been a preacher or a high school principal. He meant well. Charlie could see that. Hoover had meant well, too. And what did it get him? Shantytowns named after him, and a smashing electoral defeat.

"I am a man of the people," Landon said in his acceptance speech. "Someone needs to be for them, because Joe Steele has turned against them. The Populists came out of Kansas when I was a boy. If you like, I am a Populist myself."

Charlie liked that fine. Quoting Ambrose Bierce was even more fun than quoting Mr. Dooley. Gone but not forgotten, Bierce defined a Populist as *A fossil patriot of the early agricultural period, found in the old red soapstone underlying Kansas; characterized by an uncommon spread of ear, which some naturalists contend gave him the power of flight, though Professors Morse and Whitney, pursuing independent lines of thought, have ingeniously pointed out that had he possessed it he would have gone elsewhere. In the picturesque speech of his period, some fragments of which have come down to us, he was known as "The Matter with Kansas."*

He hadn't thought to do anything more than have fun with *The Devil's Dictionary*. But sometimes a phrase sticks. Sometimes people will make it stick if they think that will do them good. After the Democrats came together to re-nominate Joe Steele and John Nance Garner, they started calling Alf Landon "The Matter with Kansas," too. Every ad for the ticket used the phrase.

"If I am 'The Matter with Kansas,' then Joe Steele is what's the matter with the whole country," Landon declared. He proudly wore a Kansas sunflower on his lapel. But he was about as exciting as oatmeal with skim milk. His campaign bounced and rattled. It never took off and flew.

The Literary Digest took a poll. It predicted that Landon would win twice as many electoral votes as Joe Steele. Charlie asked Stas Mikoian what he thought about that. "We aren't voting about literature," the wily Armenian answered.

People swarmed to the polls on election day. As soon as the polls started closing, it became obvious that *The Literary Digest*'s poll couldn't touch the real results with a ten-foot pole. In 1932, Joe Steele had beaten Herbert Hoover by a landslide. Everybody said so at the time. That made headline writers grope for a new word to describe what he did to Alf Landon. *Avalanche* was the one they hit on most often.

An avalanche it was. Joe Steele won forty-six of the forty-eight states. As MAINE GOES, SO GOES VERMONT, one wag of a newspaperman wrote. The President took more than sixty percent of the popular vote. His coattails gave the Democrats even more Senators and Representatives than they'd had before.

Over Christmas, Charlie and Esther went up to New York City to visit family and friends. Chanukah had ended on the sixteenth, but Esther's mother made latkes for them when they got there. Charlie loved latkes. The only problem was . . . "Gawd, I feel like I swallowed a bowling ball," he said as the two of them staggered out of Istvan and Magda Polgar's apartment.

"An onion-flavored bowling ball," Esther said.

Charlie burped. "Yeah, that, too."

With the Polgars, he didn't have to worry about anything but overeating and heartburn. Things got trickier when he and Esther went out to dinner with Mike and Stella. "Well, your guy got another four years," Mike said even before they sat down in the steakhouse. "Looks like you *can* fool most of the people most of the time."

"Mike, I'm gonna tell you two things about that," Charlie answered. "The first one is, Joe Steele ain't my guy. I just work out of Washington, so I write a lot about politics."

"You suck up to those California gangsters, is what you do," Mike said.

Charlie held up a hand, and held on to his temper. "The other thing is, we came up here to see people we care about—"

"People we love," Esther broke in.

"People we love." Charlie nodded. "That's right. We didn't come up here to wrangle about politics. That's not a whole lot of fun. Okay?"

Mike was scowling. Charlie wondered if he'd had a drink or three before he came over here. Stella put her hand on his arm. He started to shake her off, but seemed to think twice. With what looked like a real effort, he made himself nod. "Okay, Charlie. We'll do it that way. For auld lang syne, and all."

"For auld lang syne," Charlie agreed gratefully. He *didn't* want to fight with his brother, especially out in public. He was in New York for a good time, not a row.

He got a T-bone. Esther chose a New York strip. Each cut off a bite and passed it to the other. Mike and Stella did the same thing with his sirloin and her veal chop. Marriage had all kinds of advantages. You got to try two different entrees whenever you went out to eat together.

But, except for the food, the dinner wasn't a success. Charlie sighed once he and Esther got back to their hotel room after good-byes and handshakes and hugs. "Even if we didn't talk about it, the elephant was still in the room," he said.

"The elephants are all lying on their backs with their legs in the air," Esther said.

He made a face at her. "You know what I mean. He thinks I'm a sellout. He might not've said it, but he still thinks it. And the way it looks to me is, he's so buggy about Joe Steele, he doesn't like anything the man does. And he has done some good, doggone it."

"Some, maybe," Esther said judiciously. "But everything comes with a price. And now we've got four more years to see how expensive it is."

March, people said, came in like a lion. If March did come in like a lion, then January, 20, 1937, was . . . what? A *Tyrannosaurus rex*, maybe. The Twentieth Amendment had moved Inauguration Day forward by six weeks, but it hadn't moved the weather.

The day was about as nasty as Washington ever got, in fact. Close to a quarter of a million had come into the nation's capital to watch Joe Steele take the oath of office for his second term, and Charlie was sure just about all of them wished they'd stayed wherever they came from. Several thousand holed up in Union Station and never got any farther. They might have been the lucky ones, or the smart ones.

It was cold. It was wet. It was miserable. It started raining before sunup and it didn't stop all day. In the morning, some of the rain was freezing and some turned to sleet. By noon, the mercury did climb above freezing: one whole degree above freezing. Shivering in a topcoat under an umbrella, Charlie would sooner have been home in bed. Much sooner.

Joe Steele went ahead with the ceremony as if it were seventy-five degrees and not a cloud in the sky. Joe Steele, from everything Charlie had seen, always went ahead with what he'd already planned to do, no matter what. If people got in his way, he went through them or ran over them. If the weather got in his way, he just ignored it.

That meant Charles Evans Hughes also had to go ahead with the ceremony. The Chief Justice was in his mid-seventies. Watching water drip from the end of his nose and from his beard, Charlie hoped the poor old man wouldn't come down with pneumonia and die. Hadn't that happened to somebody, to one of the Presidents? Was it William Henry Harrison? He thought so, but wasn't sure without looking it up. (Was Joe Steele, on the other hand, hoping Hughes did die of pneumonia so he could name a pliable replacement? Charlie told himself that was the kind of thing Mike would think.)

The President took the oath of office about twenty past twelve. It was raining harder than ever. A Secret Service man held an umbrella over Joe Steele's head. Another held one above the microphone. Charlie watched that with some apprehension. Wouldn't you fry yourself using the mike in this weather?

It didn't bother the President. Or if it did, Joe Steele didn't show it. Not showing he was bothered was another of his strengths. Not far from Charlie, Lazar Kagan and Stas Mikoian both looked miserable. Even Scriabin might have wanted to be somewhere else, and his pan was almost as dead as his boss'.

"We have finished the first Four Year Plan. We will go on with the second Four Year Plan." Joe Steele made his program seem as implacable as he was. "The first Plan laid the foundation for moving forward with reconstructing our country. Now we will build on that foundation. The powerful who have become powerful by tricks and by guile have tried to stop me, but they have failed. The people see through their lies. We will move forward, and we will have better days ahead."

He paused for applause. He got some, but it was tepid and muffled. Almost everybody was too soaked to show much enthusiasm—and the steady rain drowned the sound of clapping.

"I will work without rest to make this great nation more secure both at home and abroad," the President said. "No wreckers will be allowed to stand in the way of progress or to sabotage it. No foreign foe will be allowed to challenge our strength. We defy Reds and Fascists alike. Neither disease will ever touch these shores!"

Another pause for applause. Some more soggy handclaps. Charlie thought the inaugural address would read well, but nobody except perhaps Gypsy Rose Lee would be able to excite this crowd—and Gypsy Rose Lee would freeze to death if she came out in what she usually almost wore.

Joe Steele plowed ahead. He promised jobs. He promised food. He promised dams and highways and canals. He promised warships on the seas, warplanes in the skies, and tanks on the ground. The microphone didn't electrocute him. Charlie couldn't have said why it didn't, but it didn't.

And after the speech was done, Joe Steele stood on an open-air reviewing stand while soldiers and tanks and marching bands rolled past. No one held an umbrella over his head there. He had his familiar cloth cap, and that was it. According to the program, bombers were supposed to have flown by overhead, but that bit of business did get canceled. Nobody could have seen the planes through the thick, dark clouds.

When he went back to the White House, it was in the same open car that had brought him to the Mall. Charlie was also in an open car, eight or ten vehicles behind the President's. People lining the streets waved to him and the other shivering, dripping reporters, thinking they were dignitaries. A couple of them waved back. Charlie didn't have the energy.

Secret Service men hurried the reporters into the White House. Going past the President's car, Charlie saw that it had something like a half inch of water sloshing around in the bottom of the passenger compartment. The one he'd ridden in must have, too.

Colored cooks and servants set out hot coffee and tea and snacks. A Negro bartender in a tux waited for business. If he didn't get rich from the tips the grateful gentlemen of the press gave him, they were even cheaper than they got credit for.

"I may live," Charlie said after he got outside of a cup of coffee and a shot of bourbon.

"I must get out of these wet clothes and into a dry Martini." Another newspaper man shamelessly cribbed from a movie script.

Charlie was contemplating another bourbon—as antifreeze, of course—when Lazar Kagan came up to him. The chunky Jew had put on a dry jacket, but his shirt still clung to him under it. "The President would like to talk to you for a few minutes," he said.

"He would?" Charlie wondered how much trouble he was in. Joe Steele was not the most forthcoming President the country had ever had. He seldom talked for the sake of talking.

Kagan led Charlie from the press room to the President's Study, the oval chamber above the Blue Room. Joe Steele sat behind a massive desk made from California redwood with a granite top. The President puffed vigorously on his pipe. He'd had to do without it while he was watching soldiers and musicians squelch by. No one could have kept it lit out there.

"Hello, Sullivan," Joe Steele said, voice friendly but eyes hooded as always.

"Mr. President," Charlie said cautiously. He tried something more: "Good luck on your new term, sir."

"Thank you. Thank you twice, in fact. You helped some with 'The Matter with Kansas.'"

"It wasn't mine, you know. I just hauled it out and used it." *Better I tell him myself,* Charlie thought.

"Oh, yes." Joe Steele nodded. Even relaxed and smoking, he radiated danger as a banked fire radiated heat. "But you did haul it out, and it stuck to Landon like a burr. One of the easiest ways to beat a man is to make him look ridiculous."

"Yes, sir." Charlie knew that, as any reporter did. But reporters didn't make it sound clinical, the way Joe Steele had.

The President leaned forward, toward Charlie. "Yes, I have you to thank, to some degree. I do not thank your brother, though." For a moment, the fire wasn't banked, and the danger fairly blazed.

Gulping, Charlie said, "Mr. President, I don't know what I can do about that."

"No? Too bad." Joe Steele made a small, flicking gesture with his left hand. Charlie left the study. Charlie, if you want to get right down to it, fled.

X

Even a President who wasn't the most forthcoming did have to come forth now and again. Modern politics demanded it. If you stayed in Washington all the time, people would forget about you. Or, if they remembered, they would think you were hiding out there for a reason. Radio and newsreels helped some, but they couldn't do it all. Real people had to see a real President, or else he might stop seeming real.

And so Joe Steele took a train from Washington to Chattanooga to celebrate the completion of one of the dams that would ease flooding in the Tennessee River Valley and bring electricity to millions who lived nearby. Charlie was one of the reporters who got invited to travel with him. The President . . . noticed Charlie these days. As with the fellow who found himself tarred and feathered and ridden out of town on a rail, if not for the honor of the thing, Charlie would rather have walked.

He played poker and bridge with the other reporters on board—and with Mikoian and Scriabin. Mikoian played better bridge than poker. Vince Scriabin was a shark at both games: his expressionless face was good for all kinds of things. "The government doesn't pay you enough?" Charlie groused after the Hammer squeezed out a small slam in diamonds.

"When it comes to money or power, is there ever such a thing as enough?" Scriabin replied. Not having a good answer for that one, Charlie kept his mouth shut.

Along with cards, *Gone With the Wind* killed time. Charlie had resisted since the novel came out the summer before, even though Esther went crazy for it along with the rest of the country. But a train ride, and especially one down into the South, left him with no more excuses. Nothing like a good, fat book to make you forget you were rattling down the rails. Unlike a deck of cards, a book wouldn't even cost you money after you bought it.

And he did keep turning pages. He would have kept turning them had he been sitting in the overstuffed front-room rocking chair in his apartment. He could see why everybody had swallowed the book whole.

Well, almost everybody. He ate supper in the dining car sitting across the table from Stas Mikoian. He had Swiss steak, which could have been worse but also could have been better. As one of the colored stewards carried his plate away on a tray, he remarked, "I wonder what *he* thinks of *Gone With the Wind*."

"I saw you were reading it," Mikoian said. "I went through it at the end of last year, when I could come up for air after the election. She can write—no two ways about that."

"She sure can. But what *do* you suppose Negroes think about it?"

Mikoian answered the question with another one: "What would you think, if you were a Negro?"

Charlie contemplated that. "I think I might want to punch Margaret Mitchell right in the snoot—only they'd string me up if I did."

"Yes, they would," Mikoian agreed . . . sadly? "Segregation in Washington was an eye-opener for me when I came from California. For you, too, I'm sure, since you're from New York City."

"It's strange, all right," Charlie said. "After the Civil War, the South figured out that it had to let Negroes be free, but it didn't have to let them be equal. And that's where we've been ever since."

"We are, yes," Mikoian said. "Whether we still should be after all this time—that's a different story."

"Are you speaking for Joe Steele?" Charlie asked, pricking up his ears. He hadn't been able to think of anything that would cost the President much of his enormous political clout. Trying to get equal rights for Negroes in the Deep South might turn the trick, though.

"No, just for Anastas Mikoian." Joe Steele's aide quickly shook his head. "I'm an Armenian, remember. In Armenia, my people were niggers to the Turks. It was wrong there, and it's wrong here, too. Armenians, Negroes, Jews—it shouldn't matter. We're all human beings. We all deserve to be treated that way."

"Won't get any arguments from me," Charlie said.

"That's what draws people to the Reds, you know," Mikoian went on. "If they really followed through on 'from each according to his abilities, to each according to his needs,' they'd have something going for them. But they don't, any more than the Nazis do. That's one of the reasons Joe Steele hates Lenin and Trotsky so much. They just found themselves a new excuse to be tyrants. Instead of doing it in the name of one people like Hitler, they say they do it for all humanity—"

"—and they end up doing it to all humanity," Charlie finished for him.

Mikoian flashed a smile. "That's right. They do."

"What about the people who say Joe Steele is doing the same thing to the USA that Lenin and Trotsky have done to Russia?" Charlie asked.

"They're full of shit, that's what," Stas Mikoian said. Charlie must have blinked, because the Armenian let out a sour chuckle. "I'm sorry. Wasn't I plain enough for you?"

"Oh, you might have been." Other questions jumped up and down on the end of Charlie's tongue as if it were a springboard: questions about Franklin Roosevelt, about Huey Long, about the Supreme Court, about Father Coughlin. They jumped up and down, yes, but they didn't dive off. The swimming pool under that springboard had no water in it, not a drop. You'd smash into the concrete bottom, and you would break, and it wouldn't.

With about 120,000 people in it, Chattanooga struck Charlie as a hick town. Then again, Washington also struck him as a hick town. When you grew up in New York

City, the only other place in the world that might not strike
you as a hick town was London. That most of the people in
Chattanooga talked like Southerners—which they were—
did nothing to make them seem less hickish.

Joe Steele stayed at the Road House Hotel, a couple of
blocks from Union Station. (Charlie did wonder whether,
had the South won the Civil War, it would have been called
Confederate Station.) The hotel dated from the boom of
the mid-1920s. The lobby was paneled in walnut, to show
how ritzy it was. The building was twelve stories high, which
made it one of the tallest in Chattanooga. Definitely a hick
town.

The restaurant was decent, and surprisingly cheap.
Charlie ordered sturgeon, which he'd never had before.
"Straight outa the Tennessee River, suh," the waiter said.
"Mighty good, too." It tasted fishy, but not quite like any
other fish he'd eaten before. He didn't think he would have
called it mighty good, but it wasn't bad.

A motorcade took the President and his aides and the
reporters who covered his doings to the Soldiers and Sailors
Memorial Auditorium, where he would speak. The motorcade didn't take long to get where it was going: the auditorium lay only about four blocks northeast of the hotel. Still,
some people stood on the sidewalk to watch the President
roll by. It was a mild spring day, nothing like the dreadful one
on which Joe Steele's second term started.

Here and there, a man or a woman or, most often, a child
would wave an American flag. Most of the thin crowd
seemed friendly, though one man shouted, "Who killed
Huey Long?" as the President's car went by. Charlie
watched a cop run up and give the man a shove. The car he
was in kept him from seeing what, if anything, else happened to the heckler.

The auditorium took up a whole city block. It wasn't
Madison Square Garden, but it wasn't small, either—the
main hall had to hold more than five thousand people. It
was filling up fast, too. The President didn't come to Chattanooga every day. Charlie wondered if a President came to
Chattanooga every decade.

With the other reporters, he had a seat on the stage.

They were off to the side and dimly lit, so the crowd would look at the man behind the lectern and not at them. Charlie noticed a low, broad wooden stool in back of the lectern. The crowd wouldn't see that, but Joe Steele would seem taller than he really was. He chuckled quietly. Reporters noticed such things, but they didn't write about them. Politicians got to keep some illusions.

Reporters also had the sport of watching the people who watched the President. The *Washington Times-Herald*'s Presidential correspondent nudged Charlie and whispered, "Check the soldier in the first row. He's so excited, he's about to wet his pants."

He was, too. He was a young officer—a captain, Charlie thought, seeing the overhead lights flash silver from the bars on his shoulders. He wiggled like a man with ants in his pants. His eyes were open as wide as if he'd gulped eighteen cups of coffee. Even from a good distance away, Charlie could make out white all around his irises.

"And Joe Steele's not even out there yet," Charlie whispered back. "I wonder if he's an epileptic or something, and getting ready to throw a fit."

"That'd liven up the day, wouldn't it?" the *Times-Herald* man said.

"Be nice if something could," Charlie said. He'd been to too many speeches.

Out came the mayor of Chattanooga, to welcome the audience and the President. Out came the engineer who'd been in charge of the local dam, to tell everyone how wonderful it was. Unfortunately, he talked like an engineer—he was so dull, he might have exhaled ether. People applauded in relief when he stopped.

And out came Congressman Sam McReynolds, who'd represented Chattanooga and the Third District of Tennessee for years. He wasn't—Charlie had checked—related to the late Justice James McReynolds; that worthy had come from Kentucky. Only a sadist would have made the brother or cousin of a man he'd executed introduce him to a crowd.

Introduce Joe Steele Congressman McReynolds did. "He pays attention to Tennessee!" McReynolds said, as if announcing miracles. "He pays attention to the little people, the forgotten people, of Tennessee. And here he is—the President of the United States, Joe Steele!"

By the oomph he put into it, he might have been bringing out Bing Crosby or some other popular crooner. And the crowd responded almost as if he were. That Army captain bruised his palms banging them together. No smooth, handsome, debonair crooner came to the lectern, though. It was just Joe Steele, hawk-faced, fierce-mustached, wearing a black suit that might have come straight off the rack at Sears.

He looked out over the audience from behind the lectern. Charlie could see the sheets with the text of his speech, though the people in front of the stage couldn't. Joe Steele raised a hand. The applause died away.

"Thank you," the President said. "Thank you very much. It is good to remember that the people care about me, no matter what the newspapers claim." He won a few chuckles. That dry, barbed wit was the only kind he owned. "And it's good to come to Chattanooga, because—"

"I'll show you what the people think about you, you murdering son of a bitch!" the Army captain screeched. He sprang to his feet, pulled the service pistol from the holster on his hip, and started shooting.

Charlie thought the .45 barked twice before Secret Service men returned fire. He was sure the captain got off at least one more shot after he was hit. Red stains appeared on the front of his tunic. He fell over backward and fired one last time, straight up at the ceiling.

Several people near him in the crowd were shrieking and bleeding, too. Charlie had no idea how many Secret Service men tried to kill the would-be assassin, or how many rounds they fired doing it. One thing was all too obvious: not all those rounds struck the man they were aimed at. A bullet from an excited, hasty gunman was liable to go anywhere.

Joe Steele slumped down to one knee behind the lectern. "Jesus Christ!" the *Times-Herald* man said. "If that bastard killed him, John Nance Garner's President, and God help us all!"

Charlie hardly heard him. The gunfire'd left him paralyzed. He hadn't even had the sense to flatten out on the stage when the shooting started to make himself a smaller target—he didn't have combat reflexes drilled into him from the Great War, since he'd got to France after the shooting ended. He'd just sat there gaping like everybody else. Now he made himself get up and run over to Joe Steele.

The President had both hands pressed to the left side of his chest. Between his fingers, Charlie saw blood on his white shirt. After a moment, he smelled it, too, hot and metallic. "Mr. President! Are you all right?" he bleated—the usual idiot question.

To his surprise, Joe Steele nodded. "Yes, or I think so. It grazed me and glanced off a rib. That may be broken, but unless I am very, very wrong it did not go in."

"Well, thank heaven!" Charlie said. "Let me see it, please?" Scowling, Joe Steele took his hands away. Sure enough, his shirt had a long tear, not a round hole. Charlie unbuttoned a couple of buttons and tugged aside the President's undershirt. There was a bleeding gash below and to the left of Joe Steele's left nipple, but his furry chest wasn't punctured.

"Did they get the asshole who shot me?" he asked—not a line that sounded Presidential, maybe, but one that was plainly heartfelt.

"Yes, sir. He's got more holes than a colander," Charlie said. "Some of the other people by him got hit, too."

Joe Steele waved that back, as being of no account. "He's dead? Too bad. Alive, he could have answered questions." Charlie would not have wanted to answer questions of the kind that burned in the President's eyes.

Somebody grabbed Charlie from behind and yanked him away. He landed on his tailbone on the waxed planks of the stage. It hurt like hell—he saw stars. But he bit down on the yip he wanted to let out. For one thing, the Secret Service guy who'd thrown him aside was only doing his job. For another, he was a long, long way from the worst hurt here.

"Is there a doctor in the audience?" the agent by Joe Steele yelled. Some medical men were there. Looking out,

Charlie saw them doing what they could for the wounded close by the assassin. At the call, a tall man with a cowlick jumped up on the stage and hurried to the President's side.

"Take a gander at this," one Secret Service man said to another. "Look how the waddayacallit here has these chromed bars for reinforcement or decoration or whatever the hell." He was pointing at the lectern. "And the bullet caught one of 'em and slewed, like. Otherwise, it might've hit the boss dead center."

"That woulda been all she wrote, sure as hell. You *don't* want to meet up with a .45, not square on you don't," his friend replied.

"Who was the guy who fired at the President?" Charlie asked.

They seemed to remember he was in the neighborhood. "No idea yet," one of them said. "But we'll find out, and we'll find out who was behind him, too. Oh, yeah. You bet we will."

The assassination attempt spawned screamer headlines around the country—around the world, in fact. It also spawned the biggest investigation since the Lindbergh kidnapping. J. Edgar Hoover growled out new little nuggets of fact—or of what he said was fact—to the press almost every day.

No one doubted that the gunman was Captain Roland Laurence South, of San Antonio. He was thirty-one years old, a West Point graduate who'd got his second bar just ten days before his fated, and fatal, encounter with Joe Steele. He'd done very well at the Military Academy. People said he was a general in the making, or he had been till politics started eating away at him.

Hoover was a busy beaver. He gnawed down tree after tree of rumor to bring in twig after twig of fact. The twigs led upward in the chain of command. Like a lot of men who seemed to have a bright future ahead of them, Roland South had made friends in high places. Plenty of men of rank much higher than captain had known him or known who he was.

By all accounts, Captain South hadn't been shy about saying what he thought of Joe Steele. None of his friends in high places had reported him for expressing opinions like that.

"It makes you worry," J. Edgar Hoover said. "It truly does. They claim they didn't report him because talk was cheap and they couldn't imagine he would take out a gun and try to murder the President. But you have to wonder— did they keep quiet because they agreed with him?"

Joe Steele took to the airwaves to say, "People of America, I want you to hear with your own ears that I am alive and doing well. X-rays show that one bullet Captain South fired cracked a rib. I believe that. It hurts like anything when I cough. But the doctors say I will make a full recovery in about six weeks. Captain Roland Laurence South was just one more wrecker who tried to put a roadblock on America's path to progress."

"That's twice in a minute he called him *Captain South*," Esther said as she and Charlie listened to the President in their apartment. "He wants people to remember South was in the Army."

"Uh-huh." Charlie nodded. "And he and his men have talked about wreckers before, but he kind of bore down on it there."

Meanwhile, Joe Steele was continuing, "We have already seen too many wreckers in high places. Wreckers corrupted the workings of the Supreme Court till we set it right. Although Senator Long was murdered before he could be tried, all the evidence points to his being a wrecker, too. Father Charles Coughlin wrecked the teachings of his church to try to tear down the American way of life. And this attempt on my life shows that wreckers may also have infiltrated the highest ranks of our military. The force that should defend our beloved country may want to turn against it."

"Uh-oh," Esther said.

"*Uh-oh* is right," Charlie agreed. "Sounds like the gloves are coming off."

So they were. "We must get to the bottom of this," the President said. "We must be able to rely on our courts, our legislators, and our soldiers to do their duties the way they should. I have appointed Mr. J. Edgar Hoover of the Justice Department to head a new Government Bureau of Investigation—the GBI, for short—to investigate wrecking and to root it out wherever he finds it."

"Wow," Charlie said.

His wife put it somewhat differently: "Yikes!"

"Not all wrecking is in high places, either. We all know that," Joe Steele went on. "The businessman who gouges customers, the farmer who waters his milk before he sells it, the newsman who spreads anti-American lies, the auto builders whose machines start falling to pieces a week after they come off the showroom floor? They're all wreckers, aren't they? Of course they are. And the GBI will have the authority to go after them all."

"Yikes!" Esther said again. "Hitler has Himmler, Trotsky has Yagoda, and now Joe Steele's got J. Edgar Hoover."

"I don't think it's that bad. I hope it's not." But Charlie's mind was a jackdaw's nest. What sprang out of it was the last line of an Edgar Allan Poe story: *And the Red Death held illimitable sway over all.*

As usual, his wife was more pragmatic: "He talked about reporters, Charlie. He singled them out. If you write a story he doesn't like, will somebody from this brand-new super deluxe GBI grab you and give you a shovel and put you to work digging a canal across Wyoming?"

"I . . . hope not," Charlie said slowly. He gnawed on the inside of his lower lip for a few seconds. "All the same, I think I'd better pay a call on the White House tomorrow morning and find out what's going on."

"Good. I was going to tell you I thought you should," Esther said. "I'm glad you've got the sense to see it for yourself."

"Yes, dear," Charlie said, which was never the wrong answer from a husband.

When Charlie went to the White House, he asked to see Scriabin. He thought he might as well hear the worst, and the Hammer would give him that with both barrels. But he got shunted to Lazar Kagan. The receptionist said,

"I'm sorry, Mr. Sullivan, but Mr. Scriabin is otherwise engaged for the time being."

Which was more polite than *Go peddle your papers*, but no more helpful. Kagan was a little more helpful than *Go peddle your papers*, but not a whole lot. Scratching his double chin, he said, "The way it looks to me is, you personally haven't got a thing to worry about, Charlie."

Charlie wasn't sure whether that was good news or bad news. "I'm not here just on account of myself. There's a swarm of people in my racket. And, last time I looked, nobody's repealed the First Amendment."

"Nobody's even talking about repealing it, for heaven's sake." Kagan spread his fleshy hands, appealing for reason. Then he wagged a finger under Charlie's nose. "People can't go around yelling 'Fire!' in a crowded hall, either, though. You need to keep that in mind."

"Yeah, yeah. But somebody can say the President's wrong, or even that he's full of malarkey, without yelling 'Fire!' You don't go to jail for something like that, not since the Alien and Sedition Acts you don't."

"We'll fight wrecking wherever we find it," Kagan said, which might mean anything or nothing. "Politics is rougher than football these days. If we're soft, we'll lose."

"Politics has always been rougher than football," Charlie said. "I'll tell you why, too — there's more money in politics." He waited. He didn't get a rise out of Lazar Kagan. When he decided he wouldn't, he took a different tack: "What's Vince up to right now?"

"You mean, that's more important than seeing you?" Kagan chuckled to himself, pleased at zinging Charlie. "As a matter of fact, he's putting his head together with J. Edgar Hoover. We *are* going to set our house in order."

"Our house as in Washington or our house as in the whole country?" Charlie asked.

"Set Washington straight and leave the rest of the country the way it is and in two years' time Washington will be a mess again," Kagan said. "Set the country straight and Washington will stay all right because the people will choose the best public servants."

"Good luck!" Charlie blurted.

"Thank you." Lazar Kagan sounded placid and happy and confident. He sounded so very placid and happy and confident that Charlie wondered if he had a case of reefer madness.

He also sounded so placid and happy and confident that Charlie got out of there as fast as he could. Then he made a beeline for the nearest watering hole. He didn't usually drink before lunch, but the sun was bound to be over the yardarm somewhere. After Joe Steele's speech and after his own little talk with Kagan, he needed some liquid anesthetic.

He'd been in this dive before. He'd run into John Nance Garner in this dive before, too. As best he could remember, the Vice President was sitting on the same barstool now as he had been then. Garner might well have been wearing the same suit, too, though the cigarette smoldering between his fingers now was probably different from the one he'd been smoking back in Joe Steele's first term. Charlie couldn't prove he'd moved off that barstool since then.

Garner raised an eyebrow when Charlie ordered his double bourbon. "Getting to be a big boy, hey, Sullivan?" he drawled.

Charlie refused to rise to the baiting. "I need it today," he replied. When the barkeep gave it to him, he raised the glass in salute. "Down with reporters and other riffraff!" he said, and down the hatch the drink went. Like a big boy, he didn't cough.

"I'll drink to that." John Nance Garner fit action to words. "'Course, I'll drink to damn near anything. That's all a Vice President is good for—drinking to damn near anything. Beats the snot out of presiding over the Senate, let me tell you."

"Oh, I don't know." The bourbon was hitting Charlie like a Louisville Slugger. "You almost wound up with the top job a little while ago."

"Nah." Garner shook his head in scorn. "No stupid little worthless shit of an Army captain was gonna punch Joe Steele's ticket for him, even if he did come from San Antone. Joe Steele, he'll be President as long as he wants to, or till the Devil decides to drag him back to hell."

"*Back* to hell?" That was an interesting turn of phrase.

"Hell, Fresno, it don't make no difference." How long and how hard had the Vice President been drinking? Long enough to lose his grammar, anyhow. He pointed a nicotine-yellowed forefinger at Charlie. "I know what's wrong with you. You been listenin' to the radio, an' you're in here drowning your sorrows."

"Now that you mention it," Charlie said, "yes."

"It's a crazy business, ain't it?"

"A scary business."

"The thing of it is," John Nance Garner said as if Charlie hadn't spoken, "Joe Steele, he's gonna do what he wants, and ain't nobody gonna stop him or even slow him down much. You see that, you see you can't change it so's you ride with it instead, you'll be all right. I'm all right now—I'm just fine. You bump up agin' him, though, your story don't got no happy ending." He raised that forefinger to ask for another drink without words.

"You've got it all figured out, don't you?" Charlie said.

"Joe Steele, he's got it all figured out," Garner answered. He got to work on the fresh bourbon. Charlie raised his index finger, too. One double wasn't enough, not this morning.

It was summer. Under the sun, under the humidity, Washington felt as if it were stuck in God's pressure cooker. Thunderheads boiled up out of the south. Not even rain, though, could drain all the water from the air.

The baseball Senators wallowed through a dismal season. They weren't last, where the old jingle put them, but they weren't going anywhere, either. They'd brought back Bucky Harris to manage them a couple of years earlier, but it didn't help. The then-boy manager had led them to two pennants in the Twenties. Whatever magic he'd had in those days was as gone now as the soaring stock market.

The Senators who played their games in the Capitol also weren't having a great year. Every so often, Joe Steele would put in a bill to tighten up on this or to make that a Federal crime. The Senators and Representatives passed them in jig time, one after another. Joe Steele signed them into law. A lower-court judge who declared a couple of them unconstitutional ended up in a wheelchair, paralyzed from the waist down, after a terrible car crash. Andy Wyszynski appealed his rulings while he was still in the hospital, and a district court overturned them. Things hummed along.

Charlie and Esther started talking about children. As far as Charlie was concerned, using rubbers was a sin. That didn't stop him; it just gave him something to confess. He didn't go to church as regularly as his mother would have liked. Of course, if he had gone as regularly as Bridget Sullivan liked, he would hardly have had time to do anything else.

Summer was the slow news season. The Japanese bit big chunks out of China, but who could get excited about slanties murdering other slanties? Nobody in America, that was for sure. Hitler was shouting at Austria, and at Czechoslovakia for the way it treated Germans in the Sudetenland, but who on this side of the Atlantic knew, or cared, where the Sudetenland was unless his granny came from there?

And then Charlie's phone rang early one morning, so early that he was just sitting down to coffee and three of Esther's great over-medium eggs. Esther was dressed for work, too—she rode herd on an office full of idiots studying to be morons, at least if you listened to her.

"What the heck?" Charlie said. Either something had gone wrong in the world or it was a wrong number. Grumpily hoping it was a wrong number, he picked up the telephone and barked, "Sullivan."

"Hello, Sullivan. Stas Mikoian." No, not a wrong number. "If you show up at the Justice Department Building at ten this morning, you may find something worth writing about."

"Oh, yeah? Anywhere in particular or sorta all over?" Charlie asked, only slightly in jest. Justice Department headquarters had gone up on Pennsylvania Avenue, half a dozen blocks from the White House, at the start of Joe Steele's presidency. The building was enormous. If the birds ate the bread crumbs you left to mark your trail, you might never get out again.

"Go to the GBI's exhibition center, room 5633," Mikoian said. "I hear that Mr. Hoover will have something to exhibit, all right."

"Like what?"

"That would be telling," the Armenian answered, and hung up.

Charlie swore as he slammed the handset into the cradle. Esther clucked and laughed at the same time. "What's going on?" she asked.

He told her, finishing, "He knows I've got to show up, the miserable so-and-so. It'll probably be some Carolina moonshiner, or else a pig poacher from Oklahoma."

"Well, you've got time to finish breakfast first," Esther said.

Sure enough, Charlie went over to the Justice Department and with plenty of coffee keeping his eyelids apart. He wasn't completely amazed to run into Louie Pappas on the way to room 5633. "Who tipped you off?" Charlie asked.

"One of the White House guys called AP," the photographer said. "So something's going on, and they want pictures of whatever it is."

Checking his watch, Charlie said, "Whatever it is, we'll know in fifteen minutes."

"Hot diggety dog." If Louie was excited, he hid it well.

J. Edgar Hoover, by contrast, was as bouncy as a chunky man could get. He kept looking down at his own wrist so he could time things to the second. Either his watch ran slow or Charlie's was fast, because Hoover got going at 10:02 Charlie Standard Time.

"The reason you are here today, folks," Hoover told the reporters who fidgeted on folding chairs, "is that the GBI wishes to announce one of the largest and most important series of arrests in American history." He gestured to several men cradling Tommy guns. Hoover, from what Charlie had seen, liked telling armed men what to do.

His henchmen led in ten or twelve dispirited-looking fellows, all of them middle-aged or older. Three wore dark blue; the rest were in khaki. The clothes might have been uniforms, but no rank badges or decorations or emblems remained on them.

"These," J. Edgar Hoover said in portentous tones, "are some of the leading generals in the U.S. Army and admirals in the U.S. Navy. We arrested them last night and this morning. The charge is treason: namely, conspiracy with a foreign power to assassinate the President of the United States. We expect to make further arrests within the military shortly. The accused will be tried before military tribunals. The penalty upon conviction is death."

"Is this connected with Captain South?" Charlie called.

"That is correct," J. Edgar Hoover said while Louie and the other lensmen snapped away at the disgraced officers. More reporters bawled questions. Hoover held up a well-manicured hand. "I don't wish to comment any further at this time. I would say the arrests speak for themselves. I wish I did not have to bring you here on such an unfortunate, embarrassing occasion, but that is what the country has come to."

"Like fun you wish that," Louie muttered out of the side of his mouth. "You're having the time of your life up there."

Hoover gestured to his troops again. They herded the generals and admirals out of the big room and back to wherever they were being confined. The reporters ran for telephones. Had anyone been timing them, some of the sprint records Jesse Owens had set in Berlin the year before would have fallen.

Charlie had to wait for a pay phone this time. The pause helped him organize the story in his mind a little better. He wasn't so stunned as he had been when the Supreme Court Four were accused of treason, or when it was the turn of Huey Long and Father Coughlin. When things happened over and over, they lost some of their power to shock.

But what would the Army and Navy do without their top commanders? Whatever it was, how well could the armed forces do it? One thing he was sure of—Joe Steele didn't worry about it. The President wanted men loyal only to him, and didn't care what he needed to do to get them.

A reporter came out of a phone booth. Charlie elbowed his way into it. He stuck in some nickels, waited till he got an answer, and started talking.

XI

Mike Sullivan slid a half-dollar under the ticket-seller's grill. "Two, please," he said.

The girl dropped the coin into her cash box and handed back two green tickets. "Enjoy the show," she said listlessly.

"I don't know about the show, but I'll enjoy the air-conditioning," Stella said. New York sweltered, but she had a sweater on her arm. Air-conditioning came with two settings: not working at all and way too cold. There was no happy medium.

"I don't know about the show, either." Mike also carried a sweater. "We'll see how it is, that's all." It was a fight film called *Kid Galahad*, with Bogart, Bette Davis, Edward G. Robinson, and a new actor named Wayne Morris in the title role. Despite the strong cast, it had been out for a while without setting the world on fire.

A youngster with a straggly try at a David Niven mustache took their tickets and tore them in half. Mike got popcorn and Good & Plentys and sodas at the snack counter. Popcorn and licorice didn't exactly go together, but what the hell? They didn't exactly not go together, either.

He and Stella went inside and found seats. They passed the goodies back and forth while they put on the sweaters. Yeah, the air-conditioning was going full blast. Two seats over from Stella, a woman hadn't thought to bring a cover-up. She shivered, and her teeth chattered like castanets.

Down went the house lights. The projector turned the big screen to magic. Mike had thought of movies like that ever since he saw his first silent picture when he was a short-pants kid, and a little short-pants kid at that. Movies weren't just bigger than life, they were *better* than life.

Even coming attractions for films that would be forgotten five minutes after their runs ended seemed more interesting than the sweaty world outside the theater. Then the newsreel came on. The Japs pushed forward over heaps of Chinese corpses. Nationalists and Loyalists banged heads in Spain, Hitler and Mussolini fighting Trotsky by proxy.

"And in news closer to home . . ." the announcer boomed. The screen showed more officers tied to the conspiracy against Joe Steele—or what Joe Steele and J. Edgar Hoover said was the conspiracy against the President. "The first batch of military traitors have already been executed," the announcer said, sounding indecently pleased about it. "More severe punishments will be handed down against anyone who plots against America."

A card flashed the name of a city: PHILADELPHIA. The newsreel showed GBI men loading unhappy, unshaven, badly dressed men—plainly ordinary working stiffs, not lieutenant colonels or brigadier generals—into paddy wagons and a couple of big trucks that might have been taken from the Army.

"The crackdown on wreckers continues in the civilian world as well," the announcer said. "These men will labor to help rebuild the country's midsection after they are judicially processed."

"Processed?" Mike made a face as he whispered the word to Stella. "Sounds like they're gonna turn them into bratwurst, doesn't it?"

"Hush," she whispered back. Mike did, but he still wasn't anything close to happy. *Judicially processed* came a lot closer to the truth than *tried* did. People accused of wrecking barely got a trial. They went before a judge—often before a guy styled an administrative law judge, who didn't do anything but deal with wreckers. The men (and women, too) administrative law judges saw got their papers rubber-stamped and went off to do a term in a labor encampment in New Mexico or Colorado or Montana.

Due process? Due process was either a joke or a memory. Mike knew he wasn't the only person who saw that so much of what went on didn't come within miles of being constitutional. But judges willing to say so were thin on the ground; too many had found that unfortunate things happened to those who tried to go against the President.

They said the Devil could quote Scripture to his purpose. Joe Steele quoted past Presidents. He'd used Lincoln repeatedly. He knew Andrew Jackson, too. Whenever a court decision went against him and he didn't feel like killing or crippling the judge right away, he would echo the man on the double sawbuck: "'John Marshall has made his decision. Now let him enforce it.'" Then he would go on doing whatever the judge had told him not to.

A lot of men who pulled a stunt like that would have looked down the barrel of the impeachment gun. Joe Steele had an enormous majority in both houses of Congress. He'd swept to reelection less than a year before. He was still popular with everybody but *The Literary Digest*'s pollsters . . . and the wreckers. If they were wreckers.

Mike knew darn well reporters weren't. The people in his racket might or might not like the President. They universally liked, even loved, their country. As far as he could see, nobody knew of any wreckers in his own line of work. Almost everybody, though, figured there had to be some in other trades. That struck Mike as crazy, but there you were. And here he was.

He paid no attention to the sports highlights, even though the Yankees were knocking the American League to pieces and the Giants were in the race in the National. He hardly watched the two-reeler, either. He could take Westerns or leave them alone.

His political moping carried all the way through the feature. The only point to going out, as far as he could see, was that he was cold and gloomy here, where he would have been hot and sticky and gloomy back in the apartment. Oh, and going out made Stella happy. That counted.

But when they got home he went straight to his portable typewriter—it weighed half a ton instead of a regular machine's full ton—and started banging away. Stella looked miffed. "What are you doing?" she asked. Yes, she sounded miffed, too.

"Trying to tell the truth," he answered, not looking up from what he was doing. The line he'd written at the top of the piece in progress was WHERE IS OUR FREEDOM GOING? "Trying to tell as much of it as I can, anyhow. As much of it as I know."

"Well, do you have to tell it all right this minute? Why don't you come to bed first?"

Not without a pang, Mike stood up. Some suggestions you ignored only at your peril—and at your marriage's. That "first," though, gave him the excuse to go back out to the front room afterwards and start typing again. After a few minutes, Stella closed the bedroom door. Maybe that was to keep the typewriter's noise from bothering her. Or maybe she was making a different point.

Mike took what he'd written to the *Post* the next morning. He kept at it there, pausing twice to go down to the morgue to check on just when Joe Steele had jumped up and down on the Constitution in a particular way. He wanted to make sure he had his facts straight. When he was satisfied, he stashed a carbon in the locking drawer of his desk and took the original in to the managing editor.

"What have you got there?" Stan Feldman asked him.

"An ice-cream cone," Mike answered, deadpan.

"What if I want chocolate, not vanilla?"

"This ain't vanilla, I promise."

"Yeah, that's what they all say." Stan started reading. He didn't say another word till he finished. It was a long story; Mike took the silence as some of the highest praise he'd ever won. At last, the editor looked up. "Well, I just have one question for you."

"What's that?"

"Are you only trying to get yourself hauled away for wrecking, or are you angling to get the *Post* shut down, too?"

"It isn't that bad," Mike said. "I didn't say anything in there that isn't true. I can document everything I did say— which is a hell of a lot more than Joe Steele or J. Edgar Vacuum Cleaner can claim."

"Heh." One chuckle and a brief baring of teeth: Stan gave the gibe all the appreciation it deserved. "What's truth got to do with anything? The only way to stay safe these days is to keep your head down and to hope the wolves don't notice you."

"And if everybody keeps his head down and hopes he doesn't get noticed, by the time Joe Steele runs for a third term—and he will, sure as the Devil—he'll have the whole country sewed up tight, the way Hitler's got Germany."

Stan stood up and closed the door to his office. Mike couldn't remember the last time he'd done that. Walking back to his beat-up, messy desk, the editor said, "I won't tell you you're wrong. In a theoretical way, I mean. But you know what happens to the people who stick their necks out." The edge of his hand came down on a pile of papers like an axe blade.

"If nobody stands up to those people, we all get it in the neck," Mike replied.

Stan did a drumroll on the story with his fingers. "I'm not going to print this on my own hook. Too many careers go on the line if I do. I'm not kidding, Mike. I don't want that on my shoulders. But I will take it upstairs to the publisher. If Mr. Stern says it's okay, we roll with it. If he doesn't . . . It's a fine piece of work, don't get me wrong. So is an artillery shell. That doesn't mean you want one on the coffee table."

J. David Stern had bought the *Post* a few years before. He'd swung it to the left. It had backed Joe Steele on the whole, through his reelection. Now . . . Now it tried not to bang his drum or to say anything bad about him. Mike sighed. "Do whatever you think you have to do. We'll see what he says, and then I'll go from there."

If Stern said no, Mike feared he would have to go from the *Post*. He wondered whether any paper would hire him after that. They'd ask why he'd left. Either he'd have to lie or he'd have to say something like *I tried to tell the truth about Joe Steele.* Yeah, that would make anybody who was thinking of using him jump for joy, all right. Wouldn't it just?

The Daily Worker *might still take me on,* he thought. The

Worker followed Trotsky's line no matter how much it zig-zagged. On Joe Steele, it didn't zigzag much. Trotsky liked the President no better than the President liked him. There were only two things wrong with working there that Mike could see. They didn't pay for beans. And, even if he couldn't stand Joe Steele, he wasn't a Red.

No, there was one thing more. Mike had heard that a couple of men who'd written for the *Daily Worker* were currently breaking rocks or digging canals or doing whatever else people at a labor encampment had to do.

Of course, if J. David Stern did decide to run his story, he might find out about that for himself. Life was full of fascinating possibilities, wasn't it?

For the next few hours, Mike went through the motions of being a newspaperman. His heart wasn't in it. Most of his head wasn't, either. But, as he'd found, he could write some stories simply because he knew how. They wouldn't be great, but they'd do. Nobody expected Hemingway when you were writing about a pistol-packing punk who'd stuck up a delicatessen.

He was about to go to lunch when Stan called, "Hey, Sullivan! C'mere!" and gestured to the doorway to his office.

Bringing the holdup story with him, Mike came. "What do you need?" he asked—it might not have been about WHERE IS OUR FREEDOM GOING?

But it was. "Mr. Stern says we'll go with it," the editor told him. "We're gonna run it on the first page, in fact. You get the byline—unless you don't want it."

There it was, a chance to hit back at the Steele administration without putting himself in quite so much danger. He shook his head. "Thanks, but that's okay," he said. "They wouldn't need long to figure out it was me, anyhow. Not like I never swung on 'em before."

"I told Mr. Stern you'd say that." Stan looked pleased, or as pleased as an editor ever did. "If the paper stands behind the story, the guy who did it ought to stand behind it, too."

"That's my take on it." Mike felt brave and self-sacrificing, like a doughboy about to go over the top when the German machine guns were stitching death across the shattered landscape. The doughboy had a bayoneted rifle. They said the pen was mightier than the sword. This came close enough to make a good test case.

"Mr. Stern said you had it straight," Sam went on. "He said we need to hit Joe Steele six ways from Sunday while we can still do it. He said he was proud he had people like you working for him. And he said to bump you up ten bucks a week."

Mike grinned. "I like the way he talks." Stella would like the raise, too. Every bit helped. They were getting by, but they were a long way from Easy Street. How much Stella would like a story that called Joe Steele an American tyrant and gave chapter and verse to explain why . . . Mike tried not to think about that.

Charlie was having lunch at a sandwich place when another reporter said, "You're Mike Sullivan's brother, aren't you? The guy who writes for the *Post* in New York?"

"That's me." Charlie took another bite of corned beef on rye. "How come?"

"On account of he just went after the President like Ty Cobb stealing third with his spikes sharp and high." The other reporter was in his fifties, old enough to have watched the Georgia Peach at his most ferocious.

"Oh, yeah?" Charlie wasn't surprised that Mike had gone after Joe Steele one more time. Mike had it in for the President, and had had it in for him ever since the Executive Mansion in Albany burned down with Franklin Roosevelt trying to wheel his way out.

He was surprised he hadn't got one of those early-morning calls from Kagan or Scriabin or Mikoian. *I'm in Washington, so they yell at me when they're mad at Mike,* he thought. Only they hadn't this time. Had they decided it didn't do them any good? Or had they just given up on hoping Charlie could talk sense into Mike?

"Yeah," the other reporter said, derailing his train of thought. "He really tore into him. Said he was a cross between Adolf and Leon, with a little Benito thrown in like mustard on your corned beef there. Said he was lying and sneaking his way to tyranny. Added up all the things he'd done since even before he got elected the first time, and said he didn't fancy what they came to."

"How about that?" Charlie had thought his sandwich was pretty tasty. It suddenly lost its flavor. He might as well have been chewing cardboard.

"*How about that?* is right. The *Post* has a big circulation, and other rags pick up pieces from it. This'll raise a big old stink."

"I hope Mike's ready for it," Charlie said. He wondered whether putting in a word for his brother would immunize Mike against Joe Steele's wrath or make it worse. The latter, he feared. He'd already defended Mike to the President's henchmen too often, and even to Joe Steele himself. They knew what he thought.

Unfortunately, he also knew what they thought. The gloves had come off after Roland South shot at—shot—Joe Steele. This whole campaign against wreckers never would have got going the way it had if the country hadn't been shocked by what was almost the fourth assassination of a President in a lifetime. But it was rolling now, and showed no signs of slowing down.

The other reporter said, "Can your brother take a boat to Cuba or Mexico or something? Or the train to Toronto? Or one of those clipper planes to England?" He chuckled to show he was kidding, but none of those sounded like a bad scheme to Charlie.

He was damned if he would show it, though. "It'll blow over. People have been writing nasty stories about Presidents since George Washington. Before that, they wrote nasty stories about George III instead."

"Hope you're right," the older man said. He dug in his pocket and set four bits by Charlie's plate. "Here. Lunch is on me." He bailed out of the eatery before Charlie could either thank him or push the money back.

Charlie stared at the quarter, the two dimes, and the nickel. The other guy had to be telling him he didn't think Mike's chances were good. Charlie muttered to himself. He didn't think his brother's chances were so hot, either. He didn't want to think that, so he tried not to think anything at all. He did some more muttering. *Not* thinking wasn't so easy.

He went back to his desk, hoping he would find a message from the White House. That would let him call back without looking like a beggar. There was a message—from his wife, asking him to pick up a loaf of bread and a cabbage on his way home. He started to crumple it up and throw it out. Then he stuck it in an inside jacket pocket instead. That might help him remember.

Nobody from the White House called all afternoon. It wouldn't be that they hadn't seen or heard about Mike's piece. They didn't miss such tricks. No. Plainly, they'd washed their hands of him. They were going to do whatever they were going to do, and they didn't give a damn what Charlie had to say about it.

He did bring home the bread and the cabbage. He also brought home a fifth of Old Grand-Dad. Esther raised an eyebrow when she took it out of the bag. Charlie explained. She grimaced and hugged him. That made him feel a little better, but not nearly enough. After supper, the bourbon helped, too—but also not nearly enough.

People who'd escaped Trotsky's Russia and Hitler's Germany talked about the knock on the door at midnight, with the secret police waiting outside to grab you as soon as you opened up. The midnight knock had been a staple of spy novels since the Great War ended, if not longer. The movies used it all the time, too. Of course they did—it was suspenseful as all get-out.

But, no matter what, you never thought it could happen to you. That was an enormous part of what made Joe Steele's campaign against wreckers so effective. Nobody ever thought it could happen to him till it did. By then, it was too late.

Even Mike didn't really believe it could happen to him. Oh, he knew he'd poked the bear in the White House with a stick. He knew the bear had teeth and claws, too. He also knew, though, that there was such a thing as the First

Amendment. Freedom of speech and freedom of the press were enshrined in the Constitution. He assumed that still mattered.

Nothing was wrong with his knowledge. His assumptions, now, his assumptions proved sadly out of date.

When the knock came, it was actually closer to one in the morning than to midnight. It wasn't a very loud knock. Whoever was out there didn't aim to wake everybody up and down the hall. But it was very insistent. Knock, knock, knock . . . Knock, knock, knock . . . Knock, knock, knock . . .

It got to Stella first. "What's that?" she mumbled, still half asleep.

Her words made Mike open his eyes. Knock, knock, knock . . . "Somebody at the door," he said. He scowled, there in the warm dark. *Therefore never send to know for whom the bell tolls; it tolls for thee* ran through his mind. John Donne had it pegged, all right.

"Whoever it is, tell 'em to get lost." No, Stella wasn't with it yet.

Mike was. For better or worse, he woke quickly and completely. "I'll give it my best shot," he said, and padded out to the front room in his bare feet. He shut the bedroom door behind him before he turned on a light out there. Blinking, he asked the obvious stupid question: "Who is it?"

"Government Bureau of Investigation, Sullivan," a gruff voice answered. "Open up. You're under arrest."

"What if I don't?"

"We break the door down or else we shoot through it and then break it down," the voice said. "So open up. If you don't, we tack on resisting and everything you catch gets worse."

He believed the guy out there. He'd been doing his job when he wrote the article that tore into Joe Steele. The GBI men out there were convinced they were just doing their job, too. You could hear it in the way that fellow talked. You could also hear that he'd done this plenty of times before.

Numbly, Mike opened the door. Three men in cheap suits stood out there, one with a Tommy gun, one with a revolver, and one smacking the palm of his left hand with a blackjack held in his right. "Smart fella," he said. "C'mon. Quiet. No fuss."

"Can I get some regular clothes?" Mike gestured at his seersucker pajamas. "The closet's right here."

The Jeebies looked at one another. "What the hell—go ahead," said the one with the cosh. He'd been doing all the talking. "Make it snappy, though."

Pants, shirt, jacket, shoes . . . Those were all easy. Socks were back in the bedroom. Mike decided to do without. If the goons weren't inclined to bother Stella, he didn't want to give them ideas. "I'm ready," he said, one of the bigger lies he'd ever come out with.

"Awright." They took him away. Stella didn't come out screaming and fighting. That was nothing but a relief to Mike. It would have done no good, and it might have got her hurt or seized with him. Maybe she fell back to sleep.

A man down the hall opened his door, saw what was happening, and slammed it shut again. He might have been keeping demons away. The GBI men took Mike down the stairs and out to a car waiting not far away.

"When we get to jail, I want to call a lawyer," he said as he bent to get in.

The Jeebie with the blackjack used it then. Later, when Mike could think clearly again, he decided the guy would have clobbered him even if he hadn't said a word. Knocking a prisoner over the head was just part of the process of getting him under control. If he was loopy, he couldn't cause trouble.

Loopy Mike was. Everything about his ride in that car—except the stink of tobacco, sour sweat, and old puke—stayed blurry ever after. They didn't go to a police station. They went to the Federal Building on the Lower West Side. They got there ridiculously fast. There was next to no traffic at that time of night. Even with his brains rattled, Mike noticed that.

"Another wrecker, huh?" a security guard outside the building said as the Jeebies hauled Mike out of the car and kept him on his feet. They treated him more like a sack of beans than a man. He felt more like a sack of beans, too.

"You betcha," answered the GBI agent with the black-jack. To his comrades, he said, "Bring him on in. We'll get him processed and go out for the next bastard on the list."

Processed Mike was, like a side of beef. Some kind of official demanded his name. He had to think twice before he could give it. They searched him. They fingerprinted him. They photographed him. He doubtless looked like hell, but they didn't care.

They gave him a number: NY24601. Someone wrote it on a piece of cloth with an indelible pen and stapled it to his lapel. For good measure, the man yanked the jacket off him and wrote it on the lining. "Don't forget it," he said. "From now on, that's you."

Since Mike had trouble with his name just then, he wasn't sure about stowing the number in his pounding head, but he had help with it. They hauled him up in front of a fellow with a nameplate on his desk that said MORRIS FRUMKIN and below it, in smaller letters, ADMINISTRATIVE LAW JUDGE. "Charges?" Frumkin asked in a bored voice.

"Wrecking, to wit, libel against the Administration and its enlightened policies," replied the man with the enlight-ened blackjack.

"Oh. He's *that* Sullivan." Morris Frumkin made a check mark on a list held in a clipboard. "Well, we don't need much of a hearing for him, do we? He obviously did it. Sullivan, as administrative punishment for wrecking, you are transferred to a labor encampment in the Deprived Areas"—even groggy, Mike heard the capital letters thud into place—"for a term not to be shorter than five years and not to exceed ten. Transfer to take place immediately, sentence to be counted from arrival at the encampment." He gabbled that out by rote and nodded to the men who had charge of Mike. "Put him in the holding cells till the next paddy wagon goes to Penn Station."

They did. Half a dozen men already waited there. They were all the worse for wear. A couple had blood on their heads and shoulders—the Jeebies who clouted them hadn't been so smooth as Mike's captor. And one was all bloody and bruised. He'd put up a fight before Joe Steele's agents could subdue him. What had it got him? Fifteen to twenty instead of five to ten. He was proud of the longer term, as he was of his lumps.

Mike's head started pounding like a steel mill. One of the other wreckers slipped him two aspirins from a little tin the GBI men had missed. That was sending a baby to do a man's job, but every little bit helped.

Another man got tossed in. Then the Jeebies herded them into a van. They went to Penn Station, and down to a level Mike had never imagined, much less seen. The splendid imitation of the Baths of Caracalla on the ground floor might as well not have existed. This wasn't Roman. It was all bare, angular concrete and hard metal benches without backs. Mike sank down onto one and held his poor abused noggin in his hands. Several other wreckers assumed the same pose.

A train clattered in. The noise hurt, the way it would have with a hangover. Guards chivvied them into the front two cars. Those were already crowded. Most of the guys in them talked with New England accents. The guards didn't care that they were only making the crowding worse.

"Don't worry about it none, you sorry shitheads," one of them said. "Time you get where you're goin', whole fuckin' train'll be packed." He laughed. Mike didn't think it was funny, not that the guard gave a damn.

The whistle screamed. That hurt, too. The train pulled away from that subterranean stop. Mike was bound for . . . somewhere.

The telephone rang. Charlie did his best to jump through the ceiling. When the phone goes off in the middle of the night, it means one of two things. Either some sleepy operator has made a wrong connection at the switchboard or something horrible has happened to somebody who thinks you're important.

"Gevalt!" Esther said.

"No kidding." Charlie rolled out of bed and headed for the living room. He hit his toe on the door frame and his shin on the coffee table before he could grab the phone. "Hello?"

"This is the long-distance operator," said a prim female voice. "I have a call for you from Stella Sullivan in New York City. Will you accept?"

"Yeah," Charlie answered. Something horrible had happened, all right, and he was only too sure he knew what it was.

"Go ahead, Miss Sullivan . . . excuse me, *Mrs.* Sullivan," the operator said. To Charlie, her voice seemed muffled—she was really talking to Stella at the other end of the connection.

"Charlie?" Stella said through pops and clicks.

"Yeah, it's me, all right." He wasn't sleepy any more. Hoping against hope for a miracle, he asked, "What's cooking?"

"Oh, my God, Charlie! They grabbed Mike! They came for him and they took him away and I don't know what they did with him and I just stayed in the bedroom all scared and shivering till I knew they were gone and then I called you and oh my God Charlie what am I gonna do?" Stella didn't usually talk like that. She didn't usually have any excuse *to* talk like that.

Charlie let out a long, long sigh. "Oh . . ." he said, and stopped right there. His father's hard hand applied to the side of his head had taught him not to swear in front of women. *On the phone with* counted as *in front of.*

"What will you do, Charlie?" Stella said. "Can you do anything?"

"I'll try," Charlie said. "I don't know what they'll say. I don't *think* trying will make it any worse for Mike. I don't know if it'll make things any better, either. But I'll try. The worst they can tell me is no. I'm pretty sure that's the worst they can tell me."

"Thank you, Charlie. God bless you!" Stella said. "I'm gonna go light a candle in church right now."

"Can't hurt." Charlie feared it was liable to do as much good as he could with Kagan or Scriabin or Mikoian.

He said his good-byes with Stella and stumped back to the bedroom. Esther had turned on the lamp on her nightstand, so he didn't injure himself during the return trip. "Was that . . . ?" she began. She didn't go on, or need to.

"Yeah, that's what that was." Charlie made a fist and hit the mattress as hard as he could. Then he hit it again. It didn't accomplish anything, but it made him feel a tiny bit better. Darwin had it straight—men were only a small step from apes banging on stumps with branches. "They've got Mike."

"Can you do anything about it?"

"I told Stella I'd try. I'll go to the White House when it gets light. I'll go hat in hand. I'll wear dark glasses and wave a tin cup around. In the meantime, turn out the lamp again, okay?"

"Sure." As she did, she asked, "Do you think you'll go back to sleep?"

"No, but I'll give it a shot." He lay down on his back and stared up at the blackness under the ceiling. He tried to count sheep. In his mind, they all turned to mutton chops and legs of lamb. Eventually, after what seemed a long time and no doubt was, he did drop into a muddy doze that left him almost more tired than if he'd stayed awake.

When the alarm clock clattered, for a bad moment he thought it was Stella on the phone again. He'd never killed it with more relief. Esther set something on the table in front of him. He ate breakfast without noticing what it was. He did realize she kept his coffee cup full, and her own. He went on yawning in spite of all the help the java could give him.

He visited AP headquarters before heading for Pennsylvania Avenue. People were quietly sympathetic when he told them where he had to go. They knew Mike had gone after Joe Steele with brass knucks. They also knew what happened to anyone who did something so foolhardy. Talking about such things was bad manners, but everybody knew.

Even the guard outside the White House expected Charlie. "Mr. Mikoian told me you'd likely stop by this morning, Mr. Sullivan," the Spanish-American War veteran said. "You go straight to his office. He'll see you."

Charlie went straight to Mikoian's crowded little office. He had to cool his heels outside, but only for fifteen minutes. The Assistant Secretary of Agriculture came out with a worried look on his well-bred face.

Charlie stuck his head in. "Come on, sit down," Stas Mikoian told him. "Close the door behind you."

"Thanks." Charlie did. After he sank into his chair, he said, "I got a call from my sister-in-law in the middle of the night. They arrested Mike and took him away. I don't like to beg, Stas, but I'm begging. If there's anything you can do, please do it. I'll pay you back some kind of way." If that meant writing fawning stories about Joe Steele for as long as he stayed President, Charlie would do it, and count the cost later.

But Mikoian shook his head. "I'm sorry. There isn't anything I can do." He actually did sound sorry, where Kagan would have said the same thing with indifference and Scriabin might have gloated. Shaking his head again, he went on, "My hands are tied. The boss says he's taken enough fleabites from your brother. He made his bed. Now he can lie in it."

"Will he . . . talk to me?" Charlie had to lick dry lips halfway through the question. He didn't want to have to talk to Joe Steele, not about anything like this. But Mike was his brother. For flesh and blood, you did things you didn't want to do.

"No," the Armenian answered. "He knew you'd be coming around. He keeps track of everything, you know. He has for as long as I've worked for him, since right after the war. I don't know how he does it, but he does. He told me to tell you this was once too often. And he told me to tell you that if he didn't care for what you did it would have been once too often a long time ago now."

"If I can guarantee that Mike will keep quiet—"

"You know you can't. Keeping that kind of promise isn't in him, any more than a drunk keeps promises to sober up. Your brother would fall off the wagon in a month, tops."

No matter how much Charlie wanted to call him a goddamn liar, he couldn't. Mikoian was too likely to be right. Voice dull with hopelessness, Charlie asked, "What am I supposed to tell Stella?"

"Tell her you did everything a brother could. You know I have a brother in California. There are wreckers among the engineers and scientists, too. I understand your trouble. Right now, it's the country's trouble. We'll be better for it in the end." Mikoian seemed to mean that, too. Charlie wondered how.

XII

The train wheezed to a stop. They were somewhere west of Livingston, Montana. Mike had seen the sign announcing the name of the town through the shutters the guards had put over the windows. He was convinced that wasn't because they didn't want the prisoners seeing out. No—it was because they didn't want ordinary people looking in and seeing what they were doing with the men they'd arrested for wrecking.

He'd thought this car had been crowded when he stumbled into it under Penn Station. Well, it had been, and it got more and more so. You couldn't go to another car to use the toilet. They had honey buckets in here. By now, the buckets were overflowing. Nobody'd bathed. There was barely enough water to drink, let alone to use for getting clean. The stink of unwashed bodies warred with that from the buckets.

There hadn't been much food, either. They gave out stale chunks of bread and crackers and sheets of beef jerky hard enough to break a tooth on. All of it was like the free lunch at a saloon just inside hell's city limits. It made everybody in the car thirstier—not that the guards cared.

Some men simply couldn't take it. They gave up and died. The prisoners had passed the guards two bodies at different stops. From the way the air was starting to smell, somebody else had cashed in his chips, too, and was going off. If the guards wanted to let the prisoners know that nobody cared any more about what happened to them, well, they knew how to get what they wanted.

A guard banged on the locked and barred door at the front of the car. He kept banging on it till the cursing, moaning prisoners quieted down some. Then he shouted, "My buddy an' me, we got Tommy guns with full drums. We got reinforcements, too. We're gonna open this door. You fuckers come out slow, in good order. *Slow*, you hear? You all come chargin' out at once, we're gonna kill a whole bunch o' you. Nobody'll give a shit if we do, neither. So do like we tell you or get ventilated. Them's your choices."

He waited to let that sink in. Then, slowly and cautiously, he did open the door. As slowly and cautiously as they could, the wreckers came out: hungry, thirsty, whiskery, frightened men. Mike was angry as well as scared. He would have bet some of the other prisoners were, too. But the guards hadn't been lying about their firepower. Charging Tommy guns with your bare hands was just a way to kill yourself, and maybe not quickly.

Sunlight made him blink and set his eyes watering. It had been gloomy in the car after they mounted those shutters. Montana. What did they call it? Big Sky Country, that was the name. It deserved the handle, too. The sweep of sky was wider and bluer than anything Mike had seen back East. The train stood on a siding in what could have been the exact middle of nowhere. A four-lane blacktop road paralleled the tracks. Not a car coming, not a car going.

"Line up in rows of ten!" a guard with a Tommy gun yelled. "Stand at attention if you know what that is. If you don't, pick somebody who looks like he does and do like him."

Mike took his place in one of those rows. All his other choices seemed worse. A drill sergeant would have cussed him out for his stand at attention—stab at attention would have been closer. But as long as the wreckers stood up straight and held still, the Jeebies didn't fuss.

A breeze tugged at Mike's uncombed, sweat-matted hair. It felt dry, and smelled of pine and grass. The mercury couldn't have been over seventy-five. Along with everything else, he'd left New York City's heat and humidity behind.

"Fuck!" somebody in back of him said softly. It sounded more like a prayer than an obscenity. The word dropped into a spreading pool of silence and disappeared. No traffic noise. No elevators going up and down in the building—no buildings, not as far as the eye could see. No radios blatting. No nothing.

More and more wreckers stumbled out of more and more train cars and formed more and more rows of ten. Along with the rest of them, Mike stood there, trying to stay on his pins while he waited to see what happened next.

He didn't see it. He heard it. Some of the men at attention didn't turn their heads to the left as soon as they caught the noise, for fear of what the guards would do. Others did, either taking the chance or not knowing better than to move without permission while at attention. When they got away with it, the rest, Mike among them, also looked.

A convoy of khaki-painted Army trucks was rumbling up the road toward them. Wherever they were going next, it was somewhere the railroad didn't run. Mike wondered if there'd be any food and water at the end of the truck trip. All he could do was hope.

"Board the trucks till they're full. I mean *full*!" a guard shouted after the big snorters stopped. "Don't get cute. It's the last dumb thing you'll ever do. Somebody *will* be watching you at all times."

Mike scrambled into the back of a truck. A canvas canopy spread over steel hoops kept out the sun and prying eyes. Pretty soon, the truck got rolling again. Out the back, he could see a little of where he'd been, but not where he was going.

"We oughta jump and run," said the mousy little man shoehorned in next to him.

"Go ahead," Mike answered. "You first."

The mousy guy shook his head. "I don't have the nerve. I wish I did. This is liable to be nothing beside whatever we're going to."

"It's a labor encampment. They'll work us. How bad can it be?"

"That's what I'm afraid of—how bad it can be."

Since Mike had no answer to that, he kept quiet and looked out the back of the truck. From a sign facing the other way, he discovered they were on US 89. He saw half a dozen cranes standing in a field near the road. They looked even bigger than the herons that hunted in pools and streams in Central Park. There was something wrong about a bird as tall as an eleven-year-old.

After half an hour or so, the trucks turned off the road and onto a dirt track. It went up into the mountains. Mike's ears popped several times. It got colder as they climbed, too. He began to wish for something heavier than the jacket he'd grabbed when the GBI goons got him.

Pines crowded close to the track. Every so often, branches would swish against the canvas canopy. They weren't going fast at all now. You might be able to jump out without ruining yourself. But if you did, could you get back to civilization before you starved or froze or got eaten by a bear—or did wolves prowl these mountains? Mike didn't try to find out. Neither did the mousy little man or anyone else.

At last, the trucks stopped. "Everybody out!" someone shouted. "On the double!" The wreckers were too worn from their journey to move on the double, but out they came.

Behind Mike was the pine forest through which they'd been driving. The trucks had stopped near the edge of a clearing hacked out of the woods. Ahead of them lay the camp where they'd stay.

It put him in mind of the prisoner-of-war stockades he'd seen in books of photos about the Great War. There was the same barbed-wire entanglement around the square perimeter. Guard towers stood at the corners and near the middle of each side. He could see machine guns atop some of the towers, and didn't doubt that the others also held them.

Inside the perimeter, the barracks and other buildings were made of the local pine, and so new the wood's bright yellow hadn't begun to fade. One of the buildings was a sawmill. Mike could hear a big saw biting into logs. A raven flew off a rooftop, grukking hoarsely. *Nevermore to you, too,* Mike thought.

Men ambled about within the barbed wire. Their clothes were shapeless and colorless. More than a few of them wore beards. One waved at the truck convoy. Whether that was greeting or sarcasm, Mike couldn't have said.

He didn't wave back. He didn't want to do anything the

guards might not like. He hadn't been a prisoner long, but he'd learned that lesson in a hurry.

Armed guards in uniforms that weren't quite military but weren't what cops would wear, either, moved prisoners away from the gate by gesturing with their weapons. Then they opened it. "Go on in!" one of the GBI men who'd ridden with the convoy barked. "I hope you rot in there, you fucking wreckers!"

Not too far from the front of one line, Mike inched ahead, up into a building with ENCAMPMENT ADMINISTRATION over the door. In due course, he came before a clerk who said, "Name and number?" in a tone that announced he couldn't care less.

"Sullivan, Michael, NY24601." Giving them that way was another thing Mike had learned fast.

"Sullivan . . ." The clerk flipped through an alphabetical list. "Here you are. Five to ten, is it?"

"Yes." Mike didn't show what he thought of that. Showing anything you didn't have to was dangerous.

"Okay, Sullivan NY24601. Go out that door and turn right. They'll tend to you further in the infirmary."

"Huh? What about food?" Mike asked. The clerk just pointed. Mike went.

In the infirmary, he bathed with a dozen other men in an enormous tin tub whose steaming water stank of disinfectant. As soon as he was dry, though still naked, a barber in those shapeless, colorless quilted clothes—a wrecker himself, Mike realized: his number was IL15160—snatched him bald and hacked off his sprouting beard.

"Go to the building next to this one and get your camp duds," the barber said when he finished. The slash-and-burn didn't take long.

"What do I do with the stuff I wore on the way here?" Mike had those clothes under his arm.

"Hang on to it. Try not to let anybody steal it," the wrecker answered. "It gets cold at night now. Pretty soon, it'll be cold all the goddamn time. You'll be glad for whatever you've got. Now get moving—somebody's behind you."

Mike got moving. They issued him a cotton shirt, a

quilted jacket, long johns, quilted pants, wool socks, and boots as hard as iron. Nothing except the boots fit well. They did give him the right size with those, but he had no idea how long the boots would take to break in. For all he knew, his whole term. They also gave him a tin mess kit.

They used stencils and black indelible ink to mark NY24601 on the front and back of the jacket and on the seat of his pants. Then one of them said, "Go to Barracks Seventeen. Find a bunk there. Get used to it. You'll be in it one fucking long time."

Everyone in the encampment seemed to take profanity for granted, the way cops and soldiers did. Mike came out of the supply building and went looking for Barracks 17. Each building was plainly marked, so he didn't need long to find it. He walked inside.

The bunks were four high. You slept on wooden slats—no mattress, no sheet, no blanket. In the center of the hall was an open space around a potbellied iron stove out of a Currier & Ives print. The stove burned wood. Billets of chopped pine were piled near it.

All of the bunks closest to the stove had old clothes or boots or something on them to show they belonged to somebody. Mike wondered what would happen if he moved someone's stuff and put his own in its place. He didn't wonder long—chances were he'd have a fight on his hands.

Not wanting one, he threw his junk on the best-sited empty bunk he could find. Some other new wreckers wandered in and staked their own claims. Mike lay down. The bunk was barely long enough for him, and he wasn't tall. After the trip across the country in the jammed railway car, he didn't complain. He sure had more room here than he'd had there.

Using his wadded-up slacks for a pillow, he fell asleep, mattress or no mattress. He hadn't slept more than a few minutes at a time on the train. Who could have? It wasn't much more than luck that they hadn't handed him out to the guards feetfirst. He was hungry, too, but he would worry about that again when he woke up.

When he did wake, it was with a start. He almost banged his head on the slats of the bunk above his. More people were coming into the barracks. Their talking was what had roused him. The light had shifted. Night was coming on. It wasn't dark yet, but even a city fellow like him could tell it wouldn't be long.

"We got us some new scalps here," said a man standing in the narrow aisle near the bunk. He nodded to Mike. "How the hell are ya, scalp?" His voice had a Western twang. The number on his jacket was WY232. Wyoming didn't hold many people, but the GBI hadn't wasted any time getting its hands on him.

"I'm hungry. I'm thirsty. I'd murder somebody for a cigarette. My head still hurts from where they blackjacked me. Leave all that out, and I'm fine," Mike said. "How the hell are *you*?"

"I'm okay," the other man answered. "Wasn't a bad day today. Nobody in the work gang got hurt or anything. We did what they told us to do, and now we're back. Lineup soon, then supper. They call me John."

"I'm Mike, Mike Sullivan." Mike's mouth twisted. "Sullivan, Michael, NY24601."

"Dennison, Jonathan, WY232." John shrugged. "Mostly we don't bother with any o' that shit 'cept for first names." He was in his early thirties, a few years younger than Mike. He wasn't a scalp—he had longish brown hair and a gingery beard with a few white hairs in it. His forehead was wide, his chin narrow. If he hadn't seen everything, his pale eyes didn't admit it. He pulled a small suede drawstring pouch from a trouser pocket. "Let's find some paper. You can get a smoke, anyways."

The paper came from a six-month-old newspaper. Mike had never rolled his own before. With unflustered patience, John showed him how. Mike suspected nothing came for free. He wondered what Dennison would want from him. Right now, he had nothing to give. He'd worry about that later, too. He smoked like a drowning man coming up for air.

"That was *wonderful*," he said.

"Glad you liked it," John answered easily. "You'll learn the ropes quick, believe me. C'mon outside now. They have to count us before they feed us, make sure nobody's run off.

With all you new scalps here, they'll screw it up a few times before they get it straight." He spoke with calm, resigned certainty.

Sure enough, the guards went through the count four times before they were satisfied. Then the wreckers hurried to the kitchen. Everyone got a chunk of brown bread. In New York City, Mike would have turned up his nose at the coarse, stale stuff. After days of worse, it made him think of manna from heaven.

Once they'd grabbed their bread, the inmates walked past cooks who ladled stew into their mess tins. "Hey, Phil," John said to one of the men: like the rest, an inmate himself. "Give my pal Mike here something good, okay?"

"Natch," Phil said. "Just like the fuckin' Waldorf." He filled Mike's tin, then jerked his thumb toward the rough tables. "Gwan, get outa here."

Mike gobbled the bread. He spooned up the stew. The gravy was thin and watery. In it floated bits of potato and turnip and cabbage and a few strings of what might have been meat. He would have stomped out of any place that dared charge even a penny for it. Right here, right now, it seemed terrific.

He'd got his tin almost perfectly clean before he thought to wonder, "What kind of meat was that, anyway?"

John Dennison was eating more slowly. "Some questions here, you don't ask. You don't ask what somebody did to wind up here. He can tell you if he wants to, but you don't ask. And you don't ask what the meat is. It's there, is what it is—when it *is* there. If you knew, maybe you wouldn't wanna eat it. And you gotta eat here, or else you fold up and die."

"Okay," Mike said. All kinds of interesting possibilities went through his mind. Bear? Coyote? Skunk? Squirrel? Stray dog? He wouldn't have ordered any of those at a greasy spoon back home. But he wasn't about to pick them out of his tin, either. He tried another question: "Can I ask you what you did for a living before you got here?"

"Oh, sure. I was a carpenter." John chuckled. "I know the wood a hell of a lot better now than I did then. I know it with the skin on, I guess you'd say. How about you?"

"I wrote for a newspaper," Mike said.

"Did you?" John Dennison chuckled again. "Then I bet I don't have to ask how you wound up here." He held up a hasty hand. "And I'm *not* asking. You don't got to say anything if you don't feel like it."

"I don't care," Mike said. "That's what happened, all right. I bet I'm a long way from the only reporter here."

"Won't touch that one. I'd lose," Dennison said. "Me, I got drunk and stupid and I told off Joe Steele. I think the bastard who turned me in was the guy who wanted my building, only he couldn't get it from me. So he ratted on me to the Jeebies, and I won my five to ten, plus a big old knot on the side of my head. They still do that when they grab you?"

"Oh, hell, yes. I already told you I got blackjacked." Mike rubbed his own bruise, which was sore and swollen yet. "Sort of a welcome-to-the-club present."

"Welcome-with-a-club present, you mean," John said. Of all the things Mike hadn't expected to do in a labor encampment, laughing his head off stood high on the list. He did it now, though.

Charlie had to call Stella back and tell her he couldn't do anything for Mike. She burst into tears. "What am I gonna do without him?" she wailed. He didn't know what to say to that. He didn't think anybody could say anything to that.

And, just to make his joy complete, he had to call his folks and tell *them* he couldn't help Mike. His mother answered the telephone. Bridget Sullivan didn't take the news well. "Why didn't you stop him?" she demanded bitterly. "Why didn't you keep him from writing that stuff about the President? Then he wouldn't have got in trouble."

"What was I supposed to do, Mom? He's a grown man. Should I have held a gun to his head? Or maybe an ether cone over his nose?"

"I don't know," his mother said. "All I know is, you didn't stop him, and now he's in one of those horrible places people don't come back from." She started crying, too.

He got off the phone as fast as he could, which wasn't nearly fast enough. Then he walked into the kitchen, pulled an ice-cube tray from the freezer, put rocks in a glass, and poured three fingers of bourbon over them. "Boy, that was fun," he said, coming back to the front room.

"Sounded like it," Esther said.

He took a healthy swig. "Whew! That hits the spot! Good for what ails me, all right." He looked from the glass to his wife and back again. "Sorry, hon. I'm being rude and crude. Want I should fix you one, too?"

"No, thanks," she said. "Bourbon hasn't tasted good to me lately."

"What do you mean? It's Wild Turkey, not the cheap stuff they scrape out of the barrel and have to fight into a bottle with a pistol and a chair."

"It hasn't tasted good anyway," Esther answered. "Coffee doesn't taste right, either, or even tea. Must be because I'm expecting."

"Exp—" Charlie got half the word out, and no more. He wasn't astonished—he knew when her monthlies were due, and they hadn't come. But it was still a big thing to hear officially, as it were.

She nodded. "That's right. We wanted to. Now we're going to. I did a little thinking when I decided I was sure I was going to have a baby. If I worked it out right, Junior will be in the high school class of 1956. Can you believe that?"

"Now that you mention it, no," Charlie said after trying and failing. "He'll probably fly to school in a rocket car, carry his phone in his shirt pocket, and go to the Moon for summer vacation."

Esther laughed at him. "I think you let that Flash Gordon serial last year soften your brain."

"Maybe—but maybe not, too," Charlie said. "Look where we were twenty years ago. Nobody had a radio. Model T's were as good as cars got. People had iceboxes—when they had iceboxes—not refrigerators. You put out a card to tell the iceman how much to leave. Airplanes were made out of wood and cloth and baling wire. Can you imagine what they would've thought of a DC-3 if you stuck one in a time machine and sent it back?"

"Flash Gordon," Esther said again, but this time her

tone was thoughtful, not amused and mocking. She changed the subject: "What do you want to name it?"

"If it's a boy, *not* Charlie, Junior," he said at once. "Let him be whoever he is, not a carbon copy of his old man."

"Okay," Esther said. "I was thinking the same thing. Jews don't usually name babies for someone who's still alive. I would've gone along with it if you wanted to, but I'm not sorry you don't."

"How about if it's a girl?" Charlie said.

"Sarah? After my mother's mother?"

"Hmm . . ." He savored the name. "Sarah Sullivan. That might be okay, even if it sounds like it's out of *Abie's Irish Rose*."

"*We're* out of *Abie's Irish Rose*, only with him and her turned around," Esther said. "You could fill the Polo Grounds four or five times with all the couples out of *Abie's Irish Rose*. And the ones who aren't are Jewish and Italian or Italian and Irish or Irish or Russian and Irish or, or anything under the sun. The New York Mutts, that's us."

"Sounds like a pretty good ballclub." Charlie snapped his fingers. "Now I gotta call my folks again. They'll be glad to hear from me this time, I bet. *Hey, Ma? Guess what? You're gonna be a grandma!* Yeah, she'll go for that. And you gotta call yours, too. We'll run up the bill, but who cares?"

He dialed the long-distance operator once more. When the call went through, his mother started yelling at him again. He might as well not have left the line. She started crying again, too.

Finally, he went, "Mom, will you just—hold on a second?" You couldn't tell your mother to shut up, however much you wanted to. Well, you could, but you wouldn't make yourself popular if you did.

"Why should I?" she wailed.

"So I can get a word in edgewise and let you know you're gonna be a grandmother, that's why."

"But you let them take your own—" His mother wasn't the swiftest at shifting mental gears. The stop, when it came, must have lasted for ten or fifteen seconds. Then she asked, "What did you say?"

"I said you'd be a grandmother. Esther's going to have a baby."

More tears. More yelling. They were happy tears and joyful yells. She said they were, anyway. They sounded pretty much the same to Mike. She shouted for his father, so he got congratulated twice. Then Pete Sullivan said, "You still have to fix things for your brother, Charlie."

"I'm doing everything I know how to do, Pop. I can't make them do what I tell 'em, you know."

Like his mother, his father knew nothing of the sort. Charlie got off the line as fast as he could. Esther sent him a sympathetic look. "You did your best," she told him.

"Yeah, and a fat lot of good it did me. They listened to me the same way Mikoian did. If I'd told 'em that, they would've hit the roof. It's true anyhow." He gestured invitingly toward the telephone. "Your turn now. Your folks will be glad to get the news."

While she made the call, he went back to the kitchen and fixed himself another drink. He understood why his parents felt the way they did. He felt that way himself. Nobody wanted to see a loved one carted off to a labor encampment. He blamed himself even more than his mother and father blamed him. He didn't need them to shovel guilt down on top of him. He already felt plenty guilty. Did they understand that? Did they understand anything?

He scowled and drank some more Wild Turkey. By the evidence, they didn't.

In the front room, Esther was chatting excitedly with her mother. Every so often, she'd slip out of English and into Magyar, of which Charlie knew not a word. He got, and used, some Yiddish. Anybody from New York did. Esther certainly did. But she'd learned the Hungarians' language even before English. She'd told him the hardest thing she had to do was stop rolling her r's. To this day, she could sound like a lady vampire when she wanted to.

But then she said, "Yeah, that's right. I didn't know you'd heard about it." A beat, and then she went on, "Of course he's doing everything he can." After that, she added something in Magyar that sounded as if it ought to sterilize frogs.

Charlie hoped she wasn't saying anything that sounded like that about him. She must not have been, because after she said her good-byes she gave him a kiss and told him, "That's from my mother."

"How about one from you, babe?"

"How about that?" she said. The second kiss was a good bit warmer than the first. But she made a face afterwards. "I don't like bourbon—or bourbon doesn't like me—now even secondhand."

"That's a crying shame." Charlie liked bourbon just fine. And two stiff drinks put more pathos in his voice than he could have got without them. "A whole bunch of things are crying shames."

"Let's put you to bed," Esther said firmly, and steered him in that direction.

"How do you mean that?" he asked over his shoulder.

"We'll both find out," she said, and they did.

Mike looked at the palms of his hands in amazement and dismay. He'd done so much typing that he'd worn the fingerprints off the tips of both index fingers. He'd had a writer's callus, too, next to the nail on his right middle finger. But for those, his hands had been soft and smooth.

They had been. They weren't any more. Swinging an axe and working with a variety of saws had turned his palms all blistered and bleeding. John Dennison advised him to rub them with turpentine as often as he could. Dennison even called in a favor to get some so he could. It sounded horrible, but the stuff cooled and soothed the burning.

"I wouldn't have believed it, not in a million years," Mike told him.

He shrugged. "That's one I knew before I got here. They didn't send us here to have fun, but we don't got to make it worse'n it already is."

"I guess not. It's bad enough anyway." Mike yawned. He was always tired. No, he was always exhausted. They didn't give you enough time to sleep. When he first saw the bare bunks in Barracks 17, he'd wondered if he could sleep on slats. Now he was convinced that, if they told him he had to hang by his feet like a bat, he'd still get as much shut-eye as they let him have. He'd never worked so hard or so long in his life.

He was always hungry, too. They didn't feed the wreckers enough for the labor they had to do. Watery oatmeal in the morning, a cheese sandwich on bad bread to take to the woods, stew and more bad bread in the evening. Sometimes the stew had bits of creature in it; sometimes it was full— but not full enough—of beans. Mike had to hold up his pants with a length of rope.

The only thing that ever made him forget being hungry was how tired he was. The only thing that made him forget being tired was how hungry he was. They rigged things so you couldn't win.

Here he was, for instance, in some of the most beautiful country God ever made. The encampment wasn't far from Yellowstone National Park. There weren't geysers and hot springs and such things here, but there were mountains and trees as far as the eye could see. The sky was as enormous as Montana's nickname promised.

And Mike hardly ever saw, or got to pay attention to, any of it. A mountain was something he had to stumble up and down, not something he could admire from a scenic distance. Trees were things he had to knock over and chop up, not things he could look at and savor. The sky? He didn't have time to see the sky. The guards growled if you slowed down for anything.

The guards in the camp were easygoing. They could afford to be. They carried guns. The wreckers had nothing. Out on work details, things were different. The men doing the labor needed tools. They weren't beavers, to chop down trees with their front teeth. They had to have those axes and saws.

But tools were also weapons. A wrecker who decided he had nothing left to lose could start swinging an axe and try to chop down some guards before they filled him full of holes. From what Dennison said, they'd got a few guards right after the encampment opened up. The GBI bastards hadn't figured out all the angles then themselves.

They had now. Any time a wrecker approached, he had

to come slowly and not get too close. Mike got used to having a Tommy gun aimed at his brisket, even when he was asking for something as harmless as permission to go behind a pine and crap. The guards didn't know he was just going to do that. They didn't take chances, either.

Now . . . Now Mike rolled a cigarette. He still wasn't as good at it as John, but he was a lot better than he had been. *Custom hath made it in me a property of easiness,* he thought. *Hamlet* still sprang to mind, here where the nearest hamlet that wasn't a labor encampment was miles away.

He offered John the makings, too. He kept his tobacco in a metal box that had held throat lozenges. "Thanks," Dennison said. "Nice box. Where'd you get it?"

"Found it by the infirmary," Mike answered. "A doctor must've chucked it out a window or something." No wrecker would have been so prodigal. You could use a little metal box for all kinds of things.

John didn't ask where Mike had got the tobacco. That was just as well. His pride had gone before a smoke. In the outside world, he wouldn't have dreamt of polishing another man's boots. Here, he'd made a guard's shine almost as if by a light of their own. And he'd got his reward. The guard, one of the more nearly human ones, didn't even make him beg like a dog getting up on its hind legs in hopes of a scrap.

Another guard, this one from the venomous school, scowled at the two of them. "Playtime's over, youse guys," he said. "You better finish that trunk by the time we go back if you know what's good for youse."

"Sure thing, Virgil." John didn't sound angry or flustered. He just wanted to get along with as little trouble as he could.

After Virgil went off to inflict himself on some other wreckers, Mike asked John a low-voiced question: "How do you let that asshole roll off your back like that? It was everything I could do to keep from giving him the finger and telling him to go fuck himself."

"Thing of it is, you're still a scalp," John answered placidly. Mike ran a hand through his hair. He could do that again; he had enough hair to run a hand through it. But the man with WY232 on his jacket and pants just chuckled. "You're still a scalp inside your own head, I mean. You let things get under your skin like a tick's mouth. Virgil ain't worth getting excited about."

"Not to you, maybe," Mike said.

"Well, shit, what can you do about him that won't get you killed? Nothin', that's what. So you can roll with the current or you can try and buck it. Rollin's a lot easier."

That made good, logical sense. When you wanted to see your axe bite into the back of someone's head instead of lopping branches off a fallen lodgepole pine, logic went only so far. Come to that, Mike was just glad his axe hadn't bitten into his own leg or foot. He was better with it than he had been when he got here, but not so much better as he was at rolling cigarettes. Rolling cigarettes mattered to him. How good he was with an axe mattered only to the guards. To be fair, axe work was also harder than cocooning tobacco in paper.

He and John chopped away at the pine. John could make an axe do everything but stand up and sing "Let Yourself Go." But he didn't move any faster than he had to, and he didn't do much more work than Mike (though he wore himself out much less doing it). He'd mastered the age-old, glacial pace of the prisoner . . . or the slave.

Mike hadn't. He didn't want to. He still felt he ought to be fighting, not coasting through the days. As John Dennison reminded him, he was still a scalp, a greenhorn, a beginner.

XIII

When Charlie got home after another day chasing around Washington after stories that might or might not mean anything to the rest of the country, he found Esther bouncing around as if she had springs in her shoes. She waved a small cardboard rectangle at him. "Look!" she squealed. "Look!"

"I can't," he said irritably—he was beat. "Hold it still, why don't you?"

She did. It was a plain postcard, creased and battered. But the message was welcome. *Hey, Charlie*, the familiar script said. *Just a note to let you know I'm doing all right here. Hard work, but I can do it. Let Stella and the folks know I'm okay, please. I get one card a month. Wrote Stella last. Your brother, Mike.* Under that was an unfamiliar number: NY24601.

Stella hadn't let Charlie know she'd heard from Mike. The earlier card might not have got to her. Or she might still have been mad at Charlie for not getting Mike out of the labor encampment. Wouldn't she have told his folks, though? Of course, they might not have been happy with him, either. Everybody thought he had more pull with the administration than he really did.

"It's good news," he said to Esther. "Or it's news as good as you can get when the news is bad."

She nodded. "That's just what it is." Then she tapped the number with the red-painted nail of her right index finger. "Isn't this terrible? It's like they've taken away his name."

Charlie hadn't thought of it like that. "It's for the file clerks," he said. "Plenty of guys named Mike Sullivan—some parts of some towns, about one in five. But there's only one NY24601."

"It's like a prisoner's number. It *is* a prisoner's number. I think it's disgusting," Esther said.

Since he couldn't tell her she was wrong to feel that way, he did the next best thing: he changed the subject. "How are *you* doing, babe?" he asked.

She answered with a yawn. "I'm sleepy. I'm sleepy all the time," she said. "And I tossed my cookies about twenty minutes after you left, just before I was gonna go out the door."

"Well, they call it morning sickness," Charlie said.

"I don't care what they call it. I don't like it," Esther answered. "I wasn't doing anything much. But I just barely made it to the bathroom in time. I've done more puking the last couple of months than in my whole life before, I think."

He had no idea what to say to that. He was only a man. Morning sickness was as much a mystery to him as anything else that had to do with pregnancy. Cautiously, he asked, "Do you think you'll be okay for dinner?" Calling it morning sickness didn't mean it couldn't come on any old time. He'd found that out. So had Esther, from painful experience.

She shrugged now. "Who knows? I was fine till about half a minute before I had to heave this morning. Then I was running for the pot."

She did manage to keep the dinner down. It was ground round without onions. Sometimes anything spicy would make her give it back. Sometimes she'd give back the blandest food. Sometimes she could eat anything at all and stay fine. Her insides might understand why, but she didn't. Neither did Charlie.

He called Stella while Esther did dishes. He'd done more long-distance calling since Mike got sent West and Esther found out she was in a family way than ever before. It was expensive, but it was quick.

"No, I didn't get that card," Stella told him. "I would've let you know if I did."

"Okay," Charlie said, and some of the weight of worry fell from his shoulders. His sister-in-law didn't hate him as much as she might have, anyhow. "Maybe the next one will be to you, too. He says he gets one a month."

"That's awful," she said. "Is there a return address or anything, so I can write to him?"

"Lemme see." Charlie picked up the card. "It just says 'National Labor Encampment System.' If you write care of them, maybe he'll get it. I bet it'd help if you put his number on the card."

"His number?" Stella echoed in dismay.

Charlie gave it to her again—he'd read it when he read the rest of the message, but it must not have sunk in. Then he said, "Listen, I'm gonna get off the line. I've got to call Mom and Pop, let them know what's going on."

"I'll do it if you want, save you the money of another long-distance call," Stella said.

"Would you? Thanks!" Charlie didn't want to talk to his mother, who would probably answer the phone. She'd just start crying again. And he pinched pennies harder than ever now that Esther was going to have a baby. You never knew what would happen day after tomorrow. The economy wasn't as bad as it had been at the bottom of the Depression, but it was a long way from booming. Lose a job and God only knew when you might land another one.

There were other things to worry about, too. That NY24601 pretty much summed them up. A couple of people had vanished from the AP office into the encampments. Charlie didn't think either Scriabin or Joe Steele disliked him enough to send the Jeebies after him. His stories about the administration stayed upbeat. Unlike Mike, he knew where the line was and didn't try to cross it.

But you never could tell.

A guard tossed Mike a big burlap sack. "Thanks," Mike said. His voice was less sardonic than he wanted it to be. The guard checked his number off the list on his clipboard. He jerked a thumb at an enormous, fragrant pile of sawdust from the mill. Mike went over to it and started filling the sack with a shovel. Blowing sawdust made his eyes water and went up his nose to set him sneezing. He didn't care. He worked away with more vim than he ever showed felling trees. That was for the camp and for the government that had stuck him in the camp. This was for himself.

"Don't get it too full!" a guard shouted, as he did every couple of minutes. "You'll need to flatten it out, remember!"

"Yes, Mommy," John Dennison muttered from a couple of feet away. No guard could have heard him. Mike hoped his own giggles didn't set the screws wondering what was up.

When they'd finished filling their sacks, they tied them shut with lengths of twine another guard doled out. Then they went into the supply building in a ragged line, each wrecker with his sack full of sawdust slung over his right shoulder. Yet another man inside also checked off each man's number before reluctantly issuing him a blanket.

Mike's was thinner than he wished it were, and almost as coarse and scratchy as if it were woven from steel wool instead of the kind that came off a sheep. Again, though, he said "Thank you" with more sincerity than he'd intended to show. The bastards who ran the camp didn't want the wreckers to freeze to death—or at least not all of them, not right away.

Back to Barracks 17 he and Dennison went. Snow still lingered in places that didn't get much sun. It had started in early October, which was horrible enough. Pretty soon, from what the man with WY232 on his clothes said, it wouldn't melt back. It would just stay there, most of the way through spring. Mike had seen cold weather before, but not cold weather like that.

It would get down below zero, too. And it might stay that way for days if not for weeks. So . . . blankets and these sacks of sawdust. Mike laid his on the slats where he'd been sleeping since the Jeebies sent him here. He thumped and pounded on the burlap to get it as even as he could. Then he climbed into the bunk to use his body as a steamroller to flatten the cheap makeshift mattress some more.

Cheap. Makeshift. Thin. Lumpy. All those words applied. Still, this was the most comfortable he'd been in there since he came to the camp. He wasn't the only one who thought so, either. "Welcome to the fucking Ritz!" another wrecker exclaimed.

Mike lay back. He put his hands behind his head, fingers interlaced. Another minute and he would have fallen asleep.

He could sleep anywhere these days, even, sometimes, standing up while the prisoners were being counted.

He didn't get the minute. A guard thumped in. The Jeebies' boots sounded louder than the wreckers'. Mike didn't know why, but they did. "Come on, you lazy, good-for-nothin' bums!" the guard yelled. "Y'all don't git the goddamn rest cure this mornin'!"

Like a lot of the GBI men at the encampment, this guard came from somewhere between North Carolina and Arkansas. Mike couldn't have said why the Jeebies got so many volunteers from that part of the country, but they did. The Southern guards were often rougher on the men they held than Jeebies from the other side of the Mason-Dixon Line, too.

Nobody told this fellow where to go. Doing that to somebody with a Tommy gun wasn't the smartest stunt you could pull. Even an insult would set some guards shooting. Mike had never yet heard of any Jeebie getting in trouble, no matter what he did to a wrecker. And a wrecker's word was worth nothing when set against a guard's.

Out the men came. Mike sent a longing, fretful look back toward his bunk. Just because the wreckers had so little, that didn't keep them stealing from one another. Things you didn't keep an eye on had a mysterious way of walking with Jesus.

They were taken to the woods to hack down more lodgepole pines. Snow lingered there more than it did inside the encampment. It crunched under Mike's boots. He and John attacked a tree.

"You know," Mike said between strokes with the axe, "we shouldn't take stuff from each other. We should be solid. We should make a waddayacallit, a popular front—us on one side, the Jeebies on the other."

"We should do all kinds of shit," John Dennison said. "One of the things you should do is run your mouth less, y'know? All kinds of finks who'll rat on you for half a pack o' Luckies." *Thunk!* His axe bit into the trunk. The sap smelled halfway between turpentine and maple syrup.

Mike spat. He swung the axe again. He didn't blister so much any more; calluses were forming where the blisters had been. "They should have an accident or something," he said. "Yeah, or something."

"Sometimes they do, when they get bad," Dennison said. "But then somebody new starts feedin' the GBI the dope. That's a bad time, 'cause you don't know who to trust or whether you can trust anybody."

The lodgepole creaked. It started to sway. Dennison pointed the direction in which it would fall. Mike sang out: "Tim-berrr!"

Wreckers scrambled back. Down came the tree, pretty much where John Dennison had said it would. Snow flew up off its branches and from the ground. After the cloud subsided, Mike and John started lopping branches off the trunk.

"I don't want to do this," Mike said.

"Nobody wants to do this," Dennison answered.

"I know that. I mean, I don't want to do it now. I want to go back to the barracks and see what sleeping on a mattress feels like."

"Why? You won't sleep any longer or any harder than you did without the goddamn thing," John Dennison said.

He was bound to be right about that. Mike couldn't sleep any longer, because he'd have to tumble out of his bunk when reveille sounded tomorrow morning. And he could only sleep harder if he died after the lights went out and before reveille drove him upright again.

"I'll be more comfortable. I won't be so cold," he said.

"That counts a lot for the half a minute before you fall asleep and for the five seconds between when you wake up and when you got to get up," John said. "Otherwise, you won't notice. So why get excited about it?"

"Gotta grab all the fun here you can," Mike answered. Most of the time, John Dennison was a quiet man who didn't draw attention to himself. Now he laughed like a loon. After a minute, so did Mike. When you got right down to it, the idea of fun inside the labor encampment was, well, pretty goddamn funny.

Wire and radio reports poured in from the other side of the Atlantic. Adolf Hitler's *Wehrmacht*—renamed as he entrenched himself in power—had marched into Austria, joining it to Germany. The *Anschluss* wasn't violent. By the way things looked, most Austrians who weren't Jewish loved it. Violent or not, though, it rearranged the map of Europe. The new, enlarged Germany was the biggest country west of Russia. It was also the strongest. And now it surrounded western Czechoslovakia on three sides. With the *Führer* screeching that he wanted to annex the Germans in the Sudetenland, too, that wasn't good news for the little Central European democracy.

Charlie tried to make sense of the fast-breaking story. He tried to break it down into pieces that Americans in, say, Kansas, many of whom couldn't have found Czechoslovakia on a map if their lives depended on it, might possibly understand. He feared it was a losing effort, but he did his best.

The phone on his desk jangled. He grabbed it. "Sullivan, AP."

"Hello, Sullivan, AP. This is Sullivan, your wife. Things have started. I just called a taxi. I'm heading for the hospital."

"Oh, God," Charlie said. He'd known the day would come soon. But you're never ready, especially not the first time. "Okay, hon. I'll see you there. Love you."

He finished the story he was working on. Luckily, he was almost done. He took it out of the typewriter and set it on his editor's desk. Then he said, "I'm gone, boss. Esther just called. She's on her way to the hospital. I'll see you in a few days."

"Okay, Charlie," the editor said—an advantage of being able to set things up in advance. "Shame it has to happen just when all hell's breaking loose in Europe."

"I know, but . . ." Charlie shrugged. "It's not our fight, and it is my kid. I'll worry about the world again when I get back."

"I hope it all goes well for your missus and the baby," his editor said. "And if you have a boy, for God's sake bring in some good cigars, not the stink bombs the last couple of guys with sons handed out."

Laughing, Charlie said, "Promise." He grabbed his hat

and topcoat and hurried away. He flagged down a cab without much trouble.

At the hospital, he filled out papers promising he wouldn't spirit away mother and baby without paying his bills. They allowed that he would be able to pay things off on the installment plan. That would spread his pain, as opposed to Esther's, over some considerable stretch of time. He didn't like the installment plan, but he liked digging deep into his savings even less.

Once papers were signed and hands shaken, they led him to a waiting room. Two other almost-fathers already sat there. One looked barely old enough to shave, and was shaking in his shoes. The other, close to forty, smoked a cigarette and leafed through a magazine. "This is our sixth," he said. "Not like we never done it before."

"I guess not," Charlie said. "Just my first, though."

The guy about his age waited till the nurse went away, then pulled a half-pint of scotch from his jacket pocket. "Have a knock of this, buddy. It'll calm you down."

Charlie didn't go for scotch most of the time. Today, he made an exception. "Thanks," he said, and swigged. It tasted like medicine, the way he remembered. It *was* medicine right now.

By the time anyone came into the room for him, the dose had long since worn off. He'd stepped out to buy more cigarettes, having gone through the ones with him, and to eat lunch and dinner at the hospital's sorry cafeteria. If that place was any indication, all the nasty cracks people made about hospital food were not just true but understatements.

Kid number six for his benefactor turned out to be a girl, which evened his score at 3-3. Kid number one for the nervous youngster was a boy. The nervous guy let out what had to be the closest thing to a Rebel yell since Appomattox. Another father-to-be came in and stared at the pale green walls with Mike.

Just before midnight, a tired-looking doctor came in with his face mask down around his neck and said, "Mr. Sullivan?"

"That's me!" Charlie jumped to his feet.

"Congratulations, Mr. Sullivan. You have a fine, healthy

baby girl. She's twenty and a half inches long, and she weighs seven pounds, nine ounces. Your wife is doing well, too. She's worn out, but that's to be expected."

"A girl," Charlie said dreamily. "We're gonna call her Sarah."

"Yes, that's what your wife said." The doctor nodded.

"Can I see them?" Charlie asked.

"That's one of the reasons I came in here. Follow me, please." The doc held the door open so Charlie could. They walked down the hall to a room with MOTHERS AND NEWBORNS neatly stenciled over the door. The doctor opened that one, too.

Charlie went in. Esther lay on one of those hospital beds where you could crank up the top or bottom half. The top half was partway up. She had the blanket-wrapped baby cradled in her left arm, and was giving it her breast.

"How you doin', babe?" Charlie asked, trying not to sound nervous. She looked as if she'd just run five miles and gone a few rounds with Max Schmeling. Sweat matted her hair. She was pale as cottage cheese, except for dark circles that made you think she had a mouse under each eye.

The baby, or what Charlie could see of it, didn't look all that hot, either. Sarah was kind of pinkish purple, with squashed features and a funny-shaped head. A little hair crowned that head, but not much.

"Like I got run over by a truck, that's how," Esther answered. "And hungry enough to eat a horse, too. They wouldn't give me anything except some water while I was in labor, and hardly any of that, either. They said if I had anything much in my stomach I'd throw it up."

As if on cue, a nurse came in through a side door with a tray. The roast beef on it looked tough enough to have been peeled off an auto tire. "Here you are, dear," the nurse said, as proud as if she'd brought something that was actually good.

"Thanks," Esther said, and then, "Can you hold the baby, Charlie, while I eat?"

"I guess so," he said warily. The nurse helped him, showing him how to support the baby's head. Esther attacked the overdone roast beef and squashy boiled vegetables like a lion devouring a zebra. They disappeared in nothing flat. Sarah kicked and wiggled and screwed up her face and started to cry.

"I'll take her," Esther said. Charlie quickly gave her back. He knew he'd get used to holding a baby, but he hadn't done it yet. His wife went on, "You know what? That was the best lousy dinner I ever ate."

"Our dietary department has a good reputation." The nurse sounded offended.

Esther laughed. "Heaven help the places they're comparing it to, in that case. But I don't care. How long will I be here?"

"Usually a week or so, if there are no complications after birth," the nurse replied.

"Okay. I won't complain about the food again—promise," Esther said. "And Charlie will have the chance to get everything ready for when I come home . . . and when Sarah does."

"Yeah." Charlie made himself nod. When he saw the baby there in Esther's arms, the notion of being a father turned real. A roll in the hay wasn't always just a roll in the hay. Sometimes it had consequences nine months down the line. In a week or so, a squawky, wiggly consequence would be coming home. *High school class of 1956,* Charlie remembered. Try as he would, he still had trouble imagining that.

Not quite idly, he wondered whether Joe Steele would still be President.

It was April. By the calendar, it was supposed to be spring. Trees should have been turning green. Flowers should have been popping out here and there. Birds should have been singing their heads off.

As far as Mike could tell, this stretch of Montana had never heard of calendars. He couldn't prove it knew anything about spring, either. The lodgepole pines were the same almost-black color they'd always been. No flowers. No birds except ravens and a few gray jays.

No letup from winter, either. It was still snowing, with no sign of rain or even sleet ahead. The snow was wetter now than it had been in January. It didn't sandpaper your face the way it had when it blew then. The wind didn't howl down out of the north quite so savagely. But it still hadn't warmed up to even a bad New York City winter's day.

One man from Mike's gang got lost when they went out to chop wood in a blizzard. The guards and bloodhounds found him three days later. He was frozen hard. A couple of other wreckers had just quietly lain down on the job and died. If you gave up here, you wouldn't last long.

Mike had been tempted now and again. Freezing seemed a pretty easy way to go. You were cold, then you stopped caring, then you were dead. It probably didn't hurt much. You might not even have the energy to stay scared for long.

But he didn't want to give Joe Steele the satisfaction. He wanted to get back to the world outside the labor encampments. And he wanted to spit in the President's eye when he did.

Of course, he knew he would have to stand in a long line to get what he wanted. He also knew Joe Steele would be soaked—if not drowned—by the time he got to the front of the line. He didn't care. He was ready to wait his turn and take his best shot when it came.

Most of the other wreckers in the labor encampment felt the same way. He knew that, even if there wasn't a whole lot of talk about it. You never could be sure about who would squeal on you to the guards. And what the bastards who ran the encampment called *willful failure to reform* could add years to your stretch here. Not even the most dedicated masochist wanted that.

Most of the wreckers couldn't stand the President, no. But there were a few . . . Four or five guys in Barracks 17 were certain their sentences were just what they deserved. "I love Joe Steele," insisted a sad-eyed little bookkeeper named Adam Bolger. "I just couldn't do the work my firm needed from me. If that doesn't make me a wrecker, I don't know what would."

"What don't you put a fucking sock in it, Bolger?" somebody in a top-tier bunk called. "Nobody wants to listen to your shitass sob stories."

"All of us are guilty," Bolger said. "Nobody works as

well as he ought to all the time. That makes everyone a wrecker."

"Then they should chuck everybody into one of these goddamn encampments, let all the people see how they like it," his critic said. "Me, I'm in here on account of some ass-hole told the Jeebies lies about me. Ain't no other reason."

Several other men chimed in with loud, obscene agree-ment—in the encampment, there was usually no other kind. If you admitted you'd done anything to make yourself belong here, you won the GBI's battle for it. So Mike thought, along with the majority.

He didn't chime in tonight. They'd be blowing out the lanterns pretty soon. He lay in his bunk, atop the joke of a mattress and under the joke of a blanket. The stove was hot, but not much warmth reached this far. The only clothes he'd taken off were his boots. They made a crappy pillow, but they were the only pillow he had—he'd wrapped his tattered Outside clothes around his feet to help keep them warm.

He yawned. He wondered how Stella was doing. Every once in a while, most of the time when he least expected them, loneliness and horniness pierced him like a stiletto. More often than not, though, he was too weary or too hun-gry or—most of the time—both to conjure up anything but a shadow of the feeling he knew he ought to have. The slow extinction here reminded him too much of the beginning of death.

The other choice, of course, was an extinction not so slow. A man who'd had all he could take would try to sneak through the barbed wire without trying very hard to be sneaky. Or he'd go after a guard with an axe or a rock or his bare hands. And he'd wind up dead, most of the time with-out laying a glove on the Jeebie. Some wreckers said guards got bonuses for killing wreckers. That, Mike didn't believe. Were it true, a lot more of the sorry so-and-sos with num-bers on their clothes would have been holding up a lily.

Even with all the snow on the ground, some optimists—or jerks, depending on how you looked at things—ran away when their work gang went out to the woods. Then, of course, the evening count was off. As soon as the count was off, the search was on. Mike had never yet heard of anybody who got away.

Some people died trying. As long as the guards found the bodies, that didn't worry them. A body made the count work, too. Some would-be escapees realized how far they were from any human beings who didn't live in labor encampments. They gave themselves up. That also made the count work.

As far as Mike could see, dying was better. The encampment had a punishment barracks next to the administration building. The cells there were too small to stand up or lie down in. The punishment barracks had no stoves for heat. Rations were bread and water—piss and punk, in the jailhouse slang that lay behind so much encampment lingo. They didn't give you much, either. By the time they let you out, you were like an inner tube with a permanent slow leak.

Mike yawned again. But what could you do? Not much, not so far as he could see. John Dennison had the best way. Take it one day at a time, get through that, and then do it again when reveille sounded the next morning. Mike leaned out of his bunk for a second. He couldn't spot the carpenter from Wyoming, not in the dim red lamplight.

A guard banged a steel bar hanging from a rope with a hammer. That was the lights-out signal. The wreckers blew out the kerosene lamps. Only the hot embers in the stove reminded the barracks that darkness wasn't absolute. Mike thrust his hands into the pockets on his jacket to keep them as warm as he could. His eyelids came down like garage doors. He slept.

Hitler kept screaming about the Sudetenland. As far as Charlie could see, Hitler screamed about everything, like a three-year-old throwing a tantrum. Nobody'd paddled his fanny for him when he *was* a three-year-old, so he still thought he could get away with that kind of nonsense. The Rhineland and the *Anschluss* with Austria sure hadn't shown him he was wrong.

The only way he wouldn't jump on Czechoslovakia with both feet in hobnailed boots to get back his pet Germans was if somebody either stopped him or handed him those Germans on a silver platter. The countries that would have to stop him, if anyone did, were France and England. Neither had its heart in the job.

Joe Steele and Leon Trotsky cheered them on from the sidelines. If war broke out, Red Russia and the USA wouldn't have to get sucked into the fighting. Russia bordered neither Czechoslovakia nor the Third *Reich*; Romania, Poland, and the Baltic republics shielded Trotsky from consequences. And not only the broad Atlantic but also the Western European democracies stood between the United States and the *Führer*.

Charlie thought it was funny that the President and the guy the papers called the Red Czar were both cheering for the same thing when they loathed each other so much. Here more than twenty years after the Russian Revolution and the Bolshevik takeover, the United States still refused to recognize the Reds as Russia's legitimate government. That pretty much meant the USA recognized nobody as overlord of the biggest country in the world. The real Czar and his family were dead, deader, deadest. Kerensky remained in exile in Paris with so many other Russian émigrés, but not even Joe Steele, Trotsky-hater though he was, could take Kerensky seriously.

Charlie thought Joe Steele and Trotsky singing in chorus was funny till Daladier and Chamberlain, instead of fighting to save Czechoslovakia, *did* hand Hitler the Sudetenland on a silver platter at Munich. Hitler promised it would be his last territorial demand in Europe. If he was telling the truth, *wunderbar*. If he wasn't, things didn't look so good.

But all that was a long way away. Charlie had other things on his mind, things closer to home. Sarah was teething, which left him and Esther both even lower on shuteye than usual. And a couple of more desks near him had nobody sitting behind them. Two reporters had vanished almost without a trace. Where were they now? Somewhere between New Mexico and North Dakota—that was as much as anybody knew.

His telephone rang. He picked it up. "Sullivan, AP."

"Scriabin, White House." The Hammer could be viciously sardonic. "The President wants to see you."

"About what?" Charlie asked, in lieu of a gulp.

"He'll tell you. If he wanted me to do it, I would," Scriabin said. "Are you coming?"

"I'm on my way," Charlie said. If the Heebie Jeebies were going to grab him, they could do it here or at his apartment. Or, of course, if Joe Steele felt like watching J. Edgar Hoover's men in action, they could do it at the White House. But Charlie couldn't say *I don't want to see him.* The President and all his men had long memories for slights.

When Charlie got to 1600 Pennsylvania Avenue, a steward took him up to the oval study above the Blue Room. Joe Steele sat behind that big redwood desk, puffing on his pipe. "Sullivan," he said with an abrupt nod.

"Mr. President." Charlie tried not to show how nervous — hell, how scared — he was. "What do you need, sir?"

"Here." Joe Steele shoved typewritten pages across the desk at him. "I am going to issue a statement saying how wrong France and England were to appease Hitler over the Sudetenland. None of the drafts from my writers is any damn good. You throw words around. Let's see what you can do." He waved Charlie to the chair on the other side of the desk.

Sinking down into it, Charlie wondered what the stakes were. If Joe Steele liked what he did, would Mike come out of the labor encampment? If Joe Steele didn't like it, would Charlie go into one and leave another AP desk vacant? Those were . . . interesting questions, weren't they?

He pulled a pen from his shirt pocket and got to work. Joe Steele was right about one thing, anyway: as it stood now, the statement was muddy and opaque. Charlie thought of himself as a good editor and polisher. Now it seemed to be put up or shut up.

The statement wasn't very long. He spent fifteen minutes noodling and nipping and tucking. Twice, he needed to ask the President just how specific and how sharp he wanted to be. Between puffs, Joe Steele told him.

"Here you go, sir." Charlie passed the statement back. He waited for the sky to fall.

Joe Steele put on glasses to read what he'd done. The President used them, but seldom let himself be photographed wearing them. His hair was grayer than when he first took office. After two or three minutes, he looked at Charlie over the tops of the spectacles. As always, his eyes were unreadable.

But then, out of the blue, he smiled. Like a snake with a bird, he could be charming. "This is excellent!" he said. "Much better than anything my hacks turned out. I'll use it, or something very close to it."

"Thank you, Mr. President," Charlie said. The lady, not the tiger.

"How would you like to work here?" Joe Steele asked. "I can use someone who doesn't write English like a foreign language. I'll raise your pay two thousand dollars over what the Associated Press gives you. With a baby in the house, money comes in handy, doesn't it?"

One brother in a labor encampment, one working in the White House? Wasn't that insane? *But what will he do if I say no?* Charlie didn't want—didn't dare—to find out. "Thank you, sir. I'm honored," he muttered. *Honor or not, I'd still rather walk.* Walking, though, wasn't a choice Joe Steele had offered him.

XIV

Not even a year after German troops marched into Austria, not even six months after German troops goose-stepped into the Sudetenland (and after the *Führer* swore he had no more European territorial demands), the *Reich* annexed Bohemia and Moravia, the Czech parts of what had been Czechoslovakia. The Slovak part became "independent" under a bunch of homegrown Fascists headed by a priest.

Charlie got the wire-service feeds in the White House, the same as he had while he was still working for the Associated Press. He pulled an atlas off the shelf in his little office and eyed the map of Central Europe. With the revisions, it didn't look so good, not if you wanted the world to stay at peace.

A cigarette in the corner of his mouth, Stas Mikoian stuck his head into the office. "What are you looking at?" he asked.

"The next world war, that's what," Charlie answered gloomily.

"I hope it's not as bad as that," Joe Steele's aide said.

"I hope so, too, but it damn well is. C'mere and see for yourself," Charlie said. When Mikoian did, Charlie pointed to the map. "Look. Now the Nazis can put soldiers in Slovakia, not just the Sudetenland. With East Prussia, they've got Poland in the same kind of nutcracker they squeezed Czechoslovakia with after they grabbed Austria."

Mikoian studied the Rand McNally, no doubt filling in the new borders for himself. He grunted thoughtfully. "Yeah, it looks that way to me, too. And if we can see it, the brass at the War Department will see it, too."

That made Charlie grunt. Some of what had been the

top brass in the Army and Navy had been shot for treason. Other officers were serving long prison terms. Still others were breaking rocks or cutting down trees or digging ditches or doing whatever else wreckers did in labor encampments. Newer, younger men Joe Steele trusted further—not that Joe Steele trusted anybody very far—sat in those emptied chairs. Were they smart enough to see such things? *They'd damn well better be,* Charlie thought.

But Stas Mikoian hadn't finished: "And if we can see it, the brass in Paris and London can also see it. And the brass in Moscow, not that they wear much brass there." Charlie nodded—the Reds had leveled things so thoroughly, even generals' uniforms were hardly fancier than those of private soldiers.

Another thought crossed Charlie's mind. "I bet they're having spasms in Warsaw," he said. "Poland grabbed a little chunk of Czechoslovakia, too, when Hitler moved into the Sudetenland. I wonder how they like the taste of it now. Talk about shortsighted!"

"You said it," Mikoian agreed.

"What's the boss going to do about it?" Charlie asked. Before Joe Steele's aide could answer, the telephone rang. Charlie picked it up. "Sullivan." He still sometimes had to remind himself not to add *AP* after his name.

"Yes." That rasp belonged to the President. "Put together a draft for me. I want to let the people know that this latest German move pushes Europe closer to war. I want them to know that we have to move closer to being able to defend ourselves no matter what happens, but that I don't want or aim to get drawn into a fight on the other side of the Atlantic. Got that?"

"Sure do." Charlie had scrawled notes while Joe Steele talked.

"Then take care of it." The phone went dead.

"Was that him?" Mikoian asked. Charlie nodded. The California Armenian gave forth with a crooked grin. "Well, now you know what he's going to do about it, in that case." He nodded and left. He probably expected his own call any minute, or that he'd have to respond to one that came while he was talking with Charlie.

That was how Joe Steele worked. He'd hand several people the same assignment, take what he liked most from each man's work, stir those chunks together, and use them as his own. It gave him the best from each member of his staff. It also kept the men he relied on competing against one another for his favor. One thing he knew was how to wrap people around his finger.

Charlie ran two sheets of paper sandwiched around a carbon into his typewriter and started clacking away. He bore down hard on keeping America out of the fight. Going to war again in Europe was pure political poison, nothing else but. Joe Steele could—and did—do pretty much what he wanted inside the borders of the USA. Halfway through his second term, the Constitution was what he said it was. Anybody who didn't go for that would soon be sorry. But not even the Jeebies could ship everyone who didn't fancy a war to the closest labor encampment. Spacious as the encampments were, they couldn't begin to hold all those people.

And Charlie bore down hard on what a lying, cheating SOB Hitler was. Kagan and Mikoian and Scriabin and whoever else was working on this would also emphasize that. Everybody knew Joe Steele couldn't stand Hitler. You couldn't go wrong calling him names.

Charlie wondered how much of his draft Joe Steele would use. He was the new kid on the block. He hadn't been on the staff since Joe Steele was a Congressman nobody outside of Fresno—and not many people in the town—had ever heard of. In a way, having a fresh approach gave him an edge. But the old-timers often teamed up against him, as much to remind him he *was* new as for any reason important in and of itself.

Office politics worked that way. They did in a bank, at the Associated Press, and here in the most important office in the country. Sometimes Charlie remembered that, and didn't let slights get him down. Sometimes, instead, he remembered that, if Joe Steele turned against him, firing was the least of his worries. If Joe Steele turned against him, it could be the firing squad. Or they could chuck him into a labor encampment and forget he was there. On days like that, he bit his nails and gnawed his cuticles till they bled.

On days like that, he also went to the watering hole near the White House, the one where the Vice President held court. Joe Steele never asked John Nance Garner for drafts of speeches. He never asked him what he thought about the great storm rising in Europe, or about the troubles that still dogged the United States.

And John Nance Garner wasn't sorry that he didn't. "I ain't got a thing to worry about," the Vice President declared one afternoon when he'd taken on enough bourbon to pickle his grammar. "Joe Steele don't give a damn about me. Long as I stay out of the way and keep my trap shut and don't kick up no trouble, he'll leave me alone. You should be so lucky, Sullivan."

"Yeah." Charlie was morose that day. Joe Steele had talked about strikes, and how to keep the country producing in spite of them. He hadn't used many of Charlie's ideas. If Charlie had to guess, most of the ideas he had used came straight from J. Edgar Hoover, with maybe a few from Vince Scriabin. The speech hadn't had any compromise in it, in other words.

The Vice President leered at him like a fox eyeing a bunny. "Just recall, son—you *volunteered* for this," Garner said.

"Yeah," Charlie said again, more morosely yet. Then he eyed Garner in turn. "Now that I think about it, so did you."

"Uh-huh." The Vice President's sigh was so high-proof, it was a good thing he wasn't smoking—he might have impersonated a blowtorch. "Too late to fret none about it now. You grab the tiger by the ears, you got to hang on for the ride. Long as you're on his back, he can't eat you."

Joe Steele didn't literally devour followers who displeased him. No, not literally. But when you had the most powerful job in the country and you took it three or four steps further than any other President had ever gone . . . Maybe the times demanded that. Maybe the times conspired with Joe Steele's nature. However that worked, even a metaphorical devouring could leave a man bloodied or dead.

Charlie held up his hand to ask for another drink.

*   *   *

It was summer—summer high in the Rockies. It got up into the sixties, sometimes into the seventies. Nights stayed chilly as the warmth of the day fled after sundown. Chilly, yes, but they didn't drop below freezing.

Mike enjoyed the good weather, knowing it wouldn't last. Even in summer up here, winter lay right around the corner. Winter always lay right around the corner . . . except when it sprang out and clasped you in its frigid embrace.

One day at a time, though. *Right around the corner* didn't mean *here*. He'd been in the labor encampment for a couple of years now. He had its measure, as much as anyone could. Even inside his own head, he was NY24601, wrecker, more often than he was Mike Sullivan, *New York Post* reporter.

He leaned on his axe, there in the woods. He was scrawny and dirty and shaggy and shabby. He also had harder muscles than he'd ever dreamt of, to say nothing of owned, before the Jeebies grabbed him. Nietzsche might've had it straight after all. What didn't kill you honest to God did make you stronger.

Sometimes it did kill. Too many men had left the labor encampment in pine boxes. They couldn't do the work. Or they couldn't stand the food. Or they simply despaired. If you gave up, you didn't last long.

"Spare any alfalfa?" Mike asked John Dennison.

The carpenter pulled out his tobacco pouch. When he did have some, he was always ready to share with friends. If they didn't share in turn, they didn't stay friends long. Mike understood that. "Get your paper ready," Dennison said.

Mike tore a cigarette-sized piece off a wad of newspaper he kept in his pocket. He could wipe his ass on the rest when he had to shit. By what the papers printed these days, that was about what they were good for. They all sucked up to Joe Steele like you wouldn't believe. Or, considering how many reporters were in labor encampments these days, you might believe it.

Even smoking, even wiping your ass, you had to watch yourself. If somebody finked on you for burning up a newsprint photo of Joe Steele or getting it brown and stinking, you'd do a stretch in the punishment cells. Insulting the President was a serious business.

John Dennison poured the cheap, harsh tobacco onto the paper. Machine-made cigarettes with the tasty stuff inside them were as good as money in the encampments. As often as not, they were too precious to smoke. This nasty junk just kept you from getting the no-cigarette jitters. That was all Mike cared about, that and the excuse for a short break.

Dennison rolled one for himself, too. He sucked in smoke, blew it out, and looked around. "By the time they turn us loose," he said, "won't be a goddamn tree left in this part of Montana."

"I wouldn't be surprised," Mike said, and then, after a puff of his own, "If they ever turn us loose."

"Sooner or later, they'll get sick of us," John Dennison said. "Wonder if I'll know how to fit in anywhere but a place like this by then."

"Mmm," Mike said—not a happy noise. He'd had the same worry, and the one on its flip side: whether Stella would want anything to do with him once they did let him go back to New York City and civilization as he'd known it. Plenty of the wives of wreckers at the encampment had already divorced them. Some of those ladies had found new men, not caring to wait for their husbands to return.

And others had filed for divorce to cleanse their own names. If you were married to a wrecker, something had to be wrong with you, too, didn't it? If you were looking for work, wouldn't whoever was hiring pick somebody reliable instead? If your son was applying for college, wouldn't they admit someone from a loyal household in his place? If you needed a loan, wouldn't a bank decide you made a poor risk because you might go off to an encampment yourself?

Mike had no reason to believe Stella was anything but faithful and one hundred percent behind him. But he hadn't heard from her for several months now. He didn't know whether that was because the Jeebies were sitting on his mail (or just tossing it in the trash) or because his wife couldn't find anything to say to him.

He didn't spend every waking moment brooding about

it. He wasn't Hamlet, to brood about every goddamn thing that happened to him. Besides, during most of his waking moments he was too busy or too tired. Every so often, though, most often when he paused for a smoke, the worry bubbled back to the surface.

"What I really want to do," Dennison went on, "is pay back the skunk who told the Jeebies about me. Yeah, that son of a bitch, he's gonna have hisself an accident or three."

"Mmm," Mike repeated. Nobody'd needed to point him out to J. Edgar Hoover's thugs. The way he'd gone after Joe Steele, he'd done everything but shine a searchlight on himself. He'd been asking for it, and he'd got it.

The trouble was, he hadn't realized fast enough how much the rules had changed. Back in the old days—before Joe Steele's first inauguration—the First Amendment still meant something. If you behaved as if it did when it didn't . . . you ended up on a mountainside in Montana, leaning on your axe while you smoked so you wouldn't have to work for a few minutes.

A couple of hundred yards away, another lodgepole went over with a rending crash. A wrecker let out an excited yip. Some people could get worked up about whatever they wound up doing, even if it was only a short piss away from slave labor. Mike didn't have that knack. They could make him do it, but they couldn't make him get excited about it.

A guard came toward Mike and John Dennison. He was smoking a Camel; guards could burn their machine-mades whenever they got the urge. Sure as hell, the bastard looked at what was left of the wreckers' roll-your-owns. Had he spotted Joe Steele's mustache on either one, there would have been hell to pay.

Since he didn't, he just said, "Okay, kids—playtime's over. Get it in gear and knock down some wood."

"Sure thing," Mike said. You couldn't tell 'em to piss up a rope. But you could look busier than you were. Slaves had known that trick before the Pyramids rose. In the outside world, most of the wreckers had been hard workers. Not here, not when they didn't have to. What was the point? Mike didn't see any at all.

*　　　*　　　*

Sometimes things happened too fast for outsiders to keep up with them. Watching Europe through August, Charlie had that feeling. Every day seemed to bring a new surprise, each one more horrible than the last.

Hitler shrieked about the Polish Corridor the way he'd shrieked about the Sudetenland the year before. It had belonged to Germany. Germans still lived there. The Poles were mistreating them. Therefore, the Corridor had to return to the *Reich*.

But the year before, he'd sold France and England his bill of goods. They weren't buying this time around. The way he'd gobbled up Bohemia and Moravia after pledging he wouldn't finally persuaded them they couldn't believe a word he said. They told him they would go to war if he invaded Poland.

They still weren't eager about it, though. In the war against the Kaiser, Russia had done a big chunk of the Entente's dying. France and England wanted Russia on their side again, even if it was Red, Red, Red. They sent delegations to Moscow to sweet-talk Trotsky into bed with them.

Charlie had always thought Trotsky looked like a fox, with his auburn hair, his knowing eyes, his sharp nose, and his pointed chin whiskers. He listened to what the French and English diplomats and military envoys said—and what they didn't or wouldn't say. He listened, and he made no promises, and he waited to find out whether he heard from anyone else.

When he did . . . At the start of the last week of August, Maxim Litvinov flew from Moscow to Berlin. The Jew ruling Red Russia sent his Jewish foreign commissar to the world's capital of anti-Semitism. Litvinov and Ribbentrop put their heads together. The very next day, with Adolf Hitler beaming in the background, they signed a nonaggression treaty and an enormous trade package.

The news burst like a bomb in Paris and London . . . and in Warsaw. Whatever the Russians would do, they wouldn't fight to keep the Germans out of Poland. Russians didn't think Poles were *Untermenschen*, the way the Nazis did. But an independent Poland affronted Moscow almost as much as it outraged Berlin.

Lazar Kagan was the first important aide Charlie ran into after the story broke. "What do we do about this?" Charlie asked him, feeling very much like a jumped-up reporter. "What *can* we do?"

"I don't know." Kagan sounded as stunned as Charlie felt. When Charlie realized the large, round man was thrown for a loop, too, something inside of him loosened. This wasn't just too big for him. This was too big for everybody. After a moment, Kagan went on, "There's probably nothing the United States can do except to tell France and England to stick to their guns. We're too far away from what's going on to influence Germany and Russia one way or the other."

"I guess so." Charlie hesitated, then asked, "Have you seen the boss?"

"Yes, I've seen him." Kagan managed a nod. "He . . . isn't very happy."

And that would do for an understatement till a bigger one rolled down the pike. If Charlie was any judge, none would any time soon. The two world leaders Joe Steele despised more than any others had suddenly made common cause. Charlie found one more question: "How long does he think Poland's got?"

"Days. Not weeks—days," Kagan answered. "The Poles say they'll fight. It's just a question of how well they can. They have a lot of men in uniform—a lot more than we do. Maybe Hitler has bitten off more than he can chew. Maybe." He sounded like a man trying to talk himself into believing it but not doing very well.

"Okay. Thanks—I guess." Charlie went back to his office and wrote a statement condemning the Nazis and Reds for joining in a pact "obviously aimed at the nation between them" and hoping that the remaining European democracies "would remain true to their solemn commitments."

When Joe Steele spoke on the radio that night, he used Charlie's phrases unchanged. Listening, Charlie felt satisfaction mixed with dread. Joe Steele had the air of a doctor standing outside a sickroom, going over things with the relatives of a patient who wouldn't pull through.

But Sarah grinned and banged her Raggedy Ann doll on

the coffee table. Charlie watched to make sure she didn't bang her head on it—at not quite a year and a half, she didn't have walking down pat yet. She also didn't know what was going on across the Atlantic. Even if she had known, she wouldn't have cared.

Plenty of much older Americans didn't care, either. They or their ancestors had come here so they wouldn't have to worry about Europe's periodic bouts of madness. Another war, so soon after the last one? You had to be crazy to do something like that. Didn't you?

Crazy or not, just over a week later Germany invaded Poland with tanks and dive-bombers and machine guns and millions of marching men in coal-scuttle helmets and jackboots. France and England sent ultimatums, demanding that Hitler withdraw. He didn't. First one and then the other declared war.

But that was all they did. They didn't attack Germany the way Germany was attacking Poland. There were a few small skirmishes along the *Reich*'s western frontier. Past that, nothing. Meanwhile, before the fighting farther east was more than a few days old, it grew crystal clear that the Poles were in way over their heads. Shattered by weapons and by doctrine they couldn't start to match, they reeled back or charged hopelessly. Charlie read reports about mounted lancers attacking tanks.

"Yes, I've seen those, too," Vince Scriabin said when he mentioned them. "It's very brave, but it isn't war, is it?"

"What would you call it, then?" Charlie asked.

"Murder," Scriabin answered. He had on his desk just then a typewritten page full of the names of men condemned for wrecking and other kinds of treason. It was upside down, but Charlie could read things that way—a handy skill for a reporter to pick up. Scriabin had written *HFP—all* in red in the narrow margin above the names.

Charlie did his best not to shiver. *HFP* abbreviated *Highest Form of Punishment*. In other words, that was a page full of the names of dead men. On how many other sheets had Scriabin scribbled those same three ominous letters? Charlie had no idea, but the number couldn't be small.

He didn't see Mike's name on the sheet. That was something: a small something, but something. If he had seen it, the sentence would already have been carried out. Nothing to do then but kill himself or take his best shot at killing Scriabin and J. Edgar Hoover and Joe Steele.

Well, he didn't have to worry about that, thank God. All he had to worry about was a new world war. Next to what happened to his brother, it didn't seem like so much.

Then, with Poland on the ropes, Trotsky jumped what was left of it from behind. His excuse, such as it was, was as cynical as anything Joe Steele could have come up with. He blandly announced that, since Poland had fallen into chaos, Red Army troops were moving in to restore order.

And to split the country's corpse with Hitler. Nazi and Red officers shook hands at the new frontier (which Litvinov and Ribbentrop had agreed to in advance). A British cartoonist turned out what became a famous drawing of Hitler and Trotsky graciously bowing to each other over a body labeled POLAND. The smirking *Führer* was saying, "The dirty Jew, I believe?" to which the smiling Red leader was replying, "The assassin of the workers, I presume?"

Joe Steele made a speech before the National Press Club. That wasn't what it had been back in the day. If you didn't like the President—if you insisted on saying you didn't like the President—you weren't at the banquet in a suit and tie or a tux. No, you were somewhere farther west, eating plainer grub and not much of it, and wearing less elegant attire.

Or, if you were less lucky still, you'd gone West for good. You'd shown up on one of those sheets that crossed Scriabin's desk, or maybe Joe Steele's, and the aide or the boss had written *HFP* on it, and that was all she wrote. You'd never come back to the land of the free and the home of the brave.

Those were damn depressing thoughts to have while you were downing candied carrots and mashed potatoes and rubber chicken. Charlie tried to improve his attitude with bourbon. It helped some, even if he did stagger when he went to get his last couple of refills.

Attorney General Wyszynski introduced Joe Steele.

That was enough to make the reporters pay attention all by itself. If you didn't merely end up on a bureaucratic list, if you needed to be tried, Wyszynski and his pet prosecutors were the ones who would send you up the river.

Everyone applauded the President. Everyone watched everyone else to see how hard the others were applauding. Everyone tried to applaud harder than the people near him. You couldn't just like Joe Steele. You had to be seen—and heard—to like him.

The President ambled up to the lectern. He had a rolling, deliberate walk that would have seemed more at home in a vineyard than in the corridors of power. Charlie didn't expect much from the address, even if he'd helped draft it. Joe Steele was a decent speaker, but that was all he was.

He outdid himself that night. Maybe he was speaking from the heart. (Yes, Charlie knew some people denied that Joe Steele had a heart. Sometimes, he was one of those people himself. Sometimes, but not that night.) The President's talk got remembered as the Plague on Both Your Houses speech.

"Half the troubles in our own country come from the Nazis. The other half come from the Reds," he said. "Now they lie down together. They are not the lion and the lamb. They are two serpents. If we were lucky, each would grab the other by the tail. They would swallow each other up till nothing was left of either one. But we are not so lucky, and there are more players in the game than Germany and Russia alone."

He paused to puff on his pipe. It stayed close at hand all the time, even when he was making a speech. "For the second time in a generation, war tears at the vitals of Europe. We will not let it touch us here. This fight is not worth the red blood of one single American boy. No one over there has a cause that was worth going to war for. No, gentlemen. No one. All they have in Europe are hate and greed.

"For the United States, for the land we all love, the greatest dangers lurk in insidious encroachments for foreign powers by fanatics. We must and we shall step up our vigilance against them—Reds and Nazis will both try to ensnare us. As long as we stamp them out at home, everything will go well here. And as long as we steer clear of Europe's latest stupid war, everything will be fine—for us—there."

He dipped his head and stepped back. The hand he'd got before the speech was pragmatic, politic. The one he got after it? The reporters meant that one. He'd told them what they wanted to hear, and he'd done it well. Later, Charlie decided the difference was something like the one between a stage kiss and a real kiss.

Sitting next to Charlie was the *Los Angeles Times'* Washington correspondent. "He keeps talking like that, he won't have any trouble getting a third term," the man said. Chances were he meant it and wasn't just currying favor. The *Los Angeles Times* was firmly in Joe Steele's back pocket.

"Wouldn't be surprised if you're right," Charlie said. He expected Joe Steele to run again, and to win again. Why wouldn't he? Not just the *L.A. Times* was in his back pocket. These days, the whole country was.

News of the war reached the labor encampment, of course. Few men there got excited about it. They had more important things to worry about. Another Montana winter was coming on. If they didn't do everything they could to get ready for it, they wouldn't see spring.

A couple of scalps, guys who'd been in only weeks or months and still sometimes thought of themselves as free men, tried to volunteer for the Army. The Jeebies who ran the encampment only laughed at them. "The bastard said, 'Why do you think the Army needs wreckers in it?'" one would-be soldier reported indignantly.

Mike listened. He sympathized. He didn't get up in arms, though. You had to take care of Number One first. After more than two years, his old jacket had got too old and tattered for even the best tailor in the encampment to keep it in one piece. That didn't necessarily mean they'd issue him a new one, though. Wreckers didn't have to get replacements for such things. Who was to say they hadn't wrecked the old, ratty ones?

He'd spent weeks running errands for a sergeant in the

supply cabin. He'd buttered the man up as if he were basting a Thanksgiving turkey. He'd let the sergeant get a good look at the cotton quilting coming out at the elbows of his old jacket and at the seams across the back.

And he'd got a new one. The Jeebie had actually thrown the new one at him, growling, "Get your number on this, front and back, quick as you can. Make sure the ink dries so it doesn't run."

"I'll do it!" he'd said happily. "Thanks!" And he did.

Now he had to keep that sergeant sweet with more small favors for another few weeks. He'd ease off a little at a time, so gradually that the sergeant didn't notice. Or maybe he wouldn't ease off at all. His boots were wearing out, too. A new pair would mean he didn't have to plug holes with rags and cardboard to keep his toes from freezing.

From somewhere, John Dennison had got his hands on a wool watch cap, the kind they wore in the Navy. Jacket, pants, and boots were all uniform items. The Jeebies didn't get their knickers in a twist about what you put on your head. Oh, they'd kick your ass for you if you wore a turban like Rudolph Valentino in *The Sheik*. But they'd cut you some slack if you didn't do anything too stupid.

"What I really crave is one of those Russian fur hats with the earflaps," John said. "But this is the next best thing."

"You're better off with what you've got, you ask me," Mike told him. "If you put on one of those fur hats, sure as hell a guard'd steal it. The GBI doesn't give them anything that nice."

"Huh," Dennison said thoughtfully. "Well, you've got somethin' there. I didn't look at it like that."

Winter had some advantages. The latrines stank less. Flies and mosquitoes disappeared till the weather warmed up again. Even fleas grew less annoying for a while. Bedbugs and lice . . . Bedbugs and lice didn't care what the weather was like. They'd get you any which way.

A nearsighted wrecker used a sharp chunk of volcanic glass to carve louse combs out of wood. Mike got one with some tobacco. The craftsmanship was amazing; the comb looked as if a machine had shaped it. And the teeth were close enough together to rout lice from his hair and even to peel off nits. You couldn't ask for a better tool.

Three days after he started using it, Mike suddenly burst out laughing in his bunk. "What's so funny?" four or five other men asked, more or less in chorus. In the encampment, anything funny was precious.

He held out the elegant piece of woodcarving. "Look!" he said. "It's a fine-toothed comb!"

A couple of wreckers swore at him. The others laughed along. But Mike kept staring at the carved marvel. Damned if it *wasn't* a fine-toothed comb. Back in the days before bathtubs and showers grew common, people needed fine-toothed combs to fight back against the pests that lived on them. When you searched with one of those, what were you searching for? Lice, that was what.

He caught one, too, and crushed it between his thumbnails. He'd almost puked the first time he found a small, pale louse in his hair. Now all he felt was satisfaction when he killed one. Familiarity bred contempt, all right.

The encampment had other kinds of adventures besides pest control. There was mail call, for instance. The Jeebies didn't let in everything everybody wrote to you—nowhere close—but they did let in some mail. You always wanted to hear from people you loved, even if a censor's scratchouts sometimes showed you weren't the first one to set eyes on what they wrote.

Mail call also had another side to it. It was a gamble. Sometimes you won, sometimes you lost. If the bastard with the sack didn't call your name, good form said you had to turn away without showing how disappointed you were. It was like not showing that a wound hurt you in the last war . . . or, Mike supposed, in this new one. Since Stella's letters stopped coming, he'd got good at it.

One cold day—a day colder than he would have thought possible with the sun shining brightly—the guard bawled, "Sullivan! NY24601!"

"I'm here!" Mike pushed his way through the other wreckers and held out a mittened hand. The Jeebie gave him an envelope, then called out another name and number.

It wasn't a letter from anybody Mike knew. It was one of those cellophane-windowed envelopes businesses used. The return address was printed: Hogan, Hunter, Gasarch & Hume, with an address not too far from where he'd lived in the half-forgotten days before he came to Montana.

He opened the envelope and unfolded the letter. Hogan, Hunter, Gasarch & Hume turned out to be a firm of lawyers. And the letter turned out to be a notification of divorce proceedings against him. The cause was given as abandonment. *In view of the circumstances,* the letter finished, *no alimony is sought in this case.* A signature that might have been Gasarch's lay under the typewritten words.

Mike stared at the piece of paper. Like so many wreckers' wives, Stella'd had enough. She was getting on with her life without him. The Catholic Church didn't recognize divorces. The state of New York damn well did, though. Stella might think about the world to come, but she lived in this one.

"Fuck," Mike muttered, breathing out fog. No, he wasn't the first guy here whose wife ran out of patience with being on her own. He knew he wouldn't be the last. That didn't make the hurt, the loss, or the sense of betrayal any easier to take. He crumpled up the paper and tossed it over his shoulder. It was too thick and firm to be good around a cigarette or for anything else.

XV

"I'm going to work, sweetie," Charlie told his daughter. "Come give me a kiss bye-bye."

"No." Sarah was just past two. She said no at any excuse or none. Then she came over, wrapped her arms around him, and kissed him.

"Okay. My turn now," Esther said after Sarah disentangled herself from her daddy.

"No," Sarah said again.

Taking no notice of her, Esther stepped into Charlie's arms. They kissed. He counted his blessings every time he held her. One of the big ones was that he wasn't in a labor encampment. If he were, would Esther have dumped him the way Stella'd dumped Mike? He hoped not, but how could you know?

Stella and Esther had stayed friends in spite of everything. "It's not that she didn't love him," Esther'd tried to explain to Charlie. "It's just that he wasn't there and he couldn't be there and finally she got so she couldn't stand being by herself any more and watching the world pass her by."

Charlie still resented it. "What about that 'in sickness and in health, for richer, for poorer' stuff?" he'd asked.

"What about 'to have and to hold'?" Esther had returned. "She couldn't have him, she couldn't hold him, not for years. That's why she talked to a lawyer. Who knows when they'll turn him loose? Who knows whether they'll let him come back to New York City if they do?"

He'd had no retort for that. Some wreckers had been released from labor encampments, but on condition they stayed in the empty states that held the encampments. If

they broke the deal and got caught where they weren't supposed to be, back behind barbed wire they'd go, and for a
longer stretch this time around.

He squeezed Esther extra tight before heading out the
door. He hoped she wouldn't drop him and run as if from a
grenade with the pin pulled if he did get thrown aboard a
train and shipped to the prairie or the mountains. And he
hoped the Jeebies never knocked on his door at midnight.
Even when you worked in the White House, even when
you talked to Joe Steele almost every day, hope was the
most you could do.

A short-pants kid was hawking papers at the corner
where Charlie caught the bus. "Extra!" the kid shouted.
"Nazis invade Low Countries! Read all about it!"

"Oh, God!" Charlie said. The other shoe had finally
dropped, then. The Germans had taken Denmark at a gulp,
and hadn't had much trouble in Norway, either. But Scandinavia was just a sideshow. Everybody knew it. The main
event would be in the west, the way it had been the last
time around. Now the bell for that one had rung. Charlie
tossed the newsboy a nickel. "Lemme have one of those."

"Here you go, Mister." The kid gave him a paper.

He read it waiting for the bus, and then on it on the way
to the White House. The Nazis weren't doing anything halfway. They hadn't just violated Belgium's neutrality, as the
Kaiser did in 1914. They'd trampled Holland's neutrality,
too. And Luxembourg's, not that anybody gave a damn
about Luxembourg. The only reason it seemed to be there
was to get it in the neck.

The *Luftwaffe* was bombing the hell out of the Low
Countries, and out of France, too. Göring had shown what
it could do as far back as the Spanish Civil War. He hadn't
let up in the attack on Poland. He wasn't letting up now,
either.

And Neville Chamberlain was out as British Prime Minister. He'd underestimated Hitler over the Sudetenland.
He'd said the Nazis had missed the bus even as they were
devouring Scandinavia. He'd "won" a vote of confidence by
a margin much smaller than the Tories' majority in
Commons—even they hadn't had much confidence in him.

Now he was gone. Winston Churchill would have to measure himself against the *Führer*.

Charlie carried the paper into the White House. Seeing it, Stas Mikoian pointed at it and said, "Everything's going to hell in a handbasket over there."

"Sure looks that way, doesn't it?" Charlie agreed. "Hitler's shoved all his chips into the pot."

"So has everybody else," Mikoian answered. "Now we see what the cards are worth."

Over the next month, they did. The fighting was really decided in the first few days, when the Nazis' tanks and troop carriers punched through the weak French defenses in the Ardennes and raced for the Channel. That only became clear looking back, though. What was obvious at the time were the surrenders of Holland and Belgium, the headlong French retreat, and the way the best French and British troops got cut off and surrounded against the sea at Dunkirk.

Most of them managed to cross the Channel to England. From the perspective of anyone who didn't root for the Nazis, it looked like a miracle. Churchill bellowed eloquent defiance at Hitler on the BBC.

And Joe Steele summoned Charlie to the oval study above the Blue Room. The smell of the sweet pipe tobacco he favored hung in the air, as it always did there. "We need to keep England in the fight," the President said bluntly. "Hitler is already on the Atlantic in France. If England goes down, too, America will face the whole continent united under a dictator."

"Yes, sir," Charlie said, in place of *Takes one to know one*. He knew who and what he was working for. He just didn't know how not to work for him. Well, he knew some ways, but they all struck him as cures worse than the disease.

Still blunt, Joe Steele went on, "England is running out of money to buy war supplies from us. They can't turn out enough to fight off the Germans on their own. If we don't give them credit—or give them what they need now and worry later about getting paid back—they'll fold up. So get me a draft of a speech saying that's what we'll do. I'll run a bill through Congress to keep it legal."

He would, too. Congress was as much under his muscular thumb as the courts were. Congressmen who made him unhappy found themselves with legal troubles—or with scandals exploding in their districts.

Charlie wrote the speech. Joe Steele used some of it on the radio. People didn't jump up and down about the idea of taking a step closer to war. They didn't do much complaining where anyone else could hear them, then. You never knew who might tell a Jeebie you were a wrecker. Labor encampments always needed fresh backs. Joe Steele's bill sailed through Congress.

Across the Atlantic, Churchill took note of the new law. "Once again, America is too proud to fight," he said. "But, luckily, she is not too proud to help us fight. Well, fair enough. Give us the tools, and we will finish the job. If the Devil opposed Adolf Hitler, I should endeavor to give him a good notice in the House of Commons. Thus I thank Joe Steele."

"Did I just hear that?" Esther exclaimed after Churchill's speech crackled across the sea by shortwave. She sounded as if she couldn't believe her ears.

"Yeah, you did, 'cause I heard it, too," Charlie said. "I wouldn't go on about it with your friends or anything, though."

She made a face at him. "I know better than that."

"Okay." Charlie left it there. He needed a shortwave set. In his job, he had to hear the news as soon as he could. It wasn't against the law for anybody to have that kind of radio and to listen to whatever he pleased. But Churchill wasn't the only foreign leader who threw darts at Joe Steele over the airwaves. If you repeated them, you could find yourself in more trouble than you really wanted.

Was Joe Steele listening to the Prime Minister's speech? Charlie had no way of knowing. Sometimes Joe Steele slept in the middle of the day and stayed up all night—and made his aides and anyone who needed to do business with him stay up all night, too. Sometimes he kept the same hours as anybody else. He was a law unto himself.

Whether the President was listening now or not, he would hear about the gibe. Charlie was sure of that. And, sooner or later, Joe Steele would find a way to make Churchill pay. Charlie was sure of that, too.

The Republicans gathered in Philadelphia to pick someone to run for President. Charlie wondered why they bothered. They might not know they wouldn't win, but everybody else did. A couple of Senators wanted a crack at Joe Steele. So did Tom Dewey, the young Governor of New York. He'd been a crusading district attorney. To Charlie, he looked and sounded like a GBI man.

They didn't nominate him. Maybe they thought he was too young. Maybe they thought he acted like a Jeebie, too. They also didn't nominate either Senator. They chose a dark horse, a newcomer to politics—and to the Republican Party—named Wendell Willkie.

"I used to be a Democrat," Willkie declared in his acceptance speech. "I used to be, till Joe Steele drove me out of the party. He's driven everybody who cares about freedom out of the party. Now it's time to drive him out of the White House! Nobody's ever had a third term. Nobody's ever deserved one. He sure doesn't. Let's put this country back together again!"

All the Republicans in the hall cheered and clapped. Coming out of the radio in Charlie's front room, the noise was like the roar of heavy surf. He had no doubt that J. Edgar Hoover's men had already compiled a dossier for every delegate and alternate. Chances were, a list of all those names had already crossed Vince Scriabin's desk. Beside how many of them had the Hammer scribbled *HFP*?

Three weeks after the GOP tapped Willkie, the Democrats convened at the Chicago Stadium. Charlie hadn't been back there since the convention in 1932. He wondered if that diner near the Stadium was still in business. He didn't try to find out. He also made damn sure he didn't remind Scriabin about it.

Things were different now. He was working for Joe Steele, not covering his nomination. There wouldn't be any fight at this convention, either. It would do what Joe Steele wanted. It would, and it did. It nominated him and John Nance Garner for third terms.

"I thank you," the President told the Democratic politicos (and chances were the Jeebies had files on them, too). "I thank you for your trust. If the world were not in such disorder, I might not run again. But the country needs an experienced hand on the wheel. I will do my best to keep us going in the right direction, and I will do my best to stay at peace with the whole world."

They cheered him. Charlie applauded with everybody else. You couldn't sit there like a bump on a log. And the sentiment was worthwhile. The only question was whether Joe Steele, or anyone else, could live up to it.

Wendell Willkie charged around the country. He had energy. He'd make a speech wherever a couple of dozen people gathered. Joe Steele didn't campaign nearly so hard. He told people he didn't intend to go to war. He asked them if they wanted to change horses in midstream.

And his organization carried the ball for him. The only way *somebody* wouldn't tell you to vote for Joe Steele was if you climbed a mountain, lived in a cave, and ate bugs. Even then, one of his men might try to recruit you for a HERMITS FOR JOE STEELE club.

Charlie wrote the speeches Joe Steele told him to write. Hitler did his best to get the President reelected. The savage air attacks against England and the U-boats terrorizing shipping in the Atlantic warned against picking a rookie to try to run things.

In the last six weeks before the election, J. Edgar Hoover came to the White House almost every day. He might have been briefing Joe Steele about Reds and Nazis doing their dirty work somewhere inside the country. He might have, but Charlie didn't think so. Every time he saw the GBI boss, J. Edgar Hoover was grinning. Smirking might have been the better word.

Like any bulldog, J. Edgar Hoover usually looked as if he wanted to take a bite out of whoever got near him. A happy J. Edgar Hoover made Charlie wonder how and why such a prodigy could happen. A happy J. Edgar Hoover also scared the hell out of him.

Joe Steele often smiled after he talked to Hoover, too. The President showed amusement more often than the Jeebies' head honcho did. He would have had trouble showing amusement less often than J. Edgar Hoover did. But a smiling Joe Steele, like a smirking J. Edgar Hoover, made anyone who saw him wonder what was going on behind that upcurved mouth.

People who lived in Washington, D.C., all the time didn't have the right to vote for President. Joe Steele retained his California registration. He had himself photographed dropping an absentee ballot in the mailbox so it would arrive in good time.

And then election day rolled around. Joe Steele had trounced Herbert Hoover fair and square (as long as you didn't dwell on how he'd won the nomination, anyhow). He hadn't pulled any funny business clobbering Alf Landon, either. He hadn't needed any.

Charlie would have liked to stay with Esther and Sarah and listen to the returns on the radio. When you wrote speeches for the President of the United States, nobody cared what you liked to do, not on the first Tuesday after the first Monday in November of a year divisible by four. He went to the White House instead.

Colored cooks brought in trays of ham and fried chicken and sweet potatoes and string beans. Colored waiters served the men who served Joe Steele. A colored bartender had set up shop in a corner of the East Hall.

"Bourbon over ice," Charlie told him.

"Yes, suh," the barkeep answered with a smile. That was an easy one: no mixing, no thinking. Charlie tipped him a dime anyway. The bartender smiled again. So did Charlie. He used bourbon the way a knight of old used his shield: to hold trouble at a distance.

Joe Steele's California cronies were in the East Hall, of course. So was J. Edgar Hoover. So was Andy Wyszynski. So were a good many other men who'd helped the President run the country since 1933. Everybody seemed confident.

And, when the polls in the Eastern Time Zone closed and returns started coming in, they found they had reason to be confident. Joe Steele ran up percentages even higher than he had against Alf Landon. He'd got past sixty percent in 1936. This year, he looked to be winning by almost two to one.

"I figured he'd get his third term," Charlie said to Stas Mikoian. "But Willkie ran hard. I thought he'd make a better showing than this."

Mikoian's eyes, dark as black coffee, narrowed under bushy eyebrows. "You never know, do you?" he said blandly. "That's why they have the election—so you can find out."

"Uh-huh," Charlie said. Something lay behind the clever Armenian's words, but Charlie couldn't unravel it. He'd had enough bourbon to shield himself from thought as well as trouble.

By eleven o'clock, polls on the West Coast were closing, too. Joe Steele's rout had swept clean across the country. Most of the candidates he liked for the House and Senate were comfortably ahead, too.

He and his wife came down to the East Hall a little before midnight. Maybe he'd been working. Maybe he'd been sleeping. You never could tell. Everybody cheered when the President and First Lady walked in. Joe Steele waved and dipped his head and looked as modest as a not very modest man could look.

He walked over to the bartender. "Apricot brandy, Julius," he said.

"Comin' up, suh. Congratulations, suh," the man said.

Apricot brandy was one of the few bits of his heritage Joe Steele left on display. As far as Charlie was concerned, the stuff made good paint thinner or flamethrower fuel, but you needed a stainless-steel gullet to toss it down the way the President did.

Betty Steele asked Julius for a scotch and soda. She mostly kept to herself around the White House; Charlie seldom saw her. She was anything but an active First Lady, the way, say, Eleanor Roosevelt might have been. She still had her usual air of quiet sadness.

People hollered and pointed at the radio. "Wendell Willkie has conceded defeat," the announcer was saying. "His statement has just reached us. He claims there were certain voting irregularities in some areas, but admits they were not enough to change the result. He extends his best wishes to the President for leading the country through this difficult and dangerous time."

"Well, you can't get much more gracious about it than that." Stas Mikoian seemed in a mood to be gracious himself. He commonly showed more class than the other men who'd come east from California with Joe Steele.

Vince Scriabin, by contrast, laughed like a hyena, laughed till tears streamed down his face from behind his spectacles, when he heard Willkie's concession statement. Charlie gaped at him, hardly believing his own eyes. He couldn't remember seeing the Hammer smile, though he supposed he must have. He was positive he'd never seen Scriabin laugh. He hadn't imagined the pencil-necked little hardcase had laughter in him.

"Voting irregularities!" Scriabin chortled. "Oh, good Lord!" He dissolved into fresh hilarity.

Joe Steele and J. Edgar Hoover thought that was pretty goddamn funny, too. "You know what Boss Tweed said, don't you?" the President asked the head of the GBI.

"No. What?" Hoover asked, as he was meant to do.

"'As long as I count the votes, what are you going to do about it?'" Joe Steele quoted with great gusto. He jabbed a thumb at his own chest. "And I damn well do!" He and J. Edgar Hoover both thought that was the funniest thing they'd ever heard.

"Now, Joe," Betty Steele said, but she was chuckling, too.

Charlie also laughed, along with everybody else close enough to the President and the GBI boss to hear the exchange. Boss Tweed had been dead for a hell of a long time. And anyone who repeated Joe Steele's crack anywhere outside of this room was much too likely to end up the same way in short order.

Charlie went over to the bartender, who waited expectantly. "Let me have another bourbon, Julius," he said. "Why don't you make it a double this time?"

"You got it, suh," Julius said. Charlie inhaled the drink, and then another double after it, and another one after that. No matter how pickled he got, though, and no matter how drug through a knothole he felt the next morning, he couldn't forget what Joe Steele said.

*   *   *

Another lodgepole tottered, crackled, and fell, landing in
the snow within a few inches of where Mike had thought
it would drop. He'd turned into a pretty fair lumberjack
since they chucked him into this encampment. He hadn't
intended to, but he had anyway. As with anything else, practice made good if not perfect.

Of course, working alongside John Dennison for more
than three years now went a long way toward making good,
too. The man with WY232 on the front and back of his
jacket came over to stand next to Mike and admire the
downfallen tree for a moment before they started lopping
branches off it. "Nice job," Dennison said.

"Thanks." Mike grinned. Praise from the carpenter
counted for more than it did from most people, because he
never came out with it unless he meant it.

But Dennison hadn't finished. Barely moving his lips,
pitching his words so no guard could possibly hear them, he
went on, "Help fuck up the count tonight, okay?"

"Oh, yeah?" Mike answered the same way. That prison-
yard style of talking was one more thing he hadn't known
he'd pick up when they shipped him here from New York
City. But he had, all right. As with dropping trees where he
wanted them to fall, he'd got good at it, too.

"Uh-huh." John didn't nod. He didn't do anything to
draw the Jeebies' notice toward Mike and him. The guards
weren't paying them much attention now anyway. They'd
just cut down a tree. That showed they were working. And
they were veterans of the encampment by now. The bastards with the Tommy guns trusted them as far as they
trusted anybody. The scalps, the guys who didn't know how
things worked and who still had the taste of freedom in
their mouths, those were the dangerous people. Or so the
guards thought.

"Okey-doke," Mike said through a mouth that stayed
still. He tramped over to the top of the trunk and started
trimming the branches and cutting the main growth into
manageable lengths. When the work gang knocked off for
the day, he and John dragged a sledge full of wood back to
the encampment with ropes over their shoulders.

Mike's usual place in the count was third row, seventh man from the left. But he could slide into another slot in the next row farther back as soon as the Jeebie with the clipboard walked past him. Everything got to be routine for the guards after the encampment had run smoothly for a while. They didn't think any harder than they had to.

He kept his head down when he was standing in the row behind his assigned position. He kind of scratched at his chest with his mittened hand to obscure his number from the guard. You were supposed to stand at attention while the count was going on, but everybody had itches that needed scratching. The screws had long since quit getting excited about it.

He didn't look around to see if other wreckers were helping to wreck the count. He also didn't look around to see who wasn't there. What he didn't know, they couldn't pull out of him no matter how long they left him in a punishment cell.

As soon as he could, he slid back to his proper place. Footprints in the snow would give him away for a little while, but not for long. As soon as everybody else started moving around, the tracks would get wiped out.

"Dismissed to dinner!" the lead Jeebie shouted. Whatever stunt the prisoners had pulled, it worked this time. It would unravel. All the shabby, dirty, skinny men tramping through the snow toward the kitchen understood as much. Well, all the wreckers who knew something was going on did, anyhow.

They got through the next morning's roll call. Somebody answered for every number and name the Jeebie called out. Whether the man who answered was always the man to whom that number and name belonged . . . Mike had no way of knowing. Neither John nor anyone else asked him to sing out for somebody who wasn't there to sing out for himself.

But the morning count went wrong. Mike didn't know how. As far as he could tell, no one noticed his shuffle from his proper place to his improper one. Still, at the end of things, the boss guard said, "We gotta do it again." He sounded disgusted, at his men as well as at the inmates. It was an article of faith among the wreckers that the Jeebies couldn't count to twenty-one without reaching into their pants. Smart people didn't want work like that. No—smart people who ended up in an encampment landed there with stretches on their backs.

"No moving around, you assholes!" a guard shouted when they tried again. He kicked somebody who'd started to switch spots too soon. Not wanting a boot in the belly, Mike held his place.

The other wreckers who'd been playing games must have done the same thing, because at the end of the count the boss guard clapped a hand to his forehead in extravagant disbelief and despair. "Holy fucking shit!" he howled. "We got four o' these pussies missing! Four! God only knows how long the turds been gone, too!"

They got no breakfast that morning. Instead of food, they got interrogations. Mike said "I don't know" a lot. He said, "I didn't know anybody was missing till the count came out wrong." He said, "Could I get something to eat, please? I'm hungry."

"You're a lying shitsack, is what you are!" The Jeebie who was grilling him slapped him in the face. But he did it only once, and with his hand open—it was a slap, not a punch. That told Mike the guards didn't really suspect him of anything. This guy was just knocking him around on general principles.

They put him in a punishment cell for two days. He got bread and water—and not much bread. They didn't give him a blanket. He rolled himself into a ball, shivered, and hoped he didn't freeze to death.

Three days after he got sent back to Barracks 17, the Jeebies brought in two live wreckers and a corpse. "This is what happens if you run away from your deserved punishment," the camp commandant said. Then the guards beat the surviving escapees to within an inch of their lives while the rest of the wreckers watched and listened. After the stomping, the men the Jeebies had recaptured didn't go to the encampment's infirmary. No, they went into the punishment barracks, and for a stretch a lot longer than two days. If they recovered and came out, that was all right.

And if they didn't, the guards wouldn't lose a minute of sleep over them.

But four men had run off. The Jeebies got hold of only three. Mike clung to that, the way a man bobbing in the sea after a shipwreck would cling to a wooden plank. Maybe the fourth wrecker was dead, frozen meat somewhere high up in the harsh Montana mountains. Maybe bobcats and cougars were scraping flesh from his bones with their rough tongues right now.

Maybe he'd got away, though. Four had escaped the labor encampment. One still wasn't accounted for. Maybe he was free. Maybe, right this minute, he was back in Ohio. Or if he was still in Montana, maybe he was shacked up with a rancher's pretty sister.

Mike sure hoped so. And he knew he was a long way from the only wrecker who did.

As 1940 groaned into 1941, the war seemed to pause to catch its breath. The Nazis still bombed England and torpedoed every ship they could, but it seemed plain the swastika wouldn't fly from Buckingham Palace any time soon. The RAF raided Germany night after night. Goebbels screamed about terror flyers the way a calf screamed when the branding iron seared its rump. But the *Luftwaffe* hadn't broken the Londoners' will to keep fighting. It also seemed plain the British bombers wouldn't scare the Berliners into abandoning Hitler.

Charlie got drunk again after Joe Steele's third inauguration. Even toasted, he knew better than to say what he was thinking. If he came to the White House with a hangover the next morning, the President's other aides—and the President himself—figured he'd hurt himself celebrating, not for any other reason.

On the home front, Esther got Sarah potty-trained. "Thank God!" Charlie said. "If I never see another dirty diaper as long as I live, I won't miss 'em one bit." He held his nose.

His wife sent him a quizzical look. "You don't want to have another baby one of these days before too long?" she asked.

"Um," Charlie said, and then "Um" again. Knowing he'd stuck his foot in it, he added, "Well, maybe I do. But I still don't like diapers."

"Nobody likes diapers except the people who make them and the companies that wash them," Esther said. "You need 'em, though. Nobody likes babies peeing and pooping all over everything, either."

"You got that right, babe," Charlie agreed—a safe response, he thought.

"I didn't want to have two kids wearing diapers at the same time," Esther said. "That's enough to drive anybody squirrely. But Sarah will be close to four by the time I have another one. She may even be past four if I don't catch right off the bat."

"Catch right off the bat?" Charlie said. "Do you want to have another baby or sign up with the Senators?" Esther made a horrible face, so he could hope she'd forgiven him.

She didn't catch right off the bat, the way she had when they started Sarah. The little girl turned three. Out in the wider world, the Germans pulled Mussolini's chestnuts out of the fire by invading Yugoslavia and Greece. In the North African desert, the German Afrika Korps also helped the Italians keep their heads above water against England.

And in the Far East, Japan took bite after bite out of China. The Japs had occupied airfields and naval bases in the northern part of French Indochina the year before— fallen France was in no position to tell them they couldn't. Now they pressured the Vichy regime to let them move into the whole region.

Churchill didn't want them doing that. It put fresh pressure on British Malaya and Singapore. Joe Steele didn't like it, either. Indochina was too close to the Philippines, which belonged to the USA. Douglas MacArthur was one of the few senior officers Joe Steele hadn't purged in the 1930s. He was already in the Philippines by then, helping the natives build their own army against the day when they won independence. The local authorities gave him the rank of field marshal. He was the only American ever to hold it, even if it wasn't with his own country's forces.

When Joe Steele didn't like something, he did something

about it. Here, he summoned Charlie to his study and said, "I am going to stop selling Japan oil and scrap metal. All they do with it is use it against China. Before you know it, they'll use it against us, too. And I am going to freeze Japanese assets in the United States. They need to understand that I will not put up with them going down the road they're on."

"Yes, sir." Charlie hesitated, then asked, "Isn't that only about a step away from declaring war?"

"Farther than that." Joe Steele puffed on his pipe. He didn't say how much farther it was. He did say, "When I announce the news, I want to sugarcoat it as much as I can. I don't want Tojo any angrier than I can help, and I don't want Americans getting all hot and bothered about it, either. So give me a draft that leans in that direction. I'll want it by this time tomorrow."

Instead of shrieking in despair, Charlie nodded. "I'll have it for you." Being in the newspaper racket for as long as he was had got him used to impossible-seeming deadlines. And Joe Steele commonly used them as tests for his people. He remembered when you passed them. And he remembered when you didn't. You might get by with booting the ball once. If you did it twice, you wouldn't stay at the White House.

Again, Charlie wouldn't be the only one working on how to put Joe Steele's idea across. He knew that. But neither Vince Scriabin nor Lazar Kagan knew much about sugarcoating anything. Mikoian might—Charlie admitted that much to himself. Just the same, he expected the President to use big pieces of what he wrote.

And Joe Steele did. Even when he tried to speak softly, you saw the big stick he was holding. He took after Theodore Roosevelt that way. In some other respects, perhaps a little less.

The speech, and the howls Japan let out right after it, were front-page news for four days. Papers didn't print much that risked the Jeebies' displeasure these days. They couldn't ignore a speech from Joe Steele, though, or the foreign response to it.

On the fifth day, everybody from Washington State to Florida forgot all about it. That was the day Hitler invaded Russia.

Joe Steele summoned his top military men to see what they thought of the new, titanic war. George Marshall was a three-star general now, not a colonel sitting on a military tribunal. Although that wasn't exactly a previous acquaintance, Charlie buttonholed the stone-faced soldier. "What do you think Trotsky's chances are?" he asked.

"I'll tell you the same thing I told the President," Marshall answered. Of course, he would have been insane to tell Charlie anything different. If Joe Steele found out he had, he wouldn't keep those stars on his shoulders long. He went on, "If the Russians last six weeks, I'll be surprised."

"Okay," Charlie said—he'd heard much the same thing from map readers (and tea-leaf readers) of less exalted rank.

Marshall shook his head. "It isn't okay. If Hitler holds everything from the Atlantic to the Urals, he's a deadly danger to the whole world. The way the President put it was, 'I want to see lots of dead Germans floating down the river, each one on a raft of three dead Russians.'"

"Heh," Charlie said. That sounded like Joe Steele, all right. His sense of humor, such as it was, was grim. Then again, he wasn't kidding here, or he was kidding on the square. And he hated Trotsky just as much as he hated Hitler.

Six weeks later, the Reds were still fighting. They'd given up a lot of ground and lost a ton of men, but they didn't show their bellies the way the French had. They kept slugging. Charlie presumed Marshall was surprised. He knew *he* was.

XVI

A little more than a month after the Nazis jumped on the Reds, Winston Churchill came to North America to confer with Joe Steele. He flew from England to Newfoundland, then cruised down to Portland, Maine, in a Royal Navy destroyer.

Vince Scriabin expressed sour satisfaction about that. "Churchill wanted Joe Steele to come to Newfoundland or Canada," he told Charlie. "We told him no. He's the one who's hat in hand. If he needs something from us, he can damn well do the traveling and the begging."

"Doesn't make any difference to me one way or the other," Charlie answered. Diplomacy reminded him too much of what went on on elementary school playgrounds. The smaller kids had to do what the bigger kids said. Every so often, fights started. The trouble was, there were no teachers to break them up and paddle the punk who'd started things.

"Have you ever been to Portland before?" Scriabin asked.

"I've been to the one in Oregon. I don't think I've been to the one in Maine," Charlie said.

"Well, pack a suitcase. The boss wants you along," Scriabin said. "Throw in a sweater or two. We'll be out on the ocean some of the time, and it's not warm even in the middle of summer."

As he was packing, Esther said, "Can I send you a wire while you're there?"

"I don't think you'd better," Charlie replied. "This is supposed to be hush-hush, you know? How come? What may not keep till I get back?"

"Well, I'm more than a week late now," she said. "I'm not sure yet, but I've kinda got the feeling, if you know what I mean."

"All right!" He squeezed her till she squeaked. He knew he hadn't sounded thrilled about the idea of a second kid when she put it to him. He tried his best not to make the same mistake twice.

"I do think it's good that they're bringing you along," Esther said.

"Yeah, me, too." Charlie nodded. "Means—I hope it means—they've decided they trust me after all."

He'd always had the fear Joe Steele had asked him to work at the White House not least to keep an eye on him. Mike had provoked the administration enough to get tossed into that damned labor encampment. No wonder they'd figure Charlie was liable to be another dangerous character. And, of course, nine years ago now Charlie had walked past Vince Scriabin when the Hammer was telling whoever was on the other end of the line to take care of something tonight, because tomorrow would be too late.

Even now, he didn't *know* that Scriabin had been arranging Governor Roosevelt's untimely demise. He'd never once mentioned it to the Hammer in all the years since. Keeping his mouth shut about it felt like paying life-insurance premiums. Scriabin *might* laugh—not that he was the laughing kind—and tell him he was full of baloney. But he also might not. If Franklin D. Roosevelt could have a tragic accident, Charlie Sullivan sure as hell could, too.

He kept his mouth shut on the train trip up to Portland. He had no tragic accidents on the way or after he got there. The President and his entourage traveled in far higher style than an AP stringer on the way to cover a trial or a grain-elevator explosion.

They rode a U.S. Navy destroyer out to meet the Royal Navy warship. The two vessels made an interesting contrast. The British ship was painted a slightly darker gray than its American counterpart. But it was a *war*ship in ways the U.S. Navy destroyer wasn't. Everything not essential had been stripped away from it. The Royal Navy sailors and officers wore uniforms that had seen hard use. Their expressions said *they'd* seen hard use, too. They eyed the non-combatant American sailors and officials with faint—or sometimes not so faint—contempt.

Pink and round-faced, Churchill looked like a pugnacious, cigar-smoking baby. He and his advisors met Joe Steele and his followers in the officers' mess.

"You've come a long way," Joe Steele said after a silent steward served drinks—Royal Navy ships weren't dry. "What can I do for you?"

"This side of fighting, you're already doing all you can do for me," the Prime Minister answered. In person, his voice seemed even more resonant than it did on the radio. "Now I want you to do—I need you to do—the same thing for Trotsky and Russia."

Joe Steele scowled. "I knew you were going to say that. If I wanted to do it, I would have done it already."

"Whether or not you want to do it, you need to do it," Churchill said. "Trotsky may rant about world revolution, but that's all it is—ranting. Red Russia is a nation other nations can deal with."

"Pfah!" Joe Steele said. The United States had no embassy in Moscow, nor did the Reds have one in Washington. Kerensky had got out of Paris just before the Nazis marched in. He was in New York these days. The USA still didn't recognize him, either. As far as American diplomacy was concerned, a sixth of the globe's land area was only a blank space on the map.

"Oh, but you must," Churchill said, as if the President had spelled all that out for him instead of making a disgusted noise. "Russia, as I told you, we can deal with. Not well, perhaps, nor smoothly, but we can. Hitler's Germany, on the other hand, is not a state at all. It is a cancer on the world's body politic. Unless it is cut out, it will spread without limit. That is what cancers do. You need not love Trotsky to see that Hitler is the more dangerous of the two."

"Pfah!" Joe Steele said again. This time, he added real words: "He's turned that whole country into a prison camp."

Churchill looked at him. "And you have not, in yours?"

For a bad moment, Charlie thought Joe Steele would walk out of the officers' mess, off the Royal Navy destroyer, and away from anything resembling friendship with England. No one in the United States talked to Joe Steele that way. No one talked about him that way, not any more, not where the Jeebies might get wind of it.

The President looked stonily back at the Prime Minister. That look said nothing here would be forgotten—or forgiven. But Joe Steele's reply sounded mild enough: "The ones who go into my encampments deserve it. That's the difference between me and Trotsky."

"Well, you may be right." By the way Churchill said it, he didn't believe it, not even slightly. But he went on, "And I assure you I am right about aid to Trotsky and Russia. Hitler may win that fight anyhow. But anything you can do to keep him from winning it, you should do. No, you must."

"You are not well positioned to tell me what I must do," Joe Steele said.

"Because your country is bigger and richer than mine, do you mean?" Churchill contrived to make that seem of no account. "If you want to stay that way, you could do worse than to listen to me. America's knowledge of the international arena is sadly limited by your good fortune in having broad oceans—and the Royal Navy—to shield your shores. Britain, now, has been in the arena, of the arena, for centuries. My country and I have more experience than you and yours. What I tell you now springs from the depth of that experience."

He spoke to Joe Steele as a man speaks to a boy. No one in the United States did that, either. The President's glower said he didn't fancy it. But he didn't tell the Prime Minister where to head in. He said, "Have supper with me aboard my ship. We can talk more about it then."

"As long as I may take over certain liquid refreshments," Winston Churchill said. "I know of your Navy's abstemious habits, you see."

"You can do that, yes." Now Joe Steele seemed amused. "You can even try some apricot brandy from California, if you care to."

Churchill smiled. "I look forward to it. As commander-in-chief, you not only make the rules, you may break them as you please." And maybe he was still talking about bringing apricot brandy aboard a U.S. Navy ship, and maybe he wasn't.

Back aboard the American destroyer, Joe Steele commandeered the officers' mess for himself and his followers. "He still feels England is the greatest country in the world," the President growled. "Maybe not here, but here." He tapped first his forehead, then the center of his chest.

"Arrogant bastard," Vince Scriabin said.

"He is, yes. You don't go far in politics without that," Joe Steele said. "Arrogant or not, is he right? Is Nazi Germany dangerous enough for the United States to help keep Russia in the game?"

"Trotsky made his bed. Then he pulled Hitler into it with him," Stas Mikoian said. "He deserves whatever happens to him."

"I agree." Scriabin nodded.

Lazar Kagan kept quiet. Trotsky and a swarm of the Reds who ran Russia under him were Jews. Joe Steele would know that, considering how the Nazis persecuted them, anything Kagan said wouldn't be objective.

Speak now or forever hold your peace, Charlie thought. But it wasn't peace. It was a war even bigger than the one they'd hopefully called the War to End War. Taking a deep breath, he said, "I think we ought to give Russia a hand. If Germany takes Russia out, she'll flatten England after that. And if she does, the ocean isn't wide enough to keep her away from us."

Joe Steele puffed his pipe. Scriabin sent Charlie the kind of look the President had given the Prime Minister. Scriabin was good at not forgetting, too.

That evening, Churchill remarked on how neat and tidy and clean and new everything aboard the American destroyer was. It was one more way of saying *We're fighting and you aren't.* He praised the roast beef in the same style, which didn't keep him from eating three helpings of it. Whiskey and the President's brandy improved the meal.

Smoke from pipe, cigar, and cigarettes filled the mess. Joe Steele said nothing about Russia. He did his best to make his demeanor a riddle wrapped in a mystery inside an enigma. Churchill also was a man who didn't show all he was thinking, but his advisors began to fidget. So did Charlie. He hoped no one noticed.

At last, Churchill took the bull by the horns and asked, "Have you made up your mind about Trotsky?"

"I made up my mind about Trotsky more than twenty years ago, and nothing you've said has done one damn thing to make me change it," Joe Steele answered. He waited till Churchill began to slump in his seat before continuing, "But I'll send him toys to shoot Germans with. You talked me into that, you and one of my men." He nodded toward Charlie.

That nod won Charlie Winston Churchill's grave regard. "Jolly good," the Prime Minister said. "You have men of sense in your service."

"Well, I hope so," Joe Steele said. Charlie knew what that meant. If helping the Russians went well, the President would take the credit for it. He'd deserve credit, too; he was the man responsible for the choice. But if it went badly, the blame would fall on Charlie's head.

If, for instance, Hitler declared war on the USA because of this, Charlie figured he would find out more than he ever wanted to know about cutting down trees or digging ditches or turning big ones into little ones. Or maybe they'd strap him to a bomb and drop him on Germany. He hoped to go out with a bang one of these years, but not like that.

Joe Steele didn't say anything about his change of policy toward Russia. He just quietly started shipping Trotsky planes and guns and trucks and telephone cable and high-octane fuel and anything else the Red Czar's little heart desired. The Russians still had no embassy in Washington. They had one in Ottawa, though, and huddled with the Americans there.

Joe Steele's try for secrecy didn't last long. Trotsky didn't mind not mentioning the goodies he would get. As long as he got them, keeping quiet about them was a small price to pay. But Winston Churchill trumpeted the news like a town crier. He *wanted* the rest of the world to know the United States disliked the Nazis even more than the Reds. He wanted the rest of the world to know he'd helped start the aid, too.

Hitler, predictably, screamed bloody murder. He screeched that the USA wasn't neutral, never had been neutral, and never would be neutral. He shrieked that Jews and subhumans were running the United States. He promised to do unto Jewish capitalism in America as he was doing unto Jewish Bolshevism in Russia.

He didn't declare war, though, to Charlie's relief. German U-boats did fire torpedoes at American freighters in the Atlantic and sank a few, but they'd been doing that for a while now. War? Only unofficially. It stayed unofficial even when an American destroyer sank a Nazi sub, and when another U-boat blew the stern off an American light cruiser and killed two dozen sailors.

Charlie wondered whether the U.S. help for Russia would prove too little, too late. German armies laid siege to Leningrad in the north and Sevastopol in the south. They captured Kiev. And they captured Smolensk, which Charlie had never heard of till it showed up in the war news but which was apparently the main strongpoint protecting Moscow itself.

Summer passed into fall. Esther had morning sickness with the new baby, the same way she had carrying Sarah. Sarah started learning the alphabet. She had wooden blocks for all the letters and numbers, and played with them all the time.

Fall in Russia meant rain. Outside the big cities, Russian roads were only dirt tracks. When the rain fell, they turned to mud. German tanks and motorcycles and foot soldiers bogged down. Neat, orderly Germans were used to neat, orderly paved roads. They didn't do so well without them.

If there were fall rains in the Far East, they didn't bother Japan. The Japs went on pounding China. They finished occupying French Indochina. That made Winston Churchill fuss, because it brought their bombers within range of the British colonies farther south and west.

Joe Steele called Japan almost as many names as Hitler was calling the USA. The Japs paid hardly more attention than America did. As winter neared, General Tojo finally sent Foreign Minister Kurusu to Washington to see if the two countries could work something out.

Kurusu knew what he wanted. He wanted Japanese assets in America unfrozen. And he wanted the United States to start selling his country raw materials again. Joe Steele asked him whether Japan would clear out of China if the USA did that.

Unlike the talks with Churchill, Charlie didn't get invited to these. He wasn't broken-hearted. He had nothing to say about Japan or to the Japanese. He heard about what was going on from Vince Scriabin.

"That slant-eye flat-out said they wouldn't pull back," Scriabin reported. "He said America held an empire and Russia had one and England had one, and now it was Japan's turn to take one if she was strong enough—and she was. He thinks he's as good as a white man, is what he thinks." By the way Scriabin rolled his eyes, that was an opinion he didn't share.

"Yeah, Japan's strong enough, as long as they get our scrap metal and our oil," Charlie said. "But what happens when they run out of oil?"

"Everything they've got with a motor in it grinds to a stop, that's what." Scriabin sounded as if he was looking forward to it. "From what the War Department brass says, they'll have trouble lasting a year on their own."

Charlie had heard the same thing. He didn't let on; the dumber you acted, the more interesting things other people said to you and around you. "How long has it been now since the President slapped that embargo on them?" he asked. Again, he knew the answer, but this way the Hammer could feel superior for a little while.

"Just about five months," Scriabin said. "So they've got to be feeling the pinch already. That stupid Kurusu will be singing a different tune the next time he comes here, I promise you."

"He sure will." Charlie had about as much trouble taking Orientals seriously as Scriabin did. He liked Chinese food, though he'd never found a place in Washington he enjoyed as much as Hop Sing's back in the Village. That was as far as it went. He no more thought Asians deserved to put themselves on an equal footing with whites than the

Hammer did. The idea seemed too silly for words. So did a lot of Orientals, come to that.

One chilly Sunday morning, Charlie and Esther and Sarah went out to breakfast at a waffle place not far from their apartment. Esther had the waffles, and cut up some for Sarah. Charlie got pancakes and a side of bacon. One slice went to his daughter. Sarah made it disappear.

After they got home, he read the papers and goofed around and eventually turned on the Redskins–Eagles game on the radio. If the Redskins won, they'd finish third in the Eastern Division with a 6-5 mark. If they lost, they'd finish third at 5-6. The Eagles, the team behind them, had only two wins all year. Charlie figured their chance of breaking .500 was pretty good.

In spite of their crappy record, the Eagles took the early lead. The Redskins had the ball when the signal cut out for a moment. Before Charlie could do more than start to turn his head toward the radio, it came back. "We interrupt this broadcast for a special news flash!" said a different announcer, one who had to be back at the radio station's headquarters. "The White House reports that Japanese planes have bombed the American naval base at Pearl Harbor, Hawaii, in an unprovoked attack. Casualties are believed to be heavy. That is all that is known at this time. We now return you to our regularly scheduled program." The football game came back on.

"Oh, God!" Esther exclaimed.

"Couldn't put it better myself," Charlie said. The Redskins had picked up another first down while the bulletin ran, but he didn't care any more. He wondered how long it would be before he could care again about something as silly as a game of football or baseball. He grabbed his shoes and put them on. "I better get over to the White House right now."

The telephone rang. Esther picked it up. "Hello?" she said, and then, "Yes, he's here." She thrust the phone at Charlie, mouthing *Mikoian*.

He nodded. "Hello, Stas," he said.

"You need to come over right now," Mikoian said without preamble.

"I was already on my way. I just heard the news flash," Charlie said. "All hell must be breaking loose."

Stas Mikoian's chuckle was perfect gallows. "It's nowhere near that quiet. We haven't announced it yet, but the Japs have attacked in the Philippines, too. Doesn't look good there, either."

"Happy day!" Charlie exclaimed.

"Now that you mention it," Mikoian said, "no."

"Right," Charlie said. "I'll see you as soon as I can." He hung up. Then he called for a taxi. He didn't want to waste forty-five minutes standing on the corner waiting for a bus. They didn't run as often as usual on Sundays. He kissed Esther and Sarah—who, luckily, couldn't have cared less about Pearl Harbor—and hurried down to the street.

"The Japs've gone crazy," was what the cabby greeted him with.

"I've heard," Charlie said. "Take me to the White House. Step on it." He hadn't wasted time putting on a tie. His brown checked jacket didn't go with his gray pants. It was the one he'd pulled out of the closet, that was all.

But his voice must have carried the snap of authority, because the driver said, "You got it, Mister." He touched the patent-leather bill of his cap in an almost-salute as the Chevy shot away from the curb.

Charlie gave him a buck and didn't wait for change, though the fare was only sixty cents. Reporters stood on the White House lawn, waiting and hoping for more news. When they spotted Charlie, they converged on him like ants going after a forgotten picnic sandwich. He fended them off with both hands. "I don't know any more than you guys do," he said. "I was listening to the football game with my wife and little girl. I had Sunday off, or I thought I did. Soon as I heard the bulletin, I figured I'd better come in."

Some of them wrote that down. White House speechwriter Charlie Sullivan was somebody who made news, not somebody who reported it. Charlie knew that was true, but it still struck him as crazy.

He got through the crowd and into the White House. Vince Scriabin said, "We have a Cabinet meeting set for half past eight. Some Senators and Congressmen will join in at nine."

"Okay," Charlie answered. His guess was that most of the decisions would get made before the meeting convened. Except perhaps for Andy Wyszynski, Joe Steele's Cabinet members were there to tell the lesser folk under them what to do, not to shape policy. Joe Steele figured that shaping policy was his bailiwick, no one else's.

"We'll declare war on Japan, of course," Scriabin said. "The boss will need to make a speech in front of Congress before they ratify the declaration. You may want to start thinking about that."

"Gotcha," Charlie said. In fact, he'd already started thinking about that. But showing up Scriabin in any way, small or large, was one of the dumber things anybody in the White House could do. Like him or not, the unpleasant little man was Joe Steele's right hand and a couple of fingers of the left. Charlie asked, "Do we know any more than we've told the radio and the papers?"

"Not much," Scriabin answered. "It's bad in Hawaii, and it's not good in the Philippines. Oh, and I just now heard that the Japs have started bombing the English in Malaya, and Japanese troops have crossed the Malayan border from Siam. They're going all out."

"Misery loves company," Charlie said. Scriabin's mouth twisted, though his mustache made the motion hard to see. It came closer to a smile than Charlie had expected.

Joe Steele met with his unofficial aides (the Pain Trust, people sometimes called them, though not where the GBI could hear) before the Cabinet meeting. He was not a happy man. "We got caught with our pants down around our ankles in Hawaii," he growled. "I will want the admiral and the general who were in charge there recalled for interrogation. They should have had more on the ball."

"I'll take care of that, boss," Lazar Kagan said. Charlie wondered whether anyone else would see those officers after Joe Steele's interrogators got through with them. He wouldn't have wanted to be in their shoes.

"Well, we're in the war at last," the President said. "We didn't start it, but we'll finish it. By the time we get through with the Japs, there won't be one brick left on top of another on those islands."

The Cabinet meeting was the same thing on a larger scale. Charlie sat off to one side, listening. When he heard a phrase he liked, he noted it to toss into the draft he'd give the President. Kagan talked to the Secretary of War and the Secretary of the Navy in a low voice. Neither man looked thrilled at what Joe Steele's aide told them, but they both nodded.

Charlie was up late, finishing the draft for the speech Joe Steele would give when he asked a joint session of Congress for the formal declaration of war against Japan. Millions of people across the country would hear that speech when the President gave it. They might not love Joe Steele—he was one of the least lovable men Charlie had ever known. But when foreign enemies attacked the country he led, who wouldn't rally behind him?

With Senators crowding in along with Representatives, the House chamber was packed for the joint session. Charlie counted himself lucky to get a seat in the visitors' gallery. You didn't watch and listen to history being made every day.

The ferocious roar with which the members of both houses greeted Joe Steele and the way they sprang to their feet to applaud him even before the Speaker of the House could introduce him told Charlie there'd be no trouble over the declaration of war. He hadn't expected any, but finding out you were right always felt good.

"Members of the Congress of the United States, people of America, yesterday the Empire of Japan attacked Pearl Harbor and the Philippines without warning in time of peace," the President said. "This act of vicious treachery will never be forgotten. Because of it, I ask the Congress to declare that a state of war exists between the United States and the Empire of Japan."

More roars. More cheers. Joe Steele went on, "A grave danger hangs over our country. The perfidious Japanese military attack continues. There can be no doubt that this short-lived military gain for the Empire of Japan is only an episode. The war with Japan cannot be considered an ordinary war. It is not only a war between two armies and navies, it is also a great war of the entire American people against the Imperial Japanese forces.

"In this war of freedom, we shall not stand alone. Our forces are numerous. The arrogant enemy will soon learn this to his cost. Side by side with the U.S. Army and Navy, thousands of workers, community farmers, and scientists are rising to fight the enemy aggressors. The masses of our people will rise up in their millions.

"To repulse the enemy who used a sneak attack against our country, a National Committee for Defense has been formed, in whose hands the entire power of the state has been vested. The Committee calls upon all people to rally around the party of Jefferson and Jackson and Wilson and around the U.S. government so as self-denyingly to support the U.S. Army and Navy, demolish the enemy, and gain victory. Forward!"

Forward they went. Two Representatives and one Senator voted against the declaration of war. Nothing, it seemed, was ever unanimous, but that came close enough.

When Charlie got back to the White House, Stas Mikoian greeted him with a long face. "The Japs just smashed our planes on the ground at Clark Field, outside of Manila," Mikoian said.

"Wait," Charlie said. "They did that today?" Mikoian nodded. "A day after the fighting started? On the ground? Flat-footed?" Mikoian nodded again. Charlie found one more question: "How, for Chrissake?"

"That, I don't know," the Armenian answered. "The boss doesn't, either—he just found out, too. But he'll want to know. He'll have some interesting questions for General MacArthur, don't you think?"

"I wouldn't be surprised," Charlie said. Douglas MacArthur was five thousand miles from the American West Coast. The big naval base between the West Coast and the Philippines had just been blown to hell and gone. All things considered, though, Charlie figured MacArthur was much safer fighting the Japs where he was than he would be if he had to come home and answer those questions from Joe Steele.

Three days after the United States declared war on Japan, Germany did—and overdid—an ally's duty and declared war on the United States. Charlie thought Hitler did Joe Steele a favor. The President hadn't declared war on the Nazis, even though the U.S. Navy and German U-boats had been skirmishing for months. Now the *Führer* had done it for him.

Three days after that, Admiral Kimmel and General Short arrived in Washington. Husband Kimmel looked handsome in his gold-striped sleeves. Charlie remembered Walter Short from the days when he'd sat on a military tribunal. Now he and Kimmel found themselves on the wrong end of one of those proceedings.

The questions the officers who served as judges asked the admiral and the general were the obvious ones. Why hadn't somebody spotted the Japanese fleet before the carriers started launching planes? Why were so many American planes lined up on the runways almost wingtip to wingtip? Why didn't more of them get airborne once the authorities realized the war was on?

Admiral Kimmel said, "We searched the areas where we thought the enemy was most likely to appear. Our patrols to the west and to the southwest of Pearl Harbor were thorough and diligent."

"But you had no airplanes searching to the north, the direction from which the Japs really came?" a judge asked.

"No, sir," Kimmel answered somberly. "We did not look for an approach from the North Pacific. We thought the weather and the waves at that time of the year made it too dangerous for the Japanese to attempt."

"You were mistaken, weren't you?"

"So it would seem, yes, sir." Husband Kimmel sounded more somber yet.

"I ordered the aircraft grouped in a compact mass to better protect them against sabotage," General Short said when they asked him about that. "Something like one civilian in three on Oahu is a Jap. Too many of them are loyal to the place they came from, not the place where they live now."

"Was there any sabotage by Hawaiian Japanese during the enemy attack?" a judge inquired.

"Not that I am aware of," Walter Short answered unwillingly.

"Was there any sabotage by Hawaiian Japanese before the enemy attack?"

"Not that I am aware of."

"Has there been any sabotage by Hawaiian Japanese since the enemy attack?"

"Not that I am aware of."

Charlie wondered why he attended the tribunal. He knew what would happen before it did. Kimmel and Short might not, but that was their hard luck. Anyone who'd been around the White House and seen what kind of mood Joe Steele was in didn't need a crystal ball to see what was coming.

And Charlie had been to tribunals before. The United States was a secular country. It didn't have anything like the old Spanish auto-da-fé. These tribunals, with the verdicts scripted in advance, were about as close as it came.

Substandard performance. Dereliction of duty. Neglect of duty. During the last war, during any war, those were charges that would blight any officer's career, even if they were made but not proved. The judges needed only a few minutes to find both men guilty and to deliver the sentence: death by firing squad.

In spite of everything, Walter Short was astonished. "What? You can't do that!" he shouted.

Admiral Kimmel hung his head. He knew too well that they could. He might not have expected it, but he recognized the possibility.

"By passing sentence on you, we remind other officers in the military service of the United States that they must be diligent in the pursuit of their duties at all times and under all circumstances," the judge who'd announced the verdict declared.

"Pour encourager les autres," Kimmel murmured.

"I beg your pardon?" the judge said. "I don't speak French."

"It doesn't matter," Admiral Kimmel replied. Charlie was sure he was right. The judge would never have heard of Admiral Byng. Chances were he'd never heard of Voltaire, either.

"This is an outrage!" Walter Short certainly sounded outraged. "I'll appeal this—this travesty of justice!"

As a matter of fact, that was just what it was. Even so, Charlie was sure appealing wouldn't do General Short one red cent's worth of good. The judge didn't say that, not in so many words. He said, "You have the right to appeal, yes. The President will personally review this proceeding and will pass judgment on all appeals springing from it."

"Oh," Short said in a sick voice. Reality suddenly crashed down and hit him on the head, the way the acorn—and maybe the whole sky—had hit Chicken Little. He wouldn't be able to talk his way out of the blame for Pearl Harbor. He might or might not deserve all of it, but it had landed on him. Husband Kimmel had figured that out faster.

In the end, they both appealed. Kimmel must have thought he had nothing to lose, and how could anyone tell him he was wrong? He also had nothing to gain. Neither did Walter Short. Joe Steele rejected both their appeals and ordered the tribunal's sentence carried out.

Charlie didn't go to watch the executions. No one was paying him now to witness men's deaths. It had sickened him when he did it. Yes, some died more bravely than others. What difference did that make, though? Brave and not so brave ended up equally dead.

Word came back to the White House that both Short and Kimmel met their final moments with as much courage as anyone could want. "I didn't have them shot for cowardice," Joe Steele said. "I had them shot for stupidity—a much more serious failing in an officer." His pipe sent up smoke signals. Neither Charlie nor any of the President's other aides had any reply to that.

XVII

Mike approached the encampment's administration building with trepidation. *No, dammit, I'm a writer. Forget the
fancy talk,* he thought. *I'm approaching that place with fear.*
Like any wrecker, he had good reason to stay as far away
from the administration building as he could. It was full of
Jeebies, and nobody in his right mind wanted anything to
do with those bastards.

Snow crunched under his boots. The air he breathed in
stung his nostrils. He breathed out fog. It was goddamn
cold. It was dark, too. The encampment lay on about the
latitude of Bangor, Maine—far to the north of the New
York City cycles he was used to. When winter neared, night
slammed down early and stayed late.

Not surprisingly, the administration building lay next to
the punishment block. The GBI men needed to keep an eye
on the luckless fools they jugged. Also not surprisingly, the
administration building, unlike the rest of the encampment
(well, except for the searchlights in the guard towers), had
electricity. A gasoline-powered generator inside chugged
away. It sounded like a distant truck engine idling rough.

A guard in a fur hat frowned and hefted his Tommy gun
when Mike came inside the circle of light the bulb above
the entryway threw into the darkness all around. "Who are
you? What do you want?" the Jeebie asked, his voice harsh
and suspicious.

"Sullivan, Michael, NY24601, sir. Barracks Seventeen."
Mike identified himself the way a wrecker should. He exhaled more vapor before he went on, "I want to ask permission to join the Army, sir."

"Oh, Jesus! Another one!" But the guard didn't tell Mike

to get lost, the way he would have before the Japs hit Pearl Harbor. The United States was at war now. A wrecker who volunteered for the Army wouldn't necessarily have it easier than one who served out his stretch inside an encampment. All kinds of bad things could happen to you in these places, sure. But unless you ran away or the guards were feeling uncommonly mean, they weren't likely to shoot you. Japanese and German soldiers might prove less considerate.

"Yes, sir." Mike stood there and waited. He didn't come any closer. Doing that before the guard said he could might make the SOB decide he was dangerous. He didn't want that. Oh, no.

After a few seconds, the Jeebie gestured toward the door with his Tommy gun. "Well, come on, then," he said gruffly. His breath smoked, too. "They're putting together some kind of asshole list in there. You wanna stick your name on it, you can. Guy you wanna see is Lopatynski. Room 127—turn left when you get inside and go halfway down the hall."

"Thank you, sir!" Mike knew most of that from other wreckers, men who already had their names on the list. But you had to keep the guards buttered up. They'd make you pay if you didn't. Sometimes they'd make you pay even if you did.

The Jeebie patted him down before letting him inside. He had a knife, one made from part of a big can of corn and patiently sharpened on granite. Most wreckers had them. They used them as tools more than as weapons. He'd made sure to stash his in his miserable sawdust-stuffed mattress before coming here, though. No matter how common they were, they were also against the rules.

Bright lights and heat clobbered him inside the building. He unbuttoned his jacket, something he hadn't done since early fall except for the weekly scrub in disinfectant soap. Wreckers shivered through about eight months of the year. Not the Jeebies. They had it soft.

Aloysius Lopatynski was a warrant officer. Not a sergeant. Not a lieutenant. Betwixt and between. He had a specialty that made him useful, but not enough general wonderfulness for them to turn him into a full-fledged officer. He was typing some sort of report—respectably fast—

when Mike stood in the doorway to room 127 and waited to be noticed.

He didn't have to wait long. Lopatynski looked up and said, "Who are you? What do you need?" Not *What do you want?*—an interesting variant, especially from a Jeebie.

"Sullivan, Michael, NY24601, sir. Barracks Seventeen." Mike went through the ritual again. Then he said, "Jonesy outside told me you were the one to see about joining the Army."

"Right now, no one from any encampment is joining the Army. No wrecker, I mean—several guards here have enlisted," the warrant officer said. "What I am doing is putting together a list of people who may be interested in volunteering if and when that's permitted."

"Okay, that's what I need, then." Mike gave his information to Lopatynski once more. The Jeebie entered it on that list. Then Mike said, "My stretch is five to ten. I got here in 1937, so they could be turning me loose in a few months."

"You were an early bird, weren't you?" Lopatynski remarked.

"Well, kinda," Mike answered with a certain pride. He wasn't an early bird next to somebody like John Dennison, but far more wreckers had come in after him than before. He went on, "If they do turn me loose next summer, can I go straight into the Army then?"

"That's an interesting question. I'm not sure of the answer. Of course, you also don't know if they'll turn you loose at the short end of your stretch. But if they release you while the war is still going on . . . I don't know what your obligation would be. I don't know if you can volunteer, either. You can try, and find out what happens."

"All right. I'll do that when I get the chance. If I get the chance." Mike hesitated before adding, "Thanks." He said it to the guards all the time. It didn't mean much to them, though; he was just another wrecker trying to keep the screws sweet. Saying it when he did mean it came harder.

"You're welcome," Lopatynski said. "Now you'd better hustle to your barracks. I know it's cold out there."

Not cold in here, Mike thought. But he didn't come out with the sarcastic crack. As far as he could tell, Lopatynski just didn't want him freezing. He gave back a brusque nod and walked away. Getting reminded that even a GBI man could be a decent human being was one of the more disturbing things that had happened to him lately.

The U.S. Army and Navy had known for years that they might have to fight Japan. Like other armed forces the world around, they made plans against the day. Anyone, even generals or admirals, could see that the Philippines, American-ruled but close to the potential enemy, were an area the Japs would try to overrun as soon as they could.

Holding the entire island chain wasn't practical or even possible, not with the relatively small American garrison and the larger but less trained native Philippine forces. The plan, then, was for most of the Americans and as many locals as could join them to hole up on the Bataan Peninsula and hang on for as long as they could.

By holding out there, they denied the Japs the use of Manila's fine harbor. And, if everything went according to plan, they might still be holding out when the Pacific Fleet steamed west from Hawaii and met the Imperial Japanese Navy in a sea battle that would make Jutland look as if it were fought in a bathtub by toy boats.

But things didn't go according to plan. The Pacific Fleet wouldn't be coming. Too much of it lay at the bottom of Pearl Harbor. The soldiers holed up on the Bataan Peninsula could still deny Manila's harbor to Japan. Nobody was coming to their rescue, though. Sooner or later, they would have to throw in the towel.

Meanwhile, they fought bravely, Americans and Filipinos alike. They held back the Japanese week after week, month after month. They took a moniker that they wore with a kind of upside-down pride—the Battling Bastards of Bataan. A reporter wrote a limerick about them, one of the few good clean ones:

"We're the Battling Bastards of Bataan,
No Mama, no Papa, no Uncle Sam,
No aunts, no uncles, no cousins, no nieces,
No pills, no planes, no artillery pieces,
And nobody gives a damn!"

That last line, as Charlie knew all too well, wasn't true. Joe Steele did give a damn about the men fighting in the Philippines, and about what losing the islands would mean. But there was a difference between giving a damn and being able to do anything about it.

The difference got underscored in the middle of February, when England surrendered Singapore to the Japs. Wanting to hang on was one thing. Being able to was another. Joe Steele started sending Douglas MacArthur messages urging him to leave Bataan and come back to Washington for consultation about his next assignment.

Charlie polished up the President's messages and smoothed them as much as he could. Joe Steele was angry at the distant general, and it showed in anything that came from his pen. Despite the smoothing, MacArthur remained cagey. One of his replies read *I wish to share the fate of the garrison. I know the situation here in the Philippines and unless the right moment is chosen for this delicate operation, a sudden collapse might occur.*

"He doesn't want to come back," Charlie said to Lazar Kagan after that one came in.

Kagan looked at him, expressionless as usual. "Would you?" Remembering what had happened to Short and Kimmel, Charlie had to shake his head.

Finally, Joe Steele stopped dickering and ordered MacArthur to leave Bataan, go to Australia, and from Australia come to Washington as quickly as he could. MacArthur still hesitated. Joe Steele had George Marshall send a cable to the U.S. commander in the Philippines, reminding him that refusing to obey orders was a court-martial offense.

That did the trick. A PT boat plucked MacArthur, his family, and his entourage off the peninsula and took them to the island of Mindanao, which was also in the process of falling to the Japs. Three B-17s came up from Australia and landed on a dirt strip to take the general and his companions to safety.

A roundabout air route got MacArthur to Honolulu. He dropped a wreath into the oily water of Pearl Harbor before flying on to San Diego. Soldiers, sailors, Marines, and civilians there gave him a hero's welcome and put him on a cross-country train. He made speeches at half the stops, sounding more like a political campaigner than a military man.

Spring had already sprung by the time he got to Washington. Along with Vince Scriabin and Stas Mikoian, Charlie was at Union Station, not far from the Capitol, when the train pulled in.

A platoon of soldiers waited on the platform with them. There were no ordinary civilians around, nor any reporters. "I hope this isn't *too* ugly," Charlie said to Mikoian as the train rolled to a stop.

"So do I," the Armenian answered, "but it will be."

Scriabin waved such worries away. "He won't get anything he doesn't have coming to him," the Hammer said. Like Joe Steele, he never seemed afflicted by doubt.

A door in the side of one of the Pullman cars opened. A colored porter set down a contraption with three wooden steps to ease getting down from the train to the platform. Then the Negro stepped back, and Douglas MacArthur stood in the metal doorway.

He was tall and thin and craggy. His uniform hung loosely on him. By the way he looked around, he was expecting at least a brass band and maybe a ticker-tape parade. The corncob pipe jerked in his mouth when he saw he wouldn't get them. He eyed the soldiers. They weren't pointing their weapons his way, but they looked as if they could any second now.

"What kind of welcoming committee is this?" he asked, sounding like a man who didn't really want the answer.

A spruce young captain stepped toward him out of the ranks. "You are Douglas MacArthur?" he asked in turn, his voice formal. He didn't give MacArthur his rank. He didn't say *sir*. He didn't salute.

"You know damn well I am, sonny," MacArthur said roughly. "Who the hell are you?"

"I am Captain Lawrence Livermore," the young officer said. "You are under arrest. The charge is failure to defend the Philippine Islands properly, in that the bombers under your command were caught on the ground and destroyed by Japanese aircraft a full day after fighting began in Hawaii. The charge includes negligence and dereliction of duty. I am ordered to bring you before the military tribunal that will judge your case."

MacArthur stared at him. "Fuck you. You hear me? Fuck you, you little prick! Fuck your goddamn military tribunal. They're going to shoot me—that's what you're saying. Oh, and fuck Joe Steele, too, up the asshole with a cactus."

Whoever'd chosen Captain Livermore had chosen him not least because he didn't rattle. He didn't even redden when MacArthur swore at him. He just turned back to his men and nodded. Their front rank dropped to one knee as they aimed their rifles at the suddenly disgraced general. The men behind them aimed at him, too, over their heads.

"Either you come with us quietly," Livermore said, "or we'll need to hose down this platform before we can use it again."

No one had ever claimed MacArthur lacked courage. His right hand flashed to his belt. But he remembered with the motion only half made that he wasn't wearing a sidearm. His hand fell back to his thigh. He looked up at the roof—and at the heavens beyond it—and said, like Charles Coughlin before him, "'Father, forgive them; for they know not what they do.'"

"You aren't Him," Captain Livermore said. "Last chance. Come before the tribunal . . . or don't come before the tribunal."

Charlie thought MacArthur would make them kill him right there in the train station. But MacArthur's shoulders slumped. "I'll go to your damned tribunal," he said. "You can shoot me. Just leave my family alone, you hear?"

They took him away. Captain Livermore didn't say anything about what would happen to his family.

The tribunal was brief and to the point. Had those planes been on the ground a day after Pearl Harbor? Had the Japs bombed them and wrecked them before they could get airborne? Not much doubt about either question.

MacArthur didn't bother appealing to Joe Steele. When you'd suggested buggery by cactus, you couldn't expect much sympathy. From what Charlie heard, MacArthur died well.

Joe Steele went on the radio the day after the execution. "I know this may seem hard. I know it may seem cruel," he said. "If you tell me Douglas MacArthur was a brave man, I will agree with you. But he made the same kind of stupid mistake General Short and Admiral Kimmel did. Theirs cost us the disaster at Pearl Harbor. His has gone a long way toward costing us the Philippines. We will not win every battle. I understand that. But we should not lose battles because we are stupider than our enemies. *That kind of failure will not be tolerated.* And that is why Douglas MacArthur is dead."

Listening to the speech with his very pregnant wife, Charlie wondered how things would have gone if Joe Steele had paid less attention to Hitler, who couldn't reach American fighting men, and more to Tojo, who could—and had. Charlie was sure of one thing: nobody would haul Joe Steele up in front of a tribunal to judge him for his mistakes.

No, he was sure of something else, too. He couldn't say such a thing to anybody, not even to Esther. Keeping your mouth shut seemed to be one of the hardest things anybody could do. He did it.

One of the expectant fathers in the waiting room paced up and down, hands clasped behind his back, as if he'd escaped from an animated cartoon. Charlie wanted to trip him every time he went by. He didn't. He pretended to read a magazine. He smoked cigarette after cigarette. In the delivery room, Esther was going through all the horrible things a woman had to go through to have a baby. He was stuck out here, waiting.

A doctor walked into the room. All the men stared at him. Behind his mask, he could have been anybody's obstetrician. He said, "Mr. Lefebvre?" Everybody except the pacing guy slumped.

He at least stopped. "It's *Le-fehv*," he said; the doctor'd pronounced it *Le-fever*. "How's Millie doing?"

"Your wife is fine, Mr. Le-fehv," the doctor said. "If you

want to come with me, you can see them now. Congratulations!"

Lefebvre went with him. The other men in the waiting room went back to waiting. At least he wasn't pacing back and forth any more. Ten minutes later, the door opened again, but it was only another worried-looking dad-to-be. An hour went by. Another doctor came in. "Mr. Sullivan?"

Charlie jumped to his feet. "That's me!" You couldn't mess up Sullivan.

"It's a boy, Mr. Sullivan—eight pounds on the nose. *Mazel tov!*" The doctor wasn't Irish.

"Thanks." Charlie had White Owls in his jacket pocket. He gave the doctor one and tossed one to each man in the waiting room. Churchill smoked cigars, but he'd cut out his tongue after a White Owl, or maybe before. *Too bad,* Charlie thought. He'd bought some Havanas, too, but he figured he'd save those for when he went back to the White House.

"Come with me, and you can visit with your wife and your new son," the doctor said.

Esther looked as trampled as she had the first time, even though this labor had moved a little faster. The baby was a funny color, and his head was a weird shape. That didn't alarm Charlie; Sarah had looked the same way. He kissed Esther's sweaty forehead. "How are you?" he said.

She shook her head. "Did you get the license number of that truck?"

He looked at the baby again. "He's a big boy."

"He sure felt big coming out!" Esther said. She stroked the little bits of fine hair splayed across the top of the baby's head. "Patrick David Sullivan." He was named for Charlie's father's father and her mother's father.

"When they throw me out of here, I'll go call Mrs. Triandos and let her know she can tell Sarah she's got a new baby brother." The family across the hall, who had two little kids of their own, were tending to Sarah till Charlie got back.

Patrick—or would he be Pat?—started yelling. It was one of those what-the-devil's-going-on? cries newborns let out. The world was a confusing enough place after you'd lived in it for a while. When you'd just arrived, you had no idea what was happening, or why.

"Here. Shut up and have some milk." Esther put the baby on her breast. He might not know much yet, but he knew how to go after the good stuff. Esther had nursed Sarah for a year. She planned to do it again. No matter what the baby-food companies said, it was simpler and cheaper than bottles and formula.

"A son," Charlie said dreamily. It wasn't that Sarah wasn't wonderful. She was. But boys and girls were different, dammit. They'd do different things. They'd think different ways. If not for the differences between boys and girls, this old world wouldn't have much point, would it?

"After you call Irene, you need to tell our families," Esther said.

"I was thinking I'd wait till I got home to do that. It'd be a lot cheaper than doing it from a phone booth."

"Oh." Esther thought about it, then nodded. "Well, okay. That makes sense. You can let the White House know, too." She laughed. "When I married you, I never thought I'd say anything like that after I had a baby."

"Life isn't what you think you're gonna get," Charlie said. "Life is what happens to you while you're looking out for what you think you're gonna get."

"That sounds good. Does it mean anything?" Esther yawned. "I'm so beat up, I don't care if it means anything or not. Go call Mrs. Triandos. If Junior here lets me, I'm gonna sleep for a week. After I eat something, I mean. I'm starved. Having a kid is hard work. They don't call it labor for nothing. You'd better believe they don't."

Looking at her, all pale and exhausted, Charlie didn't see how he could do anything but believe her. He kissed her again, and kissed Patrick David Sullivan, too. New babies had a fresh-baked smell that wasn't like anything else in the world. Charlie'd been sad when Sarah lost it and started smelling like an ordinary little kid. Now here it was again, the odor that said something new had been added to the world.

There were phone booths (Charlie wondered why they weren't phone beeth, which said something about how tired he was) in the lobby downstairs. He called Irene Triandos. She squealed when he gave her the news. Then she called Sarah to the telephone.

"Daddy?" Sarah said.

"Hi, sweetie. You've got a new little brother. Mommy had a baby boy."

"It's a boy! It's a brother!" Sarah told Mrs. Triandos, who already knew.

Talking on the phone with little kids was always an adventure. When Sarah started paying attention to the voice in her ear once more, Charlie asked her, "Do you remember what we were gonna name the baby if it was a boy?"

"'Course I do, silly! Patrick David Sullivan!"

"That's right. So you've got a little brother named Patrick."

"Patrick brother! Brother Patrick!" Sarah was still kind of hazy about how those things worked. Pretty soon, though, she'd discover that one of the things younger brothers were for was driving older siblings nuts. Charlie was a younger brother. He'd been good at it. He was sure Patrick would follow in his footsteps.

Just as winter nights in Montana seemed to stretch like saltwater taffy, nights in summer were hardly there at all. That was how it felt to Mike, anyhow. The sun disappeared behind the Rockies. Next thing you knew, it was coming up again on the other side of the sky.

He realized with a small shock, or maybe not such a small one, how used he was getting to the rhythms of the sun here, and to the rhythms of encampment life. This was where he'd been, this was what he'd done, for the past five years. He'd served his stretch. It felt that way to him, anyhow. Yeah, the administrative law judge had slapped him with five to ten, but weren't five years of this enough for anybody?

Some people with stretches like his got out after five. He'd seen it happen. The Jeebies gave them clothes without numbers and twenty bucks, then put them on a bus to Livingston, usually with orders to stay inside the Rocky Mountain and Midwestern states. He didn't know what would happen if you went back to, say, New Hampshire and they caught you there. You'd probably get another term, a longer one.

They didn't seem about to turn him loose. John Dennison hadn't gone anywhere, either. Dennison dealt with the encampment better than anyone else Mike had ever seen, himself included. Whatever happened, it rolled off his back. He had the measure of the place. He didn't like it—who could?—but he dealt with it.

And just because some people got out, that didn't mean others didn't come in. These days, the labor encampments were full of Japanese-American scalps. Joe Steele had ordered everyone of Japanese descent on the U.S. mainland seized. Women had encampments, too. Those were probably also loaded with black-haired, almond-eyed people. The Jeebies here came down extra hard on the Japs. They blamed them for starting the war. Why not? Plainly, Joe Steele did, too. Mike wondered how many Japanese would get turned loose, or if any ever would.

He also wondered if he ever would. Curiosity made him brave the administration building again. He told himself the worst they could do was say no. How was he worse off if they did? (Actually, the worst they could do was beat the crap out of him and stick him in a punishment cell for a few weeks, but he preferred not to dwell on such things.)

A sergeant pulled his file and examined it. "Well, your record's not *too* bad, and you put in your enlistment request pretty early," the man said. "That's one more point for you. Let's see what Captain Blair thinks."

"Okay. Let's." Mike figured he hadn't struck out, anyhow. Whether he was just getting in deeper, he'd have to find out.

Captain Blair had a patch over his right eye socket. Mike guessed that made him a Great War veteran—no, with a new war in town, now they were calling it World War I. He bent low over the papers to examine them, which meant his remaining eye was nearsighted. Then he looked up at Mike.

"Normally, you'd serve your full ten. At least your full

ten," he said. "Sergeant Sanders didn't notice some of the coding in here. But there is a way for you to get out of the encampment, if you want to."

"Tell me," Mike said.

"We can take you to Livingston—straight to the recruiting station there. You can volunteer to serve for the duration of the war. Your service will be in what's called a punishment brigade. It will have men from the encampments and disgraced officers trying to get their good name back. It will go in wherever things are hottest. It will keep doing that as long as the war lasts. If you live, you'll be released then. If you don't, well, so it goes."

"Oh," Mike said, and then, "You don't pull any punches, do you?"

"You can't say you didn't know the score before you played the game," Blair answered. "You can take your chances—and they aren't too good." He touched the patch to emphasize that. "Or you can stay here a long time. You must have ticked off somebody with clout."

"I ticked off Joe Steele," Mike said proudly.

"I hear all kinds of bullshit from wreckers. You, I almost believe. So what'll it be?"

John Dennison would have stayed. Dennison *was* staying. Mike didn't want to let another five years go by here, or another ten. He'd look up and find he'd worked here longer than he had for the *Post*. He wouldn't be able to imagine a life beyond the barbed wire and the chopping details, let alone live one. They'd try their best to kill him if he joined the Army? They were killing him here, only in slow motion.

"Take me to Livingston," he said.

"You'll go in the morning, after roll call and breakfast," Captain Blair said. "Believe it or not, I wish you the best of luck. I tried to get back on active military duty, but they wouldn't take me. The limeys used Admiral Nelson even though he was shy an eye and an arm. These are modern times, though. I don't cut the mustard for the real war. I'm stuck here."

Making war on Americans instead, Mike thought. But he didn't say it. Blair had been square with him, as square as anybody could be. What he did say was "Thank you." It felt as unnatural as it had when he'd said it to Lopatynski the winter before.

Charlie got a card from Mike announcing he'd joined the Army. *The hardest part is, I have to learn a new number for myself,* his brother wrote. *I've been NY24601 a long time. But I'm someone else these days.*

He didn't know whether the card was good news or bad news. Mike hadn't gone overseas the last time around. He'd worked in a munitions plant instead. At the labor encampment, he was reasonably safe. In the Army, he wouldn't be. On the other hand, the powers that be were more likely to let him out of the Army than to release him from the encampment.

Out in the wider world, the war ground on. Charlie remembered Admiral Spruance from his days on one of Joe Steele's military tribunals. He hadn't been an admiral then. Now his ships smashed the Japs near Midway: one more place Charlie'd never heard of till it got splashed all over the newspapers.

In Russia, the Germans couldn't attack along the whole vast front, the way they had the year before. They pushed forward in the south and hung on in the center and north. Plainly, the drive was aimed at the Caucasus and the oilfields there. Oil had always been a problem for the Germans—they didn't have enough. If they could grab the Russians' fields, they'd help themselves and hurt the Reds at the same time.

Rostov-on-the-Don fell. The Germans had taken it in 1941, too, but the Red Army drove them out then. Now they hung on to it and even advanced. Trotsky sent his faltering troops an order: not one step back! Order or no order, the Russians kept retreating.

The Nazis couldn't just roll into the Caucasus. That would leave them with a long, unprotected northern flank. They had to take more of southern Russia. There was a city on the Volga that, in the days before the Revolution, had been called Tsaritsyn. The Reds couldn't leave it with a reactionary name like that. Now it was Trotskygrad: Trotsky's town.

Something like 40,000 people died when the *Luftwaffe* hammered it from the skies. Panzers and foot soldiers stormed across the steppe toward the shattered city. They stormed into it. But the Russians defended Trotskygrad block by block, factory by factory, house by house, room by room. Getting in, Hitler discovered, was much easier than clearing the Reds out.

Hitler had thought he would knock Russia out of the war in a hurry. Well, General Marshall had thought the same thing. Nobody was right all the time. Now the *Führer* had a much bigger war on his hands than he'd wanted. He had a much bigger war than he could fight by himself, in fact. Romanians and Hungarians and Italians and Slovaks and even a division of Spaniards joined the *Wehrmacht* in Russia.

Wehrmacht soldiers, though, had better gear and better training than their allies. (That the Hungarians and Romanians hated each other worse than either hated the Russians didn't help.) That fall, the Red Army sliced through Hitler's foreign flunkies in two places and cut off the big German force still grinding away in Trotskygrad.

Even Joe Steele said, "I commend the Russian Army's endurance and bravery. This stroke has dealt the Nazis a heavy blow."

Vince Scriabin's comment to Charlie was more cynical: "I wonder how many generals Trotsky shot before the Red Army started doing things right. More than we have here—I guarantee you that."

"You've got to be right," Charlie said—if he told Scriabin he was wrong, he'd get shot himself, or at least end up in a labor encampment. He wasn't saying anything he didn't believe. Trotsky might have been even more ruthless than Joe Steele, and he'd held on to the reins longer. Charlie added, "I wonder how many Hitler's gonna shoot now that the Germans aren't doing so hot."

He actually got a smile out of Scriabin. "I like that!" the Hammer said. "I really like that! So will the boss. And I'll tell him you said it, too. I won't steal it from you."

"I wasn't worried about it." Again, Charlie told the truth. If Scriabin did steal his nice line, what could he do? Nothing. Luckily, he had sense enough to see as much.

"When the boss asked you to come to the White House, I wasn't sure you'd work out here," Scriabin said. A sentence like that carried any number of possibilities for disaster. Scriabin had the authority to act on his doubts. Who would miss a reporter-turned-speechwriter? Well, Esther would. Who with any power, though? The question answered itself. But the Hammer went on, "You've done all right since you got here. Maybe I was judging you by your brother."

"Glad I could be useful." Charlie left it right there. He didn't tell Scriabin that Mike had gone from that labor encampment to the Army. Scriabin could find out in seconds if he decided to. If he didn't feel like finding out . . . Mike was bound to be better off.

"Useful. Yes." Scriabin bobbed his head on his thin neck and hurried away. If Charlie was any judge, Joe Steele's aide had embarrassed himself by acting somewhat like a human being.

A few days later, American troops under Omar Bradley—another man who'd sat on a tribunal or two—landed in North Africa with the British. They didn't trap the Germans retreating out of Egypt through Libya so neatly as they planned. Grimly, the Nazis hung on in Tunisia.

So things weren't perfect. In his forties now, Charlie didn't expect or even much hope for perfection. Things could have been worse. For a middle-aged man, that would do.

XVIII

In Washington, the war seemed like voices from another room even after more than a year. The Germans surviving in Trotskygrad threw down their guns and surrendered early in 1943. They marched off into Red captivity with their hands clasped on top of their heads. Seeing Russian photos of those glum, dirty, starving men, Charlie wondered how many of them would ever get back to the *Vaterland*. Precious few, unless he missed his guess.

For a while, it looked as if the Nazis' whole position in southern Russia would unravel. But the *Führer*'s generals still knew what they were doing. They let the Red Army outrun its supplies, then counterattacked. Pretty soon, the Russians, not the Germans, were the ones hoping the spring thaw that stopped operations for weeks would come early. They'd hurt Hitler, but they'd got hurt in turn.

In the Pacific, Eisenhower's soldiers and Nimitz's sailors and Marines won control of the Solomons. It was neither easy nor cheap, but they did it. The Japs fell back in New Guinea, too. Like the Germans, their reach had exceeded their grasp. Now they were finding out what hell was for.

And in Washington, people grumbled because gasoline for civilians was rationed, tires were hard to get, and you couldn't buy all the sugar or coffee you wanted. Nobody starved. Nobody went hungry who hadn't been hungry before the war. Fewer people were hungry these days. With factories open and humming, jobs were easy to get.

Sarah turned five. Patrick turned one. Charlie wondered how that had happened. He hadn't aged a day since his first child was born. Eyeing Esther, he was sure no time had passed for her, either. But Sarah would be starting kindergarten in the fall, and Patrick was saying *dada* and *mama* and connecting the noises with the people they belonged to.

Joe Steele's henchmen in the White House seemed contented if not happy. "A year ago, things looked terrible," Stas Mikoian told Charlie. "The Germans were going crazy. They were smashing the Russians. They were sinking everything in sight on the Atlantic. Hell, in the Caribbean, too. It looked like they might take the Suez Canal. The Japs were running wild, too. We couldn't slow 'em down, let alone stop 'em. Neither could England or Holland. The boss was really worried we might lose the war."

"It won't happen now," Charlie said.

"Nope. It sure won't," Mikoian agreed. He and Scriabin had more gray in their hair than they did when Charlie came to work at the White House. So did Joe Steele. Lazar Kagan didn't. Charlie suspected him of discreetly touching it up. If he did, though, only his barber knew for sure.

"How long do you think it'll take?" Charlie asked, and then answered his own question: "Somewhere between one year and three, I bet. Peace again in 1945 or '46—maybe '44 if we get lucky."

"That sounds about right," Mikoian said. "I mean, unless something goes wrong somewhere. All things considered, the war may be hard on the rest of the world, but it's good for us."

"Funny—I was thinking the same thing not long ago," Charlie said. "When everything's done, the Japs and the Nazis'll be knocked flat. The Russians are doing all the dying against Hitler, so they'll be a while getting back on their feet, too. England can't fight Germany without us, 'cause we make so much of what she needs. We make what everybody needs, and Hitler and Tojo can't get at us."

Mikoian nodded. He smiled. He had an inviting smile, one that urged you to come and be amused, too. "And the war lets Joe Steele finish getting the country properly disciplined without a bunch of people grousing all the time."

"Properly disciplined . . ." Charlie tasted the phrase. "Is that what he calls it these days?"

"Oh, no. You've got to blame me for it. It's my line," Stas Mikoian said. "But that's about the size of it, you know.

When the boss took over, everything was a mess. Everybody was screaming at everybody else like a bunch of monkeys in a cage. The government didn't have the power to do anything."

"Hey, c'mon. Only us chickens here, okay?" Charlie said. "When you say the government, you mean the President."

"Well, sure." Mikoian didn't even try to deny it. "Who else? Congress? What were they but the loudest monkeys around? The Supreme Court? If Joe Steele hadn't taken care of the Supreme Court, we'd still be screwed up. All they ever said was no. So who does that leave? If the President doesn't do it, nobody would."

"Yes, but if he goes overboard, how do you stop him?" Charlie asked—not the least dangerous question in the White House. He wouldn't have asked it of Scriabin or Kagan. He sure as hell wouldn't have asked it of Joe Steele. But he trusted the Armenian—a little bit, anyhow.

Mikoian smiled again. "I know what's eating you—your brother went to a labor encampment."

"That's sure some of it," Charlie admitted.

"But we need labor encampments. They're good for discipline, too. They keep people from being stupid. They keep people from being careless. My brother works with Douglas, remember. There were wreckers among the aeronautical engineers, believe it or not."

"You've said that before, but your brother didn't get a term," Charlie said harshly.

"He could have. If they'd put a case together against him, he would have. Do you think being my brother would have made any difference? You don't know Joe Steele very well if you do."

After Charlie did think about it, he decided Mikoian was right. Anybody could get a term, anybody at all. It was just something that happened, like getting a toothache. "How long do you suppose he'll be President?" Charlie asked, not quite out of thin air.

Stas Mikoian looked at him as if he'd come up with a really stupid question. "As long as he wants to be, of course," the Armenian said. Charlie nodded. That *had* been a stupid question, sure as hell.

*   *   *

Mike had been in the Army for months now. He still
couldn't decide whether he'd been smart to trade the
wrecker's shabby uniform for the soldier's sharp one. You
had to keep a soldier's uniform neat. They gave you grief if
you didn't. They gave you grief for all kinds of stuff the
Jeebies didn't give a damn about.

The thing of it was, the Jeebies were making it up as they
went along. The Army had ways of doing things that went
back to George Washington's day. Hell, the Army probably
had ways of doing things that went back to Julius Caesar's
day, if not to King Tut's. And most of those ways of doing
things were designed to make sure you did exactly what your
superiors told you to do, the second they told you to do it.

Saluting. Marching. Countermarching. Going through
intricate maneuvers on the parade ground, all in perfect
step. Keeping your uniform, well, uniform. Making your cot
just so, with the sheets tight enough so you could bounce a
quarter on them.

The cot's mattress was softer than the sawdust-filled burlap sack he'd had in the wintertime—much softer than the
bare slats he'd slept on during the summer. It still felt funny,
wrong, to him after five years in the labor encampment. He
wasn't the only wrecker who bitched about that—nowhere
close.

He also wasn't the only wrecker who bitched about the
weather. The Army encampment—no, the Army just called
them camps—was right outside of Lubbock, Texas. The
weather came as much of a shock as the discipline. After five
years in the Montana Rockies, he'd forgotten there was
weather like this.

One thing hadn't changed a bit: they were still behind
barbed wire. This was a punishment brigade. The War Department officials who'd created it figured anyone who got
stuck in it might light out for the tall timber if he got half a
chance.

As a wrecker, Mike had become a good lumberjack. As
a soldier, he became a good killer. He surprised himself by
proving a pretty fair shot. They gave him a marksman's
badge. He wore it with more pride than he would have ex-

pected. A top sergeant a couple of years older than he was taught bayonet fighting.

"This is what I learned last time around," the noncom told his pupils. "I'm gonna work you guys harder than I would with most troops. Places you're going, things you'll do, you'll need it."

A younger fellow, a limey who wore his chevrons upside down, taught them the tricks of the trade with a different toy: the entrenching tool. You could, it turned out, do some really horrible things with an entrenching tool, especially if you ground down the edges to get them sharp.

They marched. They dug foxholes and trenches. They ran. They exercised. They trained against one another. Mike got a scar on his arm blocking a knife thrust that might have gutted him like a trout. Not at all by accident, he broke the other guy's nose with an elbow a split second later. Then he said, "You fucking jackass."

"Ah, your mudder," the other man said. He didn't have a speech impediment—only a rearranged snoot.

They went to the infirmary together. Mike got half a dozen stitches. A doc put the other soldier's nose back roughly the way it had been before Mike broke it. A couple of burly attendants had to hold the fellow while the doctor attended to it.

The one thing the punishment brigade didn't do was go fight the Germans or the Japs. Mike bitched about it to his company CO. Captain Luther Magnusson was a gloomy Swede. He'd been brought back from North Africa in disgrace after getting his company cut up when he gave stupid orders because he was drunk.

He still drank; Mike could smell it on him while he was complaining. Magnusson's pale eyes were tracked with red. They could have shot him for screwing up the way he did; Joe Steele's Army didn't have many soft spots. Or they could have given him a sledgehammer to make big ones into little ones for the next thousand years.

Instead, he had one more chance. He would redeem himself or die trying. That was what punishment units were all about. His mouth quirked. "Why do you think they haven't shipped us out?"

"I was hoping you'd know, sir," Mike said. Military courtesy was one more thing they'd drilled into him. "You've been in this racket longer than the rest of us."

"Yeah, I have, and a hell of a lot of good it's done me," Magnusson said. "But I can answer that one. So can you, if you think a minute. You're no dope, Sullivan—I've seen that."

"Thanks—I think." Then Mike did think. He didn't need long, once he remembered what a punishment brigade was all about. Like Luther Magnusson, they'd all redeem themselves or die trying. Odds were the stress lay on the last three words. "They still haven't found any place that's hot enough to make it worth their while to throw us in?" he suggested.

"I can't prove a thing, you know, but that's sure as hell the way it looks to me," Magnusson said.

Mike shrugged. "Hey, it's something to look forward to, right?" He won a chuckle from the dour, disgraced captain.

A troopship packed men together even tighter than the bunks in a labor-encampment barracks. Mike wouldn't have thought it was possible, but there you were. And here he was, out on the Pacific. A faint whiff of vomit always hung in the air. Some guys' stomachs couldn't stand the motion. Mike didn't think it was too bad, but that distant stink didn't help his own insides settle down.

He wore two stripes on his left sleeve, two stripes and a P that announced what kind of outfit he was in. A T under your stripes—or between chevrons and rockers if you were a senior sergeant—meant you were a technician. That P meant you were vulture bait, assuming any of the miserable islands out in the Pacific boasted vultures.

He didn't care about being a corporal. Oh, he was modestly pleased they didn't think he was a screwup. He hadn't joined the Army just to get out of the labor encampment. He'd joined because he honest to God wanted to fight for the United States in spite of the murderous tyrant infesting the White House.

But making corporal wouldn't help him stay alive. That was going to be a matter of luck any which way. He'd need a big dose of it to come out the other side.

He made a few dollars more every month now, but he wasn't jumping up and down about that, either. Were things different, he might have sent Stella some money. But things weren't different. Part of him hoped she'd found somebody else and was happy. Part of him hoped she was sorry she'd dumped him every minute of the day and night.

Before they'd boarded the train to San Diego, they'd gone into Lubbock for a spree. He'd had about ten minutes with a Mexican-looking gal in a nasty crib—the first time he'd laid a woman since the Jeebies grabbed him. It was— what did they say?—more a catharsis than a rapture. Afterwards, he'd clumsily used the pro kit they issued him. Either the hooker was clean or the kit worked. He hadn't come down with a drippy faucet.

Every fifteen or twenty minutes, the ship would zigzag to confuse any Jap subs that might be stalking them. More soldiers seemed to throw up when they headed straight into the swells. Waves hitting the bow tossed the ship up and down, up and down. You felt as if your stomach was going up and down, up and down, too.

They got to Hawaii ten days after they set out. The camp where they stayed was on the island of Maui. Except for the port, it might have been the only thing on the island of Maui. It was the only part of the island the punishment brigade saw, anyhow. A couple of guys had been to Honolulu. They talked with awe in their voices about the chances for debauchery there. On Maui, nobody got so much as a beer.

The ship took on fuel, food, and fresh water. Then it sailed on, west and south. Every passing minute took the men closer to the time and the place where Uncle Sam—or was it Uncle Joe?—would start using them up. Most of them didn't seem to care. The poker games started up as soon as the men got back aboard. The dice started rolling, too.

Mike didn't gamble much. He lay in his bunk, plowing through paperbacks. He hadn't had much chance to read in the labor encampment. He was trying to make up for lost time. These cheap little books were great for that.

It got hotter and stickier every day. When they crossed the Equator, the sailors summoned the soldiers topside and drenched them with fire hoses. King Neptune and his court magically transformed the polliwogs to sturdy shellbacks.

They disembarked at Guadalcanal. The scars in the jungle were already healing, but the place still looked like hell. They went into an encampment that made the one outside of Lubbock seem like a Ritz-Carlton by comparison.

There'd been mice in the barracks in Montana. Some of the guys there, with nothing else to give their affection to, had made pets out of them. No mice scurrying over these bunks. There were cockroaches instead: cockroaches almost as big as mice. You couldn't tame them. All you could do was squash them, and they made a mess when you did.

Ordinary soldiers, Mike quickly discovered, weren't allowed to mingle with men from punishment brigades. No fraternization—that was what the Army called it. That was why they had the P on their sleeves. They were soldiers, and then again they weren't.

Time dragged on. The brass still didn't seem to have decided how best to dispose of them. Some men cooked up a nasty brew from fruit and sugar and whatever else they could promote that would ferment. A fellow from South Carolina who swore he'd been a moonshiner rigged a still. What came out of it was even fouler than the undistilled product. Mike sampled both, so he had standards of comparison.

Captain Magnusson hunted him up when he was still feeling the aftereffects. "One thing about this year," the company CO said. He'd been putting away rotgut, too; his breath stank of it.

"What's that, sir?" Mike was discovering that heat and humidity didn't improve a hangover. He wished Magnusson would go away.

But the captain had tabbed him as somebody he could talk to. "We go into action before it's over, that's what," he said. "And we see how many of us get to say hello to 1944, let alone 1945."

"You always know how to cheer me up, don't you, sir?"

As if he hadn't spoken, Luther Magnusson went on. "And you know what else? I'm still looking forward to it." Almost in spite of himself, Mike nodded. He was, too.

*   *   *

Charlie looked out of the hotel at Basra. The smells coming in through the window would have told him he wasn't in America any more even if he couldn't have seen any of the Iraqi city. No town in the United States had smelled like this since the turn of the century, maybe longer. Neither the locals nor the British, who'd grabbed hold of Iraq after the First World War (and who'd hung on to it despite a pro-Nazi uprising) seemed to have bothered with putting in flush toilets or sewer lines. The canals near the river only added to the stink.

Right by the Shatt al-Arab Hotel was a little England, at least to the eye. Rich people, limeys and their wog flunkies, lived in those rose-gardened houses. Farther away, most of the buildings he could see were made of mud brick, with flat roofs. He could have found the like in Albuquerque or Santa Fe; he'd done a good bit of knocking around the country in his AP days. But nowhere in the USA would he have seen domed mosques with minarets spearing up toward the sky. Just looking at them made him think of the *Arabian Nights*, or of Douglas Fairbanks buckling a swash in a silent movie.

Basra wasn't silent. The mosques weren't even close to silent. They had PA systems to amplify the muezzins' wailing calls to prayer. The first time Charlie heard one, he knew he wasn't in Kansas any more.

The hotel, like its surrounding district, was a little bit of England dropped into the Middle East. The elevator—the lift, they called it—creaked. The beer was warm. The dining room served roast beef and Yorkshire pudding although, even in October here, Basra was hotter than London ever got.

Charlie didn't know how many Tommies were protecting the hotel from any mischief the natives or even the now-distant Germans could brew up. He did know the number wasn't small. And the security was needed. Charlie wouldn't have come a quarter of the way around the world if Joe Steele hadn't come. The President had his own guards under J. Edgar Hoover, who was also along.

Joe Steele wasn't just playing tourist. He hadn't come to ride in one of the almost-gondolas that plied the canals.

He'd come here to meet with Winston Churchill, and with Leon Trotsky. They needed to plan how the rest of the war would go, and to talk about what the world might look like once it didn't hold crazy Nazis and fanatical samurai.

Churchill had greeted Joe Steele when he and his followers flew in from Cairo. Trotsky was due at the airport any minute now. He'd said he didn't want to be greeted. He would meet the leaders of the Western democracies when he got to the hotel.

How many people around the world would have wanted to be in the room to witness the first confrontation between Trotsky and Joe Steele? Millions. Millions and millions, for sure. *I get to be one of the lucky ones who do it,* Charlie thought. The reporter he had been quivered in anticipation.

Someone knocked on the door. Charlie opened it. There in the wildly carpeted hallway stood J. Edgar Hoover. "I just received word that Trotsky has arrived safely. The President and the Prime Minister will greet him in the Grand Ballroom on the first floor." He made a face. "What the limeys call the first floor. It'd be the second floor to us."

"Gotcha. Thanks," Charlie said. To an Englishman, the American first floor was the ground floor. *Two countries separated by the same language.* Charlie couldn't remember who'd said that. Whoever it was, he'd known what he was talking about.

He walked down the stairs to the Grand Ballroom. He didn't trust that lift. He wouldn't have trusted it if they'd called it an elevator. The ballroom was a garish horror. It was a bad English imitation of Arab decor that was bad to begin with. Low couches, footstools, silk brocade, cloth-of-gold . . . Put it all together and it spelled tasteless. The British crystal candelabra with light bulbs in place of candles only added to the surreal gaucheness.

Churchill and his entourage sat on the right side of the chamber as you came in. Joe Steele and his were over to the left. Charlie headed that way. In the center would be Trotsky and his followers. Only a few hard-faced Red security men stood there now. They eyed the decadent capitalist imperialists to either side of them with an odd and—Charlie was to learn—very Russian mix of fear and contempt.

Lazar Kagan nodded to Charlie as he came over. So did General Marshall. Scriabin ignored him. Mikoian and Joe Steele were whispering back and forth. The President chuckled at something Mikoian said.

J. Edgar Hoover strode in. He'd only grown heavier and jowlier in the years since Charlie first met him when he seized the Supreme Court Four. He took his place with the rest of the Americans. "Any minute now," he said.

A British military band outside the hotel struck up "The Internationale." That had to be one of the more bizarre moments of Charlie's life. It also had to mean the boss Red was here.

When the lift worked, you could hear it all over the building. Charlie listened to it now. Into the Grand Ballroom strode Trotsky, accompanied by a couple of generals, by Foreign Commissar Litvinov, by a skinny little man who had to be his translator, and by some more tough-looking Russian security men with submachine guns. The three leaders' guardsmen could have themselves quite a little war if things went south.

But they didn't. "My dear Leon—a lion indeed!" Churchill said warmly. He'd met Trotsky before—he'd gone to Moscow a couple of times after England and Russia both found themselves fighting the Nazis. Now he walked up to the Red leader carrying, of all things, a sword. "Allow me to present to you the Sword of Valor, given to you in the name of the Russian people by his Majesty, King George VI."

Trotsky murmured something in Russian. The translator sounded as if he'd gone to Oxford (maybe he had): "He says this is not how he ever expected the ruler of the world's biggest empire to give him the sword."

Charlie laughed in surprise. Even translated, that showed wit. Well, Trotsky looked as foxy as ever, with that shock of graying red-brown hair, the red-brown chin beard—also graying—the nose that did duty for a muzzle, and the clever eyes behind glasses a lot like Scriabin's. Chances were he hadn't risen to the top in the dog-eat-dog world of Red politics by accident.

Winston Churchill laughed, too: a booming chortle that invited everyone who heard it to join in. "Politics is a strange business, all right," he said. "But anyone who opposes Adolf Hitler passes the most important test." He glanced over his shoulder and saw Joe Steele coming up. "And now let me introduce you to the President of the United States, whom you have not met before."

Joe Steele and Leon Trotsky sized each other up. Plainly, there was still no love lost between them. But when, after two or three seconds, Trotsky stuck out his hand, Joe Steele took it. The President spoke first: "Churchill has it right. We will beat Germany and Japan first, and worry later about everything that comes later."

As a matter of fact, Russia and Japan had a neutrality treaty. Russian freighters crossed the Pacific, loaded up on American weapons to shoot at the Germans, and steamed back to Vladivostok to put them on the Trans-Siberian Railway without worrying about Japanese submarines. As Churchill said, politics was a mighty strange business.

Trotsky's smile didn't quite reach his eyes. "Well, we can start worrying about them now, but we won't let them stand in our way," he said.

"Fair enough," Joe Steele said. The two men took a step back from each other, both at the same time.

Joe Steele was short and lean. Leon Trotsky was short and had a middle-aged man's potbelly, but wasn't really heavy. Winston Churchill was short and roly-poly. Charlie didn't know what that meant, or whether it meant anything. From what he'd heard, though, Adolf Hitler also wasn't exactly a skyscraper. *The short shall inherit the earth, or at least order it around?* Since Charlie didn't have a whole lot of inches, he found himself liking the idea. Vince Scriabin probably would, too.

As the leaders chatted, Trotsky through his interpreter, their entourages warily mingled. Among the Russians, Litvinov spoke good English. He'd been Red envoy to England and, Charlie found out, had an English wife. Lazar Kagan knew enough Yiddish to get by, and it was close enough to German to let him talk with a couple of the Red generals.

At the banquet that evening, Trotsky drank vodka as if it were water. Churchill poured down whiskey the same way. Joe Steele had but one liver to give for his country, and manfully kept up. Charlie had not been unacquainted with strong drink in the course of his life. He put down enough that evening to know he'd be sorry in the morning. Scriabin was doing a good job of knocking them back, too. Charlie didn't know where the little man put all the booze, because he didn't show it. Maybe he had a hollow leg. He and Litvinov got into a row about the Second Front. The Russians had wanted England and the USA to invade France in 1943. It hadn't happened, and they were still steamed about that. Just to make matters worse, Scriabin and Litvinov seemed to love each other as little as Joe Steele and Trotsky did.

From everything Charlie'd seen, Churchill had stalled the landings on the Channel coast more than Joe Steele had. Churchill remembered too well the bloodbath in France from the last war. He didn't want England to go through that again. Meanwhile, the Russians went through a bigger bloodbath of their own.

Charlie took three aspirins before he finally hit the hay that night. He woke up with the jimjams anyway. He sent more aspirins down the hatch, then headed for the ballroom in search of coffee. The kitchen had gone native to the extent of offering an Arab-style brew: thick as mud, clogged with sugar, and served in tiny cups. Charlie drank three, one after the other. They didn't cure him but, along with the little white pills and the hair of the dog that had mauled him, they left him functioning.

Other men from all three great powers staggered down, most of them a good deal the worse for wear. Yanks, limeys, Ivans—it didn't matter. A hangover hurt just as bad no matter who had it. A couple of the worst sufferers walked with great care, as if afraid their heads would fall off. Charlie wasn't quite so damaged, but he sympathized.

When Churchill came down, he seemed fresh as a daisy. He greeted Charlie with "Ah, the Irishman!" and went on to guzzle tea and eat a hearty breakfast. Trotsky also showed few signs of all he'd drunk the night before. If you were going to run Russia, you had to be able to hold your liquor. Joe Steele was sallow and scowling, but he was always sallow and often scowling, so that proved nothing.

After breakfast, the leaders and their top military and political men sat down together to hash things over. Charlie wasn't a big enough wheel to be invited to that get-together. He knew why Joe Steele had brought him along: to help draft the statement the President would release when the conference ended.

In the meantime, he could see a little of Basra. He bought a copper-and-glass water pipe at a bazaar. He likely paid four times what it was worth, but it was still cheap. Some of the filth and poverty . . . The worst Hoovervilles at the Depression's lowest ebb hadn't come within miles of this. He went back to the Shatt al-Arab Hotel with a new respect for Western civilization.

At the banquet that evening, Scriabin whispered to him: "Trotsky! That son of a bitch is the stubbornest man in the world."

"Is he?" Charlie whispered back. He'd always thought the Hammer was in the running for that prize, and Joe Steele with him. Saying so didn't seem smart. Scriabin nodded. He probably figured he was a reasonable fellow, which only proved not everybody knew himself.

After dinner, the booze came out. People made toasts. "To the bravery of the Red Army!" Joe Steele said. Everybody drank.

"To the heroic U.S. Navy!" Churchill said—he was, as he was fond of noting, a former naval person. Everyone drank again.

Trotsky stood up. He raised his glass. "God save the King!" he said in English. He tossed back the vodka with a virtuoso flip of the wrist. Laughing, everybody drank to that one, too.

General Marshall took his turn. "To victory!" he said, and drank with soldierly aplomb. The rest followed suit. It was going to be another long night.

Air Marshal "Bomber" Harris said, "May American planes treat Japan as the RAF is treating Germany." That one would take a while to fulfill. American planes weren't in range of the Home Islands yet. People drank anyhow.

Marshal Koniev, Trotsky's top general, spoke in Russian.

"Death to the Hitlerites!" the interpreter said. Nobody could resist such a toast.

It went on and on. It got bleary out. Eventually, Charlie lurched to his feet. Then he realized he had to say something. "To truth!" he blurted, and drank.

"Hear! Hear!" Churchill downed the toast. As soon as he did, the others drank, too. Charlie sagged down into his seat again.

The statement that came out of the Basra Conference promised independence for the captured nations of Europe and the Far East and punishment for the German and Japanese warlords who'd plunged the world into chaos for the second time in a generation. It promised an international organization with enough teeth to make the peace last.

It didn't talk about the deals the Big Three cut among themselves. Joe Steele got Trotsky to agree that, when the time came, the Red Army would help the United States invade Japan. At that point, Trotsky said, the neutrality treaty would be old galoshes. The translator helpfully explained that was Russian slang for a used rubber.

Trotsky wanted Russian hegemony over every square inch of Eastern Europe and the Balkans. After some effort, Churchill talked him into yielding dominant influence in Greece to England. Scriabin told Charlie how he'd done it: "He said to Trotsky, 'There's not an acre of the country the Royal Navy's guns can't reach. Your bloody Red bandits would have no place to hide.' That did the trick."

"I guess it would," Charlie said. "Good thing we're all on the same side, isn't it? We'd have even more fun if we were enemies."

"Strength matters to Trotsky. He's like the boss that way," Scriabin said. "And we'll all stay friends till this war's over. Hitler's too dangerous for us to do anything else."

Charlie nodded. "You said it. Some of the things the Russians are finding now that they're taking back land the Nazis held for a while . . . That stuff would make Genghis Khan lose his lunch."

Of course, the Nazis screeched about the way the Reds

fought the war, too. And in the Pacific, neither the Japs nor the Americans seemed interested in taking prisoners. The Japs would kill themselves before they surrendered. And the Americans had learned the hard way that it was better not to land in a Japanese POW camp.

It was, Charlie thought, better not to land in anybody's prison camp of any variety. He was sure his brother could go on in far more detail on that theme than he could. Every once in a while, though, you were better off *not* knowing a subject exhaustively. This seemed like one of those times.

XIX

Mike had scrambled down the netting thrown over the side of the troopship. He and a good many other men bobbed in the amphibious tractors—amtracs, everybody called them—clustered by the troopships like ducklings around their mothers. They should have already been chugging toward the beach. The attack was supposed to go in at 0830.

But the Jap emplacements on Tarawa were supposed to have been silenced, too. The Japs were still shooting back with guns as big as eight inches. Somebody'd told him they'd hauled those here from Singapore. He didn't know about that. He did know the shells kicked up enormous splashes. He didn't want to think about what a hit would do to a ship.

At 0900, after more shelling from the Navy and bombing from carrier-based planes, the amtracs and other landing craft did get going. The Japs had smaller stuff, too, and started turning it loose as soon as the Americans came into range. Machine-gun bullets clattered off the amtrac's armored bow.

"Those fuckers're trying to shoot us!" Mike said. The surprise he put in his voice was a joke, but a grim one.

The amtrac clawed its way over a reef just at the waterline, then scrambled up onto the beach. Down came that armored front. "Out!" the sailors screamed.

Out Mike went, straight into hell on earth. They'd come ashore near a pier at the south end of the island. The beach was . . . sand. Tarawa wasn't much higher inland. There was grubby jungle—and there were Japs.

A bullet cracked past his head. As he'd been trained, he got as low as he could and crawled forward. Another bullet hit in front of him and spat sand in his face. Ice-blue Japanese tracers, very different from the red ones Americans used, sprayed across the beach.

He saw movement ahead. No Americans had got that far. He fired two quick shots with his M-1. Whatever was moving went down. Maybe he'd killed somebody. Maybe he'd just made a Jap hit the dirt.

Mortar bombs whispered in and blew up with startling crashes. Soldiers screamed for corpsmen. Not all the landing craft could make it over the reef. Marines and punishment-brigade soldiers waded ashore in the waist-deep water of the lagoon. Mike had thought of the amtracs as ducklings. Those poor wading bastards were sitting ducks. One after another, they slumped into the warm sea, wounded or dead.

"Keep moving!" Captain Magnusson shouted through the din. "We've got to get off the beach if we can!"

That made sense. There was cover ahead, if they could reach it. They'd all get shot if they stayed here on the sand. But there were Japs ahead, too. They already had the cover, and they didn't want to give it up.

Machine-gun fire came from a dugout just inland from the beach. The American bombardment had swept off some of the sand that protected the roof of coconut-palm logs. It sure as hell hadn't wrecked the position, though. No, that was left for the guys with the P's on their sleeves.

Mike waved to a couple of men with submachine guns to give him covering fire. He scrambled closer to the dark opening from which the machine guns blinked malevolently. He tossed two grenades into it, lobbing them in side-arm so he could raise up off the ground as little as possible.

Screams came from inside when the grenades went off. The machine guns fell silent. There was a back door—a Jap burst out of it, his shirt in shreds and blood running down his back. One of the Americans with a grease gun cut him down.

Other dugouts lurked farther inland. The Japs had spent a lot of time and effort fortifying Tarawa, and it showed. Every position had another position or two supporting it. If you cleaned out a strongpoint and stood up to wave your buddies forward, a Jap in the next dugout along would kill you.

As usual, Tojo's soldiers didn't, wouldn't, surrender. If you wanted to get past them, you had to kill them. You had to make sure they were dead, too. They'd play possum, holding on to a grenade that they would use to take some Americans with them when they joined their ancestors.

Mike hadn't known how he would react to killing people. He was too busy trying to stay alive himself to worry about it much. And the Japs hardly seemed like human beings to him, not with the savage way they fought to the death. It felt more like clearing the island of dangerous wild beasts.

Night came down with equatorial suddenness. Tracers and artillery bursts lit up the darkness, but the enemy didn't mount a big counterattack. Noticing he was ravenous, Mike gulped rations. When he smoked a cigarette, he made sure no sniper could spot the match or the glowing coal.

Captain Magnusson came by, taking stock of his company. "How're we doing?" Mike asked, adding, "All I know is what's going on right in front of me."

"We're still here. They didn't throw us off the island," Magnusson said. "Not all of us are still here, though. They've already chewed us up pretty good." He chuckled harshly. "This is what we signed up for, right?"

"Maybe what you did," Mike said. "Me, I signed up 'cause I was sick and tired of cutting trees down in the Rockies in the snow." He managed a chuckle of sorts. "Ain't fucking snowing here, even if it would be there. End of November? Oh, hell, yes."

"Get whatever sleep you can," the company CO told him. "If it doesn't pick up tonight, it will come sunup. More Marines will land then, up at the other end of the island."

"Oh, boy," Mike said.

He did get a little rest. The Japs didn't attack during the dark hours, though they were known for that elsewhere in the Pacific. They must have decided they could make the invaders pay a higher price by sitting tight.

Things did pick up at first light. The Marines made it onto the beaches farther north, putting the Japs in a nutcracker. From then on, it was bunker-busting and dugout-clearing and fighting from one foxhole to the next. Mike's bayonet had blood on it. He wore a field dressing on his left arm where a bullet had grazed him. Unless it started dripping pus or something, he didn't figure he'd bother the medics about it.

Fighting lasted two more days. It stopped only when no more Japs were left to kill. The Americans captured fewer than two dozen Japanese soldiers, all of them badly wounded. A hundred Korean laborers, maybe even a few more, gave up. The rest of the enemy were dead.

So were close to a thousand punishment-brigade men and Marines. Some of the leathernecks stayed on Tarawa to garrison the miserable place. The P-brigaders got shipped back to the replacement depot on Espiritu Santo to refit, to get their table of organization filled out with fresh recruits, and to get ready to hit the next beach.

Mike thought longingly of lodgepole pines. If he lived a while in the Pacific, he'd see a lot of things. Not lodgepoles, though. He was about as far from lodgepole pines as a man could get.

When the phone in Charlie's White House office rang, he grabbed it. "Sullivan."

"This is the long-distance operator. I have a call for you from Thelma Feldman in New York City."

He started to tell her he didn't know anybody called Thelma Feldman. But hadn't Mike's editor at the *Post* been named Stan Feldman? On the off chance this was a relative, he said, "Put her through. I'll take the call."

He heard the operator tell the person who'd made the call to go ahead. She did, in a strong New York accent: "Mr. Sullivan?"

"That's right," Charlie said. "Are you Mrs. Feldman?"

"I sure am. Mr. Sullivan, the Jeebies, they grabbed my husband. They grabbed him and they took him away. You gotta help me, Mr. Sullivan! You gotta help me get him free!"

"I . . . don't know what I can do, Mrs. Feldman." Charlie hated calls like this. He got more of them than he wished he did. One would have been more than he wished he got. Reporters and their friends and relations knew he worked in the White House. They figured he had enough juice to square things when one of them got in trouble. The problem with that was, most of the time they were wrong.

"*Vey iz mir!*" Thelma Feldman screeched in his ear. "You gotta try! He didn't do nuttin'! Nuttin' bad! They came and they grabbed him!"

"Why do you think I can help your husband when I couldn't help my own brother? They arrested him years ago."

"You gotta try!" Mrs. Feldman started to bawl.

Charlie hated women who cried. It was so unfair. Not only that, it worked. "Give me your number, Mrs. Feldman," he said wearily. "I'll see what's what, and I'll call you back."

"You're an *oytser*, Mr. Sullivan. An absolute *oytser*!" she said. That wasn't a Yiddish word he knew; he hoped it meant something good. She gave him her phone number. He wrote it down. Then he hung up.

"Fuck," he muttered. He wished he had some bourbon in his desk drawer. Anesthesia would be welcome. He wouldn't have been the only man in history to stash a bottle like that, but he hadn't done it. Shaking his head, he trudged down the hall to wait on Vince Scriabin.

He had to wait for him as well as waiting on him. After half an hour, J. Edgar Hoover came out of Scriabin's office. "Hey, Sullivan." He bobbed his head at Charlie and walked on. You always thought he went through doorways more or less by accident, and that he was just as likely to bull through a wall.

"Well, Charlie, what is it today?" Scriabin asked when Charlie went in. It was always *something*—that was what he seemed to be saying.

Sighing, Charlie answered, "I just got a phone call from Thelma Feldman, Stan Feldman's wife. You know, Stan's the guy on the *New York Post*."

"Oh, sure. I know of him," Scriabin said. "So?"

"So the GBI has arrested him. His wife's upset. You can understand that. She wanted to know if there was anything

I could do for him. I've met him a few times. He's a nice enough guy. So"—Charlie spread his hands—"I'm seeing if there's anything I can do for him."

"No." Scriabin's voice was hard and flat. "We should have dealt with him a long time ago, but we finally got around to it."

"You must have figured everything the *Post* put out was Mike's fault." Charlie didn't bother to hide his bitterness.

"It wasn't that. The paper stayed unreliable long after your brother, ah, left. It still is. With luck, it will be less so now." As usual, Scriabin had no give in him at all.

"Do this one as a favor for me. Please. How often do I ask?" Charlie loved begging as much as anyone else would have. He did it anyhow, more as a backhand present for Mike than for Thelma Feldman.

"You could be worse." From the Hammer, that was no small concession. "Take it to the boss if you want to. Tell him I said you could. If he decides it's all right, then of course it is." As far as Scriabin was concerned, anything Joe Steele decided was right.

But begging from Joe Steele was even worse than doing it from Vince Scriabin. Again, Charlie wished for a shot of Dutch courage. He went upstairs. He had to wait for the President, too. Joe Steele received him in the oval study. He wasn't smoking, but it smelled of his pipe tobacco anyhow. "Well?" he said without preamble.

"Well, sir . . ." Charlie explained—again—what he wanted.

Before replying, Joe Steele did fill his pipe and light it. Maybe he used the time to think. Maybe he just let Charlie stew. Once he had the pipe going, he said, "No. Feldman is a troublemaker. He's been one for years. Some time in an encampment may straighten him out. I can hope so, anyway. We're too soft on these wreckers, Charlie. We aren't too rough on them."

"His wife asked me to do what I could," Charlie said dully. "I figured I owed her that much."

"Now you can tell her you've done it, and tell her with a clear conscience." Joe Steele sent up another puff of smoke. "Or is there anything more?"

"No, sir. Nothing more." Charlie got out of there. The

Jeebies could come for him, too, even now. Did Joe Steele have a clear conscience? If he didn't, he never let the world know. That came close enough, didn't it?

Charlie telephoned Thelma Feldman. He told her he'd talked to Scriabin and to the President, and that he'd had no luck. She screamed and wailed. He'd known she would. He said he was sorry, and got off the phone as fast as he could. Then he went to the watering hole around the corner from the White House and got plastered. It helped, but not nearly enough.

"**W**e have landed in Europe." Static on the shortwave set made General Omar Bradley's voice go snap, crackle, pop. "American, British, Canadian, and Polish troops have secured a beachhead in Normandy and are moving deeper into France. German resistance, though ferocious in spots, is lighter than expected. The Second Front has come."

"About time," Charlie said. Leon Trotsky wasn't the only person who thought so. Americans had been expecting the invasion for months. The Germans must have expected it, too, but they couldn't stop it.

Charlie hadn't known when the landing would come. If somebody told you something big like that, fine. If no one did, it was because you didn't need to know ahead of time. Charlie didn't love military security, but he saw the need for it.

"About time is right," Esther said—they were listening to the BBC in their front room. "Now we can give it to the Nazis like they deserve. I just hope some Jews in Europe will still be left alive by the time we knock them flat."

"Me, too, babe," Charlie said. "I've bent the boss' ear about it whenever I get the chance. Kagan does the same thing. And Trotsky's warned Hitler he's got no business killing people on account of religion."

"Hitler really listens to Trotsky, of course," Esther said. Charlie flinched. She went on, "And Trotsky never killed a Jew in his whole life."

"He didn't kill them because they were Jews. He killed them because they weren't revolutionary enough to suit him," Charlie said.

"Are they any less dead that way?"

"Um—no."

"Well, then." Instead of rubbing Charlie's nose in it some more, Esther changed the subject: "If we're finally on the Continent, that means we can see the end of the war, even if we can't touch it yet. And if the war looks won, that makes Joe Steele's chances for a fourth term better."

"Looks that way, yeah." Charlie figured Joe Steele would win the election in November unless the Nazis invaded Massachusetts—maybe even then. He might not get the most votes, although, with the war going well and more jobs than there were people to fill them, he was likely to. But whether he did or not, he would be recorded as winning. The people who counted ballots were in his pocket. Or enough of them were, in enough places in enough states.

"Dewey for the Republicans this time?"

"Looks that way," Charlie said again. "If their mustaches were running, Joe Steele's would win every state."

His wife giggled. "You're right about that. Say what you want about Joe Steele, but he's got a real mustache. Dewey looks like a lounge lizard. You can't take him seriously."

"I sure can't," Charlie said. He suspected part of the problem was that he and Dewey were about the same age. He still wanted to think of the President as something like a father. A father couldn't be the same age you were.

Of course, Joe Steele was the kind of father who took his country behind the woodshed with a strap. You had a tough time loving a father like that. People had always had a tough time loving Joe Steele. But they respected him, and he kept them on their toes.

Sarah came in to hear the last of that exchange. She seemed bigger and more grown-up every time Charlie looked at her. *How did she get to be six?* he wondered with a father's bemusement. "What's a lounge lizard?" she asked.

Charlie and Esther looked at each other. "You used it," Charlie said. "You explain it to her."

"Thanks a lot." Esther gave him a dirty look. She screwed up her face as she thought for a second. Then she said, "It's old-fashioned slang—"

"Are you and Daddy old-fashioned?" Sarah broke in.

"I wouldn't be a bit surprised," Esther said, which set Charlie laughing. She went on, "It's old-fashioned slang for someone who hangs around in bars and thinks all the girls are in love with him because he's so wonderful."

"But he really isn't?" Sarah wanted to make sure she had things straight.

"That's right." Esther nodded. Charlie made silent clapping motions. She'd done better with the explanation than he could have.

Patrick wandered in after her. He was carrying a picture book. He climbed up into his father's lap and said, "Read!" At two, he still talked like a telegram—the fewest words that would get the job done.

"Okay," Charlie said. "This is the story of Curious George and the Man with the Pink Pantaloons. They—"

He didn't get any further. "Read right, Daddy!" Pat said irately.

"Sorry," said Charlie, who wasn't. He'd played this game with the book ever since they got it. It made things more fun for him and drove his kid bonkers. Who could ask for better than that? "Well, anyway, Curious George and the Man with the Orange Socks—"

"Daddy!"

"Okay, okay. Now the Man with the Yellow Hat"— Charlie waited for Pat to smile in relief, then sprang his sneak attack—"knew that George was a curious little hippopotamus, and he—"

"Daddy!"

Mike smoked cigarette after cigarette as the amtrac rattled toward the next island. This one was called Saipan. The punishment brigade had spent more than six months waiting for another call. They had replacements for every casualty they'd taken on Tarawa. Mike wondered whether the new guys, who didn't know what they were getting into, were more or less nervous than the ones who'd lived through Tarawa and seen the kind of fight the Japs put up.

Mike didn't know the answer. He did know how nervous he was. The Japs wouldn't give up, no matter what. They fought till you killed them, and you had to be goddamn sure they were dead. You called them slanties and slopes and yellow monkeys so you wouldn't have to remind yourself they were men, and tough men at that.

Everything from destroyers to battleships to bombers had given Saipan a once-over the past few days. You wouldn't think an ant could have lived through that pasting, let alone an army. But they'd hit Tarawa with everything but the kitchen sink, too. As soon as soldiers got close enough for the Japs to start shooting them, they did. Mike figured it would be the same way here.

He spat out the butt of one Camel and lit another. The best he could hope for, he figured, the absolute best, would be to lose something like a foot or an arm and not be able to fight any more. Otherwise, they'd keep throwing him in till he got killed or the war ended, and the war didn't look like ending any time soon.

Was it worth it? he wondered. *If you had it to do over again, would you still have written those stories about Joe Steele?* Years too late to worry about it now, of course. One thing was plain: he'd underestimated how ruthless the man could be. He'd taken it for granted that the First Amendment and the whole idea of freedom of the press shielded him from anything a politician might do. He'd never dreamt he—or the country—would run into a politician who cared no more for the First Amendment than he did for the rest of the Constitution.

Then the amtrac's belly scraped on sand. The water drive stopped. The tracks churned. A bullet slammed into the steel, then another one. Mike stopped caring about the Constitution, too. All he cared about was living through the next five minutes—with luck, about living till tonight.

Down thumped the steel unloading door. "Get out!" yelled the sailors who crewed the ungainly beast. They wanted to get out of there themselves, and who could blame them?

Mike yelled like a fiend when he charged onto the beach. It wasn't to scare the Japs. It was to unscare him a little bit. He saw jungle ahead, more than he'd seen on Tarawa. That just meant the little yellow men here had more hiding places. They'd know how to use them, too.

Next to him, a guy from his squad folded up like an accordion and added his screams to the din all around. *That could have been me,* Mike thought. A bullet tugged at his trouser leg like a little kid's hand. It pierced the cotton, but not his flesh. If that was anything but dumb luck, he couldn't see what.

A couple of Americans with machine guns sprayed bullets into the bushes ahead. You didn't want to run in front of them, or they'd shoot you, too. Mike swerved to the left.

A Jap with a rifle popped up out of nowhere right in front of him. They stared at each other in horror for a split second, then fired at the same time. They couldn't have been more than a hundred yards apart, but they both missed. Shooting when your heart was pounding two hundred beats a minute and your mouth was dry with fear was no easy test. The Jap frantically worked the bolt on his Arisaka. Mike just pulled the trigger again. The semiautomatic M-1 fired. The Jap clutched his chest. He managed to get off another shot, but it went wild. He fell back into whatever hole he'd popped out of.

Of course, if Mike's first shot had been the last one in the magazine, it would have popped out with a neat little clink—and the Jap would have plugged him instead. One more time, the luck of the draw.

He crawled up to where he could see the opening in the ground the Jap had come from. He threw in three grenades, in case the son of a bitch had company in there.

Fighter planes raked Saipan with heavy-caliber machine guns and rockets. Bombers dropped more high explosives on the Japs' heads. The fleet offshore kept pounding away with everything up to fourteen-inch guns. And the American soldiers had tanks and flamethrowers along with their other toys.

Tojo's boys had no air support. No warships gave them a hand. But Japan had owned Saipan since the end of the First World War. The Japs had dug in but good, and camouflaged all their bunkers and dugouts and strongpoints. Anybody who wanted them dead had to come kill them, and they commonly took a deal of killing.

Still, once the Americans got off the beach and into the jungle, it was only a matter of time, and of how big the U.S. butcher's bill would be. American officers used the punishment brigade instead of Marines where things were hottest. That was what punishment brigades were for.

Mike acquired a flesh wound on his leg, another on his arm, and an abiding hatred for all American officers except the ones in his outfit. His hatred for the Japs, oddly, shrank each day as he killed them and they tried to kill him. They were in the same miserable boat he was. They had to stand and fight. He had to go to them and fight. If you didn't go to them, you either got shot on the spot by MPs who trailed the punishment brigade or you earned a drumhead court-martial and the services of a firing squad. If you went forward, you might make it. Mike went forward.

He lived. So did Luther Magnusson, despite a shrapnel gash along the side of his jaw. But the brigade, despite being built up again after Tarawa, melted away like a snowball in Death Valley.

Puffing greedily on a cigarette from a C-ration pack, Magnusson said, "I think the Germans are better professional soldiers than these guys. The krauts, they have the doctrine down like you wouldn't believe. Everybody does, generals down to privates. They know what to do, and they know how."

"These guys, all they do is mean it," Mike said. The wound on his arm didn't hurt, but it itched like a bastard. He scratched the bandage. You weren't supposed to do that, but everybody did.

"Yeah. That's about the size of it," Magnusson agreed.

Just how much the Japs meant it, he saw a few days later. Japanese soldiers with nowhere left to go charged the Americans behind a great red flag. Anyone who could walk, wounded or not, armed or not, went to his death hoping to take some of the enemy with him. And, since Japan had held Saipan for so long, there were civilians on the island, too. Thousands of them leaped to their deaths from cliffs on the eastern coast rather than yielding to the Americans.

"What can you do with people like that?" Mike asked when it was finally over.

"Damned if I know." After watching women throw children off a cliff and then jump into the Pacific after them, Captain Magnusson had the air of a man shaken to the core. Mike understood that; he felt the same way himself. It was like getting stuck inside a nightmare where you couldn't wake up and get away. As a matter of fact, combat in general was a lot like that. Luther Magnusson shook his head and spat. Quietly, he repeated, "Damned if I know."

Paris fell. Charlie heard there were practically orgies in the streets when the Allies entered the long-occupied French capital. The stories varied, depending mostly on the imagination of who was telling them. The Germans in France skedaddled toward the *Reich*.

In Italy, the Allies ground forward. The Germans there were stubborn. They'd hold a line as long as they could, then fall back a few miles and hold another one. The rugged terrain worked for the defenders.

And the Russians! Trotsky's men drove the Nazis back over the frontier they'd had before the Eastern Front exploded. Finland bailed out of the war. Romania switched sides with treacherously excellent timing. Bulgaria bowed out, too. Sure as the devil, Trotsky was going to gobble up most of the Balkans. Red Army tanks rolled all the way to the Vistula, to the suburbs of Warsaw.

Hitler still had a few cards up his sleeve. When Slovakia rebelled, he squashed it before the Russians could help. And he stopped Hungary from asking for an armistice by kidnapping the admiral who'd run the landlocked country and putting in a passel of Hungarian Fascist fanatics horrible enough to satisfy even him.

But the writing was on the wall. Most of the world could see it, even if Hitler couldn't or wouldn't. The Allies were going to win the war. The Axis was going to lose. It would happen sooner, not later.

In the United States, anybody who wanted work had it, and was probably making more money than he (or she—especially she) ever had in his (or her) life. Quite a few people who might not have wanted work were working hard anyway, in one or another of Joe Steele's labor encampments. By now, those had been around long enough, most of the country took them for granted. Why not? Most folks knew somebody or knew of somebody who'd got himself (or, again, herself) jugged.

Tom Dewey rolled and sometimes flew across the country as if his pants, or possibly his hair, were on fire. He promised to do better with the war and less with the labor encampments than Joe Steele was doing.

He couldn't say much else. But it would have been hard to do better with the war than Joe Steele was already doing in the fall of 1944. Anyone who paid any attention at all to the headlines or listened to the news on the radio could see that. And the labor encampments were old news. People took them in stride, the way they took bad weather in stride. You tried not to say anything stupid where some squealer could overhear it and pass it on to the Jeebies. And you got on with your life.

Charlie found Thelma Feldman's address in a New York City phone book. He put a hundred-dollar bill in an envelope with a sheet of paper folded around it so no one would know what it was. One Sunday, he told Esther he had to go in to the White House. Instead, he went to Union Station and took a train up to Baltimore. When he got there, he left the train station so he could drop the envelope in a street-corner mailbox. Then he turned around and went back to Washington.

He didn't want the editor's wife to know from whom the money came. He also didn't want anybody from the White House or the GBI to know he'd sent it. That kind of thing wasn't illegal, which didn't mean it couldn't land you in the soup.

Esther wouldn't have minded. If she'd known what he was doing, she would have kissed him or maybe even dragged him off to the bedroom to show what she thought of it. But not even the Jeebies could pull what she didn't know out of her.

Sometimes Charlie remembered the days when he didn't need to worry about things like that. He also remembered millions of people out of work, and his own fears of winding up in a bread line. So parts of life were better now, even if other parts were worse. Life was like that. If you got something, you mostly had to give up something else.

Joe Steele wasn't going to give up the White House, not to the likes of Tom Dewey. Charlie was convinced the President would win an honest election, maybe not so easily as he had against Alf Landon, but without any trouble. With the apparatus he had in place, chances were he wouldn't lose even if he told people to vote for the other guy.

He seemed to feel the same way. He asked for only a few campaign speeches from Charlie. His theme, naturally, was winning the war and staying prosperous after peace came. None of that was exciting, but Charlie could see it was what he needed to say.

With time on his hands—and with his conscience none too clear in spite of sending Thelma Feldman that C-note—he visited the watering hole around the corner from the White House more often than he had been in the habit of doing.

Every so often, he would run into John Nance Garner there. Garner was a drinker's drinker. He rarely seemed out-and-out drunk, but he rarely seemed sober, either. By all the signs, he started as soon as he got up and kept on till he went to bed. Not too much at once, but never very long without, either.

"Congratulations, sir," Charlie told him one afternoon. "You're the longest-serving Vice President in American history."

John Nance Garner glared at him. "Ah, fuck you, Sullivan. It don't mean shit, and you know it as well as I do."

Since Charlie did know, all he could say was, "I didn't mean it like that."

"Hell you didn't. It don't mean *shit*," Garner repeated with mournful emphasis. "Only way it means shit is if I'm still around when Joe Steele kicks the bucket. And you know what else? That ain't gonna happen, on account of I'm more than ten years older'n he is, an' on account of I bet he's got a deal with the Devil, 'cause he just don't get no older."

That wasn't true. Joe Steele was grayer and more wrinkled than he had been in 1932. But he hadn't aged as much as Garner since then. He also hadn't drunk as much. Charlie said, "I hope you both last a long time." Garner had to be more pickled than he looked to talk at all about Joe Steele dying. You couldn't pick a less safe subject.

He must be sure I won't rat on him, no matter how plastered he is, Charlie thought. That was a compliment, and not such a small one. It made Charlie feel better for the rest of the day.

When the election came, Joe Steele trounced Dewey. "I wish the President well," Dewey said in his concession speech, "because wishing the President well means wishing the United States well, and I love the United States, as I know Joe Steele does." Listening in the White House, Charlie glanced over at the President. Joe Steele didn't even smile.

XX

It was over. Half of it was over, anyhow. Along with every-body else in Washington, Charlie had gone nuts with joy over reports from German radio that Adolf Hitler had died fighting against the Russians in the blazing ruins of Berlin. Shortly afterwards, Radio Moscow claimed he'd done no such thing—he'd blown out his own brains in his fortified bunker when it finally dawned on him that the Nazis wouldn't win their war and the *Reich* wouldn't last a thou-sand years.

A few days later, the Germans surrendered uncondi-tionally. A reporter wound up in trouble for breaking the story before it became official. As an ex-reporter with a brother who'd got in trouble for what he'd reported, Char-lie sympathized. He still thought the guy was a prime jerk, though.

Slippery to the last, the Germans tried to give up to the Americans and English but not to the Russians. On Joe Steele's orders, Omar Bradley told them they could do it the way the Allies wanted or they could go back to fighting everybody. They did it the way the Allies wanted. They even staged a second ceremony in Berlin for the Red Ar-my's benefit. Marshal Koniev signed the surrender there for Leon Trotsky. The guns in Europe fell silent after almost six years.

Joe Steele went on the radio. "This is victory, victory in Europe, V-E Day," the President said. "And victory is sweet, no doubt of that. It is all the sweeter because it came against such a cruel and heartless foe."

Charlie grinned when he heard that. He'd suggested it. The reports on what the Nazis had done in their prison camps and their death camps still seemed impossible to believe. How could a famously civilized country go mad like that? But photos of skeletal corpses piled like cordwood had to be real. No one could be sick enough to imagine such things. No one except Hitler's thugs, anyhow. And they hadn't just imagined them. They'd made them real.

"And it is all the sweeter because it comes after so much pain and heartache," Joe Steele went on. "And so we deserve to celebrate—for a little while. Only for a little while, though. Because our job is not done. Japan still fights against the forces of freedom and democracy."

He could say that with a straight face, because Russia and Japan remained neutral to each other. Trotsky had promised Joe Steele and Churchill he would enter the war against the Japs. Of course he would—he wanted to grab as many goodies from the chaos convulsing Asia as he could. But he hadn't done it yet.

"Unless the Japanese follow the German lead and yield to our forces without conditions, we will treat their islands as we have treated Germany." Joe Steele sounded as if he looked forward to it. "We will rain fire and destruction from the skies upon them. We will make a desert, and it will be peace. If the Emperor of Japan and his servants do not think we are determined enough to follow through, they are making the last and worst in a long string of disastrous mistakes. The fire-bombing of Tokyo month before last was only a small taste of what they have to look forward to."

Charlie whistled softly. Beside him in the front room of their apartment, Esther nodded. Hundreds of B-29s had dropped tons of incendiaries on Tokyo in March. They'd burned—cremated was a better word—more than ten square miles in the heart of the Japs' capital. Tens of thousands died. Outside of Japan, nobody could be sure how many tens of thousands. Charlie didn't know if anyone inside Japan could be sure, either.

"So celebrate, Americans, but carry on. I know we will fight as well and as bravely in the Pacific as we did in Europe. I know that victory will be ours there as well," Joe Steele said. "And I know our country will be a better place once peace returns. Thank you, and God bless America."

"Like he said, one down, one to go," Charlie said.

"The big one down, as far as I'm concerned. Hitler wanted the whole world, and he came too close to getting it," Esther said. "I had cousins and aunts and uncles in Hungary. I don't know how many of them are still alive. I don't know if any of them are."

"Mike's still in the Pacific somewhere," Charlie said quietly. "If the Japs don't quit, we'll need an invasion that'll make the one in France look like a day in a rowboat on the Lake in Central Park."

"There is that," she said. "I hope he's all right, too. But that's all we can do, hope, same as with my kin. The Japs are never going to beat the United States, though, never in a million years. Hitler . . . If he'd flattened Trotsky fast, the way he tried, he might have got England, too. Then it would have been our turn. Oh, maybe not right away, but he wouldn't have waited real long."

That all sounded disturbingly likely to Charlie. Likely or not, though, it wouldn't happen now. Because Hitler couldn't do what he'd wanted to do, other things would happen instead. Charlie said, "Instead of Hitler, Joe Steele's watching Trotsky and the Reds."

"And Trotsky's worth watching." Esther sounded sad. "Nothing big will happen between us and the Russians till we KO Japan. We need each other till then. After that, watch out."

"Looks the same way to me." Charlie smiled a crooked smile. "And now that we've tied up all the world's problems in pink string and put a bow on them, what do you say we make some lunch?"

"Sounds good," Esther said. "We've still got some fried chicken from the other night in the icebox."

"Yum! But what will you eat?" Charlie said. Laughing, she poked him.

Mike gnawed on a D-ration bar. They were what the Army gave you to eat when you didn't have anything else. They were slabs of chocolate made to keep pretty much forever. They tasted something like a Hershey bar and something like a birthday candle. The wax or tallow or whatever it was made them chew like no chocolate bar you'd eat if you didn't have to.

Rain poured down. Mike's foxhole had six inches of water in it. It had started raining on Okinawa several days earlier, just after soldiers and Marines had beaten back a Jap counterattack from the Shuri Line. By all the signs, it could keep right on pouring for the next week, too. The downpour didn't make the war move any faster.

He'd heard about men who drowned in foxholes like this. His other choice was to stand up. If he did, the Japanese soldiers still in the Shuri Line would shoot him. They'd given up most of Okinawa without a big fight, but they were hanging on ferociously here in the mountainous south. The Americans had to dig them out one foxhole, one strongpoint, one tunnel at a time—and to pay the price for doing it.

Tarawa. Saipan. Angaur. Iwo Jima. Now Okinawa. Gnawing away on the hard, waxy chocolate, Mike thought, *I am a fugitive from the law of averages*. He had a Purple Heart with two oak-leaf clusters. He couldn't imagine going through the fights he'd been through without getting hurt. The miracle was, he'd come through them without getting maimed for life or killed. Damn few of the guys he'd trained with outside of Lubbock were still in there fighting. They'd been used, and they'd been used up.

Miracles did happen, of course. They didn't always happen to the good guys, either. Hitler had been a runner during the last war. He'd taken messages from the officers to the front-line trenches and back again, the kind of thing you had to do before there were radios and field telephones in every company. The usual life expectancy for a runner was measured in weeks. Hitler had done it all through the war. He'd got gassed once, not too badly, but that was it.

And much good it did him in the end. He was sure as hell dead now, and the Nazis had thrown in the sponge. Mike had heard that just before the last Jap counterattack. He'd been dully pleased, and that was about it. The enemy in front of him was not in a surrendering mood.

Eventually, the rain would stop. Eventually, the fighting would pick up again. Eventually, in spite of everything the

Japs here on Okinawa could do, they'd be exterminated. The Americans had too many men, too many guns, too many tanks, too many planes, too many bombs.

Suppose I'm still alive and in one piece when that happens, Mike thought. *What comes next?*

Motion seen from the corner of his eye distracted him. He swung his grease gun towards it. He'd picked up the submachine gun on Iwo. For the kind of close-quarters fighting the punishment brigade did, it was better than an M-1. If you sprayed a lot of lead around, some of it would hit something. That was what you wanted. (He'd also picked up his third stripe on Iwo, not that he cared.)

But this wasn't a Jap. "Jesus fucking Christ, Captain!" Mike burst out. "Get down in here! I almost drilled you!"

Luther Magnusson slid into the hole with him. He was all over mud. The Japs couldn't have seen him. But moving around above ground this close to the Shuri Line was dangerous. Machine guns and mortars meant they didn't have to see you to kill you. They could manage just fine by accident, or by that goddamn law of averages.

"Good," Magnusson said. "I was looking for you."

"Oh, yeah? How come?" A lot of the time, you didn't want an officer looking for you. But Magnusson was all right, even if he did still drink like a fish every chance he got. By now, they'd been through a hell of a lot, and a lot of hell, together. So many familiar faces gone. Magnusson was lucky, too, if you wanted to call this luck.

"Got something for you." The captain pulled a brand-new twenty-pack of Chesterfields, the kind you bought in the States, out of his breast pocket. The cellophane around the paper kept them dry and perfect. "Here you go."

"You didn't have to do that!" Mike yipped, which was an understatement. Magnusson had risked his life to deliver these cigarettes.

"No big deal," he said. Considering life as they lived it, he might not have been so far wrong.

"Well, smoke some with me, anyway." Mike draped a dripping shelter half over their heads so the downpour wouldn't drown their cigarettes. Magnusson's Zippo—painted olive drab to keep the sun from shining off the case and giving away his position—worked first time, every time. They puffed through a couple of fresh, fragrant, flavorful Chesterfields apiece. Then Mike said, "Those were terrific! Where'd you get 'em?"

Magnusson jerked his thumb back toward the north. "Took 'em from a colonel—no P, natch. He didn't need 'em any more. I figured they might as well not go to waste."

Yeah, real colonels got all kinds of goodies men in punishment brigades never saw. Fat lot of good that had done this one. He'd been brave to come up to the front with his men. Now he wasn't brave. Now he was just dead.

After one more cigarette, Mike asked, "How many of the old guys you think'll be left after we invade Japan?"

Magnusson looked at him. Along with being dirty, his face was also stubbly. So was Mike's. The closer you got to the front, the less time you had to worry about stupid things like how you looked. "You sure that's the question you wanna ask?" the captain said at last.

"Uh-huh." Mike nodded. "It's what I was thinking about when you went and dropped in at my mansion here." Franklin D. Roosevelt had lived in a mansion for real just about his whole life. And what had that won him? An end even nastier than most soldiers got, which was really saying something.

"Mansion, huh?" Mike squeezed a short chuckle out of Luther Magnusson. After a beat, the company CO went on, "Well, a few of us may still be hanging around. Or else none of us. Me, I'd bet on none, but I could lose. War's a crazy business."

"Man, you got that right," Mike said. "Okay, thanks. Pretty much the way I read the odds, too, but I wanted to see what somebody else thought. Other side of the coin is, we may all be gone before Okinawa's over with."

Magnusson leaned toward him under the shelter half and kissed him on the cheek. Mike was so caught off guard, he didn't even slug him. "I couldn't resist," the captain told him. "You say the sweetest things."

Mike told him what his mother could do with the sweetest things. To manage all of it, she would have needed more native talent, as it were, and more stamina than God issued to your garden-variety human being. "In spades," Mike added. "*You* can get off this fucking island with a Section Eight."

"Nah." More seriously than Mike had expected, Magnusson shook his head. "It's as near impossible as makes no difference for anybody from a penal brigade to get a psych discharge. The way the head-shrinkers look at it is, if you weren't crazy already, you never woulda signed up for an outfit like this to begin with."

"Oh." Mike chewed on that, but not for long. He nodded. "Well, shit, it's not like they're wrong." From behind them, American 105s threw death at the Shuri Line. A short round might take out this foxhole instead. Mike didn't waste time worrying about it. He couldn't do anything about it, so what was the point? The rain drummed down. He wondered if he could dig a little channel so it wouldn't get too deep in the hole. He pulled his entrenching tool off his belt. That, he might actually manage.

A couple of weeks after the Army announced the fall of Okinawa, Charlie got a card from Mike, addressed to him at the White House. It was a dirty card, not because it had a naked girl on it but because somebody's muddy bootprint did its best to obscure the message.

Charlie had to hold the card right in front of his nose to read it. It was short and to the point. *Call Ripley!* it said. *Still here—believe it or not.* Underneath that was a scrawled signature and *NY24601*. Charlie laughed. In spite of himself, the card sounded like his brother. So did sending it where he had.

"That's good news!" Esther exclaimed when he showed it to her. "Nice somebody's getting some." She and her folks weren't having much luck finding out if any of their Hungarian relatives survived. Magyar officials cared little for Jews. Their Red Army occupiers and overlords cared even less for letters from the United States.

"Half an hour after the mailroom clerk put the card on my desk, Scriabin walked in," Charlie said. "He asked me, 'How do you like having a hero for a brother?'"

"What did you tell him?"

"I said it was nice there was one in the family, anyhow. He kind of blinked and went away. Now I've got to call my mom and dad. I don't know how many cards they let those guys send."

It turned out that the elder Sullivans had also heard from Mike. Their card announced that he was alive and well and doing fine. It was the kind of card you sent to your parents, as the one Charlie had got was the kind you sent to your brother.

"Did you tell Stella?" Charlie asked his mother, figuring she'd miss no chance to rub it in with her ex-daughter-in-law.

But Bridget Sullivan said, "No. Hadn't you heard? She's engaged to one of those draft-dodging sheenies she works for."

"Mom . . ." Charlie said. No, his mother and father had never warmed to Jews, no more than they had to.

"Esther is all right," his mother said. "But the ones Stella works for, that's just what they are."

"Whatever you say." Charlie got off the phone as soon as he could. He relayed a censored version of his mother's message to Esther.

By the way his wife lifted an eyebrow, she could read between the lines. "Stella didn't tell me, but I suppose she wouldn't, all things considered. I hope she ends up happy, that's all. She never would have dumped Mike if the Jeebies hadn't taken him."

"I guess not." Charlie didn't want to think anything good about the gal who'd left his brother. Esther was probably right, but that had nothing to do with the price of beer, not to him.

"Let's hope they knock Japan for a loop before Mike has to go in," Esther said.

"Amen!" Charlie said. "The Japs, they're like a boxer on the ropes taking a pounding. The B-29s are flattening their cities one at a time. God only knows why they won't give up and say enough is enough. Joe Steele doesn't get it—I'll tell you that."

Esther's mouth narrowed into a thin, unhappy line. "I

don't know how you can stand to work at the White House," she said. "I can't understand why it doesn't drive you nuts."

He shrugged helplessly. "When I started there, all my other choices looked worse. And you know what? They still do. If I walk away, just tell 'em I quit, you think I won't go into a labor encampment inside of fifteen minutes? I sure don't think I won't. You want to raise two kids on what you'd make without me?"

"I don't want to do anything without you," Esther answered. "But I don't want your job to wear you down the way this one does, either."

Charlie shrugged again. "I like to think I do some good once in a while. Stas and me, we're the ones who can slow Joe Steele down sometimes. Not always, but sometimes. Scriabin and Kagan and J. Edgar Hoover, all they ever do is cheer him on. If they get a new speechwriter, you can bet your boots he'd be another rah-rah guy. That'd leave Mikoian even further out on a limb than he is already."

"How does he manage to hang on if he doesn't see eye-to-eye with most of the people in the White House?" Esther asked.

"Funny—I asked him pretty much the same thing once," Charlie said. "He looked at me, and he smiled the oddest smile you've ever seen in your life. 'How?' he said. 'I'll tell you how. Because if I go somewhere without my umbrella and it's raining when I come out, I can dance my way home between the raindrops. That's how.'"

"Nice work if you can get it—if you can do it, I guess I should say. If he can, good for him," his wife said. "But when *you* go out in the rain, you come home dripping wet like a normal person. And I wish you didn't have to."

"Well, so do I," Charlie said. "Now wish for the moon while you're at it."

Mike's pack weighed him down as he trudged along the wharf to the waiting troopship. He'd landed on Okinawa in April. Here it was six months later, and he was finally getting off the miserable island. That was the good news. The bad news was that the punishment brigade, rebuilt yet again, was going somewhere that promised to be even worse.

Operation Olympic, the brass was calling it. Kyushu. The southernmost Home Island. If Tojo's boys wouldn't say uncle, the United States would go in there and take their own country away from them. It would cost a lot of American lives. As one of the Americans whose life it was likely to cost, Mike knew that much too well. But the number of Japs who were going to get killed beggared the imagination.

And if Operation Olympic didn't convince the Emperor and Company the lesson Joe Steele wanted them to learn, Operation Coronet was waiting around the corner. That would seize Honshu, the main island. From what Mike had heard, something like a million men would go in if they needed that one. How many dead would come out was anybody's guess.

Mike had a section of his own now—a couple of dozen men to ride herd on. They'd all come into the brigade after he had. Captain Magnusson was still here. Or rather, he was here again. He'd taken a bullet in the leg, but by now he'd had time to recover and risk getting one in a really vital spot.

As the soldiers settled themselves on the crowded bunks, one of them asked, "Hey, Sarge, is it true what Tokyo Rose says?"

"Jugs, if Tokyo Rose says it, bet your ass it ain't true," Mike answered. "Which pile of bullshit are you wondering about in particular, though?"

Jugs was properly Hiram Perkins, a Southerner who'd wound up in a labor encampment because—he said—somebody with connections had taken a shine to his wife. It was possible; people went into the encampments for all kinds of reasons. Mike wouldn't have cared to guess if it was true. The way Perkins' ears stuck out gave him his nickname. He said, "The one where she says the Japs'll spear us if they don't shoot us."

"You've got a grease gun, don't you?" Mike said.

"No, Sarge. Got me an M-1."

"Okay. Either way, you can shoot anybody who comes after you with a spear before he sticks you, right?"

"I reckon so, yeah."

"Well, all right, then. You won't get speared unless somebody catches you asleep in a foxhole or something."

Jugs worked that through. Mike could practically see the gears turning inside his head. They didn't turn very fast; Jugs wasn't the brightest ornament on the Christmas tree. He finally said, "That makes sense. Thanks, Sarge. I purely don't like me no pig-stickers."

"Other thing is," Mike said, "if the Japs do come at us with spears, it's because they don't have enough rifles to go around. So let's hope they do. The easier they are to kill, the better I like it."

He wondered how many kamikaze planes the enemy had left. They'd been troublesome around Okinawa. Mike figured the Japs would throw everything they could at a force invading the Home Islands.

Later, he also wondered if he'd jinxed things. Less than half an hour after kamikazes crossed his mind, the troopship's antiaircraft guns started bellowing. Down in the bowels of the ship where the enlisted men waited out the passage from Okinawa to Kyushu, they swore or prayed, depending on which they thought would do more good.

In the bunk across from Mike, another Catholic worked a rosary. Mike still more or less believed, but not that way. God was going to do what He was going to do. Why would He listen to some stupid human who wanted Him to do something else instead?

No flaming plane with a bomb under its belly slammed into the troopship. Either the gunners shot it down, or it missed and smashed into the sea, or the pilot was aiming at some other ship. The Japs were terribly, scarily, in earnest. The way their soldiers fought showed that. But kamikazes? Didn't you have to be more than a little nuts to climb into a cockpit and take off, knowing ahead of time that you weren't coming back? The things some people would do for their country!

Mike started to laugh. What *he'd* done for his country was volunteer for a punishment brigade. And his country had rewarded him how? By sending him to hell five different times. It hadn't managed to kill him off yet, so here he was, going in for a sixth try at suicide. What was he but a slow-motion kamikaze pilot?

The guy who was telling his beads paused between one Our Father and the next. "What's so funny?" he asked.

"Nothing," Mike said. "Believe me, nothing."

"Too bad. I could use a yock," the other soldier said, and went back to the rosary.

When they scrambled down nets from the troopship to the landing craft, that green to the north rising up out of the sea was the Japanese mainland. The punishment brigade was going in on the west side of Kagoshima Bay, a little south of the middle-sized city of Kagoshima. Orders were to push toward the city once they got off the beach. Those orders assumed they *would* get off the beach. That had to mean the fellow who wrote them was a damned optimist.

To be fair, the USA was doing everything it knew how to do to keep its men alive, even the ones in punishment brigades. Warships shelled the coast, sending clouds of dust and smoke into the air. Fighter-bombers raked the landing zone with machine guns, rockets, and firebombs made from jellied gasoline. From farther overhead, heavier bombers flying out of Okinawa and Saipan and other islands bloodily taken from the Japs dropped high explosives on the enemy.

Mike had been through the preliminaries too many times before to think they'd murder all the Japs waiting to murder him. No matter how much hellfire you rained on the bastards, you killed only a fraction of them. The rest would require more personal attention.

Even now, the Japs were trying to fight back. Shells kicked up waterspouts among the wallowing landing craft. Just by the luck of the draw, a few of those would be direct hits, and God help the poor fools in those boats.

The landing craft mounted .50-caliber machine guns as token antiaircraft protection. Suddenly, all of them seemed to start going off at once. Tracers stitched across the sky.

Some kamikazes went after the bigger warships and freighters. Some pilots decided they'd be doing their duty for the Emperor if they took out a landing craft's worth of Americans. They weren't so far wrong, either—if they could do it. A lot of them got shot down trying, or else missed their intended targets and went into the drink.

One flew terrifyingly low over Mike's landing craft, so low he got a split-second glimpse of the young pilot's face. Then the kamikaze was gone. Whatever he did, Mike never found out about it.

A swabby manning the .50 that had been banging away at the Jap flyer sang out: "Beach just ahead! Good luck, you sorry assholes!"

Mike would be happy to take all the good luck he could get. The Japs knew the Americans were coming. Kagoshima Bay was the closest part of the Home Islands to Okinawa. You didn't have to be a military genius to see what that meant. All you had to do was look at a map.

So they'd put mines in the beachside water. A couple of landing craft hit them and went up with a boom. But the one Mike was riding made it onto the sand of Kyushu. Down went the landing gate.

"Come on, you fuckers!" Mike shouted to the men he would lead for as long as he could. He dashed out. They followed. His boots scuffed across the Japanese beach.

People were shooting at him again. That seemed to happen every goddamn time he visited a new island. The only polite thing to do was to shoot back.

A Corsair roared in at just above treetop height, almost as low as the kamikaze had passed over the landing craft. It machine-gunned and napalmed the ground in back of the beach. Mike whooped when the fireball from the napalm sent black, greasy smoke into the sky. He whooped again when he realized a lot less Jap fire was coming in. That Navy plane had done some good.

"Keep moving!" he called. "The farther off the beach we get, the better off we are." He didn't know that was true, but he hoped like hell it was.

Enemy fire picked up again. The Japs were doing everything they could to drive the invaders into the ocean. As if to underline that, a soldier stepped on a land mine. What happened next reminded Mike of an explosion in a butcher's shop. He had nightmares often enough as things were. That memory would only make them worse.

Pretty soon, his boots were thumping, not scuffing. Whenever he saw anything moving ahead, he squeezed off a burst. He assumed anyone alive here would try to kill him with even a quarter of a chance.

You weren't supposed to shoot civilians. Then again, they weren't supposed to shoot at you, either. A gray-haired man in farmer's clothes fired a rifle at him. The range wasn't long, but the fellow missed. A big puff of white smoke poured from his weapon. Mike greased him before he could duck back into his hole. Then he ran up to make sure the guy was dead.

He was, or he would be in a few minutes. Half his head was blown off. Mike stared at the piece he was carrying more than he did at the horrible wound. It looked like something a farmer might make for himself. The Jap had a powder horn with black powder in it. He had percussion caps. His bullets were half-inch lengths cut from an iron bar. When Mike looked down the barrel, he saw it wasn't even rifled. It looked to have been made from ordinary metal pipe. The whole setup belonged to 1861, not to 1945.

But by the end of the day he'd seen three or four more of those smoothbore muskets, all in the hands of civilians. Jap soldiers here carried Arisakas, the same as they did everywhere else he'd been. Those weren't as good as M-1s, but they were reasonable military weapons. The muskets . . . You could make stacks of them in a hurry and pass them out to anybody who wanted to use them.

They wouldn't do much good. They weren't a whole lot more dangerous than the spears Jugs had heard Tokyo Rose talking about. When you fired one, the smoke that burst from the muzzle yelled *Here I am!* to the world. With a smoothbore, you'd hit a man out past fifty yards only by luck.

What the makeshift weapons did say was that the Japs aimed to fight to the last man. Their soldiers had done that everywhere Mike had seen. He remembered the women on Saipan throwing their children off the cliffs and then jumping after them. Here in the Home Islands, it would be even worse.

And it was. Some of the people with those muskets weren't old men who hadn't gone overseas. Some were young women and girls. You had to shoot them, or they would shoot you. Mike hadn't puked since Tarawa, but killing a musketeer in a kimono damn near did it for him.

A guy in his section, a burly fellow who went by Spider from a tattoo on his left forearm, didn't kill one of those lady musketeers. He just wounded her. When he went up to see if he could save her and take her prisoner, she waited till he got close, then blew herself up with a grenade, and him with her.

From then on, the guys in Mike's section shot first and didn't ask questions even afterwards. That had to violate the laws of war. He didn't worry about it. The Japs weren't playing by the rules, either. If they armed civilians and sent girls into battle, they had to take their chances.

American Sherman tanks clanked forward. Mike was happy to trot along behind one for a while. It was like having a shield that also blew things up and killed things for you. The Japs had only a handful of tanks, and the ones they did have were no match for Shermans. Mike had heard that Shermans were death traps against German panzers, but they were almost unstoppable on this side of the world.

Almost. Something exploded under the one Mike was following. Fire and smoke burst from the hatches. A couple of crewmen got out. The rest . . . didn't. Mike peered under the Sherman's flaming carcass. An arm hung out of a hole in the ground. A Jap had been in there with an antitank mine or an artillery shell. He'd killed himself when he set it off, but he'd killed the tank, too.

"Fuck," Mike muttered. He lit a cigarette, wishing he had whiskey in his canteen. How were you supposed to fight people like this? Most military planning assumed that the other guy wanted to live as much as you did. The Japs tore up that rule and danced on it.

Fighting barely slowed down when night fell. The Japs kept coming, wave after wave of them. Mike snatched a little sleep like an animal, curled up in a hollow. Nothing this side of getting wounded would have woken him.

Firepower let the Americans push forward. The only planes in the sky had stars on their wings and fuselages. The Japs fought for Kagoshima street by street, house by house, just the same.

Eating C-rations behind a wrecked building, Mike said, "This must be what Trotskygrad was like."

One of his men nodded wearily. By then, the section was down to seven guys: less than a squad's strength. The tired soldier said, "That reminds me, Sarge. I heard the Russians are finally fighting the Japs with us."

"About time," Mike said between bites of canned ham and eggs. The ration wasn't bad if you heated it. You could eat it straight from the can, the way he was, but you'd like it less. He went on, "I sure as hell wish they'd come fight the ones we got here."

"There you go," the soldier said.

Something blew up near them. "Here we go," Mike said, and made sure he had a full magazine on his grease gun.

XXI

Charlie had put a *National Geographic* map of the Home Islands on the wall in his office. Blue pins measled Kyushu. Nothing at all was left of Nagasaki, near the westernmost part of the island. B-29s full of incendiaries had annihilated the old port city even more thoroughly than they'd leveled Tokyo. Kagoshima? Fukuoka? Miyazaki? Likewise names for places that were no longer there.

Also no longer there were too many thousands of American soldiers. As far as Charlie knew, Mike was still okay, but he didn't know how far he knew. Japanese casualties, military and civilian? Nobody had any idea, not to the nearest hundred thousand.

Farther north, red pins measled Hokkaido the same way. The Russians had swept through the southern half of the island of Sakhalin, which they'd lost in the Russo-Japanese War. They'd swept across the Kuril Islands. They'd roared into what had been Japanese Manchukuo and Chosen, and what were now nominally part of China (though still under Trotsky's thumb) and the People's Democratic Republic of Korea under a native Red called Kim Il-sung, which was every bit as independent as Father Tiso's Slovakia had been under the Nazis.

And the Red Army had invaded Hokkaido, the northernmost Home Island. The Russians had had just as much fun there as the Americans had in Kyushu. The Japs fought as if there were no tomorrow. For them, there mostly wasn't.

But they wouldn't quit. They had no idea how to quit. The Emperor and his generals ruled only Honshu and Shikoku. They still bellowed defiance at the rest of the world. The rest of the world responded with incendiaries and high explosives. The Japs shot back when they could. They sent raiding parties to harass the Allies occupying Kyushu and Hokkaido.

So Coronet was on—was, in fact, only a couple of weeks away, from what Charlie'd heard. With it would come a Russian invasion of northern Honshu. The whole campaign would be an enormous, bloody mess. Everybody knew it. But how else could you knock out an enemy who wouldn't quit on his own?

As Charlie didn't know for sure that Mike was all right, he also didn't know whether his brother's punishment brigade was part of the invasion force for Operation Coronet. He feared it was, though. You served in a punishment brigade for the duration: yours or the war's. Usually, it was yours. Mike still had a chance of coming back, though.

Charlie was studying the map and trying to stay hopeful when Lazar Kagan came in and said, "Got a question for you."

"Shoot," Charlie said. Whatever Kagan asked him, it would help take his mind off the bad reflections the map of the Home Islands stirred in him.

"What do you know about uranium?" Kagan said.

Charlie stared. As a matter of fact, Charlie gaped. "I don't know what the hell I thought you'd ask me, but I could've guessed for a million years before I came up with that one," he said. "Why?"

"I'll tell you why in a minute. Tell me what you know first." Kagan sounded serious. Charlie couldn't remember the last time Kagan hadn't sounded serious. He had none of Mikoian's occasional impishness. To give him his due, he also wasn't so nasty as Vince Scriabin.

"O-kay." Charlie flogged his brains. He got tiny little bits from high school chemistry he'd done his best to forget over the intervening quarter-century and more, and a few others from science stories before the war. "It's an element. Is it ninety-one or ninety-two? Ninety-two, I think. And it's—what's the word? Radioactive, that's it. Like radium, only it doesn't glow in the dark, does it? And—" He stopped with a shrug. "And that's about it. How'd I do, Mr. Baker?"

"Heh," Kagan said. Phil Baker had hosted *Take It or*

Leave It, the radio quiz show with questions that kept doubling in value till they got to sixty-four dollars, since before the Japs hit Pearl Harbor. After a moment, though, Kagan grudged a nod. "You did pretty well. Better than Vince and me, better than Hoover, about as well as Stas."

Mikoian's brother knew science, being an engineer. Maybe some had rubbed off on Joe Steele's aide. "Now you've got to tell me why you asked me," Charlie said.

Lazar Kagan nodded again. "All right, I will. But it goes no further. Not even your wife, you hear? I'm serious about this. So is Hoover. So is the boss. If you don't think you can do that, forget I ever asked you."

"I know when to keep my mouth shut. I'll keep it shut now." Charlie would have liked to tease Kagan, but that didn't look like a good idea, not if he wanted to find out what was what.

Even as things were, Lazar Kagan hesitated. He must have seen he'd gone too far to stop, though. "You're right—uranium's radioactive. But that's not all. It turns out you can *split* the right kind of uranium atom. When you do, you release energy—a lot more than you can get from dynamite or TNT. I mean, a lot more, enough so one bomb could blow up a whole city. The Germans were working on this during the war, we've found out. They didn't get too far, thank God, but they were trying."

One bomb, one city? Charlie's mind spun dizzily. It sounded like one of those stories you read in the pulps with the robots and the little green men on the cover. But Kagan sounded as serious as he ever did, which was saying something. "The Germans were working on this, you say?" Charlie asked. Kagan nodded yet again. Charlie found the next question with no trouble at all: "How come we weren't, too? If we weren't."

"We weren't." Kagan spoke the words like a judge passing sentence. "As to why we weren't . . . It is possible that there have been wreckers inside the scientific community."

Charlie didn't burst out laughing. He remembered that Mikoian had said his brother had said the same thing. He hadn't believed it then, and he didn't believe it now. But he didn't want to cut his own throat, either.

And it was just as well that he kept his mouth shut and his features still, for Lazar Kagan went on, "Einstein is coming down from Princeton to discuss this with the boss. Since you know a little something, maybe you should sit in on the meeting—it's tomorrow at ten. I'll talk to the boss. Unless I tell you otherwise, you're in."

Once more, Charlie didn't laugh in Kagan's face. A little something was what he knew about uranium, all right! Accent on *little*. Before he went home that night, he stopped at the public library, yanked the *Britannica* off the shelf, and read what it had to say about uranium and radioactivity. He took no notes; if the Jeebies found them, he figured they'd shoot him before they questioned him. The encyclopedia said nothing about splitting any kind of uranium atoms. Well, that made sense—it wasn't exactly common knowledge.

As ordered, he didn't tell Esther anything about uranium or Einstein. She noticed he had something on his mind, even if she didn't know what. "You okay?" she asked him. "You're kind of not quite with it tonight."

"Work stuff," he answered, as lightly as he could. "I can't talk about it yet."

"Oh." She left it there—she respected that. She wasn't the kind of person who tried to pry business out of him, for which he was duly grateful.

When he took his seat in the conference room the next morning, three places down from Joe Steele, he wondered how much he remembered of what he'd read. And he wondered how much what wasn't in the encyclopedia made what he did remember obsolete.

Also sitting in with the President were his three California cronies, J. Edgar Hoover, and a scholarly-looking Navy captain named Rickover. A White House staffer led Einstein in a few minutes after ten. "Mr. President," the physicist said in good but accented English.

"Professor Einstein," Joe Steele replied. "Sit down, please. Do you want coffee or anything like that?" His voice was under tight control. His face showed nothing at all.

"Thank you so much, but no," Einstein said as he slid into a chair across the table from the President.

"All right, then," Joe Steele said. "I have learned that the

Germans were trying to make a bomb, a very powerful bomb, from uranium. They don't seem to have tried too hard, but some of my military men who reviewed their work"—he nodded toward Captain Rickover—"tell me this might be possible."

Einstein nodded sadly. Sadness seemed to live naturally on his face. "Yes. This is possible, I am sorry to say. I have understood that it is possible since I learned of the Hahn-Meitner experiments at the end of 1938 or the beginning of 1939." Charlie'd never heard of the Hahn-Meitner experiments. They weren't in the *Britannica*. Plainly, Rickover had; he leaned toward the President and whispered something.

Joe Steele waved his words aside. He turned the full force of his will on Einstein. "You knew of this for so long, but you said nothing about it?" The question was all the more fearsome for being so soft.

"Yes, sir." If it put Einstein in fear, he didn't let on.

"Why?" Joe Steele asked, more softly yet.

"Because I was afraid you would build this bomb, sir. Because I was afraid you would use it." Einstein didn't say *Mene, mene, tekel, upharsin*. The words tolled inside Charlie's head all the same. *Thou art weighed in the balances, and art found wanting.*

And the writing was on the wall for Albert Einstein, too. Just for a moment, Joe Steele's calm mask slipped and showed the raw, red rage underneath. Charlie flinched away from the President, as he would have flinched away from a furnace door that suddenly opened and blasted heat in his face.

"You deprived the United States of a weapon that might have won the war sooner?" Joe Steele hissed.

"I tried to stop, or at least to delay, the birth of a weapon that may destroy the world," Einstein said calmly.

Joe Steele swung toward J. Edgar Hoover. "Tend to him. He's not just a wrecker. He's the king of wreckers."

Hoover nodded. "I'll take care of it." He bounced to his feet and hustled out of the room. Einstein watched him go with what looked like mild interest. As the President did, the physicist smoked a pipe. He took it out and started charging it with tobacco.

He never got the chance to finish. Hoover came back with four burly Jeebies. Had they been waiting outside for a moment like this? They must have. They hauled Einstein out of the chair and hustled him away. The pipe fell on the floor. One of the GBI men picked it up and stuck it in his pocket on his way out.

As if such things happened at the White House every day, Joe Steele asked Captain Rickover, "With what you know now, can you go on and finish the job?"

"Yes, sir, I think so," Rickover said. "There will be engineering issues to overcome, but it should be doable."

"How long? Six months? A year? You'll have whatever resources you need."

"I fear it may take longer than that, sir. We'll be doing things no one has ever done before, you know. The Germans barely even opened the door. We have to go through it."

"You will not waste time." Joe Steele sounded like Moses coming down from Mount Sinai hurling *Thou shalt not*s at the children of Israel. "The Reds will know about this, too. So will the English, for that matter."

"If you think you can find someone better to run the project, sir, put him in charge instead of me," Rickover said. "If you don't, I'll do the best I can."

"That will do. I hope that will do," Joe Steele said.

"Whatever resources I need, you said?" Rickover asked him.

"That's right." The President gestured impatiently. "What about it?"

"Some of the people who could help me a lot on this project are serving terms in labor encampments on one charge or another," Rickover said. "If I can get them released—"

"You can use them," Joe Steele said. "They'll be released if they do what I need fast enough. In the meantime, we'll set up your project as a special labor encampment. If they do any more wrecking, we'll dispose of them. Be plain about that when you recruit them, understand me?"

"Yes, sir. I will do that, sir," Rickover said.

"All right, then. Go ahead."

Charlie took his courage in both hands and asked, "Sir,

what will you do with Einstein? He's too famous just to bump off."

"We took him in when he had to run from Hitler. This is how he thanks us? By keeping quiet about something so important?" Joe Steele shook his head. "I said it before—he is the king of wreckers. He will get what he deserves. Any of the others we took in who also kept still about this, they will get it, too." His eyes warned that, if Charlie said one more word, he would get some, too.

He even had a point . . . of sorts. But Einstein might have said more had he thought more of the man to whom he would be saying it. As one of that man's aides, Charlie was in no position to point out such things. He kept quiet. *Poor Einstein*, he thought.

Mike squatted in a cratered field, stripping and cleaning his grease gun. Not far away lay the highway that ran from Kyoto to Tokyo. American forces were supposed to have cut the road already. They had cut it, in fact. A Jap counterattack had opened it again, at least for a little while.

Several men from Mike's company stood guard while he cared for his weapon. He was still a sergeant, but he headed a company anyhow. Nobody who'd been a scalp in an encampment would ever make officer's rank, even if he commanded a regiment. Captain Magnusson had commanded a regiment till he picked up another leg wound. He was on the shelf again, but he was supposed to get better.

Here on Honshu, they actually had fought girls carrying spears. Jugs would have laughed if he hadn't stopped a machine-gun round with his nose outside of Nagasaki. Mike hadn't thought it was funny. He didn't want to kill those high school kids. They sure as hell wanted to kill him, though. Sometimes you didn't get many choices, not if you wanted to go on breathing.

He clicked the magazine back into place and chambered a round. "Okay," he said. "Let's get moving."

One of his men, a nervous little greaser named Gomez, pointed west along the highway. "Maybe we better hold up a second, Sarge," he said. "Looks like something's comin' towards us."

"Well, shit," Mike said mildly. "When you're right, you're right. I don't wanna fuck with Jap tanks."

The Japs didn't have many. They never had. The ones they did have weren't as tough as American Shermans. That didn't mean they were anything foot soldiers wanted to face, though. Mike could have yelled for one of the company's bazooka teams. But stalking the tanks wouldn't be easy—there wasn't much cover close by the road. He lit a cigarette instead. He'd done plenty of fighting for his country. He knew he'd do more, but not right this minute.

There were four tanks: two, then a gap, then two more. And in the gap . . . "Well, will you look at that?" Mike said. "I wonder who the big shot is." In the gap, plainly being escorted by all that armor, came a plain black car. A Japanese flag fluttered on a small staff—it could have been a radio aerial—sticking up from the right front fender.

"Some general, I betcha," Nacho Gomez said.

He didn't suggest going after the important Jap. The men with Mike hadn't seen as much as he had. But they'd all seen plenty, even if the landing west of Tokyo was their first and not their third or their sixth. They were still ready to fight. Nobody was eager any more. Sooner or later—probably sooner—those tanks would run into American armor. That would take care of that.

As a matter of fact, that got taken care of even sooner than Mike expected. Half a dozen Hellcats screamed down out of the sky. Flame rippled under their wings as they fired air-to-ground rockets at the tanks and the car. Their heavy machine guns hammered away, too.

Tanks were hideously vulnerable to strikes on the engine decking and on top of the turret. Their armor was thinnest there, not that Japanese tanks carried real thick armor anywhere. Tank designers didn't worry—or hadn't yet worried—about their creations being attacked from the air.

Three of the tanks burned like torches. So did the passenger car. The fourth tank didn't seem badly damaged. It stopped just the same. The whole crew—all five men—

jumped out and ran to the blazing car. They paid no attention to anything else in the world.

"Come on, boys," Mike said. "Let's see what they've got ants in their pants about."

Disposing of the tank crew was the easiest thing he'd done since hitting the beach at Tarawa two and a half years before. A brass band, complete with high-kicking majorettes, could have come up to the Japs and they never would have noticed. The Americans shot four of them before the last one finally spun around, pistol in hand. He managed to fire once, wildly, before he went down, too.

Mike finished him with a shot to the head at point-blank range. Then he said, "What did they think was more important than watching their backs?"

The Japs had managed to drag one man out of the car. The pants on his good Western suit were still smoldering, but it didn't matter. Two heavy machine-gun bullets from a Hellcat had caught him square in the middle of the chest. Shock alone might have killed him. If it hadn't, those .50-caliber rounds, big as a man's thumb, had torn up his heart and lungs but good—he was dead as shoe leather.

He'd been in his mid-forties, on the skinny side, with buck teeth and a mustache. Ice walked up Mike's back as he recognized him. The only Japanese face that might have been more familiar to an American was Tojo's, and Tojo had died in battle leading troops against the Coronet landings.

"Holy shit," Nacho said softly, so Mike wasn't imagining what he thought he was seeing.

"Fuck me up the asshole if this isn't Hirohito. We—the planes, I mean—just sent the goddamn Emperor to his goddamn ancestors." Mike kept staring at the scrawny little corpse.

So did the rest of the Americans. "If the Japs don't quit now, with him dead, they ain't never gonna," Nacho Gomez said.

That they wouldn't quit even now struck Mike as much too likely. But they might. Clobber somebody hard enough and often enough and the message had to get through sooner or later . . . didn't it? He could hope so, anyway.

"If they quit . . ." He had to try twice before he could get it out: "If they do quit, the fuckin' war's over." His stunned wits started to work again. "Nacho!"

"Yes, Sergeant?" Nacho couldn't have sounded so crisp since escaping from basic training.

"Haul ass back there and bring up somebody with a radio or a field telephone. We gotta let the brass know pronto," Mike said. Nacho nodded and started to dash away. Mike held up a hand to stop him. "Hang on, man! Bring up all the reinforcements you can grab, too. If the Japs find out what happened to Hirohito, sure as hell they're gonna want his carcass back, and we'll have a big fucking fight to worry about."

"I'm on it, Sergeant." The greaser took off toward the rear at a dead run. Mike envied his speed. Well, the kid was less than half his age and probably hadn't been in an encampment all that long before he decided a punishment brigade made a better bet.

He might even have been right. Who would have imagined that even half an hour earlier?

Mike pulled his entrenching tool off his belt and started digging a foxhole. Any time you were going to stay in one place longer than a few minutes, any time you thought you'd have a fight on your hands, a hole in the ground was your best buddy. Even a shallow scrape with some dirt in front of it helped. The more time you had, the deeper you dug. It was that simple.

The rest of the Americans followed his lead. It was just as well they did, too, because Japanese soldiers did start coming up to see what had happened to their tanks—and to the car those tanks were escorting. The Americans' rifle and grease-gun fire kept them at a distance till . . .

The cavalry came to their rescue. It wasn't quite like a Western serial, but close enough. Some of the soldiers who hurried up with Nacho Gomez did ride in jeeps and half-tracks. Those tough little vehicles came as close to the days of the Old West as anything in modern warfare.

A lieutenant colonel who didn't have a P on his sleeve crawled up to look the corpse over for himself. He might not serve in a punishment brigade, but the way he moved said he'd been around the block a time or three. He nodded to Mike, whose foxhole lay closest to Hirohito. "That's him, all right," he said. "I was posted to our embassy here in the late Thirties. I saw him several times at parades and such, once or twice up close. No doubt about it."

"Yes, sir," Mike said. "People know what he looks like."

"They sure do." The officer didn't treat him like a nigger because he *did* wear a P, which was nice. The man gestured someone else forward: a photographer, who started immortalizing the fact that the Emperor of Japan was mortal.

"Sir, what do you think the Japs will do now?" Mike asked.

"Damned if I know," the light colonel answered. "I hope they give up, but who knows? What have they got left to fight for?" He pointed north. "It isn't just us, either. It's the Russians, too. We smashed the Germans between us till there was nothing left. If we have to, we'll treat the Japs the same way."

"Here's hoping we don't have to." Mike had had enough war for any hundred men.

"Yeah, here's hoping," the officer said. "But we'll just have to wait and see."

"My God!" Charlie stared out the window of the President's airliner in awe and disbelief. "Will you *look* at that?"

Lazar Kagan sat beside him. "Lean back a little so I can," Kagan said. Charlie did. Kagan looked, then shook his head. "Not much left of the place, is there?"

"Hardly anything," Charlie said. They were flying low over what was left of southern Honshu. Till Hirohito bought a plot, the Japanese had fought with everything they had, from tanks and fighter planes down to teeth and fingernails. They'd killed hundreds of thousands of Americans, and probably a similar number of Red Army men. Whether you called that surpassing bravery or surpassing insanity depended on how you looked at things. Japanese casualties ran way up into the millions, and that was just talking about deaths. Then you added in the maimed, the crippled, the blinded . . . Not much was left of what had been a great country, even if you didn't like it.

Only after Hirohito was dead, and was known to the Japs to be dead, did they despair at last. American officers had sensibly kept ordinary American soldiers from mistreating the corpse. They'd put it on ice, in fact, to keep it as fresh as they could. And, when the Japs asked for it, they gave it back under flag of truce so it could be cremated.

That polite gesture also helped spur the surrender. Farther north, Trotsky's men hadn't done anything so accommodating. But even the Japs could see they had no chance to resist the Russians once they'd yielded to the United States. The brigadier general who'd signed that surrender document slit his belly immediately afterwards to atone for his shame, but the surrender remained in force.

The airliner was descending toward the small, no-account town of Wakamatsu. No-account or not, it was the biggest place on the Agano River, which marked most of the border between American-occupied Japan to the south and Russian-occupied Japan to the north. Joe Steele had come halfway around the world and Leon Trotsky was coming a quarter of the way around the world to talk about what they wanted to do with Asia.

Trotsky was already making his ideas all too clear. He had his Red boss in Korea, which his troops had taken from the Japs. Manchukuo went back to being Manchuria and to belonging to China, but the Red Army handed it—and all the Japanese weapons captured there, and no doubt some Russian weapons as well—to Chinese Red Mao Tse-tung, not to Chiang Kai-shek, the U.S.-backed President of China. Mao and Chiang had been squabbling long before the Japs swarmed into China. Now that the Japs were gone, they could pick up where they'd left off.

And the Russian half of Japan had been tagged the Japanese People's Republic. Trotsky'd found some Japanese Reds the *Kempeitai* hadn't hunted down and murdered. They were puppets for Field Marshal Fyodor Tolbukhin, who gave the orders—well, after he got them from Trotsky.

American-held Japan—the southern half of Honshu, Kyushu, and Shikoku—currently wore the clumsy handle of the Constitutional Monarchy of Japan. Hirohito's son, Akihito, was not quite thirteen. He was the constitutional monarch, though the constitution hadn't been finished yet. As the Japanese Reds took their marching orders from Marshal Tolbukhin, Akihito's main job was to do whatever General Eisenhower told him to do.

Clunks and bumps announced that the landing gear was lowering. The plane landed smoothly enough. The runway was brand new, made by U.S. Army engineers. Wakamatsu had been bombed—Charlie didn't think any towns in Japan hadn't been bombed—but the surrender came before it saw an infantry battle. Some of the buildings were still standing, then.

Humid late-summer air came in when the airliner's door opened. Charlie wrinkled his nose; that air held the stench of death. He'd smelled it even more strongly down on Kyushu, where the plane had stopped to refuel. It was older there, but the fighting had been worse.

Trotsky's plane landed an hour after Joe Steele's. Watching it come in, Charlie thought it was a DC-3. But it wasn't: it was a Russian model no doubt based on the Douglas workhorse, but one that sported a dorsal machine-gun turret.

Joe Steele greeted Trotsky on the runway. This was between the two of them. Clement Attlee, the new British Prime Minister, had no horse in this race. And Russia and the USA were the countries that counted in this brave new postwar world.

Photographers Red and capitalist snapped away as the two leaders shook hands. "The war is over. At last, the war is over," Joe Steele said. "I thank you and the Red Army for your brave aid in the victory against Japan."

"We were glad to help our ally," Trotsky replied through his translator. *We were glad to help ourselves,* Charlie realized that meant. But the Red leader hadn't finished yet: "And I thank you and the U.S. Army for your brave aid in the victory against the Hitlerites."

Joe Steele started to say something else, then stopped when he realized he'd been given the glove. He sent Trotsky a glare that should have paralyzed him. Trotsky smirked back. Joe Steele couldn't order him to a labor encampment. He had labor encampments of his own. He had more of them and he'd had them longer than the President.

"Let's do what we can to make sure that neither one of us has to fight again for many years to come," Joe Steele said after a pause for thought.

"That would be good," Trotsky agreed.

"Even revolution needs a vacation, eh?" The President tried a jab of his own.

"Revolution never sleeps anywhere." Trotsky might have been quoting Holy Writ. As far as he was concerned, he was.

Joe Steele, by contrast, liked quoting past Presidents. He did it again now: "Yes, Jefferson said 'The tree of liberty must be refreshed from time to time with the blood of patriots and tyrants. It is its natural manure.' We've rid the world of savage tyrants these past few years."

"So we have." Trotsky nodded—and smirked once more. "We've rid it of a good many patriots, too."

Dinner that evening was at the Army base by the runway. The food was American style. The toasts were drunk Russian fashion: stand up, say your say, and knock it back. This time, unlike in Basra, Charlie was ready. "To peace between North Japan and South Japan!" he said when his turn came, giving the half-nations their newspaper names instead of the clumsy official titles.

Russians and Americans drank to that. No doubt the Japs would have, too, had any been invited. But this was a gathering of the victors, not the vanquished.

Trotsky seemed more easygoing than he had while discussing European affairs. When Joe Steele proposed a three-mile-wide demilitarized zone between the parts of Japan the great powers held, Trotsky waggled his hand as if to say it wasn't worth arguing about. "You took the Balkans seriously," Joe Steele teased.

"Oh, yes." Trotsky turned grave again. "The fight against Hitler was a struggle for survival. Another such fight in Europe would be, too." He eyed the President before finishing, "But this over here? This was only a war."

The longer Charlie thought about that, the more sense it made. A professor or a striped-pants diplomat would have said Japan didn't affect Russia's vital national interests the way Germany did. Trotsky got the message across saying what he said. He got his own cold-bloodedness across, too.

Joe Steele never mentioned uranium. Charlie didn't know how Rickover was doing with the project that had cost Albert Einstein—and, from small stories in the paper, several other prominent nuclear physicists, one here, one there, one now, one then—a discreetly untimely demise. Charlie couldn't very well grab the President by the lapel and ask, *Say, how's that uranium bomb coming?* If Joe Steele wanted him to know, he'd know. If Joe Steele didn't, he'd find out with everybody else, or he'd never find out at all.

Of course, Leon Trotsky never mentioned uranium, either. Was that because he'd never heard of it? Or was it because he also had scientists and engineers slaving away? There was a fascinating riddle, especially after Charlie had tossed down enough toasts to get toasted.

He didn't ruin himself the way he had in the Iraqi city. Despite aspirins and Vitamin B12, though, he still felt it the next morning. He slouched toward coffee (mandatory) and breakfast (optional). As he left the Quonset hut he'd shared with Kagan, a trim young first lieutenant said, "Excuse me, Mr. Sullivan, sir, but there's a noncom who'd like to speak to you."

"There is?" Charlie said in surprise.

There was. A lean, tough-looking sergeant who looked as if he'd been in the Army for a million years came up. Only when he cocked his head to one side did Charlie realize who he was. "Hey, kiddo! How the hell are ya?" Mike said.

Hangover forgotten, Charlie threw himself into his brother's arms. "Mike!" he blubbered through tears while the lieutenant gawped. "What in God's name are you doing here, Mike?"

"Well, the Japs couldn't kill me, not that they didn't try a time or two . . . dozen," Mike answered. "But why I'm here in Hey-Sue-Whack-Your-Mama or whatever they call this rotten joint, I'm here on account of Joe Steele's gonna pin a medal on me for knowing that dead Jap was Hirohito. Is that funny, or what?"

"That," said Charlie with deep sincerity, "is fucking ridiculous. Come on and have some breakfast with me. I bet we get better grub than you do."

"I haven't groused since I left the encampment," Mike said. "Long as there's enough, I take an even strain."

But he went into the fancy mess hall with Charlie. He filled a tray, demolished what he'd taken, and went back for seconds. He disposed of those, too. While he was doing it, Joe Steele paused on his own way to the chow line.

"Ah, the brothers Sullivan," he said. "Have any good stories about me now, Mike? I wondered if you were that Sullivan. Now I know." He couldn't have thought about Mike more than once in the nine years since his arrest . . . could he? Whether he had or not, he remembered everything, just the way Mikoian said he did.

"I'm that Sullivan, all right, sir. NY24601." Mike recited his encampment number with quiet pride.

"Well, if you run into WY232 again, give him my regards, not that he'll appreciate them." With a nod, Joe Steele went off to get some bacon and eggs and coffee.

Mike stared after him. "Christ!" he said hoarsely.

"What?" Charlie asked.

"He even knows who my best friend in the encampment was. He's a son of a bitch, but he's smarter than I thought he was, and I never pegged him for a dope."

Leon Trotsky came in with two Red bodyguards and his interpreter. "Here's another smart SOB," Charlie said in a low voice. "And between the two of 'em, they've got the whole world sewed up."

"Ain't life grand?" Mike said. They both started to laugh.

XXII

Mike stayed in the Army after what they called peace came. All his other choices seemed worse. They made it plain to him that, as someone who'd served a stretch in an encampment, he could live legally only in the Midwest and Rocky Mountain states. What would he do there? Asking the question answered it. He'd starve, that was what.

Who would hire a reporter who'd got jugged for going after Joe Steele? No one in his right mind, even if the President had personally given him a Bronze Star with V for valor. The other trade he knew was lumberjack. He hadn't enjoyed doing it for the Jeebies enough to want to keep doing it on his own.

After a bit, he realized he'd also got good at one other thing. But how much demand for a button man was there in places like Denver or Salt Lake City or Albuquerque? Not enough, chances were, to support him in the style to which he'd like to become accustomed. And, as with cutting down trees, cutting down people was something he could do when he had to but not something he wanted for a career.

So he kept the uniform on. They promoted him to first sergeant—getting a medal from Joe Steele's own mitts carried weight with them. And they mustered him out of the punishment brigade and into an ordinary infantry unit. He felt a pang of regret when he took off the tunic he'd worn so long, the one with the P on the sleeve. Part of the regret came from remembering how many guys he'd liked who'd worn that P with him weren't here to take it off. Getting rid of guys like that—guys like him—was what punishment brigades were all about. It just hadn't quite worked in his case.

He could have lied about his past and said he'd come from some other ordinary unit. When they cut his new orders, they even offered to give him a fictitious paper trail: probably one more consequence of getting the Bronze Star from Joe Steele. But he said, "Nah, don't bother."

He was proud of his stretch in the punishment brigade. He was proud of the four oak-leaf clusters on the ribbon for his Purple Heart. He was proud of his stretch as a wrecker, too. A lot of the poor bastards in the encampments got their time because somebody sold them out. Not him. He'd earned a term as honestly as a man could.

And when he went to the brigade near the demilitarized zone, he found that the men there were in awe of what he'd lived through. He'd seen more hard fighting in more bad places than any four of them put together. Most of them wanted to go home as soon as they could and start reassembling the lives they'd had before they put on the uniform.

Mike had nothing left to reassemble back in the States. He'd liked seeing Charlie. But they'd gone their separate ways even before the knock on the door at one in the morning. Charlie'd come to terms with Joe Steele. Mike hadn't and couldn't. In the United States these days, no chasm gaped wider.

So Mike figured he was better off an ocean away from the United States. Now that he wasn't trying to kill the Japs, he discovered they could be interesting. They bowed low to the American conquerors whenever they walked past. A lot of soldiers accepted that as no less than their due. Mike wondered what would happen if he started bowing back.

Old men stared as if they couldn't believe their eyes. Younger men—often demobilized soldiers, plainly—also acted surprised, but a few of them grudged him a smile. And women of any age went into storms of giggles. He couldn't decide whether he was the funniest thing in the world or he embarrassed them.

They also giggled when he learned a few words of Japanese and trotted them out. He liked being able to ask for food and drink without going through a big song and dance. Beer—*biru*—was easy. He learned the word for *delicious*, too, or thought he did. That set off more laughter than anything else he said. He wondered why till a Jap with bits of English explained *oishi* meant something lewd if you didn't say it just right. He did his best after that and used it a lot, because he liked Japanese food more than he'd thought he would.

He liked soaking in a Japanese bath, too. Other Americans ribbed him when he said so. "I like bathing by myself, thanks," one of them told him.

"Hey, this beats the shit out of climbing into a tub full of disinfectant with a bunch of smelly scalps," Mike answered. As far as he knew, the other soldier had never been within a hundred miles of an encampment. But the guy understood the slang. Joe Steele left his mark on America all kinds of ways.

He'd left his mark on Japan, too. Everyone was desperately poor. The Japs scrounged through the base's garbage without shame. Old tin cans, scraps of wood, and broken tools were all precious to them. So was cloth, because they had so little of their own.

Not surprisingly, a black market sprang up. Some things passed from the base to the natives in unofficial ways. Americans wound up owning little artworks that hadn't got ruined in the fighting. A village druggist rigged up a still that would have made a moonshiner proud during Prohibition. Mike had drunk plenty of worse white mule back in the States.

And, of course, some of the women paid for what they wanted in the oldest coin of all. If that bothered them, they showed it less than their counterparts in the West would have. It was, their attitude seemed to say, all part of a day's work. Mike liked that better than the hypocrisy he'd grown up with.

Some of the men resented the Americans for beating them. There were places in South Japan where soldiers had to travel in groups so they wouldn't get bushwhacked. The island of Shikoku was especially bad for that. It had been bypassed, not overrun and ground to sawdust. The Japs there hadn't been licked the way the ones on Kyushu and Honshu had.

Up here near the demilitarized zone, the locals gave the

Americans far less grief. Bad as things were on this side of the Agano River, all the Japs had to do was look over the border into North Japan to know they could have had it one hell of a lot worse.

The Americans were at least going through the motions of trying to get the Japs in their half of the prostrate country back on their feet. The Russians? They treated North Japan the way they treated East Germany: as a source for what they needed to rebuild their own ravaged land. Factories and mills got broken down and shipped by sea to Vladivostok for reconstruction somewhere in Russia. Farmers were herded together into agricultural collectives (Mike saw little difference between those and Joe Steele's community farms, but nobody asked him so he kept his mouth shut).

Anyone in North Japan who complained vanished—into a reeducation camp or into an unmarked grave. Of course, anyone in South Japan who complained could find himself in big trouble, too. But there was a difference. More people tried to flee from the north to the south than the other way round. When it came to voting with their feet, the Japs preferred the U.S. Army to the Red Army.

Days flowed by, one after another. Winter along the Agano was tougher than it had been in New York City—storms blew down from Siberia one after another. But it was a piece of cake next to what it had been like in the Montana Rockies. Mike laughed at the men who complained.

He laughed more than he had since before the Jeebies took him. Next to being a wrecker in a labor encampment, next to hitting beach after beach in a punishment brigade, this wasn't just good—this was wonderful. He hoped he'd remember how wonderful it was after he got more used to it.

For a little while after the war ended, Charlie had hoped real peace would take hold in the world. People had felt the same way after the First World War. They'd called it the War to End War. And they'd been all the more bitterly disappointed when history didn't come to an end with the Treaty of Versailles.

Having seen his hopes blasted once, Charlie was less surprised when they came a cropper again. Trotsky really believed in world revolution, or acted as if he did. Red regimes sprouted like toadstools in Eastern Europe. Italy and France bobbled and steamed like pots with the lids down too tight. Korea and North Japan were good and Red, too. In China, Mao was ahead of Chiang on points, and looked to be getting ready to knock him out.

Before the war, J. Edgar Hoover's GBI had chased Nazis, Reds, and people who were neither but didn't like Joe Steele, all with about equal vigor. Now the Jeebies seemed intent on filling labor encampments with Reds. If you didn't hold your nose and run away when you heard Leon Trotsky's unholy name, you'd find out more about lodgepole pines than you ever wanted to know.

Charlie thought the USA would do better, both abroad and at home, if it looked at why so many people wanted to chuck out the governments they had and put in new ones, even if the new ones were Red. You could still think such things. J. Edgar Hoover had no mind-reading machines, though he might have been working on them. But if you opened your mouth . . .

He tried to imagine saying something like that to Vince Scriabin. How long would he stay free if he did? As long as the Jeebies took to get to his office after the Hammer called them. Or maybe Scriabin would just grab some White House guards and handle it himself.

That cheered Charlie up so much, he knocked off halfway through the afternoon and headed for the bar near the White House where John Nance Garner drank away his terms. Sure enough, the Vice President was there smoking a cigarette and working on a bourbon.

"Well, hell, it's Sullivan!" he said. "They let school out early today, Charlie boy?"

"Time off for bad behavior," Charlie answered. He nodded to the bartender. "Let me have Wild Turkey over ice."

"You got it, suh," the Negro answered, and in a moment Charlie did. He sipped. This wasn't one of the bad days where he had to get smashed as fast as he could, but he needed a drink or three. At least a drink or three.

John Nance Garner watched him fortify himself. With a small shock, Charlie realized the Veep had to be close to eighty. Drinking and smoking were supposed to be bad for you, weren't they? He couldn't have proved it by Garner, who was still here and still had all his marbles, even if he wasn't what you'd call pretty.

"I expect the boss is gettin' ready for term number five," Garner said.

"Hasn't he talked about it with you?" Charlie asked.

The Vice President guffawed. "You reckon I'd be tryin' to find out if I knew? The less Joe Steele's got to say to me, happier I am."

"Shall I tell him you said so?"

"Shit, sonny, go ahead. It's nothin' he don't know already. You think he wants to talk to me? If he did, he'd do more of it—I'll tell you that."

"Why—?" Charlie began, but he let the question die unasked.

"Why don't he dump me if he feels that way?" John Nance Garner answered the question whether Charlie asked it or not: "On account of I don't make waves. I don't make trouble. I do what he tells me to do, and I don't give him no back talk. He knows he don't got to worry about me while he's lookin' some other way. Japan cornholed him but good while he was makin' faces at Hitler an' Trotsky. I just sit there in the Senate or I sit here in the tavern. He can count on that, an' he knows it."

It made sense—if you looked at it from Joe Steele's point of view, anyhow. Hitler's flunkies hadn't disobeyed him till the war was good and lost. Trotsky's henchmen were loyal or they were dead. Joe Steele needed people he could rely on, too. He didn't need much from the Vice President, but what he needed John Nance Garner delivered.

What does he need from me? Charlie wondered. *Words.* The answer formed itself. He'd given Joe Steele words, and the President had used the ones he wanted. But there was more to it than that. Putting Charlie in a White House office while Mike was in a labor encampment was the kind of thing that amused the President. It was a nasty sense of humor, but it was what Joe Steele had.

Charlie turned to the quiet man behind the bar. "Let me have another one, please."

"I will do that, suh," the barkeep said.

Wild Turkey was safer than thought. To keep from dwelling on Joe Steele's sense of humor, or the part of it that had bitten him, Charlie asked the Vice President, "What do you think of all the fuss about the Reds?"

"They're no bargain. Unless you're a Red yourself, you know that. Trotsky says he wants world revolution, but what he's really got in mind is all those revolutions dancing to his tune," Garner replied, which was safe enough. Then he added, "Now, J. Edgar Hoover, he's a nasty little pissant any way you look at him."

I couldn't have put it better myself. But Charlie lacked the nerve to come out and say so.

John Nance Garner must have seen the look on his face. The Veep laughed, coughed, and laughed some more. "They ain't gonna take me away," he said. "You reckon Joe Steele don't know Hoover's a nasty little pissant? Don't make me laugh! 'Course he knows. But Hoover's *his* nasty little pissant, like a mean dog that'll lick the face of the fella who owns it. He don't got to fret about him any more'n he's got to fret about me."

And what would the none too modest J. Edgar Hoover think of that? Charlie was curious, but not curious enough to find out. The less he had to do with the head of the GBI, the better off he'd be.

He bought some Sen-Sen on the way home that night, but it didn't help. Esther screwed up her face when she kissed him after he walked in. "How many did you have before you got here?" she asked.

"A few," he said. "I'm okay."

"Are you?" She didn't sound so sure. Jews were often harder on people who put it away than the Irish were. *Shikker iz a goy. The gentile is a drunk.* When you learned some Yiddish, you learned phrases like that. Esther when on, "You've been drinking more lately than I wish you were."

"I'm okay," Charlie said again. "Honest to Pete, I am. I'm holding the bottle. It isn't holding me."

"It hasn't been. I don't want it to start," Esther said. "After a while, you can't walk away from it. Maybe you should try while you're still ahead of the game. I don't mean quit cold—I don't think you have to go that far. But you should cut back."

"Well, maybe. Hard to do that in Washington, but I guess I can give it a shot." If she wasn't going to push it as hard as she might have, he wouldn't dig in his heels the way he could have done. He kissed her again, saying, "You take good care of me, babe."

She smiled against his cheek. "It's a filthy job, but somebody's got to do it."

The kids hadn't come out to say hello—a returning father wasn't an inspiring spectacle—so he pawed her a little. She squeaked—softly, remembering that they were around. He said, "You want filthy, wait till later tonight." He nibbled her earlobe.

She pushed him away, but she was still smiling. "We'll see who's awake," she said. Anyone listening to them would have thought they'd been married for a while.

Artillery boomed, off to the north. Looking across the Agano River, Mike said, "Christ, what are the Russians up to now?"

Officially, Captain Calvin Armstrong commanded the company. Unofficially, he leaned a lot on his first sergeant, who was twice his age. That was what experienced noncoms were for. "What do you think it is?" he asked.

"Who the hell knows with them, sir? As long as nothing comes down on our side of the line, we can't make it our business."

"I understand that." Armstrong looked no happier. "I hope they don't have an uprising up there, though. That's the kind of thing that could spill over to here."

"Yes, sir." Mike hoped the same thing. South Japan wasn't so much a powder keg as North Japan, but the locals didn't exactly love their conquerors, either. They especially resented seeing Emperor Akihito reduced to the status of General Eisenhower's mouthpiece. Cartoons showed Akihito as a ventriloquist's dummy sitting on Eisenhower's lap with Eisenhower's hand reaching into him from behind. You could get into piles of trouble for posting those flyers, but the Japs did it anyhow.

"Do you think they'd tell us if they did have an uprising?" Captain Armstrong asked.

He wasn't a dope. He found interesting questions. "I doubt it, sir," Mike said slowly, "unless things got out of hand and they couldn't squash it or something. Near as I can see, the Russians don't tell anybody anything as long as they can help it."

Armstrong nodded. He looked more as if he belonged on a college campus than here looking toward North Japan. He might have been a college kid before he went into the service, and raced through OCS to get christened a ninety-day wonder. Most of those guys stayed second looeys, though. If he was one, he must have impressed some people to win not one but two promotions.

"Maybe I'll ask Major Dragunov at the monthly meeting, if I remember," he said. "Too bad the next one's three weeks away." Local commanders from the two sides of the demilitarized zone did still get together to hash over problems that could cross from one to the other.

The big guns boomed again, off to the north. "Well, sir, if that goes on from now till then, you sure won't forget about it," Mike said.

It did, on and off. Dragunov and Armstrong met at the river, unarmed. It was Dragunov's turn to cross to the American side, which he did in a putt-putt of a motorboat. He didn't speak English; Armstrong knew no Russian. They got along in a schoolboy mishmash of French and German. Since neither was fluent, both gestured a lot. Mike could follow bits and pieces, though his French was of much less recent vintage than Calvin Armstrong's and his German was New York City Yiddish, also none too fresh these days.

He certainly knew when Armstrong asked about the artillery fire. Dragunov didn't answer right away, not in a language the Americans could understand. Instead, he spoke in Russian with his assistant, a lieutenant whose blue arm-of-service color and know-it-all air said he came from the NKVD. Mike didn't know exactly what the initials stood for. He did know that *NKVD man* was how you said *Jeebie* in Russian.

After making sure he could open his mouth without catching hell for it, Dragunov went back to German and French. He said something that sounded to Mike like *the popular army of the Japanese People's Republic*.

Captain Armstrong asked what seemed like the next logical question: "This popular army, it is composed of Japanese?"

"Oui," Dragunov admitted reluctantly. More back-and-forth with the NKVD lieutenant. Then mostly French again: "How not? The Japanese People's Republic has the necessity of being able to defend itself."

"Defend itself? Against whom?" Armstrong asked, which also seemed like a good question.

"Why, against warmongers and imperialists, *aber natürlich,*" Major Dragunov answered, switch-hitting with the German phrase. "Those are the enemies a peace-loving state has the need to be on guard against."

"I don't think there are many warmongers left in South Japan," Armstrong said. "We killed most of them."

"It could be that you are right." The Red Army man didn't sound as if he believed it for a minute. "If you are, no doubt we will march well. But one must prepare for every possibility, is it not so?"

They talked about other, less important, things for a few minutes. After a sharp exchange of salutes, Major Dragunov and his—minder?—got back into their boat and chugged over to the North Japanese side of the river.

"You better get on the horn with the brass, sir," Mike said. "If they don't know about this, they sure as hell need to, and right away."

"You're reading my mind, Sullivan," Captain Armstrong answered. "We just spent all that time and blood smashing the Jap Army flat, and now they're putting together a new one? Jesus wept!"

"If their Japs have guns, our Japs'll want guns, too," Mike said. "And how are we supposed to tell them no?"

"Beats me." Calvin Armstrong stared after the motor-boat with the Russians in it as it crossed to the far side of the Agano. "The only thing I'm glad about is, I'm not the one who has to figure out the answer."

Joe Steele eyed Charlie. "I am looking for a way to say something important," he said. "I know the idea, but I do not have the words I need yet. Words are your department. Maybe you can come up with some."

"I'll give it my best shot, Mr. President," Charlie said, as he had to. Yes, Joe Steele did get words from him. "What's the idea?" He couldn't say *What's the big idea?*, not to the President. You needed a working sense of whimsy to smile at that. Joe Steele would have scowled instead.

"I want to talk about how the Reds are clamping down wherever they've taken power, how they aren't letting us help them rebuild the countries that the war tore to pieces, how they just want to take with both hands but not give with either." Joe Steele gestured in frustration. "That's the idea. But it sounds like nothing when I say it that way. I want it to sound as important as it is. If I can make other people see it the way I do, maybe we won't have to fight a war with Russia in a few years."

No matter how much Charlie longed for peace, he could see that war looming ahead, the way anyone with his eyes open in 1919 could have seen that Germany would have another go as soon as she got her strength back. Plenty of people *had* seen the seeds of World War II. Charlie remembered the cartoon that showed a weeping baby outside Versailles as the Big Four emerged from signing the treaty. The baby's diaper was labeled CONSCRIPTION CLASS OF 1940. That guy'd hit it right on the nose.

So would the United States and Red Russia square off in 1960 or 1965? Charlie wanted to do whatever he could to head that off. Joe Steele did, too. Say what you would about the man, but he deserved credit for that.

"Let's see what I can do, sir." Scratching the side of his jaw, Charlie went back to his office, locked the door, and took the phone off the hook. When the dial tone annoyed him, he stuck the handset in a desk drawer and closed it. Then he settled down to think.

What was it that made the Reds so hard to work with?

You could never tell what they were going to do till they did it. No one had dreamt Litvinov would sign a treaty with the Nazis till he hopped on a plane, went to Berlin, and signed the damn thing. No one had dreamt his name on the dotted line would cost so much blood, either.

The Reds wrapped a blackout curtain around everything they did. Charlie wasn't sure that was because they were Reds. It might just have been because they were Russians, or Jews who'd grown up among Russians. Why didn't matter. The phrase did.

Blackout curtain? That wasn't bad. It was on the way to what Joe Steele wanted. Charlie didn't think it was there. Red-out curtain? He wrote it on a piece of scratch paper. It didn't make him stand up and cheer—it was too cute. But it was something he could offer if he didn't come up with anything better.

He pulled his trusty Bartlett's off the shelf. It was one of the speechwriter's best friends. People had said a lot of clever things over the past few thousand years. Here they were, ready for the taking. Or for giving you a new idea, and with luck a better one.

Nothing sprang out at him. He still liked the notion of the curtain, though. Not the blackout curtain. Black was the wrong color for Trotsky's regime and for the ones he backed. Red-out curtain still sounded silly.

"Red Curtain?" Charlie muttered to himself. Then he said it again: louder, more thoughtfully. He wrote it down. Yes, that might do. It just might.

He ran a sheet of paper into the typewriter. Maybe his fingers could do the rest of his thinking for him. Only one way to find out: turn 'em loose and let 'em rip.

From the Adriatic to the Baltic, from Leipzig to Sapporo, a Red Curtain has fallen over a quarter of the world, he wrote. *Behind it lie governments that are not really governments at all, but organized conspiracies, every one equally resolute and implacable in its determination to destroy the free world.*

He looked at that. If it wasn't what Joe Steele was trying to say, he'd misunderstood what the boss wanted. It was worth taking a chance on. He pulled it out of the typewriter and took it up to the President's oval study.

This time, he had to wait a little while before he got to see Joe Steele. Andy Wyszynski came out looking serious. "How are you, Sullivan?" the Attorney General said with a nod.

"I'm all right. Yourself?" Charlie answered. He got tired of the flat, flavorless speech of Joe Steele and his California cronies. Wyszynski had a big-city accent different from his own, but at least it was a big-city accent.

"Well, Sullivan, what have you got?" Joe Steele asked when Charlie went in. Charlie handed him the typewritten paragraph. The President perched reading glasses on the arched bridge of his nose. "Red Curtain . . ." He shifted his pipe to the side of his mouth so he could bring out the phrase. Then he puffed, tasting the words as well as the tobacco. He ran a hand through his hair. It was still thick, though he'd gone very gray. "Red Curtain . . ." He nodded, as if he meant it now. "Every once in a while, you earn your paycheck, don't you?"

"I try, Mr. President," Charlie said. Joe Steele offhand and insulting was Joe Steele as friendly as he ever got.

Newspapers all over the United States seized on the Red Curtain when the President used it in a speech about Russia. Charlie would have been prouder of that if American newspapers weren't in the habit of seizing on anything Joe Steele said and trumpeting it to the skies. When papers in Canada and England and even one in New Zealand picked up the phrase, he really started to think he'd earned his pay that day.

J. Edgar Hoover arrested spies in the War Department and in the State Department and even in the Department of the Interior. They were working to sell America down the river to Leon Trotsky, he declared. The way he stuck out his jaw dared anyone in the world to call him a liar.

Andy Wyszynski pounded the lectern when he told the world—or at least the reporters, nearly all of them American, at the press conference—what a pack of scoundrels the men seized because of spying for Trotsky were. "They want to drag the United States behind the Red Curtain!" the Attorney General shouted furiously. "They've already dragged too many countries behind it, and not a one of them has come out free yet!"

"Ouch!" Charlie said when he heard Wyszynski's tirade on the news that night. "I didn't mean it like that."

"And so?" Esther said. "People take things and make them mean whatever they want, not what you wanted."

"Tell me about it!" Charlie said ruefully. He'd felt proud when Joe Steele called the part of the world led from Moscow the part behind the Red Curtain. He'd felt even prouder when people used the line wherever English was spoken.

When Andy Wyszynski used it the way he did . . . Charlie might have been less proud if he'd seen *Red Curtain* scribbled on a privy wall, or perhaps as the name of a whorehouse. On the other hand, he also might not have.

He wanted a drink. Some bourbon would clean out the nasty taste the Attorney General left in his mouth. His thigh muscles bunched as he started to get up from the couch and go to the kitchen. But then he eased back again. He was trying to be a good boy and not grab the whiskey bottle whenever he got the yen. It didn't always work, but it did some of the time. He was drinking less than he had before Esther called him on it.

It worked tonight. Instead of a drink, he had a cigarette. Esther smiled at him. She must have known what he wanted to do. They'd been together a good many years now. Chances were she understood how he ticked better than he did himself.

Sarah came into the front room. She made a face at seeing her boring old parents listening to the boring old news. At going on ten, she was convinced they were as far behind the times as Neanderthal Man or the Republican Party. What she would be like when that high-school class of 1956 graduated—not nearly so far away now!—Charlie shuddered to think.

"Can someone *please* help me with my arithmetic homework?" she said. As far as she was concerned, the news existed only to keep her from getting the help she needed. She would have made a pretty good cat.

"What are you doing?" Charlie asked.

"It's long division. With decimal places, not remainders." By the way she said it, that ranked somewhere between Chinese water torture and the Black Hole of Calcutta when measured on the scale of man's inhumanity to students.

"Well, come on to the kitchen table and we'll have a look." Charlie found a new reason to be glad he hadn't had that bourbon. It wouldn't have helped him do long division even with remainders.

Sober, he didn't need long to see why Sarah was having trouble. She'd multiplied seven by six and got forty-nine. "Oh!" she said. "Is that all it was?" She snatched the paper away and ran off to do the rest of the work by herself.

"That was fast, Einstein," Esther said when Charlie came back.

"I'm not Einstein," Charlie said. "I'm the one who's still breathing." With his wife, he could still come out with things like that. He never would have had the nerve with anybody else. He wondered how Captain Rickover and his scalps were doing with uranium. Joe Steele hadn't told him anything about it. He didn't go out of his way to ask, which was putting it mildly. If anyone decided he needed to know, he'd find out. If nobody did . . . Maybe no news was good news.

The treason trials helped liven up a dreary winter. Andy Wyszynski outdid himself in some of the prosecutions. He would scream at the luckless men and women the GBI had grabbed: "Shoot these mad dogs! Death to the gangsters who side with that vulture, Trotsky, from whose mouths a bloody venom drips, putrefying the great ideals of democracy. Let's push the animal hatred they bear our beloved Joe Steele back down their throats!"

Shoot those mad dogs, if they were mad dogs, government firing squads did. Things had got simpler and quicker in the justice system year by year after Herbert Hoover went out and Joe Steele came in.

An assistant attorney general also made a reputation for himself in the spy trials. He was a kid from California, only in his mid-thirties, with a Bob Hope ski-slope nose and crisp, curly black hair. He didn't rant like Wyszynski. He just pounded away, relentless as a jackhammer. "Are you now or have you ever been a Red?" he would demand of each defendant in turn, and, "What did you know, and when did you know it?"

He got convictions, too, about as many as his boss. Joe Steele smiled whenever his name came up. Charlie wondered if the President saw something of his own young, ambitious self in that graceless, hard-charging lawyer.

It was going to be another election year. It got to be February 1948 before Charlie even remembered. He laughed at himself. Back in the day, Presidential races had been the biggest affairs in American politics. The only thing that would keep Joe Steele from winning a fifth term now was dying before November rolled around.

And that wouldn't happen. Joe Steele had disposed of swarms of other men, but he showed no sign of being ready to meet the Grim Reaper himself.

XXIII

"Hup! Hup! Hup-hup-hup!" Mike watched the company of South Japanese troops parade. They wore mostly American uniforms, though their service caps were the short-billed Imperial Japanese style. Most of them were survivors from Hirohito's army. Jobs were hard to come by in South Japan, especially for veterans. The American authorities discouraged employers from hiring them. So the newly formed Constitutional Guard—no one wanted to call it an army—had no trouble finding recruits.

But they weren't *good* recruits. They knew what to do; it wasn't as if they were going through basic. Giving a damn about doing it? That was a different story.

Mike turned to Dick Shirakawa. Dick was his interpreter, a California Jap who'd gone into a labor encampment after Pearl Harbor and eventually into a punishment brigade. His unit, full of Japs, had fought in Europe. The powers that be had figured ordinary American soldiers in the Pacific would shoot at them first and ask questions later. For once, Mike figured the powers that be got it right.

Like him, Dick had stayed in the Army after the war ended and got the P out from under his corporal's stripes. Since he spoke the language, they'd decided he'd be most useful in Japan once the shooting stopped. Mike was glad to have him. His own bits of Japanese, while they helped him, weren't enough to let him ride herd on these clowns.

"Ask 'em what's eating them, will you?" he said to Shirakawa now. "They should make better soldiers than this."

Dick palavered in Japanese with three or four guys who looked to have a few brain cells to rub together. They had to go back and forth for a while. Mike had learned that Jap notions of politeness involved telling you what they thought you wanted to hear, not what was really on their minds. You had to work past that if you were ever going to get anywhere. When Shirakawa turned away at last, his face wore a bemused expression.

"So what's cookin'?" Mike asked him.

"Well, I found out how come they don't take us serious," the American Japanese said. "I found out, but I'm not sure I believe it."

"Give." Mike had already had some adventures of his own unscrewing the inscrutable.

"You know what the trouble is?" Dick said. "The trouble is, we're too fucking nice. I shit you not, Sergeant. That's what they tell me. Their own noncoms slugged them and kicked them whenever they pulled a rock. We don't do any of that stuff, so the way it looks to them is, we don't give a rat's ass. To them, we're just going through the motions. That's all they think they need to do, too."

"Fuck me." Mike lit a cigarette. He'd imagined a lot of different troubles, but that wasn't any of them. "You know what they sound like? They sound like a broad who's only happy when her husband knocks her around, 'cause that's how she knows he loves her. He cares enough to smack her one."

Shirakawa nodded. "That's about the size of it. What are we supposed to do? Our own brass would court-martial us—hell, they'd crucify us—if we treated these guys the way *their* sergeants did."

"I'll talk with Captain Armstrong about it, see what he thinks," Mike said. "In the meantime, tell 'em it's not our custom to beat the crap out of people who didn't really earn it. Tell 'em that doesn't make us soft, any more than surrendering or taking prisoners does. Remind 'em we won the war and they damn well didn't, so our ways of doing things work, too."

"I'll try." Shirakawa harangued the company in Japanese. Mike got maybe one word in ten; he never could have done it by himself. The Constitutional Guardsmen listened attentively. They bowed to the corporal and then, more deeply, to Mike. After that, they marched a little better, but not a lot better.

When Mike talked with Calvin Armstrong, the young officer nodded. "I've heard other reports like that," he said, frowning. "I don't know what to do about them. If we treat the Japs the way their old army did, aren't we as bad as they were?"

"If we don't treat 'em that way, will the new army—"

"The Constitutional Guard."

"The Constitutional Guard. Right. Sorry. Will the goddamn Constitutional Guard be worth the paper it's printed on? Is the idea to be nice to them or to get them so they're able to fight?"

"I can't order you to rough them up. My own superiors would land on me like a ton of bricks," Armstrong said unhappily.

"Yes, sir. I understand that," Mike said. "But I'll tell you one thing."

"What's that?"

"The sorry bastards in the North Japanese Army, they don't ever worry that the Russians telling 'em what to do are too fucking soft."

Armstrong laughed what might have been the least mirthful laugh Mike had ever heard. "Boy, you've got that right," he said. "The Red Army's just about as dog-eat-dog as the Japs were."

"They may be even worse," Mike said. "Their officers have those NKVD bastards looking over their shoulder all the time."

"Uh-huh." Armstrong nodded. "Wouldn't it be fun if the Jeebies kept an eye on our guys like that?"

"I never really thought about it, sir," Mike answered. He liked Calvin Armstrong. He respected him. But he didn't trust him enough to say anything bad about the GBI where the younger man could hear him. He didn't want to wind up in a labor encampment again if Armstrong reported him. No, the Jeebies didn't put political officers in U.S. Army units, or they hadn't yet, anyhow. That didn't mean they had no influence in the Army. Oh, no. It didn't mean that at all.

Esther had got a call from the elementary school where Sarah and Pat went. She had to go in early and bring Pat home. He'd landed in trouble on the playground at lunchtime. Esther told Charlie the story over the phone, but he wanted to hear it from the criminal himself. Not every kindergarten kid could pull off a stunt like that.

"What happened, sport?" Charlie asked when he came back from the White House.

"Nothin' much." His son seemed not at all put out by landing in hot water.

"No? I heard you had kind of a fight."

"Yeah, kind of." Pat shrugged. No, it didn't bother him.

"How come?"

Another shrug. "I had on this same shirt"—it was crimson cotton, just the thing for Washington's warm spring—"and Melvin, he asked me, 'Are you now or have you ever been a Red?'"

"And so?"

"And so I bopped him in the ol' beezer," Pat said, not without pride. "Everybody knows Red is a dirty name. But he got a bloody nose, and he started crying all over the place. I guess that's why they sent me home."

"'Everybody knows Red is a dirty name,'" Esther echoed.

"When the five- and six-year-olds throw it at each other, you know it's sunk in pretty deep, all right." Charlie turned back to Pat. "From now on, don't hit anybody unless he hits you first, okay?"

"Okay," Pat said with no great enthusiasm.

"Promise?"

"Promise," Pat said, more reluctantly yet. But Charlie and Esther had taught him that promises were important, and that if you made one you had to keep it. With any luck at all, this one would keep Pat from becoming the scourge of the schoolyard—or from getting his block knocked off if he goofed.

Not long after dinner, the phone rang. Thinking it might be someone from the White House, Charlie grabbed it. "Hello?"

"Mr. Sullivan?" a woman's voice asked. When Charlie admitted he was himself, she went on, "I am Miss Hannegan, the principal at your children's school. I'm calling about what unfortunately happened this afternoon."

"Oh, sure," Charlie said. "We gave Pat a good talking-to. I don't think you'll have any more of that kind of trouble out of him."

"I'm glad to hear it." Miss Hannegan didn't just sound glad. She sounded massively relieved. "I wanted to be positive you weren't angry at Miss Tarleton for bringing Patrick to my office, and to remind you that *of course*"—she bore down hard on that—"Melvin Vangilder had no idea what you do, or he never would have said what he said to your son."

"Uh-huh. If you hadn't called, I never would have thought of that," Charlie said. Miss Hannegan seemed more relieved than ever. He said his good-byes as quickly as he could and hung up.

Then he fixed himself a drink. Esther gave him a look, but he did it anyway. The principal had called to make sure he wasn't an ogre. She assumed that someone who worked at the White House had but to say the word and Miss Tarleton (who taught Pat's kindergarten class) would disappear into a labor encampment. So would Melvin Vangilder's mother and father. So would Melvin himself, and never mind that he might or might not have had his sixth birthday. She might not have been wrong, either.

"But doggone it, I'm *not* an ogre," Charlie muttered when he'd finished the drink—which didn't take long.

"What?" his wife asked.

"Never mind." The real trouble was, he understood why Miss Hannegan had been so worried. If he were an ogre, she couldn't stop him from doing whatever he wanted to Miss Tarleton and to the Vangilders. All she could do was beg him. If he didn't feel like listening, what would he do? He'd pick up the phone and call J. Edgar Hoover. The Jeebies would take it from there.

He'd never used his influence that way. It hadn't occurred to him, which he supposed meant that his own parents had raised him the right way. He wondered whether Lazar Kagan, say, had got even with somebody who beat him up on a school playground back around the turn of the century. He couldn't very well ask the next time he bumped into Kagan in the White House. And, all things considered, he was bound to be better off not knowing.

*   *   *

When American soldiers in Japan got some leave, they often went to Shikoku. Yes, the natives there resented their presence more than Japs in other parts of South Japan did. But the cities and towns of Shikoku had just had the hell bombed out of them. They hadn't had the hell bombed out of them and then been fought over house by house. It made a difference.

Along with Dick Shirakawa, Mike took the ferry from Wakayama on Honshu to Tokushima on Shikoku. The ferry was a wallowing landing craft, the kind he'd ridden towards unfriendly beaches too many times. The only part of Wakayama that had much life, even now, was the harbor, and Americans were in charge there.

Tokushima . . . wasn't like that. It was the friendliest beach Mike had ever landed on. It was, in fact, a quickly run-up, low-rent version of Honolulu. The whole town, or at least the waterfront district, was designed to give servicemen a good time while separating them from their cash.

You could go to the USO and have a wholesome good time for next to nothing. Or you could do other things. You could gamble. You could drink. You could dance with taxi dancers who might or might not be available for other services, too. You could go to any number of strip joints — Japanese women, even if most of them were none too busty, had fewer inhibitions about nakedness than their American sisters did. Or you could go to a brothel. The quality of what you got there varied according to how much you felt like spending, as it did anywhere else.

MPs and shore patrolmen did their best to keep the U.S. servicemen from adding brawling to their fun and games. They also stayed alert for Jap diehards who still wanted to kill Americans even two years after the surrender. Japs not in the Constitutional Guard or the police forces weren't supposed to have firearms. Mike knew what a forlorn hope that was. Before the American invasion, the authorities had armed as many people in the Home Islands as they could. You could get your hands on anything from one of those sad black-powder muskets to an Arisaka rifle or a Nambu light machine gun with no trouble at all.

You could also get your hands on what American soldiers still called knee mortars. You couldn't really fire them off your knee, but you could lob the little bombs they threw for most of a mile. Every so often, Japs in the suburbs would shoot at the bright lights of the waterfront. They were only a nuisance—unless you happened to be standing where a bomb went off. The Americans seldom caught anybody. Knee mortars were too easy to ditch.

Nobody fired anything at Tokushima while Mike and Dick were in town. The days were hot and muggy: a lot like New York City in the summertime. Nights were warm and muggy. A lot of the eateries by the harbor featured hamburgers and hot dogs, or steaks if you had more money.

But you could find Japanese food, too. Mike was the only round-eye in the place he and Dick went into. He'd got halfway decent with *hashi*, which made the serving girl giggle in surprise. When Americans did come in here, they usually asked for a fork, not chopsticks. Between pieces of sushi, Mike said, "Before I crossed the Pacific, I never would've touched raw octopus or raw fish or sea urchin. I guess I know better now."

"We mostly ate American food in L.A.," Dick said. "Except for the rice—my mom always made sticky rice. But oh, yeah—this is good, too."

Mike held up his empty glass. *"Biru, domo."* He went back to English: "Beer washes it down great."

"You got that right," Shirakawa said.

They also tended to other pleasures, and went back to Wakayama four days later, lighter in the wallet but sated and otherwise amused. Mike signed for a jeep in the motor pool there, and he and Dick started north again, back toward the Agano River and the increasingly nervous demilitarized zone. Almost all of the traffic was American jeeps and trucks. That was a good thing. The Japs had driven on the left, British-style, before the occupation. Sometimes—especially when they'd had a snootful—they forgot the rules had changed. Head-on collisions with American-driven vehicles happened all too often.

A flight of F-80s screamed overhead, racing north. A few minutes later, more of the jets roared by. "Wonder what's going on," Dick Shirakawa said.

"Beats me," Mike answered. "Goddamn, but those jets are noisy! Just hearing 'em makes me want to ditch the jeep and dive into a foxhole. If you didn't know what they were, just the racket might scare you into giving up."

They were still south of Tokyo when they got stuck behind a column of tanks, Shermans and a few of the newer, heavier Pershings, all on the way north. There was just enough southbound traffic to make Mike hesitate about pulling into the other lane and trying to pass the column. Bends in the road showed it was long. He fumed instead, crawling along at fifteen miles an hour.

An MP at a crossroads waved the jeep over to the shoulder. "Show me your papers, you two!" he barked. He kept not quite pointing his M-1 at Dick Shirakawa. Seeing a Japanese man in an American uniform made him jumpy, even if most of the Constitutional Guard wore them. He examined both sets of leave documents with microscopic care, Dick's even more than Mike's.

Finally, Mike got fed up and said, "What's the story, anyway?"

The MP stared at him. "You haven't heard?"

"I haven't heard jack shit, man. If I had, would I be asking you?"

"You guys are fucking lucky you weren't back at the border—that's all I've got to tell you. The North Japanese are attacking South Japan. They've got tanks and big guns and I don't know what all else. No warning, no nothin'. One minute, everything was quiet. The next one, all hell broke loose."

Mike and Dick looked at each other in consternation. "We've got to get back up there," Mike said. "Our buddies are there. So are the Jap troops we were training."

"Good luck—that's all I've got to tell you." The MP liked the phrase. "Here's what you do. Go on in to Tokyo. Get your orders there. Draw some weapons there, too. You sure as hell ain't safe without 'em."

Being unarmed hadn't worried Mike till then. Riding in a jeep, he'd felt safe enough. Not if there was a new war on, though. He nodded tightly. "We'll do that, then."

American authorities in sad, ruined Tokyo seemed as

discombobulated as if they'd taken a right from the Brown Bomber square in the kisser. They hadn't expected an attack from North Japan. Mike didn't know why not. Captain Armstrong had been sending in worried reports for weeks. So had other commanders near the demilitarized zone. Had anybody here believed them, or even read them? It sure didn't look that way.

Getting weapons was easy. The armory issued Mike and Dick grease guns and as many magazines as they could carry. Getting orders . . . Dick got his right away: to sit tight in Tokyo. The captain who told him to do that sounded apologetic but firm. "Corporal, I understand what you are. I understand what you've done for your country," he said. "But I don't want our own guys getting a look at you and filling you full of holes because they think you're a North Japanese soldier in an American uniform."

"You think our men are really that dumb, sir?" Dick Shirakawa asked.

"You tell me," the harried captain replied. Dick thought it over. He didn't need long. He stayed in Tokyo.

Mike scrambled into a halftrack that was part of a patched-together regimental combat team. Hardly anybody in the machine knew anybody else. That worried him. One of the reasons men fought well was to protect their buddies. Another was to keep from seeming yellow to those same buddies. How well would these guys do if they didn't care about the men with them and those men didn't give a damn about them?

For a while, it just seemed like a training ride. Then, off to the north, the rumble of artillery began to make itself known above the different rumble of the halftrack's engine. Smoke stained the horizon. War and fire went together like pretzels and beer.

They stopped for the night before they found the action, or it found them. Some of them didn't know the first thing about digging a foxhole or setting up a perimeter. They were draftees who'd been doing garrison duty, not soldiers with combat experience. Mike took charge of them. He had a first sergeant's stripes and a manner that said he knew what he was doing.

In the morning, they went forward again. It started to be stop-and-go traffic. Refugees clogged the roads: Jap civilians who didn't want to live under North Japan's Rising Sun with the gold Hammer and Sickle inside. Mike didn't blame them, but they sure didn't make getting up there to defend South Japan any easier.

Then Mike saw other Japs getting away from the North Japanese invasion. Some wore American uniforms, some that of the old, dead Imperial Army. A lot of them had thrown away their rifles so they could retreat faster. The Constitutional Guard, or big chunks of it, didn't seem eager to guard the shiny new constitution. A few of those soldiers were wounded, but only a few. The rest were just bugging out.

Mike started worrying in earnest.

As far as the White House was concerned, the Japanese War couldn't have come at a worse time. The Republicans had just nominated Harold Stassen. Hardly anyone outside of Minnesota had ever heard of him. The way it had looked, he would have been a token candidate, and Steele and Garner would have rolled to a fifth term.

Now? Now Joe Steele had to work again. He was almost seventy. Some of the old energy was gone. Charlie could see that. The President seemed not just insulted but amazed that Trotsky's followers in North Japan dared try to upset the applecart.

At his orders, the Americans in South Japan tried to bomb them back to the Stone Age. B-29s thundered over North Japan, the way they'd thundered over the whole country when Hirohito still ran it. But the Imperial Japanese air defenses had been flattened before the Superfortresses rolled in.

It wasn't so easy now. North Japan flew Gurevich-9 fighter jets. The Gu-9s weren't as good as American F-80s. They were Russian versions of the German Me-262, probably built with the help of captured Nazi engineers and technicians. Even if they couldn't match the American jets, though, they were far more than B-29s had been designed to face. Daylight air raids over North Japan lasted only a few days.

Had they gone on any longer, there would have been precious few B-29s left to make more.

And . . . Charlie went up to the oval study to ask Joe Steele a question: "Sir, is it true a lot of those Gu-9s have Russian pilots?"

"It's true," Joe Steele answered. "But there's no point to saying anything about it." He knocked dottle from his pipe into a favorite ashtray: a brass catcher's mitt.

"Why not?" Charlie exclaimed. Propaganda points danced in his head.

Joe Steele looked at him the way he looked at Pat when his son asked a child's question. "Well, Sullivan, do you suppose the Japs are flying all those F-80s and B-29s?"

Charlie deflated. "Oh," he said. Then he brightened. "But North Japan invaded South Japan. We're helping the South Japanese defend themselves. Trotsky's pilots are helping the aggressors."

"If you can do something with it, go ahead." The President still sounded like a man humoring a little boy. He scratched his mustache. "What we really have to do is stop the bastards before they take Tokyo. That wouldn't look good at all. Can't let it happen." He nodded in a way that said there would be some dead generals if it did happen.

Seeing that Joe Steele didn't have anything else to tell him, Charlie got out of there. He fiddled around with the news that the Russians were flying planes for North Japan. Fiddle around was as much as he did. He couldn't manage to bring it out in a way that didn't show the Americans were doing more than just flying planes for South Japan. If not for American boots on the ground, the whole fragile Constitutional Monarchy of Japan might get swept away.

And one pair of those boots belonged to Mike. Charlie hoped his brother was okay. Hope was all he could do; he hadn't heard from Mike since the fighting broke out.

Idly, or not so idly, he wondered what kind of dope J. Edgar Hoover had on Harold Stassen. Whatever it was, it would poison the well during the campaign. Joe Steele might be slowing down, but he hadn't stopped. He wasn't about to lose an election, not if he could help it. And, as Charlie had reason to know, he damn well could.

*   .   *   .   *

Utsunomiya was one more medium-sized Japanese town, about as important, or as unimportant, in the scheme of things here as Omaha was in the States. It was also one of those places that might find its way into the history books by getting drenched in blood.

If the North Japanese broke through at Utsunomiya, Mike had no idea what would stop them this side of Tokyo. He was only a first sergeant, of course. He had a bug's-eye view of the battlefield, not a bird's-eye view. But, by the way the brass kept piling American troops and the steadier units of the Constitutional Guard into the fight, they felt the same way.

He and his section were dug in on the northern outskirts of Utsunomiya. If they had to fall back, they had orders to fight inside the town, too. Mike hoped they wouldn't have to. Where they were now marked the deepest penetration into South Japan the North Japanese had made.

Enemy bodies swelled in the sun in the fields north of town. That sickly-sweet stench was horribly familiar to Mike. It didn't just fill your nostrils. It soaked into cotton and wool, too; you brought it with you when you left the battlefield.

A killed T-34/85, a hole in its side armor, sat not far from his foxhole. He eyed the steel corpse with a healthy respect. One T-34/85 could make two or three Shermans say uncle. The Russian tank was faster than its American foe, it had better armor, and its gun was more powerful. The Sherman did have better fire control—a Sherman's gunner was more likely to hit what he aimed at. But if the round didn't get through, what good was a hit? This particular T-34/85 hadn't been lucky.

Or maybe a Pershing had got it. Pershings were definitely the big kids on the block, but there weren't enough of them to go around. Mike hoped like anything more were on the way.

Cautiously, he stuck his head up out of the foxhole. The North Japanese had pulled back a couple of miles, probably to gather themselves for one more push. He could see them moving around in the distance, but not what they were up to. He wished American artillery would hit them harder.

Then flames rippled from trucks parked over there. Lances of fire stabbed up into the sky. "Hit the dirt!" Mike yelled to his men. "Katyushas!"

He'd heard that the Red Army's rocket salvos scared the Nazis worse than anything else. He believed it. They sure as hell terrified him. He huddled in his hole as the rockets screamed down. They burst with deafening roars. Blast made breathing hard. Fragments of hot, sharp steel screamed through the air. Katyushas could devastate a whole regiment if they caught it out in the open.

But the Americans weren't out in the open. And the rocket barrage seemed to wake up the U.S. gunners. As the North Japanese tanks and foot soldiers surged forward, 105s and 155s started dropping shells among them. Purely by luck, one scored a direct hit on a T-34/85. It went up in a blaze of glory as all its ammo blew at once.

A Sherman clanked up and sat behind the dead Russian tank near Mike. Using the T-34/85 as a shield, it pumped high-explosive rounds at the enemy infantry. It couldn't kill enemy tanks till they got closer, and sensibly didn't try.

Mike held his fire. A grease gun was a murder mill inside a couple of hundred yards. Past that range, it was pretty much useless.

Corsairs and Hellcats roared in low, pounding the North Japanese troops with their machine guns and dropping napalm on their heads. The prop-driven Navy planes were obsolete for air-to-air combat, but they still made dandy ground-attack machines.

The North Japanese came on anyhow. They had a few old Russian fighters, but not so many planes as the Americans did. No one could say their foot soldiers weren't brave. Mike wished he could say that. He wouldn't have been so nervous.

Before long, he was banging away with his submachine gun. He greased one Jap who was about to throw a grenade his way. That was as close as the enemy got. Try as the North Japanese would, they couldn't bang their way past the defenders and into Utsunomiya.

Sullenly, they pulled back again as the sun went down in blood to the west. Mike discovered he had a gash on one arm. He had no idea when he'd got it. It didn't start to hurt till he realized it was there. He dusted it with sulfa powder and slapped on a wound bandage. If an officer noticed before he healed up, he might get another oak-leaf cluster for his Purple Heart. If not, he didn't care enough to make any kind of fuss.

He lit a cigarette. The smoke made him feel better for a little while. "Fuck," he said wearily. "I think we held 'em."

Joe Steele's voice came out of the radio: "It looks like we have stabilized the front in Japan. Now we have to clear the invaders from the Constitutional Monarchy and drive them back across the border they violated. I am sorry to say this may not be quick, easy, or cheap. But we will do it. We have to do it. The peace of the whole world demands that we contain Red expansion wherever Trotsky's minions try it. Like Nazism, world revolution is an idea whose time has come—and gone."

He went on to talk about rooting out Red spies and traitors at home, and about the way the economy was booming. Charlie listened with reluctant but real admiration. "There's life in the old boy yet," he said.

"It seems that way." Esther never went out on a limb to show what she thought of Joe Steele, but Charlie had no doubts on that score. She eyed him. "How much of the speech is yours?"

"Bits and pieces," he answered honestly. "Half a dozen people feed him words and ideas. He stirs them all together, takes what he likes, and adds his own stuff. The bit about containing the Reds—I came up with the word. It's something he wants to do. Maybe we can make it work in Japan and in Europe."

"How about in China?" Esther asked.

"How about that?" Charlie said, deadpan. Mao kept gaining ground; Chiang kept giving it. "Mao won't win before the election, anyway. It's only two weeks away. That will give us a while to figure out what to do about China going Red."

"If Joe Steele wins," his wife said.

"Oh, he'll win." Charlie sounded sure because he was sure. He agreed with both John Nance Garner and Stas Mikoian: Joe Steele would be President of the United States as long as he wanted to be.

Esther eyed him again. "How much *do* the election results they announce have to do with the real ones?"

She'd never asked him that before, not in all the years he'd been at the White House. Maybe she hadn't wanted to know. Charlie didn't know himself, not exactly. Approximately? Well, yes, he knew that much. And, because he knew, he replied, "Tell you what, hon. If you pretend you didn't say that, I'll pretend I didn't hear it."

Sometimes something that wasn't an answer turned out to be an answer after all. Esther sighed. This time, she was the one who got up, walked into the kitchen, and came back with a drink in her hand. Charlie could have used that as an excuse for one of his own. He would have not too long before. Now he was finding he felt better when he drank less. They'd run him out of the Hibernian Hall if he ever told them so, but it was true just the same.

He stayed at the White House for election night. Esther could have gone over to listen to the returns come in, but keeping an eye on Sarah and Pat gave her the perfect excuse to stay home. Since she had it, she used it.

Maine went for Stassen. New Hampshire and Vermont joined it. So did Maryland and Delaware. Lazar Kagan swore when losing Maryland became certain. Charlie did get himself a drink then. Somebody from the state out of which the District of Columbia was carved would catch hell for not stuffing the ballot boxes better.

But the big states, the states with the piles of electoral votes, stayed in Joe Steele's camp. New York, Pennsylvania, Illinois a little later on—they all backed the fifth term. The South stayed Solid behind the President. That was what the radio announcers said, anyhow. If the actual results were different from the announced totals, nobody was going to prove it.

Some of the states with lots of labor encampments and lots of resettled wreckers swung Harold Stassen's way. They might have been sending a message, but it wasn't loud enough. They didn't have many electoral votes.

More people lived on the West Coast. All three states there remained in Joe Steele's pocket. He didn't win so overwhelmingly as he had in 1936, 1940, or 1944, but Stassen's challenge wasn't serious.

About fifteen minutes after his lead in California grew too big to overcome, the President and Betty Steele came downstairs. Charlie joined in the applause. People would have noticed if he hadn't. Joe Steele waved to his aides and henchmen. "Well, we did it again," he said, and got another hand. "We'll keep on setting the country to rights, and we'll make sure the world doesn't go too crazy, too."

He was telling stories with Andy Wyszynski and the young assistant attorney general when Charlie came over to congratulate him. "Thanks, Sullivan," Joe Steele said. "You know what I wish we'd done when we went to Japan?"

"What's that, sir?"

"I wish we'd shot down Trotsky's plane. The Reds might've had themselves another civil war, trying to sort out who'd follow him." The President shook his head in annoyance. "Too late now, dammit. I'll never get such a good chance again."

"Sorry, sir." As soon as he could, Charlie hurried to the bar. He had a drink or three. Even if he didn't need them all the time any more, sometimes he did.

XXIV

Mike hunkered down behind a rock in the snow. A bullet spanged off the front of the rock. He shivered both from fear and from the cold. If Japanese summers reminded him of the ones in New York City, winters here came straight from Montana. It could get good and cold. It didn't always, but it could—and it had.

He was farther north than he had been this past summer, too. The fighting was north of what had been the border between North Japan and South Japan, but only by a few miles. He'd heard that Russian pilots flew North Japanese fighters. He wasn't even sure it was true. He hadn't seen any of the Russian occupiers fighting on the ground.

The North Japanese sure had a lot of fancy new Russian equipment, though. Trotsky was doing the same thing as he had in the Spanish Civil War, and Hitler and Mussolini with him. He was letting some other people try out his latest and greatest toys to see how they worked.

One of those new toys was a rifle of a kind Mike had never seen before. It spat bullets like a submachine gun, but you could still hit things with it out to a quarter of a mile. Some guys who'd fought in Europe said the Germans had used a piece like it right at the end of the war. For Mike and for most of the American troops on this side of the world, though, the AK-47 came as a nasty surprise.

Motion off to the left made Mike's head whip that way. Were the North Japanese trying to outflank his men? But it wasn't a Red Jap. It was a brownish gray monkey, its fur dusted with snow. It carried some kind of root in one startlingly human hand.

"Get the hell outa here, monkey!" Mike called softly. He

gestured with his grease gun. Damned if the monkey didn't lope away. The words or the movement seemed to make sense to it. Most of the critters that lived in Japan didn't look too different from ones you'd see in the States. Not everything was just the same, but most came close.

And then there were the monkeys. None of those in New York City, not outside of the zoos. The males were as big as two-year-olds, and had much sharper teeth. They were half tame; the Japs didn't bother them. And, just like their human cousins, they would steal anything that wasn't nailed down. He'd even seen them eat cigarette butts. If he'd done that, he would have heaved up everything he'd eaten for the past week. It didn't seem to bother the monkeys one bit.

He wondered how many of them had got killed in the American and Russian invasions. It wasn't as if—he hoped it wasn't as if—soldiers killed them on purpose. But monkeys, just like soldiers, could wind up in the wrong place at the wrong time.

Mike hoped he wasn't in the wrong place at the wrong time . . . again. He did have that fifth oak-leaf cluster for his Purple Heart now. What he didn't have any more was the bottom of his left earlobe. The wound had bled like hell. He didn't much care. Four inches to the right and that round would have caught him between his nose and his mouth.

A kid in a white winter suit with a radio on his back crawled up to Mike and said, "Sarge, they're gonna start shelling the Japs in half an hour. When they let up, they say we're supposed to go in and clean 'em out."

"They do, huh? Happy fucking day," Mike said. The brass always figured artillery would do more than it really could. But no help for it, not when he couldn't pretend he hadn't got the order. Sighing, he went on, "Tell 'em we'll give it our best shot."

The barrage came in on schedule. He peered around his rock and watched dirt and snow fly as the 105s thudded down one after another. You thought nothing above bug size could live when you watched something like that. But you'd be wrong. Human beings proved tough to kill, time after time.

Like me, for instance, Mike thought. He hoped he'd be tough to kill one more time. They hadn't got him yet. Nobody said they couldn't, though.

As soon as the barrage stopped, he bounced to his feet. "C'mon, guys!" he yelled. "We'll hit 'em while they're groggy!" He wanted to close with the North Japanese troops as fast as he could, so his grease gun would stand a better chance against those new automatic rifles.

Bullets snapped past him no more than a few seconds after he started running forward. Not all the enemy soldiers were groggy, dammit. He fired a burst of his own to make them duck.

They didn't have much barbed wire up—only a few strands. Younger men who ran faster had cut it by the time he reached it. A North Japanese wearing a Russian helmet popped out of his hole like a prairie dog to see what was going on. Mike shot him in the face. He fell down again with a bubbling wail.

Clearing trenches was a nasty business. They'd learned that in the American Civil War, and in World War I, and one more time in World War II. The Shuri Line on Okinawa had taught Mike more than he'd ever wanted to learn. But here he was, still at the same old trade. A grease gun was a good thing to have along. An entrenching tool was another. He'd have to clean his off when he got the chance.

The North Japanese had no more quit in them than their brothers and cousins had had in places from Wake Island to the borders of India. They wouldn't surrender, and they didn't want to retreat. So they died. Trotsky would have been proud of them, or perhaps just amused. A few Americans fell, too, for some frozen acres that would never mean much to anybody.

Charlie had the *Geographic* map of Japan back on his office wall at the White House. He'd drawn in what had been the demilitarized zone between Trotsky's North Japan and Joe Steele's South Japan. These days, the pins showing where the recent fighting was went into territory north of that borderline.

But he wasn't sure where all the pins should go. Some of

the places that had seen bitter fighting carried handles like Sukiyaki Valley or Mamasan Ridge or Hill 592. They must have owned other names, too, names that might have shown up on his map. Whatever those names were, though, they hadn't made it across the Pacific.

In Japan, Joe Steele's plan was to train and arm the Constitutional Guard till it could go up against the North Japanese forces on something like equal terms. Trotsky's Japs meant it. The ones fighting and dying for Akihito as constitutional monarch didn't. They weren't eager to go forward, or to fight if they did happen to advance.

One reason for the trouble was that the Constitutional Guard was full of Red infiltrators. Trotsky's backers must have started that the minute Hirohito bought a plot, or maybe even before. They spread distrust of officers and of Americans and a reluctance to obey orders far and wide.

That was something Joe Steele knew how to handle—or he thought he did. The trouble was, treason trials and harsh punishments for anyone who even looked unhappy did nothing to improve the Constitutional Guard's morale.

So Americans kept doing most of the Constitutional Monarchy's fighting and most of the dying in Japan. Next to the battles there before World War II ended, even next to the fighting in Europe, the stubborn positional war going on now was small potatoes. But it was like an infected sore that wouldn't stop oozing casualties. News of young American men killed and young American men maimed wouldn't go away. Spring passed into summer. Places christened Geisha Gulch and the Valley of the Shadow of Death showed up in the newspapers. They weren't the kind of names that won popularity contests.

Charlie went to Stas Mikoian, who was the most reasonable of Joe Steele's longtime cronies. "You know, if the boss wants to get reelected in 1952, he's got to do something more about the Japanese War," he said.

Mikoian smiled at him. "If the boss wants to get reelected in 1952, he'll get reelected in 1952, and you can take that to the bank."

"He'll have to cook the books harder than usual to make sure nothing goes wrong," Charlie said.

"Nothing will go wrong." Stas Mikoian kept smiling. Was it an I-know-something-you-don't-know smile? Charlie didn't especially think so at the time. At the time, all he thought was that Mikoian should have paid more attention to him. Afterwards, though, he wondered.

And the Japanese War and its misfortunes weren't limited to the far side of the Pacific. A few days after Charlie talked with Mikoian, he saw a little story in the *Washington Post* some AP stringer in New Mexico had filed. *An ammunition dump exploded in the desert about a hundred miles south of Albuquerque*, it read. *The blast, which took place in the predawn hours, lit up the bleak countryside and could be heard for miles. The cause is still under investigation. No casualties were reported.*

Casualties or not, somebody's head will roll, Charlie thought. *Sounds like it was a big boom. Good thing it was off in the middle of nowhere. That's where they need to keep ammunition dumps.* He read the story again. That *bleak* argued the reporter wasn't from New Mexico. He smiled to himself, there in the office. If his life hadn't got tangled up with Joe Steele's, he might have written the paragraph in the paper himself.

He wondered if he would be happier now had he kept on writing for the Associated Press. It wouldn't have been hard to arrange. If he'd taken a leak a few minutes earlier or a few minutes later in that Chicago greasy spoon in 1932, so he didn't hear Vince Scriabin talking to, well, somebody . . . Those few minutes, the chance filling of his bladder, made all the difference in the world to his life, and to Mike's, too.

You could drive yourself clean around the bend if you started wondering about stuff like that. What if Joe Steele's folks had stayed in the old country instead of coming to America? What would he have become over there? A priest? A Red? Nothing very much? That was the way to bet. The United States was the land of opportunity, the place where a man could rise from nothing to—to five terms in the White House.

People always liked to believe they were the masters of their souls and the captains of their fate. But just because you liked to believe it didn't make it true. It seemed at least as likely that people bounced at random off the paddles of God's pinball machine, and that they could as easily have bounced some other way.

In a similar vein, hadn't Einstein said God didn't play dice with the universe? Something like that, anyhow. But Einstein himself had crapped out before his appointed time, so how much had he known?

No. That wasn't a problem of physics or quantum mechanics or whatever you wanted to call it. That was Albert Einstein misreading Joe Steele. Einstein had been mighty good with a slide rule. With people? Not so hot. With Joe Steele, you got only one mistake. Einstein made a big one, and paid a big price.

What went through Charlie's mind was *I'm still here*. Einstein had done more while he was around. Charlie knew that. But Einstein was a genius, and Charlie didn't fill the bill there. He knew that, too. Genius or not, he was still around to do the things he could do, while Einstein wasn't. That also counted. As far as Charlie could see, it counted for more than anything else.

Mike sat in the ruins of Yamashita, on the east coast of North Japan, as the sun went down. Red propaganda posters still decorated the walls and fences that the fighting hadn't knocked down. Workers and peasants marched side by side into a sunny future. Happy tractors—they were smiling cartoons—plowed fields. He couldn't read the script, but the pictures spoke for themselves.

He spooned beef stew out of a C-ration can. It wasn't one of his favorites, but it beat hell out of going hungry. Down in South Japan, they were trying to make the Japs use the Roman alphabet all the time. The idea was to link them to the wider world. Whether they wanted to be linked that way . . . Eisenhower didn't bother to ask. He just followed Joe Steele's orders.

Trotsky was supposed to be the one who tore everything up by the roots. But the Russians hadn't tried to change the way people in North Japan wrote. What did it say when Joe Steele was more radical than Mr. World Revolution?

A soldier came over to Mike and asked, "Hey, Sarge, are we gonna move up toward Sendai tonight?"

Sendai was the next real city, about ten miles north of Yamashita. It held about a quarter of a million people. It was also the place where the North Japanese were digging in for a serious stand. All the same, Mike shook his head. "Doesn't look that way, Ralph. Our orders are to sit tight right where we are."

"How come?" Ralph said. "If we hit 'em when they're off-balance, like, maybe we can punch through 'em an' get this goddamn stupid useless fucking war over with."

Mike chuckled. "Tell me again how you feel about it. I wasn't quite sure the first time." He held up a hand. "Seriously, though, all I do is work here. You want to get the orders changed, go back to Division HQ. That's where they came from."

"Oh, yeah. They're gonna listen to a PFC." Ralph patted his single stripe. "But I still say we're missin' a good chance."

"I think so, too, but I can't do anything about it, either. Maybe we'll bomb 'em tonight or something." Mike paused to slap at a mosquito. There weren't nearly so many of them now in August as there had been during spring, but Japan seemed to be without them only when it was snowing.

Ralph slapped, too. "What we ought do is bomb *this* place with that new shit, that DDT," he said. "Beats the bejesus out of Flit and like that. I mean, it really kills the little sonsabitches."

"Yeah." Mike wasn't lousy. He didn't have fleas. He got sprayed every week or two, and the pests couldn't live on him. "It's the McCoy, all right."

He walked around his section's perimeters, making sure the sentries were where they needed to be and stayed on their toes. The main North Japanese force was up at Sendai, sure. But those bastards liked to sneak men in civilian clothes, sometimes even women, back into areas they'd lost and have them toss grenades at the Americans and try to disappear in the confusion afterwards. Whenever you fought Japs, you needed to stay ready all the time or you'd be sorry.

About half past ten, Mike was getting ready to roll himself

in his blanket. He'd learned to sleep anywhere at any time in the labor encampment. That came in handy for a soldier, too.

Before he dropped off, though, bombers droned overhead, flying from south to north. They really were going to hit Sendai, then. They hadn't used the B-29s all that much lately, even at night. North Japanese fighters and flak made the big planes suffer.

The ones tonight were flying so high, he could hardly hear their engines. Considering how much noise B-29s made in the air, that was really saying something. The North Japanese in Sendai knew they were coming, though. Their antiaircraft guns sent a fireworks display of tracers into the sky. Mike hoped the crews would come through safe.

He twisted in his hole. Like a dog or a cat, he looked for the most comfortable way in which to sleep. He'd just found it and closed his eyes when a new sun blazed in the north.

Even in the hole, even with his eyes closed, the hideous glare tore at his sight. He clapped his hands to his face. That wouldn't have helped, either, if the light hadn't faded quickly. As it faded, a thunderous roar, like that of every artillery piece in the world going off at once, left him half deaf. Wind whistled past him for a moment, though the night had been calm till then.

He scrambled to his feet. Now he could bear to look to the north. He gaped at what he saw. Lit from within, a cloud of gas and dust and God knew what rose high into the sky, higher and wider every moment. It had a terrible and terrifying beauty unlike anything he'd ever dreamt of.

Even though it was so far away, he felt heat against his face, as he would have from the real sun. What had happened to Sendai, right under . . . whatever that was? What had happened to the North Japanese troops crowding Sendai? Whatever had happened to them, he was sure he didn't need to worry about them any more.

Joe Steele's voice came out of the radio: "Yesterday, August 6, 1949—a day which will live in history—the United States of America harnessed the power that lights the stars to bring peace between the two warring nations that now share the Home Islands of Japan."

Charlie beamed. He beamed so much that Esther smiled, too, and asked, "That's your opening, isn't it?"

"You bet it is," Charlie said. The news was big enough that what Joe Steele had to say about it was bound to wind up in Bartlett's. The President would get the credit, but Charlie would know where the words came from even if nobody else but his wife did.

"A B-29 dropped an atomic bomb on the city of Sendai last night," Joe Steele went on. "It was a legitimate military target because of its factories and because North Japanese troops were massing there for a fresh attack against American forces at Yamashita, ten miles to the south. This one bomb had the explosive power of twenty thousand tons of high explosive. It was two thousand times as strong as the biggest bomb that fell on Germany during World War II.

"We used this terrible weapon with reluctance. But it has become clear that the North Japanese and their Russian backers cannot be made to recognize the legitimacy of the Constitutional Monarchy of Japan by anything but extraordinary measures. And so we have now turned to those measures. To the leaders of North Japan and to all who prop them up, I give a warning they would do well to heed. Enough is enough."

"That sounds like we have more of those atomic bombs piled up somewhere ready to go," Esther said.

"It sure does," Charlie said. "But you can't prove anything by me. I didn't know we had the one till it went off." He had known Rickover and his pet physicists and engineers were working on it, but not that they'd succeeded. The eggheads Rickover had pulled out of the regular labor encampments and into his special one probably wouldn't have to break any more rocks or pave any more roads.

"Here's hoping this means your brother gets out of the war in one piece," Esther said.

"That would be good. That would be wonderful, in fact," Charlie said. "As far as I know, Mike hasn't been on this side of the Pacific since he shipped out in—God!—1943."

Esther looked and listened to make sure Sarah and Pat couldn't hear what she had to say. Charlie not only recognized the gesture, he used it himself. Satisfied, she said, "He probably doesn't want to get any closer to Joe Steele than he can help."

"No, he probably doesn't." Charlie sighed and started to take a Chesterfield out of the pack. Then he decided he didn't have the urge that badly; he could wait a little longer. After another sigh, he went on, "Not everything Joe Steele's done has been bad. We're the richest, strongest country in the world now. We sure weren't when he took over. We were out on our feet like a fighter who walked into a left hook."

His wife checked again. Only after that did she say, "Well, you're right. I can't argue. But we used to be the freest country in the world. I don't think we are now. Do you? Is what we got worth what we've lost?"

"I can't begin to tell you," Charlie said. "When the kids' kids are all grown up, ask them. Maybe they'll have an answer."

"What's that thing in the New Testament?" Esther snapped her fingers in frustration, trying to remember. "Something about, What does it profit—?" She shook her head; she couldn't finish the quote.

But Charlie could: "'For what is a man profited, if he shall gain the whole world, and lose his own soul?'"

"That's the one! It's a darn good question, isn't it? Even if it's goyish, I mean." She sent him a crooked grin of the kind he was more used to feeling on his own face than to seeing on hers.

"It is a good question," he said. "But that's not how I look at things. For me, it's more like 'Render unto Caesar the things which are Caesar's; and unto God the things that are God's.'"

"This Caesar's done a lot of rendering, hasn't he?" Esther said. "Mike would think so."

"Yeah, I guess he would," Charlie agreed. "But so would all those North Japanese troops at Sendai. They got rendered down in spades."

Esther made yet another check to be sure the children couldn't hear. She dropped her voice all the same: "What happens when he dies, this term or next term or the one after that? What do we do then? Do we turn back the clock and try to pretend he never happened? Or do we go on the way . . . the way he's shown us?"

Charlie whistled tunelessly between his teeth. "Babe, I have no idea." The only person who'd ever mentioned to him the possibility of Joe Steele dying was John Nance Garner, and the Vice President hadn't believed it would happen—certainly not soon enough to do him any good.

Scriabin, Mikoian, Kagan, Hoover, Wyszynski, Marshall . . . They all had to know the boss was mortal. And they had to know that acting as if they knew would send them crashing down in ruin.

A couple of days went by. The first Americans got into Sendai, breathing through masks and wearing lead-lined clothes. Pictures were horrific. The one that particularly made Charlie shudder was of a man's shadow, printed on the sidewalk by the flash of the bomb. The shadow was the only thing left of the man who'd cast it. He'd gone up in smoke a split second later.

While the Americans were bombing Japan during World War II, a handful of damaged B-29s that couldn't get back flew on to Russia instead. The Reds interned the crews: for most of the war, they hadn't been fighting the Japs. They also kept the planes. They kept them and they copied them, the same way they copied DC-3s. Russian Tu-4s looked and performed almost the same as their American models. The North Japanese flew a few bombing raids with them early in the Japanese War: or, more likely, Russian crews handled the flying for them. Those raids didn't do that much, and pretty soon they stopped.

On the night of August 9, a lone B-29 flew high over Nagano, a medium-sized city in South Japan. No one paid any special attention to it. There was a war on. Warplanes came by every now and then. Only this one wasn't a B-29. It was a Tu-4. A bomb fell free. The plane made a tight turn and got out of there as if all the demons of hell were after it.

And they were. Not quite a minute later, Nagano was incinerated the way Sendai had been three days earlier. Radio Moscow's shortwave English-language broadcast explained the whys and wherefores: "The capitalist jackals of

South Japan demanded American aid in their unjust struggle against the peace-loving Japanese People's Republic. Recently, that aid became destructive to an unprecedented and barbarous degree. In response, the peace-loving Japanese People's Republic called on its fraternal socialist ally for assistance against imperialist aggression. That assistance has been proffered.

"President Steele, the arch-aggressor of the postwar world, declared that enough was enough. As the leader of the Red vanguard of world revolution, Leon Trotsky agrees. Enough *is* enough. These devastating bombs can fall upon the territory of countries other than the two Japans. The world struggle may prove painful, but we shall not shrink from it."

When photos from Nagano began coming out, they looked just as dreadful as the ones from Sendai. The only difference was, some of the ones from Nagano had mountains in the background, while some of those from Sendai showed the Pacific. The dead, the melted, the scorched, and, soon, the people dying of radiation sickness in both cities looked pretty much the same.

"What are we going to do?" Charlie asked Stas Mikoian. "How many bombs do we have? How many has Trotsky got? Do we want to start playing last-man-standing with him?"

"That's about what it would come down to, all right, only I don't know if anybody'd be left standing. I don't know just how many bombs we have, either," Mikoian said. Charlie took that with a grain of salt, not that he could do anything about it short of calling Mikoian a liar. The Armenian went on, "And I have no idea how many Trotsky has. I didn't know he had one till he dropped it."

"What does the boss think? I haven't had the nerve to ask him."

Mikoian scowled. "He wants to kill Einstein all over again, that's what. I've got a hard time blaming him, too. If we'd started on the bomb in '41 instead of '45, we would have kept the whip hand on the Russians for years."

Maybe that was what Einstein was afraid of, Charlie thought. If Joe Steele had the atomic bomb and Leon

Trotsky didn't, wouldn't he have held it over Trotsky's head like a club, or else bashed him with it? Sure he would have. But saying as much to Mikoian wouldn't be Phi Beta Kappa. Charlie hadn't been Phi Beta Kappa himself, but he could see that.

He found one more question: "What'll we do about the Japanese War now?"

"Wind it up as quick as we can. What else are we supposed to do?" Mikoian said. "If we keep going like this, pretty soon there won't be any Japanese left alive to fight over."

"Makes sense to me," Charlie said. That had looked obvious to him since the news came out of Nagano. He was damn glad it looked that way to Joe Steele and his other henchmen, too.

Mike climbed into the back of an olive-drab Army truck with nothing but relief. "And so we bid farewell to lovely, romantic North Japan, to its quaint natives, and to its curious and exotic customs," he said. Even after so many years as a wrecker and a dogface, he still liked slinging words. It was a hell of a lot more fun than, say, slinging hash.

He thought so, anyhow. The other soldiers boarding the truck with him jeered and hooted. "Cut the bullshit, Sarge," one of them said. "Only good thing about the fuckin' natives is, they didn't manage to shoot me."

"I can't even say that," Mike replied.

"Oh," the soldier added, "and we didn't get blown up by the atomic whoozis."

"That wasn't the North Japanese. That was us," Mike said.

"Well, what if the flyboys had missed? Then it woulda come down on our heads and blown us to the moon instead of the Japs. Coulda happened, I bet. Them bomber pilots, they can fuck up a wet dream."

"Yeah." Mike couldn't even tell him he was full of it. Maybe he wasn't. It wasn't as if Mike hadn't had to dive into a hole a time or three himself to escape his own side's ordnance. But that big a screwup wouldn't have been easy, and it hadn't happened.

Another soldier said, "Us and the Japs, we sure wasted a lot of time and blood and sweat to call it a tie and all go back to where we started from."

"Status quo ante bellum," Mike said. He wasn't sure whether that came from being a reporter or straight out of Catholic school. Either way, he'd had it a long time.

It just confused the soldier from his section. "What the hell does that mean, Sarge?" the man asked.

"The same thing as what you said, only in Latin."

"Latin? La-de-da!" the guy said. Mike gave him the finger. Everybody laughed. If Mike hadn't shown he was as tough as anybody half his age, his men might have decided he was a fairy. He'd seen that soldiers often prided themselves on how ignorant they were, and distrusted anybody who knew anything that didn't have to do with killing. The only worse group for that he could think of were Jeebies.

The driver slid over from behind the wheel to look back through the little window in the partition that separated his compartment from the bigger one behind it. Seeing the truck was full, he said, "Okay, we're gonna get outa here." The men in the back gave him a hand. Mike joined in along with the rest.

Down the coast road from Yamashita they went. Looking backward—the only way he could look out—Mike was reminded of the truck ride he'd taken from the railway siding to the labor encampment in the Rockies. The fields on either side of that highway hadn't been pocked with shell craters, though. And, once that truck got up into the mountains, the air had been crisp, and smelled like pines. Now it was hot and muggy and held the faint but unmistakable whiff of death.

Before too long, they left North Japan and went back into South Japan. The two countries that were unhappily learning to divide the Home Islands between them had already set up border checkpoints on the road. The two flags flew on poles of exactly the same height. Even though nobody on either side of the frontier bothered the truck convoy, Mike was glad to get out of the country that put the hammer and sickle inside the meatball and into the one that left the old Japanese flag alone.

Not far south of the border, an enormous American processing center had sprouted, rather like a ring of toadstools after a rain. One advantage of being a sergeant was that Mike stood in a shorter line before the rear-echelon clowns who decided what to do with him.

He showed a personnel sergeant his dog tags. "And where were you stationed before the fighting broke out?" the man asked.

"On the demilitarized zone. Right outside of Wakamatsu, about fifteen miles east of the mountains."

"Really?" The personnel sergeant lifted an eyebrow. "You were . . . lucky, weren't you?" That was a polite way of saying *How come you're still alive? Did you run like Red Grange?*

"Mac, you don't know the half of it," Mike answered. "I was coming back from leave on Shikoku when things went kablooie. My buddy and me, we'd just about made it to Tokyo when we got the news." He wondered how Dick Shirakawa was doing. With his looks, Dick had a built-in excuse, one even the Army recognized, for staying behind the lines.

"I see," the personnel sergeant said. Mike wondered how he'd managed to steer clear of the fighting. The guy wore a clean uniform. He hadn't missed any meals. He might as well have been in an insurance office back in Bridgeport. Now he asked, "Would it suit you if I send you to that area again?"

"I guess so," Mike answered. "I liked being there before. Christ only knows what it looks like these days, though, or how many of the people I knew last year are still there." *Are still alive,* he thought, but he didn't say it.

"We'll do that, then. Wakamatsu, you said?" The personnel sergeant seemed glad to solve a problem so fast. Mike wasn't so sure he was glad to be going back. But now he had orders, so all he had to do was follow them.

The processing center had its own motor pool. A buck private wouldn't have been able to promote a jeep, but a veteran first sergeant with a chestful of ribbons (Mike made sure he put them on before he went over) had no trouble at all. They also might have given him a bad time had they known he'd served in a punishment brigade, but he hadn't worn the P on his sleeve for a while now.

Country around the demilitarized zone hadn't been smashed up so badly as the rest of Japan during the Second World War. The Japanese War made up for that, and then some. All the damage here was fresher than it was farther south. And the North Japanese had kidnapped lots of people and taken them over the border. Others, they simply shot. Not many of his old friends greeted Mike when he made it back. The only thing that made him sure he'd come to the right place was his road map.

On the far side of the zone, he got glimpses of far-off North Japanese soldiers laying barbed wire and digging tank traps. They'd invaded the Constitutional Monarchy, but now they were getting ready for somebody to invade them. Mike just scratched his head. He didn't follow that kind of logic, if it was logic.

Joe Steele would, he thought, and laughed quietly to himself.

XXV

Only a couple of months after atomic fire seared Sendai and Nagano, Mao ran Chiang off the Chinese mainland. Chiang and his Nationalists Dunkirked across the Formosa Strait to the island of the same name (though most maps also called it Taiwan). Without any navy to speak of, Mao's Reds couldn't follow them. Chiang declared that the Nationalists still were the legitimate government of all of China, and that one fine day they'd go back to the mainland for another few rounds with Mao.

Joe Steele recognized Chiang as rightful President of China. Some of America's allies did, too, but not all of them. Charlie wasn't particularly surprised. Joe Steele hadn't recognized Trotsky as ruler in Russia till they ended up on the same side in the war against Hitler.

He did remark to Stas Mikoian, "I wondered if the boss was going to use some more A-bombs in China to give Chiang a helping hand." Not by word or by inflection did he let on about how much the idea scared him. Showing that anything the boss might do scared you was an invitation to the Jeebies to come pick you up. The only way you could mention such things was with a neutrality more scrupulous than Switzerland's.

Mikoian nodded. "There was some discussion of it," he answered, also as coolly as if he were talking about how much vermouth to put in a Martini. He was smoother with that tone than Charlie was. As far as Charlie could tell, Mikoian was smoother with it than anybody. He might have been lightly amused as he continued, "Remember when Gromyko visited last month?"

"Sure," Charlie said. The Russian ambassador always

looked as if he had a poker shoved up his behind. The Great Stone Face was his Washington nickname. He made Vince Scriabin seem jolly by comparison, and that wasn't easy. "Why? What did he say?"

"He said that if we dropped anything on Shanghai or Peiping, for instance, he couldn't answer for what might happen to Paris or Rome."

"Oh," Charlie said. After that, there didn't seem to be much more *to* say. A moment later, Charlie did find one more question: "He persuaded the boss he meant it or Trotsky meant it or however you want to put that?"

"He must have, or the bombers would have flown," Mikoian answered. "Myself, I thought they were going to. But the world can probably live through one atomic bomb from each side. Once you start throwing them around for every little thing, pretty soon there's not much left to throw them at. Chances are there's not much left of you, either."

"Is that you talking, or are you quoting Joe Steele?"

"I'm quoting what I told him. General Marshall said the same thing," Mikoian replied. "He thought it over, and he decided we were right."

"I see," Charlie said, in place of the *Thank heaven!* he felt like shouting. He added, "You know, there are times it doesn't break my heart that I'm not a big enough wheel to sit in when you guys talk about stuff like that."

"I don't know what you're talking about." The glint in Mikoian's eye gave his sardonic words the lie. With a wry chuckle, he said, "I didn't expect I'd need to worry about blowing up the world when I came to Washington with Joe Steele right at the end of the First World War. All you can do is roll with the punches the best way you know how."

"Hey, I didn't think I'd wind up here, either. I figured I'd write stories for the Associated Press the rest of my life, or maybe get good enough at what I did so a paper like the *Boston Globe* or the *New York Times* or the *Washington Post* would pick me up," Charlie said. "But here I am."

"It hasn't worked out too badly," Mikoian said.

Charlie couldn't even tell him he was wrong. He'd done well for himself here. But the quote from Matthew that Esther hadn't quite been able to remember kept coming back to mind. He hoped he hadn't lost his soul. He thought things were better here with him than they would have been without him. He hadn't exactly stood up to Joe Steele, though. He'd gone along with some things he wished he hadn't.

It was cold and rainy and getting close to Christmas when GBI men swooped down on half a dozen scholars of Chinese history, literature, and culture and dragged them off their campuses (in one case, straight out of a lecture hall) and into prison. The charge was aiding and abetting the fall of mainland China to the Reds.

"We know who lost China for Chiang Kai-shek!" Andy Wyszynski boomed at a press conference. "Yes, we know, and those people will pay the price for their disloyalty!"

"Haven't we heard this song before?" Esther asked.

"We aren't just hearing it—we're watching it," Charlie said. And they were. The television set seemed an awful lot of cabinet—and an awful lot of money—for not much screen, but there was the Attorney General, bellowing away right in their living room.

"Those treacherous fools deserve the long prison terms we will impose on them!" Wyszynski shouted, pumping the air with his clenched fist.

When he said that, Esther raised an eyebrow. "What? He's not going for the death penalty? Is Joe Steele getting soft?"

Charlie gave one of those let-me-check-the-children looks. Then he said, "I don't think he's getting soft. I think he's getting old. He really is slowing down some now that he's passed seventy."

"About time, wouldn't you say?" Esther made sure she kept her voice down.

A commercial came on: a smiling blond girl who wore a costume that covered her torso with a rectangular cigarette pack pranced around in fishnet stockings while a background chorus sang about how wonderful the brand was. Charlie clucked sadly. "Boy, I didn't think anything could be dumber than radio advertising, but this TV stuff shows me I was wrong."

"It's pretty bad, all right." Esther didn't return to talking about Joe Steele. Charlie wasn't sorry. Talking about the President had been dangerous at any time during his long, long administration. It seemed all the more so now that he was visibly starting to fail. He might lash out to show that his sand wasn't really running out after all.

Or he might live, and stay President, another ten years. Just because he was slowing down, that didn't mean he had to stop soon. If he had any reason to live on, wasn't it to spite John Nance Garner?

Every few weeks, a technical sergeant with a Geiger counter drove a jeep along the southern edge of the demilitarized zone, checking radiation levels from the bomb that had fallen on Nagano—and also, Mike supposed, from the one that had fallen on Sendai. The United States and Russia had both added to Honshu's postwar misery.

"How does it look?" Mike asked the guy, whose name was Gary Cunningham. "I mean, besides cold?"

"I'm from Phoenix, Arizona. Not the weather I grew up with—that's for goddamn sure." Cunningham waved at the snow on the ground. "Didn't have to worry about crap like this. But the radiation? It's going down—seems to be dropping pretty much the way the slide-rule boys figured."

"Is it dangerous?" Mike asked.

"I don't think so, not where it's at now. I mean, the smart guys don't think so," Cunningham answered. "All I do is, I get the numbers they want, and then I listen to them going on about what the shit means."

Mike suspected he was sandbagging. Plainly, he was nobody's dope, even if he wasn't a scientist himself. He would have seen enough and heard enough to make some pretty good guesses of his own. "I was in Yamashita when we dropped the one on Sendai," Mike said. "What's that going to do to me over time?"

"So you were as close as anybody American," Cunningham said. It wasn't a question: he was putting a card in his mental filing cabinet. He went on, "You didn't come down with radiation sickness, right? Your hair didn't fall out? You didn't start puking?"

"No, nothing like that," Mike said.

Cunningham nodded. "Haven't heard that any of us there came down with it. Some Americans who were too close to Nagano did."

"Some Americans who were in fucking Nagano, there's nothing left of them now. Nothing left of a big old pile of Japs, either," Mike said.

"Well, you've got that right. I don't know how many Russians we toasted in Sendai, either," Gary Cunningham said. "But getting back to you . . . The short answer is, nobody knows what the radiation dose you picked up will do to you ten, twenty, thirty years down the line. You're a guinea pig. If you die of cancer, maybe you can blame it on being too close to the bomb. Or maybe it would have happened anyway. I can't tell you. Right now, I don't think anyone can. The docs'll be studying you and the other soldiers and the Japs who were in the neighborhood, and when your son's as old as you are maybe they'll know what's what."

"I don't have any kids. My wife deep-sixed me when I was in an encampment," Mike growled. "Suppose I meet somebody now. Do I need to worry about what the bomb did to my nuts?"

"I don't know the answer to that, either. I can't even begin to guess, so I won't try, okay?" Cunningham said. He cocked his head to one side and studied Mike. "So you were a scalp, too, huh?"

"Damn straight. Sullivan, Michael, NY24601. I was up in Montana, chopping down trees. How about you?"

"Cunningham, Gary, AZ1797. I dug irrigation ditches in New Mexico and Colorado." Cunningham took off the gloves shielding his hands from the cold. His palms were all over calluses, even after what had to be a good length of time away from forced labor. "They turned me loose in '44, and I got drafted right afterwards. I liked the Army better than anything I could do on Civvy Street, so I stayed in. What's your story?"

"I volunteered in '42 to get out of the encampment," Mike replied.

"Wait . . ." Cunningham eyed him again, in a different way this time. "Guys who did that went straight into a punishment brigade."

"Uh-huh," Mike said dryly.

"But . . . Fuck, they told me what the odds were if I went into an outfit like that. I stayed in till my stretch ended on account of it. How many other guys who started out with you are still here?"

"The ones who went all the way through everything and didn't get maimed early on? My company CO did it. I know of two, three others. They weren't people I was tight with or anything."

"Damn!" Cunningham said. "Now I feel like I've seen the Great White Whale. My hat's off to you, man." He doffed it. It was a fur cap with earflaps, the kind the guards in Montana would have drooled over. Mike didn't think it was Army issue; he wondered if Cunningham had scavenged it from a dead North Japanese soldier or a Russian.

"Yeah, well, that and a couple of yen'll buy me some sake. Want to go into Wakamatsu and buy some sake?" Mike said. "You go through weather like this, you understand why the Japs drink it hot."

"That's a fact," Cunningham said. "I'll buy you a couple. I'm honored to. You don't run into many guys who went through everything you did and came out in one piece."

"Well, almost." Mike rubbed the bottom of his left earlobe, which was most of an inch higher than the bottom of his right ear. "But thanks—I'll take you up on that." After so much terror and pain, serving in that punishment brigade had finally paid off—a couple of shots of sake's worth, anyhow. What the hell? You took what you could get.

After Esther discouraged him from drowning his sorrows whenever he got the urge, Charlie didn't go to the tavern near the White House anywhere near so often as he had before. He felt better for staying away, too . . . most of the time. Every once in a while, often on days when he'd had more of Vince Scriabin than he could take, he needed a Band-Aid for his brain. Bourbon did the trick better than anything else he knew.

When he did go in there, he commonly found John Nance Garner perched on his usual barstool. Joe Steele ran the country. Joe Steele, in fact, ran most of the world that wasn't Red. The USA was the only big power that hadn't had its economy ravaged by war. The American economy had boomed louder than American guns. Anyone who wanted help had to keep the President happy.

John Nance Garner presided over this tavern and the United States Senate. Comparing the time he spent in the Cabinet to the time he spent here, Charlie knew which part of his little domain mattered more to him. Well, with things as they were in Washington during Joe Steele's fifth term, the bartender here held more power than the Senate did.

When Charlie walked in on a mild spring afternoon, Garner greeted him with, "Hey, if it ain't Charlie Sullivan! How are things out in the real world, Sullivan?" A cigarette in his hand sent up a thin strand of smoke. The full ashtray in front of him said he'd been here a while. So did the empty glasses.

"The real world? What's that? I work in the White House," Charlie said, and then, to the bartender, "Wild Turkey over ice, please."

"Comin' right up, suh," the Negro replied. Charlie slid a half-dollar and a dime tip across the bar. Prices had climbed after the war; not even Joe Steele could keep them down, any more than King Canute had been able to hold back the tide.

Garner puffed, chuckled, and puffed again. "Hell, I wouldn't know. Damned if I remember the last time I went inside there. Joe Steele don't want me around. I'm a poor relation. I embarrass him."

"If you embarrassed him, he wouldn't put you on the ticket every four years," Charlie said. He didn't think that was the problem at all. The need to have a Vice President reminded a President of his mortality. These days, Joe Steele's own body was giving him reminders like that. He didn't need John Nance Garner around to rub them in.

"Sonny, the only reason I stay on there is 'cause he knows I don't make waves," Garner said. It had to be one reason; Charlie didn't think it was the only one. The Veep went on, "If he put me out to pasture back in Uvalde, wouldn't break my heart, not one bit."

"Oh, come on. I don't believe that," Charlie said. "You'd

been in Washington a long time before you started running with Joe Steele. You have to like it here, or at least be used to it."

"I'm used to it, all right." Garner screwed up his face. "That don't got to mean I like it, though."

"Okay. Sure." Charlie wasn't going to argue with him. If he said anything about protesting too much, Garner would just get mad. He finished his drink and held up a forefinger to show he wanted another.

Garner had another one, too. After so many, what was one more? After the Vice President died, if he ever did, they really needed to take out his liver and donate it to the Smithsonian. It was a national treasure, if not a national monument.

"Another term," Garner said with a maudlin sigh. "And then another term after that, and maybe another term after *that*." By the way he used the word, he might have been talking about stretches in a labor encampment, not the country's second highest elected office.

But the difference between highest and second highest was even starker in politics than it was in sports. Charlie was pretty sure he could rattle off every World Series winner from 1903 to this past October. He was much hazier on the teams that had lost. Who wasn't?

The difference between President and Vice President, though, wasn't the difference between winning and losing. It was the difference between winning and not getting to play. Joe Steele could order two-thirds of the world around. John Nance Garner could order . . . another bourbon. And he had.

Shakespeare chimed in Charlie's head, as Shakespeare had a way of doing.

Tomorrow and tomorrow and tomorrow,
Creeps in this petty pace from day to day,
To the last syllable of recorded time;
And all our yesterdays have lighted fools
The way to dusty death.

He didn't come out with the quotation, though he expected Garner would have known it if he had. Anyone who'd been educated in small-town Texas before the turn of the century would have been steeped in Shakespeare the way a tea bag was steeped in hot water.

Before Charlie could say anything at all, Garner went on, "I never reckoned I'd be in this slot so long, you know? When I said I'd run, I thought I'd have me a term or two, and that'd be it. Joe Steele would lose, or he wouldn't run for a third term, or whatever the hell. Shows what I knew, don't it? The things I've seen since . . ." He shook his big head. "The things I've seen my whole life, I should say. I was born three and a half years after the States War ended. Ain't many left who can say that."

"No, there aren't." Charlie grinned at him. "Most of the ones who can would call it the Civil War."

"Damnyankees, the lot of 'em," Garner said without heat. "Weren't any cars or planes or phones or radios or records or *tee*vees or movies or lightbulbs or any o' that crap when I was a boy. We had trains an' the telegram an' gaslamps, an' we reckoned we were the most modern folks on the face of the earth. An' you know what else? We *were*."

"I guess so." Charlie had grown up with most of the things Garner had seen coming in. But he remembered what a prodigy radio seemed like, and how the switch from silents to talkies changed film forever. Now, of course, television was changing the world all over again. That had only started. He could see as much, but he had no idea how it would turn out.

"Tell you somethin' else, though," John Nance Garner said after a pull at his latest bourbon. "I got goin' on eighty-two years on me now, an' in all my time on earth, I ain't never seen nothin' like Joe Steele. And Sullivan?"

"What?" Charlie said.

"You can take that to the fuckin' bank."

Mike walked into Wakamatsu. By now the castle, which had been bombed by the USA in World War II and shelled by both sides during the Japanese War, was looking pretty much like its old self again. The Japs worked hard at putting their shattered homeland back together again. At least they did here in South Japan, where American aid helped them repair what American firepower had smashed. Things on the other side of the demilitarized zone were tougher. Trotsky cared more about what he could get out of North Japan than he did about putting anything into it.

Because of that, Mike heard gunfire along the demilitarized zone every few days. Some North Japanese voted with their feet to show what they thought of their regime. Or they tried to, anyhow. Getting past the fortified border would have been tough even without the trigger-happy guards. With them, you literally risked your life. And, singly and in small groups, those Japs did.

The other interesting thing was that not all refugees from North Japan were welcome on this side of the line. Not everyone who came over the border was fleeing Red tyranny. Some of the people who crossed were spies and agitators doing North Japan's business in South Japan. And figuring out who was who with so many records burned or blown up or otherwise lost wasn't easy, either.

A woman walking up the street politely bowed to Mike as he came down it. He returned the bow, saying, *"Kon-ichiwa."*

She smiled, covered her mouth with her hand, and burst into a storm of giggles. He hadn't said or done anything funny. As he'd seen before, that was what Japanese did when you caught them by surprise. After she got over it, she returned the *good-day*.

"Genki desu-ka?" he asked. He didn't mind the chance to trot out more of his bits of Japanese with her. He thought she was in her mid- to late thirties, though it was often hard to be sure with Japanese women. However old she was, she wore it well. She had on a white cotton blouse and a black skirt: better in this hot, sticky summer weather than his uniform.

In reply to his *how-are-you?* (actually, it meant something like *Are you bouncy?*—*genki* was a tricky word), she spoke in pretty good English: "I am fine, thank you. And how are you?"

"Just great, thanks." Mike almost giggled himself; she'd caught him off-guard. He asked, "Where did you learn to speak so well?"

"I am to teach English here in Wakamatsu. I studied it for years before the war. I am glad you think I speak well. For a long time, I did not use it much. You understand why?"

"Hai." Mike nodded. During the war, anything that had to do with America was suspected because America was the enemy. Even baseball, which the Japanese had enthusiastically taken to, got sidelined for the duration.

Of course, the Japs hadn't sent tens of thousands of Americans into labor encampments, the way Joe Steele had with Japanese in the States. Then again, the Japs hadn't had the chance to do anything like that. Had they had it, chances were they would have taken it.

The English teacher smiled at him now as if he was a human being, not just a curiosity. "How much of my language do you know?" she asked.

"Sukoshi." He held his thumb and forefinger close together. In English, he went on, "I didn't know any before I, uh, got here." *Before I jumped out of my landing craft and started killing people.* That was what it came down to.

"You must have a good ear, then. Is that right? You say, a good ear?"

"Yes, that's what we say. And thank you. *Arigato.*"

"You are welcome," she said gravely.

"I haven't seen you here before. Are you new in Wakamatsu?" he said. The place was big enough that she might not be, but he thought he would have noticed a nice-looking English teacher who'd lived here for a while.

She nodded, though. "Yes. I am new here. I come from Osaka. With the new law that every city must teach English to the children, I came here. Not so many in the north of the Constitutional Monarchy speak well enough to teach. There is a needage for more."

She meant *need*, but he wasn't about to turn editor. He saw the uses of the law. Hardly anyone outside Japan spoke Japanese, while English went all over the world. Learning English was also one more way to bind South Japan to the USA, of course. On the other side of the demilitarized zone, the North Japanese were probably having to come to terms with Russian.

"Do you mind if I ask what your name is?" Mike asked.

"No. I am Yanai Midori—Midori Yanai, you would say. We put family name first, personal name last. And you are . . . ?"

"I'm Mike Sullivan." Mike smiled. This was as much talking as he'd done with a woman since the Jeebies jugged him. Other things, yeah, but not talk.

"I am happy to know you, Sergeant Sullivan." She'd been around enough Americans to have no trouble reading chevrons. "Now please to excuse me. I am so sorry, but I must go." She said that last with worry in her voice. If he didn't feel like letting her leave, what could she do about it? Getting in trouble for abusing the natives wasn't impossible, but it also wasn't easy.

But all he said was, "May I ask you one more thing before you go?"

She nodded warily. "What is it?"

"Are you married?" He held up a hasty hand. "I'm not proposing. I'm just asking."

She smiled at that—not very much, but she did. The smile didn't last long, though. "No, I am not married. I am a widow, or I am sure I am. My husband was stationed in the Philippines. He did not come home. He was not one of those who laid down their arms in the surrenders after the Emperor died." She cast down her eyes when she spoke of that.

Some Japanese units in the Philippines had held out till the fighting in the Home Islands ended. They were a sideshow; the Americans hadn't pushed hard after driving them from the bigger towns. "I'm sorry," Mike said, and then, "I was never in the Philippines." He didn't want her to think he could have had anything to do with her husband's death.

"I understand," Midori Yanai said. "I really do have to go now, so sorry. Please excuse me. Maybe we will see each other again. Good-bye." She started away.

"*Sayonara,*" Mike called after her. She looked back over her shoulder to show she'd heard and wasn't ignoring him. He stood there watching her till she disappeared around a corner. Then he kicked a pebble down the street. He felt like a sixteen-year-old kid trying to figure out how the whole business of women worked.

Well, no man would ever figure out the *whole* business of women, not if he lived as long as Methuselah. But godalmightydamn, wasn't trying to unravel it the best game in the whole wide world?

Charlie walked out of Sears with a sour expression on his face. He kept not-quite-cussing under his breath. Esther set a hand on his arm. "It's okay, honey," she said.

"Like fun it is," he said. "The TVs they've got in there have bigger screens and better pictures than the one we bought a little over a year ago—and they cost a hundred and fifty bucks less. We wuz robbed!"

"No, we weren't. We just got one as soon as we could." Esther was more reasonable than he was. She went on, "It worked the same way with radios and refrigerators, too, and cars when we were little kids. They all got cheaper and better in a hurry."

"Maybe we should have waited, then." He still felt like grumbling.

"Why? Okay, we paid more money. But we had the television, and we've been watching all the shows on it since we bought it. If we'd waited, yeah, we would have bought it cheaper, but so what? We could afford it, and we wouldn't have got to see all that stuff."

"Wait a minute," Charlie said. "Remind me again which one of us is the Jew."

She poked him in the ribs. For good measure, she added, "If you were a Jew, Buster, I would know it."

Charlie's ears heated. He wasn't circumcised. Pat was, not only because he had a Jewish mother but also because these days they pretty much did it to a baby boy unless you told them not to. They said it was cleaner and healthier. Maybe they were right, but Charlie liked himself fine just the way he'd come out of the carton.

When they got home, Pat was watching *Tim Craddock—Space Cadet*. He didn't care that the TV set cost too much or that the picture was little. He'd grow up with television, and probably take it for granted in a way Charlie never did. He would have trouble remembering a time when it wasn't around to give him something to do.

It was giving him something to do right now. Whether he'd done everything he was supposed to do . . . "Have you finished your homework?" Charlie asked him. "Tomorrow's Monday, remember."

"Aw, Dad!" Pat said. "After the show, okay?"

"Okay—this once," Charlie said after a moment's thought. "But from now on, you get it done before you start goofing off, you hear? You had all weekend to take care of it. Instead, you'll have to rush through it at the last minute, so it won't be as good as it oughta be."

He felt Esther's eyes on him when he came out with that. He had trouble saying it with a straight face. As a reporter and as a speechwriter, he'd worked to the tightest of deadlines. Getting it done by 7:45 was more important than prettying it up. Well, if *Do as I say, not as I do* wasn't a parent's oldest rule, it ran a close second to *Because I said so, that's why!*

Pat's face lit up. He didn't care about the lecture. He cared about Tim Craddock and the Martians with antennae pasted to their foreheads. "Thanks, Dad! You're the greatest!"

Charlie wasn't so sure about that. He feared he was an old softy. But hearing it did make him feel pretty good.

When Charlie walked into the White House the next morning, a plump doctor was coming out. Tadeusz Pietruszka was Joe Steele's physician. Charlie hadn't seen him for a couple of years—in spite of moving slower than he had, both mentally and physically, Joe Steele never even came down with a sniffle. So Charlie heard the surprise and worry in his own voice when he asked, "What's up with the boss?"

"Nothing serious." Dr. Pietruszka touched the brim of his fedora and went on his way.

He might be a good doctor. If he took care of the President, he'd better be a good doctor. But he would have flopped as a politician. He made a lousy liar.

Instead of going to his own office, then, Charlie headed for Vince Scriabin's. He asked the Hammer the same thing he'd asked the doctor: "What's up with the boss?"

Scriabin sent him an *Et tu, Brute?* look. "It isn't anything much," he said. Charlie stood there and folded his arms. For once, Scriabin wasn't going to be able to wait him out. "All right!" The Hammer sounded impatient. "He came down with a headache in the middle of the night. He took some aspirins, but it wouldn't go away. Betty talked him into calling the doctor."

"Good thing somebody did! What did Pietruszka have to say?"

"That he had a headache. That his blood pressure could be lower, but he's not a young man." Scriabin bared his teeth in what looked nothing like a smile. "None of us here is a young man any more."

Since Charlie had a bald spot on his crown and was graying at the temples, he could hardly call the Hammer a liar. He asked, "Did he do anything besides take his blood pressure?"

"He gave him a sleeping pill. And he told him to call if he didn't feel better when he woke up." Scriabin bared his teeth again. This time, he didn't even try to smile. A cat that looked like that would have been about to bite. "Not a word about this to anyone. I shouldn't have to tell you that, but I will anyhow."

"You know I don't bang my gums," Charlie said. "Did I start telling the world about uranium?"

"Let people start worrying about whether the boss is well, and that will blow you up higher and faster than a pipsqueak thing like an atomic bomb." Scriabin turned away to show the discussion was over.

Charlie slowly walked to his own office. He should have been working on a speech about how much the community farms were producing and how everybody who worked on them was part of one big, happy family. It was drivel, of course, but a familiar kind of political drivel. He couldn't make himself care about it. His deadline was still two days away, and he had other things on his mind.

Sometimes a cigar was only a cigar. Sometimes a headache was only a headache, too. Sometimes it wasn't. Sometimes it meant you were having a stroke. Charlie's uncle had complained of a headache just before he keeled over. Two days later, he was dead.

Joe Steele wasn't dead. He came down late that afternoon. If he looked pale and puffy, well, he could still be feeling the pill. The pill could account for the way he groped after words, too. He still had his marbles—he asked Charlie how the speech was coming.

"It'll be ready when you need it, Mr. President," Charlie said.

"Of course it will." Joe Steele blinked at the idea that Charlie could suggest anything else was possible. Stroke or not, sleeping pill or not, he was pretty much his old self, in other words.

By the time he had to deliver the speech, he *was* his old self. He'd never been an exciting speaker. He still wasn't. But he'd always got the job done, and he did once more. Charlie let out a sigh of relief—in his office, with the door shut. One of these days, it wouldn't be a false alarm. This time, it had been.

XXVI

Days would go by at the White House; Charlie would look back at them and try to remember what he'd done, only to discover he had no idea. Sometimes his head would come up after what he thought were a couple of days, and he would look at the calendar and see three weeks had passed. Where did they escape to? What had he been dealing with while they slipped through his fingers?

He noticed Christmas of 1951—he spent that time with his family. But the only way he really noticed it was 1952 was by peeling the cellophane off the calendar a White House clerk left on his desk. Another year! Not just another year, but another election year. Joe Steele had already had five terms. It was like talking about five drinks. Once you'd had that many, what was one more?

"He *is* going to run again, then?" Esther asked when Charlie came home with the astonishing news that 1952 had arrived after all.

"I sure don't see any signs that he won't," Charlie said. "But you know, going in these days is the strangest thing I've ever done."

"How do you mean?"

"It feels like riding on a merry-go-round," Charlie answered. His wife gave him a quizzical look, or maybe just one that meant he was full of hops. "It does," he insisted. "That's the best way I know how to put it. You climb on, and it starts to go, and pretty soon it's up to speed. You spin round and round, and round and round, and round and round some more."

Esther's finger spun round and round, by her right ear. Charlie stuck out his tongue at her. "Sorry," she said—a lie if he'd ever heard one. "But you aren't making any sense."

"You didn't let me finish. So the merry-go-round turns at that one speed for most of the ride. But when it's heading toward time for your bunch to get off and the next bunch to get on, the merry-go-round doesn't stop all at once. It slows down a little bit at a time. And when you're on it, at first you don't even notice, 'cause you're still moving. But then you see things going around in slow motion instead of regular speed, and you know what's going on. And *that's* what the White House feels like these days."

"Oh. Okay, now I see what you mean," Esther said. "Well, we've had twenty years of King Stork. A term or two of King Log might not be so bad." Aesop's fables had been a hit with Sarah and then again with Pat. Reading the stories over and over lodged them in Esther's head and Charlie's, too.

"Maybe," Charlie said. "Or maybe he'll go on another kick instead. For a while, I thought *who-lost-China?* would be it, but he seems to have lost interest in that."

"I'll tell you the one that scared me," Esther said. "Einstein . . . died, and then some of the other physicists who Joe Steele thought didn't speak up, they . . . died, too."

"I remember," Charlie said unhappily. That discreet pause conveyed a world of meaning.

"But I don't know if you were paying attention to the names. Oppenheimer—a Jew. Van Neumann—a Jew. Szilard—a Jew. A Hungarian Jew, in fact, poor man."

"Enrico Fermi wasn't Jewish," Charlie said.

"No, but he had a Jewish wife," Esther returned. Charlie hadn't known that. She went on, "For a while there, I thought Joe Steele would decide Hitler'd had a good idea about what to do with the Jews. To the Jews, I should say."

"He got rid of those guys because he was sore at them, not because they were Jewish." Before coming to the White House, Charlie'd never dreamt he could sound so calm about murder, but here he was. And here those physicists weren't. He added, "Besides, Captain Rickover—well, he's Admiral Rickover now—he's a Jew, too. And so were some of the guys he grabbed from the labor encampments. Teller, Feynman, Cohen, I don't know how many other wreckers."

"I know that now. I didn't know it then," Esther said.

"And they made the bomb work, and fried all the Japs in that city. Suppose it didn't, though. Suppose Trotsky made his first. What would Joe Steele have done to the wreckers then? Or to all the Jews?"

That was a good question, wasn't it? Charlie decided he was better off not knowing the answer—and so was Esther. Much better. "It didn't happen," he said. "That's what you have to remember. It's just something you worried about. It's not anything that came true."

"I know. But my folks came to America so they wouldn't have to be afraid of pogroms any more, and so I wouldn't, either," Esther said. "That was what America stood for— being able to get along no matter who you were. But it didn't exactly work out that way, did it?"

"Oh, I don't know. Not too long ago, I heard a shoeshine man talking with a janitor when they didn't know I was listening." Charlie didn't say the men he was talking about were colored—with those jobs, what else would they be? He continued, "One of them said, 'That Joe Steele, he done more for equality than any other four Presidents you can think of.' 'What you talkin' about?' the other fellow said. And the first guy told him, 'He treats everybody jus' the same way—like a nigger.'"

Esther laughed and looked horrified at the same time. "That's terrible!"

"It sure is," Charlie agreed. "What's for dinner tonight?"

Mike walked into the classroom with his usual mix of excitement and dread. He supposed actors felt the same way as the curtain rose. He got a better reception than actors commonly did. All the kids in the room jumped to their feet, bowed, and chorused, *"Konichiwa, Sensei-san!"* Then they said the same thing in English: "Good morning, teacher!"

When Mike returned the bow, he didn't go as low as they had. They were just middle-school students, and he was a grown man. He didn't grasp all the details of how Japanese bowed to one another; he wondered if any foreigner did. But he got the broad outlines, and they forgave his blunders because he *was* a foreigner and couldn't be expected to know any better. As with a three-legged dancing bear, the wonder was that he did it at all, not that he did it well.

"*Konichiwa!*" he said, and "Good morning!" Then he bowed to Midori Yanai as one equal to another and told her, "*Konichiwa, Sensei-san!*"

Her bow was slightly lower than his: the bow of woman to man. The Constitutional Monarchy wrote women's equality into its laws. Mike had no trouble playing along. For someone like her, who'd been raised in the old ways, change came harder.

"Good morning, Sergeant Sullivan," she said in English. Hanging around with him the past couple of years had made her better at distinguishing the *r* sound in his title and the *l* sound in his name. She went back to Japanese to talk to the class: "Sergeant Sullivan has come here today to help you learn his language."

"Thank you, Sergeant Sullivan!" the boys and girls sang out in English. Most of them said *Surrivan*; Japanese didn't use the *l* sound, and they had trouble hearing it, let alone saying it. Quite a few of them said *Sank you*, too; the *th* sound was another one their language didn't own.

"I am honored to be here," Mike said in Japanese. He used that phrase whenever he visited a classroom. They took honor seriously here. Because he used it a lot, he said it well. When he went on, he didn't sound so smooth. He knew his Japanese was bad. He didn't worry about it. Because he'd hung around with Midori for a while, he had enough to do what he needed to do here—and she'd help him if he stumbled. "When I speak your language I am *ichiban baka gaijin*." They giggled—the A-number-one stupid foreigner was admitting what he was. He continued through the giggles: "But when you speak my language, *you* are *ichiban baka gaijin*."

That brought them up short. They weren't used to thinking of themselves as foreigners. That another language had its own native place was an idea they needed work on.

"I try to speak Japanese better each time I do it," Mike said. "You should try to speak English better each time, too."

He led them in touching their tongues to the backs of

their front teeth to make *l* noises, and to putting their tongues between their top and bottom teeth for *th*. Because he'd been making those sounds since he was a baby, he was better at showing how to do it than Midori Yanai was. For her, they were as foreign as they were to the kids.

He went through conversation drills with them, letting them hear what a native speaker sounded like. Then he asked for questions in English. A boy raised his hand. Mike nodded to him. "Why English the verb not at the end puts?" he asked.

"Why does Japanese put it at the end?" Mike answered. The kid blinked; that was water to a fish to him. Mike went on, "I don't know why. Why, I don't know." He grinned. The kid just frowned. He didn't get wordplay in English yet. So Mike continued, "But Japanese is wrong with the verb in the middle. English is wrong with the verb at the end." It wasn't always, but they were still learning rules. They weren't ready for exceptions.

They bowed him out of the classroom with a singsong *"Arigato gozaimasu, Sensei-san!"* He killed time in Waka-matsu till school let out. Then he went back there to meet Midori.

"Thank you," she told him. "I think that went well today."

"Good. I thought so, too, but you know better than I do." Mike didn't hug her or give her a kiss. Men didn't show women affection in public here. Things like that were starting to catch on with youngsters who imitated the Americans they saw in person or in the movies, but Midori kept the ways she'd grown up with. Mike didn't push it, which was one of the reasons they got along.

After they walked side by side, decorously not touching, for a while, they went to a restaurant. It was more than a greasy spoon, less than fancy. She had *tonkatsu*: breaded pork chop fried and cut into bite-sized slices, with a thick, spicy sauce. He ordered a bowl of *ishikari nabe*. It was a Japanese take on salmon stew that he'd learned to enjoy.

Once they'd eaten, they went to her little apartment. The building was new since the Japanese War. It was made of bricks and concrete, not wood and paper. "My only fear,"

Midori had said, "is that it will not stay up in an earth-quake."

Mike had felt several since coming to Japan. He hadn't been in one strong enough to knock down buildings, but he knew they had them. He'd said, "I hope it stays up, too." What else could you say?

The apartment was bigger than a jail cell, but not much. It would have driven Mike crazy. Midori took it in stride. She made the most of the space she had by not putting a lot in it, and by making sure everything stayed in its proper place if she wasn't using it.

She didn't even have a bed. She had futons—floor mats. The Japs had been using them forever. Rooms here were so many futons long and so many wide. If you piled two or three together, well, that was pretty nice when you felt like fooling around.

Lazy and happy in the afterglow, Mike said, "You're wonderful, you know that?" He tried to say the same thing in Japanese, too.

"I am also happy with you," she said. "Sometimes I feel I should not be, but I am."

"You shouldn't be? How come? Because I'm American?"

"Hai." She nodded. "I am sorry. I am so sorry, but it is true. You are a good man, but you are a *gaijin.* You cannot fit here for the rest of your life."

She was bound to be right about that. Sooner or later—sooner, since he was well past fifty—they'd muster him out of the Army and ship him home. And then he'd have to face all the nasty choices he'd ducked in 1946 by leaving the uniform on. Montana? New Mexico? Wyoming? Colorado? Reporter? Tree feller? People feller? Go back East and risk the Jeebies jugging him again, this time for what would be a life stretch?

With Midori, there might be other possibilities. "Do you think you could fit in in the United States, in a country full of round-eyed barbarians?"

He said it as a joke, but he knew that was how she thought of Americans in general. After a moment, she asked, "How do you mean that?"

Mike took a deep breath. "Do you want to marry me?" he asked. When Stella, or her lawyers, told him she was cutting him loose, he'd never dreamt he would ask that of another woman. But that letter had come to the labor camp more than a dozen years ago now. Stella had long since found somebody else: a booking agent named Morris Cantor. Why shouldn't he?

"I would like to do that, yes," Midori said slowly, "but how hard will it be?"

"I don't know. I'll find out." Mike did know they didn't make it easy. But he thought he could manage it. He'd done everything the USA asked from him and then some the past ten years. The USA might manage a little something for him. And the rules about getting together with local women were easier now than they had been right after the big war. Fraternizing then might land you in the guardhouse.

"It is good to know you care about me for more than this." Still naked in the warm night, Midori touched herself between the legs for a moment. "I thought so, but it is still good to know."

"Good to know you care about me—you love me—too." Mike's voice sounded rough even to himself. Americans who took up with Japanese women often wondered if their lady friends cared or if they were only meal tickets.

"I did not expect you to propose to me tonight." Midori laughed.

Hearing that laugh made Mike feel better. "It's about time, you know?" he said. She nodded. He could have said *It's now or never*, and that would have been every bit as true. It sounded better this way, though. He still had a bit of writer in him after all.

When the Republicans gathered in Chicago, they nominated Robert Taft. He aimed to be the first man since John Quincy Adams to follow his father into the White House. Before they nominated him, they talked about drafting Omar Bradley or Dwight Eisenhower.

The conqueror of Western Europe and the architect of victory in the Pacific both turned them down. "Politics is no place for soldiers," Bradley said. George Washington, Ulysses S. Grant, and Zachary Taylor, among others, might have come out with a different view of things. But Washington, Grant, and Taylor hadn't served under Joe Steele.

Casually, Charlie asked Vince Scriabin, "Do you know how the two generals happened to say no?"

"Yes," the Hammer answered, and not another word. Charlie was left to his own imaginings. He hoped they were juicier than what really happened, but he had no guarantees.

Three weeks after the GOP cleared out of the International Amphitheatre, the Democrats came in to renominate Joe Steele and John Nance Garner. Charlie always felt funny about going back to the Windy City for a convention. This one, at least, was in a different building from the one they'd used to pick Joe Steele the first time. Banners hanging from the rafters shouted TWENTY YEARS OF PROGRESS!

In his acceptance speech, Joe Steele said, "When I first became the Democratic candidate in 1932, the United States suffered in the grip of the Depression. Many of you can remember that. Now we are the greatest, the strongest, the richest country in the world. Every one of you knows that. I am not braggart enough to claim I had everything to do with that. But I am not modest enough to claim I had nothing to do with it, either."

Delegates laughed and applauded. So did Charlie, up on the podium. Most of the words were his. The delivery was the President's, and he could have done better. He stumbled over a few phrases; it was almost as if he were sleepwalking through the speech.

It wouldn't sound too bad over the radio, though, and he hadn't wanted TV here. The Republicans had had it, and it played up a vicious floor fight. The Democrats didn't have those brawls, not under Joe Steele they didn't. But that might not have been why he vetoed the cameras. He wasn't young any more. He also wasn't well any more. But he was still shrewd enough to realize he would do better not to show the country how old and unwell he was.

Taft went around the United States arguing that it would be better to bring American troops home from Europe and from South Japan. "If they want our weapons to defend themselves, that is one thing," he said. "But haven't we spent enough lives outside our borders to pay the butcher's bill for the rest of this century?"

"We are part of the world whether we like it or not," Joe Steele replied. "Even if we go away from it, it won't go away from us. Bombers with atomic weapons can already reach our shores. One day soon, rockets will fly halfway around the world in minutes. We have enemies, countries that hate and fear and envy our wealth and safety. We have to hold them back wherever we can."

"Not a bad speech," Esther said to Charlie. "How much did you do?"

"The line about being part of the world whether we like it or not, that was mine," he said.

"Sounds like you," she agreed.

"But the rest . . . I don't know where the writing came from," Charlie said. "The ideas are what he's been talking about since we got into World War II. Except for the rockets, I mean. I don't know who fed him that one, or whether he came up with it himself. But it's pretty silly, wherever it came from."

"I guess so." Esther's chuckles sounded nervous. "You never can tell with that Buck Rogers stuff, though, not any more. Who would have believed an atom bomb was possible before they dropped that one on Sendai?"

"Well, Trotsky would have, or he wouldn't have had one ready to drop on Nagano," Charlie said. Esther made a face at him. He spread his hands in half an apology. Even so, he went on, "I'll believe in rockets that can go halfway around the world when one comes down on Washington."

"If one ever does, God forbid, you won't believe in it for very long." Esther didn't usually insist on getting the last word, but she did that time.

As he'd done every four years since 1940, Charlie stayed late at the White House on the first Tuesday after the first Monday in November. As she'd done every four years since 1940, Esther stayed home on election night. Sarah was fourteen now; Patrick was ten. She could have left them alone. But the less she had to do with Joe Steele and the men who did his bidding, the happier she was. Charlie didn't even ask her to come any more. He knew how she felt. To not such a small degree, he felt the same way. But she had a choice. He didn't. He'd made his choice not long after Joe Steele jugged Mike, and he'd had to live with it ever since.

"A whole generation has grown up knowing no President of the United States but Joe Steele," a radio commentator said. He made sure he sounded as though that was a good thing. Had he sounded any other way, his mellow voice would have traveled the airwaves no more. In Joe Steele's America, everybody made choices like that and lived with them . . . or didn't.

New York went for the President. So did Pennsylvania. So, Charlie noted, did Maryland—whatever Kagan had done to fix things there after 1948, it had worked. Ohio didn't, but Ohio was Taft's home state. When Central Time Zone results came in, Illinois swung Joe Steele's way, too.

"By the time the President completes the sixth term he now seems sure to win, he will have led the country for almost a quarter of a century," the commentator said. "It will be many years before anyone comes close to that astonishing record."

Robert Taft conceded a little before midnight. Joe Steele didn't come down to celebrate with his crew. That was different from the way things had gone the past three times. Julius, the colored bartender, told Charlie, "He's gonna take it easy tonight, suh. I did send a bottle o' that nasty apricot brandy he likes to the bedroom for him and his missus."

"That should work," Charlie said. Yes, the boss was getting old. Julius had gray in his hair, too, and he sure hadn't when Charlie first met him. And Charlie knew too well that he wasn't any younger himself.

Midori oohed and ahhed when the Golden Gate Bridge loomed out of the fog. "So big! So beautiful!" she said.

"It's something, all right. I remember when they finished it, almost twenty years ago now." Mike realized this was the first glimpse of American soil—well, American ironmongery—

he'd had in nearly half that time. He'd sailed out of San Diego in 1943, and here 1953 was only a month away. *Time flies when you're having fun,* he thought vaguely. The trouble was, time also flew when you weren't.

The freighter they'd boarded in Yokohama let loose with its foghorn. It had been sounding the horrible thing every couple of minutes for hours now. Other mournful blasts came out of the mist every so often. Mike hated the racket, but he did approve of not colliding with another ship.

He smiled at Midori. "Well, Mrs. Sullivan, I've seen a lot of your country. Now you've seen some of mine, anyhow."

"Yes, Mr. Sullivan, that is true. *Hai—honto.*" She said the same thing in English and Japanese. Then she spread the fingers of her left hand. Her ring was just a plain gold band, but not even a ten-carat diamond could have sparkled in this gloom. *Hey, it's the thought that counts,* Mike thought. And as long as she felt the same way, everything was fine.

After the freighter docked in San Francisco, they had to go through customs and Immigration and Naturalization. Mike had a manila folder to accompany his passport. It held papers that included his Army discharge, his official permission to marry a Japanese national, and records pertaining to his Purple Heart, all the oak-leaf clusters, and his Bronze Star. There was a note attached that Joe Steele himself had presented the Bronze Star—the first time his acquaintance with the President had ever been worth anything to him. Midori also carried an impressive collection of documents in English and Japanese, though hers was thinner than Mike's.

"Everything seems to be in order," the Immigration and Naturalization clerk said after he'd gone through it all. "However, I do need to check your passport number against one other list." He started to turn his swivel chair towards a file cabinet.

Mike knew exactly what that list would be. "Don't bother," he said quietly. "It's NY24601."

"Ah, thank you." The clerk nodded. "You do understand the restrictions imposed on former inmates of labor encampments?"

"Oh, yeah," Mike said. "But it's kinda hard to take a ship from Japan to Montana or Wyoming."

"Indeed. If I give you ten days' incoming authorization to remain outside the restricted zone for former inmates, will that be adequate?"

"That should be plenty. Thanks. I know where we're gonna go, and yes, it's inside the zone." Mike had wondered how the authorities would handle an ex-wrecker. He might have known they would have procedures in place. He wasn't the first of his kind to come home to the good old USA. He wouldn't be the last, either.

"We'll do it that way, then," the clerk said. They had procedures, all right. One of the stamps he used on Mike's passport had a number of days he could adjust as required. If Mike was still in San Francisco and had to show that passport more than ten days from now, his story wouldn't have a happy ending.

For the time being, he said, "Can you point us to a hotel not too far from here? With luck, one close to a Western Union office? I need to send a couple of wires, let people know I'm back."

The clerk mentioned a couple. One was only a block away. Mike and Midori walked there with their worldly goods. Midori stared at the streets, and at all the cars on them. "Everything is so rich, so wide, so open!" she said.

"Sweetie, you ain't seen nothin' yet," Mike told her.

She exclaimed again at the hotel room, which was bigger than her apartment in Wakamatsu. Mike went out and sent his telegrams. When he came back, he asked the desk clerk about nearby restaurants. He splurged and took Midori to a steakhouse.

How much she got amazed her all over again. "This is too much for three!" she said, which didn't keep her from making a big dent in it. Mike finished what she couldn't.

They had an American honeymoon at the hotel for a couple of days. Then they took a cab to the train station. Mike bought tickets. He hadn't made much in his Army time, but he'd spent even less. He had plenty of money for now. Once he'd got the tickets, he sent one more wire.

By dumb luck, the train left in less than an hour. They

went to their seats. The roomy car and big, snorting engine impressed Midori, too. She squashed her nose against the window as the train pulled out. After they left town and got out into the open, she mashed it even tighter.

"So much space!" she breathed after a while. "So much! I knew America was wide, but I had no idea how wide. Our generals must have been crazy to think they could fight so much."

She said the same kind of thing several more times as they rolled east. The more of America she saw, the bigger it seemed. The farther east they went, the colder it got, too, as they left the mild coastal climate behind. Snow, though, unlike broad open spaces with no people in them, Midori was used to.

They changed trains in Salt Lake City. Sunrise on the snow-covered salt flats outside of town was one of the most beautiful things Mike had ever seen. Midori was dozing, though, and he didn't want to wake her.

From Utah, they went into Wyoming and crossed the Continental Divide. The prairie on the far side of the Rockies astonished the woman from Japan all over again. Then the conductor called, "Casper! All out for Casper!"

"That's us, babe," Mike said. He and Midori hurried out.

John Dennison waited on the platform. He might not have aged a day in the ten years since Mike had last seen him. A slow smile stretched across his face as he stuck out his hand. "Howdy, scalp," he said.

Joe Steele took the Presidential oath of office for the sixth time on a cool, cloudy day. Chief Justice Prescott Bush administered it. Bush was as pliable a Chief Justice as even Joe Steele could want. He wasn't a lawyer, but he was friendly and gregarious and smart enough not to say no to the man who'd appointed him.

At the lectern, the President fumbled with the text of his latest inaugural address. Charlie watched from the bleachers behind the lectern. These days, he always wondered how well Joe Steele would get through a public event. Sometimes he was fine. Sometimes, he wasn't.

Today, he pulled himself together. It wasn't a great

speech, but he never gave great speeches. He gave speeches that got the job done. "Man's power to achieve good or to inflict evil surpasses the brightest hopes and the sharpest fears of all ages," he said. "We can turn rivers in their courses, level mountains to the plains. Nations amass wealth. Labor sweats to create—and turns out devices to level not only mountains but also cities. Science seems ready to confer upon us, as its final gift, the power to erase human life from this planet.

"The Reds know no god but force, no devotion but its use. They tutor men in treason. They feed upon the hunger of others. Whatever defies them, they torture, especially the truth."

Charlie carefully didn't wonder about accurate election returns from the last few years divisible by four, and from the ones divisible only by two. That took work, but he did it.

"Freedom is pitted against slavery; lightness against the dark," Joe Steele went on. "It confers a common dignity on the French soldier who dies in Indochina, the British soldier killed in Malaya, the American life given in Japan. The strength of all free peoples lies in unity; their danger, in discord. We face the Red threat not with dread and confusion, but with confidence and conviction."

He waited for applause, and he got it. He went on to talk about the need to keep America prosperous and to boost trade around the world. And he finished, "Patriotism means equipped forces and a prepared citizenry. Moral stamina means more energy and more productivity, on the farm and in the factory. Love of liberty means the guarding of every resource that makes freedom possible. This is the work that awaits us all, to be done with bravery, with charity, and with prayer to Almighty God."

He stumbled a little turning away from the lectern. He caught himself before he fell, though. He was shaking his head as he went to the limousine that would take him back to the White House. Getting old had to be a terrible business. You could feel your grip slipping day by day, but you couldn't do anything about it.

Charlie didn't go to any of the inaugural balls and banquets. He never had. Esther didn't enjoy them. More to the point, she didn't enjoy the people she would run into at them. Going to a ball by himself wasn't Charlie's idea of fun. It wasn't like election nights. His absence at the social gatherings might be noticed, but he wouldn't be missed.

After January 20, things went back to normal in a hurry. With so many under his belt, one more Inauguration Day was only a formality for Joe Steele. He kept the lid on at home and dueled with Trotsky by proxy around the world. Trotsky was no spring chicken, either—he was the President's age, give or take a few months.

"I'm waiting for him to drop dead," Joe Steele said at a meeting of his aides. He had held more of those the past couple of years than he'd been in the habit of doing before. Chuckling, he went on, "That place will fall to pieces as soon as his hand comes off it."

No one wondered out loud what might happen to this place as soon as Joe Steele's hand came off it. Anyone who did wonder out loud about such things wouldn't stick around long enough to learn the answer.

Joe Steele called another one of those meetings on a bright almost-spring day in early March. The general in charge of U.S. forces near the Japanese demilitarized zone had complained that his troops didn't have enough ammunition in reserve if the North Japanese came over the border. Eisenhower seemed to think General Van Fleet was worrying over nothing.

Even though the President had summoned his henchmen, he had trouble acting interested in what they said. He kept frowning and raising his left hand to rub behind his ear. Finally, Charlie asked him, "Are you all right, sir?"

The frown deepened into a scowl. "I have a terrific pain in the back of my head," Joe Steele said. He started to bring up his left hand again, but never finished the gesture. His eyes widened, then slid shut. He slumped forward, his chin hitting the table hard.

His aides all jumped up, shouting and cursing. "Get him to the couch next door!" Scriabin said urgently. "And for Christ's sake call Doc Pietruszka!"

Charlie helped carry the President out of the conference

room. "Be careful," Joe Steele muttered, half conscious at best. They laid him on the couch, as the Hammer had suggested. Mikoian loosened his tie. His breathing still sounded bad: slow and irregular and harsh. He looked bad, too. He was pale, almost gray. Charlie fumbled for his wrist to take his pulse. It felt weak and much too fast.

"What is it?" Kagan asked.

"I wasn't counting, but I don't think it's good," Charlie answered.

"What do we do now?" Mikoian said.

"Wait for Pietruszka and hope he can help," Scriabin snapped.

By Mikoian's expression, that wasn't what he'd meant. "We'd better let Betty know," he said.

Joe Steele's wife waited with the aides, all of them shivering and numb, till Dr. Pietruszka got to the White House. It took less than fifteen minutes, but seemed like forever. Joe Steele had gone grayer yet by then. The aides described what had happened. The doctor took the President's pulse and peeled back his eyelids to examine his pupils. "He's had another stroke, a bad one this time," he said. That answered whatever questions Charlie might have had about the headache a couple of years before.

"Is there any hope?" Mikoian asked.

Before Dr. Pietruszka could reply, Joe Steele groaned. He inhaled one more time. Then he simply—stopped. No one who saw him could doubt he was dead. To Charlie's own horrified humiliation, he burst into tears.

XXVII

Charlie's humiliation lasted no more than seconds. Then he noticed everyone in the room was sobbing with him. Betty Steele, of course, had every right to weep for her dead husband. But Dr. Pietruszka was crying, too. So were Stas Mikoian and Lazar Kagan, the one who'd boasted of being able to dance between drops of water and the other who seemed to have no feelings of any kind. And even Vince Scriabin's rock of a face was a rock wet with tears. He took off his glasses so he could dab at his eyes with a handkerchief.

"What will I do?" Betty Steele wailed.

"What will the country do?" Mikoian asked. No one had an answer. For a day longer than twenty years, no one had had to wonder about the United States without Joe Steele at the helm.

A minute or so after that, a look of utter astonishment spread over Lazar Kagan's broad face. He clapped a hand to his forehead. "My God!" he exclaimed, and then, as if that wasn't enough, *"Gottenyu!"* A moment later, he explained why he was shocked enough to fall back into his childhood Yiddish: "Now look! That damned cowboy Garner is President of the United States!"

They stared at one another. For a day longer than twenty years, John Nance Garner had been the country's spare tire. He'd lain in the trunk, in the dark, all that time. Now they had to bolt him into place and pray he hadn't gone flat.

"How horrible," Scriabin muttered. If Charlie hadn't been only a few feet away from him, he wouldn't have heard the words. Even if it creaked, the Constitution might need to start working again.

"We'd better call him." By the way Mikoian said it, he

would have been happier going to the dentist for a root
canal without novocaine. But no one told him he was
wrong. He called the Capitol. Wherever the Vice President
was, he wasn't presiding over the Senate. He called Garner's Washington apartment—he had to look up the number, which showed how often he needed it. He spoke briefly,
then put down the handset with a disgusted look. "He's not
there. It's cleaning day, and I got the maid."

A flashbulb went off inside Charlie's head. "I know
where he is!" he exclaimed. All the others in the room
looked at him. Well, all but Joe Steele. Even dead, he
seemed impossible to leave out of consideration. Charlie
had to tear his gaze away from those set features before he
could make himself walk out.

"Where are you going?" Kagan called after him.

"I'll be back soon," he threw over his shoulder, which
both was and wasn't an answer. Once he made it out of the
room where Joe Steele had died, he moved faster. Even if
he hadn't, it would have made little difference. He wasn't
going far.

"Sullivan!" John Nance Garner said when he walked
into the tavern near 1600 Pennsylvania Avenue. "You're
early today, son." He'd already been there a while. A couple
of empty glasses, a full one, and a half-full ashtray sat in
front of him on the bar.

"Sir . . ." Charlie had to work to bring the words out, but
he did: "Sir, you need to come back to the White House
with me."

"I need to do what?" In all the years they'd known each
other, Garner had never heard anything like that from
Charlie before. He started to laugh. Then he got a look at
Charlie's face. "Oh, sweet Jesus," he whispered. He gulped
the fresh drink, then got to his feet. "Let's go. I'm . . . as
ready as I'll ever be, I reckon."

They walked to the White House side by side. Garner
was, if anything, steadier on his pins than Charlie. He was
used to bourbon; Charlie still felt the shock of Joe Steele's
death. As they walked, he told the Vice President—*no, the
President now*: he still had to remind himself—what had
happened. "So you're it, Mr. President," he finished.

"I never dreamt the day would come," John Nance Garner said, partly to himself, partly to Charlie. "He'd just go on forever. Only he didn't, did he?"

"No. I can't believe it, either." Charlie's eyes still stung.

When they came up the walk, the guards at the entrance stiffened to attention. "Mr. President!" they chorused. Word was spreading, then.

In walked Garner. *In walked President Garner,* Charlie thought, trailing him. Yes, that would take some getting used to.

Kagan, Mikoian, and Scriabin waited just inside the doors. They also said "Mr. President!" as if with one voice.

Garner nodded to them. "Take me to Mrs. Steele, if you'd be so kind."

"This way." Kagan gestured. "She's with—him."

Betty Steele sat on the couch where her husband had died. There was room for her and for his body; he hadn't been a big man. She started to stand when Garner came in. He waved her down again. "Ma'am, I am sorrier than I have words to tell you," he said. "He was one of a kind, and that's the truth."

She gestured toward the corpse. "I can't believe—I won't believe—that's all that's left of him. The rest has to be in a better place." She started to cry again.

"I hope you're right," Garner said. Charlie hoped so, too. Hoping and expecting were different beasts. The new President went on, "You don't need to move out right away or anything. I can sleep in one of the guest bedrooms for a while. Take some time to get myself up to speed on what all needs doing, but I reckon I'll manage."

"We'll do all we can to help you, sir," Mikoian said.

"Oh, I just bet you will." Garner's eyes were gray and cold and hard. They might have been chipped from some ancient iceberg. He paused to light a cigarette. "First things first. We got to let folks know what's happened, and we got to arrange a funeral that says good-bye the right way."

No one said no. He hadn't known he was President for half an hour yet, but he already saw it took a lot to make anyone say no to the man with the most powerful job in the world.

*   *   *

Casper, Wyoming, had twenty or twenty-five thousand people in it. It sat, about a mile up, on the south bank of the North Platte River. To the south rose pine-covered mountains that reminded Mike too much of the ones where he'd learned the lumberjack's trade. When he said so at a coffee shop or diner, he often got knowing chuckles; quite a few middle-aged men there were wreckers who had few choices about where they lived.

To him, it was . . . a place. To Midori, it was a spark of light in an ocean of darkness. The wide-open spaces of the American West awed her till they scared her. She didn't like to go out of town. Just a few miles, and any sign that humans inhabited the planet disappeared. Japan had next to no places like that. Too many people, not enough land . . . That was what the fight between Japan and America sprang from, right there. Here in Wyoming, it was the other way around—too much land, with not enough people to fill it.

Mike worked with John Dennison some of the time. He wasn't a great carpenter, but he could do most of what he needed to do. All those years in the encampment and in the Army had skilled his hands into learning things in a hurry. He did a little woodcutting to bring in extra cash.

And he bought an old typewriter and banged out a few stories. He submitted them under a pen-name. The first one came back with a note scrawled on the form rejection. *Too hot for us,* it said. *You can write, but you've got to tone it down if you want to sell.*

He swore. He *wanted* people to know what it was like to survive as an ex-wrecker in Joe Steele's America, dammit. But editors didn't want to wind up in encampments. After a while, he realized he could write stories that had nothing to do with barracks and thin stew and punishment brigades, but that his attitude toward those things would come through anyway.

So he wrote stories about Greenwich Village in the Thirties. He wrote stories about breakups where the abandoned party couldn't help what happened and was left feeling sideswiped by life's unfairness. He sold a couple of them, not to top markets and not for top money, but he sold. Little checks helped, too. So did the chance to drain bitterness from his spirit, even if he had to do it less directly than he cared to.

And then Joe Steele died. Mike and John found out about it when they knocked off for lunch and walked from John's shop to the diner down the street. (John was back in the place he'd used before he became WY232. The fellow who'd denounced him had been denounced in turn, and had died in an encampment. "Who says there's no such thing as justice?" John would ask—but only with the handful of people he trusted.)

Snow crunched under Mike's Army boots. Casper's climate was less rugged than the labor encampment's had been. Casper was both lower and farther south. But the first week of March here belonged to winter, not spring.

The waitress who brought their menus was about their age. John Dennison had known her since they were kids. She got her blond hair out of a bottle these days. She was brassy and usually unflappable. Today, mascara-filled tears drew streaks down her face.

"Good Lord, Lucy!" John exclaimed. "Tell me who did it to you, and the son of a gun is dead." By the way he said it, he meant it.

But Lucy answered, "He *is* dead," and started crying some more.

"Who's dead?" John and Mike asked together.

"You haven't heard?" She stared at them, her eyes wide and red. "The President is! Joe Steele!" She wept harder than ever.

Mike started to let out a war whoop of pure joy. He started to, but he didn't. The counterman was sniffling, too. So were almost all the customers. Mike knew one guy sitting at the counter was an old scalp. He kept dabbing at his eyes with a Kleenex, too.

Even John Dennison looked stunned. And he'd gone into the encampments for what he said about Joe Steele, the same way Mike had.

"What are we gonna do?" Lucy asked, possibly of God. "He's been running things so long! How'll we get along without him?" She blew her nose, then grabbed her order pad. "What d'you guys wanna eat?"

They told her. She went away. "I don't believe it," John said, shaking his head in wonder. "After all these years, I just don't believe it."

"Let's see if we get some freedom back now," Mike said.

"You don't get freedom. You have to take it," John Dennison replied. "I wonder if we know how any more."

That was a better question than Mike wished it were. He was having trouble getting used to what freedom he had. For fifteen years, Jeebies and soldiers of higher rank had told him what to do and when to do it. Figuring out how to use time on his own was harder than he'd expected. For twenty years, Joe Steele had told the whole country what to do and when to do it. Maybe picking up where it had left off wouldn't be so easy.

When Mike asked to knock off early that afternoon, John let him. He ambled around Casper, listening to what people were saying. *Anybody'd figure I was a reporter or something,* he thought, laughing at himself.

But he didn't keep laughing long. Everybody he listened to—in a park and at a gas station, in a general store and at the public library—seemed shocked and saddened that Joe Steele had died. It wasn't just words. Words were easy to feign. Tears came harder, especially for men. Mike saw more red eyes and tear-streaked cheeks than he ever had before.

The two things he heard most often were *He was like a father to all of us* and *What will we do without him?* He wanted to scream at everybody who said either one of those. He wanted to, but he didn't. Joe Steele might be dead. Flags might fly at half staff. The labor encampments were still very much going concerns. Anybody who'd been through them once never wanted to see them twice.

When he went back to the house he and Midori were renting, he found she'd heard the news on the radio. "This is what Japan felt, first when General Tojo was killed, then when we learned the Emperor was dead," she said. "We thought the world was coming to an end."

Mike had never told her he'd been the first American

soldier to recognize the dead Hirohito. He didn't tell her now, either. You tried not to hurt the people you loved. He did say, "General Tojo may not go down in history too well. Neither will Joe Steele."

"Who is President now? They say Garner, but I do not know anything about Garner," Midori said.

"We'll all find out," Mike answered. "He's an old man. He's been Vice President since 1933. He's from Texas. He used to be in Congress. Now you know as much about him as I do. I don't even know if he can hold on to the job."

"Will someone try to take it away from him?" Midori asked. "Can they do that here in America?"

"If you'd asked me before Joe Steele took over, I would've laughed myself silly and then told you no," Mike said. "Now? Now, babe, all I can tell you is, I haven't got any idea. We'll all find out."

Joe Steele lay in state in the Rotunda of the Capitol. Flower arrangements made a U around the bronze casket. Photographers had snapped pictures of Washington dignitaries—the new President, the California cronies, J. Edgar Hoover, Attorney General Wyszynski, Chief Justice Bush, Secretary of War Marshall, and a few Senators and Congressmen—standing by the coffin. Charlie wasn't sorry not to be included in those photos. He would have bet all the politicos were suspiciously eyeing the men closest to them. And he would have bet that Joe Steele, dead or not, dominated every picture.

After the dignitaries withdrew, ordinary people started filing through the Rotunda to pay their last respects to the man who'd been President longer than any two of his predecessors. Nobody had to come. Nobody had to wait in the long, long line that stretched out of the great marble building and down the Mall, doubling back on itself several times. The Jeebies wouldn't haul you away if you stayed home. People came because they wanted to or because they needed to. They came by the thousands, by the tens of thousands, by the hundreds of thousands.

That outpouring of respect and grief made Charlie wonder whether Joe Steele would have won all his elections even if he hadn't left anything to chance. He might well have. But he'd never been one to risk anything he didn't have to. He'd always assumed the deck would be crooked. If he didn't stack it, someone else would. He made damn sure nobody else did.

They'd planned to let him lie there one day, till eight p.m. The crowds were so large, they kept the Capitol open all day and all night . . . for three days in a row. When they closed it at last, disappointed mourners threw rocks and bottles at the police and Jeebies who tried to clear them away.

Joe Steele went into the ground at Arlington National Cemetery, on the Virginia side of the Potomac. His final resting place wasn't far from where he'd executed the Supreme Court Four and other adjudged traitors. Charlie wondered how many besides him would think of that. Most of the reporters covering the funeral hadn't been in the business when Joe Steele started ordering people shot.

John Nance Garner delivered the memorial address. He started by adapting Shakespeare: "I come to praise Joe Steele, not to bury him. For all he did will live on in this country for years to come. He lifted us out of the Depression by our bootstraps. Not everyone now remembers how bad off we were then. He led us through the greatest war in the history of the world. And he made sure the Reds wouldn't be the only ones with atom bombs. We're as free as we are on account of him."

The new President paused. He looked as if he wanted to light a smoke or take a drink. But this was the time and place for neither. He drew in a deep breath and went on: "Some will say we ought to be freer than we are. Maybe they're right, but maybe they're wrong. Maybe this is the way things have to be if we're going to stay even so free. I don't know the answer to that yet. I'll be working on it, the same as Joe Steele was."

Another pause. "The President we used to have is dead. I'm sorry as all get-out. I wish I wasn't standing here in front of you making this speech right now. But even with Joe Steele gone, the United States of America is still in business. God bless America, and God bless each and every one of you." He stepped away from the microphone.

By the graveside, Betty Steele gently wept. Most of Joe Steele's cronies and Cabinet members, as well as the Senators and Representatives and Supreme Court justices who'd served under him for so long, also sobbed. Charlie sniffled a little himself. He couldn't help it. Had he not been there when Joe Steele died, he might have thought they were all hypocrites shedding crocodile tears. He understood better now. Some losses simply were too big to take in. This was one of them. They could worry later about whether Joe Steele and all he'd done were good or bad. What mattered now was that the man was gone. His passing couldn't help leaving a void inside everyone who remained.

Cemetery workers lowered the bronze casket into the ground. They took hold of shovels and began to fill in the grave. Dirt thudding down on the coffin lid was the most final sound Charlie knew. TV cameras brought the funeral to the whole country.

Dignitaries walked back to their Cadillacs and Lincolns and Imperials and Packards. Some men drove themselves away. Others let chauffeurs take care of the work. Armed GBI guards on motorcycles escorted the small convoy of expensive Detroit cars Charlie rode in: the one that went back to the White House. People filled the sidewalks, many with handkerchiefs pressed to their faces as they mourned. Nobody under thirty-five had any idea what the country'd been like before Joe Steele won his first national election in 1932.

John Nance Garner (*President* John Nance Garner—sure enough, that still had just begun to sink in) stood waiting by his limousine as Charlie came up to him along with Scriabin and Kagan and Mikoian. "Mr. President," Charlie murmured. The other aides nodded, all of them in their somber mourning suits.

"Gentlemen," Garner said. He suddenly seemed taller and straighter than Charlie remembered. Going from Number Two to Number One would do that, even if Garner hadn't looked to be President. He went on, "Gentlemen, I would like to talk with all of you in the conference room in fifteen minutes."

They all nodded again, though the look Kagan sent Scriabin said nobody but Joe Steele had any business ordering them around like that. Who did John Nance Garner think he was, the President or something? By the way he stood next to the Cadillac, that was just what he thought.

Charlie hadn't been in the conference room since Joe Steele had his stroke there. He shivered when he walked in. The place still overwhelmingly reminded him of the dead President. The lingering aroma of Joe Steele's pipe tobacco rammed the memory home—smell was tied in with emotion and evocation more than any of the other senses.

John Nance Garner was smoking a Camel, not a pipe. A drink sat on the table in front of him, but he didn't pick it up. "Hello, Sullivan," he said. "Who woulda figured it'd come to this?"

"I know I didn't, sir." Charlie glanced at the clock on the wall behind the new President. If Joe Steele's California henchmen didn't hustle, they'd be late.

They weren't. They came in together, on time to the second. "Mr. President," they chorused as they slid into their usual seats.

Garner slid sheets of paper across the table at them and at Charlie. "These are letters of resignation," he said. "They're for form. I'm getting them from the Cabinet, too."

Charlie signed his and passed it back. If John Nance Garner wanted someone else putting words in his mouth, he was entitled to that. Charlie didn't know just what he'd do if the new President let him go, but he expected he could come up with something. He might wind up poorer—no, he would wind up poorer—as a newspaperman, but he might be happier, too. He wondered if he remembered how to write a lead any more. Chances were it would come back to him.

The glances Mikoian, Scriabin, and Kagan sent him were all distinctly hooded. But they couldn't very well refuse to sign letters like that. One by one, they scrawled their names. Kagan needed to borrow Scriabin's pen so he could put his signature on the underscored line.

John Nance Garner set reading glasses on his nose and examined each letter in turn. He clucked his tongue between his teeth and sighed. Then he said, "Mikoian, Kagan,

Scriabin—I'm going to accept your resignations, effective immediately. Sullivan, you can stick around a little longer, anyways."

Joe Steele's henchmen stared at him in disbelief too theatrical for any director to use. "You can't do that!" the Hammer exclaimed.

"You don't dare do that!" Kagan added.

"Oh, yes, I can, and I damn well do dare," John Nance Garner replied.

"Why are you doing this?" Mikoian asked. Charlie also thought that was a pretty good question.

Garner answered it: "Why? I'll tell you why. Because for the past twenty years you whistleass peckerheads have pretended I'd never been born, that's why. That's easy when you're messing with the Veep. But I'm not the goddamn Veep any more. Now I call the shots, and I'll keep the company I want to keep, same as Joe Steele did before me. Tell you what, though—I'll make it easier on you, so it doesn't look quite so much like I'm kicking you out the White House door."

"How do you mean?" Scriabin demanded, hard suspicion curling his voice.

"Well, I was thinking I'd name Mikoian here ambassador to Afghanistan, and Kagan ambassador to Paraguay," Garner said. "I don't reckon I'll have any trouble getting the Senate to confirm those."

"What about me?" the Hammer asked.

"Don't you worry about a thing, Vince. I got a place for you, too," John Nance Garner replied. No one called Scriabin *Vince*, not even Joe Steele. No. No one had. Smiling, Garner continued, "I'll put you up for ambassador to Outer Mongolia. Have fun with the camels and the sheep."

"You won't get away with this." Scriabin would have sounded less frightening had he sounded less frigid.

"No, huh? People like you, they serve at the President's pleasure. Well, the pleasure ain't mine. Now get the hell out of the White House, before I call the hired muscle to throw you out."

They stalked from the conference room, Mikoian serene as always, Kagan scowling, and Scriabin shaking his head in tightly held fury. That left Charlie alone with the new President. "What about me, sir?" he asked. But that wasn't the question he wanted to ask. After a moment, he got it out: "Why didn't you fire me, too?"

"Like I told you, you can hang around if you want to," Garner said. "And here's why—you remembered I was a human being even when Joe Steele didn't. You'd drink with me. You'd talk with me. More'n Joe Steele or those three puffed-up thugs o' his ever did. You know how I found out there was such a thing as an atom bomb?"

"How?" Charlie asked.

"When I heard on the radio we dropped one on that Sendai place, that's how," John Nance Garner growled. "Nobody said a word to me before. Not one goddamn word, Sullivan. I was Vice President of the United States, an' they treated me like a dirty Red spy. Did *you* know about the bomb ahead of time?"

"Well . . . some." Charlie wondered whether Garner would show him the door for telling the truth.

"I ain't surprised. I wish I was, but I ain't." The President lit another cigarette. "You wrote some pretty good words for Joe Steele. You might've done even better if he'd wanted you to, too. So we'll see how it goes, if that suits you. If I don't like it, I'll toss you out on your ear."

"All the way to Outer Mongolia?" Charlie asked.

Garner chuckled hoarsely. "Shit, even that ain't far enough for Scriabin. I'd send him to the far side of the moon if only I could get him there."

"I'll stay for a while, Mr. President," Charlie said. "But you'd better keep an eye on the Hammer before he leaves. He's had the office in here a long time. He won't want to give up everything that goes with it."

"Now tell me something I didn't know. I'll have J. Edgar's boys watching him every second. Oh, you bet I will." John Nance Garner muttered to himself. "Now who do I get to watch Hoover?" He knew the questions that needed asking, all right.

Charlie looked for something, anything, more to say. The best he could do was, "Good luck, sir."

"Thanks," Garner said. "I'll take whatever I can get."

*   *   *

Mike stuck a nickel in a machine and took out a copy of the *Casper Morning Star*. He wondered why he bothered. It was a thin, anemic sheet compared to the *New York Post*. Compared to the *New York Times*, it was barely a newspaper at all.

But it was what Casper had for a morning paper. The evening *Herald-Tribune* was no better. That a town as small as Casper had both a morning and an evening paper said something, though Mike wasn't sure what. He shrugged as he folded the *Morning Star*, stuck it under his arm, and carried it into the diner where he ate breakfast most days.

"Morning," a man and a woman said when he came in. He'd been here long enough for people to know him for a regular at the joint. But the locals still thought of him as new in town. He was, of course, but they'd go right on thinking of him that way if he stayed here till he was ninety. They cut him a little extra slack because he was friends with John Dennison, but only a little.

The counterman poured coffee and gave him the cup. "You want hash browns or pancakes?" he asked. Mike almost always ate bacon and eggs over medium, but he went now with one side, now the other.

"Hash browns today," he said, adulterating the coffee with cream and sugar.

The counterman called the order back to the kitchen. Mike opened the paper and started to read. Some of the local writing was pretty good. The *Morning Star* kept the city fathers on their toes. National and world news all came from the wire services. The next time the paper sent a reporter out of Wyoming would be the first.

A story below the fold on the front page caught his eye. WHITE HOUSE SHAKEUP, the headline read. The story announced that three of Joe Steele's longtime assistants had resigned and been offered ambassadorial positions by President Garner. For a moment, Mike swore under his breath. They deserved to be tarred and feathered as far as he was concerned, if not drawn and quartered.

Then he noticed where John Nance Garner wanted to send them. You couldn't leave the USA any farther behind, not unless you did a swan dive from a B-29 into the South Pacific halfway between Australia and New Zealand.

He wanted to whoop. He wanted to holler. He wanted to jump off his stool and cut capers right there at the counter. But he just sat, reading the paper. You never could tell who was a Jeebie or who informed for the GBI. Even though a ton of scalps lived here, people had mourned Joe Steele, and mourned him yet. They might still feel something for his nasty henchmen, unlikely as that seemed to Mike. You didn't want to take chances, not in America the way it was these days.

Mike did let himself smile as he sipped from his cup. No informer could report him for that. Right next to the story about the ambassadorships to the back of beyond was one about a colt rescued from a drainage ditch. That one might have made Vince Scriabin smile. It sure would have made him happier than being named ambassador to Outer Mongolia did.

"Thanks," Mike said when the counterman set the plate in front of him. He grabbed the syrup, and was about to use it when he remembered he'd asked for the potatoes. They got salt and pepper instead, along with the eggs. After breakfast and two cups of snarling coffee, he headed for the carpenter's shop. He took the *Morning Star* with him, though he usually left it behind in the diner.

With John Dennison, he could gloat over the fall of the Pain Trust to his heart's content. The more he gloated, the more contented his heart got, too. John was less delighted than he was. "The bastards'll still be living off the fat of the land, right?" he said. "Only difference'll be, from now on it's the fat of somebody else's land."

"So what would you do with 'em, then?" Mike asked.

"Send 'em to an encampment, that's what," Dennison said with no hesitation at all. "Let's see 'em live on the thin for a change. They deserve it! Bread made out of sawdust and rye? Stew from potato peels and old cabbage and turnip greens and maybe a little dead goat every once in a while if you're lucky? A number on 'em front and back? Chopping wood when it's twenty below? How many times did they give it to other folks? Let 'em find out what it's like and see how they enjoy it."

"Only one thing wrong with that," Mike said.

"Like what?" Plainly, John didn't think it was wrong at all.

"As soon as the wreckers realize who they are, how long will they last?" Mike said. "Not long enough to get skinny, that's for sure."

"Oh." Dennison paused. Then, reluctantly, he nodded. But he also said, "You gonna tell me they don't deserve to get ripped to pieces? Go ahead, scalp! Make me believe it."

"I don't want anybody grabbing hold of them when I'm not there to help," Mike said. "I'd dig up Joe Steele if I was back East and tear him to bits along with his flunkies."

"He got you as bad as anybody, didn't he?" John said. "The stretch, the punishment brigade, two wars, and now internal exile. You sure as hell didn't miss much."

"He didn't have me shot," Mike said. "He figured the Japs would take care of it for him, but they fell down on the job."

Midori understood American politics in Japanese terms. After Mike got home, still full of the news, she said, "The new Prime Minister always shakes up the cabinet. Sometimes it matters. Most of the time?" She shook her head.

"Yeah, that makes sense." Mike wanted to keep talking about it. Seeing bad things happen to Scriabin, Mikoian, and Kagan pleased him almost as much as learning Joe Steele was dead had done. But Midori hardly seemed interested. Because Mike was so excited about what he'd read in the *Morning Star*, he needed longer to notice than he might have. After a while, though, he asked, "Are you okay, honey?"

"I am very okay." Even after she'd come to the States and started using it all the time, her English had a few holes in it. Or so Mike thought, till she went on, "Dr. Weinbaum says yes, I am going to have a baby."

Mike's jaw dropped. He could feel it drop, something he never remembered before. "Oh, my God!" he whispered. He hadn't really thought that would happen. She'd turned forty the summer before. You never could tell, though. He forgot all about Vince Scriabin, Lazar Kagan, Stas Mikoian, and even — miracle of miracles! — Joe Steele himself. "That's wonderful!" He hugged her. He kissed her. He said, "If it's a little girl, I hope she looks just like you!"

She smiled a bit crookedly. "So you would want another Sullivan with black hair and slanted eyes?" She was joking, and then again she wasn't. There were no more than a handful of Orientals in Casper. Most of the others were Chinese who wanted nothing to do with her. Though the war'd been over for years, whites could still be rude, sometimes without even meaning to.

"You're darn tootin', I do!" Mike meant that. He could bring it out quickly, and he did.

"I am glad that you are glad." She sounded relieved. If she'd wondered . . . Try as they would, how well could two people truly know each other in the end? How well could one person know himself? Or even herself?

"A baby!" Part of him, part of her, would go down through the years after all. That baby would be years younger than he was now when the odometer turned over and the twenty-first century started. And that baby, lucky kid, would know about Joe Steele only through history books.

XXVIII

For a little while, things went on without Joe Steele very much as they had while he was President. His widow moved back to Fresno. No one had paid much attention to Betty Steele while she was the First Lady. No one paid any attention to her once she went into retirement.

At the White House, John Nance Garner made a less demanding boss than the man he succeeded. Charlie had trouble conceiving of a more demanding boss than Joe Steele. The new President carried out the policies he found in place when he took over. He was in his mid-eighties. How many changes could he try to make, even if he wanted to?

Kagan went to Paraguay. Mikoian went to Afghanistan. "I'm sure I'll get as many thanks there as I ever did in Washington," he quipped to reporters before boarding the airliner that would start him on his long, long journey.

Scriabin didn't go to Outer Mongolia, at least not right away. Like someone waking from a drugged, heavy sleep, Congress needed a while to realize Joe Steele's heavy hand no longer held it down. Members didn't automatically have to do whatever the President said or else lose the next election or face one of those late-night knocks on the door. John Nance Garner didn't carry that kind of big stick.

And the Hammer still had clout of his own in the Senate. It was a pale shadow of Joe Steele's clout, but it was enough to keep him out of Ulan Bator. It wasn't friendship. Except perhaps for Joe Steele, Scriabin had never had any friends Charlie knew of. Charlie didn't know what it was. Blackmail didn't seem the worst of guesses.

John Nance Garner had accepted the resignations of all his Cabinet members except the Secretary of State and the

Secretary of War. Dean Acheson was a reasonably able diplomat, while George Marshall had kept himself respectable despite serving Joe Steele for many years.

Acheson was due to speak at an international conference on the Middle East in San Francisco. The DC-6 he was riding in crashed as it went into its landing approach. Forty-seven people died. He was one of them. It was tragic. Despite all the progress in aviation over the past twenty years, things like that happened more often than they should.

Charlie didn't think it was anything more—or less—than tragic till a week later, when Marshall got up to make an after-the-dinner speech during a cannon-manufacturers' convention. He strode to the lectern with his usual stern, erect military bearing. All the newspaper reports that came out of the convention said he stood there for a moment, looking surprised. Then he turned blue—"as blue as the carpeting in the dining room," one reporter wrote—and keeled over.

Several doctors were in the audience. One gave him artificial respiration while another injected him with adrenaline. Nothing helped. Both medicos who tried to save him said they thought he was dead before he hit the floor.

But Charlie found out most of that later. The morning after it happened, John Nance Garner summoned him to the oval study Joe Steele had used for so long. The old President's desk was still there. So was the pipe-tobacco smell that everyone who knew Joe Steele associated with him.

"Some no-good, low-down, goddamn son of a bitch is gunning for me, Sullivan," Garner growled when Charlie came in.

"Sir?" Charlie said. He wanted another cup of coffee.

"Gunning for me," Garner repeated, as if to an idiot. "I'm President. Ain't no Vice President. Presidential Succession Act of 1886 says, if the President dies when there's no Vice President, Secretary of State takes over, then the other Cabinet fellas. Ain't no Cabinet now, either. Senate ain't confirmed anybody. If I drop dead this afternoon, who runs the show? God only knows, 'cause the law sure don't. In the Succession Act of 1792, it was the President *pro tem* of the Senate and then the Speaker of the House, but the 1886 rules threw that out. So like I say, God knows."

Two vital Cabinet deaths inside a week swept Charlie's thoughts back more than twenty years. "I bet Scriabin set it up," he blurted.

"Oh, yeah?" Garner leaned forward. "Sonny, you better tell me why you think so." So Charlie did, starting with what he'd heard before the Executive Mansion fire cooked Roosevelt's goose, and Roosevelt with it, in 1932. When he finished, the President asked him, "How come you never said anything about this before?"

"Because I could never prove it. Hell, I still can't. And when my brother did kick up a stink, what happened to him? He wound up in an encampment, and then in a punishment brigade. But when two more die like that—"

"—and when Joe Steele ain't around any more," Garner broke in.

Charlie nodded. "That, too. I figured you'd better know."

"Well, I thank you for it," John Nance Garner said. "I expect Vince Scriabin ain't the only one who can arrange for people to have a little accident."

"That's good, Mr. President," Charlie said. "But if we're gonna start playing the game by banana-republic rules, there's something else you'd better think about."

"What's that?"

"All your guards here belong to the GBI. How far do you trust J. Edgar Hoover?"

Garner's eyes narrowed as he considered the question. "You and me, we go back to the days when they'd've strung up anybody who even talked about them labor encampments, never mind set 'em up. Himmler killed himself when the limeys caught him. How long you reckon Yagoda'll last once they finally stuff Trotsky and stick him next to Lenin in Red Square?"

"Twenty minutes," Charlie said. "Half an hour, tops."

"That's how it looks to me, too—unless he's quicker on the trigger than all the bastards gunning for him." Garner scowled. "But what am I supposed to do about J. Edgar? Who do I get to watch this place except for the Jeebies?"

"Soldiers?" Charlie suggested. "You think the Army can't add two and two? They'll have a pretty good notion of what happened to Marshall, and why."

"Maybe." But John Nance Garner didn't sound happy about it. "That would really take us down to South America, wouldn't it?"

"Which would you rather have, sir? The Army protecting the President or a putsch from the head of the secret police?"

The telephone on the desk that had been Joe Steele's for so long rang. Garner picked it up. "Yeah?" he barked, and then, "*What?*" His face darkened with rage. "All right, goddammit, you've let me know. I'll deal with it. How? Shit, I don't know how. I'll work something out. Jesus God!" He slammed the handset back into place.

"What was that, sir? Do I want to know?" Charlie asked.

"Those fucking pissants in the House." Garner had been one of that number for many years, but he didn't care now. And he had good reason not to: "They've introduced a motion to impeach me, the stinking dingleberries! Says I'm 'complicit in the many high crimes and misdemeanors of the Joe Steele administration.'" He quoted the lawyerese with sour relish, even pride. "I bet Scriabin put 'em up to it, the cocksuckers."

Charlie knew perfectly well that Joe Steele's administration had committed high crimes and misdemeanors past counting. He also knew perfectly well that John Nance Garner wasn't complicit in any of them. Joe Steele hadn't let him get close enough for complicity. But the House and Senate wouldn't care. They couldn't put a bell on Joe Steele; he'd been too strong, and now he was too dead. Garner, both weaker and still breathing, made an easier target.

Something else occurred to Charlie. "If they throw you out of office, who comes in to take over for you?"

"Beats me." Now Garner sounded almost cheerful. "The law we've got now doesn't say, not in the spot we're in here. Constitution says Congress can make a law picking who comes after the President and Vice President, but a law is something the President signs. How can you have a new law if you ain't got no President?"

"I have no idea, sir." Charlie's head started to ache.

Mike turned on the television. He'd bought it second-hand. The screen was small and the picture none too good, but some inspired haggling had brought the guy who was getting rid of it down to forty bucks. Now he could watch Lucille Ball and Sid Caesar and baseball games with everybody else—or so it seemed.

And he could watch the news. Washington kept boiling like a kettle of crabs. Nobody seemed to remember how to play politics the old-fashioned way, the way people had done things before Joe Steele was President. The new game, when seen from close to two thousand miles away, seemed a lot bloodier. They were playing for keeps—for keeps all kinds of ways.

As it went in the United States, so it also went in the wider world. The East Germans rioted against their Russian overlords. Trotsky preached world revolution, but not revolution against him. The news showed smuggled film of Red Army tanks blasting buildings and machine-gunning people in the streets of East Berlin.

"President Garner has issued an executive order eliminating the restricted zone for people released from labor encampments," the handsome man reading the stories announced. "GBI Director J. Edgar Hoover publicly deplored the move, stating that it endangers the nation's safety. And leaders of the impeachment drive in the House say the order will have no effect on their insistence that Garner be removed. More after this important message."

Music swelled as the commercial started. Over it, Midori said, "I understand that right? He says wreckers can now live anywhere in the country?"

"That's what he said." Mike thought about going back to New York City. Hell, he didn't even know if the *Post* was still in business. He'd been away more than fifteen years. Picking up the city's frantic pace after so long wouldn't be easy.

"You want to go somewhere else?" she asked.

"I was just thinking about that. I don't know," Mike said. Midori might like the Big Apple. If any place in America could remind her of her crowded homeland, New York City would be it. "How do you feel about it?"

"Where you go, I will go," she said. She wasn't a Christian; she'd never heard of *Whither thou goest, I will go.* If you had that thought, though, the words would follow directly.

Before Mike could reply, the newsman came back. Next to him was a photo of a familiar face. "Vincent Scriabin, Joe Steele's longtime chief assistant, died last night at the age of sixty-three. He was struck and killed by an automobile while crossing the street after eating dinner at an Italian restaurant in Washington. Because Scriabin was not in a crosswalk, the driver, who police said showed no signs of intoxication, was not held."

"Oh, my," Mike said softly as the fellow went on to the next story.

"Nan desu-ka?" Midori asked.

How could you explain the Hammer to somebody who hadn't been here while Joe Steele was President? Charlie might have been able to. Why not? Charlie'd worked side by side with him for years. Mike reminded himself he needed to let his brother know Midori would be having a baby. He'd had that thought before, had it without doing anything about it.

How accidental was Scriabin's death? As accidental as Franklin D. Roosevelt's? Probably just about. Scriabin hadn't gone off into exile without any trouble, the way Kagan and Mikoian had. He'd stayed in Washington and kicked up a fuss. John Dennison guessed he was behind the House's stab at impeaching Garner. It wouldn't have surprised Mike. Like the man he'd served for all those years, the Hammer went in for revenge.

Mike realized he hadn't answered his wife's question. "He was one of Joe Steele's ministers," he said, which put it in terms she'd get. "The new President didn't want to keep him. He didn't like that. Now he's dead. He walked in front of a car—or the guy in the car was hunting him."

Midori's eyes widened. "I did not think American politics go that way?"

"They didn't used to," Mike said. "Now? Who knows now? Everything is all different from the way it used to be." He'd been away from politics since early in Joe Steele's second term. In political terms, that was a lifetime, if not two.

"People would kill politicians on the other side all the time in Japan," Midori said. "It made politics too dangerous for most people to try. The ones who did always had bodyguards with them."

"It may wind up like that here, too," Mike said. "English has a word for killing people in politics. When you do that, you *assassinate* somebody."

"Assassinate," Midori echoed. "I will remember. Assassinate. If English has this word, it needs it, *neh?*"

"*Hai,*" he said. *Neh?* meant something like *Isn't that right?* Japanese used it all the time. He wished English had such a short, handy word for the same phrase. It would have been useful.

As far as Mike knew, Charlie was still at the White House, working for John Nance Garner. The new President hadn't canned him, the way he'd canned Joe Steele's California cronies. To Mike, that said something good about his brother, anyhow. Working for Joe Steele hadn't made all of Charlie's soul dry up, turn to dust, and blow away. Hard to believe, but it could be true.

"You say—you have said—you lived in New York City." *Whither thou goest* or not, Midori came back to it. "You do not want to go back to New York City, now that law says you may?"

"No, I don't think so, not unless Casper drives you crazy," he said.

She shrugged. "It is a strange place, but to me any place in America is strange. It starts to seem not so strange. If you want to stay here, we can stay here."

"We'll do that, then," Mike said. Fighting for work against guys half his age didn't appeal to him. Joe Louis had stayed in the ring too long, and got badly beaten up several times on account of it. And, after being away from New York City for so long, going back might make his head explode. He nodded. "Yeah, we'll do that." He got up, went into the kitchen, pulled two bottles of beer from the icebox, opened them with the blunt end of the church key, and brought them back to the TV.

John Nance Garner sounded disgusted. "You know what the trouble is?"

Sure I do, Charlie thought. *The House is gonna impeach you, and then the Senate is gonna convict you and throw you out on your ass. After that, you can spend all your time at the tavern around the corner again.* But that wasn't what Garner needed to hear. "What is it, Mr. President?" Charlie said dutifully. "Is it anything you can fix?"

"I only wish I could," the President said. "But I don't hardly know anybody in the House any more. That's what's wrong. None of the boys I was in there with is still around, or damn few, anyways. Some lost. Some got old and died. Some went into the encampments. And some of the ones who're still there, them bastards never did cotton to me."

"Hoover could clean them out," Charlie remarked. Had Joe Steele ever found himself in this predicament, the Jeebies *would* have cleaned out the House. But Joe Steele had intimidated Congress too much for it to rise against him. The new President didn't.

"Nah." John Nance Garner shook his head. "I ain't gonna do that. If I did that, Hoover'd be running the show, not me. Fuck him, Sullivan. I may go down, but by Jesus I'll go down swinging."

"Okay." Charlie was more glad than angry. He thought a deal with J. Edgar Hoover was a deal with the Devil, too. But he and Garner had made deals like that before. The one who hadn't made a deal was Mike. And how did virtue get rewarded? He'd gone through years of hell in the encampments, years of worse hell in the Army, and now he was living in Casper goddamn Wyoming married to a Jap. All things considered, the wages of sin seemed better. Charlie asked, "Can you give them anything to get them off your back?"

"Christ, I already gave 'em Mikoian and Kagan and

Scriabin. Wasn't enough. They say, 'You're as bad as they were. You gotta go, too.'"

"Shame about Scriabin," Charlie remarked.

"Ain't it?" Garner chuckled, coughed, hawked phlegm, and chuckled again. "I wonder if anybody came to his funeral."

"Don't know. I wasn't there." Charlie thought he would have gone had Mikoian died before heading for Kabul. He might have gone for Lazar Kagan. But Scriabin? It would have been too much like attending the memorial service for somebody's pet rattlesnake.

"But I mean, how're they gonna impeach me and convict me? How can they do that?" Garner dragged his mind away from pleasure and back to the business at hand. "If they do, they shoot the whole executive branch right behind the ear. I'm all there is of it, for Chrissake. They can't make laws by their lonesome, not if there's nobody to approve 'em. Not even the chickenshit Supreme Court Joe Steele left us'd let 'em get away with that."

"Mr. President, every single word you just said is true." Having told John Nance Garner what he wanted to hear, Charlie also told him once more what he needed to hear: "But you know what else? I don't think Congress gives a damn. They've got the atom bomb, and they're gonna drop it."

"I only wish I could tell you you were full of crap. That's how it looks to me, too, though," Garner said gloomily. "What happens if they throw me out and twenty minutes later, Trotsky, he starts somethin' in South Japan or West Germany? Who's gonna give our soldiers orders then? If somebody does, why should the soldiers do what he says?"

"I have no idea." Charlie figured Trotsky had to be laughing in his beer, or more likely his vodka. He'd outlived his American rival, and now the USA was in a hell of a mess. The only thing that might hold him back was the fear of reuniting America—against him. That was a thin, weak reed to lean on.

"Me, neither." John Nance Garner reached into a desk drawer and pulled out a bottle of bourbon. He didn't bother with ice, or even a glass. He just swigged. Then he slid the bottle across the stone desktop to Charlie. Charlie had a belt, too. He needed one. Garner went on, "But I don't know what I can do to make 'em see it. I don't know what I can do to make 'em show any common sense. They look at me, and all they see is, they're givin' Joe Steele one in the eye. Biting the hand that fed 'em, half the time. Hell, more'n half."

"Joe Steele's dead," Charlie said roughly.

"I thought so, too, when we planted him," Garner said. "But right after Antony talks about burying Caesar, not praising him, he goes, 'The evil that men do lives after them,/ The good is oft interred with their bones.' Boy, did old Will hit *that* nail square on the head. We'll still be untangling ourselves from Joe Steele when your kids get as old as I am now."

That had the unpleasant ring of truth. "Do we need a Constitutional crisis straight off the bat, though?" Charlie asked.

"Need one? Shit, no, sonny. It's the last goddamn thing we need. But we've sure got one." Garner stood up, leaned across the desk, and retrieved the whiskey bottle. He took another stiff knock. "This here, this is what I need."

Drunk and sober, he politicked as long and as hard as he could against the impeachment charges. Charlie wrote speech after speech, trying to sway public opinion against the proceedings in the House. None of that did any good. Charlie hadn't really expected it would.

The House Interior Committee reported out three articles of impeachment, passing them by votes of 37-1, 33-5, and 31-7. The whole House passed them by almost equally lopsided margins. For the first time in eighty-five years, a President was impeached. The case went to the Senate for trial.

Chief Justice Prescott Bush presided with the look of a man who acutely wanted to be somewhere, anywhere, else. An Associate Justice who was a real lawyer sat at Bush's elbow to guide him through whatever legal thickets might crop up. The President's attorneys tried to make the thickets as impenetrable as they could. The Chief Justice ruled in their favor whenever he could without making himself look completely ridiculous.

It didn't matter. The three Congressmen who managed the push for conviction dealt with legal thickets by driving over them with a Pershing tank and crushing them flat. Joe Steele had committed all kinds of impeachable offenses. Everybody knew it. Nobody'd done, nobody'd been able to do, a thing about it while he was alive to commit them. Now that he was dead, John Nance Garner made a handy scapegoat.

When the Senate voted on whether to convict, the tallies on the three articles were 84-12, 81-15, and 73-23, all well over the two-thirds required. Watching from the visitors' gallery, Charlie saw Prescott Bush lick his lips before stating the obvious: "President Garner has been convicted of the three articles for which he was impeached. Accordingly, he is removed from office and disqualified from holding and enjoying any office of honor, trust, or profit under the United States. He remains liable to indictment, trial, judgment, and punishment according to law." He banged his gavel. "These proceedings are concluded."

"Who runs things now?" someone yelled from the gallery. Two cops grabbed him and hustled him away. Nobody answered the question.

Charlie got back to the White House just in time to hear a young reporter ask John Nance Garner, "What do you think of your conviction and removal, sir?"

"Fuck 'em all," Garner said.

The kid turned red. Whatever he put in his story, that wouldn't be it. Gamely, he tried again: "What will you do now?"

"Go on home to Uvalde and eat worms," Garner answered. "You reckon the country was goin' to hell with me, just watch how it goes to hell without me." And that was the end of the press conference.

"I'm sorry, sir," Charlie told him.

"Me, too, Sullivan." John Nance Garner shrugged. "What can you do, though? Let's see how those damn fools run this damn country, that's all. Like I told that little punk, fuck 'em all. If it wasn't for the assholes who done this to me, I'd be glad for the excuse to leave."

"Good luck," Charlie said. They shook hands. Charlie hoped nobody would throw Garner in jail for however much time he had left. He'd been in Joe Steele's administration, but not of it. The policies weren't his fault. Of course, he also hadn't done anything to stop them.

Well, neither did I, Charlie thought uncomfortably. If they were still on the prowl after scapegoats, he was around.

After finishing his good-byes with John Nance Garner, he went home. "What are you doing here at this time of day?" Esther asked in surprise.

"Honey, I'm a presidential speechwriter in a country without a President," he said. "What's the point to sticking around?"

"Will they pay you if you don't show up?" Yes, she was the practical one.

"I dunno. To tell you the truth, I didn't worry about it. As long as they don't arrest me, I figure I'm ahead of the game."

"Arrest you? They can't do that!" Esther made a face. "Or I guess they can if they want to. That's what you get for working for that man for so long."

Charlie sighed. "Yeah, I guess that is what I get. What I'm liable to get, anyhow. But we both know I would have got it a lot sooner if I hadn't gone to work for him."

"It isn't fair," Esther said. "What can you do when all your choices are rotten?"

"The best you can. That's all you can ever do." After a moment, Charlie continued, "My senior year with the nuns, we did some Tacitus. You know—the Roman historian. God, that was tough Latin! But I remember he talked about how good men could serve bad Emperors. That crossed my mind a few times while I worked for Joe Steele. I tried to be a good man. I'm sure I wasn't always, but I tried."

Esther put her arms around him. "I think you're a good man," she said. "In spite of everything." That she added the last four words explained why they worried someone might come after him.

More out of curiosity than for any other reason, he went to the White House the next morning. There was no THIS SPACE FOR RENT sign on the front gate. He supposed that was something, at any rate. He had no trouble getting in; it wasn't as if the guards didn't know who he was. But once he was in, he had nothing to do. He sat in his office and listened to the radio.

When it was getting on toward lunchtime, he casually walked down the corridors—*the corridors of power*, he thought, *only not right now*. The offices that had belonged to Scriabin and Kagan and Mikoian were all closed and locked. Like Joe Steele, Scriabin was beyond judgment now. Charlie wondered whether the other two would ever come back to the United States.

He went home early, but not so early as he had the day before. After dinner, he turned on the television. It was a good evening for letting the box entertain him. You could watch it and not think about anything else. Not thinking seemed wonderful right now.

At half past eight, though, they cut away in the middle of a commercial. An urgent-voiced announcer said, "We interrupt our regularly scheduled broadcast to bring you this special announcement from Washington, D.C."

"What now?" Esther exclaimed.

"Don't know," Charlie said. "We'll find out, though."

And they did. In a studio presumably in Washington, a man sitting in front of an American flag stared at the camera. He was middle-aged and beefy, with beetling eyebrows and a big, strong jaw. Recognizing him, Charlie felt his heart sink down to his toes.

"Good evening, my fellow Americans," he said. "I am J. Edgar Hoover, Director of the Government Bureau of Investigation. I am speaking to you tonight because the rule of law and order in the United States has collapsed. We have no President, and no legitimate successor to occupy the White House. After removing John Nance Garner, the House and the Senate have sought to arrogate to themselves powers not granted to them by the Constitution. The rule of law, then—indeed, any sort of legal authority in the country—has entirely broken down."

"Uh-oh." Charlie had the bad feeling he knew what was coming next.

He did, too. J. Edgar Hoover went on, "This being so, it is necessary to create a new authority to preserve and protect the safety and security of our beloved nation. Until the present state of anarchy and emergency is resolved in a satisfactory manner, it becomes necessary for me to assume the temporary executive power in the United States.

"For the time being, to prevent subversion, assemblies of more than ten persons are prohibited. GBI and police personnel will enforce this measure by whatever means prove necessary. Congressional leaders responsible for the current disastrous state of affairs are being detained for interrogation and for their own protection. Obey the authorities in your local areas, proceed with your everyday affairs, and this necessary adjustment to government will have little effect on you. Red-inspired whining and revolt, however, will not be tolerated. You have been warned. Thank you, and God bless America."

"That was our new Director, J. Edgar Hoover, speaking to you from the nation's capital," the announcer said suavely. "Here is the regularly scheduled program once again."

Charlie's right arm shot up and out. "*Heil* Hoover!" he said.

Esther nodded, but she also said, "Be careful!"

"I know, I know, I know. I'm not going down to the tavern where Garner would drink and do that to make the other barflies laugh."

"Probably a good idea if you don't," his wife agreed. "But are you going to the White House tomorrow?"

After a moment's thought, Charlie nodded. "Yes, I guess so, unless you've got a good reason for me not to. They know where I live, for crying out loud. If they want me, they can come get me here. They don't have to wait till I show up at my office."

Esther did some thinking of her own. "Okay. That makes sense," she said. "I just hope everything goes all right, is all."

"You and me both!" Charlie said.

When he got to 1600 Pennsylvania Avenue the next morning, he knew right away that the place was under new management. More guards than he'd ever seen stalked the grounds, and he recognized only a couple of them. Every single man carried a grease gun and looked ready to use it. Charlie gave his name at the gate. A guard checked it off. "Go on in, Mr. Sullivan," he said. "The Director wants to see you, in fact." As with the TV announcer the night before, you could hear the capital letter slam into place.

"J. Edgar Hoover is in there?" Charlie asked. Hoover hadn't wasted much time. No time at all, in fact.

"That's right." The guard's head bobbed up and down. "I'd step on it, if I were you. The Director's a busy man with a lot on his plate."

When Charlie went into the White House, a Jeebie he'd never set eyes on before frisked him. Persuaded he was harmless, the man sent him upstairs. Now J. Edgar Hoover sat behind the heavy redwood-and-granite desk. A few days before, that had been John Nance Garner's spot (Charlie wondered if the bourbon bottle still sat in the drawer). For all the years before, it had been Joe Steele's.

"Hello, Sullivan," Hoover said.

"Mr., uh, Director." Charlie swore at himself for stumbling over the title.

"We've known each other a long time. I like the work you do," Hoover said. That could have led up to anything. But then he added, "Don't get me wrong—I do," and Charlie knew he was in trouble. The Director went on, "The sad fact is, though, that you've got too many links to the past that put us in the mess we're in now."

The mess that put you in the White House, Charlie thought. He didn't say it. Why make a bad spot worse?

"So I'm going to have to let you go," Hoover said briskly. "I'm sorry, but that's the way the ball bounces. I'm sure a man with your talent won't have any worries about finding something new. You don't need to bother going back to your office. You can pick up your last check at the door as you head out. I've put in a three months' bonus. Not much of a good-bye after such a long time here, I'm afraid, but I hope it's better than nothing."

"Thank you, sir," Charlie mumbled, when he really wanted to echo John Nance Garner's *Fuck 'em all!*

"Keep your nose clean, Sullivan," the Director said, which was dismissal. Charlie nodded, turned, and walked out of the oval study.

Charlie knew he was a nuisance around the apartment. Except on weekends, he wasn't supposed to be there during the daytime. Sometimes he went out to look for work. No one had the nerve to hire a man who'd been at the White House so long. A few people blamed him for everything that had gone wrong since 1932, the way Congress had blamed John Nance Garner.

Under a pseudonym, he tried his hand at writing fiction stories. It was different from speechwriting and reporting, but he could write. He sold the second one he turned out, and the fourth. He knew he'd never make anybody forget Steinbeck or Salinger. That didn't bother him. He brought in a little money, and the writing gave him something focused to do.

Half an hour after J. Edgar Hoover left GBI headquarters in Richmond, Virginia, a bomb blew up inside and killed twenty-six people. The Director tightened the screws on the state of emergency. The man the Jeebies arrested for planting the bomb was first cousin to a Representative who'd voted against impeaching Garner. Hoover tightened the screws on Congress, too.

Day by day, Charlie told himself. *Take it one day at a time. That's how you get through the rough patches.* By all the early signs, this might be a mighty rough patch. J. Edgar Hoover made Joe Steele seem downright friendly by comparison. Charlie wouldn't have believed anyone could.

He got a postcard from Mike, letting him know he had a half-Japanese niece named Brenda. He started making notes for a novel about brothers whose lives went different ways. His working title was *Two Roads Diverged.* Nobody didn't like Robert Frost.

He was drinking more again, but Esther didn't nag him about it. She knew what was wrong. Hoover wasn't even sixty yet—he was just a handful of years older than Charlie. He might be Director a long time yet, unless somebody like that funny-looking assistant attorney general from California brought him down while he wasn't looking. Talking about things like that, Esther started drinking more herself.

No matter what, you never thought it could happen to you. When the knock came, it was actually closer to one in the morning than to midnight.